S0-BSJ-584

DIVIDED NATIONS in a DIVIDED WORLD

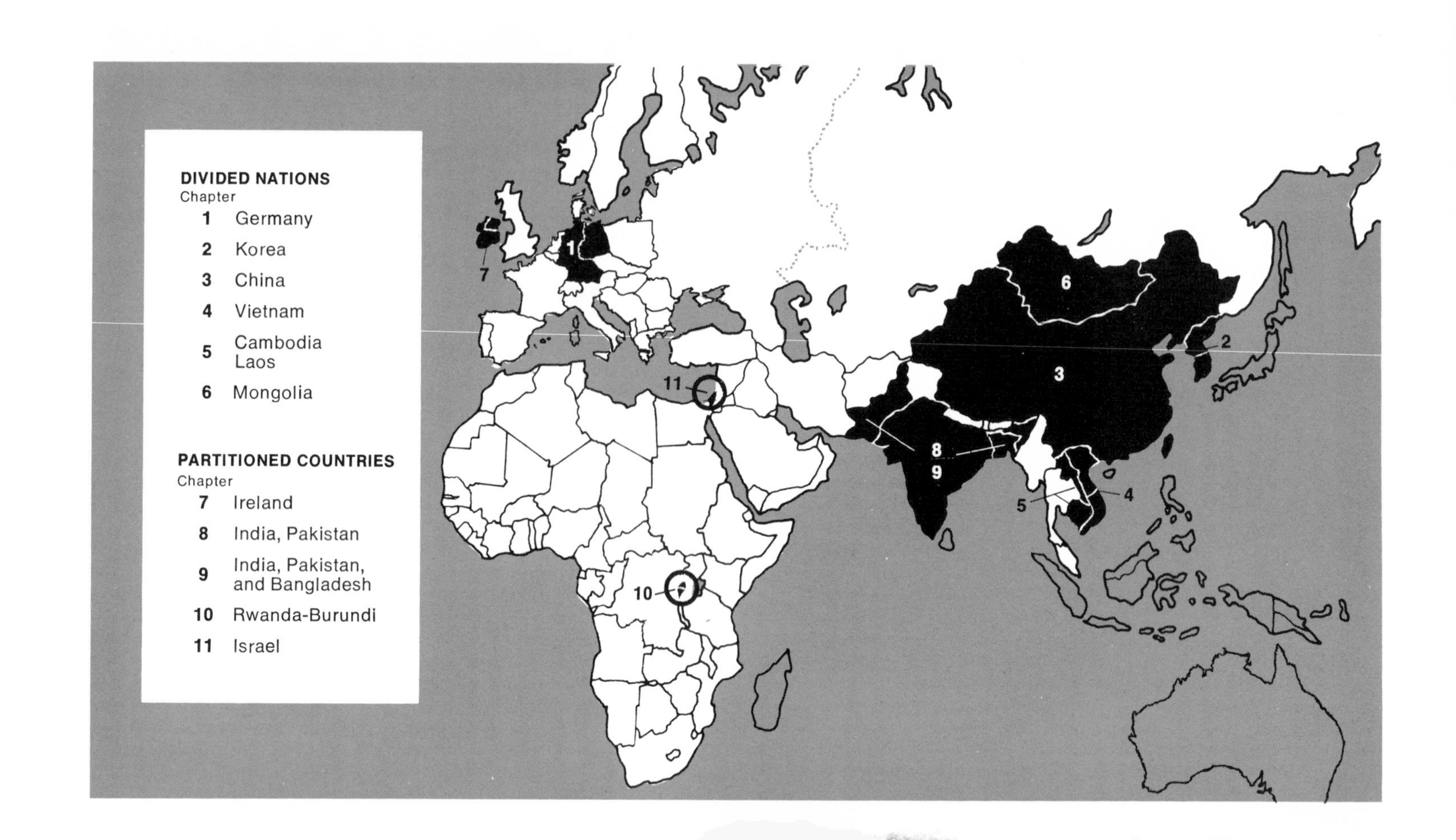
DIVIDED NATIONS
Chapter
1 Germany
2 Korea
3 China
4 Vietnam
5 Cambodia Laos
6 Mongolia
PARTITIONED COUNTRIES
Chapter
7 Ireland
8 India, Pakistan
9 India, Pakistan, and Bangladesh
10 Rwanda-Burundi
11 Israel

DIVIDED NATIONS in a DIVIDED WORLD

Gregory Henderson
Richard Ned Lebow
John G. Stoessinger

DAVID McKAY COMPANY, INC. · NEW YORK

INTERNATIONAL STANDARD BOOK NUMBER (CLOTH): 0-679-30057-0
(PAPER): 0-679-30056-2
LIBRARY OF CONGRESS CATALOG CARD NUMBER: 73-93430
MANUFACTURED IN THE UNITED STATES OF AMERICA
DESIGNED BY JUDITH LERNER

About the Authors

Craig Baxter: Foreign Service officer and presently on the faculty at the U.S. Military Academy at West Point, he authored *The Jana Sangh: A Biography of an Indian Political Party* (1967), and *District Voting Trends in India* (1967).

Bernard K. Gordon: Professor of political science and chairman of the department at the University of New Hampshire, he is the author of *The Dimensions of Conflict in Southeast Asia* (1966) and *Toward Disengagement in Asia: Strategy for American Foreign Policy* (1969).

Gidon Gottlieb: Professor of law, New York University School of Law. Representative of Amnesty International to U.N. Author of *The Logic of Choice* (1968) and contributor to leading journals, including the *Journal of International Law and Politics*, and *International Law in Vietnam*, ed. Richard Falk (1969).

Gregory Henderson: Adjunct associate professor of diplomacy at the Fletcher School, Tufts University. Research fellow, East Asian Research Center, Harvard University. Author of *Korea: The Politics of the Vortex* (1968) and editor of *Public Diplomacy and Political Change* (1973).

John H. Herz: Professor of political science and chairman of the graduate program in international relations at City College of the City University of New York, he is the author of *Political Realism and Political Idealism* (1951), *International Politics in the Atomic Age* (1959), and co-author of *Major Foreign Powers* (1972), and *Government and Politics in the Twentieth Century* (1973).

Rounaq Jahan: Associate professor of political science and chairman of the department, University of Dacca, Bangladesh, she is the author of *Pakistan: Failure in National Integration* (1972).

Richard Ned Lebow: Assistant professor of political science at City College of the City University of New York and research associate at the Institute of War and Peace Studies, Columbia University. Contributor to leading journals including the *Journal of International Affairs* and *Journal of Modern History* and author of *Between Peace and War: the Anatomy of International Crisis* (1974).

Harrison E. Salisbury: Pulitzer-Prize-winning reporter for the *New York Times*, he is the author of numerous books, among them *The Nine Hundred Days: the Siege of Leningrad* (1969).

John G. Stoessinger: Professor of political science at Hunter College of the City University of New York, he is the author of *The Might of Nations: World Politics in Our Time* (1962) and *Nations in Darkness: China, Russia and America* (1971).

Nathaniel B. Thayer: Associate professor of history and politics at Hunter College of the City University of New York and a research associate at the East Asian Institute of Columbia University, he is the author of *How the Conservatives Rule Japan* (1973).

Le Thi Tuyet: Visiting Fulbright professor of political science at College of Mount Saint Joseph-on-the-Ohio, she received her Ph.D. at the City University of New York.

Warren Weinstein: Associate professor of political science at the State University of New York, College at Oswego, he has written articles for *African Report, Africa Today*, and the *Pan African Journal*; co-author of *The Pattern of African Decolonization: A New Interpretation* (1973).

Introduction

THIS BOOK GREW FROM the twin convictions shared by the editors that political division and partition have precipitated the greatest human tragedies in the postwar world and continue to be mortal dangers to our generation and that of our children. When brother turns against brother, the struggle assumes a ferocity that strangers seldom muster. One has only to contemplate the recent histories of Vietnam, Korea, Germany, India, Pakistan, China, Ireland, and the Middle East to appreciate the vast scale and stubborn persistence of political division. In the light of this, it is startling that so little systematic research has taken place on the subject of division as a generic phenomenon. It is true, of course, to paraphrase Tolstoy, that every divided country or partitioned people is unhappy in its own particular way. But it is equally true that the phenomenon is so widespread that it lends itself to the case study approach. This in turn yields comparative analytical material, and hopefully some general conceptual conclusions. To undertake this diagnostic task in a rigorous and systematic manner in essence is the purpose of this book.

The book itself was born in a seminar that met for two years under the aegis of the Institute on the United Nations of the City University of New York. Since its inception in 1967, the Institute has attempted to build bridges between the world of thought and the world of action. Its basic purpose has been to bring together scholars and diplomats in a common forum for the purpose of analyzing in depth the most burning international issues of the day. During the two-year incubation period of this book, leading professors, diplomats, government officials, United Nations staff members, and students met regularly in informal seminars to discuss the problems of divided nations and partitioned peoples. The blending of theoretical and practical approaches, and the presence of statesmen and scholars from different nations and ideological persuasions, produced a unique intellectual climate. Diplomats who usually meet under instructions in the chambers of the United Nations got together informally under the aegis of the Institute with scholars and students who in turn enriched their own perspectives. The twin goals of the Institute have always been objective and empirical analysis and constructive quest for workable solutions.

Most of the contributors to this volume presented their case studies in draft form to their peers in the UN Institute seminar. While the final products are, of course, their own, all have benefited from this unique exposure. The cases in this book represent, in the view of the editors, the most significant examples of division and partition on the contemporary international scene. The methodology is traditional in the sense that it follows the case study method and avoids excessive quantification, but it is innovative in that it offers the insights of leading experts who have benefited from a singular and fertile international environment. A concluding chapter makes an attempt at overall conceptualization.

The editors have attempted to inject a common conceptual theme into the book while preserving the integrity of each individual contribution. Each author has collaborated beyond the call of duty and deserves special gratitude for his or her forbearance during the long process of production. If the final product meets the authors' expectations, the editors will have been well served.

In conclusion, the editors hope that this volume will appeal not only to the academic community, but also to the many statesmen, diplomats, government officials, and concerned men and women in all walks of life, who have been grappling with the problem of political division in our time.

JOHN G. STOESSINGER
Director of Seminars
Ralph Bunche Institute
on the United Nations
The City University of New York

Contents

Part 1

DIVIDED NATIONS

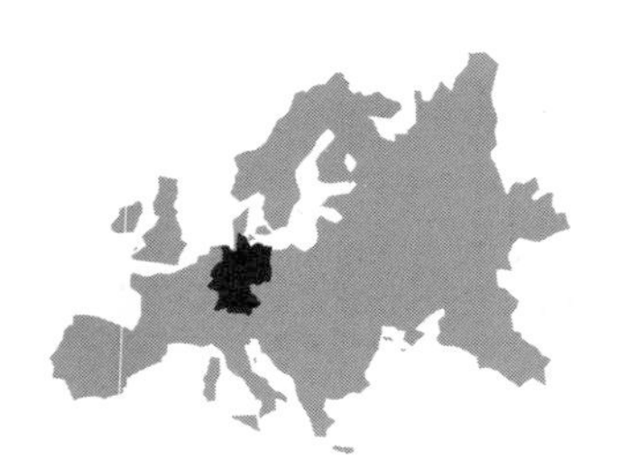

GERMANY

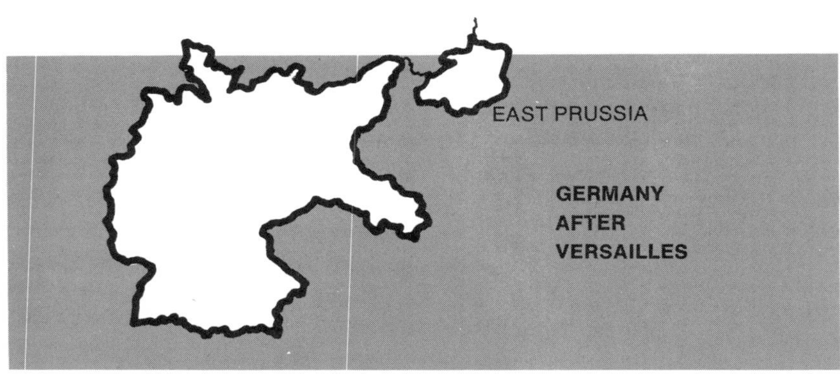
EAST PRUSSIA
GERMANY
AFTER
VERSAILLES

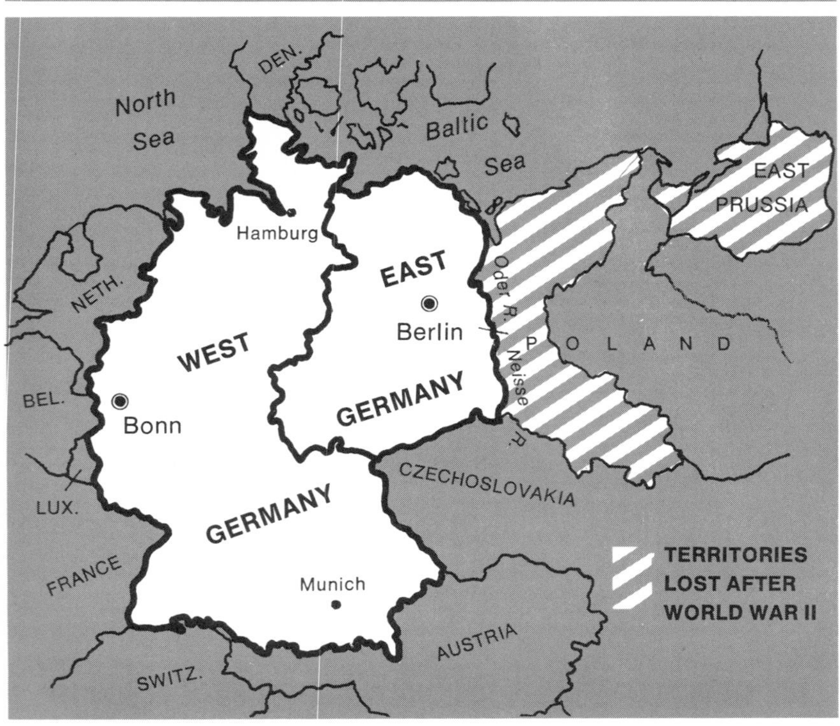
DEN.
North
Sea
Baltic
Sea
EAST
PRUSSIA
Hamburg
NETH.
EAST
Berlin
Oder R.
Neisse R.
P O L A N D
WEST
GERMANY
BEL.
Bonn
CZECHOSLOVAKIA
LUX.
GERMANY
FRANCE
Munich
AUSTRIA
SWITZ.
TERRITORIES
LOST AFTER
WORLD WAR II

1

Germany

John H. Herz

Einigkeit und Recht und Freiheit
Für das deutsche Vaterland

(Unity and Right and Freedom
For the German Fatherland)

GERMAN NATIONAL ANTHEM

Zur Nation Euch zu bilden, Ihr hoffet es, Deutsche, vergebens.
Bildet, Ihr koennt es, dafuer freier zu Menschen Euch aus!

(Vainly, Oh Germans, you hope to form yourselves into a nation.
Form yourselves, as well you can, free human beings instead)

GOETHE, 1796

AMONG THE DIVIDED NATIONS of the world Germany constitutes perhaps the most poignant case. Some countries are nations only in a dubious or ambiguous sense (are there two, or three, or a hundred "nations" in India? Do the non-Israeli Palestinians form a nation or are they part of an Arab nation?), but Germans have shared a feeling of nationhood for a long time. On that basis they had lived closely integrated in one national unit until 1945. Other divided countries had previously been under colonial rule or similar control by outside powers (with India "united" only under British rule; Indochina, under the French; Palestine, Turkish and then a mandate; Ireland, long under the British; even Korea, prior to partition, a Japanese dependency), but Germany fell from the height of national independence and power into the abyss of impotence and partition. And, while some other divided nations lie somewhat outside the centers of world politics and world conflict, Germany is located right across the two power blocs where they confront each other in a most vital area. Situated in the heart of Europe, one of the most advanced industrial nations of the world could not fail to become entangled in some of the most dangerous postwar conflicts. The division of Germany, unlike the two other (in a political sense) "East-West" divisions, those of Korea and Vietnam, has not led to actual war, but it is safe to say that war, if it should ever occur over the German issue, would involve the superpowers directly and, quite possibly, inaugurate the final holocaust.

If the "German question" has proved intractable, the reason is that Germany, on the one hand, is an undoubted "nation"; on the other hand, its involvement in the ideological and political polarization of the world renders reunification apparently unobtainable at this point. For a quarter of a century "self-determination in freedom," i.e., unification, had been the battle cry of most Germans and of many countries backing them; now it seems that acceptance of the status quo, i.e., partition, is the only way to détente and rapprochement, not only between East and West in Europe but also between Germans themselves.

Today divided nations abound. Historically, however, this is a rather new phenomenon. Prior to the age of nationalism it would have made little sense to talk in terms of, for instance, a "Germany" divided into a large number of territorial units, as it was before the Napoleonic era. But with the rise of nationalism (defined as a feeling that the "nation" was, or should be, the major political unit), the problem of German unity became one of the foremost national and international problems in Europe. What constituted the German nation, however, remained contested even after its political unification in the Bismarckian Reich. Should the German-speaking inhabitants of the Austrian Empire, for instance, be included? This doubt eventually led to World War II, to a short-lived "Greater Germany" (uniting, in many instances against their will, populations claimed by Hitlerian racialism as Germans, such as Austrians, Alsatians, Sudetens, German-speakers in Poland and other Eastern and Southeastern European countries), and in the end, to a huge loss of territory in the east and national partition of the rest.

Because of the emotional aspects of modern nationalism, divided nations are liable to become fountainheads of international unrest and instability. This is particularly true where national division coincides with, and indeed is often the result of, worldwide systemic division, such as East and West, "Free World" and Communism, etc. This is also the reason why, in the case of a divided Germany, one cannot (as one can, e.g., in the cases of India or Ireland) view and discuss the issue in more or less regional or even local terms but only in the context of global bipolarity, of which it has been a symbol, a reflection, and both a cause and a result.

There is another complication. Speaking of German division or partition, one usually thinks of the two present political units, the Federal Republic of Germany (FRG) in the West, and the German Democratic Republic (GDR) in the East. In reality there was a whole series of divisions: (1) the detachment of the territories east of the Oder-Neisse rivers (in turn divided into the major Polish part and a smaller Soviet portion); (2) the remainder split into FRG and GDR but with the exception of (3) the former capital city of Berlin, which, in turn, was divided into East Berlin (now, for all practical purposes, incorporated into the GDR, which has made it "capital city of the Republic") and West Berlin, now, on the basis of the Four-Power Agreement of 1971–72, a separate entity with close ties to but not fully part of the FRG. How all this can be construed in political and legal terms has never been clear. Theories about what happened to the postwar German Reich as legal subject in international law, or concerning the international status of FRG, GDR, and Berlin, usually reflect political attitudes and objectives. This is why we must discuss them briefly before entering into a discourse on the political problems of division. It is interesting to note that in this respect, too, different divided countries have produced widely diverging attitudes. Thus India and Pakistan (and now Bangladesh), and probably also North and South Vietnam, whatever their attitudes toward "nationhood," consider each other as separate "states" (in the sense of legal and political units). Both Chinese regimes, on the other hand, agree that China is one unit; they quarrel only over who (Taiwan or Peking) is entitled to represent it. To the Arabs (or at least to many of them) Palestine is one, with part of the area under "occupation" by an illegal regime since 1948. Some Irish construe "Ireland" in similar fashion. Attitudes in and toward Korea perhaps are somewhat more in line with those found in Germany where, until recently, the larger unit claimed to represent all of the country, while the smaller one considered the country divided into two sovereign and independent states.

Legal Status and Legal Approaches

If one asks what constitutes "Germany" today, he must be aware of the historical milestones that have marked events surrounding Germany since 1945.

Toward the end of the war, the Allied powers agreed that upon the surrender of the Reich they would assume supreme authority over all Germany, which would be divided into four zones of occupation. Joint control by the four would be exercised by an Allied Control Council (ACC) with headquarters in Berlin. For this reason, Berlin would remain outside the zones of occupation and in turn be divided into four sectors; it would be governed by an inter-Allied command (*Kommandatura*). As was made clear in the Potsdam Declaration of August 1945, rule by ACC and total occupation were not meant to annex Germany or to keep it under foreign control indefinitely but to create conditions for the eventual restoration of an indigenous German government on a democratic basis.

Despite this avowed intention, agreement on how to restore central German government proved impossible. By 1947 the Control Council had ceased to function; thereupon the Soviets, on the one hand, and the three Western powers, on the other, proceeded to establish German governments in their respective spheres: the Western powers by merging their three zones into the Federal Republic of Germany, the Soviets by presiding over the establishment of the German Democratic Republic. Both units started to function under their respective constitutions in the fall of 1949.

They were not yet entirely "sovereign," however. For another six years, supreme power remained vested in the respective occupying powers. In the West this regime terminated with the coming into force of the Paris Agreements of 1955, concluded between the three occupying powers and the Federal Republic. With the exception of certain rights "relating to Berlin and to Germany as a whole, including the reunification of Germany and a peace settlement," full sovereignty was bestowed upon the Bonn Republic, with Allied troops no longer occupation forces but forces stationed on West German territory by agreement among legal equals. A similar agreement, concluded a bit later in 1955 between the Soviet Union and the GDR, conferred sovereignty on the latter.

Berlin had been similarly divided by 1949. Following an irreparable split in the *Kommandatura* and the subsequent abortive Soviet attempt to force the Western Allies out of the city through the "Berlin blockade," the three western sectors of the city were merged into one unit. This unit was allowed close ties with West Germany but not to merge with it completely, since, for reasons of continued access to the city through Soviet-zone (subsequently GDR) territory, the Western powers preferred to maintain ultimate control. Indeed, in 1971–72, when Berlin's status was defined, or redefined, after many "Berlin crises" and confrontations, this was done by agreement of the four powers, which fixed the details of West Berlin's status pretty much on the previous basis of a self-governing unit with close ties to the FRG but legally a separate entity. Practically nothing was said about East Berlin.

There remain the Eastern territories. Under the Potsdam agreements, these were placed under Polish administration, except for the northern portion of East Prussia which was placed under Soviet control. This was done "pending a final peace treaty." Most German inhabitants were forced to leave these areas, which were settled by Poles and Russians, respectively, and have since been treated as fully integrated portions of Poland and the Soviet Union. Under the Moscow and Warsaw treaties of 1972 the Oder-Neisse boundary between Poland and East Germany (accepted as definitive by the GDR in the early 1950s) was confirmed as "inviolable" by the FRG, as was the boundary line between the GDR and the FRG itself.

These, then, were the main steps taken in the "German question" since the demise of the Nazi Reich. The problem of their legal significance and their legal consequences is not only complex but politically significant as well. Different answers can be found for legal questions such as these: Is present Germany or are any of the present Germanies identical with prewar Germany? Is one of the two present units, or are both, independent, sovereign states in the sense of international law? The answers reflect not only different doctrines but also different political interpretations of what has happened. They reveal attitudes on the part of third countries, for instance in regard to the legitimacy of postwar and present Germany; or they reflect ways in which Germans themselves have viewed their national identity and interpreted the legitimacy of postwar political establishments. Legal self-interpretation on the part of Germans is particularly important, because it has been the basis on which postwar German governments and political elites have tried to justify their policies over the last twenty-five years, whether they were aiming at unification or separation, whether they involved recognition or nonrecognition, whether they formed the basis of a Hallstein doctrine or of charges of "splittism." In doing so, Germans have grounded their theories on the rules and principles that traditional international law furnishes in connection with questions of statehood, state identity and continuity, state succession, recognition, and so forth. To understand German reactions, we must therefore briefly sketch the answers international law provides to the problems that evolved around the "German question."

First problem: How to interpret what happened to the German Reich in 1945? A prominent lawyer, Hans Kelsen, claimed at that time that with the disappearance of the Nazi regime, and in the absence of a German successor government, the Reich had ceased to exist. This theory was rejected not only by Germans but also by predominant opinion in the Allied countries. And indeed, since conquest had not been followed by annexation, one could construe the substitution of the Allied Control Council for indigenous government as fulfilling the legal requirement of central government for the continuing statehood of a Germany still identical with the Reich. As the case of Japan showed at the time, even total occupation does not exclude continuity of the occupied entity as long as *some* kind of organized central government remains. For a while, therefore, Germany was still there, with Berlin (seat of ACC) as its capital and even within its former boundaries. The Eastern territories, "pending a peace treaty," were merely "administered" by Poland and the Soviet Union, respectively. This interpretation reflected the intention of the powers to restore indigenous government to a united, hopefully democratic Germany.

But with the demise of ACC the last vestige of central government disappeared. Chances for the restoration of one central German government became dimmer and dimmer with the outbreak of the cold war and, in its wake, the establishment of two separate German political entities. Until these were granted "sovereignty" by their respective protecting powers—that is, from 1949 to 1955—they may, under international law, have been "protectorates" of the respective powers (the FRG a joint U.S.-British-French one, the GDR a Soviet one). From 1955 on, however, they fulfilled the legal requirements of statehood: people, territory, government of their own, and capacity to act in foreign affairs. They could be considered as full-fledged independent states; even the GDR now was as independent in the legal sense as any of the other East European "satellites" of the Soviet Union.

Logically, this would seem to have implied the disappearance of the Reich as a legal entity. But there were, for a while, remnants of common statehood, such as a common citizenship (asserted, to this day, by the West Germans, while the East Germans, by now, have established their own, separate GDR citizenship). Much law was still applied throughout Germany as if it were the common law of one country. There were also the rights of the powers to act for "Germany as a whole" and in regard to Berlin (reaffirmed by the four powers anent the Four-Power Agreement on Berlin and the "normalization treaty" between the two Germanies in 1971 and 1972). Did this imply continuance of an ever-so-shadowy Germany over and above the two independent German states? This, as we shall see, has been the interpretation of most West German lawyers and politicians. It makes more legal sense, however, to consider the "old" Germany as no longer existent. The rights of the powers regarding "Germany as a whole" do not require that one considers this whole Germany as a kind of superstate over and above the two German units. They can be viewed as rights of the powers vis-à-vis the two Germanies to have a say in any future settlement of German borders or in similar "all-German" affairs, with the corresponding obligation on the part of the two German states to act only in conjunction with the powers when engaging in such matters (as they did, for instance, in regard to the Berlin arrangements of 1971–72).

This interpretation makes more legal sense regarding the Eastern territories in particular. If an overarching Germany still existed, it might still lay legal claim to them. In its absence, however, the international law principle of "effectivity"—what has become firmly established over a period of time and is likely to endure (e.g., a new state or government, or an annexation or incorporation of territory) turns into a fact which the law recognizes—leads to a more realistic interpretation of conditions in the Eastern lands. Under that interpretation, those territories are by now Polish or Soviet not only de facto but de jure, while the opposite interpretation involves absurdities such as considering the Polish "corridor" separating a German East Prussia from the main part of Germany, or the "Free City of Danzig," as still in existence. That the former interpretation seems to favor the East over the West, politically, results from the fact that international law in the long run sanctions de facto situations and developments which, in this case, were accepted by the East, while the West, for a long time, remained unreconciled to the postwar territorial status of Central and Eastern Europe.

What all of this amounts to is this: the Reich has ceased to exist. Portions of it have become parts of foreign countries (Poland, Soviet Union); one part, West Berlin, still is an inter-Allied dependency with close ties to the FRG; the remainder is organized as two independent states on the territory of the former Reich (cases of state succession), with neither of them, in the legal sense, continuing the defunct Reich or being entitled to represent Germany as a whole or to act as *sole* successor to it.

If we now turn to German legal self-interpretation, we do this, as we have said, not in order to analyze a large and confusing variety of doctrines that German lawyers have developed. Their efforts would be devoid of general interest if it were not for the fact that these are no abstract games lawyers play but "ideologies" reflecting political attitudes and objectives.

One of their chief goals, undoubtedly, was to preserve—beyond defeat, occupation, and absence of German government—some legal basis for the eventual restoration of German unity. Hence their almost unanimous rejection of the above-mentioned Kelsenian theory of disappearance and discontinuity. What happened in 1945 had not destroyed Germany; it lived on, identical with the pre-1945 Reich. Almost all of the West German jurists, moreover, assert that this continuity (*Fortbestand*) doctrine applied not only to the early postwar years but holds to this very day. Thus, identity and continuity of pre-1945 Germany were not affected by the emergence of either FRG or GDR. But while the coming into existence of at least one of these (the FRG) as a full-fledged, sovereign state was not denied, it proved exceedingly difficult, logically, to combine the continuity theory with the emergence of one or even two new Germanies.

The effort to do this produced a number of mutually contradictory doctrines. According to one—which can be called "dominating" and is accepted, for instance, by the West German constitutional court—the Reich is identical with the Federal Republic. In the FRG, and only there, has the former political and legal organization of the Reich found its continuation; the FRG is the "core" of what used to be the German Reich (hence *Kernstaat* doctrine, core-state theory). But Germany at the same time is more than its "core." Although for the time being unable to function in areas beyond the Federal Republic, in some fashion it still has legal jurisdiction over territories within its prewar boundaries; although now "in suspense," it is to be restored and resubstantiated upon the conclusion of a peace treaty with its former enemies and within boundaries to be fixed by that treaty.

The above-mentioned reservations of four-power rights regarding "Germany as a whole," of course, serve this doctrine as chief evidence. Politically, the doctrine served the policies of West Germany (and of the powers supporting it) as legal underpinning for some twenty years, and particularly throughout the period of the cold war. On it could be based such claims as the "sole representation claim" (*Alleinvertretungsanspruch*), that is, West Germany's claim to be recognized as the only legitimate German unit and thus entitled to speak for all Germans, East and West. From this there also followed the Hallstein Doctrine, according to which West Germany refused to have (or would break off) diplomatic relations with any state recognizing the GDR, as well as the policy of nonrecognition of the GDR. In more general fashion, the core-state theory can be viewed as reflection of the socioeconomic and general continuity of the Federal Republic with the earlier Germany; not only was it the largest of the two new units in terms of area and population, but it also symbolized the fact that, in contrast to the East, no fundamental change in the basic institutions of Germany had taken place in the West. In the East, on the other hand, according to this view, no legitimate German unit had arisen because what had happened there had not originated in the will of the people freely expressed but in foreign dictate. Thus the core-state doctrine is based on a theory of democratic legitimacy.

Without going into its many variants, we must briefly sketch a second theory which, whether in its form as "roof theory" (*Dachtheorie*) or as doctrine of the "partial states" (*Teilstaatentheorie*), differs at least partly from the first. While likewise proceeding from the assumption of the Reich as a continuing, overarching ("roof") unit, it places two units as "partial states" beneath it. Both FRG and GDR are states within their provisional areas of jurisdiction, somewhat like "states" within a federal structure of government, or members of the European communities in their relations to the Community as such. Both the *Teilstaaten* and that elusive and shadowy "Germany as a whole" above them are held to be subjects of international law, with their respective international rights and obligations. For instance, none of the partial states can do by itself what must be left to a future united Germany capable of acting again, such as to recognize a new boundary or to conclude a general "peace" settlement. In view of the aforementioned Allied reservations about Berlin and a future all-German settlement, this theory comes closer to reality than does the core-state theory. Yet it fails to explain how an overarching Germany lacking any remnants of organization and capacity to act can be considered a full-fledged person in international law. Politically, though, this doctrine reflects another trend in postwar German affairs, a trend toward at least de facto recognition of the existence of the GDR, and toward substituting détente for cold war; a trend that came to the fore in the 1960s. Inasmuch as it recognizes two German states at least as "partial states," it comes closer to the legal interpretations current in the East, which, as we shall see, have been based since the middle 1950s on the assumption of the existence of two independent German states (*Zweistaaten* doctrine), each entitled to international status and recognition.

It should be clear from the foregoing that different legal interpretations have had important ideological foundations and political effects. These can be discussed within the framework of an outline of power politics and power interests that led to partition and of the policies under which partition assumed the structure that exists now.

The Emergence of Partition

On May 12, 1972, a treaty on traffic matters between the FRG and the GDR was initialed at Bonn. This was the first full-fledged "state treaty" between the two. It opened the way toward the conclusion of a more general and more basic treaty between the two German entities which was initialed in the fall of that year and whose chief purpose was to "normalize" the relations between the two parts of divided Germany. On the occasion of the initialing of the first treaty, the West German negotiator said:

> The state treaty on traffic questions that was initialed today is the first treaty of this sort between the two German states. It has demonstrated that only by means of negotiations among equals, with the goal of concluding agreements that are just as binding as are agreements with third states—only in this way can genuine and assured improvement be obtained for the people of both states in Germany.

Together with the ratification of the Moscow and Warsaw treaties, which put the Western stamp of approval upon the territorial status of Eastern and Central Europe as it had emerged from World War II, and with the conclusion of the "normalization" treaty between the two Germanies, whose ratification came about in 1973 after the victory at the polls of the Brandt-Scheel government on November 19, 1972, the conclusion of the first formal treaty between FRG and GDR meant sealing a process that had begun two years earlier, when the heads of government of East and West Germany had met for the first time at two official conferences. It symbolized the end of a long political process, for the new policy of rapprochement was in sharp contrast to a decades-long history of antagonism during which the rift had constantly widened. By the same token, it seemed to seal the fate of reunification. Accepting, for the time being, partition as a fact of life, one hoped to create conditions of détente under which the two Germanies and their people might come closer to each other again. But the unprecedented bitterness with which the fight over this new approach was carried on in West Germany showed also that not everything would be easy going.

If one wants to understand meaning and emergence of both the older and the more recent policies, he must start from the givens of world power relations as they existed at the end of the Second World War. In particular, he must start from the elementary and stark fact that the present territorial and political configurations of Europe still reflect the results of that war and, hence, that the partition of Germany reflects the balance between the two superpowers as it, and they, emerged from that war. As a matter of fact, the line that divides Germany today is almost exactly the one of deepest military penetration of Western and Soviet forces into Germany at the time of German capitulation. Inasmuch as it deviates from this (some penetration of American forces into what subsequently became the Soviet zone of occupation, and the initial Soviet occupation of *all* Berlin), it was based on presurrender expectations of the powers concerning what they would possess at the moment of cessation of hostilities. But by and large, what East and West had conquered became the basis for postwar distribution of power and influence among the emerging two power blocs; it also determined the communist or noncommunist character of the respective areas. As for Germany, the powers had originally intended to undo its zonal division through restoration of a central German government on the basis of the Potsdam principles. But since they were unable to agree on how to reestablish a "democratic" Germany that would be neither pawn of the West nor puppet of the East, the dividing (zonal and sector) lines in fact remained the boundaries of their respective power spheres. Both East and West came to consider their vital interests tied up with the control of their respective portions of Germany. The cold war, in part originating from the conflict over Germany and, in turn, with its mutual suspicions and recriminations reinforcing this conflict, rendered each side ever more intent on preserving its sphere of influence in Central Europe.[1]

Realistically, short of force, a change in the balance thus established could only be obtained by mutual concessions. In particular, yielding control of East Germany so that Germany could be reunited on a Western (i.e., noncommunist) pattern would have meant such sacrifice of vital Soviet interest that it could have been expected (if at all) only as quid pro quo for similarly far-reaching concessions on the part of the Western powers (e.g., military withdrawal from a non-rearmed West Germany and agreement to subsequent neutralization of all Germany). Historians will long debate whether an arrangement of this sort was possible in the late 1940s or the early 1950s, but the ensuing Adenauer-Dulles policy of "building positions of strength from which to negotiate" (i.e., integrating a rearmed West Germany into NATO) doomed any such deal. It matters little today how one interprets that policy. Was it based on the illusory expectation that the Soviets would weaken sufficiently to compel them eventually to yield their control over much of Eastern Europe in the face of overwhelming Western strength? Or was it never really expected to achieve what it purported to achieve—in which case the aim of German "unification in freedom," or that of rollback of Communism and "liberation" of satellite nations, constituted mere cold war rhetoric. In any event, by the mid-1950s cold war policies of display of force had jeopardized any hopes for a speedy solution of the "German question."

Stating it that bluntly does not mean determinism. For years, even after the emergence of the two Germanies, much in the situation had still been in flux. Especially in the East, interest remained in some form of reunification or, at least, in exploring possibilities. The GDR constitution of 1949 was not one of a typically communist state but rather resembled Germany's pre-Nazi Weimar Constitution, as if to indicate that it might function as the basis for reestablishing an all-German government. Actual totalitarian organization of society and state, while progressing fast, was not yet complete. In East-West negotiations Stalin, as late as 1952, had seemingly agreed to all-German "free elections." As mentioned, this feeler was not reacted upon by the West; negotiations were aborted over the issue of international supervision of the elections. Actually, Adenauer shied away from the risks involved, and thus nothing came of it. But even after Stalin's death the Soviets were still hesitant concerning the all-out support of an East Berlin regime such as Walter Ulbricht's, which had just shown its dependency on Soviet tanks and artillery for maintaining itself in power against a terrorized populace (workers' uprising of June 1953). As late as 1955, at the Geneva East-West summit conference (at which the two German delegations sat at little tables next to the Big Four), both Eastern and Western instructions to the negotiating foreign ministers mentioned the powers' "common responsibility for the regulation of the German question and the reunification of Germany."

By then it was too late. The Soviets subsequently veered more and more toward a policy of building "their" Germany into a bastion of the Eastern bloc and demanded from the West recognition of its existence on an equal footing with the FRG. By that time, the Federal Republic had become fully integrated into the U.S.-led Western bloc. True, Adenauer's policy had been strongly opposed by the Social Democrats who charged that the "chancellor of the Allies" was dividing Germany for good. (A strange reversal of roles compared with 1969ff., when the now-ruling SPD, standing for recognition of partition, was incessantly indicted by the opposition CDU for giving up the cause of reunification!) But the opposition was to no avail. The majority of West Germans, at that time more interested in economic reconstruction than political unity, backed the policy of Western integration which not only brought about the West German "economic miracle" but reacceptance of Germany by and into a world that recognized the FRG as "the" legitimate Germany. The FRG's rapid rise to international status and influence, coming so fast upon the disdain in which Germans had been held because of their Nazi venture, was indeed miraculous. The ostracism of the GDR and the corresponding exclusion of its 17 million Germans from the "legitimate" Germany was the price paid for this rise and this influence. For the ruling forces in the FRG it seemed a price worth paying for having gained reentrance into the community of nations.

After the mid-1950s the gap deepened. To be sure, plans for "neutralization" of Germany, alone or together with other Central and Eastern European countries, abounded. There were plans for disengagement, demilitarization, or "thinning-out" of foreign military forces, for denuclearization, and so forth; Rapacki Plan, Eden Plan, proposals by George Kennan, etc. These, however, were paper exercises devoid, for the time being, of any chance of realization. Over and against them was the reality of cold war and confrontation, of repeated, dangerous crises, especially over the status of, and access to, Berlin; the increasing isolation of the GDR and the hardening of its regime; the attitude of nonrecognition of de facto situations considered as legally invalid, in particular in reference to the existence of the GDR and the Oder-Neisse line dividing it from Poland—an attitude reflected in the Hallstein Doctrine under which Bonn refused normalization of relations with the Eastern bloc countries (with the exception of the Soviet Union). And while this policy became less effective over the years (with many countries, especially those of the Third World, dealing with the GDR through trade missions, consulates, and, increasingly, official ties), it was successful in isolating the GDR internationally, preventing her from being represented even in the more technical international organizations. As late as 1972 the GDR was not admitted to the Stockholm Conference on the Human Environment, which led to the boycotting of the meeting by the other members of the Soviet bloc.

In internal relations between FRG and GDR, certain unofficial ties continued. Thus inter-German trade ties were established sub rosa (a strange side product of nonrecognition of the GDR enabled the GDR to profit from the lowering of tariffs by the Common Market!). But such negotiations were kept on a subgovernmental level, with Bonn refusing any more formal ties. Terminology reflected attitudes: it was never to be GDR without qualification, and one proceeded only slowly from the official "SBZ" (*Sowjetische Besatzungszone*—Soviet Zone of Occupation) to "the other part of Germany," or to putting GDR between quotation marks, or prefacing the name with an "alleged" or "so-called." The East reciprocated, not so much with terminological niceties as with invective against Bonn's "militarism," "revanchism," neo-Nazism, monopoly capitalism. Western policies of intransigence met with hardening Eastern policies. Although in the earlier 1950s Soviet and GDR policies had still paid lip-service to reunification as final objective and had suggested confederation and similar devices as first steps toward that goal, subsequent "two-Germanies" policy implied giving up that objective. In practice, it meant as much separateness as possible for the "socialist German state," a state which in the 1960s acquired ever closer cultural, trade, and political ties with the East. The crudest symbol of separation was erected in 1961 with the building of the Berlin Wall. This made the GDR a hermit kingdom toward the West by cutting off the last escape route for those of its inhabitants who wanted to go West (as millions had done over the years) and, at the same time, isolating West Berlin which previously had lively ties with East Berlin but now was reduced to precarious ties with the West. Some West Germans could still visit the GDR, and an even tinier trickle of GDRers were permitted "excursions" to the West, but the 1960s constituted the acme of separateness and division, in human and personal terms as well as politically.

Yet, with all this division, separateness, conflict, and confrontation, the powers did not pursue a policy of expansionism. Both sides in the bipolar world had come to realize that such a policy would involve unacceptable risks. With the rise of the Soviet Union to nuclear parity, the West, in particular, came to be convinced that display of force could be used for deterrence only, and not for achieving a change in the existing balance of power. This realization implied mutual, if tacit, recognition of two spheres of influence in Europe and a mutual, if tacit, agreement on the part of the superpowers not to intervene in the other's sphere. (This policy of nonintervention was practiced at an early point by Stalin in regard to Greece, and subsequently by the West at the time of the East-Berlin uprising, the Hungarian revolution, and the Berlin Wall; the Brezhnev Doctrine, dealing with intervention *within* one sphere, likewise is in line with this spheric division.)

On the other hand, reunification in freedom, that is, eventual inclusion of East Germany in a noncommunist, Western-oriented united Germany, continued to be the official goal of the Federal Republic and its Western allies. This implied revisionism. Thus a clear contradiction emerged between acknowledgment of spheres, that is, recognition of status quo as between East and West, and averred policy objectives in the German question, involving essential change. For a while one could try to plaster over this discrepancy with formulas. In the end a decision had to be made. It came with the turn of the West toward policies of détente, and the break in the stalemate on the part of the FRG through *Ostpolitik* in the late 1960s.

The Emergence of Compromise

Even prior to 1969, when the new Brandt-Scheel government at Bonn took its Eastern policy initiatives, there had been signs that the long cold-war stalemate over Germany was breaking. A West German policy of "little steps" toward rapprochement with the East—such as trying to improve economic and cultural ties—had been inaugurated even before the formation of the "grand coalition" government of 1966 (in which Willy Brandt took over the foreign ministry). But it had aimed primarily at improving relations with the Eastern countries outside the GDR and could thus, correctly, be interpreted by the latter as yet another attempt to keep it in isolation. This is why minor goodwill gestures toward East Berlin ran into a stone wall of rejection on the part of Ulbricht. He established a kind of "Hallstein Doctrine in reverse," trying to persuade Moscow and the other Eastern capitals to abstain from closer relations with Bonn as long as Bonn denied full recognition to the GDR. Except for Rumania and Yugoslavia (which did establish diplomatic relations with Bonn at that time), he succeeded.

On the other hand, significant changes occurred both in the policies of the powers and in the attitude patterns of West Germans. Détente objectives, instead of the rigid cold-war posture of the 1950s, began to characterize American policy in Europe in the wake of the Cuban missile crisis. Strategies of "flexible response" and suggestions on balancing forces replaced the strategic doctrine of "massive retaliation." France, under de Gaulle, inaugurated a policy of rapprochement with the East which included official recognition of the Oder-Neisse line. The Soviets, in turn, seemed increasingly concerned with building up their domestic structure in conjunction with the other bloc countries; for this they needed peace and quiet in their Eastern European imperium. Prodded, in addition, by a perceived new threat to their security at their Eastern flank, they thus became chiefly interested in stabilizing the European situation. They now seemed ready to accept the Western-aligned Federal Republic as a fact of life, and as a tempting trade partner to boot.

Significant changes also took place in the attitudes of the West Germans themselves. Into the mid-1960s reunification had ranked as the most important issue, surpassing any domestic or other foreign policy matters. About 1967, this attitude changed. In 1963, 42 percent of those polled about what they considered the most important problem facing Germans had mentioned reunification; in 1967, only 19 percent did so. During the election campaign of 1969, educational and welfare policies ranked at the top of concern, with reunification way down the list; instead, over 60 percent ranked détente as the most important foreign policy problem. Germans seemed to turn inward, feeling more secure abroad. The same trend emerged in regard to other "foreign" issues. In the 1950s almost every West German rejected the idea of the loss of the Eastern territories (1951: 80 percent vs. 8 percent); almost half were resigned to it by 1967. Therefore, in 1968, Brandt for the first time could come out in favor of recognition of the Oder-Neisse line as an inevitable step toward reconciliation with the Poles. In the same year, referring to reunification, he could say that "German policy today is based on the assumption that overcoming the divisions of Germany will be a long process whose duration nobody can predict." When he assumed the chancellorship it seemed that a majority of Germans had ceased to consider the two Germanies as "provisional" units.

Why, then, are the new policies so important? If, inside Germany and outside, one was now more or less agreed on the acceptance of the status quo in Europe—units, boundaries, and all—why all the commotion about *Ostpolitik*?

In a way, it is true, there is less here than meets the eye. Mere confirmation of a de facto state of affairs involves less than a big policy change. Neither the Moscow and Warsaw treaties nor the new Berlin agreements affect or were intended to affect the overall strategic and political balance of power; not a square foot of actually controlled territory was to change hands; no new or changed alignments, Eastern or Western, were in the offing. Essentially, nothing much in power terms has changed or is likely to change.

Nevertheless, there are good reasons for considering the new approach significant. One concerns international stability. While a de facto peace settlement has prevailed in Europe for more than a quarter of a century, politically—and one might add, psychologically and emotionally—it had not been accepted because of the underlying revisionism in Western, particularly West German, policy objectives. And a situation is never stable when a major actor is basically interested in revision, even if by peaceful means. There is even more insecurity when units that in fact are going concerns remain unrecognized. If West Germany now, through *Ostpolitik*, signalized that she was ready finally to make peace with the East on the basis of defeat in World War II, realizing that Germans had to pay for the excesses committed by a criminal regime but also that, as Brandt put it, "nothing is given up [by *Ostpolitik*] that was not gambled away long ago [i.e., by Hitler]," this did mean creating a new basis for peace and stability in Europe. Reflecting a change in attitudes and values away from ingrained nationalism toward moderation, it was a change that a détente-minded world (including the West) might welcome.

Another reason that the new policies are important is more mundane. Even though conditions as they had shaped up over the decades in Central Europe reflected tacit agreements and entailed practices observed more or less regularly by the powers, their unconfirmed nature left the situation ambiguous and unstable in its details. Nothing, for instance, had ever been put in writing about access rights to Berlin. Recurring incidents, even the most trivial ones (e.g., the "tailgate" incident that involved the question of how many inches the tailgates of trucks carrying U.S. soldiers from West Germany to Berlin had to be lowered for inspection), crises (over Berlin, and others), and confrontations testified to the inflammable nature of a situation in which status, rights, and obligations of actors were not clearly spelled out. Hence a mutual interest of powers in a search for more clear-cut solutions in order to avoid recurring confrontations arising from the closeness of two opposed systems, the indeterminate nature of agreements, and the geographically abnormal status of Berlin.

One can perhaps best understand what happened since 1969 by asking: What, in the situation as it had shaped up by that time, bothered the respective parties most? It will then appear that, by mutual concessions about the major points of complaint, a kind of "package deal" was possible, which has in practice been enacted (or is in the process of being acted upon) through the negotiations and agreements that began in 1970. What bothered West Germany most was the uncertain status of Berlin and the access rights on which the city's survival depends. This was also important for the other Western powers, since peace has been so easily threatened by "Berlin incidents." Equally bothersome was the separation of East Berlin from West Berlin as well as, more generally, the isolation of the people in East Germany from the West. What bothered the East most was that the West, and West Germany in particular, still refused officially to recognize the "Eastern" results of World War II, that is, the territorial and boundary arrangements in Central and Eastern Europe. Particularly bothersome was the isolation, the continuing "outlawry," of the GDR. *Ostpolitik* in the broader sense (comprising not only West German but other Western powers' policies) was the attempt to deal with these concerns by compromise without jeopardizing vital interests.

The major points in the emerging package deal can be listed, somewhat schematically, in the form of the respective concessions required from the two sides. In the case of the West:

1. West German recognition of the GDR, or, at least, normalization of FRG–GDR relations. This would pave the way for other nations to establish official ties with the GDR. It would also imply dropping what remained of the Hallstein Doctrine and would enable the GDR to enter international organizations including, together with the FRG, the United Nations.
2. West German recognition of the Oder-Neisse boundary as the definitive boundary toward Poland.
3. Normalization of West Germany's relations with Czechoslovakia through a declaration that she considered the Munich Pact of 1938 invalid from the beginning.
4. West German abstention in West Berlin from actions, especially of a governmental nature, considered provocative by the GDR (e.g., holding presidential elections or parliamentary sessions there).
5. West German renunciation of nuclear ambitions through ratification of the Non-Proliferation Treaty (NPT).

The Eastern part of the deal would include:

1. Soviet and GDR recognition of West Berlin as an entity with special ties to the FRG and guaranteed independence from control or interference on the part of the GDR.
2. Guarantee of free access to West Berlin, with undisturbed air, road, rail, and similar transportation, traiffic, and communications.
3. Permission on the part of the GDR of free, or at least freer, movement of persons between GDR and East Berlin, on the one hand, and West Berlin and FRG, on the other.
4. Soviet readiness not to interfere with the resumption of diplomatic relations and the development of economic and cultural ties between the FRG and Eastern bloc countries.
5. Soviet renunciation of claimed rights unilaterally to intervene in West Germany as a former enemy on the basis of Articles 53 and 107 of the UN Charter.

Most of this has been achieved or at least initiated by the negotiations that began in the fall of 1969 and the resulting treaties and agreements. But it was by no means an easy process. Mutual distrust necessitated establishing "linkages" (*Junktims*) between what the one side and the other were ready to do. For example, the Soviets declared that there would be no Berlin agreement (in which they were supposed to make the major concessions) unless and before the Moscow and Warsaw treaties were ratified by Bonn, which led to a counter-*junktim* by the West of tying up the ratifications with a satisfactory Berlin agreement.[2] In consequence, the finalizing of the Berlin Agreement was held up from early autumn 1971 to June 1972. The delay, in part, was also caused by the necessity of having the Four-Power Agreement on Berlin implemented by agreements on details by the Germans, one between FRG and GDR and another between GDR and the West Berlin senate (governing body). All this goes to show that it was a genuine give-and-take: Western concessions were tied up with Eastern ones; the new "peace settlement" for Europe could be based only on mutuality. It shows further that conflicts of interest were not excluded even on the same side. They were minor in the West. The chief divergencies developed between the Soviets and the GDR regime. The Soviets were interested in a speedy overall settlement because it would open the way to a general European Security Conference long desired by them (consent to which, by still another *junktim*, was made dependent by the Western powers on finalization of the Berlin agreements). But for Ulbricht, the Moscow Treaty with its rapprochement between the Soviets and the so-far-suspected, revanchist, militaristic, dangerous FRG, conjured up an understandable fear of being replaced by the FRG as the "foremost" Germany, even in Eastern eyes. It is likely that his fall from power in the spring of 1971 resulted from his obstinacy in defending against the Soviets what he perceived as the "national interest" of the GDR. Subsequently, even his successor, with whom the Soviets had hoped to come to terms more easily, offered stubborn resistance to some of the concessions involved in the Berlin arrangements. After all, GDR harassment of Western access to Berlin had been the chief means for the GDR to squeeze the West. Eventually to gobble up West Berlin after its establishment as a "special entity" or "free city" (free, that is, from ties to the West) had long been one of the GDR's ulterior objectives. In the end, GDR leadership had to comply with the Soviets. In the FRG, the Bonn opposition could not afford to bring down the Eastern treaties by voting against them, so it abstained. It goes to show that relationships between the Germanies and their respective allies, especially the big "protecting" power, still contain some elements of hegemony.

The New Settlement

The new treaties ratify the three "divisions" of Germany previously mentioned: the detachment of the Eastern territories (Warsaw Treaty of December 7, 1970), the division between FRG and GDR (Moscow Treaty of August 12, 1970 and Basic, or "Normalization" Treaty of December 21, 1972), and the special status of Berlin outside both Federal and Democratic Republics (Quadripartite Agreement on Berlin of September 3, 1971).

Even prior to 1969 Bonn had offered Moscow a "renunciation of force" (*Gewaltverzicht*) agreement, which was in line with the policy of "little steps" toward détente. The Moscow Treaty goes far beyond a mere nonaggression pact. Its core article[3] contains West Germany's acceptance of the existing European frontiers, including the Oder-Neisse line and "the frontier between the Federal Republic of Germany and the German Democratic Republic" as well as of "the territorial integrity of all States in Europe within their present frontiers." The Warsaw Treaty[4] repeats this acceptance in regard to the Oder-Neisse line. This, upon its face, constitutes recognition of the Eastern and Central European status quo, including loss of territory beyond the Oder-Neisse line and recognition of the GDR within its present frontiers. Certain West German statements seem to imply reservations, however. A letter by Bonn Foreign Minister Scheel, appended to the Moscow Treaty at its signature in 1970, stated (without the Soviet Union's taking exception) that "this treaty does not conflict with the political objective of the Federal Republic of Germany to work for a state of peace in Europe in which the German nation will recover its unity in free self-determination."

By itself, this expression of intention would not seem to contradict recognition of the existing partition. Independent nations can merge or federate, as did those independent Germanic states that merged into the Reich in 1871. But this was not enough to pacify the opposition at Bonn. In order to permit it to abstain in the final vote (May 17, 1972), the Bundestag unanimously adopted a resolution which, among others, reiterated Germany's "right to self-determination" and stated that, while the FRG raises no claims to border changes, "the treaties do not anticipate a peace settlement for Germany and do not create a legal basis for the frontiers existing today." This resolution was subsequently sent to the powers, including the Soviet Union which, again, took no exception. Although they remained silent, Moscow and Warsaw, when ratifying the treaties on their part, nevertheless left no doubt that they interpreted them as final solutions of the respective problems—boundaries and all.

That Bonn, too, considered the reservations as highly theoretical and as not precluding practical implementations such as the establishment of full-fledged diplomatic relations with Poland through exchange of ambassadors was made clear soon after. Difficulties, however, seemed to develop in regard to the GDR, which, right after the ratification of these treaties (to which it, of course, was not a formal party) claimed that they implied "recognition of the GDR by the FRG according to international law." This Bonn denied. While not refusing to conclude treaties with the GDR which would be equally as "binding under international law" as any treaties concluded with third states, Bonn insists that the GDR, in relation to the FRG, is not and can never be a "foreign country." Relations between the two are therefore "inter-German"; mutual recognition in the sense of international law is not possible (although the GDR, like the FRG, *can* have such relations with third countries), and only "plenipotentiaries," not "ambassadors," should be exchanged, etc.

The Basic Treaty (Treaty on the Basis of Relations between the FRG and the GDR), initialed by the West and East German negotiators on November 8, 1972, ratified in June 1973, and intended to put the relations of the two units and their governments on a "normal" basis, reflects these hesitations and differences. On the one hand, the two parties declare in the preamble[5] that they want to proceed from the facts as they have developed historically, and, consequently, they reaffirm inviolability of frontiers, respect of territorial integrity, and exclusive jurisdiction of each unit within its domain. Each party renounces any claim to represent or act for the other German state. This would seem to imply for the FRG giving up Hallstein Doctrine, *Alleinvertretungsanspruch,* and any other exclusivist attitude, at the same time recognizing, for all practical purposes, the GDR within its present boundaries. On the other hand, the FRG insisted, successfully, upon inserting into the preamble a reference to the difference in views of the two units "on fundamental questions including the national question," clearly a reference to the hope for eventual reunification as well as the disagreement of the two regimes in regard to the question whether, despite partition, the Germans still are one nation (something the GDR leadership now denies; see below). In other words, the treaty constitutes recognition of the status quo on the part of the FRG, except for a mental reservation regarding change in the indefinite future. It further constitutes, for all practical purposes, recognition by the FRG of the GDR and its regime through the development of "normal, good-neighborly relations . . . on the basis of equality" (art. 1). For this purpose, the two agree to exchange "permanent missions" (art. 8). Even though the GDR failed in its demand to have the representatives given the rank and title of "ambassadors," this is a mere semantic concession: the "plenipotentiaries" (*Bevollmächtigte*) will represent separate, independent governments and states.

The importance of the treaty for future relations between the two German states and for future European relations in general will depend on its implementation. The decisive election victory in 1972 of its West German initiator, the Brandt-Scheel government, gave it a clear mandate to implement its policy of détente. The treaty itself provides for implementation in the form of appended and/or additional agreements on easing personal contacts, visits, renewed cultural exchanges, and so forth. Much will depend on whether the GDR regime feels secure enough to engage, on its part, in bona fide policies of détente and meaningful, far-reaching measures of rapprochement.

During the negotiations of the Eastern treaties the Soviets had stated that, when renunciation of force between the Soviet Union and the FRG had become binding, they would consider the "enemy state" clauses of the UN Charter as having become inapplicable. This takes care of "Eastern concession 5" in our earlier list. It seems that they were also ready to permit normalization of FRG relations with bloc countries (see Eastern concession 4). While this might involve certain risks of loosened intrabloc ties, the general benefits, especially for the economies of Eastern bloc countries, seem to outweigh these, and any danger of one or the other of these countries becoming too closely aligned with the West seems to be ruled out by the precedent of 1968 and the threat of the Brezhnev Doctrine. West German rapprochement with Poland has been facilitated by Poland's permitting repatriation of ethnic Germans still residing in the former East German provinces[6], a concession made upon conclusion of the Warsaw Treaty.

Taking up diplomatic relations with other bloc countries was on Bonn's agenda by summer 1972. Such normalization of relations has been most significant in regard to Czechoslovakia, the only Communist country sharing borders with West Germany. Bonn had declared that it considered the Munich Pact of 1938 (under which the Sudeten territory was detached from Czechoslovakia) as "no longer valid." Prague wanted it considered null and void "from the outset." Bonn was afraid that nullity *ab initio* might render Sudeten Germans liable to prosecution in Czechoslovakia for having committed treason (because in that case they would have remained Czechoslovakian citizens after 1938).[7] In the summer of 1973 the two countries agreed on the resumption of diplomatic relations on the basis of simply declaring the Munich agreement "void with regard to their mutual relations" and agreeing that no Sudeten Germans would be prosecuted in Czechoslovakia except for war crimes. Actual establishment of relations, delayed over disagreements concerning the FRG's right to represent West Berlin authorities, took place in December 1973.

The Berlin situation, as noted, was for the West the most precarious. After the city's split-up in the late 1940s, access to the city (except by air), upon which its survival depended, was forever at the mercy of the Soviets and/or the GDR authorities. Here the East had to make the more far-reaching concessions. The West's insistence on a Berlin solution as precondition for finalizing the Eastern treaties proved good diplomacy. After a good deal of hesitation of its own and of prodding the GDR, the Soviet Union accepted the major demands of the West. We have placed them on our list as Eastern concessions 1, 2, and 3. While the Western powers, in the Quadripartite Agreement,[8] reconfirm West Berlin's status as still under the original occupation regime and thus not a constituent part of the FRG, the Soviets admit the city's actual ties with the West as they have "grown" over the decades, as well as the general Western orientation of the city. All existing economic, cultural, legal, and other ties between West Berlin and West Germany will be "maintained and developed." As a counter concession, no "constitutional or official acts" (such as Bundestag sessions, considered "provocative" by the GDR) will be performed by West German authorities in West Berlin. Moreover, its continued status as a

Western island surrounded by Eastern territory will be safeguarded by the Soviets guaranteeing unimpeded and even facilitated transit between the city and West Germany. Details have been spelled out in subsequent agreements between the FRG and the GDR, and between the latter and the West Berlin government; they refer to sealed passage of goods by rail and road, mere formal identification of persons, and so on. But the chief political advance is that the Soviets are committed to see to it that the GDR acts in conformity with these rules. There can no longer be a threat (as there was in the past) of the Soviets, by agreement with the GDR, transferring their rights to control access to the latter, leaving the GDR to do as it pleases. The powers agreed that "the situation which has developed in the area shall not be changed unilaterally." It means a Soviet commitment to détente, as far as Berlin is concerned.

The Soviets further conceded that Bonn may represent West Berlin in international organizations and conferences, that West Berliners may travel to Eastern countries on West German passports, and that treaties made by the FRG may be extended to West Berlin. In return, the Soviet Union was permitted to open a consulate in West Berlin (with a limited number of persons allowed to serve in it). Regarding movement of persons, the agreements likewise open up new possibilities. The Wall becomes more permeable, at least in the West-East direction, with West Berliners, upon application, permitted visits to East Berlin and the rest of the GDR for a maximum of thirty days a year, an increased number of crossing points, improvement of telephonic communications, etc. GDR citizens are still excluded from West Berlin, but there will be improved contact between GDR and FRG. West Germans will be allowed into the GDR more easily than heretofore, and the GDR has promised to permit GDR citizens to travel to the FRG "in cases of urgent family matters" and to lower the age limits from sixty-five to sixty for those, pensioners, already permitted to visit relatives in the FRG. This is not much, but it is a beginning. The wall in Berlin (and the corresponding barbed wired and mined boundary between GDR and FRG) will vanish only with the complete normalization of relations between the two states. Until the difficulties encumbering that goal are overcome, the new policies, despite the progress made, cannot be said to have achieved their major objective: that of improving contacts and relations among the people in a divided country.

Our list of mutual concessions mentioned ratification by the FRG of the nuclear nonproliferation treaty. While this issue is not usually referred to in connection with problems of partition, it is easy to see its connection with general détente, and thus with *Ostpolitik.* The Soviets have long considered West German accession to the NPT a vital element in a new European settlement. Actually, it is not much of a concession. Bonn, by its treaties with the West of 1955, is already committed not to produce ABC weapons; NPT would only add a commitment not to obtain them from others. Some German nationalists, however, have at times voiced dreams of

West German access to such weapons, e.g., indirectly upon and through European federation. But no one, including the Western powers, can be happy about Germans, directly or indirectly, getting their fingers on the nuclear trigger. And Germany, of all countries, can least afford to have such ambitions. Strategically, whatever protection through deterrence is possible, they have already in the "big" deterrent of the United States. Since Bonn has signed the treaty and seems satisfied regarding the problems that arose in connection with international inspection, it seems reasonable to expect ratification in the near future.

Arguments Surrounding Present Policies

Before discussing effects of partition and policy prospects, we must deal with a few major arguments that have surrounded *Ostpolitik* and related policies. It is important to understand the objections that have been raised against their underlying assumptions, especially when leveled by a West German opposition which, although reduced in strength by the 1972 election, is still a force to reckon with. Together with hesitations in the East, the charges could threaten the effectiveness of the new settlement.

1 One argument, raised against the Moscow and Warsaw treaties in particular, is to the effect that there was no genuine give and take: West Germany, while "legitimizing" the GDR and, indeed, the entire Eastern setup by foregoing its "rightful claims" to reunification and a better territorial settlement through an eventual peace treaty, got nothing in return. This argument overlooks several factors. One refers to "rightful claims." However "rightful," claims that cannot in practice be realized are worthless currency in the diplomatic game of give-and-take. By foregoing such claims, West Germany "gave" little, if anything. By conferring "legitimacy," the West may indeed have "given" something of value to the East, but there were at least two "returns." One is in a Berlin settlement favorable to the West. The Moscow and Warsaw treaties cannot be evaluated in isolation; their counterpart is the Quadripartite Agreement on Berlin, and it is clear which side this agreement favors.[9] Second, a perhaps more elusive but potentially important "return" for the West lies in the effects which giving up revisionist claims may have on Soviet controls over bloc nations. For many years, fears of a German comeback tied countries such as Poland to the Soviet Union, the only country that could protect them against German "revanchism." Freed from such fears (probably imaginary but still real in the minds of Eastern leaders and people), these countries may become freer in their relationships with the Soviets. And in the case of the GDR, a regime that no longer feels isolated and ostracized may well be in a position to ease up on its controls over its own people.

2 Place names often serve as shorthand for significant policies and

events: Munich, Locarno, Rapallo. A frequent objection to *Ostpolitik* is to the effect that it constitutes a new "Rapallo"; that is, that it foreshadows a political realignment of West Germany, which might give up its ties with the West and draw closer to the East.[10] Some even profess fear of a full-fledged political if not military alignment of West Germany with the Soviet Union, in return perhaps for the latter's release of "its" Germany, i.e., reunification. It is almost ludicrous to expect such a radical break with Western orientation from any of the presently leading parties or groups in West Germany. The Brandt-Scheel coalition vies with the CDU opposition in professing loyalty to the West; there is anxious insistence on continuing protection by the United States and the continued stationing of American troops in Germany. A renewal of the "Eastern orientation" of the 1920s, which was based on a political alliance of rightist and leftist radicals, "geopoliticians," and so forth, is simply not in the cards. The term "Locarno" rather than "Rapallo" might be applied to present policies. Locarno had meant transforming the "truce" of Versailles into genuine peace as far as Germany's western boundaries were concerned, but there was no recognition of the boundaries with Poland, no "eastern Locarno." Now there is. As far as Soviet policies are concerned, Rapallo raises the question of their ultimate aims. To the ideologists of anticommunism these are expansionist, but more likely the Soviet leaders, presiding over a petit bourgeois, increasingly "consumerist" society, have long given up world-revolutionary aims. They seem more interested in stabilizing the present European setup than in further penetration. Even if an opportunity arose to extend controls further into Europe, one might question whether that would be in the Soviet interest. Could they hope to control a vastly strengthened, possibly reunited Germany, which, no longer tied to the West, would be free to pursue independent policies? They must have learned (from a deal datelined 1939) that alignment with a "Greater Germany" may backfire. Even in the event that Germany should turn communist, could they welcome another communist power on their flank, in addition to the one in the East? Could they afford sacrificing the GDR, either through amalgamation with the FRG or through the inevitable loss of status that would result for the "socialist German state" from an Eastern alignment of the so-much-more-weighty FRG? How would such sacrifice affect the remainder of the communist bloc?

3 Another objection, somewhat related to the "Rapallo" argument, is to the effect that present policies tend to weaken NATO, impede West European integration, and stifle the American will to defend Europe. But NATO, in a strategic-political sense, can hardly be said to exist anymore as far as the defense of Western Europe is concerned. Instead, there is an American–West German alliance. As a defensive alliance, all major groups in West Germany want NATO to continue. As for West European integration, Brandt as well as the opposition want to see it strengthened. Brandt was instrumental in securing British entry into EEC and in

obtaining the Soviets' "recognition" of the European Communities. As far as U.S. resolve to stand by Western Europe is concerned, this seems to depend more on general developments in U.S. foreign policy (e.g., a turn toward "neoisolationism") than on *Ostpolitik*. As we shall see, it might be possible *failure of Ostpolitik* that could cause America to withdraw from Europe.

4 Finally, we may mention a somewhat strange objection that has been raised regarding the two Germanies', or rather the GDR's, entrance into the UN. This, one fears, would give the latter a chance to level constant charges against the FRG, which would burden that organization with yet another conflict situation. But what, one may ask, is a peace organization for, if not for tackling major world problems? West Germans might welcome an opportunity to discuss and disprove in open forum accusations they consider unfounded. As for détente policies in general, the admission of the Germans may open the way toward that of the Koreans and possibly others. Presence of portions of divided countries not only in the UN but in other world organizations, in turn, might serve to alleviate in some measure some of the problems that arise from their partition.

Effects of Partition

The effects of the partition of Germany have now been felt for over a quarter of a century. Since Germany used to be a highly developed country with a closely integrated society, much more space than is available here would be needed to present the merest outline of all the changes that have occurred through partition. It has affected the political and social structures under which Germans in the two parts of the country live, as well as their economy, their legal systems, their educational systems, their cultural affairs, population trends, even their style of life. All we can do here is present a few highlights.

The effects of partition were profoundly influenced by the fact that the division of Germany coincided with (indeed, was caused by) the division of Europe into the two politically and ideologically opposed blocs of communist and noncommunist countries. Historically, separation of an area with basically similar institutions and way of life (such as Austria from the rest of Germany) has not usually caused as much separateness and dissimilarity as does a detachment based on the revolutionary revamping of everything. The latter occurred when the Soviets introduced into "their" Germany the politics and institutions of Soviet communism. Thus the chief effect of German partition, from which everything else flows, has been the contrast of political structure.

Consider the following: here, a one-party state, with the leadership of the Socialist Unity Party (SED) in control of all areas of political and social life; there, a liberal-democratic polity under which the basic social, economic, and general characteristics of the earlier Germany continued. Here, the attempt to fashion a "classless society" through expropriation of land estates, extinction of the feudal class of estate owners, and collectivization of agriculture; a nationalization of industries that meant the destruction of the bourgeoisie and the establishment of state-owned enterprises and a planned economy; in sum, a "workers' and peasants' state" under the control of a party-political elite. There, a "class society," with organized labor and management competing for influence in a system of "social market economy" that combines principles of free enterprise with cartel and similar restrictive tendencies as well as comprehensive welfare-state features. Here, a system based on controlled opinion and the attempt to instill one particular *Weltanschauung:* Marxism-Leninism. There, freedom of competing and widely differing opinions and attitudes within a system of multiple political parties as well as in education, the media, etc. Here, an almost complete break with the past; there, acceptance of the past which one tries to develop in agreement with the requirements of a modernized society but which sometimes, with authoritarian remnants, impinges on such development. With developments over the past twenty-five years having gone into such extreme opposites, it is hard to visualize how two so different systems *could* be reunified, even in the unlikely event that the international situation allowed for reunion. As we shall see, things have developed so far apart that the very concept of common nationhood is questionable. The best that can reasonably be expected is improvement in the relationships between the two units and their people—i.e., peaceful coexistence and increased cooperation.

In this respect, the area of the economy is perhaps the most promising. Countries with opposed systems can at least trade with each other. As early as 1951, when the GDR had hardly come into existence, "interzonal" trade agreements between the two systems had rendered inter-German trade possible. Although each unit has since become more and more integrated with its respective economic region (the FRG with the Common Market, the GDR with Comecon), this trade has increased over the years. The degree of the GDR's integration with the East is revealed by the fact that over 40 percent of its foreign trade is with the Soviet Union. Still, trade with the FRG, amounting to 10 percent, comes second. On the other hand, for the FRG, by now one of the largest trading countries of the world, trade with the GDR constitutes only 2 percent of its foreign trade volume. Considering that Germany once was one market, this is not much, but at least there is something that can be developed in the future.[11]

If we now consider, not movements of goods but movements of people, the picture is quite different. There the trend has gone from relative freedom to more and more restriction. Only lately, in consequence of *Ostpolitik,* has there been some improvement. In the beginning, there was the tremendous migration of millions of refugees and expellees[12] from the detached provinces in the East as well as other European countries and, soon thereafter, from the GDR, into the Western part of Germany. Expellees came to the FRG (in part after having been in the GDR for a while) in the immediate postwar period. Their number has been estimated at over 10 million. The number of refugees who fled the GDR, chiefly in the 1950s, amounted to over 3 million; since the building of the Berlin wall closed the last escape hatch in 1961, a mere trickle of refugees has made it to the West. With the improvement of living conditions in the GDR, renewed large-scale migration from GDR to FRG would be unlikely even if freedom of movement were restored. But in the 1950s and early 1960s the movement constituted a severe bloodletting for the GDR, in particular since many refugees were highly qualified professionals. In the West, in turn, the influx of so many millions (about one-fifth of the FRG's population) confronted the fledgling republic with severe problems of integration. But the problem turned into a blessing: economic reconstruction and the steep rise of GNP would have been impossible without the manpower and skills furnished by these millions. Politically, too, most of them were successfully integrated. An early "special interest" expellee party disappeared, its demands having been satisfied by favorable legislation. The "right to the homeland" claimed by expellee organizations was interpreted as right to regain territorially what had been lost only by a radical minority. Still, the latter's agitation for a long time rendered politically infeasible any major party's or any government's advocacy of accepting the Oder-Neisse line or of recognizing the GDR. As noted, this became feasible only with the radical change in attitudes around 1969, and it remains to be seen to what extent resentments by this group and its sympathizers will be able to impede progress toward "normalization" of the relations between the two Germanies. Over the long pull, things look promising: the young and middle-aged, through intermarriage and otherwise, are so successfully integrated with their present "homeland" that chiefly oldsters still identify themselves with their former *Heimat.* Problems remain, but on the whole the German refugee problem has been solved better than that, say, of the Indian subcontinent (let alone Palestine).

How have the personal relationships between the Germans on both sides of the line shaped up? With the new agreements of 1971–72, new possibilities have opened up. Until recently, however, impeded or nonexistent contacts have been among the most vexing problems. Germans in the GDR have been shut-in almost completely; they might travel to Outer Mongolia or Bulgaria, but only in exceptional cases would they be permitted to visit any Western country (including, of course, the FRG). In the mid-1960s an exception was made for GDR citizens over sixty-five years old. An annual 1 million have since made use of this opportunity. West Germans, who were permitted to travel to the GDR to visit relatives or for business or similar reasons, availed themselves of this possibility at the same rate, approximately 1 million a year; the annual Leipzig trade fair is a rare occasion on which the regime has made it relatively easy to get a visa. There has been no direct air connection between FRG and GDR. Postal contacts have been impeded by delays and controls, while communication by phone or telegraph has suffered from a dearth of lines. In the area of cultural contacts, the two countries have been so mutually suspicious of these being exploited for propaganda purposes that there has been almost nothing in the way of meetings of professionals or scholars, guest performances of theater groups, and so forth. Very little contact has taken place even in so "unpolitical" an area as sports. But the participation of the GDR in the Olympic games at Munich in 1972 has shown what is possible; it also showed (with its separate teams for the two Germanies, the hoisting of the GDR flag, the playing of its hymn) the separateness of the two. As far as youth meetings are concerned, there have been no student exchanges, and very little else, except for more radical West German groups occasionally visiting with their counterparts in the GDR. As long as the battle of the ideologies continues, little by way of improvement can be expected.

In the area of education and culture the degree of alienation is perhaps highest of all. The GDR leadership claims for itself custodianship of that part of historic German culture that, when it antedates Marx and Engels, they call "humanist" (e.g., Goethe and Schiller); when it is more recent, they identify with "progressivism," "socialism," etc. If they live up to these standards, contemporary West German cultural products (e.g., literary publications) are admitted; if not, they are banned as "reactionary," "decadent," and so forth. West Germany in principle admits all GDR publications in book form, but there are restrictions on newspapers. Occasionally GDR authors whose writings cannot be published in the East are published in the West. The same selectivity prevails regarding movies. As for radio and television broadcasts, Eastern ones can be freely heard and seen in the West, while Western ones are not supposed to be received by East Germans. Of course, control in this respect is difficult, and many East Germans have been able to keep up this contact with the Western world. There still is a window to the West.

In the West the traditional German class system of education still exists (reserving higher education to a relatively small group that traditionally has staffed the professions, the higher posts in public and economic life, etc.), although efforts are being made to ameliorate it; but it is a liberal system in that it allows for a great variety of subject matter, approach, and ideas. In the East, education is based on narrowly controlled indoctrination. On the other hand, higher education is accessible to all; it is tuition-free, and upper-level high school and university students are even paid salaries. It is a system "open to talent" and in this respect is more democratic than that of the FRG.

The increasing alienation of the two Germanies is, perhaps, most poignantly revealed in what happened to the German legal system. We refer here not to the way in which the administration of justice is organized (e.g., recruitment of judges, structure of the court system); here the ways of the two states parted at an early point. We refer, rather, to the substantive rules of law whose uniform codification for all of Germany had constituted one of the great achievements of the Bismarckian Reich. This legal unity in areas like civil, criminal, and family law had been preserved under succeeding regimes (Weimar, Nazi). As noted, the early postwar period continued the assumption of legal oneness, assisted by the theory that, over and above any German fragment states, there was still an overarching Germany (*Gesamtdeutschland*) with a common German citizenship, common codes of law, common legal procedures, and so on. Thus uniform law, though in many respects differently applied and interpreted, prevailed in the two parts of Germany far into the 1960s. It safeguarded a minimum of common concepts, often basic for ways and styles of life, such as definitions of major crimes, basic ideas about marriage, inheritance, etc. But this, too, has been changing. While in the FRG amendments of the various legal codes (e.g., reform of criminal law and procedure) have so far been only partial ones, the GDR has proceeded to replace one after the other by completely new codes. Thus a new code on family law revamps the entire field of marriage and divorce, paternal relations to children, etc. With the revamping of society on the basis of new "socialist" principles, this was to be expected. Inasmuch as basic legal concepts shape ways of life, the gap between the life styles of the two Germanies and their inhabitants is deepening. There still are legal contacts between the respective judicial and administrative authorities, e.g., in regard to mutual legal assistance in specific (civil or criminal) cases; there is here a remnant of the idea of not being "foreign countries" in one's relations. But this amounts to little. Basically, the ways are parting. Are Germans still one nation?

Outlook

Nationhood, today one of the strongest bonds tying groups of people together, has been defined as the feeling of belonging together, as the will to live together in one political unit, separate from and not controlled by any other. This feeling, or will, underlies all policies of "national self-determination," strivings for unification, merger, secession, as the case may be. In the case of divided countries it poses the problem of national identity. How do divided countries define their identity? Although living in separate states—and, perhaps, resigned to it—do their people (still) consider themselves one nation? Or do all or most of them, those in both units or only those in one, now consider themselves as separate nations? To what extent, that is, have new identity feelings developed? Have the attitudes of elites, or specific elite groups, in this respect developed differently from those of masses of the people?

In the case of divided Germany it is more difficult to answer these questions than one might assume. From what we have said earlier, it would appear that Germans, in their vast majority, and whatever the specific policies they advocate on the "German question," still feel one "nation-wise." They may have written off national unification as a practical policy objective but still seem to consider it the ultimate goal. Hence their insistence on an ultimate right freely to determine their fate and on the Allies' responsibility to enable them to do so; hence the insistence of their lawyers and ideologists on the concept of one Germany over and above the two states; hence the concern of those in charge of education and public opinion not to let die this feeling of national identity.

This applies in the main to West Germany, however; it has become doubtful as far as the GDR is concerned. There, developments have gone from one extreme to the other. In the early postwar period when, as noted, leading groups in West Germany were less concerned with reunification than with Western alignments and integration, GDR leadership (as well as opposition groups in West Germany, including an intellectual and religious elite) were "German nationalists" in the sense of strongly emphasizing the unity of Germans and their right to be reunited. At that time, SED leaders never tired of blaming the West for the German split, whether setting up the FRG as a separate state before the GDR "had to" follow suit, whether integrating West Germany with NATO (whereupon the GDR "had to" become member of the Warsaw Pact organization and to rearm on its part, too), or in many other ways. In other words, the East charged the West with "splitism," with being responsible for partition. Then came the time when the emphasis was shifted to the independence and sovereignty of the "two German states," but it was still to be two states in one nation. As late as 1968 the new constitution of the GDR defined the GDR as a "socialist state of German nationality" (*Staat deutscher Nation*). Since then, however, in agreement with its attempts to "set off" (*abgrenzen*) the GDR ever more sharply from its West German neighbor, GDR leadership has developed a new theory of nationhood, according to which national identity or separateness depend on social structure. The GDR has now emerged as a "socialist nation" (not merely a socialist state), and the former national identity of Germany has been destroyed by the degeneration of West Germany into "a capitalist NATO state with restricted national sovereignty." With the development not only of a separate political and economic structure but also of a separate "socialist" culture and way of life, the GDR has found its own, separate national identity.

This is now the doctrine of the political elite in the GDR. Whether and to what extent it has affected the feelings of a larger proportion of those ruled is hard to assess. The spontaneous outpouring of "German" national feeling on the occasion of Brandt's visit to Erfurt in 1970 pointed in the other direction. But one cannot write off the new policy, or doctrine, as mere propaganda. In the absence of free expression of opinion in the GDR it is difficult to establish its effectiveness. It may be that the older generation preserves more "all-German" feelings than the younger ones. One must not forget that about one-half of the present population of the GDR never witnessed another system. To some extent, the republic is "theirs." And whatever their attitude toward the regime and the system, we know that many have developed pride in its achievements, which, to a large extent, have been owing to their work, their efforts, their sacrifices. Many resent a frequently condescending West German attitude toward them and the GDR, while the materialism, consumerism, and money consciousness of the West Germans seem to lend credence to the leadership's claims of the GDR's superiority. It certainly would be premature to give full credence to the claims of new nationhood. But there *is* a problem here. The past has seen few (if any) cases in which integrated nations were split not only territorially but into completely different, antagonistic *systems.* Living under them may eventually produce what according to the rulers of East Germany exists already now: a separate nation according to the feelings of the people at large, expressed in that *plébiscite de tous les jours* which is the basis of genuine national identity. Hence the urgency, for those who want to preserve the unity of the German nation in both states, of improved relations and more frequent and intimate contacts.

Peace in our time, as stressed earlier, depends on the chief powers defending, and staying within, their mutually agreed-upon spheres, which happens to place some divided countries, such as Germany and Korea, on opposite sides. This bodes ill for reunification. Major prerequisites for German unification seem to be: (1) a foreign policy constellation under which the United States and the Soviet Union could agree to release "their" Germanies from alignment with their blocs; (2) an inter-German agreement on the kind of system (political, economic) that would prevail in a reunited Germany (since it is hard to see how two opposed systems could coexist in one political unit); and (3) all this to be achieved within a reasonable period of time, so that mutual estrangement has not gone so far as to create a separate nationhood sentiment, especially in the East. Neither of the first two conditions is likely to materialize soon; thus reunification, in all likelihood, will remain a dream.

On the other hand, acceptance of partition does not preclude détente and closer relations between the divided units. On the contrary, whatever remains of hope for coming closer to each other again is predicated upon relaxation of tension. The policies tending in that direction have already been discussed. But even though they may be embodied in solemn treaties, their effectiveness depends on the continued readiness of the parties to improve and implement an atmosphere of détente. Otherwise they will slip back into mutual suspicion, hostility, concern for "face," and confrontation. In Germany, the new approach hangs in the balance. Much, in particular, depends on domestic developments in the Federal Republic. If, following the 1972 elections, readiness for conciliation with Eastern nations such as Poland, and willingness to strengthen the ties with the Germans living beyond a no-longer "iron" curtain despite the nature of their regime prove stable and lasting, this might inaugurate a process through which the problems of division might be solved for a long stretch of time. That is, they may be solved not in the way that in the past seemed the only fashion—reunification—but by alleviating the effects of a division which, as such, seems impossible to overcome. Paradoxically, it may turn out that the way to reunite people (families, friends, others) is through renouncing political reunification and through recognizing partition. Such an outcome might well prove a lesson for all, or most, divided nations.

This leads to the final question of how developments in the German issue will affect international, and especially European, relations. We have already mentioned the linkage that has been established between the finalization of the Eastern treaties and the Berlin Agreement, on the one hand, and the holding of a European Security Conference and negotiations on Mutual Balanced Force Reduction in Europe, on the other. Now the latter two get-togethers have begun. Their outcome will affect the overall relationships between the two blocs in Europe (their strategies, NATO and Warsaw Pact machinery, etc.) but also the relations between the superpowers and their respective "clients." Thus, much is at stake in policies by and toward divided Germany. The major "stakes" can perhaps be listed as follows:

For the Federal Republic the issue is between return to nationalist revisionism and moderation; domestically, between progressivism and conservatism. For the Democratic Republic the issue is hard-line "separatism" vs. some amount of liberalization within, and restoration of ties not only with the other Germany but the world at large. For the Soviets, where Brezhnev seems to have staked a good deal of his power and prestige on success of his policies toward Germany, what may well be at stake is the influence of cold-war hard-liners vs. supporters of détente and rapprochement with the West (in particular, the United States: e.g., further arms controls). For the other Eastern bloc countries the new policies may render possible a degree of autonomy (from Moscow) and of liberalization (internally), while renewed fear of Germany would presage increased Soviet controls and "re-Stalinization" in their domestic affairs.

In the West, and particularly for the United States, failure of *Ostpolitik* and détente might result in either of two opposites. It might revive a spirit of cold-war hostility against the communist world and a policy of antagonism in which a strongly armed, strongly anti-Soviet West Germany would be a major ally but where there might also be U.S. attempts to restore a previous hegemonial position vis-à-vis all NATO allies. But intentions and success in this respect appear unlikely, and another alternative might materialize. Increasing American disillusionment with, and withdrawal from, European affairs, in which case the European countries, having to shift for themselves, might well become open to increasing Soviet influence. Successful implementation of *Ostpolitik,* on the other hand, would not only allay fears by countries such as France of revived German nationalism and revisionism but also diminish dependency on U.S. protection, thus rendering them more independent.

This leads to a last question: Might not stronger *political* integration of West European countries (especially the Nine) solve many of these problems? Might not a united Western Europe be able to stand on its own against any threats of Soviet dominance? And might not the age-old problem of German nationalism find its resolution in a merger with other nations and a common "Europeanism" overarching the somewhat petty national separateness of former big powers now reduced to lesser status? There is not, at this point, much hope that Europeans will coalesce politically and ideologically in the near future. But in the long run this might provide the best solution of the German problem. Should the GDR go its separate way toward nationhood, Germans may feel they are still one *Kulturnation* but politically separate for good (as in the case of Austrians, or German-speaking Swiss). More than a decade ago the German philosopher Karl Jaspers suggested a solution under which the Soviets would permit liberalization of East Germany against a Western commitment to continued separation and the status of permanent neutrality for the GDR on the Austrian pattern. In that or a similar event it might not be mere wishful thinking to believe that the other Germans might sometime in the future merge their national identity with their European neighbors. Something like this may evolve when, not only in Germany but all over the world, the idea of the political nation becomes less and less persuasive in the face of increasing needs for, and trends toward, international integration.

Documentary Appendix

From *Declaration by Allied Powers on the Defeat of Germany and the Assumption of Supreme Authority* (June 5, 1945)

> The governments of the United States, the Soviet Union, the United Kingdom, and the provisional government of the French Republic hereby assume supreme authority with respect to Germany, including all the powers possessed by the German government, the High Command, and any state, municipal, or local government or authority. The assumption . . . of the said authority and powers does not affect the annexation of Germany. . . .[13]

From *Potsdam Conference, July 17–August 2, 1945*

A Political Principles.

1 In accordance with the Agreement on Control Machinery in Germany, supreme authority in Germany is exercised, on instructions from their respective governments, by the commanders-in-chief of the armed forces of the U.S.A., the U.K., the U.S.S.R., and the French Republic, each in his own zone of occupation, and also jointly, in matters affecting Germany as a whole, in their capacity as members of the Allied Control Council.

2 So far as is practicable, there shall be uniformity of treatment of the German population throughout Germany.

3 The purpose of the occupation of Germany by which the Allied Control Council shall be guided are to:

4 . . . prepare for the eventual reconstruction of German political life on a democratic basis and for eventual peaceful cooperation in international life by Germany. . . .[14]

From *Basic Law of the Federal Republic of Germany* (May 23, 1949)

Preamble, last sentence: The entire people of Germany are called upon to achieve in free self-determination the unity and freedom of Germany.

Article 146: This Basic Law shall cease to be in force on the day on which a constitution adopted by a free decision of the German people comes into force.

From *Constitution of the German Democratic Republic* (1968)

Article 1: The German Democratic Republic is a socialist state of German nationality (*Staat deutscher Nation*).

From *Statement by Dean Acheson, U.S. Secretary of State, on the Illegality of the East German Government* (October 12, 1949)

The U.S. government considers that the so-called G.D.R., established on October 7 in Berlin, is without any legal validity or foundation in the popular will. This new government was created by Soviet and Communist fiat. . . . The new government is not the outcome of a free popular mandate. . . . Such a government cannot claim by any democratic standard to speak for the German people of the Soviet zone; much less can it claim to speak in the name of Germany as a whole. . . . The U.S. government and the governments associated with it will continue to give full support to the government of the F.R.G. at Bonn in its efforts to restore a truly free and democratic Germany.[15]

From *Convention on Relations between the Three Powers and the FRG* (May 26, 1952)

Article 1 The F.R.G. shall have the full authority of a sovereign state over its internal and external affairs.

Article 2 In view of the international situation, which has so far prevented the reunification of Germany and the conclusion of a peace settlement, the Three Powers retain the rights and the responsibilities, heretofore exercized or held by them, relating to Berlin and to Germany as a whole, including the reunification of Germany and a peace settlement. . . .[16]

From *Statement by the Government of the Soviet Union on Relations with the GDR* (March 25, 1954)

1 The Soviet Union establishes the same relations with the G.D.R. as with other sovereign states. The G.D.R. shall be free to decide on internal and external affairs, including the question of relations with West Germany, at its discretion. . . .[17]

From *Joint Declaration by Allied High Commission on the Status of East Germany* (April 8, 1954)

The three governments represented in the Allied High Commission will continue to regard the Soviet Union as the responsible power for the Soviet zone of Germany. These governments do not recognize the sovereignty of the East German regime, which is not based on free elections, and do not intend to deal with it as a government. They believe that this attitude will be shared by other states, who, like themselves, will continue to recognize the F.R.G. as the only freely elected and legally constituted government in Germany. The Allied High Commission also takes this occasion to express the resolve of its governments that the Soviet action shall not deter them from their determination to work for the reunification of Germany as a free and sovereign nation.[18]

From *Federal Republic, Minister of Foreign Affairs, Statement on the Hallstein Doctrine* (October 19, 1957)

The government of the Federative People's Republic of Yugoslavia, having expressed its decision to establish diplomatic relations with the so-called German Democratic Republic, the government of the Federal Republic of Germany has the honor to communicate to the Yugoslav government the following:

The federal government has never left any doubt that it would have to regard as an unfriendly act, directed against the vital interests of the German people, the establishment of diplomatic relations with the government in central Germany—which lacks all democratic legitimacy—by governments with which the F.R.G. maintains diplomatic relations. . . .

With the exception of a few states, which form one of the power blocs, nearly all the other states of the world maintain diplomatic relations with the F.R.G. alone and not with the so-called G.D.R. . . . By the decision now taken, the Yugoslav government ranges itself unequivocally on the side of the states first mentioned and identifies itself with a policy toward the German people that is pursued only by these states.

In the situation created by the unilateral decision of the Yugoslav government, the federal government finds itself constrained to terminate diplomatic relations between the Federal Republic of Germany and the Federative People's Republic of Yugoslavia.[19]

From *Allied Powers, Tripartite Declaration on Germany* (August 1957)

Twelve years have elapsed since the end of the war in Europe. The hopes of the peoples of the world for the establishment of a basis for a just and lasting peace have nevertheless not been fulfilled. One of the basic reasons for the failure to reach a settlement is the continued division of Germany, which is a grave injustice to the German people and the major source of international tension in Europe.

The governments of France, the United Kingdom, and the United States, which share with the Soviet Union responsibility for the reunification of

Germany and the conclusion of a peace treaty, and the government of the F.R.G. as the only government qualified to speak for the German people as a whole, wish to declare. . . .

1 A European settlement must be based on freedom and justice. Every nation has the right to determine its own way of life in freedom, to determine for itself its political, economic, and social system, and to provide for its security with due regard for the legitimate interests of other nations. Justice requires that the German people be allowed to reestablish their national unity on the basis of this fundamental right.

2 The reunification of Germany remains the joint responsibility of the Four Powers. . . .

4 Only a freely elected all-German government can undertake, on behalf of a reunified Germany, obligations that will inspire confidence of other countries and that will be considered just and binding in the future by the people of Germany themselves.

5 Such a government can only be established through free elections throughout Germany for an all-German national assembly.[20]

From *Letter by GDR Premier Stoph to Federal Chancellor Kiesinger* (May 10, 1967)

In his New Year message for 1967, the chairman of the Council of State of the G.D.R., Walter Ulbricht, made proposals for the next steps that should be taken in the interest of peace and relaxation of tension. . . . With these proposals in mind, I suggest that we open direct negotiations with a view to establish agreements on (1) the establishment of normal relations between the two German states; (2) the renunciation by both German states of the use of force in mutual relations; (3) the recognition of present frontiers in Europe, especially the frontier between the two German states . . . (6) the support by the government of the G.D.R. and the government of the F.R.G. of normal relations between the two German states and the other European states. . . .[21]

From *Letter by Federal Chancellor Brandt to GDR Premier Stoph* (January 22, 1970)

On behalf of the Federal Government I suggest that our governments open negotiations on the exchange of declarations on the renunciation of force. These negotiations . . . should provide an opportunity for a wide-ranging exchange of views on the settlement of all outstanding questions between our two states, among them questions on equality in relations. . . . It is my Government's wish to reach settlements that will make life easier for people in divided Germany through negotiations on practical issues. . . .[22]

From *Treaty between the Federal Republic of Germany and the Union of Soviet Socialist Republics* (Moscow Treaty) (August 12, 1970)

Article 1 The Federal Republic of Germany and the Union of Soviet

Socialist Republics consider it an important objective of their policies to maintain international peace and to achieve detente.

They affirm their endeavor to further the normalization of the situation in Europe and the development of peaceful relations among all European states, and in so doing proceed from the actual situation existing in this region.

Article 3 In accordance with the foregoing purposes and principles the Federal Republic of Germany and the Union of Soviet Socialist Republics share the realization that peace can only be maintained in Europe if nobody disturbs the present frontiers.

They undertake to respect without restriction the territorial integrity of all states in Europe within their present frontiers; they declare that they have no territorial claims against anybody nor will assert such claims in the future; they regard today and shall in future regard the frontiers of all states in Europe as inviolable such as they are on the day of signature of the present treaty, including the Oder-Neisse line which forms the western frontier of the People's Republic of Poland and the frontier between the Federal Republic of Germany and the German Democratic Republic.[23]

Letter on German Unity (handed by Federal Foreign Minister Walter Scheel to the Soviet Foreign Ministry on the occasion of the signing of the Moscow Treaty)

In connection with today's signature of the Treaty between the F.R.G. and the U.S.S.R. the government of the F.R.G. has the honor to state that this Treaty does not conflict with the political objective of the F.R.G. to work for a state of peace in Europe in which the German nation will recover its unity in free self-determination.[24]

From *Treaty between the Federal Republic of Germany and the People's Republic of Poland* (Warsaw Treaty) (November 18, 1970)

Article 1 The Federal Republic of Germany and the People's Republic of Poland state in mutual agreement that the existing boundary line the course of which is laid down in chapter 9 of the Decisions of the Potsdam Conference of August 2, 1945 as running from the Baltic Sea immediately west of Swinemunde, and thence along the Oder river to the confluence of the western Neisse river and along the western Neisse to the Czechoslovak frontier, shall constitute the western state frontier of the People's Republic of Poland.

They reaffirm the inviolability of their existing frontiers now and in the future and undertake to respect each other's territorial integrity without restriction.

They declare that they have no territorial claims whatsoever against each other and that they will not assert such claims in the future.[25]

From *Quadripartite Agreement on Berlin* (September 3, 1971)

Part I General Provisions.

1 The four governments will strive to promote the elimination of tensions and the prevention of complications in the relevant area.

2 The four governments, taking into account their obligations under the Charter of the United Nations, agree that there shall be no use or threat of force in the area and that disputes shall be settled solely by peaceful means.

3 The four governments will mutually respect their individual and joint rights and responsibilities, which remain unchanged.

4 The four governments agree that, irrespective of the differences in legal views, the situation which has developed in the area . . . shall not be changed unilaterally.

Part II Provisions Relating to the Western Sectors of Berlin

A The Government of the U.S.S.R. declares that transit traffic by road, rail, and waterways through the territory of the G.D.R. of civilian persons and goods between the Western Sectors of Berlin and the F.R.G. will be unimpeded; that such traffic will be facilitated so as to take place in the most simple and expeditious manner; and that it will receive preferential treatment.

Detailed arrangements concerning this civilian traffic, as set forth in Annex I, will be agreed by the competent German authorities.

B The Governments of the French Republic, the U.K., and the U.S.A. declare that the ties between the Western Sectors of Berlin and the F.R.G. will be maintained and developed, taking into account that these Sectors continue not to be a constituent part of the F.R.G. and not to be governed by it.

Detailed arrangements concerning the relationship between the Western Sectors of Berlin and the F.R.G. are set forth in Annex II.

C The Government of the U.S.S.R. declares that communications between the Western Sectors of Berlin and areas bordering on these Sectors and those areas of the G.D.R. not bordering on these Sectors will be improved. Permanent residents of the Western Sectors of Berlin will be able to travel to and visit such areas for compassionate, family, religious, cultural, or commercial reasons, or as tourists under conditions comparable to those applying to other persons entering these areas. . . .

Detailed arrangements concerning travel, communications, and the exchange of territory, as set forth in Annex III, will be agreed by the competent German authorities.

D Representation abroad of the interests of the Western Sectors of Berlin and consular activities of the U.S.S.R. in the Western Sectors of Berlin can be exercized as set forth in Annex IV.[26]

From *Treaty on the Bases of Relations between the Federal Republic of Germany and the German Democratic Republic* (December 21, 1972)

The High Contracting Parties, Aware of their responsibility for the preservation of peace, Anxious to make a contribution to detente and security in Europe,

Aware that the inviolability of frontiers and respect for the territorial integrity and sovereignty of all states in Europe within their present frontiers are basic prerequisites for peace,

Recognizing that, therefore, in their relations the two German states must refrain from the threat or use of force,

Proceeding from the historical facts and without prejudice to the differing views of the F.R.G. and the G.D.R. on certain basic questions, among them the national question,

Desirous to create conditions for cooperation between the F.R.G. and the G.D.R. for the benefit of the people in both German states,

Have agreed as follows:

Article 1 The F.R.G. and the G.D.R. will develop normal, goodneighborly relations with each other on the basis of equality. . . .

Article 3 . . . They reaffirm the inviolability, now and in the future, of the frontier between them and undertake fully to respect each other's territorial integrity.

Article 4 The F.R.G. and the G.D.R. proceed on the assumption that neither of the two states can represent the other internationally or act on its behalf. . . .

Article 6 The F.R.G. and the G.D.R. proceed on the principle that the sovereignty of each of the two states is limited to its own territory. They respect each other's independence and autonomy in their domestic and external affairs.

Article 7 The F.R.G. and the G.D.R. declare their readiness, in the course of normalizing their relations, to regulate practical and humanitarian questions. They will conclude agreements on the basis of the present treaty to develop and promote for mutual benefit cooperation in the fields of the economy, science and technology, transport, legal aid, postal and telecommunications, health, culture, sport, environmental protection, and others. Details have been agreed upon in an appendix to this treaty.

Article 8 The F.R.G. and the G.D.R. will exchange permanent missions. These shall be established at the respective seats of government. . . .

Article 9 The F.R.G. and the G.D.R. agree that the present treaty shall not affect bilateral and multilateral treaties and agreements concluded earlier between them or relating to them. . . .[27]

Four-Power Declaration of November 5, 1972

The Governments of the U.S.A., the French Republic, the U.S.S.R., and the U.K. of Great Britain and Northern Ireland . . . are in agreement that they will support the applications for membership in the United Nations when submitted by the F.R.G. and the G.D.R., and affirm in this connection that this membership shall in no way affect the rights and responsibilities of the Four Powers and the corresponding related quadripartite agreements, decisions, and practices.[28]

Notes

1. As for the origins of the cold war, I believe that neither the (Western) theory of communist, or Soviet, expansionism nor the (Eastern) doctrine of American imperialist aggressivity (now also embraced by the Western "revisionist" school) offers convincing explanation. I see its origin, rather, in what I have called the "security dilemma" of nations,

that is, that mutual fears and suspicions of the intentions of the opponent may beset even defensive-minded units and their leadership and cause them to resort to steps that the other side, itself defensive, interprets as "offensive," and so on, snowballing. This applies especially to bipolar situations.

2. Another *junktim* has been between the normalization of FRG–GDR relations through the Basic Treaty (*Grundvertrag*, initialed November 8, 1972) and the readiness of the powers to let the two Germanies become members of the United Nations.

3. Article 3; text in the Appendix.

4. Article 1; text in the Appendix.

5. Text of treaty in the Appendix.

6. Contrary to common assumption, an estimated 1 million ethnic Germans remained in these provinces after the vast majority of Germans had left; the exact number is hard to establish because of the difficulty in defining who is ethnically a German.

7. In this connection we may note that art. 2 of the Treaty of Basic Relations between the Republic of Korea and Japan of June 22, 1965, stipulates that ". . . all treaties or agreements concluded between the Empire of Korea and the Empire of Japan on or before August 22, 1910, are already null and void" (referring to the Protectorate Treaty of 1905 and the Annexation Treaty of 1910). The "already," in Korean interpretation, means *ab initio;* in the Japanese, only from the date of Korean independence in 1948.

8. Text of agreement in the Appendix.

9. There is a story of Soviet negotiator Abrassimov having remarked at the signing of the agreement: "Now I shall be liquidated."

10. "Rapallo" has long been used as shorthand for a German-Russian "deal" betraying the West. The original Rapallo agreement of 1922, of course, was no such thing. It provided for establishment of diplomatic relations between the Soviet Union and Germany, implying a certain assertion of independence on Germany's part but no realignment. It might be compared with the establishment of Bonn-Moscow relations by Adenauer in 1955. And inasmuch as Rapallo looked toward revision of the German boundaries with Poland, it implied the very opposite of *Ostpolitik,* which confirms the existing boundaries.

11. The trade volume between the two German states rose considerably between 1960 and 1970. In 1960 it amounted to 2.1 billion DM; in 1969, it reached 3.84 billion; in 1970, 4.5 billion. A disproportionally high percentage of this trade was in raw materials and foodstuffs, to the detriment of industrial products. Compare the above figures with those for the total trade volume of FRG and GDR with all states: FRG (1969), 212 billion DM; GDR, 37 billion.

12. "Expellees" is usually applied to those expelled from the Eastern territories and countries; "refugees" refers to those who left the Soviet Zone (later the GDR).

13. L. W. Holborn, G. M. Carter, and J. H. Herz: *German Constitutional Documents Since 1871* (New York: Praeger, 1970), pp. 5 f.

14. Ibid., p. 7.

15. Ibid., p. 11.

16. Ibid.

17. Ibid., p. 13.

18. Ibid., pp. 13 f.

19. Ibid., pp. 227 f.

20. Ibid., pp. 228 f.

21. Ibid., pp. 230 f.

22. Press and Information Office of the Government of the Federal Republic: *Erfurt, March 19, 1970, A Documentation* (Bonn, 1970), p. 5.

23. Press and Information Office of the Government of the Federal Republic: *The Treaty of August 12, 1970* (Bonn, 1970), pp. 7 ff.

24. Ibid., p. 10.

25. Press and Information Office of the Government of the Federal Republic: *The Treaty between the Federal Republic of Germany and the People's Republic of Poland* (Bonn, 1970), p. 8.

26. Press and Information Office of the Government of the Federal Republic: *The Berlin Settlement* (Bonn, 1972), pp. 7 ff.

27. Text from *Relay from Bonn*, 8 November 1972, and *New York Times*, 9 November 1972.

28. *Relay from Bonn*, 9 November 1972.

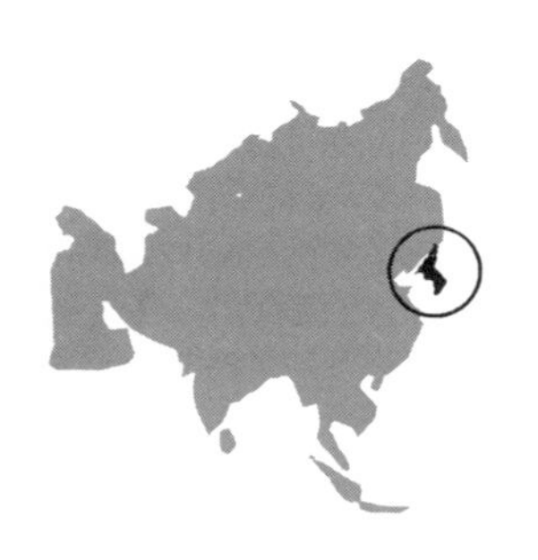
KOREA

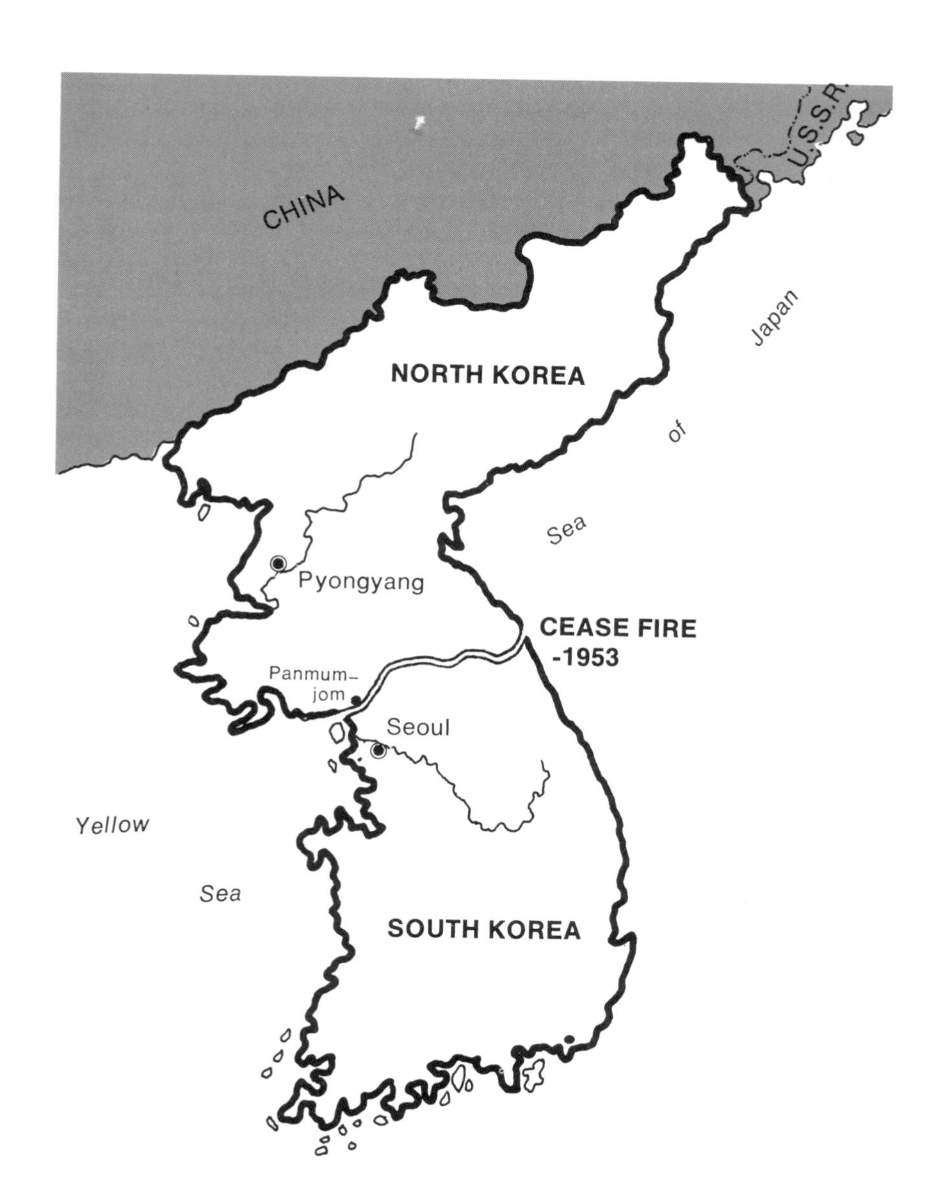
U.S.S.R.
CHINA
Japan
NORTH KOREA
of
Sea
Pyongyang
CEASE FIRE
-1953
Panmum-
jom
Seoul
Yellow
Sea
SOUTH KOREA

2

Korea

Gregory Henderson

Background

THE PARADOX OF DIVISION

NO DIVISION OF A NATION in the present world is so astonishing in its origin as the division of Korea; none is so unrelated to conditions or sentiment within the nation itself at the time the division was effected; none is to this day so unexplained; in none does blunder and planning oversight appear to have played so large a role. Finally, there is no division for which the U.S. government bears so heavy a share of the responsibility as it bears for the division of Korea.

The basic irony in Korea's division is the absence of internal factors abetting or explaining such division. Almost no national communities have been so anciently and so continuously one political, linguistic, and economic unit as Korea. Few have such strong, well-defined geographical boundaries: a peninsula whose mainland side is bounded by two mighty rivers rising in the same formidable mountain range. From A.D. 668 until 1945, with the rarest and most temporary exceptions, a united Korean state of some strength filled most—later all—of these boundaries. Even including China-Taiwan, Germany, Vietnam or, of course, Laos or India-Pakistan, no presently divided country had been previously united as an independent unit so continuously or so long.[1] Throughout two millennia of history, Korea has been united ethnically and linguistically and, since A.D. 668, has lived under the same rule, religions, and ideologies and suffered or enjoyed the same historical experience. Colonialism, strengthening north-south communications and operating with a centralism far more ubiquitously exercised than the old dynasties', reinforced rather than undermined this unity. Korea's unity as a state was, after A.D. 668, not often threatened. Severe power rivalry over a weak Korea between 1880 and 1905 brought occasional hints of a possible partition, notably between Russia and Japan. Prince Yamagata proposed such division at the 38th parallel to the Russians at the czar's coronation in 1896; Russia proposed the 39th parallel in 1903; a further, vaguer division proposal is said to have been made in 1898. These suggestions, however, arose briefly and were silenced by Japan's victory in the Russo-Japanese War.

SPARSE DIVISIVE FACTORS

The more lasting threats to Korea's internal harmony, not her unity, developed only in the last century, chiefly since 1920, out of foreign impact on Korea. Such forces operated chiefly outside the peninsula and were largely limited to several thousand persons out of Korea's population of, by 1945, 26 million.

The most potent divisive force was communism. From 1918 on, communism had made effective inroads on sizable Korean communities in eastern Siberia and Manchuria and, to a numerically smaller extent, on Koreans in North China.[2] A small Korean Communist party started within Korea in 1925 but went underground during the period of Japanese militarism (1931–45); it had at most 4,000 members organized in strong cells by the end of the Japanese regime. From 1920 on, there were constant political and a few military clashes between Korean Communists, some supported by the Comintern, and the many conservatives in the independence movement, some of whom, like Syngman Rhee, were American-based. By 1945, a second generation of expatriate Koreans, with bewilderingly varied training in communist, democratic, colonial, Japanese, or even anticommunist schools, devolved on the reawakened Korean political scene ready to play their roles.

Potential and bitter political divisiveness there was, but it had no relevance for any physical division of the peninsula by Koreans along a geographical line. Korea's small-minority communism was scattered and, if anything, stronger in the peninsula's southern cities (Seoul and Taegu) and a few southern rural areas than it was in the north. Communism and the Left would have caused considerable political trouble regardless of how Korea was liberated and governed after 1945. Without outside intervention, however, the rifts would have been those normal to many governments; they would not have been likely to generate separatism, and certainly not to force the creation of two states divided along or near the 38th parallel. Handled within the framework of one government, such potential conflict would have had far shallower roots and a narrower social base than left-right, communist-democratic divisions in other occupied states, for example, in Austria, where division was ultimately avoided.

EXTERNAL CAUSE OF DIVISION

1 THE AGREEMENTS

Korea's division resulted from the physical presence of external powers: the acceptance by the United States and the Soviet Union of the surrender of Japanese troops in Korea followed by the administration of separate occupations. Insofar as can be determined twenty-seven years after the event, however, intentions or long-range plans of the powers concerned prior to the surrender of Japan, or in the case of the United States for several years thereafter, did not support division.

The United States, Britain, and China declared in the Cairo Declaration of December 1, 1943, that, "in due course, Korea shall become free and independent." This aim was reaffirmed at Potsdam, and the Soviet Union's declaration of war on Japan on August 8, 1945, adhered to these declarations. Roosevelt proposed at Yalta a Soviet-American-Chinese trusteeship of twenty to thirty years in Korea (he had mentioned forty years at Teheran in November 1943) to prepare Koreans for self-government. Stalin merely commented, rather more sensibly, that the period should be as short as possible and, surprisingly, that the British should be invited. Both agreed that foreign troops should not be stationed in Korea; neither clarified how, under such circumstances, it would be possible to accept the surrender of many hundreds of thousands of Japanese troops or administer a nation whose political, social, and economic conditions were certain to be unstable, most probably chaotic. The formal Yalta Agreement did not refer to Korea.[3]

There was no top-level sign in U.S.–USSR discussions at Cairo, Teheran, Yalta, or Potsdam that division was intended or foreseen; nor was there the slightest surface indication of conflict over Korea. Just below the summit, Ambassador Averell Harriman privately expressed fear that the Soviets would utilize trusteeship in Korea as a means of asking for trusteeship over Hong Kong and Indo-China. Secretary Henry Stimson urged minimal troops during trusteeship on the grounds that the Soviets had one or two divisions of Soviet-Korean troops which they were likely to use to "Polandize" Korea.[4] Such reservations were confined to internal American documents and were exceedingly sparse there. Remaining documents give little evidence of serious thought by either Roosevelt, Stalin, or the middle levels of the American bureaucracy to the complexities of the Korean situation. Under these circumstances, opinions of men such as Harriman, who was crucial in handling problems with the Soviet Union, may have proved critical without ever having been fully recorded.

Warnings of the obvious dangers of separate areas of control or administration occur as early as the Yalta briefing documents and recur at Potsdam. As surrender neared without the crucial agreement on occupation, occasional references to the possibility of separate or zonal administration begin to creep into the texts; the warnings seemed to be forgotten.[5] Any such zones were intended to be temporary, replaced by a four-power "interim authority" such as trusteeship embodying "the intention of this government to assist the Korean people in the early establishment of a strong, independent nation." [6]

Unification, however wantonly sacrificed initially, was not thereafter as a policy abandoned. State Department records until the latter part of 1947 reiterate the need to achieve it. It is a leitmotiv to which State's representatives repeatedly resort to oppose Russian or conservative South Korean tendencies to perpetuate or institutionalize the existing zonal division. The Koreans must be "educated" against separate independence; Truman stresses unification pointedly in a letter to Syngman Rhee. "Our commitment to our Allies to establish a united and truly independent Korea" is strongly asserted. "Our policy is to bring about the unification of a free and democratic Korea. We intend to stay there until we have been successful in doing it." [7] The official record of the American commitment to this cause has now become quite full.[8] Once the deed was done, such protestations proved vain.

Similar Soviet documents are, of course, not available. The decisions to which Stalin agreed and the record of his conversation at Yalta reveal nothing but a desire for a joint trusteeship, as brief as possible and without much military presence. General Alexei Antonov at the Potsdam Conference invited joint U.S./USSR military action in Korea, an invitation that General George C. Marshall should have leaped to accept but failed to because of his obsession with doing one thing at a time and his preoccupation with the troop and logistical requirements of the landings in Japan.[9] No desire or plans for separate occupations are evidenced by the Soviet Union prior to September 1945. Soviet countenancing and forwarding of separate occupation in Korea and the resulting division is not verbally articulated by the Soviets thereafter, though it is clearly legible from Soviet actions.

2 *THE LACK OF AGREEMENTS*

The State Department policy document of June 22, 1945 (see note 6), adumbrates why Korea was divided against everyone's wishes. Seven weeks before the surrender of Japan, there was still no agreement on the nature of the Allied entry into and occupation of Korea; this despite the fact that a year and a half had passed since the Cairo Declaration clearly foreshadowed the probability of an occupation and trusteeship. Incredibly, from late June until August 15, no progress was made. The war ended swiftly. The Soviets, having been urged at Yalta to enter the war in East Asia, did so at the appointed time, August 8, 1945, and invaded Korea. The lack of any entry or occupation agreements proved first fatal to unity then catastrophic to peace. The United States was forced to improvise a separate, later entry and a rapid, jerry-built zonal separation with neither specific terminus nor any provision for a subsequent trusteeship. The Soviet Union, apparently through crash policy changes or formulations of its own, moved to the easy option now opened to it by the U.S. State and War Departments' decisions and took full advantage of separate occupation to perpetuate monopoly control within its zone of Korea. Thereafter, division deepened and jelled through cold-war-polarized decision making in Moscow and Washington and through the even sharper and more arresting polarization visited on and then expanded by the Koreans themselves in each zone.

No fully credible explanation for the absence of these crucial agreements with the Soviet Union on Korea has ever been made. There is no documentary evidence of Soviet adamancy on Korea before September 1945. Subordinates urged a firm agreement at Yalta; none was made. The secretary of war, writing to Acting Secretary of State Joseph Grew on May 12, 1945, asked for definite agreement with the Soviet Union that "when Korea is liberated, whether before final capitulation of Japan or after, it be placed immediately under the trusteeship of the United States, Great Britain, China, and the Soviet Union" and that "this agreement should make clear that the four trustees are to be the sole authority for the selection of a temporary Korean government." [10] Undersecretary Grew then asked President Truman on May 15, 1945, that the question of a trusteeship for Korea be immediately clarified with the Soviet Union as a matter of high priority. Truman chose Harry Hopkins for the mission.[11] Hopkins merely got confirmation of the trusteeship in principle and seems to have returned without pressing for more definite arrangements and without any explanation as to why none were obtained. Harriman accompanied Hopkins and testified twenty-five years later that "it would have been folly to push the Korea trusteeship idea further" since he knew that Stalin and Molotov would have tried to use it to acquire a Soviet occupation zone in Hokkaido.[12] This oral statement is all we appear to have. Again at Potsdam, American policy planners considered that it would be "politically inadvisable for any one of the interested countries alone to invade Korea." [13] First Molotov and then Stalin raised Korea in a trusteeship context, but this time Churchill cut them off and Truman made no attempt to restore the line of inquiry.[14] Churchill's motive, parallel with Harriman's, was apparently apprehension that Korean trusteeship would open the door to Soviet trusteeships over the former Italian colonies in Libya, thus threatening to bring Soviet power to the Mediterranean.

3 *CAUSES OF LACK OF AGREEMENTS*

One of history's important defaults of decision occurs with a complete default of explicit credible explanation. None of the memoirs or records since that time fills this gap. Korea's division was fairly clearly not an oversight. It was not even a failure of policy makers to concentrate on

Korea. An occupation over a nation of 26 million people in one of the world's most strategic locations would make such omission incredible even if we did not know, as we now do, how often decision was urged and then, at the last moment, stepped back from. Miscalculations that many months were still left before the war's end no doubt played some part.[15] Poor communication confused decision making: the Yalta decision was kept from most U.S. officials until after the end of the war and its warning briefing papers were not, apparently, read by later decision makers. As late as September 13, 1945, it was found that the British had not even been informed of a trusteeship in Korea that was to have included them.[16] The informing of the Chinese was partial and chaotic.[17] A week after Japan's surrender, the Commander in Chief, Army Forces, Pacific, not only was uninformed of the agreements arrived at regarding Korea but, in drafting a reply to him for the Joint Chiefs of Staff, the U.S. government was unable to say anything more definite than that "so far as can be ascertained, the [oral] understanding [at Yalta] . . . is the only international agreement which relates to Korea and that agreement would relate to a period and to a condition subsequent to the period of occupation of Korea." [18] The failure to establish within either the State or War Departments any group of appropriate size and leadership which could prepare for the occupation and trusteeship of Korea is also signal and unexplained.[19] So are key delays and red-tape coordination such as the study papers on Korean problems to be prepared by all the main Allies but which, on February 17, 1945, Mr. John G. Ballentine, director of the Office of Far Eastern Affairs (FE), noted calmly and without comment, "will not be available for some months." The war's end found these incomplete; meanwhile, the Department had twiddled its thumbs on Korea.

Two remarks of Ambassador Harriman and the apparent motivation of Churchill in blocking clarification of trusteeship at Potsdam may hint at a more credible, though not provable, explanation for failure to find agreement on troop entry and occupation. In brief, the hindrance to Korea decision making may have been the severe reservations felt by top policy advisers regarding the implications of trusteeship as a solution in Korea which, once started, might be applied to many other critical areas with adverse consequences for American-British positions then considered more vital.

The Yalta idea of a trusteeship for Korea was, so far as is known, a comparatively impulsive personal initiative of President Roosevelt, the implications of which in the context of more embracing postwar settlements had never been staffed out to allow full consideration by American (or British) policy advisers. Documented criticism of the trusteeship idea for Korea has not so far appeared. Strong British opposition to the general concept of trusteeship as threatening Britain's colonial position and opening the way to American hegemony is well known. Prime Minister Churchill and Ambassador Harriman—at times, Secretary Stimson also—

seem to have felt that, in essence, trusteeship for Korea was ill advised: it was almost certain to open the door for further trusteeships in still more sensitive areas such as Japan, Libya, and Hong Kong where the Soviets would, or might, demand a cotrustee role. After Roosevelt's impromptu oral agreement to an Allied trusteeship in Korea at top levels, these advisers may well have felt that the milk had been spilled and that any attempt at a new policy would only alert the Soviets and increase their demands. In addition, the Yalta agreements were known to only a very few, very busy men enveloped in a multitude of urgent problems and unable to give time to Korea's. At the same time, security hindered the delegation of planning on Korea to working-level men with the time to give to it. Under these conditions, the only course available seemed to be not to press the matter at a time when other trusteeships could be opened up but to wait until suitable dispositions had been effected in Japan, Libya, and Hong Kong and then hope that a trusteeship in Korea could still, belatedly, be pieced together. Silence was essential for it alone would forestall a Soviet protest. Whether Soviet perception of this shadow boxing and its refusal to play along with it were factors in later Soviet adamancy in Korea we do not know; desire to preserve a communist political monopoly—hence a buffer state—in North Korea is reason enough for Soviet intransigence there. Silence on the U.S. policy side was also essential for Korean public opinion which otherwise would have been quick to perceive and to resent that Koreans' own interests in their own united country had been sacrificed to power positions elsewhere—especially to those in Japan, the hated colonial master.

This speculation, if it is correct, would explain, as little else does, the otherwise baffling paralysis and inarticulateness in American decision making on Korea. It would also shed interesting light on the origins of the cold war. The foregoing remains, of course, a theory and one largely without documentary support.

4 *LACK OF ALLIED COMMUNICATION WITH KOREANS*

Until after the surrender of Japan, Koreans played no part whatsoever in planning or decision making regarding Korea's future. Except for the Cairo Declaration, they were not even informed of what fate was in store for them. A group of Chinese embassy officials, headed by Counselor Liu Chieh, suggested to the director of the Office of Far Eastern Affairs on February 17, 1945, Allied encouragement of the Korean underground movement, coordination of Korean overseas groups with the Korean Provisional Government as their focus, immediate assumption by all four powers of civilian responsibilities after the surrender, and the earliest possible establishment of a nonpartisan Korean government. No action was taken on these perceptive suggestions. Action was confined to "study papers on Korean problems" which were never produced.

In addition to their distaste for dealing with Korean groups, top-level

American decision makers or even those immediately below them also never referred to public opinion in Korea or what could reasonably have been anticipated regarding it. They had, of course, no recent sources for knowledge of it. Indirect references only are made in the State Department "Estimate of Conditions" document apparently drafted at working levels.[20] The Korean Provisional Government (KPG) in Chungking and Dr. Syngman Rhee in Washington as chairman of its Korean Commission made energetic attempts to express opinion and achieve recognition or collaborative opportunities. The State Department regarded the KPG and the Commission as not "representative of the Korean people today." It had a fixation about not consulting or recognizing such groups and spent considerable effort keeping them at arm's length.[21] It did not always even answer their inquiries.

THE EVOLUTION OF DIVISION

1 THE 38TH PARALLEL

The American policy vacuum on Korea was rapidly unmasked by the war's final days. The Soviet Union declared war on Japan on August 8, 1945, exactly as Stalin had told Harry Hopkins in May. American and Soviet military planning, meanwhile, had both come to see that, the impractical Yalta informal agreement notwithstanding, the Allies could not receive the surrender of several hundred thousand enemy troops and their arms without some Allied armed presence. Nor could such troops be present without some regard for the security conditions that would then surround them in a chaotic Korea. One occupation (or two), a word scarcely used before in civilian planning about Korea, rapidly loomed as inevitable. Without any agreement, Soviet troops were free to enter unilaterally. Soviet entry or the immediate prospect thereof triggered the American fear that the peninsula might fall wholly into Soviet hands unless U.S. troops made their own entry. A hasty ad hoc meeting was called in the night and early morning hours of August 10–11 in the office of John J. McCloy, assistant secretary of war. Two young lieutenant colonels, Dean Rusk and C. H. Bonesteel III, proposed to McCloy, James Dunn of the State Department, and Ralph Bard of the Navy that the USSR be authorized to receive the Japanese surrender north of the 38th parallel, some forty miles north of Seoul, and that U.S. troops receive it south of that line. At least as important was the added clause that, until the surrender was complete, "the administration of civil affairs" was to be "the responsibility of the respective commanders of the two zones in Korea."[22]

The decision was not, as later billed, a purely military one. The draft prepared by Assistant Secretary Dunn for the Joint Chiefs of Staff and MacArthur had important political content establishing governmental and civil functions; it was not merely surrender reception but an entire initial occupation. It was intended that, as soon as surrender was completed, "the administration of civil affairs should be combined, so that the whole of Korea would constitute a centralized administrative area" to "be placed under the command of a council made up of the Commanding Officers of the United States, Soviet and other forces participating in the occupation of Korea." [23] The surrender arrangements were hastily incorporated in General Order No. 1, cleared with the Russians, who again raised no objections relating to Korea, and sent to MacArthur.

2 *INITIAL OCCUPATION*

From this point on, events proceeded in a way which, in retrospect, was considerably less surprising than the foregoing absence of American policy.

About August 12, 1945, troops of the First Soviet Far Eastern Front entered northeastern Korea largely by amphibious landings at ports in Hamgyong Province and made rapid progress south and west. Reception of Japanese surrender was rapid; so also was the imposition of communist civilian and political controls. By the time the troops of the United States 24th Corps under General John R. Hodge arrived at Inch'on on September 8 and accepted the Seoul surrender of the Japanese forces, the mold in the north had started to set, new opportunities for communist control were being glimpsed and reported to Moscow, new policies were in motion, and such chance as may, in the first few days, have existed for a combining of the two commands went fast a-glimmering. Attempts to "establish some sort of workable agreement with the Soviets on a military level" had already by September 24 proved "almost unfruitful," and General Hodge was reporting his belief that "the current division of Korea into two occupational zones under widely divergent policies . . . poses an insurmountable obstacle to uniting Korea" and has "created a situation impossible of peaceful correction with credit to the United States unless immediate action on an international level is forthcoming to establish an overall provisional government which will be fully supported by the occupation forces under common policy." [24]

Hodge referred the problem back to Washington with urgency. Sluggishly and with no apparent sensitivity to the urgency involved, the State-War-Navy-Coordinating Committee (SWNCC) waited until October 20 before bringing forth the mouse that "present zonal military occupation . . . should be superseded at the earliest possible date by a trusteeship for Korea." A crucial month had thus been squandered without policy progress. No move to establish such trusteeship was made until the Moscow Conference of late December 1945, despite further urging from Hodge.[25] Here the United States and the USSR agreed to a four-power trusteeship to last five years (reportedly the USSR cut down a longer, U.S.-proposed period). Problems of trusteeship, economic unification and a provisional government were to be determined by a joint U.S.–USSR commission. Hodge, his political adviser, William R. Langdon, and General MacArthur opposed the solution and knew the Koreans would be unhappy with it. The Koreans were, in fact, allowed no say in preparations for the conference; they were even informed of the results late and inadequately. The Moscow Conference, born of the ill-conceived optimism of James Byrnes and Harriman that something could be worked out with the Russians, threw U.S. policy toward Korea for a costly loss.

3 U.S.–USSR OCCUPATION COMMANDS' NEGOTIATIONS

The conference of the U.S.–USSR commands, preparatory to the Joint Commission, convened in Seoul on January 16, 1946, and agreed to accords on railroad, motor, and coastal waterborne transportation; movements of certain groups of Korean citizens between the two zones; exchange of mail; radio broadcasting frequencies; and the establishment of intercommand liaison. General movement across the parallel, however, was denied, as was progress toward a uniform currency, a unified telecommunication system, or free circulation of newspapers, though all were proposed by the Americans. Even much of the above agreement, including movement by certain citizens, was not honored by the Soviets. The conference finally decided that the forthcoming Joint Commission should consist of five men from each command and should consult with democratic, political, and social organizations of North and South Korea as a prelude to the establishment of a provisional Korean government.[26]

The first Joint Commission convened on March 20, 1946. It adjourned without progress on May 8: the Soviet Union would not agree to consult any organization that had opposed the Moscow agreement which, because of its trusteeship provision, had become anathema to the chief political groups in the American zone (see below). A second Joint Commission convened on May 21, 1947, breaking down in August over a somewhat refined version of the same consultation issue.

4 UN COMMISSION AND END OF OCCUPATIONS

Convinced that a united, independent, democratic Korea could not be achieved by bilateral negotiations, the United States proposed on August 26, 1947, a conference of the USSR, the United Kingdom, China, and the United States "to consider how the [Moscow] agreement could be carried out." China and the U.K. accepted this proposal but the Soviet Union rejected it on September 4 as not being within the Moscow agreement's scope.[27] A few days later, the Soviet delegation to the Joint Commission in Seoul proposed the simultaneous withdrawal of Soviet and U.S. troops from Korea during the beginning of 1948, a proposal reiterated by the Soviet foreign minister on September 17, 1947.

Frustrated in quadrilateral negotiations, the United States laid the question of Korean independence before the second regular session of the General Assembly of the United Nations. On November 14, the Assembly adopted a resolution for Korean independence, establishing a nine-nation UN Temporary Commission on Korea (UNTCOK) which should observe elections to be held throughout Korea for a National Assembly that would establish a national Korean government and would then arrange for the withdrawal of the occupying powers within ninety days. The USSR opposed this resolution on the grounds that the Korean question did not fall within the jurisdiction of the United Nations.

UNTCOK arrived in Seoul in January 1948 and was refused admission to North Korea by the Soviet commander, an attitude which Andrei Gromyko, the Soviet permanent representative to the UN, then fully supported. UNTCOK referred the problem of its nonadmission into North Korea to the Interim Committee of the General Assembly which adopted a resolution on February 26, 1948, stating that UNTCOK should proceed with observation of elections in as much of Korea as was accessible to it and carry out there the program of the UN General Assembly. Elections held on May 10, 1948, under the U.S. command in South Korea, were observed by UNTCOK which then adopted a resolution declaring their results a valid expression of the free will of the two-thirds of the Korean people who live in the part of Korea accessible to the Commission. The representatives thus elected met on May 31 as a National Assembly, leaving one-third of the seats vacant for future North Korean representatives. They drafted and adopted a constitution on July 12, and on July 20 elected Syngman Rhee president of the Republic of Korea. The government of the Republic of Korea (ROK) was inaugurated on August 15, 1948, on which day the U.S. military government in Korea terminated. At its third session, the UN General Assembly adopted on December 12, 1948, a resolution declaring that "there has been established a lawful government . . . and that this is the only such Government in Korea." The government was then recognized by the United States and some thirty-seven other nations. Its application for membership in the United Nations was vetoed by the USSR on April 8, 1949, the first of several such vetoes.

In the north, the Democratic People's Republic of Korea was proclaimed on September 9, 1948, by a Supreme People's Council elected on August 25 without outside observation. On September 18, 1948, the Soviet Union announced that all its troops would be withdrawn by the end of December 1948. Though unobserved, this was apparently carried out. The DPRK applied for UN admission on February 9, 1949, but its application was not considered because of the UN decision that the Republic of Korea was the only lawful government in Korea.

Plans for the withdrawal of American troops were made shortly after the May 10 elections, over strong South Korean objection. After excessively hasty attempts to ready the South Korean defense forces, withdrawals of

U.S. forces began in May 1949 and ended, under UN observation, on June 29, 1950. UN Commissions have succeeded themselves, confined to the Republic of Korea, ever since, without progress toward unification. Each year the Korean Commission and its report is a profitless bone of contention at the General Assembly.

5 *THE KOREAN WAR*

Within a year of troop withdrawals, on June 25, 1950, North Korean troops invaded the Republic of Korea. The decision making behind the invasion remains unknown. The withdrawal of American troops and the inadequate arms and training of the fledgling Korean Army left the young republic essentially undefended. The initial defeat of the Korean aid bill and Secretary Acheson's Press Club statement, both in the opening weeks of 1950, strongly implied a lack of U.S. military or civilian intention of coming to the effective aid of South Korea. The republic was, however, gathering economic strength and was successfully quelling all subversive elements. Kim Il-song was apparently able to convince the aging Stalin that chances of success were good and that North Korea's attack should be supported. If the Khrushchev memoirs can be believed, such decision was as little staffed out within the Soviet government as Roosevelt's trusteeship flyer was within the American. The extreme nature of the risk taken displays how high the stakes of division in Korea were held to be.

The UN Commission reported the invasion immediately to the UN secretary-general. On the same day, in the absence of the Soviet Union, the Security Council called for a cessation of hostilities and on all members "to render every assistance to the United Nations." President Truman quickly authorized supporting use of U.S. naval and air forces. On June 27, the United States tabled a resolution that "the Members of the United Nations furnish such assistance to the Republic of Korea as may be necessary to repel armed attack and to restore international peace and security in the area." The resolution passed. A UN Command under General MacArthur was established, and sixteen UN member nations contributed armed forces. They defeated the North Korean forces in South Korea in September 1950 and were then poised to pursue a demoralized enemy into the North. On the urging of the UN commander, the UN General Assembly then adopted a resolution of October 7, 1950, recommending that all necessary acts be taken "for the establishment of a unified independent democratic government in the sovereign state of Korea" and that "all appropriate steps be taken to ensure conditions of stability throughout Korea." After calling for the surrender of the North Korean forces on October 1 and October 9, the UN commander ordered his forces across the 38th parallel and reached the northern border at several points within three weeks.[28] Deep in North Korea, the UN forces were then met by Chinese Communist "volunteer" forces on November 5, 1950, and were pushed southward by them toward an eventually stabilized line near the 38th parallel. After 400,000 ROK casualties, 142,000 American casualties (including 33,000 dead), 17,000 casualties of other UN forces, and 1.5 million estimated enemy casualties with dead of, probably, several hundred thousand, negotiations of twenty-five months established an armistice, signed on June 27, 1953, along a 4,000-meter-wide demilitarized zone which passed in the vicinity of, but an average of 25 miles north of, the old 38th parallel. This, with a Military Armistice–Neutral Nations Supervisory Commission apparatus for maintaining the armistice by meetings held at Panmunjom, continues until today, after hundreds of recriminatory meetings.

The once casual, even careless division of Korea had turned into a nightmare of separate, hostile regimes bringing one destructive war and threatening a worse one. In an intensely hostile peninsula, unification receded ever farther.

Economic Disruption

The economic disruption of halving a united peninsula at its waist is as severe as the political trauma of division.

Exact measurement of the costs involved is elusive—downright impossible—and has, so far as the author knows, never been attempted in depth in a public document. It is certain that costs were and remain high, probably higher and more serious than for any other divided country with the possible exceptions of Germany and of the far larger lands split within the Indian subcontinent.

The economies of both South and North Korea, perhaps especially the former, were devastated in the wake of the division of 1945. Industry, commerce, and transportation ground to a virtual halt. Inflation was awesome: retail prices rose 1000 percent between August 1945 and December 1946; monthly food costs rose from 8 yen before the war to 800 yen by September 1946. The South Korean interim government believed that half the labor force of 10 million fully employed in 1944 remained gainfully employed by 1947.[29] Administration was tighter in the North, the population smaller, and a heavy flight of the well-to-do provided a cushion for those remaining; but chaos, disruption, and suffering were likewise endemic.

North-South division was probably a less significant, though still important reason for this devastation. The more basic cause was the abrupt and complete schism of Korea from the economy of Japan and of her Co-prosperity Sphere which had absorbed 97 percent of Korea's pre-1945 trade and capital needs; Korea's break with the colonial power was sharper than that of any other former colony. The two schisms, coming at precisely the same moment, tended to obscure each other's separate effects.

The economic disruptions of national division, however, were and remain great. Korea had always been one economic unit. Japan's intensive colonization greatly tightened this unity. First, by building 6,362 kilometers of railroad (considerable additional mileage was from 80 percent to 90 percent finished in 1945), 20,000 miles of road (servicing 500 bus companies), 230,000 tons of shipping, 1,031 post offices, 5,600 miles of telegraph lines, 7,100 telephone lines and 15 radio stations, Japan bound all parts of Korea more closely together than the peninsula had ever dreamed of being before.[30] The North-South bonds were, in fact, particularly stressed, especially in the road and railroad network; from 1931 until 1945, the length of the Korean peninsula was used more than its breadth as a funnel through which Japanese troops and supplies poured northward into Manchuria and North China. Except for radio, all these communication lines were severed close to their midpoint in 1945.[31] Korea's urban population, which has increased rapidly since 1931, 20 percent living in communities of over 20,000 by liberation and over one-third to one-half today, would well have utilized the economic girdings of unity.

Such severing had immediate and lasting economic cost. Postal, telephone, telegraph, and radio systems were all profit-making until the end of the war; within weeks all were incurring sharp deficits because of steep declines in the volume of business and the lag in the increases in rates behind those in costs. Such deficits lasted generally until or well into the 1960s and are even today not entirely solved.

Korea was not only a united and close communication system. It had also been developed as a semimodern industrial, mining, and manufacturing unit responsive to Japan's escalating needs for a continental supply and manufacturing base from the time of the Manchurian incident in 1931 until World War II's end.

The peninsula was and is fairly evenly divided: 47,071 square miles or more (55 percent) are now in the North; 38,022 square miles (44.6 percent), in the South; and 487 square miles, in the demilitarized zone between the two.[32] By 1945, some 14,856 factories in Korea employed 549,751 workers; of the largest of these, mostly in the North, 2 percent had 40 percent of the employees.[33] Korea's industrial assets were, of course, not so evenly divided between South and North as was its territory (see Appendix 1). Of the peninsula's hydraulic resources 85 percent lie in the North along the great northern Yalu and Tumen rivers. A predominance of mine and forest resources and greater proximity to Japan's new Manchurian and North Chinese empire also dictated the emplacement in the North of greater power production, power-intensive industries, mining, metals processing, and heavy industry. The South, with some two-thirds of the population, had not only more agriculture but also more consumer- and machine-fabricating industry. The popular myth of "the agricultural South and the industrial North" is, however, not an accurate generalization as the distribution in Appendix 1 tends to show.

Nevertheless, the economies were to a large extent complementary.

Heavy industries in the North lost fabricating facilities and markets in the South. In the North, 70 percent of the output of the nitrogenous industry, one of the most developed in the Far East at the time, was used by agriculture in the South, where the need for chemical fertilizer had grown enormously since the mid-1920s. The South also lost the chief source for its requirements of bituminous coal, iron and steel, wood pulp, chrysolite, asbestos, cobalt, and other chemicals.[34] The North, in turn, lost the 75 percent of Korea's foodstuffs, 87 percent of textiles, 69 percent of light consumer goods, and 85 percent of machinery manufactured in the South.[35] The power break undoubtedly constituted one of the most frappant economic hardships directly and almost immediately induced by any division situation. Almost completely dependent for its electricity on the North, the South was thus constantly subject to potential blackmail. After long negotiations, the U.S. military government assembled considerable equipment in payment for this power. Finally, in May 1948, power was completely shut off, plunging South Korea into a memorable darkness until light was restored by emergency power from two U.S. power barges and maintained by rushed plant construction. The separate buildup of power facilities in the Republic of Korea proceeded for twenty years at a cost, through 1968, of $290.1 million in foreign loan or investment before supply and demand were in balance. Meanwhile, for some years, at least, there was a surplus in the North. At present, there may be a surplus in both parts of Korea, with 16.5 million kilowatt hours produced in 1970 in North Korea. Additionally, in North Korea much power is wastefully devoted to illuminating underground factories and fortresses deemed necessary only because of the tensions of division.[36]

Desperate personnel needs were also aggravated by division. The 700,000 Japanese residents of Korea in 1945 comprised almost all the managerial and technical personnel of Korea; 70,000 were employed by the Government-General alone. Almost all were repatriated within six months; all, except for a few technicians in North Korea, were gone within a year. Such repatriation was a major factor in the collapse of industry and of difficulties in all other sectors. For North Korea the problem was compounded by division. From August to December 1945 alone, 500,000 refugees fled to South Korea. Among these were almost all the managerial personnel and a high proportion of North Korea's professional and higher technical workers. Many of these people became key managers and technicians in South Korea. North Korea had to start almost from scratch; they imported some experts from the Soviet Union, engaged in crash training programs, and suffered industrial hardships until extensive training could fill the gaps. Even today, a labor shortage exists in North Korea which makes welcome the importation of Koreans from Japan, 100,000 since 1959, while South Korea has consistently had a labor surplus.[37] Many skilled workers have been trained in North Korea, the number of "engineers" having increased from 1,964 (plus 4,721 assistant engineers) in

1945 to 425,700 in 1967.[38] But North Korea still lacks sufficient very highly, theoretically trained cadres, especially those with the type of training that is obtainable only abroad. Kim Il-song himself has called efforts toward a technical revolution poor and said that "technical innovation has not been accomplished." He has acknowledged, for example, that the DPRK produced tractors from drawings of foreign models and only after several failures. The apparent failure of the recent North Korean seven-year plan of 1961–67 to achieve more than 72 percent of its objectives may in some part be traceable to this lack of highly trained personnel.[39] Meanwhile, thousands of Koreans from South Korea, including hundreds of Ph.D.s and large percentages of well-trained scientists and engineers, elect to remain abroad in the countries where they received their advanced education because of perceived lacks of opportunities in South Korea.

To assay the large economic costs of division with any exactness can certainly not be done here—if it can be done anywhere. Some general notions of the dimensions involved might be obtained from a few summary observations. Before 1945, Korea had an average trade deficit of some $67 million, with imports of some $303 million and exports of $236 million.[40] In the postwar era, trade deficits for the Republic of Korea alone, made up by foreign aid, averaged $259 million from 1954–56, $330 million from 1957–61, $376 million from 1962–66, $676 million in 1967, $1,007.1 million in 1968, and $1,201.1 million in 1969. They remained at more than a billion dollars until 1972 when the deficit fell to $737 million.[41] These deficits have been incurred in substantial degree because of the unusually heavy dependence of South Korean industry on imported raw materials, some of which are available in North Korea. Since relief and aid expenditures during the American military government period totaled about $1 billion in four years, South Korea's deficit might be considered to have run at a yearly rate of $250 million during that period.

All in all, from 1946 through FY 1972 Korea has received, according to official figures, a total of $5,743,000,000 in military assistance and sales; and economic assistance from 1946 until 1973 of $5,704,000,000. This plus private U.S. investment of $112,300,000. Total U.S. military and economic aid to South Korea from August 1945 through FY 1973 thus totals just over $12 billion. Had Korea not been divided, the United States might possibly have given her military and economic aid of about $3 billion. Thus the costs to the United States that are attributable to the division might well be considered to run about $9 billion. North Korea continues to spend over half a billion dollars a year (15 percent of 1973 budgetary expenditures) on her own armed forces, a heavy continuing burden on her society.

Pre-1950 costs were especially closely connected with the effects of division; those in the 1950s are more closely related to the costs of reconstruction from war damage—also a fruit of division; those since 1960 are attributable to the buildup for a modern economy, a minority part of which are the costs of building facilities in two countries which would be redundant if the two countries were one. Economic aid to North Korea from the Soviet Union, while substantial, has been much less. Even so, North Korean deficits in commodity trade with the USSR totaled $36,698,000 during 1955–68 and with Eastern European communist countries came to $133,934,000 during 1955–67. Grants of $250 million from the USSR, of $265 million from Eastern European countries, and of $200 million from the People's Republic of China, all given in 1953, were used for economic reconstruction and relief purposes. These were followed by smaller amounts of loans and credits, sometimes canceled, some of which were used for military purposes.[42]

Even without the costs of war, the costs of division are great. In South Korea scores of millions of dollars were poured into the building of coal-consuming power plants to replace cheaper and abundant hydraulic sources in North Korea. Current (1972–74) economic programs in the ROK increase costs of duplication there by strong emphasis on a heavy chemical industry which is one of North Korea's chief industrial resources. Years of importing fertilizer, at some $50 million per year, were followed by many more millions invested in fertilizer plants in South Korea while substantial and cheaper plants, which had once serviced the South, existed in North Korea.[43] Iron and bituminous coal was imported for South Korean steel and industry while such supplies were abundant in North Korea; imports of iron and steel ($13.5 million in 1958 alone), of which North Korea also had large supplies, were followed by the investment of scores of millions of borrowed funds in a South Korean iron and steel industry of dubious economic feasibility which has so far earned large deficits. There were imports of other chemicals and metals in South Korea, too; while North Korea exported them in quantity to other countries. And South Korea imported 30 percent of her needs of wood while abundant resources existed in the North. Deficits in major communication industries in South Korea are also due partly to loss of the North Korean markets.

On the North Korean side, one must count the unavailability of consumer goods which has held the North Korean population to very modest consumption levels of frequently poor quality, 60 percent reportedly produced by cottage industry; imports of machinery, some of which the South could fabricate; and occasional food needs while a small surplus was formerly and occasionally available in the South. Perhaps greatest of all North Korean losses has been the lack of a sufficient supply both of ordinary labor, of the highly trained researcher and theoretician, and, in former periods, of managers. Even today, despite the fact that two independent economies have been created out of halves that once complemented each other within a unity, many economic savings could still be achieved by unification. The wastes and disruptions outlined above have already run into the billions of dollars. Of course, if one adds to this the costs of refugees, of the Korean war, and of the maintenance for twenty-five years of two large and expensive military establishments, the costs of division would escalate into large numbers of billions. Such losses correlate in large part with the costs included within the aforementioned U.S. aid figures. Total damages to the ROK economy are estimated at $1.8 billion, roughly equivalent to the ROK's gross national product for 1949; total damage to the DPRK was probably even greater. Homes destroyed, 400,000 for the ROK, may well have totaled over a million for the entire peninsula. Over 40 percent of all industrial facilities in the South and well over 60 percent in the North were damaged or destroyed.[44]

In short, the economic costs of Korea's division and the economic distortion and duplication these have brought are of impressive—and distressing—dimensions. As modern industrial economies grow in both Koreas, arguments for integration increase and are important among the causes for revived contact today.

Refugees

The entry of Soviet occupation troops into North Korea touched off a major flow of refugees from North to South Korea. The flow was almost as immediate as, and eventually more impressive proportionately than, that which the entry of Soviet occupation forces into East Germany started toward the West.

The reasons for the Korean refugee flight were not dissimilar to those for the German, although shallower in historical depth. Koreans had received extensive propaganda from the Japanese indoctrinating them against Russian aims in the Far East in general and communism in particular. The indoctrination was easily absorbed: the Koreans were a homogeneous people with strong in-group feelings while the Russians were a completely alien group, historically new in Korea; contact between the two was sparse and difficult. Misunderstanding and rumor regarding Russian and communist harshness was thus easily implanted. Soviet Far Eastern troops had experienced little fighting and privation compared to the Soviet conquerors of Germany; but their educational, cultural, and behavioral standard did not impress the Koreans as high, and fear of them was widespread. It was soon compounded by the extreme propaganda and by violence against property holders, former officials and independent-minded students on the part of local communists and those joining their bandwagon. Besides the propertied classes, there were many Christians. North Korea, especially in the northwest, had been a rich area of Christian proselytizing—one of the richest in mission annals anywhere. Most Christians fled South, reaching for a future with a "Christian democracy."

No firm statistics are possible; none on refugees in Korea has ever been made. By the end of 1945, however, 500,000 refugees—a rate of 4,000 every day—had already come. By mid-1947, some 17 percent of the North Korean population, or approximately 1.8 million persons, had fled from

North Korea, with 120,000 more coming from China and Manchuria.[45] From October 1950 on, especially during the fall of 1950, ROK sources claim that upward of 2 million refugees fled or were evacuated from North Korea in the wake of the occupation by UN forces. A 1961 North Korean source claims, however, that the total reduction in the northern population from 1949 until 1953 was 1.13 million, or some 12 percent of 1949's 9.6 million population. Counting births and deaths, especially deaths in war, would place refugee outflow at, roughly, the 1.2-million to 1.4-million level.[46] In sum, the South thus estimates that upward of 5 million refugees, or over one-third of North Korea's present population, have fled. The North's statistics are far more modest, and it is probable that some watering of ROK estimates took place for propaganda purposes. Total refugees may actually number closer to 3 million. Almost all came in the first six years of liberation. In addition, prior to 1950, 1,108,047 Koreans, mostly war workers, returned from Japan.

The returnees from Japan went mostly to their original homes in southern Korea, mostly Kyongsang and Cheju provinces. The refugees from the North stayed briefly in refugee camps but, unlike refugees in Germany, they were soon absorbed through Korea's extended-family system or housed in structures abandoned by the Japanese. The refugees were rapidly integrated into South Korean communities. This rapid integration created an important communication system, spreading the hostilities of the refugees and their adverse experiences in the North throughout most of the society, especially in Seoul and other opinion centers. The refugee flow removed from the North most of those discontented with communism. In the South, many communists fled North, many more sympathizers (or suspected sympathizers) were killed by South Koreans in the extensive witch hunts following the communist occupation; elimination of communism from the South was ruthless and as complete as it is possible to be. The population disruption created was proportionately one of the most major within any nation of the widely disturbed postwar world. The departure of so many people from the North and their incorporation into the society of the South constituted an immense force for hostility and polarization. No separate refugee party was ever formed, but refugees, particularly those from northwestern Korea, have been prominent in the Democratic party, in the regime of Prime Minister Chang Myon (1960–61), and in the new Democratic opposition party. Apprehension regarding this group and its political-social power is believed to have been one factor behind the declaration of martial law and the extreme political measures imposed by President Park on October 17, 1972.

The large number of refugees in the ROK has given rise to the view that refugees in Korea live only in the South. This is not entirely true. Communists and leftists were originally more numerous in South Korea, and their numbers swelled as soon as the stern and ubiquitous restraints of the Japanese colonial government vanished. From 4,000 members at liberation, indigenous communist chief Pak Hon-yong claimed 29,000 by March 1946. Even the U.S. military government estimated from 15,000 to 20,000 communists in South Korea during this period. Communist affiliates and front groups numbered in the thousands and claimed millions, though the allegiance of most was evanescent. When first the U.S. military government and then the Rhee government cracked down, from 1947 on, many communists fled to the North. Others, crypto-communists or communist sympathizers and collaborators with the North during its June–September occupation of Seoul and other parts of South Korea, fled north with the defeated communist forces or were killed. The total of such refugees appears not to be known; it would certainly number in the thousands, perhaps as many as 20,000. A large percentage of these people were intellectuals and their families. Their ultimate influence in the DPRK is not presently assessable. Most ROK and American sources incline to the feeling that the downfall of the native communist movement around Pak Hon-yong deprived his followers of power as well. The truth, when known, may not be as clear-cut as this.

Another group is significant in North Korea, although it does not fall within the normal definition of refugees: Koreans emigrating to North Korea from Japan. The DPRK has assiduously cultivated the loyalty of the 600,000 Koreans in Japan, many of whom have been discriminated against and underemployed. North Korea has contributed some $25 million since 1951 to an extensive educational system for Koreans in Japan, stressing communist texts and values. Needing both skilled and unskilled labor, North Korea negotiated through its Red Cross with the Japanese Red Cross an agreement concluded in August 1959 under which Koreans could "repatriate" to the DPRK if they so chose (though 98 percent of those born in Korea came from the South). Under this agreement, some 100,000 Koreans have repatriated since 1959, the great majority of them in 1960–61. More than half of these repatriates were born after 1940 and were thus educated in the North Korean schools in Japan. Transplanted to North Korea's intensely closed society, this group, brought up in a far freer world, may have had considerable effect in North Korea, but its extent and nature are unknown.[47]

Political Structure

Each occupying power attempted to establish a government in its zone of Korea that reflected its own views of governance. The communists did so with infinitely better preparation and far more systematically, constructing a communist regime of Stalinist totalitarian ilk which has long outlasted its model in the Soviet Union but has, in its own ruthless way, proved effective thus far. With no preparation and considerably less conviction, the Americans took less effective but still definite steps to encourage free electoral process, a parliamentary body, political parties, and some other aspects of democratic rule. Although this system has shown some signs of flourishing and has attracted considerable support, it has proved less effective, has become less democratic, and has in the last months of 1972 and the first months of 1973 been replaced with an authoritarian system in which popular participation promises to be allowed no more than a minor and closely controlled role. With the hostilities of division, as with others, the Clausewitz dictum appears to stand: Enemies imitate each other.

From the beginning, the establishment of democracy in South Korea was scarcely fullhearted. The country was for two years in chaos. The economy broke down completely, unemployment and inflation skyrocketed, four thousand refugees a day hurled themselves against this broken system, and crime and political unrest rose to the heights of a serious insurrection on October 1, 1946. Communists and their sympathizers were at first the strongest and most articulate political force; chaos tended to abet their power, and only the police with brutal and authoritarian methods stood athwart the path to communist control. The Japanese had not allowed political parties; none existed in August 1945, and the scores that started in subsequent weeks lacked roots or cohesion. This background did not encourage thoroughgoing political or legal reform of the kind needed to implant the seeds of democracy on soil previously fallow of notions of political freedom, nor was the American military government equipped with the democratic zeal or the political subtlety to perform so difficult a task.

The start was not auspicious. On June 29, 1946, the military commander, General John Hodge, proposed a legislature to make laws, review appointments, and be a forum for free discussion. All decisions were, however, to be subject to the military government's review. The ninety members of the legislature were to be half elected and half appointed by the military governor, roughly in the manner characterized by the previous Japanese county, island, and provincial councils. Since there had been indications that if full suffrage were allowed, the Left would triumph, suffrage was limited: each hamlet, village, and district "elected" two representatives to serve as provincial electors. Many were simply appointed since Japanese legislation restricting suffrage to taxpayers remained on the books. The electors sent provincial representatives to a Korean Interim Legislative Assembly (KILA), which met from December 1946 to the middle of 1948. In all that time, it passed only eleven laws, several of them trivial and others badly drawn. It debated a constitution which was vetoed and never used. For most of its brief life, it was boycotted and cantankerous. The public lost interest.[48]

The second National Assembly, known as the first (regular) National Assembly, was established as a result of UN observation and the U.S. military government's electoral laws described above. Markedly greater effort went into this election and it was correspondingly more successful, despite considerable political unrest and violence which resulted in the deaths of 589 persons and the police "processing" some 10,000 persons in the ten days leading to the polling. This Assembly elected Dr. Syngman Rhee president and passed the constitution, a land-reform law, and much other important legislation.

Since the Assembly had been the initial basis of government, there was considerable discussion about creating a cabinet-responsible system. The assemblymen, however, knew little of constitutional law and embodied in themselves no national consensus on the kind of government to be created. They were therefore swayed by Dr. Rhee to change the draft to a strong presidential system with the prime minister retained only as "an assistant to the president."[49] Dr. Rhee had the clout to persuade this change: he emerged as premier politician and certain front-runner for the presidency; though American-educated, he was a strong-minded authoritarian figure with a very limited tolerance for democratic opposition.

The text of the 1948 constitution pronounced many democratic rights and freedoms, though most civil rights were made subject to the specifications of law to be enacted. It provided some checks and balances between the Executive and the Legislature, including the right of the latter to elect the president. The Judiciary was less independent and armed with fewer checks; its judges were subject to executive reappointment after ten years, and its constitutional review was subject to a constitutional committee (which was never appointed). The president appointed all top officials unilaterally except for the prime minister and chief justice who required Assembly approval; all could be removed by the president alone. The Assembly did have the right to pass legislation over presidential veto. In a manner reminiscent of the Weimar constitution, the Korean president was given emergency powers "to issue orders having the effect of law."

The margin of executive domination was great. Predictably, it was insufficient for President Rhee. When the Assembly in 1949 began passing legislation over his veto, he arrested and tried thirteen of its members. He turned back an amendment to secure a clear-cut cabinet system in 1950. When another such amendment was backed by over two-thirds of the assemblymen and his own reelection was threatened in 1952 by a hostile Assembly, he again arrested forty-five opposition members, releasing them only to vote on amendments taking his election out of the legislature and making it direct and popular. Further amendments of 1954 removed the two-term restriction on presidential tenure and provided for national referendum on constitutional amendments. The position of the president them seemed almost Caesaristic; it was nothing to what was, after a brief democratic interlude, to come.[50]

Such concentration of power brought its own corruption. The presidential elections of March 1960 became so crucial that they were crudely rigged, triggering violent student demonstrations which turned to revolution and brought the government down, April 19–25, 1960. The long-suffering constitution, already three times amended, was amended again, this time extensively. The presidential system was abandoned in favor of a cabinet system, civic rights were strengthened and no longer made subject to later provisions of law, political parties were given constitutional recognition, and the right to legislate during emergencies was hedged. The Assembly was to have two Houses which were to elect the president, now "head of State" instead of "head of the Executive Branch of the Government."

The democratic constitution was to have tragically short duration. The Second Republic was beset with unrest, especially among the students. And since they had brought the republic into being, they could not easily be quelled by it; at one point, student demonstrations forced a patently undemocratic, ex post facto, retroactive deprivation of civil liberties law. Parliamentary government also resulted in excessive party competition; an almost even split of the ruling Democratic party into two separate parties caused more quarrels about power than about policy. To achieve support, Prime Minister Chang Myon felt it necessary to carry out cabinet reshuffling on an average of every three months. Student initiative toward unification, while small in scale and probably harmless in nature, brought great apprehension. Economic and social problems, undertaken with dedication, seemed overwhelming when processed through lengthy parliamentary debate in two houses.

Gradually, by the spring of 1961, progress was being made toward greater public security and even to widening parliamentary majorities for the government. But the repressions of the Rhee government had led to expectations that the cumbersome processes of democracy could not easily satisfy. A divided country that had just fought a major war also felt keener apprehensions in the face of social disorder and the security problems than governments in peaceful and undivided countries are likely to feel.

As a result, a group of roughly 3,500 men, assembled around a core of 250 officers within a 500,000-man army, staged a coup under Major-General Park Chung-hee originally planned against the Rhee regime. It rapidly succeeded in bringing the surprised government down; with it ended, until today, Korea's brief experiment with liberal democracy.

The succeeding government has, of course, widely propagandized "the failure of democracy" during this period. Whether democracy of this ilk could or could not have succeeded in the longer run, no man can know. The government was making progress; there were important defects and unsolved problems. Only a longer time would have enabled judgment of success or failure. In the end, the democratic regime failed in the sense that it insufficiently guarded against coups: in a broader sense, it did not fail; it was overthrown.

The military coup shut down both Houses of the Assembly, and ruled by a junta which banned all political or demonstration activity; disbanded political parties; closed much of the press and controlled the rest; passed a "Law Regarding Extraordinary Measures for National Reconstruction" which superseded the constitution in essential respects and appropriated executive, legislative, and judicial powers to itself; and arrested and tried thousands of prominent persons. Return to civilian control was promised, but only after extensive further revisions of the increasingly battered constitution. These revisions, so extensive as to constitute an essentially new constitution, were passed by the junta's Supreme Council on November 3, 1962, and "ratified" by popular referendum on December 17. "Return to civilian control" was now interpreted to mean control by coup leaders in civilian instead of military uniform, and General Park edged out his political opponents in a closely fought election on October 15, 1963, for a four-year term as president.

The essentially new 1962 constitution predictably made the position of the president stronger than it had ever been relative to the other branches of government. The cabinet was downgraded to a consultative body; the president was to appoint the prime minister without the National Assembly's concurrence, and to appoint the cabinet ministers on the prime minister's recommendation. All were removable at the president's discretion, though the National Assembly might "advise" such removal. There is no vice-president. The National Assembly was unicameral, its sessions limited in length and the government empowered to continue defraying expenses in accordance with the previous budget until the Assembly passed a new one. The president also appointed the justices of the Supreme Court on recommendation rather than, as before, confirming electoral choices by a body of judges. Candidates for the National Assembly are required to be members of a political party and lose their seats if they leave or change parties during their tenure. Authorization of some censorship, government prescription for the standard of publication and the facilities of a newspaper or press, and a stipulation that "the press or publication" shall not "infringe upon public morality and social ethics," absent from former constitutions, appeared in these amendments as did strong provisions for emergency presidential powers and proclamation of a state of siege during which freedoms of speech, press, assembly, and association may be totally suspended.[51]

A further 1971 amendment to the constitution allowed President Park to run for a third term.

In the last months of 1972, the sixth major rewriting of the Korean constitution in twenty-four years has brought into being a new form of government. It promises to complete the long process, temporarily interrupted in 1960–61, whereby democratic procedures and some system of checks and balances are replaced by increasingly uncurbed executive domination. It is now hard to see how presidential dictatorship can be carried much farther in any modern constitutional form.

The amendments drafted by the State Council, announced in October 1972 and ratified by popular referendum in December 1972 now make peaceful unification a supreme constitutional aspiration, providing for the election by direct ballot of a National Conference for Unification comprising 2,359 delegates who will "without discussion" elect the president for a six-year term (to which he can be reelected without limit) and also, on the president's recommendation, will elect one-third of the National Assembly. The National Conference will also have power to discuss and confirm any amendments to the constitution proposed by members of the National Assembly and "will become a representative body for national consensus on matters concerning national unification." [52] Its members are not permitted to join political parties.

New general elections on February 27, 1973, prematurely replacing those of the year before, chose 146 new members of the National Assembly to six-year terms after campaigns with a limited degree of political freedom and even more limited press freedom. President Park's 73 appointees were dutifully "elected" by the National Conference for Unification on March 7, and the ninth National Assembly was formally inaugurated on March 12. All appointed members belong—apparently automatically and unanimously—to a new *Yujonghoe* (Revitalizing Reforms Political Fraternity Group). There are 71 elected Government party members, 52 members of a mild opposition and 2 of an extreme opposition group, and 21 independents.

The Assembly can be in session for a maximum of 90 days plus two extraordinary sessions of 30 days unless summoned by the president to discuss only his agenda. The president also has the power to dissolve the National Assembly. The Assembly has the right of concurrence in the appointment of the prime minister and to adopt a resolution on his removal and that of individual cabinet members. A provision for national referendum of important issues is newly inscribed. Constitutional amendments introduced by the National Assembly must now surmount the added hurdle of approval by a two-thirds' majority in the National Conference, a rubber-stamp body for the Executive.

The Judiciary is again weakened by having determination of constitutionality removed from it and given to a nine-man Constitution Committee appointed by the president, three selected by the National Assembly, three upon recommendation of the chief justice and three directly by the president. Judges are appointed by the president and, in accordance with subsequent regulations, can be dismissed by him. The equivalent of habeas corpus in the old Korean constitution is eliminated. Protection against conviction on the basis of confessions obtained by torture is summarily dropped, thus ending even the pretense of civil rights.

The rights and freedoms in the constitution are further weakened by being made subject to law "in individual cases."

The new constitution, while constantly professing democracy, bears few traces of it. Rather, it appears to combine the easily guided power of mass bodies divorced from free political parties, which characterizes communism, with the mingling of appointment and election to partially consultative bodies, which characterized the Japanese colonial system. The stage seems set either for an indefinite, essentially dictatorial congealing of political process or for its overthrow by violent coup or revolution. Unification, even along essentially undemocratic, authoritarian lines, does not appear to be any nearer. Article 3 still claims for the republic "the Korean peninsula and its adjacent islands." Agreement among dictators is not necessarily—or frequently—encouraged by the narrowing of the distance between the systems over which they preside.

The fate of political parties in South Korea has somewhat paralleled that of constitutions. The republic started with amorphous, schismatic political groups, constantly merging and disappearing. Out of these, from 1949 until 1952, an increasingly strong opposition Democratic party developed. This party forced President Rhee to abandon rule-through-atomization and to construct his own government Liberal party from the end of 1951 on. The two parties, despite bristling internal factions, developed what, from 1956 until 1960, and despite great attempts to limit and quell the opposition, was essentially a strong two-party system. Attempts to form third parties of socialist persuasion were—and continue to be—frustrated. The Liberal party effectively disappeared with the overthrow of the Rhee regime in 1960. During the Democratic administration, the Democratic party, which had a substantial majority in both Houses, split along factional lines. Disillusionment with this split was an important factor in the overthrow of the democratic regime and in the imposition of rules for party representation established in the first Park constitution. The military government then secretly formed its own party, in the beginning through organization captained by the Central Intelligence Agency. The resulting Democratic Republican party has been, in many ways, a revival with military personnel and somewhat different civilian elements of the type of government party represented by the Liberal party. It also has been threatened with "splitism." Opposition splits have twice been responsible for the failure to defeat President Park. The resurgence of the opposition New Democratic party in the 1971 elections, where it won 89 seats to the DRP's 113, has been a major factor behind the government's October 1972 martial law and amendments: lacking a two-thirds' majority, the government evidently felt it could not hope successfully to conclude accords with the North Koreans when it had to submit them to the 1971–72 National Assembly. Though 73 nongovernment candidates were elected in 1972, compared to the government's 71, opposition members are submerged by the president's appointive power and the creation among these 73 appointees of a third "executive political group" designed to check both popular parties. The September 1972 split in the New Democratic party and its evident infiltration by government agents has been a further cause of deep popular disillusionment with the once-popular party system and has probably induced the Park regime to feel that the Korean public will stomach the drastic downgrading in the political and functional role of parties that is so signal a part of the post-October 1972 South Korean political system.

The political vortex pattern which has induced unbounded competition for access to power regardless of issues, vested interests, or ideology, has maximized the divisiveness of political parties and, on the whole, has thus far minimized their contributions to Korea. The expense of this competition has also mounted alarmingly. The current steps to downgrade parties are probably neither fortunate nor do they represent any national consensus. Yet the problem remains essentially unsolved. Patience will be needed, as the political history of many countries illustrates; it is especially needed in Korea since political parties are hard to anchor in vortex societies.

The political structure of the Republic of Korea was thus jerry-built and has proved highly unstable and lacking in political continuity. With the exception of the democratic interlude in 1960–61, the tendency toward authoritarianism to end unbounded chaotic and expensive competition for central power has been strong. Currently the trend to authoritarianism has seemingly ended—hopefully temporarily—any meaningful democracy in Korea, an experiment in which much hope and many lives had been, and perhaps still will be, invested. The division of the country and the need to compete with a massive communist system and its chronic efforts at infiltration are one element—an overtly expressed one—behind this authoritarian trend. To this observer, the communist threat, a well-prepared-for constant, is a comparatively minor reason, a pretext used by the wielders of authority rather than the genuine cause of authoritarianism. Part of that cause lies within the nature of authority within the Korean family and educational systems, systems ingrained in the socialization of the Korean child. Even more important is the fundamental political pattern of an ancient and unmitigated centralism which provides no alternate values to the possession of government authority, hence subtly shattering all other cohesions not based on such possession. A third cause lies in the authoritarian-military background and convictions of present government leaders. The result in a divided country is a system triply brittle because it provides insufficient political contrast to the authoritarian North; because it lacks a consistent or convincingly implemented ideology; and because its discontinuity robs it of experience in operation or of the sustained buildup of popular confidence. Whether the political system now being put into operation will acquire legitimacy is dubious. The results of the February 27, 1973, elections and fall demonstrations show that it has not yet done so.

Neither discontinuity nor lack of ideology infect the political system of the Democratic People's Republic of Korea in the north, though the imposition of the original system was here far more clear.

Soviet occupation forces moved into North Korea after only one week of fighting. Their command had had long years to ponder the future, and though little is known of their preparations, it is known both from direct observation and from the means they used that prepare they did, unlike their American opposite numbers.[53] In these preparations they had the great advantage of controlling an ethnic Korean population of several hundred thousand; in contrast, only about 10,000 Koreans, mostly the descendants of fieldhands on Hawaiian sugar plantations, then lived under the American flag. Soviet commanders also had standard communist doctrine and procedure for political takeover, which were considerably more effective than Hodge's field manuals and lack of instructions. They had the added advantage of better information—a large Soviet Consulate-General had operated in Seoul throughout the war. The Soviet and U.S. commands in the Pacific theater had operated entirely separately, with no joint operations or liaison. The mutual perception of hostility was thus less mitigated, the basis for even limited rapport smaller, than in Europe.[54]

The Soviet occupation forces hence were able to bring into North Korea some 30,000 Soviet-Koreans, thoroughly indoctrinated and, in part at least, apparently quite well trained.[55] They also brought back in a Soviet major's uniform a former guerrilla force leader named Kim Song-ju who had taken the nom de guerre of Kim Il-song. He was introduced as a hero on October 3, 1945, was quickly made first secretary of the North Korean Central Bureau of the Korean Communist party, emerged as the main link between the Soviet-established Korean administration and the occupying forces, and has ever since been the unrivaled leader of North Korea. Virtually unknown inside Korea until liberation, the reasons behind choosing him are a closely held communist secret. Like most Koreans, he was not prominent within the Soviet Union; less prominent, certainly, than one or two other Korean-born leaders. If he was chosen for his obedience to Soviet authorities, they might originally have felt a satisfaction later to be disillusioned.

The incoming Soviets found more communists to work with than the Americans did confirmed democrats, but the number was still small—a few thousand—and the forces were divided into those who had worked only within Korea, those returning with the Korean leaders from Yenan, those exiled in the Soviet Union, and those born and raised there. These forces rapidly created the North Korean branch of the Korean Communist party, and knowing generally what was expected of them, they worked with a will to establish local people's committees. A puppet North Korean Provisional People's Committee began to function in February 1946 as the highest administrative organ under the Soviet forces. Kim Il-song was its chairman. A year later, after single-slate, open-ballot "elections," a convention of People's Committees created a Supreme People's Assembly and elected a Presidium and Supreme Court. A North Korean Workers' party was formed from the merger of Kim's Communist party and the Yenan group's old Korean Independence League (newly redesignated the New People's party). A further merger in June 1949 of the North Korean Workers' party with the old South Korean Labor party, the native communist group, united all communists within the all-powerful Korean Workers' party and brought the political bases of rival communist leaders firmly under Kim Il-song. From this base plus his continuing hold on administration, the previously obscure Kim Il-song achieved in less than three years what it took Stalin seventeen years to do—he became the leader of both party and state. From this position, he has successively eliminated all other communist factions and has ruled without known threat since 1958.

On August 25, 1948, a new "national election" was held to form a new Supreme People's Assembly, always a rubber-stamp body. The Assembly ratified a new constitution and proclaimed the establishment of the Democratic People's Republic of Korea (the DPRK) on September 8, 1948. Kim Il-song was named premier on September 10.[56] The new government was recognized by the Soviet Union on October 12 and became more fully independent when Soviet troops were withdrawn at the end of 1948. For a few years, the Soviets continued to exercise substantial control both through the occupation of some two hundred critical positions, including most vice-ministerships, by Soviet-Koreans and through its embassy and numerous advisory personnel. By the middle 1950s, the Soviet control apparatus was greatly decreased; the DPRK has long ceased to live under significant foreign controls. Indeed, relations with the USSR and other communist countries have sometimes been subject to strain, and recent visitors to North Korea report that feeling on neither side is warm or especially close.

The first constitution, ratified on September 8, 1948, outlined a formal governmental structure, declared that state power belongs to the people, provided for popular election of officials, and included guarantees of equal rights. It was largely window-dressing. Power in the state lay institutionally with the Korean Worker's party whose programs constituted the country's real law. The party lies outside the constitutional framework. For all practical purposes, Kim Il-song, as head of party and government, is the real source of law and its enforcer.[57] On October 30, 1972, the official North Korean press agency declared that the draft of a new DPRK constitution had been completed to prepare for the reunification of the peninsula, paralleling the new constitutional amendments being adopted in the South, perhaps by real or tacit agreement. The new constitution, ratified December 27, 1972, did increase DPRK centralization; it distinguishes between achieving "the complete victory of socialism in the northern half" and driving out foreign forces from and peaceful democratic unification of the southern half; and it claims Pyongyang and not, as previously, Seoul as its rightful capital.[58]

The educational system, one of the most extensive of any nation, is a monopoly of the state. Since November 24, 1966, an overall nine-year compulsory technological education law has been in effect which not only links education with productive labor in an increasingly advanced industrial nation but continues heavy indoctrination in the Korean version of the communist system. It emphasizes national achievement, the state system, and the thought, predominance, and virtually holy status of Kim Il-song.[59] An extremely large university system of some 78 universities with around 100,000 students carries technological training and indoctrination to higher levels. Very few students are allowed to study outside Korea and, since 1959, almost only in the Soviet Union with perhaps a few in China.

The political system of the DPRK is one of the most monolithic, exacting, and centralized systems of control ever instituted over a large human group. It is proud of and, for a socialist system, outstandingly insistent on its own independence. It is also one of the most isolated of all polities; North Korean citizens are perhaps more sedulously sealed from foreign contact than any other major educated people on earth. It is, therefore, not possible to judge directly what legitimacy the government has acquired since its earlier days when the flow of nearly one-third of its population southward was symptomatic of widespread fear and distaste. Signs of instability or overt dissatisfaction have, however, been absent or successfully concealed for years. The dominance, the virtually complete monopoly of power, by Kim Il-song and his personal followers and family has constantly escalated. It is probably rivaled in the present-day world, if at all, only by Albania; even there cultism is less overpowering. The services of an entire, well-organized state reinforce constantly the social and political system and its leadership. Education also unites technology and political indoctrination. Despite certain factional undercurrents from 1945 until 1958, and some changing external relations, the continuity of the political system and its leadership has been massive, surpassing not only South Korea by far but almost all other states in the world except Spain, Ethiopia, and Iran as well. The industrial and other achievements of the country betoken the capacity to obey and produce under the system with considerable individual sacrifice. The insulation of North Korea from outside observation makes accurate judgment impossible. On the whole, however, a fairly broad North Korean feeling of considerable legitimacy and conviction in the system, plus experience in its extended operations, must be assumed until and unless closer contact brings indications to the contrary.

Identity and Hostilization

Korea provides one of human history's most interesting and astonishing examples of the process and strength of hostilization and an arresting instance of the related process of identity formation.

As mentioned earlier, the original cause of the division of Korea had no relationship to any issue within Korea. Not only did Koreans themselves play no part in the original division, but the evidence fails to show that the occupying powers intended to divide Korea or had strong original motivations for so doing. The reason why entry and occupation was not joint appears to lie in considerations external to Korea and partly practical: in the speed with which the war was concluded and the differing alacrity with which each side could respond to the situation which war's end brought to Korea.

Granted this, and the enormously strong factors of history, common political experience, language, culture, and economic development binding Koreans together, one would logically expect to see not only sentiment—which has always existed—but a powerful native movement insisting on the overcoming of these barriers and acting to quell their obstacles.

Instead, in the course of the first fifteen weeks of division, one sees the formation of political movements within each part of Korea insisting, sometimes more powerfully than the occupation authorities themselves, on making unification conditional on political terms difficult for the other side and frequently opposing or refusing cooperation with the efforts of the occupying powers to negotiate an end to division. In the South, attempts by responsible leaders even to meet with their recent colleagues in the independence movement, who were now in the North, were met with accusations of almost treachery to which those who tried compromise sacrificed their political careers. In a few weeks, each of the two commands intentionally or unintentionally created in each zone a group cast in—or caricaturing—its own image, a group so hostile to the other that, for twenty-six years, until the late summer of 1971, no directives or policies could bring them together. Nor was the hostile division thus invoked even enclosed within the peninsula; it spread at once to Korean communities abroad, especially to the more than 600,000 Koreans in Japan who have remained irreparably sundered.[60]

How could the strong, homogenizing work of thirteen centuries be reversed in so brief a time and chiefly by foreign influence? Even if language and basic culture survived, how could ideology and the aims and organization of politics be so quickly reshaped and loyalties shattered and reconstructed? How can brothers in a closely knit culture be so instantly recast into enemies?

History is not the culprit; neither is language; nor religion, although Christians generally fled the North and concentrated in the South. The communist/anticommunist split in the independence movement created hostilities that played a role and became magnified; yet this role was confined to a few thousand persons at most and was probably not primary. Ideology played a larger role: conservatives had been heavily indoctrinated against communists, while Korean Communists saw hostile images both in the incoming American troops and in the Korean police and conservatives who rallied to them. Even so, the proportion of Koreans then deeply aware of either communism or democracy was extremely small, perhaps one percent. Its role could not be compared to that played by Catholicism and Protestantism in the sixteenth century in dividing Czech or German populations which lived almost entirely by these religions. One can assume that power politics played an important role in the drawing of the 38th parallel, the entry of American troops as far north as then thought possible, and in the Soviet decisions not to permit communication or compromise between the two zones. To the extent that Soviet-American hostilities were important on a personal negotiatory level, they perhaps derived from assumptions of power politics. Even here, they are largely inexplicit and sometimes appear only partly intentional. Yet even when such factors played roles, they are more background of the conflict than the conflict itself. None explains adequately how the occupying powers communicated their hostilities—or their hostile politics—so rapidly to the Koreans, and in the American zone so largely unintentionally, as to pulverize the unifying forces of thirteen Korean centuries.

The answer appears to lie chiefly in the nature of group formation and in the psychology that operates when groups form. That no trusteeship, and above all no central government, either foreign or domestic, was provided for in the first fifteen weeks deprived the occupation of a common goal and of the forces of merger and compromise. Without calculating the consequences, each side's military was given carte blanche to create its own system. The policy card may have been blank, but not the culture which animated the systems. Large and active armed forces moving as rulers without the restrictions normally imposed on foreign nationals, by their daily action, directed or undirected, stamped each zone with an image. Strengthened by the organization inherent to armies and the cultural self-confidence bestowed by victory, the administration of each zone rapidly forged two Korean groups with incompatible political, economic, and international orientations and openly hostile intentions toward each other. These groups quickly graded themselves in terms of fidelity or hostility to communism or the Americans instead of by linguistic, historical, or ethnic ties. Such cultural ties suddenly became no more obstructive to hostility than were ancient ethnic, linguistic, and historical ties to the enmity between Tories and revolutionaries on the American East Coast in 1775.[61]

True, if Korea had had the communication system of, say, Ethiopia and had never known, even remotely, modern political systems or a rightist-leftist split, schism would have formed far more slowly and probably very differently. The nature of the communication system within Korean society permitted the imposed systems to be internalized with alarming effectiveness. This communication system needs explanation, for the communication of hostility is a basic component of Korea's division.

Korea's communication system has sociohistorical roots. Korea had long been a peculiar and extreme society: a relatively homogeneous environment in which a paucity of interest groups and local power was capped by a highly developed centralism that neither had nor tolerated rivals. This central power had long been the instrument for transmitting foreign systems and models. The central structure also outweighed all others by incorporating organization and techniques of administration designed for imperial China's continent-wide needs. The resulting overwhelming strength of the center had several implications. Once central power in Seoul or Pyongyang had been captured, its messages could be broadcast with peculiar amplification downward. Receptivity to the broadcasts of centralism was great: nothing competed with government; nothing blocked, compromised, or qualified its terms.

This alone meant that whoever was in power tended to dispose of effective communication channels. Added to this, however, were the social derivatives of the communication system. Such unopposed central power tended to create its own social dynamic. Since no other aggregates came close to rivaling central power, men tended not to cohere in intermediate groups but each man of ambition sought central power through his own individual channel or in incohesive groups set up only for the temporary purpose of lodging oneself in the top of the wall. Such atomized citizenry, lacking the experience of unity in intermediate groups, tended to incorporate rivalry, jealousy, and hostility more easily than it did solidarity and mutual cooperation. The structure of society showed a lack of connection among the parts that hindered coagulation into interest expression or opposition, even opposition to foreign occupiers.

In 1945 such atomization was at peak levels. The Japanese government's always stern centralization had increased in wartime. War had also required forced industrialization and mass mobilizations. Koreans by the hundreds of thousands were knocked from their rural niches and social settings and herded into new environments in both Korea and, through wartime corvée, in Japan. Rootless, they were prey to the mass "populist" movements of workers, contributors, volunteers, and "patriots" of Japan's last militarist days. Japan had also been the overweening model for Korea's modernization. When Soviet and American occupiers suddenly stood in the still-warm Japanese boots, Koreans looked to them for models, for direction, even for mobilization. The occupiers, half aware, found under them a society with a surface malleability beyond their expectations. This capacity for mobilization was used by the Soviet forces with far greater skill than by the Americans. In the South, however, what the Americans lacked, the new politicians and their instant youth groups partially provided. Even the anticipation of mobilization prepared people to listen. Hence the two diverse governing models had amplified divisive effects.

These divisive effects were heightened by other aspects of the communication system. Though not nearly so literate as both Koreas were soon to become, Koreans were already nearly 60 percent literate and lived in a relatively developed environment of communications, enjoying many newspapers, journals, and radio stations.[62] The communists with their trained cadres commandeered and effectively utilized these media to spread the communist system. They even published their own newspaper in Seoul for weeks until Hodge—who never operated a U.S. military government newspaper—closed it. The U.S. command did, however, use radio; the South Korean press carried its statements and Korean managers, newly appointed by military government to run Japanese-owned media, were somewhat responsive to the Occupation. Conservative landlord elements controlled the chief Korean-language newspapers which blossomed into being important instigators of a campaign opposing the communists and joint control with them through trusteeship and supporting a separate South Korean government. The role of the media was vital in highlighting the differences between the two systems, criticizing what was deemed hostile and rallying support for campaigns and demonstrations which, erupting almost daily in those days, were themselves important media.

Refugees were another vital component in hostility communication. Not only did 1.8 million, or 17 percent, of the North Korean population flee between 1945 and 1948, but they remained very briefly in refugee camps. Rapidly integrated into the malleable world of Korean opinion formation, the refugees created their own communication systems, spreading their hostilities and adverse experiences in the North through most of the society, especially in Seoul and other opinion centers.

Equally vital were the groups created by both sides as instruments of real or perceived policy. Cadres of largely Soviet-Koreans built local communist cadres on all levels. The language of communism used in these groups provided a new reference through which the eager youth could view what were rapidly emerging as new friends, new enemies. The language specifically stressed such dichotomy. Communism's strong ideological explanation seemed a firm anchor at a time when the regnant Japanese values had been swept away, a dynamic substitute for Confucianism's worn but impressive holism. The groups themselves were impressive socializing instruments and, formed into hierarchies, led toward the ancient dream of participation in central government. Such organizational effectiveness inspired noncommunist groups also to organize and to develop hostile countering propaganda.

Anticommunist groups of every hue soon formed in the more diverse South Korean milieu: youth groups attached to prominent politicians; youth groups attached to the police or to neighborhoods in a postwar world rife in crime; youth groups sometimes also communist or leftist operating for the first two years in the South. Each socialized its members to its own views; fights broke out; men formed loyalties and convictions hardened in demonstrations, violence, and street donnybrooks; compromise was viewed as disloyalty to the group; leadership arose reflecting, then increasing, the trends established. Each college and secondary school reverberated to these struggles, even down into rural settings. Through such opinion-forming mechanisms anticommunist opinion became more extreme among Koreans than it was in the American command, and a split that was at first wholly unnatural soon became the accepted watchword of a society. It was also in this way, in North and South, that separate identities became established and all too rapidly confirmed.

Building on such networks of feeling, Dr. Syngman Rhee established his political hegemony. He and those around him quickly began to oppose any cooperation with the communists. Groups manned demonstrations which, as the fall of 1945 deepened into winter, violently opposed the idea of trusteeship and then the Moscow decision of December 28, 1945, which embodied trusteeship. These networks gave Rhee the power to distance himself from Hodge's attempt to set up a coalition political group that could cooperate with the Joint Commission. Finally, it was this brand of politics and leadership which, when all attempts of Joint Commission negotiation for trusteeship failed, triumphed in a rightist, anticommunist, separatist government.

The split has persisted for a quarter of a century. A different vocabulary has gradually crept into a once united language so that, for dealing with the North Koreans, a new dictionary has been considered. Each side knows different gods. No deity for the South compares with Kim Il-song, though, as the South moves to resemble the North, a personality cult for Park Chung-hee is now starting. Urban apartment living has sprung up in both countries, but the structure of society and the life style differ. The South knows a far more vast panoply of consumer goods; the North is more Spartan but the standards it has achieved are more evenly spread, its defensiveness to outside influences and Western living styles much greater, its sexual freedom far more restricted. Individualism in life style or expression is a sin against the northern system; in the South this trend is perhaps only now beginning. Controls in both Koreas are now ubiquitous, but those in the North are far greater, especially in the economy.

The years from liberation until August 1971 were marked by nothing but hostility. Each side claimed lawful jurisdiction of the whole peninsula; first the North, then the South warred to make good this claim.[63] War brought the bitterest dregs of hostilization. Those who saw hostilities closest—the Koreans especially—noted that no conscious cruelties were so great on the part of either the Communist Chinese or the Allied troops as those which the Korean forces of both sides visited upon each other, and especially upon defenseless civilians. Another 2 million refugees added their stories to South Korean resentment. Education and propaganda on both sides were relentless until the agreement of July 4, 1972, began a slight mildening. This increased on November 4, 1972, by an agreement to cease propaganda broadcasts against one another. Even abroad, contact and civility were strictly avoided. ROK policy was governed by the Hallstein doctrine that relations with any state that recognized the DDR would be terminated. The ROK suspended its diplomatic relations with both the Republic of the Congo (Brazzaville) in 1964 and Mauritania in 1965 when these nations recognized Pyongyang. In Burma, Pakistan, India, and Egypt consular relations were kept after these nations established relations with

Pyongyang, but common habitat was more arouser than assuager of hostility.[64] Recent weeks have opened new diplomatic possibilities for divided Korea. In accordance with the principle agreed upon in March 1973 among five Nordic countries to recognize both Koreas, Sweden announced in early April that it would recognize North Korea and Denmark, Finland, Norway, and Iceland are following suit. Malaysia, India, and others joined later. Seoul's ambassadors in such countries were at first called home, without, however, rupturing relations. They returned by January 1974. Seoul's controlled press has counseled flexibility. There is thus some prospect that sooner or later Korea will make into the path recently taken by Germany and that, as a result, North Korea will be a little less isolated from the noncommunist world and the two Koreas from each other.

The Question of Korean Unification

The question of Korean unification, long one of the more dormant questions, has since August 1971, and especially since July 4, 1972, taken forward steps that have focused world attention on it for the first time since October 1950. As of the moment of writing, what has actually happened remains extremely small in terms even of increase in contact, let alone steps toward unification itself. The latter seems distant, even questionably attainable. Nevertheless, the change in attitude toward contact if not unification has been, especially on the part of the ROK, marked, and the radical nature of the internal changes now being undergone in the ROK in the name of unification bring with them some pressure for more important results.

Following the failure of U.S.–USSR Joint Commission efforts, of the Moscow Agreement, of the UNTCOK effort to observe elections throughout the peninsula, of the North Korean effort to unite Korea by force, of the United Nations effort to do likewise, and of abortive UN efforts of December 1950 and January 1951 to arrange a cease-fire, the line of battle stabilized in the vicinity of the 38th parallel. In June 1951 negotiations began between the UN and the communist commands to fix a line of demarcation militarily more defensible than the 38th parallel had been, provide maximum reasonable assurance against renewed aggression, and arrange for exchange of prisoners. Two years of negotiations ended in an armistice signed on July 27, 1953, providing for a cease-fire, a demilitarized zone 4,000 meters wide between the opposing forces, a military demarcation line roughly parallel to and 25 miles north of the 38th parallel, and a ban on the introduction into Korea of reinforcing military personel and equipment. To supervise the implementation of the armistice agreement and deal with violations, a Military Armistice Commission, composed of officers of the UN Command and the communist forces, was established with headquarters at Panmunjom. The agreement also provided for the naming of a Neutral Nations Supervisory Commission composed of Sweden, Switzerland, Czechoslovakia, and Poland to observe, inspect, and investigate compliance with the terms of the armistice agreement relative to the introduction into Korea of reinforcing military personnel and equipment. The agreement recommended that a political conference at a higher level meet within three months and settle questions of the withdrawal of all foreign forces from Korea and the peaceful settlement of the Korean question.[65] On October 1, 1953, a U.S.–ROK mutual-defense treaty was signed pledging each "to meet the common danger" to the territories in the Pacific area of either party "in accordance with its constitutional processes.[66] North Korea signed military alliances with the Soviet Union and with Communist China in July 1961.

The political conference referred to convened belatedly in Geneva on April 26, 1954, and considered the Korean problem until June 15. On the one side were the Republic of Korea, the United States, and all other powers except South Africa that had contributed military forces to the unified command. On the communist side were the People's Republic of China, North Korea, and the Soviet Union.

At this conference South Korea presented a fourteen-point proposal for Korean unification which can, in general, be considered the official ROK position on unification.[67] The ROK advocated the holding of free elections in both North and South Korea under UN supervision on the basis of a secret ballot and universal adult suffrage; the taking of a census under UN supervision with a view to apportioning the number of representatives in a new National Assembly in exact proportion to the population in the election areas; complete freedom of movement and speech for UN supervisory personnel and for election candidates; maintenance in force of the constitution of the Republic of Korea subject to amendment by the all-Korea legislature to be convened in Seoul immediately after the elections; withdrawal of UN forces to be completed when control had been achieved throughout Korea by the unified government and certified by the United Nations; and a guarantee of the territorial integrity and independence of a unified Korea by the United Nations.[68] Ten nations expressed support for these proposals.

All communist nations rejected the competence and authority of the United Nations for the Korean question. They proposed an all-Korean commission composed of representatives of North and South Korea to be elected by their respective assemblies and including representatives of the "largest democratic and social organizations" in each area to arrange for "free elections" with an equal representation from North and South Korea on this commission and with the stipulation that decisions would be made only on the basis of "mutual agreement." The commission would draft an electoral law preparatory to the elections and develop economic and cultural ties between North and South Korea. All foreign forces were to be withdrawn within six months. "The peaceful development of Korea" should be guaranteed by "those countries most interested in the maintenance of peace in the Far East."[69] A later proposal at the conference envisaged "setting up of an appropriate international commission to supervise the holding of elections," evidently a neutral-nations' body. Already by the time of the conference it was clear that the existing Neutral Nations Supervisory Commission had become useless because of the virtual veto power exercised by the communist members. The conference broke up without agreement, essentially over the issues of a communist veto over all election and other procedures and the question of UN authority. A UN aid agency, UNKRA, and a slightly changed Commission, UNCURK, continued in Korea. UNCURK was abolished November 28, 1973, and left Korea in December. It had contributed nothing for over 15 years and even the South Korean prime minister in remarks of June 23, 1973, said that the Republic of Korea would abide by any UN decision regarding the future of UNCURK.

With the breakdown of the inspection-and-control system over the introduction of troops and equipment, it became clear that a considerable buildup was proceeding in the North. The UN side thereupon initiated buildups of its own. Troop levels and equipment have mounted almost steadily, indeed with added momentum in recent years. There are now (January 1973) approximately 650,000 ROK armed forces, sixth largest in the world; plus a home guard of some 2,000,000 in the South. The North has some 438,000 in its armed forces, twelfth largest in the world, plus a "people's militia" of 1,300,000.[70] There are still some 40,000 American troops in South Korea; no foreign troops have been in North Korea since the withdrawal of the last Chinese Communist forces in October 1958. Both sides have heavily modernized their equipment, the DPRK somewhat more than the ROK, especially in respect to planes where, with 500 modern fighter planes (*vice* 200 for the ROK) and 100 bombers, it holds a marked advantage in the air, as well as in artillery.

DPRK defense costs have been as high as $850 million, 31–35 percent of its budget (25 percent of northern GNP) though the 1972 expenditures were sharply reduced to 17 percent of the budget and those for 1973 have been announced as 1,281,526,500 won (roughly $576.7 million) or 15 percent of total budgetary expenditures.[71] The ROK has spent some 2.4 percent of its budget, 4.6 percent of its GNP, on armed forces in recent years. In 1970 it spent $238 million for defense and had a GNP of $8.7 billion, a burden of only 4.1 percent. Supplementing this, the ROK receives hundreds of millions annually in U.S. military aid; the figure in fiscal year 1972 was $396.9 million. Communist military aid is much less and North Korea's expenditure of 15 percent of her budget (close to the same percentage of her GNP) burdens her own economy. The inability of the

DPRK to make adequate economic headway and still remain reasonably independent in the face of such a military posture is presumed to have been a major factor in the recent willingness of the North to negotiate with and come closer to the ROK. Though actual northern armed forays in the South, numbering many hundreds in 1968–69, fell to nothing between September 1971 and December 1972 and have numbered only four or five in the next half year, the overblown forces and their armaments—over ten times as powerful as in 1950—have been a tremendous added hostility factor.[72] Now that the anomaly of maintaining ever greater forces in the most heavily armed territory per square mile in the world has become clearer to all in a time of declining tension, armed levels should hopefully be subject to negotiation and reduction.

The period since the Geneva Conference until August 1971 has seen little of significance in the unification policies or efforts of the two Koreas. With the exception of nine meetings which have, between May 1972 and May 1973, taken place in Pyongyang and Seoul, the two parts of Korea remain more completely riven than any divided country in the world except Vietnam; in some respects, there has been and perhaps now again is more communication between the two Vietnams. With limited and recent exceptions, the two Koreas have allowed absolutely no contact that could be prevented: no exchange of mail or other materials, no relations in international meetings (though in 1972 both Koreas appeared as competitors in Munich Olympics), no organizations which could establish bonds (except, from the summer of 1971 on, the two Korean Red Crosses). Contact has been limited to what could not always be prevented: the infiltration of agents; occasional capturing of fishing boats or planes; and radio and, more recently, TV broadcasts, reception being apparently comparatively rare. During the August 1973 World University Games in Moscow, thirty-eight South Korean athletes competed, but North Korea boycotted the games.

From time to time, suggestions for unification have been revived, more often by the DPRK. After the withdrawal of the Chinese Communist troops in 1958, the DPRK proposed complete troop withdrawals followed by elections; U.S.–UN inquiry revealed that these proposals contained no changes from those of Geneva. Kim Il-song has suggested mutual troop reductions to the 100,000 level following foreign troop withdrawal. The North has also suggested holding an international conference as well as the establishment of a variety of economic, cultural, and political ties. In August 1960, as the Sino-Soviet rift became more apparent, Kim Il-song proposed an interim North-South confederation in which the two governments would, for the time being, remain separate but would conduct a gradually increasing number of functions together under a Supreme National Council of vague function, a suggestion that since has often been publicized and reemphasized as late as fall 1973. On May 13, 1961, the

DPRK established the Committee for the Peaceful Reunification of the Fatherland, to take advantage of vocal student demands in the ROK for unification.

Three days after Seoul's military coup of May 16, 1961, Premier Kim's position hardened; he emphasized his desire to establish a Marxist-Leninist party in the South and to unite patriotic forces to expel all foreign troops from the South. The North then started a Marxist-Leninist University of the Air and a program for inciting the ROK population to organize strikes and sabotage and to overthrow the ROK government.[73] In recent years, Party Congress policy has emphasized the overthrow of the ROK by revolutionary political activity rather than by action by the DPRK. Still more recently, first in a major interview with Japanese socialist representative Kawasaki on January 11, 1972, Kim Il-song has proposed "an immediate peace agreement, and a renunciation of the use of armed force and after that the mutual reduction of armed forces under the condition that the U.S. forces withdraw." It has later been confirmed that the North does—or did—for the first time, mean by this that such steps could be taken in advance of the withdrawal of American troops. Since December 1972, however, insistence on U.S. troop withdrawal and the completion of a peace treaty (presumably ending the UN command) have revived and strengthened as the precondition for all or most other steps.

Meanwhile, until the summer of 1971, the posture toward unification on the part of the ROK remained stolidly immobile. The military government announced soon after the coup that it would not seek unification by force but through general elections throughout Korea under UN observation, the old ROK Geneva position. It made no initiatives of its own; it treated those of the DPRK with disdain. This had the effect of placing the richer, more populous, and more recognized of the two states in a position of propaganda defensiveness vis-à-vis her poorer rival.

Change was heralded by a random public-opinion poll taken in early 1970 by the ROK Board of National Reunification. This poll disclosed that among 2,014 South Koreans in 50 different districts, 35 percent favored exchange of athletes with North Korea while 28 percent opposed such exchange; 29 percent supported journalistic exchanges, with 33 percent opposed; 25 percent favored postal traffic and 14 percent thought it would not jeopardize security to permit the interchange of relatives. Their own living conditions in the South were judged better than in the North by 87 percent, and 92 percent considered their lives freer. (The remaining responses expressed no opinion or more neutral views.) The responses were elicited in an atmosphere that had regarded any contact with suspicion and under an extremely severe National Security Law with heavy penalties for contact with communists. The results were quite unexpected and proved a shock to South Koreans and the government, which had not suspected sentiment of this kind. The minister of the National Unification Board was fired. But the poll appeared to have had an effect on the ROK government.[74]

On August 15, 1970, in a speech commemorating the twenty-fifth anniversary of liberation from Japanese colonial rule, President Park stated that he was prepared to suggest "epochal and more realistic measures" to eliminate step-by-step the various artificial barriers that exist between North and South, thus laying the groundwork for unification.[75] The president asked that the North cease military provocation, including the sending of armed agents into the South. (Armed incidents had by that time decreased radically from their 1968 heights; they fell sharply further from then on.)

On August 12, 1971, within a month of the announcement by President Nixon of the Kissinger visit to Peking, the president of the Korea (ROK) National Red Cross (KNRC) proposed direct South-North negotiations to arrange for the reunion of the 10 million family members separated by the division of the country and the Korean war. Two days later, his proposal was accepted by the president of the Red Cross of the DPRK. Messengers from each side then met on August 20 for the first of five meetings at Panmunjom. On September 20, Red Cross representatives held the first preliminary meetings, agreeing to open two liaison offices connected by telephone. In subsequent preliminary meetings a proposal to hold full-dress talks alternatively in the two capitals was accepted. Thereafter it took nine months and many more meetings and working sessions to reach, on June 16, 1972, agreement on tracing the whereabouts of divided families, facilitating free visits, free meetings, and free correspondence and reunion according to their free will. By January 1974, there have still been no visits or correspondence and no reported tracing of divided families; the DPRK seems more adamant than ever.

Meanwhile, unknown to the world, Director Yi Hu-rak of South Korea's control organ, the Central Intelligence Agency, had visited Pyongyang with two aides. From May 2 to May 5 he talked secretly with Director Kim Yong-ju of the DPRK Organization and Guidance Department and also met Kim Il-song. Second vice-premier of the DPRK, Pak Song-ch'ol, on behalf of Director Kim, younger brother of Kim Il-song, then secretly visited Seoul. He held further talks with Director Lee from May 29 until June 1, and met President Park. On July 4, 1972, a historic and totally unexpected joint communiqué was published simultaneously in Seoul and Pyongyang on the agreement reached at these meetings (see Appendix). This first accord reached on a high governmental level since the establishment of the two Korean regimes agreed that unification should be peaceful and through independent Korean efforts not subject to external imposition or interference, and that it should transcend "differences in ideas, ideologies and systems." The two sides agreed not to slander or defame each other or undertake armed provocation, to restore ties and carry out exchanges, to achieve early success in the Red Cross talks, to install a direct telephone line between Seoul and Pyongyang, and to establish a North-South coordinating committee with Yi and Kim as vice-chairmen. Though some distrust and defamation continued on both sides, the "puppet regime" epithets were replaced with "north" or "south" or "Pyongyang" or "Seoul" in the respective presses; and not only was one telephone line installed between Yi and Kim, but there was evidence of many more, something totaling seventeen telephone lines. Although highly restricted, official and largely secret, communication had been reestablished.

The Red Cross talks, in turn, made progress. Agreement was reached to hold the first full-scale Red Cross meeting in Pyongyang followed by one in Seoul, the South generally succeeding in preventing these divided family talks from becoming overly politicized. The twenty-five sessions of preliminary talks ended on August 11, 1972. On August 29, thirty-four "Red Cross officials" (in effect, government representatives) and twenty Seoul newsmen reached Pyongyang for the first meeting and spent four nights there. On September 13, fifty-four North Koreans arrived in Seoul and held a meeting after entertainment on a fabulous scale. A further meeting was held in Pyongyang on October 23, a fourth, in Seoul on November 22. Then there was a complete vacuum until March 21, 1973; these being unproductive, no further meeting was called until May 9, 1973, when once more, no further progress was reported and no new meeting date was set.

Meanwhile, the first meeting of the Yi-Kim coordinating committee took place in Panmunjom on October 12; a second, in Pyongyang on November 2; and a third, in Seoul on November 30. They did not meet again until March 15, 1973, a meeting which resulted in announced disagreement over northern insistence on troop reduction and a peace treaty. A further Coordinating Committee meeting of June 12–14, 1973, foundered on the same rock. The November 2–4 meeting had agreed to organize joint machinery to arrange political, economic, and other exchanges and to promote peaceful unification; it also agreed to stop propaganda broadcasts and leaflet distribution. Mr. Yi said after the meeting that it would be possible for the two Koreas to form joint sports teams or folk music or dance troupes to be sent abroad. There was also mention of "joint development of Korea's unique traditional culture" and the promotion of "division of work in certain fields of industry," with joint resorts and some fisheries exchange being mentioned. The coordination committee is supposed to set up a joint secretariat at Panmunjom; it will have separate subcommittees on political, military, diplomatic, economic, and cultural matters and will hold a plenary session once every two or three months with a meeting of the executive officers every month alternately in Seoul and Pyongyang, or at Panmunjom when necessary.[76] None of this had, by January 1974, yet come about and a meeting on December 5, 1973, proved abortive.

After Park's "reforms," the negotiations slowed and their tone cooled. Hostile propaganda has again increased and incidents have again broken out. Communist agents have again been sent South; steps toward broadened contact have not been implemented; and the future is, as 1974 approached, clouded. Despite early and startling progress, the goal of reunification and even broadening of contact seems elusive. Indeed, in his New Year's press conference on January 12, 1973, President Park downplayed the prospects for negotiation and declared, "I cannot say that there has been any real substantial, conspicuous achievements in the talks." In the months thereafter, no progress was made and the pace of meetings slowed. No further progress was achieved up to January 1974 as North Korea jockeyed for influence at the United Nations. All concerned had hoped that in breaking down the barriers of twenty-seven years, some momentum and much expectation had been achieved which, ultimately, would prove hard to stop. Regarding even this, doubts now arise.

It is important to observe at this point a major difference between contact between the two Koreas up to now and the far more continuous and established contact between the two Germanies. Contact between the Germanies, though now marked by occasional official meetings, is overwhelmingly contact between individual, private German citizens on both sides who communicate with each other through visits, mail, telephone, and telegraph. Such contact is of course envisaged in Korea, but it has been extremely slow in coming. It appears North Korea is reluctant to engage in it and, if contact does come, it can be expected to be considerably hedged around with restrictions. Contact up to now has been only governmental, and even that remains very restricted and controlled. In fact, there has been a tendency for the talks to become increasingly secret and increasingly a monopoly concern of high leadership. Political and public discussion of them is discouraged in the South and appears to be discouraged also in the North. While titularly private, the Red Cross societies of both sides are, for purposes of these negotiations, governmental with officials of the ROK CIA and of the DPRK Organization and Guidance Department heavily infiltrated into them. No genuinely private organizations are allowed to concern themselves meaningfully with unification. The length and restrictiveness of governmental contact raises some questions as to when, how much, and under what conditions individual citizens will be trusted to further the process.[77]

This last surmise has been emphasized for the ROK by the unexpected declaration of President Park on October 17, 1972—citing the needs of unification—of martial law, the suspension of portions of the constitution, the closing of the National Assembly, the suspension of all political activity, and the closing of all universities. These actions were followed by radical amendments to the Korean constitution. These have apparently ended any effective popular or representative participation in the policies of unification, making the negotiations essentially ones between two dictatorships with political systems that, while certainly different, are now far closer in structure and concentration of power than before. This, of course, may well not make accord any easier: two dictatorships can disagree as persistently as can any other forms of government. The drastic nature of the political steps taken also raises some question about whether the measures to be undertaken will reflect popular will. If agreement is reached, the speed with which such measures could be approved and implemented might be increased. Nevertheless, impasse, hostile propaganda, armed incidents and renewed subversion since October 17 in contrast to progress between July and October 1972 raises the possibility that Kim Il-song may believe that popular opposition to the October "reforms" may reopen the path to subversion rather than negotiation as a prelude to takeover rather than to melding different systems. In this case, tension in the peninsula will again increase.

Another striking characteristic of the contact between the two Koreas in the two years since August 1971 has been its strictly bilateral character. Although the Republic of Korea still officially abides by its "unification by election under the UN" policy, absence of reference to the UN marked these years until late June 1973 excepting only the articulated determination of the DPRK to end UN involvement in Korea and the determination of the ROK to avoid UN debate on the issue.

On April 28, 1973, North Korea was voted in as a member of the Interparliamentary Union (IPU) an organization having consultative status with ECOSOC and UNESCO. Twenty days later, on May 17, Pyongyang won its greatest single diplomatic victory up to that time in becoming a member of the World Health Organization (WHO) by the not very close vote of 66–41 with 22 abstentions. In the same period, the Nordic countries decided to embark on a policy of recognizing both Koreas thus starting a trend which is, by June 1973, increasing past 58 the number of countries having diplomatic or other official relations with the DPRK. These events have led to the award to Pyongyang of observer status at the United Nations in New York and the arrival there in September 1973 of the North Korean delegation.

Responding to these pressures, President Park in a special radio and TV address on June 23, 1973, announced that Seoul "shall not object to [its] admittance into the United Nations together with North Korea" and that Seoul would not oppose North Korean participation in the UN General Assembly debate on Korea in the fall of 1973 nor to Pyongyang's admission to any organization in which South Korea is now a member. Prime Minister Kim Jong-pil, in an immediately subsequent interview, indicated that Seoul would abide by any UN decision on the disposition of UNCURK but said that the UN Command should be maintained. President Park emphasized that the new South Korean position does not mean recognition of North

Korea as a state and the Prime Minister stated that the new policy does not mean recognition of the concept of two Koreas.

President Kim Il-song in a speech a few hours later which did not refer to President Park's proposals said that North and South Korea should not enter the United Nations separately but as one state under a confederation. He proposed that the two Koreas convene "a great national assembly composed of representatives of people of all walks of life" to agree on confederation prior to unification. He did, however, say that if the Korean question were placed on the UN General Assembly agenda "the representatives of our republic should naturally be invited to take part and speak on it as the party concerned." North Korean sources in Tokyo were subsequently quoted as saying that if North Korea had the opportunity to join the UN simultaneously with South Korea such an opportunity would require "careful study" under the circumstances at the time. Pyongyang's rejection of separate admissions for the ROK and the DPRK has continued up to January 1974, however.

The November 1973 United Nation debate on Korea with both Koreas participating produced, in place of voting on rival resolutions, a concensus statement urging both Koreas to continue their dialogue for a peaceful unification "without reliance upon outside force or its interference" and agreeing to UNCURK's abolition. The UN Command remains but Korea is now removed from automatic annual debate and may revert to being primarily a four-power issue. If the UN reemerges as a major locus of debate on the unification question and on tensions within the peninsula, its new role will be less as advocate of one side. North Korea, meanwhile, has been the chief gainer and emerges as a widely accepted state in international affairs disposing of not inconsiderable weight. The prospect that this arrangement will soon conduce to more agreement and progress toward unification, however, is more debatable. There is a definite possibility that a period of enhanced rivalry may be an intermediate prospect.

The four surrounding powers have not yet been permitted to play much overt role in the events of 1971–73. It seems highly probable that both Koreas are dissatisfied with their patron states and are alarmed lest a great-power rapprochement sacrifice the entrenched Korean cold-war interests. Such client-patron strain lie behind the remarkable Korean efforts to agree and provide the basic ingredient of whatever success they have achieved so far. Seoul and Pyongyang both perceive a danger in the Sino-American, Soviet-American, Sino-Japanese, and Russo-Japanese rapprochements. This distrust unites them as little else can. Pyongyang's peace initiatives are also no doubt related to the fact that they are backed by two deeply feuding powers. It is probable that both Koreas feel or, in the South's case, may come to feel, that only by a greater degree of unity, especially in foreign relations, and by a relaxation of tension, which by reducing arms expenditures will also free them from dependencies on their allies, can they hope to adjust successfully to this new world. In addition, Japan plays in their expectations a special role and a special danger: her proximity, economic puissance, and experience in the peninsula gives her economic alliance with the South a weight for which Pyongyang can find no balance and which it accordingly fears. In the same manner, the economic role that a united peninsula could play in a milieu of vivid Sino-Japanese and Soviet-Japanese relations is too enticing for any government or system to deny. Together, these factors form powerful motivations. Political unity would not, for some time, seem among them, but a coordination of foreign and economic policies, possibly even some cautious degree of confederation, would seem possible as the longer-range object of these trends.

Policy Prospects

Whatever degree of contact may he hoped for remains uncertain. With discussion of joint athletic and cultural teams, considerably broader contact can be hoped for eventually despite current foot-dragging. Surprises have marked the past and may mark the future.

Clearly, contacts between the two Koreas are a reaction from, and an adjustment to, the trend toward thaw in the Far Eastern cold war and the rapprochement between the four great powers there. Indications are that these steps toward closer association between the Koreas have the implicit or explicit support of the four powers. What the limits of this support may be remain to be tested. It is also clear that the possibility of eventually achieving trust among Koreans has surfaced because Kim Il-song's trust in his two wrangling allies has sharply declined, and because Park's confidence in his American ally has ebbed while that of Korea in Japan suffers from severe historical trauma. In conjunction with this, declining aid and military presence or influence have greatly decreased the power of the Soviet Union and the United States in the peninsula, while the power of People's Republic of China and of Japan remain quite limited, despite the dramatic rise in the economic power of the latter in the ROK. The recent overthrow by Park of the democracy the United States tried for twenty-seven years to nurture in Korea, and the weak ineffectiveness of American response thereto, is sign and seal of great-power impotence.[78]

It follows from this that the four great powers should, and probably will, avoid inserting themselves into the Korean unification negotiations, certainly so long as reasonable progress is made. Unless severe backsliding endangers peace, this "hands-off" policy is likely to be able to last for most or all of the period when emphasis is on increased communication and trade, a period which might well take several years.

Inevitably, sooner or later, the four powers will be involved in the question of troop levels and arms supplies to each Korea. The question arises now because of renewed North Korean insistence on UN withdrawal as a prelude to further negotiations. If all goes well, it should come to serve the interests of both Koreas—as it already serves the interests of the four powers—to lower troop levels and arms within the overbristling peninsula. Any such action should involve reciprocation. As a practical matter, the United States will wish to spend less and give some signs of wishing to withdraw all or most of her remaining 40,000 troops in South Korea by 1976. If she can make a virtue of this probability by reaching informal agreement with Moscow and Peking to lower their military aid to the DPRK in the interests of harmony and increased trade, this will nudge the Korean rapprochement still further.

Participation of Japan and especially of the United States in the development of the resources of the Soviet Far East, if balanced by increasing economic involvement in mainland China, will also tend to nudge the two Koreas toward trading relations. All four powers should of course encourage and cooperate with any agreed Korean efforts to send joint cultural or sporting efforts overseas. Remaining in the background until called on for decisions relating to troop and arms levels will be the most productive policy.

Until July 1972, Korea lagged behind other divided countries in taking steps toward unification. Though still behind in many respects, a framework for contact and a degree of common motivation now exist whereby this distance could be made up, though probably not beyond the point of any actual cession of power by either side.

The United Nations constitutes another policy option. Here the UN–Korea relationship is unique, for in no other instance of a divided nation is the UN an active advocate of one side and a fighter against the other. Since such fight with North Korea can clearly lead to no victory, the UN's continued advocacy of South Korea not only blocks any UN solution to Korean unification but means that the label of UN troops and the presence of a UN Commission (UNCURK) become positive irritants and obstructions in any unification process. North Korea is quite unwilling to choose the United Nations as competent for unification in Korea nor, in international law, is there any reason why North Korea should be forced to choose an advocate in whose name forces continue to be ranged against her.

It is clearly important to end the UN troop label and abolish the UNCURK presence forthwith in Korea. It is desirable for the UN to assume on the Korean question the neutrality it preserves on Cyprus and elsewhere. This has now been started by accepting North Korea in the same observer status as South Korea, and will be continued by admitting the North, without strings, to any debate on the Korean question. Such step was, of course, not easy for West Germany and will, understandably, be harder still for South Korea. But the bitter pill has been swallowed and, after a period of acrimonius rivalry, joint presence in the UN and in a growing number of diplomatic posts may lead to a modicum of cooperative tolerance, without which progress toward peaceful unification is in any case inconceivable.

Ahead, then, far ahead, lies the question of confederation. Thus far this has been Kim Il-song's suggestion for the threshold to unification. But in the thirteen years since he proposed it, the idea has shown some signs of spreading. Joint armistice groups in the Vietnamese cease-fire agreement contain some overtones of it. The German Democratic Republic has become sufficiently wary of it to censor all references to it; for confederation is a threat to any vastly smaller partner. It seems possible that communist nations have been experimenting with some confederation ideas where military and subversive solutions no longer seem feasible.

"Confederation" covers a vast unmapped territory. It spreads from a joint archaeological publication to the joint operation of governmental organs and national assemblies. The idea of exploring this territory should be encouraged, despite the possible risks and dangers confederation may contain. It is, in fact, difficult to see how unification could take place without a stage of some jointly operating "confederative" groups.

Confederation would also be an arrangement with which the four powers could show effective cooperation when their support appeared advantageous. However desirable inter-Korean steps toward unity without foreign "interference" may be, the great powers divided Korea and, without their cooperation, reunification is unlikely. Indeed, one of the most promising long-range options for obtaining reunification remains a four-power guarantee—closely along the Austrian model—of the unity, neutrality, and independence of the Korean peninsula.

Korea was one of the first, greatest, and most innocent victims of cold-war hostility. It recently gave some signs of becoming a bellwether of cold-war thaw. The rifts of division have here run deep. If Korea can persevere and succeed in her present brave attempts to heal these rifts, she will give encouragement to every unwillingly divided people.

Appendix 1
Distribution of Assets in Major Economic Sectors Between North and South Korea in 1945.

SECTOR	NORTH KOREA	SOUTH KOREA
Heavy industry	65	35
Electric power	94	6
Coal	60	40
Ferrous and nonferrous metals	87	13
Metallurgy	89	11
Machinery and metalworking	15	85
Chemicals	90	10
Construction materials	19	81
Light industry	31	69
Paper and lumber	60	40
Textiles	13	87
Food processing	19	81
Agriculture	37	63
Commerce	18	82

(Compiled from various private and government sources.)

Appendix 2

THE SOUTH-NORTH JOINT COMMUNIQUÉ OF JULY 4, 1972

With the common desire to achieve peaceful unification of the fatherland as early as possible, the two sides in these talks had frank and open-hearted exchanges of views, and made great progress in promoting mutual understanding.

In the course of the talks, the two sides, in an effort to remove the misunderstandings and mistrust and mitigate increased tensions that have arisen between the South and the North as a result of long separation, and further to expedite unification of the fatherland, have reached full agreement on the following points:

1 The two sides have agreed to the following principles for unification of the fatherland:

First, unification shall be achieved through independent Korean efforts without being subject to external imposition or interference.

Second, unification shall be achieved through peaceful means, and not through the use of force against each other.

Third, as a homogeneous people, a great national unity shall be sought above all, transcending differences in ideas, ideologies, and systems.

2 In order to ease tensions and foster an atmosphere of mutual trust between

the South and the North, the two sides have agreed not to slander or defame each other, not to undertake armed provocations whether on a large or small scale, and to take positive measures to prevent inadvertent military incidents.

3 The two sides, in order to restore severed ties, promote mutual understanding and to expedite independent peaceful unification, have agreed to carry out various exchanges in many fields.

4 The two sides have agreed to cooperate positively with each other to seek early success of the South-North Red Cross talks, which are underway with the fervent expectations of the entire people.

5 The two sides, in order to prevent the outbreak of unexpected military incidents and to deal directly, promptly and accurately with problems arising between the South and the North, have agreed to install a direct telephone line between Seoul and Pyongyang.

6 The two sides, in order to implement the afore-mentioned agreed items, solve various problems existing between the South and the North, and to settle the unification problem on the basis of the agreed principles for unification of the fatherland, have agreed to establish and operate a South-North coordinating committee so-chaired by Director Hu Rak Lee and Director Young Joo Kim.

7 The two sides, firmly convinced that the aforementioned agreed items correspond with the common aspirations of the entire people, who are anxious to see an early unification of the fatherland, hereby solemnly pledge before the entire Korean people that they will faithfully carry out these agreed items.

Upholding the desires of their respective superiors,

HU RAK LEE[79] YOUNG JOO KIM

July 4, 1972

Notes

1. Ireland is also an ancient, homogeneous unit now divided, but Ireland has not been united in independence since the twelfth century. While paying tribute to China for many centuries, Korea under her kings exercised essentially complete internal control until annexed by Japan, 1910–45, and was hence, by normal Western canons, "independent."

2. By at least 1922, Koreans were the third largest ethnic group in the Soviet Far Eastern Republic, numbering some 200,000 to 300,000. See Suh Dae-sook, *The Korean Communist Movement, 1918–1949* (Princeton, N.J.: Princeton University Press, 1967); Chong-Sik Lee, *The Politics of Korean Nationalism* (Berkeley: University of California Press, 1963); and Xenia J. Eudin and R. C. North, *Soviet Russia and the Far East, 1920–1927* (Stanford: Stanford University Press, 1957).

3. *Foreign Relations of the United States: The Conferences at Malta and Yalta, 1945* (Washington, D.C.: Department of State, 1955), p. 770. The trusteeship idea was a favorite Roosevelt idea partly related in his mind to planning for the United Nations whose international trusteeship system was then being mapped out. Roosevelt's exaggerated concept of the length of the trusteeship period was based on a false analogy to the Philippines and on Roosevelt's personal underestimation of Korean abilities at self-government and was opposed by Koreans as soon as "Liberation" took place. It would, however, have provided a framework for a unified peninsula. Violent disagreement between the British and the Soviets and disagreement between the British and the Americans on the disposition of colonies in the postwar world underlay both the trusteeship and the Korean questions.

4. *Foreign Relations: Conference of Berlin (Potsdam)* (Washington, D.C.: Department of State, 1960) 2:260, 631.

5. See, for example, a State Department policy paper "Estimate of Conditions in Asia and the Pacific at the Close of the War in the Far East and the Objectives and Policies of the United States," in *Foreign Relations of the United States 1945: The British Commonwealth and the Far East* (Washington, D.C.: Department of State, 1969), 6:562: "Occupation and military government may be under a single power, or under two or more powers acting jointly or it may be zonal in character with responsibility . . . partitioned among several allied powers." The Yalta briefing document concerned, drafted largely by Dr. Hugh Borton, is in *Foreign Relations: Conferences at Malta and Yalta*, pp. 358–61. As connected with the top-secret Yalta meeting it was perhaps too classified to be widely available to policy makers.

6. *Foreign Relations 1945*, 6:563. The policy document is dated June 22, 1945.

7. *Foreign Relations of the United States 1947: The Far East* (Washington, D.C.: Department of State, 1972), 6:597 (quotation is from the secretary of state); references to unification abound on pp. 563, 600, 602, 603, 608, 620, ad infinitum.

8. The documents on the Yalta and Potsdam conferences have been published many years ago. More recently, the Department of State's *Foreign Relations of the United States* series has published the 1945 documents in vol. 6 for that year (*The British Commonwealth and the Far East, 1969*), the 1946 documents in vol 8, *The Far East* (1971), and the 1947 documents in vol. 6, *The Far East* (1972). Significantly, the number of pages devoted to Korea grew steadily in these volumes from 131 in 1945 to 181 in 1946 to 293 in 1947. The sharp, belated rise in official attention in the last year throws into relief the shallowness of attention given the issue in the previous years when it should have received priority attention. The quality of the work on Korea reflected in the 1947 documents is correspondingly higher. Department of State publication *The Record on Korean Unification 1943–60*, No. 7084 (October 1960), is appallingly deficient in its handling of the background for the 38th-parallel decision.

9. *Foreign Relations: Conference on Berlin*, 2:351.

10. From the memorandum of the secretary of war to Mr. Grew on May 12, 1945, and May 21, 1945, as quoted in Joseph C. Grew, *Turbulent Era: A Diplomatic Record of Forty Years, 1904–45*, ed. Walter Johnson (Boston: Houghton Mifflin, 1952), 2:1455–58, as cited in Soon Sung Cho, *Korea in World Politics, 1940–1950* (Berkeley and Los Angeles: University of California Press, 1967), pp. 36–38.

11. Grew, *Turbulent Era*, p. 1464, cited in Cho, *Korea in World Politics*, p. 38.

12. Ambassador Harriman in answer to a question from the author at a Truman Library Conference, Independence, Missouri, Fall 1970. Added confirmation that Harriman's decision related only to factors extrinsic to Korea comes from his telegram of November 12, 1945, from Moscow in which he observes that the USSR would be more likely to achieve "Soviet predominance . . . through establishment of 'independent friendly' Korean regime than through any system of international tutelage" especially since trusteeship would mean that the USSR would have one of three or four equal votes. (*Foreign Relations, 1945*, 6:1122.)

13. Secret briefing paper cited in Cho, *Korea in World Politics*, p. 41.

14. *Foreign Relations, Conference on Berlin*, 2:253, 606.

15. Secretary of War Stimson estimated even as late as the end of June, 1945, that fighting might not be over until the latter part of 1946 at the earliest (Cho, *Korea in World Politics*, pp. 40–41, citing Edward R. Stettinius, *Roosevelt and the Russians: The Yalta Conference*, New York, 1949, p. 97.) Some State officials felt the end might be later still.

16. *Foreign Relations 1945*, 6:1046–47, the text of a message from Acting Secretary of State Dean Acheson to Ambassador John G. Winant.

17. Ibid.

18. Ibid., pp. 1037–38, a draft memorandum to the Joint Chiefs of Staff referring to a JCS message from Douglas MacArthur dated August 22, 1945.

19. A pathetic reminder of the organizational inadequacy in respect to Korea is a message from Assistant Secretary of State James C. Dunn to Ambassador Patrick J. Hurley dated February 20 saying, inter alia, "The Embassy may also wish to inform the Foreign Office that, while the illness of an officer directly concerned with the work is causing some delay, the Department is proceeding with the preparation of studies (on Korean problems) based on the questionnaire." The officer concerned, Dr. George M. McCune, had been in chronic ill health since childhood yet was then the only officer within FE concentrating only on Korea. Lack of

qualified Korean experts was a problem but the U.S. government did not search out and well utilize even those who might have helped.

20. *Foreign Relations 1945,* 6:561–63.

21. Ibid., p. 1030, from a letter by Frank P. Lockhart, acting director of the Office of Far Eastern Affairs, to Dr. Syngman Rhee, dated June 5, 1945.

22. *Foreign Relations 1945,* 6:1037–40.

23. Ibid., p. 1038. Note that the British and the Chinese, included in the original Yalta agreement, are no longer specifically mentioned. It was already clear that they would not be in a position to contribute greatly to a Korean occupation or trusteeship and they had been, in any case, most inadequately consulted or even informed about participation: an interesting illustration of how rapidly the position of these two powers was deteriorating during those crucial weeks.

24. *Foreign Relations 1945,* 6:1055, a memorandum by Lieutenant General John R. Hodge to General MacArthur dated September 24, 1945. The Soviet consul in Seoul, returning on October 10, 1945, from a conference at Soviet 25th Army Headquarters, brought Hodge letters from the army commander that "There will be no negotiations on a military level concerning requests I [Hodge] have presented and that there is no prospect of any negotiations until decisions are made and relationships established between our respective governments." Ibid., pp. 1071–72.

25. U.S. governmental sluggishness, inactivity, and indecisiveness on Korea was to continue, for the most part, through 1946. On February 25, 1947, the Special Interdepartmental Committee on Korea of the U.S. government referred to this inattention: "Lack of any substantial action by the U.S. Government has apparently given many Koreans the impression, which may be shared by the Soviets, that the U.S. has no great interest in the Korean problem and has more or less abandoned General Hodge to his own devices." *Foreign Relations 1947,* 6:615.

26. For preliminary commission conference, see Cho, *Korea in World Politics,* pp. 11–17.

27. Department of State, *The Record on Korean Unification,* No. 7084, FE Series 101 (October 1960), p. 7.

28. *Record on Korean Unification*, p. 18.

29. Gregory Henderson, *Korea: The Politics of the Vortex* (Cambridge, Mass.: Harvard University Press, 1968), p. 138. There was a 60% decline in the number of persons employed in industry in South Korea between 1944 and 1947. By May 1948, Korean industry was estimated to be operating at 30% of capacity.

30. Ibid., p. 98 and references.

31. From 1946 until January 1949, some mail was exchanged across the 38th parallel in accordance with the agreement reached in the January 1946 meeting of the American and Soviet commands. This exchange was ended by President Rhee and has not yet (October 1973) been restored. Volume was apparently not major.

32. Patricia M. Bartz, *South Korea* (Oxford: Clarendon Press, 1972), p. 2, an excellent source of recent information on Korea. The Korean war added slightly to the size of the ROK and decreased that of the North but when the DMZ, nonexistent from 1945, until July 1953, is subtracted the difference is not significant.

33. Choi Ho-jin, *The Economic History of Korea* (Seoul: Freedom Library, 1971), p. 284.

34. Sung Hee Kim, "Economic Development of South Korea," in *Government and Politics of Korea,* ed. Se Jin Kim and Chang Hyun Cho (Washington, D.C.: Research Institute on Korean Affairs, 1972), p. 149.

35. Since liberation, however, the South has been a considerable net *importer* of foodstuffs, including rice, so not much would have been available for North Korea. Whatever was available would, in a united country, have relieved the DPRK's announced need to import 500,000 tons of food grains annually.

36. Kim Min-chae, "Comparison of the Economic Strengths of North and South Korea and Their Implications for the Unification of Korea," in *International* Conference on the Problems of Korean Unification (Seoul: Asiatic Research Center, 1971), p. 460. Figures for electrical project costs are from David C. Cole and Princeton N. Lyman, *Korean Development* (Cambridge, Mass.: Harvard University Press, 1971), p. 196.

37. Ibid., p. 464, claims that the unemployment rate in the ROK fell from 5% to 4.5% in 1969. Unemployment and underemployment statistics in the ROK have, however, always been vague and unreliable and such figures understate unemployment and say nothing of a high underemployment. ROK unemployment has lessened in the 1970s, however.

38. Kim Yun-hwan, "Science-Technology and Manpower Development in North Korea," in *International Conference,* p. 472.

39. For above quotations and information, see Kim Min-chae, "Comparison of Economic Strength," pp. 453–65.

40. Kim, "Economic Development of South Korea," p. 149.

41. Seung Hee Kim, *Foreign Capital for Economic Development, A Korean Case Study* (New York: Praeger Special Studies in International Economics and Development, 1970), p. 30. Statistics are mainly from *Monthly Economic Statistics,* Bank of Korea.

42. Lee Joong-koon, "Foreign Trade of North Korea, 1955–68," in *International Conference,* pp. 514–45.

43. This duplication will be increased by President Park's announced emphasis on the buildup of chemical industry in South Korea during the Third Five Year Economic Development Plan. See Presidential New Year's Message, 1973.

44. Kenneth G. Clare et al., *Area Handbook for the Republic of Korea* (Washington, D.C.: Government Printing Office, 1969), pp. 300–301.

45. *South Korea Interim Government Activities,* no. 23 (August 1947), p. 3. Rinu-sup Shinn, *Area Handbook for North Korea* (Washington, D.C.: Government Printing Office, October 1969), p. 57, places the figure at "over one million."

46. Ibid., p. 59.

47. Ibid., pp. 67–69.

48. For KILA, see Henderson, *Korea: Vortex,* pp. 153–54.

49. Rhee's words, reported by Robert T. Oliver, *Syngman Rhee: The Man Behind the Myth* (New York: Dodd, Mead and Co. 1954), p. 272.

50. For above, see Henderson, *Korea: Vortex,* pp. 155–68; and John Kie-chiang Oh, *Korea: Democracy on Trial* (Ithaca, N.Y.: Cornell University Press, 1968), pp. 39–50.

51. For above, see Kie-chiang Oh, *Democracy on Trial,* pp. 158–63.

52. "Korean News," Korean Information Office, Embassy of Korea, no. 80, 27 October 1972.

53. Wolfgang Leonhard, a prominent Soviet trainee for the Soviet occupation of Germany, reports seeing a training component for Korean cadres earlier in the war located within the Comintern school at Ula in the Bashkir Republic. See his *Child of the Revolution* (Chicago: Henry Regnery, 1964), pp. 214–15.

54. G. Henderson, "North and South Korea," in *Conflict in World Politics,* ed. Steven L. Spiegel and Kenneth N. Waltz (Cambridge, Mass.: Winthrop Publishers, 1971), p. 202.

55. Chin O. Chung, "The Government and Power Structure of North Korea," in Kim and Cho, *Government and Politics of Korea,* p. 178. This chapter is an excellent recent treatment of the subject, and I have drawn extensively thereon.

56. Kim Il-song became president of the DPRK on December 28, 1972.

57. *Area Handbook for North Korea,* p. 203. This is an excellent factual source on North Korea.

58. *New York Times,* 31 October 1972. *Korean Affairs* 2, no. 4 (January 1973) contains a translation of the DPRK text.

59. Kim Yun-hwan, "Science-Technology and Manpower Development in North Korea," in *International Conference,* p. 470.

60. Henderson, "North and South Korea," p. 203.

61. Ibid., p. 204.

62. For details, see Henderson, *Korea: Vortex,* pp. 98–100.

63. ROK Constitution, Article 3: "The territory of the Republic of Korea shall consist of the Korean peninsula and its adjacent islands."

64. *Area Handbook for the Republic of Korea,* p. 255.

65. "The Record on Korean Unification," p. 22.

66. Ibid., p. 24.

67. The ROK at first proposed that elections be held in North Korea only and, at various times during the Rhee regime, appeared to return to that position. After the overthrow of the Rhee regime in 1960, the ROK reverted to the position as articulated at Geneva.

68. Ibid., p. 26. Withdrawal of Communist Chinese troops was also specified; such withdrawal has long been completed (in October 1958).

69. Ibid., p. 28.

70. *World Military Expenditures* (Washington, D.C.; U.S. Arms Control and Disarmament Agency, 1972), as quoted in *Korea Week,* 15 November 1972, p. 3.

71. Rinn-Sup Shinn. "Foreign and Reunification Policies," *Problems of Communism* (January–February 1973): 68. For 1973 figs. see *Asian Student,* San Francisco, April 28, 1973.

72. G. Henderson, "Korea: Can Cold War Ground Thaw?", *War/Peace Report* 10, no. 7 (August/September 1970): 3–7.

73. For North Korea's unification policies through 1968, see *Area Handbook for North Korea,* pp. 245–46.

74. Henderson, "Can Cold War Ground Thaw?", p. 5.

75. *Korea Times,* 15 August 1972, p. 5.

76. *New York Times,* 5 November 1972.

77. Recent visitors to the DPRK such as Harrison Salisbury and Professor Jerome Cohen testify to the extraordinary precautions taken by North Korean authorities to prevent the slightest contact—even supervised contact—between these visitors and any private North Korean citizens.

78. Compare, for example, the American official reaction of Secretary of State Dean Acheson in May 1950 when President Rhee stated his intention simply to postpone the Assembly elections: "The United States aid, both military and economic, to the Republic of Korea has been predicted upon the existence and growth of democratic institutions within the Republic. Free, popular elections, in accordance with the constitution and other basic laws of the Republic are the foundation of those democratic institutions." Kie-chiang Oh, *Korea,* p. 31. In 1972 the overthrow by a Korean president of much of the constitution and of the entire Assembly, the radical change in the Assembly's composition, and the proposing of elections under martial law and without preceding political activity occasioned not a fraction of such reaction.

79. Hu Rak Lee was dismissed as CIA Director and co-chairman of the coordinating committee in cabinet changes of December 3, 1973. The DPRK had, in late August, demanded the removal of Lee and other CIA members from the coordinating committee and the ROK Red Cross delegation because of CIA involvement in the August 8 kidnaping from a Tokyo hotel of opposition candidate Kim Dae-chung.

CHINA

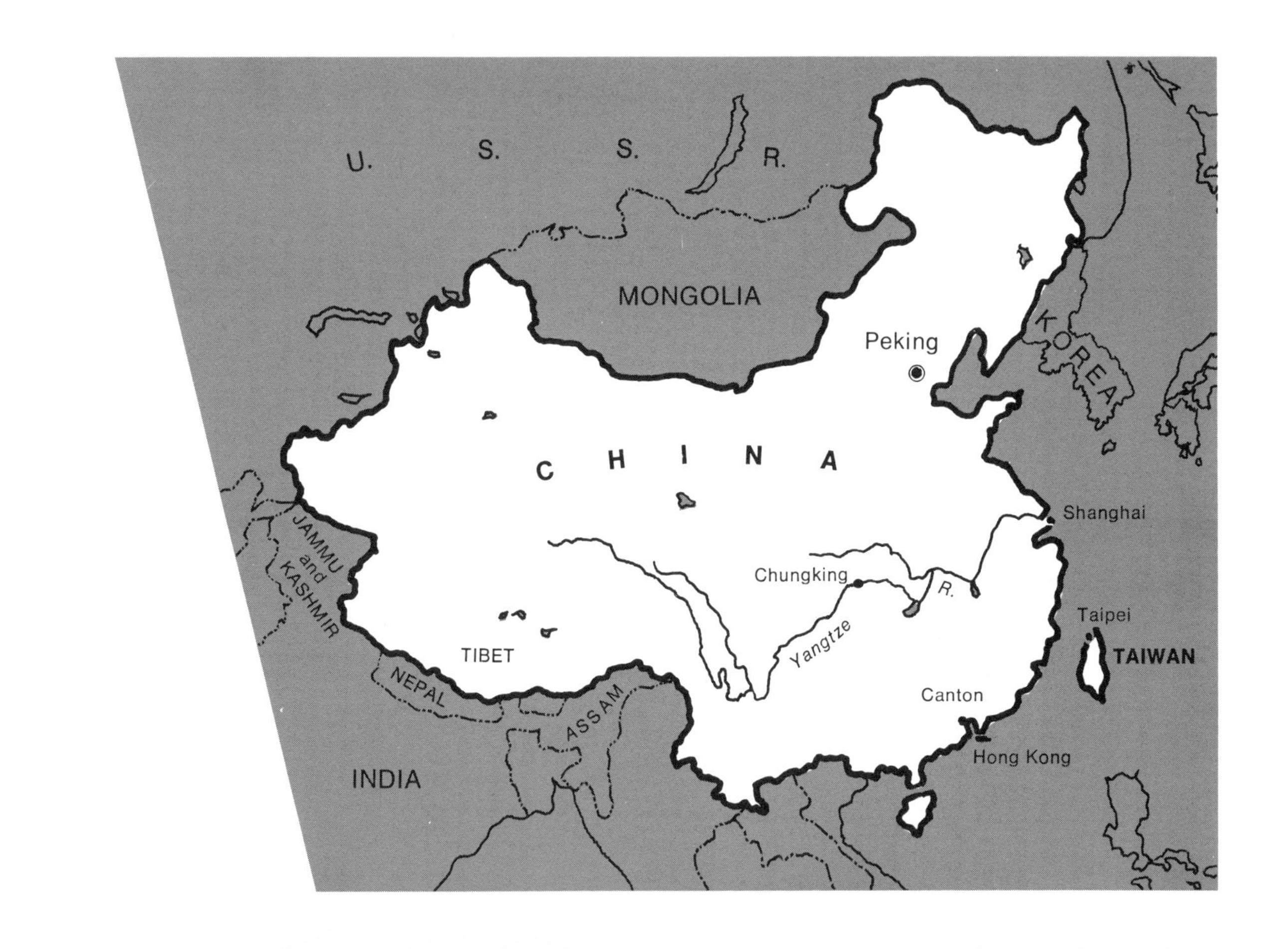
U. S. S. R.
MONGOLIA
Peking
KOREA
C H I N A
Shanghai
Chungking
R.
Yangtze
Taipei
TAIWAN
Canton
Hong Kong
TIBET
JAMMU and KASHMIR
NEPAL
ASSAM
INDIA

3

China: The Formosa Question

Nathaniel B. Thayer

FORMOSA[1] IS A TROPICAL ISLAND lying about 120 miles off the South China coast. It is about 85 miles across at its widest point and about 240 miles long. With an overall area of 14,000 square miles, it is a little larger than the Netherlands and a little smaller than Switzerland.

History

Even in its early history, Formosa had strategic value. Both Japanese and Chinese pirates used the island as a base for raids along the sea lanes, along the Chinese coast, and throughout the kingdoms of Southeast Asia. The fifteenth century brought the Europeans to Formosa: first the Portuguese, then the Spanish and the Dutch. They were interested in trading posts. In 1662, Koxinga, the son of a famous Ming pirate and a Japanese woman, expelled the Europeans and made the island his personal kingdom. Twenty years later, his grandson surrendered the kingdom to a Manchu emperor, who incorporated it into Fukien, the closest Chinese province on the mainland.

The Manchu emperors ruled Formosa from 1683 to 1895, though their administrators did not venture far from the island's garrison towns. In 1894, China and Japan went to war. The Japanese won. By the Treaty of Shimonoseki, the Chinese ceded to the Japanese Formosa and the Pescadores,[2] a group of islands lying off the west coast of Formosa. The first decade of Japanese rule was spent in pacification, the next four decades in modernization. At the start of the Second World War, Formosa was the oldest and wealthiest Japanese colony.

It was not until World War II that other nations chose to challenge the Treaty of Shimonoseki. In Cairo in 1943, Prime Minister Winston Churchill, President Franklin Roosevelt, and Generalissimo Chiang Kai-shek declared: "All territories that Japan has stolen from the Chinese, such as . . . Formosa and the Pescadores, shall be restored to the Republic of China." The Potsdam Declaration of 1945 reaffirmed this intent. When the war ended, the Supreme Commander of the Allied powers gave the nationalist government of Chiang Kai-shek authority to accept the Japanese surrender and administer the island. In the peace treaty of 1951, Japan relinquished her claim to the island, although the document did not recognize Chinese suzerainty.

Native Formosan, Japanese, and American observers claim that the Formosan population initially welcomed the arrival of the new Chinese government in 1945. Their enthusiasm was soon spent. Although the Chinese had spoken of Formosa as a lost province, the Nationalist administration treated it as occupied territory. By 1947, conditions had become so bad that the Formosans revolted. Estimates of the number of Formosans killed by Chinese troops run between 5,000 and 20,000.[3] A new Chinese governor was appointed. Although his policies were more ameliorative, he was not able to restore Formosan confidence in Chinese rule.[4]

By January 1949, the Chinese Communist armies had taken over North China, crossed the Yangtse, and started their final southern campaign. Over the next months, Nationalist troops and refugees left the mainland, and by autumn, about 1.5 million mainlanders were living among 8 million Formosans.[5] In November 1949, Chiang Kai-shek withdrew to the island and set up the Chinese Nationalist government in Taipei.

Chiang regarded his retreat as tactical. He intended to return to the mainland and reestablish his government there. But he recognized that fulfilling this goal would take time. His immediate task was to secure Formosa as a base of operations. He was faced with an independence movement, a redacted economy, and a government venal at the top and inexperienced at the bottom.

Independence Movement

Few question the existence of a Taiwanese independence movement but many find it hard to date its origins. Some enthusiasts cite Koxinga as the first Formosan leader and point to the frequent revolts during the Ching dynasty as expressions of anti-Chinese sentiment. A more common interpretation regards Koxinga as a Ming loyalist and the rebellions as the usual peasant jaqueries present throughout China's history. In 1895 a Formosan Democratic Republic was created, but this was mainly a device of the Chinese officials to avoid the terms of the Treaty of Shimonoseki.

It is easier to regard the Formosan independence movement as a product of Japanese colonial rule.[6] Industrialization created towns and cities which broke down local loyalties. New occupations changed old life styles. Better communications and transportation gave the Formosan a chance to attain a world view. Japanese rupture of migration from and travel to the mainland obstructed Formosan identification with Chinese nationalism. Finally, the Japanese attempt to export all the benefits of modernization to the Japanese home islands produced a lively sense of injustice. In the 1920s, spokesmen for this Formosan movement emerged from among the Formosan students who had studied in Tokyo. They returned to Formosa to organize workers and peasants. A Formosan Communist party sprang up and it, too, championed the movement. The Japanese authorities could tolerate the students but not the Communists. The police moved vigorously. By the 1930s they had suppressed the Formosan independence movement on the island and caused its leaders to flee to other countries.

The Formosan revolt against Chinese rule in 1947 was the first overt expression of postwar nationalism. The Chinese authorities reacted as the Japanese militarists had. They claimed Communist instigation and practiced harsh repression. Again Formosan leaders fled from the island, chiefly to Hong Kong, Japan, and the United States.

The Formosans in Hong Kong formed a League for the Reliberation of Formosa and presented a petition to the UN asking for immediate trusteeship and eventual independence. The UN did not act. Attracted by the success of the Chinese Communists, the League went to Peking. Initially, the Chinese Communists saw the League as an aid in overthrowing the Chinese Nationalist rule and supported it. Later, the Chinese Communists realized that the League would also be a threat to *their* rule, and in 1958 they purged its members as counterrevolutionaries.

The Formosans who went to Japan formed there in 1950 the Formosa Democratic Independence party. In 1955 they set up a provisional government with Thomas Liao as president. The group was most active and won a respectful hearing, particularly among powerful businessmen, conservative politicians, and the press. The Chinese Nationalists denounced the group as supported by both the Japanese and American governments, a charge the provisional government took care not to deny. The provisional government was weakened when Thomas Liao defected to the ROC government and returned to Formosa.

In the United States, the Formosan independence movement has been particularly strong on college campuses with a large concentration of Taiwanese students. These students have organized nationally: they publish magazines, they lobby, they demonstrate, they have been able to convince many members of the American academic community that their cause is just.

In recent years, particularly since the visit of President Nixon to China, both the Chinese Communists and the Chinese Nationalists have been active in wooing these overseas nationalists.[7] Their appeals appear not to have been successful.

Beyond a doubt, a strong Formosan independence movement exists overseas. The real question is, How strong is the movement on the island? A good case can be made demonstrating Formosan independence to be a potent force. An equally good case can show that a Formosan independence movement, though once strong, is now passive.

Commentators who believe that Formosan nationalism is still strong usually argue their case by relating Formosan grievances against the mainlanders.

1 Mainlanders are carpetbaggers interested only in returning to the mainland. They may sell out the Formosans to realize this interest. They require the Formosans to underwrite this interest through excessive taxation, draft into an oversized army, and support of a top-heavy government designed to rule all China.

2 Mainlanders refuse to invest in the Taiwan economy. They prefer to send their money out of the country, either to Hong Kong for a high return or to foreign banks for greater security.

3 Mainlanders occupy the best jobs in the society. They are the officers in the army. They are the top executives in industry, particularly government-owned industry. They are the principals in the secondary schools and the professors in the university.

4 Mainlanders also control the police. Their harsh and totalitarian measures prevent public expression of independence sentiments.

Commentators who believe the independence movement is no longer an important force do not deny the great differences between the mainlanders and the Formosans. But they argue that these differences are being lessened; change is rapid enough to satisfy the Formosans yet slow enough not to alienate the mainlanders.

Three important areas of progress are:

1 Language. The mainlanders spoke Mandarin, the language of government and literature, the "official" language of China. The Formosans spoke a Fukien or Hakka dialect, with Japanese as their second language. The government placed great emphasis on teaching Mandarin to everyone. They have been successful. Now at least, everyone can talk with everyone else.

2 Urban-rural division. When the mainlanders first came to Formosa, they settled in the cities. The Formosans were in the countryside. Now, mainlanders are moving to the countryside and Formosans to the city. Formosans and mainlanders no longer form separate societies.

3 Social discrimination. Chiang Kai-shek's entourage comprised

China's elite—men of high education, wealth, and cultural attainment who occupied the center of the Chinese stage. In Formosa it met with an agricultural people with only limited education, who had occupied the fringes of both Chinese and Japanese society. Inevitably, social discrimination developed. Perhaps because of the Formosans' success in commerce and industry, perhaps because of equal access to the educational system, the mainlanders' sense of superiority and the Formosans' sense of inferiority seem to be disappearing. Statistically, this leveling of society is demonstrated in the greater number of intermarriages.[8]

Perhaps William Bueler is correct. A close student of Formosan thinking, he divides the Formosans into three groups: (1) the vast majority who are politically inert, (2) a fair-sized minority who want independence but are unwilling to act, and (3) a small minority who want independence and are willing to do something about getting it. He notes that most of the last group are in prison.[9]

Prison, however, has not been Chiang Kai-shek's only tool in negating the independence movement. He has also launched an ambitious plan for economic development and a modest effort at political integration.

Economic Development

Formosa's economic development can be divided into four periods. The first period, the colonial period, lasted from 1895 to 1945. Though Japan's motive was to help the home islands, her policies did much to develop Formosa. Since Japan wanted secure sources of sugar and rice, she concentrated on agriculture. As early as 1898, the Japanese undertook a land survey that led to a thorough reform of the land laws. Later, they financed the construction of an extensive irrigation system, they improved seeds, they established farmer's organizations, they laid down a good system of communication and transportation. Under Japanese tutelage the Formosan farmer became literate and thus amenable to technological change.

Japan also undertook the industrialization of Formosa. First, the island gained a sugar-refining capacity. Shortly before the Pacific War, an electrical-power network was created for the development of chemical, oil-refining, and aluminum industries.

The second period in Formosa's economic development lasted from 1945 to 1949. During the war, the Americans had bombed the industrial plants. The Japanese had been able to rebuild only a few of them. The Chinese Nationalist troops seized them and shipped them to the mainland. Trade with the Japanese home islands broke down. Inflation was rampant. The island almost fell back to a barter economy.

The third phase of the country's development can be marked with Chiang Kai-shek's arrival on the island in 1949. The looting stopped and reconstruction began. Power and transportation were restored. Foreign trade resumed. Also conceived was a land program under which the government purchased land from the landlords with government bonds and then resold that land to tenant farmers with payment to be made over ten years. By 1953 prewar levels of production had been reached.

Substantial American aid began to flow into the island during the fourth period of development. The Chinese turned from stopgap measures to long-term development. They launched the first of their four-year plans. Since the Nationalists had lost the mainland for failing to control the countryside, they gave agriculture a lion's share of the development money. They restored the large-scale industries established by the Japanese and encouraged new industries. They solicited investment funds from overseas Chinese capitalists and passed liberal investment laws to attract other foreign capital. They turned over public industry to private enterprise, hoping competition would make it efficient. They allowed prices to respond to market conditions. They established special lines of credit for industries they particularly wanted to develop.

Each plan had its own goal: the first plan concentrated on import-substitution industries; the second, trade liberalization and manufacturing infrastructure; the third, export industries; the fourth, education; the fifth, development of industry requiring skilled labor and heavy capital.

The development plans were an immense success. The annual growth was always a two-figure percentage. By 1964 U.S. aid was no longer needed and was phased out. Among Asian nations, Formosa today has a level of development and a standard of living second only to Japan. The island is already listed among the twenty largest trading countries in the world. Predictions are that it will soon be among the first fifteen.[10]

Several points about the economy should be mentioned. It is based largely on private enterprise, relies heavily on foreign investment, and is trade oriented. Parts of its industry are integrated with industry in other nations. It is both independent of, and more highly developed than, the mainland economy.

Political Integration

Chiang Kai-shek's first political task on the island was to integrate the Formosans into a government from which they had been long excluded. During the colonial period, the Japanese had staffed all offices, from governor-general to local schoolmaster, with Japanese from the home islands. The Japanese were replaced with mainland Chinese who initially proved more interested in personal fortune than public weal. Finally, Chiang brought to Formosa the Nationalist government for all China, which he placed over the existing provincial and local government. Government on Formosa, then, has been too big, not interested in Formosan problems, and run by mainlanders.

Chiang first opened the local and provincial assemblies to the Formosans. Since 1950, all chief executive officers and members of the legislative assemblies have been chosen by direct vote. The victors in these elections have been almost entirely Formosans.

Land reform also had its political effect. Since landlords had to sell their land, they lost interest in managing local politics. They left them to their former tenants. The land program funded a farmer's association to offer instruction in modern farming techniques. Farmers who participated actively in this organization found it easy to get elected to office. By the mid-1950s, Formosans controlled local and provincial governments, and the office holders proved competent.

But how much authority do local and provincial governments exercise? Isn't the central the repository of real political power? How many Formosans participate in the representative bodies of the central government—the National Assembly, the Legislative Yuan, the Control Yuan? How many Formosans sit in the Executive Yuan? How many Formosans are in the Central Committee of the KMT, the National People's party?

The answer is: few.

Chiang faced a dilemma. On the one hand, he wished to have more Formosans in the central government to engender more popular support. On the other hand, he wished to have as many mainlanders from as many provinces as possible in government to buttress his claim that he represented all China. The claim to represent all China took precedence over the desire for popular support. Chiang allowed mainlanders, mostly men who entered office while Chiang was still on the mainland, to monopolize the central government. This political elite was certainly not representative of the Formosans. Because of its advanced age, it probably was not even representative of a cross section of the mainlanders.

The National Assembly, the highest legislative organ, is a case in point. Its last election was on the mainland in 1947. Its members average more than sixty-five years in age. In the Executive Yuan, the average age in 1970 was sixty-three. And at the Tenth Congress of the KMT, the delegates' average age was sixty.[11] In these organs were only one or two Formosans.

Recently, Chiang has tried to make adjustments. Old members of the National Assembly have been given life tenure, but supplementary elections have been held to choose new members, some of whom have been Formosans.

A similar attempt has been made to bring new members into the Executive Yuan. In the cabinet shuffle in 1972, thirteen new appointees were made in the twenty-three-man cabinet. Of the thirteen, six were Formosans. One Formosan was appointed a vice-premier and another became Minister of the Interior.

Finally, the KMT, the National People's party, has also undergone reform. Since 1970, two of the three secretaries-general have been Formosans. The Head of the Secretariat of the Central Committee is also a Formosan.

Critics point out that these reforms are only gestures. Chiang's dilemma remains. Supporters point out that Chiang has at least recognized the need to make gestures. A process has started. Although change may come slowly, it is irreversible. Future years can only bring more Formosans into the government.

Chiang's principal concern on the island has not been domestic policy. His main efforts have been directed toward overthrowing the Chinese Communist government on the mainland and keeping his Nationalist government in good standing internationally. Since the United States has been the most powerful nation in the Pacific, let us start our survey of international problems affecting Formosa with a recitation of U.S. policies and attitudes.

American Policy Toward Taiwan

American interest in Taiwan dates back to 1853, when Commodore Perry recommended that the United States annex the island for use as an outpost to maintain peace and order in the western Pacific Ocean. Washington rejected his recommendation. During World War II, the American military commanders gave considerable thought to the invasion of Formosa, but they finally concluded that this was not needed to defeat Japan. Also during the war, military intelligence and the State Department set about establishing a policy for Formosa after the Japanese were defeated. They considered three alternatives: (1) to make the island independent; (2) to transfer the island to China; (3) to provide for a period of Allied trusteeship, during which time the Formosans would conduct a plebiscite to determine their political future. It was pointed out that the Formosans' standard of living and economic development were far superior to that on the Chinese mainland and that China would need its administrators for reconstruction at home. Nevertheless, the State Department believed that the central problem was the unification of the mainland under a strong central government and that no central government could survive which did not recover the "lost province" of Formosa. On January 12, 1950, Secretary of State Dean Acheson delivered a speech that placed Formosa beyond the defense perimeter of the United States. For a century, then, American policy toward Formosa was firm. It stood on two legs: (1) Formosa was extraneous to U.S. security needs; (2) the Formosa question was part of the China question.

Our answers to the China question, however, were subject to change. U.S. authorities supported Chiang Kai-shek after World War II. But that support was not enough. By 1949, it was apparent that the Chinese Communists were going to overthrow Chiang's government. Chiang retreated to Formosa to regroup. Then, with the active support of American military forces, he hoped to launch a campaign to reconquer the mainland. President Truman had been willing to use arms shipments, economic aid, and political measures to assist Chiang so long as China was at stake. He was not willing to use American troops for what might end up as a defense of Formosa. He refused to back Chiang any longer. In January he announced: "the United States government will not provide military advice or aid to Chinese forces on Formosa." America was prepared to recognize the Chinese Communist government as the government of China—a China which included Formosa.

The Korean war proved Chiang's salvation. On June 25, 1950, the North Koreans crossed over the 38th parallel in a military attempt to take over the entire peninsula. The Americans believed that communism was monolithic; that the attack had been planned by Moscow and coordinated with Peking.

On June 27, President Truman dispatched the Seventh Fleet to neutralize the Formosan Straits. His purpose was strategic. He did not want to allow the Chinese Communists to take over the islands since this would have released Chinese troops for positions in Manchuria, thus strengthening the Communist position near the war zone. Truman also moved politically to undermine the Chinese Communists. He announced that the status of Formosa would have to "await the restoration of security in the Pacific, a peace settlement with Japan, or consideration by the United Nations." Shortly thereafter, the Truman administration started arms shipments to Chiang's armies and finally, the dispatch of a military assistance and advisory group.

At the same time, the U.S. government banned travel by American citizens to the mainland, stopped goods of Chinese Communist origin from coming into the United States, and froze Chinese assets.

In May 1951 Secretary of Defense George C. Marshall urged the United States to use its veto to keep the Chinese Communists out of the United Nations. In the same month, Assistant Secretary of State Dean Rusk announced, "We recognize the National Government of the Republic of China. . . . We believe it more authentically represents the views of the great body of the people of China. . . . That government will continue to receive important aid and assistance from the United States."

President Truman, then, though he changed U.S. policy toward China twice, ended up where he had started. Furthermore, he reopened the question of the status of Formosa. He did not rule out that the island might be Chinese territory. He just made the whole subject vague. Finally, Formosa was no longer unimportant to American security. American officials were calling it a vital outpost of the free world.[12]

President Eisenhower introduced high tension into American relations with the Chinese Communists and institutionalized U.S. support for the Chinese Nationalists. He announced his first move toward China just two weeks after assuming office. In his State of the Union message, he dropped the Truman fiction that the Seventh Fleet was designed to prevent the Chinese Nationalists from attacking the mainland as well as to prevent the Chinese Communists from attacking the island. He announced: "The Seventh Fleet shall no longer be employed to shield Communist China." Though later in the message, President Eisenhower denied aggressive intent, his move "had psychological consequences of far-reaching and lasting importance. It strengthened Chiang Kai-shek's determination. . . . It further convinced Mao Tse-tung that . . . the United States was the implacable enemy of the new China's aspirations." [13] President Eisenhower also appointed a secretary of state who refused to meet with the Chinese Communist leaders, much less negotiate with them; an assistant secretary of state for Far Eastern affairs who openly told the Congress that he intended to keep the constant threat of military action before the Red Chinese in the hope that it would bring about an internal breakdown; and an ambassador to Chinese Nationalist government who publicly admitted that his dispatches unduly supported the Nationalists. Finally, Eisenhower was willing to receive from the Chinese Nationalists a draft treaty for mutual defense.

The Chinese Communists answered American belligerence with truculence. In August 1954 Premier Chou En-lai announced the liberation of Taiwan to be a "glorious, historic mission of the Chinese people." Later in the month, he sent Chinese Communist troops to raid and bombard Quemoy, a small island a few miles off the mainland coast, which still remained in the hands of the Chinese Nationalists. These raids and bombardments continued over the next several months. The Americans responded by rushing to completion and signature the defense treaty with the Chinese Nationalists. In January 1955 the Chinese bombed the Tachen Island group and took over the small island of Yikiang. President Eisenhower asked Congress for a resolution authorizing him to employ armed forces to defend Formosa, the Pescadores, and other "closely related localities."

The Chinese Communists allowed tensions to relax slightly by allowing the Quemoy bombardment to subside and suggesting ambassadorial talks. The Americans at first laid down impossible preconditions, but finally accepted. The Americans wanted the renunciation of force in the Formosan Straits. The Chinese Communists contended that Formosa was an internal matter not subject to international agreement. The talks got nowhere.

Eisenhower's second term was much like his first. The Chinese Communists proposed an exchange of newsmen. At first the Americans refused, then attached such conditions that the Chinese were forced to withdraw the offer. In 1958 the Chinese Communists again started to bombard Quemoy but soon backed off, announcing that they would bomb only on even-numbered days. Ambassadorial talks continued inconclusively. In 1960 President Eisenhower traveled to Formosa where he told a popular rally that the United States did not accept the "claim of the warlike and tyrannical Communist regime in Peking to speak for the Chinese people." The rally didn't expect to hear anything else. That was really all the Americans had been saying for the past eight years.

Under Eisenhower, the American commitment to Chiang Kai-shek reached its zenith. That Formosa was a keystone in the structure of U.S. security was no longer a hypothesis but an article of faith. Special note should be made of the defense treaty. Although American officials were interested in strengthening Chiang Kai-shek, the treaty promised not to support his government but to defend Formosa.[14] For American officials, then, Formosa was no longer a part of China, at least not of Communist China. Formosa was an independent entity recognized by treaty. Since the treaty remains in force indefinitely, successor governments could inherit the American commitment.[15]

While still in the U.S. Senate, John F. Kennedy wanted to change U.S.-China policy. He recognized the Chinese Communist government as a permanent force, not, like John Foster Dulles, as a passing phase. He recommended that the offshore islands be abandoned because Chiang's garrison was a needless irritant to the Chinese Communists. He urged that discussion be started with the Chinese Communists about the subject of recognition.

Kennedy's slender margin of victory in the presidential elections brought second thoughts. In his first State of the Union message, he found the Chinese Communists threatening the security of Southeast Asia. In a later press conference, he found Chinese statements about the United States "malevolent." He allowed his designated secretary of state, Dean Rusk, to testify at his confirmation that he saw no likelihood of bringing about normalization of relations with China. In 1962, when the Chinese Communists again threatened the offshore islands, President Kennedy rose to say that our policy "remained just what it has been on this matter since 1954."

Kennedy's advisers have subsequently written that the President was planning changes in American China policy in his second term. But an assassin's bullet stopped the President from explaining what these changes were or how he intended to put them into practice.

It is easy to write off the thousand days of the Kennedy administration as a pause in the development of American policy toward China. Certainly Kennedy undertook the same commitments—often using the same language—as Presidents Truman and Eisenhower. But Kennedy did contribute. He thawed the Eisenhower-Dulles freeze on thinking about China and encouraged the free flow of ideas. He got the United States off the thin ice of calling Chiang Kai-shek and the Nationalists the only legal government of China. He allowed the concept of a two-China solution to be developed within the government (and was denounced by both Chinese governments for doing so). We shall return to a discussion of the two-China solution later in the paper.

Lyndon Johnson's principal concern in Asia was Vietnam. So long as that war continued, he was unwilling to listen to other problems. Policies remained unchanged. American and Chinese ambassadors continued to meet in Warsaw. A decade earlier, the United States had insisted that the Chinese renounce the use of force in connection with Formosa before agreeing to discuss any further subjects; the Chinese were willing to discuss other issues without imposing American withdrawal from Formosa. Now, Americans were willing to discuss other matters while the Chinese insisted on American surrender of Formosa before other discussion. The two nations had exchanged positions, but they were still apart. President Johnson did not bring them together. Because of the Cultural Revolution (1966) the Chinese Communists broke off the Warsaw talks and the two countries moved even farther apart.

During the Eisenhower years, Vice-President Richard Nixon had been sternest of the cold-war warriors, particularly with regard to Asia. In 1954, he had urged preemptive war. "To avoid further Communist expansion in Asia . . . we must take the risk now of putting our boys in." In debate over the offshore islands, he was against "handing over to the Communists an inch of free territory." Yet when Richard Nixon became President in 1968, he proved to be less belligerent and more flexible.

The first public indication came in a speech in April 1969 by Secretary of State William Rogers: "We shall take the initiative to reestablish more normal relations with Communist China." In July, the State Department announced ostentatiously that passports for journalists, teachers, students, doctors, scientists, and members of Congress would be automatically validated. Further, the trade embargo would be modified to allow returning citizens to bring home $100 worth of Chinese goods. Secretary Rogers said these moves could be interpreted as symbolic of the American wish for peace.

The message got through to the Chinese. Their propaganda softened. In December the Chinese chargé d'affaires in Warsaw met the American ambassador at a diplomatic reception and suggested a resumption of talks. The United States accepted the offer. As a further gesture of goodwill it permitted subsidiaries or affiliates of American firms to sell nonstrategic goods to Communist China and to buy Chinese merchandise for sale in other countries. The $100 limit was removed for tourist purchases. In his report to the Congress on foreign policy, President Nixon said that he "was prepared to establish a dialogue with Peking" and to recognize "its legitimate national interests," while continuing "to honor our treaty commitments to the security of our Asian allies."

The Chinese Communists denounced the reaffirmation of treaty ties with the Chinese Nationalists but invited an American table-tennis team to visit China for a series of exhibition games. They also admitted several American newsmen to the mainland.

The next act in the drama came in June 1971. President Nixon announced that Premier Chou En-lai had invited him to visit China and he had accepted. The meeting lasted a week in February 1972. At its conclusion the two men issued a joint communiqué.

This communiqué is different from most other communiqués. Instead of listing the areas of agreement between the principal participants and ignoring the areas of disagreement, this communiqué directs its attention principally to the areas of disagreement and slights the areas of agreement. Long paragraphs are given over to presenting each nation's position. Here we give the United States position on Formosa. It is the best public statement of current U.S. policy. Further along in the chapter I shall give the Chinese Communists' position toward Formosa.

> The United States acknowledges that all Chinese on either side of the Taiwan Strait maintain there is but one China and that Taiwan is part of China.
>
> The United States government does not challenge that position. It reaffirms its interest in a peaceful settlement of the Taiwan question by the Chinese themselves. With this prospect in mind, it affirms the ultimate objective of the withdrawal of all U.S. forces and military installations from Taiwan.
>
> In the meantime, it will progressively reduce its forces and military installations on Taiwan as the tension in the area diminishes.[16]

Later, after I have matched this part of the communiqué with the Chinese Communist position on Formosa, I shall attempt to parse this statement.

For most Americans at least, the principal actors in the Formosan drama are the two Chinese governments, the Formosans, and the Americans; the United Nations and the other nations of the world form a chorus to comment on events. Americans often ignore Japan.

Japanese Policy Toward Formosa

When the Japanese took over Formosa in 1895, their aims were frankly exploitative. They stopped migration from the Chinese mainland so that land would be available for Japanese farmers. They developed agriculture and industry primarily to supply the home islands with foods and products not produced there. They bettered the life of the Formosan so that he would become a consumer of Japanese manufactures. They maintained control of the government so that Formosans would not subvert these aims.

In the 1930s goals changed. The Japanese authorities started a policy of assimilation: they permitted marriage between Formosans and Japanese; they allowed Formosans to take Japanese names; they enrolled Formosans in Japanese universities; they granted Formosans universal suffrage. In half a century, the Japanese had: (1) created an economy far different from and far advanced over the mainland; (2) established trade patterns dependent on Japan; (3) created an efficient, Japanese-style government, but given the Formosans only limited experience in running it; (4) half convinced the Formosans that they were not Chinese, but not given them full identification as Japanese.[17]

In 1945 Japan turned over the government to the Chinese Nationalists and withdrew from the island. In 1950 Japan signed a peace treaty with the United States, and later, at U.S. insistence, signed another with the Chinese Nationalists, renouncing "all right, title, and claim" to Formosa. Thus ended Japanese political hegemony over Formosa. But social ties have continued. And economic ties have become stronger.

How do the present inhabitants of Formosa regard the Japanese? The question is not widely discussed. No formal studies have been made. But clearly, the views of the mainlanders on Formosa differ from the views of the Formosans themselves.

Many mainland leaders, including Chiang Kai-shek, studied in Japan and profess sympathy and admiration for that nation. But these men also fought an eight-year war against the Japanese, a war in which the Japanese gave no quarter, a war that many historians regard as the prime reason the Nationalists are not ruling all China today. Although Japan is no longer an enemy, she still is not much of a friend. Japan is a force to be reckoned with. Her cooperation is needed for development and a price must be paid for that cooperation. In the future, after China is developed, China will have to contest Japan for leadership among the other Asian nations and for the right to speak for these nations to the rest of the world. Today's relationship, then, is cool, commercial, and competitive.

The Formosans' view of Japan is complex. They recall that the Japanese military drafted or pressed into service more than 170,000 Formosans, of whom 34,000 died. The Japanese did nothing for the war wounded or for soldiers' widows. But this complaint is overshadowed by an enthusiasm for things Japanese. Japanese hit songs are on the radio and in the record shops. Japanese restaurants do a thriving business. The Japanese martial arts—judo and kendo in particular—have their practitioners. So does the tea ceremony and ikebana. Homes are still built in the Japanese style. Formosan students are as liable to go to Japan to study as to the United States. (Mainlander students head for the United States or Europe.) Japanese tourists are well received.

Mainland leaders on Formosa are troubled by the enthusiasm the Formosans show for Japan, and they try to dampen it. Only two Japanese publications freely enter the island; both are written in the English language. Japanese movies are also restricted and at one time were banned.

Nationalist leaders invite Japanese sport teams to participate in friendly meets, but they neither fly the Japanese flag at these events nor do they play the Japanese national anthem.

How do the Japanese view the Formosans? the Chinese Nationalists? the Chinese Communists? Again the answer is not easy to come by, though the Japanese have discussed their relations with China exhaustively and have conducted some surveys on popular attitudes.

A large Formosan colony continues to reside in Japan. It is not wealthy, and from time to time, a Formosan finds himself involved with the Japanese law. On these occasions the Japanese reveal that all vestiges of colonial superiority have not completely vanished. On other occasions, however, the Japanese feel kindly toward the Formosans. They are proud of the resurgence of Japanese culture on the island. They pay sympathetic attention to the Formosan independence movement. They would not like to see the island fall under the domination of the Chinese Communists.

The Japanese are respectful of the Chinese Nationalists. They think of them chiefly in terms of their leader, Chiang Kai-shek. Many Japanese believe that they are under obligation to him since he permitted Japanese troops to depart the mainland in peace and order without taking revenge, even though these Japanese troops had resorted to indiscriminate terrorism to pacify the Chinese peasants. These Japanese feel that their obligation can best be fulfilled by supporting Chiang in his cause against the Communists. (Some Japanese do not recognize an obligation to Chiang but support him because they find his ardent anticommunism attractive.)

Other Japanese believe that Japan should get about the business of restoring relations with the Chinese Communists. They find it foolhardy to ignore 800 million people, particularly if they have a penchant for mischief and live next door. Some Japanese admire Mao. Stubborn old men—Adenauer, de Gaulle, and MacArthur are examples—are accorded respect in Japanese society. Other Japanese are motivated by residual racism. They still hold the prewar belief that Japan's world role is to lead the yellow race against the white race. But most Japanese offer a commercial reason: Japan cannot afford to ignore the vast China market. The Chinese Communist government and its policies are unpopular. From time to time JIJI, a Japanese news service, asks nationwide which nation is most disliked. Communist China often receives the highest percentage.

Attitudes aside, Japan has been willing to follow the American initiatives toward China, particularly in matters involving international security, since the United States has undertaken the defense of Japan. In this policy the Japanese have not been slavish. Japan has been unwilling to adopt the tone of moral rectitude of John Foster Dulles. Nor have the Japanese been willing to ban all intercourse with the mainland. They have always maintained conversations, usually through private parties. They have conducted trade, though not in strategic commodities. They have extended credit, though not in amounts and on such terms that the credit could be regarded as economic aid. They have exchanged newsmen. They allow travelers, chiefly businessmen with a smattering of politicians and intellectuals, to go to the mainland.

Toward Formosa, they have maintained formal diplomatic relations. They have encouraged trade and investment. They have supported the Chinese Nationalists in their diplomatic efforts. On issues where the Chinese Nationalists and the Chinese Communists have clashed, they have supported the Nationalists.

President Nixon's Peking visit and subsequent decision to drop trade barriers and exchange liaison officers with Communist China brought a change in Japanese policy. Shortly after the Nixon visit, the Japanese prime minister visited Peking and issued a communiqué establishing diplomatic relations and announcing that Japan "fully understands and respects" the Chinese Communist position that "Taiwan is an inalienable part of the People's Republic of China."

But conditions actually changed little. In Taipei, the Japanese Embassy became the headquarters of an organization called the Interchange Association whose chief executive is a Japanese diplomat on detached service. The Japanese Consulate at Kaohsiung has become a branch office of the Interchange Association. In Japan, the Association for Far East Relations has established offices in Tokyo, Osaka, and Fukuoka; these offices are staffed by Chinese diplomats on detached service.

Both Japan and Formosa clearly wish to maintain relations with each other. The reason is not hard to find. Japan has been one of three important sources of foreign investment in Formosa and probably will become an important source again. Except for the United States, Japan has been Formosa's most important trading partner.

The three major sources of foreign investment in the Formosan economy have been the United States, the overseas Chinese, and Japan. From 1952 to 1971, Americans invested $286 million, the overseas Chinese invested $201 million, and the Japanese invested $101 million. The statistics (in millions of dollars) since 1970 are:

	1970	1971	1972
United States	$67.8	$43.7	$74.0
Overseas Chinese	29.7	37.8	26.5
Japan	28.5	12.4	7.2

The United States has consistently ranked first. During the 1950s and early 1960s, the overseas Chinese occupied the second position, but they gradually lost ground to the Japanese until, by 1970, both the overseas Chinese and the Japanese were investing about the same amount. In 1971 Japanese investment fell off sharply; in 1972 it dropped again.

Politics caused this decline. By mid-1971, most observers were aware that the United States was in the process of changing its policy toward Communist China. A short time later, Japan too began adjusting its China policy. Not until September 1972, after both the American President and the Japanese prime minister had visited the Chinese mainland, were observers assured that Formosa had not been jettisoned.

During these years of change, many circumspect businessmen, both Japanese and American, suspended Formosan investment. The American business community recovered first. Although their Formosan investments fell by one-third in 1971, they had returned to normal by 1972. The Japanese business community has been a little more cautious a little longer. Nevertheless, it would not be extraordinary to find Japanese investments returning to normal in 1973 and 1974.

Japanese trade with Formosa did not suffer even a momentary setback. The Chinese Information Service reports the 1972 trade statistics (in millions of dollars) for Formosan trade with the United States and Japan as:

	IMPORT	EXPORT	TOTAL
Japan trade	$1,080	$406	$1,486
U.S. trade	822	1,272	2,094
Total U.S.–Japan trade	1,902	1,679	3,580
Total Formosan trade	2,700	3,000	5,700

Japan accounts for better than 25 percent of the total two-way trade with Formosa, though she exports much more to Formosa than she imports. Moreover, this trade is concentrated in certain commodities. For example, Japan supplies Formosa with 19 percent of her chemicals, 14 percent of her steel, 14 percent of her machinery, and 22 percent of her electronic equipment. Japan purchases 21 percent of Formosa's agricultural exports, 11 percent of her fish products, and 16 percent of her textiles. More Japanese visit Formosa than do overseas Chinese—there were 278,000 Japanese tourists in 1972—and they constituted an important source of revenue. Finally, better than 50 percent of all Formosan trade is financed if not undertaken by the Japanese trading firms.

Today, Japanese diplomats tell other diplomats that Japan played her role in deciding the future of Formosa when she surrendered sovereignty over the island. Other powers will decide where that sovereignty lies. The statement is modest and effacing—the sort of statement Japanese diplomats like to make. Perhaps they really believe it. But other diplomats do not. Few give the Chinese Nationalists any chance of returning to the mainland. Many regard them already as remnants who will in time be reabsorbed into the Maoist empire. If the Chinese Nationalists are to survive, they must establish a new raison d'être. The Chinese mainland with its size, history, and culture hogs the political stage. The Chinese Nationalists are thus left with an economic role. Whether they are able to make Formosa into an important world economic power depends in great measure on Japan.

Formosa in the United Nations

Not only the United States and Japan but other nations as well have played a role in the deciding of the Formosa question. One of the principal stages for this international drama has been the United Nations.

The UN Charter gives China a permanent seat in the Security Council as well as seats in the General Assembly and other organs. Which Chinese government is to occupy these seats? The question was first met in the Security Council and later in the General Assembly. Other UN bodies also considered the question but deferred an answer until the General Assembly had resolved the issue.

The Nationalist government had signed the UN Declaration in 1942, had represented China at the San Francisco Conference, and had signed and ratified the Charter. It first occupied the China seats. After the Chinese Communists took over the mainland and proclaimed the People's Republic of China, they demanded the UN seats. In January 1950 the Russians introduced a resolution in the Security Council calling for the expulsion of the Chinese Nationalists.

The U.S. position toward this resolution was ambiguous. It declared that it would vote against it, but that this vote was not to be regarded as a veto. It would be guided by whatever decision the Security Council reached through an affirmative vote of seven members. The Russian resolution failed to pass. Russia walked out of the UN.

Subsequent years brought further debate on China in the Security Council. Sometimes introduced by Russia seeking to castigate the United States, sometimes introduced by the United States seeking to castigate the communists, the debate was always highly acrimonious. But the specific question of which government was to represent China devolved upon the General Assembly. That question was next raised by India in September 1950. Russia also introduced a similar proposal. By then the Korean war had started, President Truman had sent the Seventh Fleet to the Formosan Straits (and been denounced by the Chinese Communists for so doing), and the American military chiefs were wondering whether they were in the first phases of World War III. The United States was no longer ambiguous. It opposed the seating of the Chinese Communists and persuaded other nations to support its view. The Indian and Russian resolutions were defeated.

By 1951 the Chinese Communists had entered the Korean war. When the Russians introduced their resolution calling for the expulsion of the Chinese Nationalists and the seating of the Chinese Communists, the other nations expected a long-drawn and highly emotional debate, designed as much to heighten the American war effort as to denounce the Communists. They were surprised and relieved to hear an American proposal to postpone consideration until the following year. They accepted this proposal and got on with the other business of the assembly.

Next year, the Americans repeated the tactic. It seemed a good way to stall the Russian resolution indefinitely. But other nations were not willing to put off who should represent China. Each year, supporters of the American proposal grew fewer. By the time President Kennedy assumed office, American officials were aware that they needed a new strategy.

That strategy was introduced in 1961. The first step called for facing the Russians down. When they introduced their annual resolution into the General Assembly, the United States called not for a postponement but a vote. The Russians were defeated 48–37, with 19 abstentions. The second step called for the introduction of an American resolution making any future proposal expelling the Chinese Nationalists an "important question," thus requiring a two-thirds' majority for adoption. The American resolution passed 61–34, with 7 abstentions.

In 1963 the Russians stopped sponsoring the China resolution and the Albanians took over. A little later the Japanese joined with the Americans in sponsoring the important-question resolution. In 1965 the vote on expelling the Nationalists was a 47–47 tie, with 20 abstentions. In 1970 the vote was 51–49; only the two-thirds' requirement prevented adoption. In 1971 the General Assembly adopted the Albanian resolution by a decisive vote of 76–35, with 17 abstentions. The Chinese Nationalists left; the Chinese Communists took over the China seats.[18]

Throughout the 1950s and '60s, the two Chinese governments had been competing among the other nations of the world, particularly the underdeveloped nations, to secure exclusive recognition as the sole legal government of China. The Chinese Communists had been active in inviting national leaders to Peking and incorporating such statements in joint communiqués. The Chinese Nationalists had extended foreign aid, thus securing support. The change in UN recognition followed soon after by visits of the American President and the Japanese prime minister gave the competition to the Chinese Communists. Today, only the United States among the major powers and only a few nations among the middle and small-size nations continue to recognize the Chinese Nationalist government.

Communist China's Attitude Toward Formosa

The Chinese Communists seem to put Formosa in a special category. It has been the land of their enemies: it was the first Chinese territory seized by the Japanese militarists; it is the refuge of their old rival, Chiang Kai-shek. They want the island back. Since they came to power, they have been steadfast in that desire, though they have been flexible over means to achieve that end.

No sooner had Chiang Kai-shek reestablished the Nationalist government in Taipei than the Chinese Communists began preparing for an invasion. These preparations were interrupted only by the outbreak of the Korean war. When President Truman interposed the Seventh Fleet, Chou En-lai denounced the action as "constituting armed aggression against the territory of China." When President Truman announced that sovereignty over Formosa was not yet settled, the Chinese Communists responded that China had abrogated all treaties with Japan, including the Treaty of Shimonoseki, when she declared war on Japan December 9, 1941. China was exercising the right of recovery recognized in international law when she took over the islands in 1945. Sovereignty was settled.

The Chinese Communists objected to the inclusion of the Formosan question of the UN General Assembly agenda as unlawful and unjustifiable. They declared that any UN attempt to place Formosa under trusteeship, or to neutralize it, or even to investigate it would help maintain the U.S. occupation of Formosa and thus would be tantamount to "stealing China's legitimate territory."

Despite this strong rhetoric, the Chinese Communists gave up trying to liberate Taiwan forcibly. The Chinese armies, some authorities suggest, were fully occupied with campaigns, first in Korea and then in Tibet, with deployment along the Indo-China frontier, and finally with the suppression of counterrevolutionaries within China proper.

In April 1954 Chou En-lai met with John Foster Dulles in Geneva. Direct negotiations proved futile. In August the Chinese Communists began assembling men and ships along the Fukien coast. In September they began shelling the offshore islands still under Nationalist control.

These activities hastened the negotiation of a defense treaty between the United States and the Chinese Nationalists. Chou En-lai denounced the treaty as an act of aggression. He reaffirmed the Chinese Communist intent to liberate Formosa. New Zealand prevailed upon the Security Council to invite the Chinese Communists to discuss the Formosan question. Chou En-lai responded that the liberation of Formosa was an internal affair and thus not within the jurisdiction of the Security Council.

Again, the Chinese Communists' rhetoric proved more resolute than their behavior. In 1955 they changed their tactics. In March they stopped shelling the offshore islands. In April Chou En-lai announced his willingness to sit down with the United States to discuss the question of relaxing tension. The United States proposed a general renunciation of force in the resolution of international problems and a specific renunciation of force with regard to Taiwan. The Chinese Communists pointed out that Formosa was an internal Chinese problem not subject to international negotiation. They were prepared to discuss only the withdrawal of U.S. military forces, which was an international problem. Prolonged discussions ensued. By early 1956, though meetings continued, both sides recognized that agreement was not possible.

Meanwhile, the Chinese Communists had started a full-scale peace offensive against the Chinese Nationalists. They sent letters to prominent Chinese leaders who had fled with Chiang, promising both clemency and important positions on the mainland. Chou En-lai invited the Chinese Nationalists to negotiate terms for the peaceful liberation of the island. The letters remained unanswered; the invitation was spurned. The campaign ended in late 1956.

In August 1958 Nikita Khrushchev and Mao Tse-tung met secretly. Shortly thereafter, the Chinese Communists resumed bombarding the offshore islands. The American secretary of state went to Formosa to demonstrate the U.S. commitment to the islands' defense. Tension was dissolved in October when the Chinese Communists announced the bizarre policy of only shelling the islands every other day.

Since attempts to overwhelm Formosa by alternating crisis diplomacy with military action were not successful, the Chinese Communists settled in for the long haul. In September 1959 Radio Peking announced that the liberation of Formosa might take five to ten years. The defense minister said the civil war between the Communists and the Nationalists might continue for another thirty years. Mao Tse-tung declared that he could get along without Formosa for the time being.

Lest the United States conclude that the Chinese Communists had tacitly given up their campaign to liberate Formosa the Chinese Communists instructed their diplomats in Warsaw to refuse to discuss any other issue with the American diplomats.

In 1961 Communist China was mainly concerned that the United States was trying to resolve the Formosan question by creating two Chinas. President Kennedy had just assumed the Presidency, and many of the men he brought with him had advocated such schemes. Other nations also found some form of two-China solution attractive. For China, however, the crowning effrontery came from Russia. The Chinese Communists announced that Khrushchev had asked them "to agree to the United States scheme of creating 'two Chinas.' "

The third Formosan Strait crisis came in 1962. The Great Leap Forward, a radical reconstruction plan, had failed. Drought, flood, and pestilence added to difficulties. The Chinese Nationalists began calling for an uprising on the mainland. It was at this juncture that the Americans assigned a new ambassador—an admiral who had had extensive experience with amphibious landings. Only after President Kennedy informed the Chinese Communists that the United States would not support a Nationalist invasion of the mainland did the crisis dissolve.

In 1964 Chou En-lai ruled out self-determination as a solution to the Formosan question. In Chinese Communist eyes, the Formosan independence movement was a scheme conceived and financed by Japanese and American imperialists to control Formosa.

In late spring 1966, Mao Tse-tung started the Great Cultural Revolution. This great internal catharsis occupied the Chinese until 1969. In the early 1970s, the Chinese Communists returned to the task of liberating Formosa. Their offensive was diplomatic. They succeeded in having the Chinese Nationalists expelled from the United Nations and themselves recognized as the legitimate representatives of China. They played host to President Nixon. Shortly after his China visit, they caused the Japanese to withdraw formal diplomatic recognition from the Chinese Nationalists. They persuaded the British, who were signatories of the Potsdam and Cairo declarations, to acknowledge that Formosa was an inalienable part of the territory of the People's Republic of China. Here is a quote from the joint communiqué issued after President Nixon's visit. It is a full statement of the Chinese position. It also shows how little the Chinese Communists have altered their views over the years:

> The Taiwan question is the crucial question obstructing the normalization of relations between China and the United States; the Government of the People's Republic of China is the sole, legal Government of China; Taiwan is a province of China, which has long been returned to the motherland; the liberation of Taiwan is China's internal affair, in which no other country has the right to interfere; and all U.S. forces and military installations must be withdrawn from Taiwan. The Chinese government firmly opposes any activities which aim at the creation of "one China, one Taiwan," "one China, two governments," "two Chinas," an "independent Taiwan," or advocate that "the status of Taiwan remains to be determined." [19]

President Truman was the author of the statement that the "status of Taiwan remains to be determined." He made that statement when he sent the Seventh Fleet to the Formosan Straits. He wanted other nations to accept this interposition as an international act. Were Formosa regarded as Chinese territory,[20] the interposition might be regarded as interference in the domestic affairs of China. Although this took place in 1950, American diplomats have maintained that Formosa's status was not determined until President Nixon relaxed the patrols in the Formosa Straits in 1971. Since then, I have not heard American diplomats make this statement,[21] but neither have I heard them denounce it.

Most of the other solutions for a separate Formosa were actively debated during the Kennedy administration. Reviewing them one notes that the Chinese Nationalists have been just as vociferous as the Chinese Communists in denouncing them.

The two-China solution proposed that the Chinese Communist government be recognized as the government of the mainland and the Chinese Nationalist government be recognized as the government of Formosa. Academicians and newsmen had urged consideration of this solution for years. But diplomats did not begin talking about it until John Foster Dulles was no longer secretary of state and they were no longer obliged to support his contention that the Chinese Nationalists formed the sole legal government of China. The merit of this proposal was that it recognized actual conditions. The State Department pointed out its weakness: "The 'Two China' concept is bitterly opposed by Peking and Taipei. Hence, even if such a solution could be imposed by outside authority, it would not be a stable one." [22]

A variant of the two-China solution is the one-China, one-Formosa solution. Professor Robert Scalapino worked this proposal out in some detail for the U.S. Senate.[23] The proposal accepted the definition that there was only one China but excluded Formosa from that definition. It envisaged the establishment of a Republic of Taiwan, though it was not clear whether the Nationalists or the Formosans would run it. Avery Brundage, chairman of the International Olympic Committee in 1965, stated that his committee used this solution as the basis of invitations to the Olympic Games. He was roundly criticized. The Japanese have found this solution attractive but have never acted on it.

The successor-state theory is a second variant of the two-China solution. Chester Bowles authored it while he was undersecretary of state. The theory was designed for the United Nations. Both Nationalist China and Communist China were to be regarded as successor states to the China that entered the United Nations at its founding. Bowles' idea was to have the Nationalists maintain their seat in the Security Council and in the General Assembly but allow the Communists to apply to the Credentials Committee of the General Assembly for a seat. Other variations were also proposed—for example, the one-China, two-governments solution.

Another proposal involving the United Nations was offered by Adlai Stevenson, the American ambassador to that body during the Kennedy administration. He suggested leaving the status of Formosa unsettled, placing it under UN trusteeship for a specified number of years, and then holding a plebiscite of the inhabitants to determine the island's future. The idea of a Formosan plebiscite had been present in Roosevelt's thinking during World War II.

John Fairbank, a professor at Harvard University, offered a one-and-a-half-China proposal. He wished to recognize Chinese Communist suzerainty over Formosa. In return for this recognition, the Chinese Communists would make Formosa into an autonomous area with full rights to handle its own foreign affairs. The Communists would receive the Security Council seat and a General Assembly seat. The Nationalists would be limited to a seat in the General Assembly.

Richard Moorsteen and Morton Abramowitz have developed a one-China-but-not-now solution.[24] The United States and hopefully Japan would formally agree in principle that Formosa is part of China. They would point out that this statement is in accord with the official positions of both Chinese governments, but that each government placed a different interpretation on what that principle meant. Until the two Chinese governments had ironed out differences over the interpretation, the United States would continue to honor its treaty obligation to defend Formosa and the Pescadores.

Conclusions

It is hard to see how Chiang Kai-shek will realize his goal of returning to rule China. The United States will not support him in a military invasion. The Chinese Communist government may fall from misrule and Chiang may return in its stead. But were the Chinese Communist government to collapse, it would have done so during the Cultural Revolution, when the country verged on chaos. Moreover, Chiang's government was fully discredited when he was thrust from the mainland. The question, then, is not whether Chiang will return. The question is whether Formosa will exist as an independent state or will be absorbed into the mainland.

If other nations are to answer this question, Formosa will be absorbed. All major nations except the United States have recognized the Communist government and have made statements which can be interpreted as recognizing Formosa to be a province of the mainland. Japan has taken an anomolous stance. I suggest that these nations have already said all they can say about the future of Formosa and that only Japan and the United States will have any further influence on Formosa's status.

The most recent statement of American policy toward Formosa is contained in the joint communiqué between President Nixon and Premier Chou En-lai issued on February 28, 1972. The reader need not be a diplomat to recognize that this statement leaves out more than it says. It is oracular. It can be interpreted several ways. No one in authority has come forth to offer the correct interpretation.

One-China advocates can be heartened by the U.S. acknowledgment that the two Chinas maintain that there is but one China. Two-China and independent-Formosa advocates can find solace in the American refusal to join the Chinese Communist denunciation of these solutions. In fact, anybody can read whatever he wants into this statement.

That is the important point. The United States did not try to resolve the Formosa question during this meeting. It was content to get about the business of restoring relations with the Chinese Communist government without reneging on other obligations, engendering domestic debate, or changing the status quo.

In the communiqué, the Chinese Communists said that Formosa was the crucial question obstructing U.S.-China relations. *Crucial* is a strong adjective. It reveals the great pressure that China placed on the United States to resolve the Formosa question. That the United States stood pat would suggest that the United States is happy with the way things are now.

The military sentences in the American part of the communiqué also invite comment. One sentence says that the ultimate American objective is the withdrawal of all U.S. forces and military installations from Formosa. But it does not say that the United States intends to abrogate its defense treaty with the Chinese Nationalists. In fact, President Nixon has gone out of his way on another occasion to say that the United States intends to honor its defense commitments to the Chinese Nationalists. The other sentence says that the United States will progressively reduce its forces and military installations on Formosa as tension in the area diminishes. That is a polite way of saying that the forces and military installations will remain as long as tension continues.

The communiqué, then, suggests that the United States likes the status quo but will accept other solutions to the Formosa question. The only solution ruled out is a military solution.

The recent Japanese communiqué with the Chinese Communists is also murky. In that document, the Japanese "fully respect and understand the Chinese position that Taiwan in an inalienable part of China." But they do not adopt the Chinese position as their own. Nor do they offer any definition of the phrase "respect and understand." The Japanese were willing to break off political ties with the Chinese Nationalists and restore those ties with the Chinese Communists. But they were not willing to break off economic ties with the Nationalists. They are trading and investing more than ever in the island, despite Communist pressure.

The Japanese position is not far from the American position. Both nations would like a two-China solution. At least, neither nation is willing to offer more than lip service to a one-China solution. Both nations continue to permit their citizens to trade and invest in the Formosan economy. The United States shows no sign of renouncing its defense commitment. So long as these conditions obtain, Formosa will remain impervious to outside influence. The answer to the Formosa question, then, lies within Formosa.

It is hard to conceive of the Formosans reaching an accommodation with the Chinese Communists. They would only be exchanging one set of Chinese rulers for another. It is equally difficult to conceive of the Formosans seizing control from the Chinese Nationalists. If they were considering that, they should have tried it some time ago. Now the

Formosans are beginning to enter into positions in the central government. Although they may well wish the integration were faster, they will do nothing that will fundamentally alter the process.

What about the mainlanders living in Formosa? Would they be willing to accept Chinese Communist rule? A union would bring no economic benefits for them or for the Formosans. The Formosans standard of living is considerably higher than the mainland standard of living.[25] The Formosan economy is a market economy while the mainland economy is a command economy. The Formosan economy is orientated toward foreign trade and is integrated with the Japanese economy. The mainland economy is autarchic. Were the Chinese Communists to take over, the Formosan economy would certainly be integrated into the mainland economy, not vice versa. The result would only be disorder on the island.

But would economics be the major consideration? Wouldn't politics prevail? Statements from the mainland suggest the Chinese Communists think primarily in political terms. Mao has never been known for his economics. Chou En-lai has said only that the Formosan standard of living will rise if his government takes over, since he will abolish the income tax. Present mainland broadcasts offer little comment about the Formosan economy other than to call the current prosperity superficial and dependent on foreign countries.

A few years ago, the Chinese on Formosa also believed in the supremacy of politics. But no longer. In 1969 the KMT held a party congress at which it appointed an enlarged Central Committee including many men who held top managerial and technological posts both within the government and in the private sector. The Central Committee runs the KMT and the KMT runs the country. These men would probably insist that relations with the mainland make economic sense before they receive serious consideration.

Are there no political considerations? The men who rule Formosa now are Chinese and they would like to be part of China. They are from the mainland. They would like to return to the mainland. The imperatives of the middle kingdom are strong.

But these men would have to accept Communist rule. Certainly, Generalissimo Chiang Kai-shek could not do that. He has spent his life fighting Communists and will not surrender now. Neither will his son, the present premier and heir-apparent, defect. Filial piety is still a Chinese virtue. Nor could the other old men who surround Chiang defect. Their loyalty to the Generalissimo is as strong as the son's piety. They, too, have spent their lives fighting communism. Perhaps one or two might want to die in their native province and will make their individual accommodations with the Chinese Communists. The young mainlanders who are coming into the government don't have strong feelings of enmity toward the Chinese Communists but neither do they have any strong desire to return to the mainland.

The future, then, seems fairly clear. The Nationalists will talk about returning to the mainland. The Communists will talk about liberating Formosa. Both Nationalists and Communists will continue to insist that there is but one China. Each will claim to be the sole legal government. But neither will have a way of changing the status quo. Several generations will probably pass before people recognize the present reality: We shall have two Chinas—but not now.

Notes

1. *Formosa* is a word of Portuguese origin. Westerners often use it to describe the island, although *Taiwan*, a word of unclear origin, is also used. Because Taiwan can be written in Chinese ideographs and thus can be read by Chinese, Japanese, and Koreans, they use this word to describe the island. From time to time, attempts are made to attach political significance to one word or the other. For example, advocates of Taiwanese independence living in America usually use the term Formosa in an attempt to deny even a linguistic affiliation with China. Independence advocates who live in Japan, however, are obliged to use the word Taiwan if they wish to be understood. In this article, I tend to call the island Formosa. No connotation is intended.

2. The Pescadores are also known by their Chinese name, Penghu.

3. George Kerr, *Formosa Betrayed* (Cambridge, Mass.: Houghton Mifflin, 1965), p. 310.

4. *United States Relations with China* (Washington, D.C.: Department of State Publication 3573, 1949), p. 309.

5. Today, Formosa has a population of 13.5 million inhabitants. Of that number, 11 million belong to families that first came to the island before the twentieth century, 2 million belong to families that came after 1945, and 170,000 are members of aboriginal tribes. The population growth rate is 2.6 percent.

6. Maurice Meisner, "The Development of Formosan Nationalism," in *Formosa Today*, ed. Mark Mancall (New York: Praeger, 1964), p. 151.

7. *New York Times*, 31 January 1973.

8. Yung Wei, "Political Development in the Republic of China on Taiwan," in *China and the Question of Taiwan: Documents and Analysis*, ed. Hungdah Chiu (New York: Praeger, 1973), p. 95. For the social attitudes of students, see Sheldon Appleton, "Taiwanese and Mainlanders on Taiwan: A Survey of Student Attitudes," *China Quarterly*, no. 44 (October–December 1970): 38–65.

9. William M. Bueler, *U.S.-China Policy and the Problem of Taiwan* (Boulder, Col.: Colorado Associated University Press, 1971), p. 114. The *New York Times* suggests that Formosans willing to work with the Chinese Communists have recently put in an appearance. *New York Times*, 31 January 1973.

10. *New York Times*, 4 June 1973.

11. Wei, "Political Development," p. 99.

12. Foster Rhea Dulles, *American Policy Toward Communist China* (New York: Crowell, 1972), p. 95.

13. Ibid., p. 131.

14. Article V, Mutual Defense Treaty between the United States and the Republic of China, 2 December 1954.

15. Article X.

16. Communiqué between President Richard Nixon and Premier Chou En-lai, 28 February 1972, *Peking Review* 15 (3 March 1972): 5.

17. Shinkichi Eto, "An Outline of Formosan History," in Mancall, *Formosa Today*, pp. 43–58. For a good discussion of more recent events in Formosa as well as an analysis of relations between Japan and Formosa, see Toshiyoshi Wakana, *Myonichi no Taiwan* (Taiwan Tomorrow) (Tokyo: Shin Kokumin Shuppansha, 1973).

18. A complete record of the UN vote can be found in Doak Barnett, *Our China Policy: The Need for Change*, Headline Series, No. 204, February 1971, p. 41.

19. *Peking Review* 15 (3 March 1972): 5.

20. A good analysis of the status of Formosa in terms of international law can be found in Hungdah Chiu, "China, the United States, and the Question of Taiwan," in Chiu, *China and the Question of Taiwan*, pp. 112–76.

21. See, for example, the statement by Thomas Shoesmith in Jerome A. Cohen et al., *Taiwan and American Policy* (New York: Praeger, 1971), pp. 33–34. At the time, Shoesmith was the country director on the Republic of China desk in the Department of State.

22. *American Foreign Policy, Current Documents, 1958* (Washington, D.C.: Government Printing Office, 1962), p. 1143.

23. Conlon Associates Ltd., *United States Foreign Policy, Asia*, Studies prepared at the request of the Committee on Foreign Relations, United States Senate (Washington, D.C.: Government Printing Office, 1959), pp. 153–55.

24. Richard Moorsteen and Morton Abramowitz, *Remaking China Policy: US-China Relations and Governmental Decision-Making* (Cambridge, Mass.: Harvard University Press, 1971).

25. A Japanese research group, the *Chugoku Keizai Kenkyukai*, offers the following comparison of income per capita figures on Formosa and the mainland.

	Mainland	Formosa
1970	$94	$293
1971	102	329

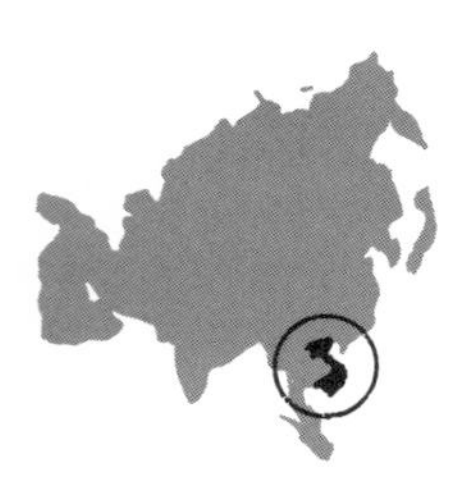

VIETNAM

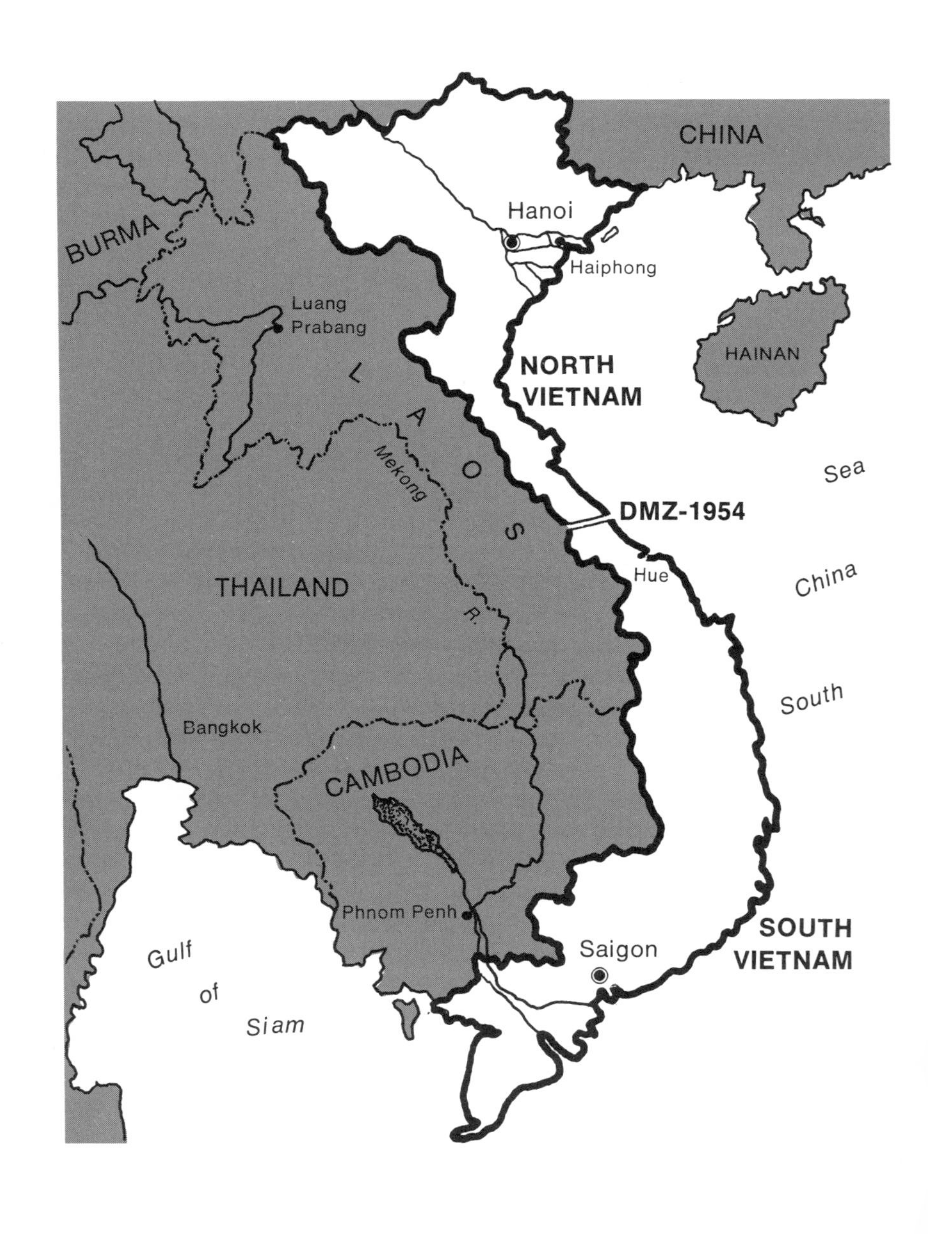
CHINA
Hanoi
Haiphong
BURMA
Luang
Prabang
HAINAN
NORTH
VIETNAM
L
A
O
S
Mekong
R.
Sea
DMZ-1954
Hue
China
THAILAND
South
Bangkok
CAMBODIA
Phnom Penh
Saigon
SOUTH
VIETNAM
Gulf
of
Siam

4

Vietnam

*Le Thi Tuyet**

Background

UNITY WITH INDEPENDENCE has been the elusive goal of the Vietnamese people for over two thousand years. Unlike any other modern divided country, Vietnam has been divided many times in its history, except for a short period (1802–58) in the nineteenth century before French colonialism took over. Put another way, the Vietnamese nation has never really been united for any length of time under one sovereign government exercising undisputed political control with a legitimate mandate over the whole country. In that regard, the division of Vietnam since 1954 has merely repeated history.

Until about 1800, when the Vietnamese expelled Chinese hegemony, expanded southward, and destroyed the Cham kingdom, independent Vietnam was constantly torn apart by dynastic power struggles and rivalries between princely families. From the fifteenth to the eighteenth century Vietnam was divided into two parts, the North under the Trinh dynasty and the South under the Nguyen dynasty. In 1620 the political division between the two families partitioned the country north of Dong Hoi—not very far above the 17th parallel demarcation line of today. In fact, a stone wall separated the South from the North.

Divided into thirds during the reign of the Tay-Son brothers (1788–1802), Vietnam was reunited by Emperor Gia-Long in 1802, only to be

* I am deeply indebted to the late Kenneth T. Young for his constructive criticisms, invaluable comments, and precious cooperation just before his unfortunate and untimely death. All responsibility for this chapter remains entirely mine, however.

divided again into three parts by the French in 1884. It was during that period that regionalism took on a new dimension. Vietnam's colonization by the French—starting in 1858—accentuated the provincial character and the geographical, economic, and political differences (rather than the similarities) of Vietnam. Politically, the French set up three separate, French-controlled administrations: one each in the South, the Center, and the North. The southern part of Vietnam, or Cochinchina, became a French colony in 1867, whereas central Annam and northern Tonkin later became French protectorates. Economically, the French created a plantation tenant-farmer economy in the South and the rudiments of an industrial economy in the Hanoi-Haiphong area. The divisiveness of French politics also intensified the political separation of the Vietnamese. For some sixty years before World War II Vietnam was divided into distinct regional entities generally known as the three "kys"—Nam-ky, Trung-ky, and Bac-ky—or, respectively, South Vietnam, Central Vietnam, and North Vietnam.

World War II resulted in a new, dual division. At the Potsdam Conference in 1945, the victorious Allies chose the 16th parallel as the line for dividing the responsibility for handling the surrender and repatriation of Japanese forces and administering the country. Chinese forces occupied the area north of that line, which had come under the de facto control of the Democratic Republic of Vietnam (DRV) founded on September 2, 1945. British forces, soon to be replaced by the French, occupied the southern half of the country.[1]

The postwar French government immediately restored French control over the southern region, at least in the cities. The authorities in Hanoi sought to negotiate a compromise with Paris, to extend Hanoi's jurisdiction over the South in return for Vietnam's association with the French Union. The March 6, 1946, agreement recognized the DRV as a "free state . . . forming part of the Indochinese Federation and the French Union" and stipulated that the unity of Vietnam would be solved by future elections: "With regard to the unification of the three ky (Nam-ky, or Cochinchina, Trung-ky, or Annam, Bac-ky, or Tonkin), the French Government undertakes to follow the decisions of the people consulted by referendum." [2]

The agreement was signed in Paris. In the field the situation looked different. In June 1946, the French high commissioner for Indochina, ignoring the agreement, established a "free republic" of Cochinchina under French control, which was later replaced by an Associate State of Vietnam, headed by Bao Dai, in mid-1949. Vietnam was politically divided again.

In December 1946 fighting broke out between the Vietminh forces and the French forces who tried to extend their military and political control over all Vietnam. After eight years of war the French did succeed in regaining the Hanoi-Haiphong area and many other cities. But Vietminh forces consolidated their control over wide areas of both North and South Vietnam. That was the complex situation at the time of the Geneva

Conference in the spring of 1954. Two separate and independent Vietnamese governments sent representatives to that conference: the Democratic Republic of Vietnam and the State of Vietnam (SVN). Each had juridical status, each was recognized by numerous states, and each was invited by the four Inviting Powers of the Geneva Conference—France, the Soviet Union, the United Kingdom, and the United States.[3] But neither Vietnamese governments recognized or dealt with the other at Geneva.

The Geneva Conference resulted in a cessation of hostilities in Indochina but, once again, in the division of Vietnam. This time the country was divided into two parts at about the 17th parallel. Before we discuss the problems of this new division it is imperative to review the main provisions of the Geneva Agreements pertaining to the division, the factors leading to the division, and the position of the protagonists and the great powers on a divided Vietnam—all of which have had a bearing on the problems of a political settlement and unification in Vietnam today.

What is generally known as the Geneva Agreements of July 1954 is a set of documents including three separate military agreements on the cessation of hostilities in Cambodia, Laos, and Vietnam; and a Final Declaration dealing with political issues. The three separate military agreements were bilateral and signed by the representatives of the Vietminh forces on one side, and the French Union forces on the other, on July 20.[4] The Final Declaration was made the next day, July 21; it contained thirteen paragraphs and was not signed by any of the nine participating members of the Geneva Conference.

The Geneva Agreement of July 20, 1954, on the cessation of hostilities in Vietnam provided for, among other things: a "provisional military demarcation line" with a "demilitarized zone" on either side of the demarcation line (Art. 1), three hundred days for regroupment of opposing forces into respective assembly zones (Art. 2), free population movements between the sides of the demarcation line (Art. 14d), and an International Commission to ensure the control and supervision of the Agreement (Art. 29).

The most crucial and controversial provision concerned the unification of the country. Yet it was casually treated, expressed in broad and general terms, and obscured among other considerations. It was not given the status of a separate agreement nor made binding in any legal sense on any party to the conference. This crucial issue was merely inscribed in the unsigned Final Declaration and not mentioned in the July 20 Agreement on the cessation of hostilities. Paragraph 6 of the Declaration stated that "the military demarcation line is provisional and should not in any way be interpreted as constituting a political or territorial boundary." Paragraph 7 stipulated that "the general elections shall be held in July 1956" and "consultations will be held on this subject between the competent representative authorities of the two zones from July 20, 1955, onwards."

Important questions which come to mind: Why partition? Who proposed it? How was it agreed to? What was its nature and scope?

As in the cases of Germany in 1945 and Korea in 1950, the partition of Vietnam in 1954 was primarily imposed on the Vietnamese by the great powers. The Geneva accords on partition and on elections in Vietnam were the products of great-power bargains rather than reflections of actual military and political conditions in Indochina.

The great powers made no genuine attempt at the Geneva Conference to negotiate the real political problems existing in Vietnam. Instead, they worked out a series of face-saving devices in exchange for other considerations beyond Vietnam and pertaining to their more immediate national interests. The British played with the idea of partition out of fear of a joint Franco-American military action in Indochina that would enlarge the war theater and endanger the Asian countries in the British-led Colombo Plan organization. The Soviet Union favored the agreements with the understanding that France would not later join the European Defense Community (EDC). China agreed to them on the assumption that the United States would stay out of Southeast Asia and not thwart the elections.

Indeed, without the great-power confrontation over the EDC issue, there would probably have been no partition. Although France was interested primarily in the disposition of the Vietnam problem, the Soviet Union and the United States had another important preoccupation on their respective agendas: the scuttling or the setting up, in each case, of the EDC.

Both the Soviet Union and the United States came to Geneva not only for Indochina but also to deal with the issue of EDC. As Gurtov indicated, Georges Bideault "warned" John Foster Dulles that "EDC would doubtless be scuttled" if the United States refused to accept the Geneva Conference *and* the participation of China.[5] On the other hand, it was revealed that "Moscow's design was to undermine the Franco-American alliance, not so much for the sake of the Communist struggle over Indochina as for the purpose of blocking a Franco-German entente in EDC."[6] In this regard, Soviet diplomacy outdid the American, because a settlement emerged on Indochina at Geneva while EDC was shelved in Paris.

Clearly, only the pressure and influence of the great powers led to the compromise on the partition of Vietnam, the determination of the demarcation line, and the date for Vietnamese elections. These were the three major painful concessions made by Hanoi, primarily in response to the pressures of the Soviet Union and China. The idea of partition was first alluded to by Pham Van Dong, to everyone's great surprise, on May 25, 1954, three days after Molotov called for a cease-fire and *military regroupment in zones* in a five-point program—quite similar to the May 8 French proposal. Dong declared in closed session:

> As far as possible, the demarcation line should follow geographical features or other reference points which are easily recognizable on the ground and it

should be drawn so as not to interfere with communication and transport within the respective zones.[7]

During the last stage of the Geneva negotiations, Dong, under the mounting pressure of an impatient Molotov and a conciliatory Chou En-lai, had to accept a major territorial compromise on the demarcation line at the 17th parallel (instead of the 13th or 14th parallel demanded by Hanoi or the 18th parallel pressed for by the French), and a considerable concession on an elections date two years after a cease-fire (instead of the six months requested by Hanoi and the eighteen months preferred by the French).

Thus, without the leverage of the EDC issue there would have been no Vietnamese partition and probably no "sudden transformation of Molotov, 'Mr. Veto,' into a virtuoso of compromise." [8]

What, then, were the positions of Hanoi, Saigon, and Washington with regard to the partition and elections agreements?

In 1954 Hanoi bought time for territory. In giving up its demand for "recognition of the sovereignty, independence and *territorial integrity* of Vietnam" and accepting a "provisional demarcation line," Hanoi was certain to get the whole territory under its control two years later, in July 1956, when the general elections were to be held. Hanoi temporarily gave up "total victory" for peace and independence. Never before in history had the sense of achieving Vietnamese unity been so close and yet so distant. And in 1956, when the Diem government refused to hold elections, the search for unity became once more elusive and illusive.

Perhaps the most unexpected and the least comprehensible attitude at the Geneva Conference was that of Saigon, especially in light of the subsequent rejection of the 1956 elections and other events. During the whole period of negotiations—public and secret—at Geneva from May 8 to July 21, 1954, Saigon consistently expressed its categorical opposition to any partition "direct or indirect, final or provisional, de facto or de jure," [9] and asked for international supervision of any cease-fire by the United Nations.

In early July, when the news of an eventual temporary partition reached Ngo Dinh Diem, he protested with indignation and reportedly said he would take no part in such a policy.[10] In Geneva, Foreign Minister Tran Van Do tried privately to persuade Pham Van Dong not to accept the partition of Vietnam—to no avail.[11]

Even after the principle of partition was accepted by the Vietminh, France, Great Britain, the Soviet Union, and China, Tran Van Do persisted on Vietnamese territorial unity. On July 18, when the nine delegations were reconvened to review the progress of the talks conducted in individual and private meetings outside the conference room, the representative of the State of Vietnam was the only one to bring a discordant note, as reported by Devillers and Lacouture:

> Suddenly, a touch of drama came from the most unlikely quarter: Tran-van-Do rose to protest, with restraint but in a voice cracked with emotion, against the partition of his country and the way in which the fate of the Vietnamese was being decided.[12]

On the night of July 20, after the military agreements had been reached and signed, Tran Van Do asked that there be no celebrations in connection with documents that would shatter the unity of his country. On the very last day of the Geneva Conference, July 21, he reiterated his solemn protest against the partition imposed on Vietnam and dissociated himself from the Final Declaration.

The American attitude on partition was an expedient one, and ambivalent to say the least. Washington did not like the idea of partition before, during, or after the Geneva Conference but could not effectively prevent it. On May 15, the U.S. delegate Walter B. Smith, officially informed Bao Dai that his country opposed partition.[13] Yet, after the DRV proposed a de facto temporary division, the Americans acquiesced. They recognized in early June that some form of partition was unavoidable, and the logical solution if France could not prevent it and if the United States could not persuade France not to accept it.[14]

The recognition of this unpleasant reality for the Americans came in the confidential agreement of June 29 between President Eisenhower and Prime Minister Churchill which was communicated to French Premier Mendès-France. In it they concurred on the principle of partition and on a demarcation line just above the 17th parallel, at Dong Hoi where the ancient wall had once before divided Vietnam. The final settlement temporarily divided Vietnam some thirty miles to the south. But the United States refused to be bound by or associated with this decision.

At the closing session the U.S. government reiterated its declaration of June 29, 1954:

> In cases of nations now divided against their will, we shall continue to seek to achieve unity through free elections, supervised by the United Nations to ensure that they are conducted fairly.[15]

A week or so after the Geneva Conference, Smith stated on a television program that the United States did not accept "the truce lines" as permanent political solutions.[16] Nevertheless, the United States has in effect accepted and furthered the paradox of "a permanent temporary partition" of Vietnam, as seen in the next section.

The demarcation line having been drawn, it is appropriate to study the nature and scope of the partition. Compared with Korea and Germany, the partition in Vietnam was more open and flexible but perhaps more ambiguous in principle. First, the idea of the demarcation line was primarily military, for the practical purpose of the regroupment forces during the cease-fire. It was not intended to be a political or economic barrier. This was the reason why it was acceptable to the Vieminh who insisted that the demarcation line was "military" and "provisional" only, and not "a political or territorial boundary."

Second, the partition was not intended as a total rupture between the two zones. On the contrary, it was supposed to be open and to allow some interaction. Article 14d of the Agreement permitted freedom of population movements for three hundred days after the armistice was signed:

> From the date of entry into force of the present Agreement until the movement of troops is completed, any civilians residing in a district controlled by one party who wish to go and live in the zone assigned to the other party shall be permitted to do so by the authorities in that district.

Also, no provisions in the Agreement forbade cultural, social, and economic exchanges. In fact, Hanoi repeatedly asked for economic exchanges with Saigon during the first seven years after the Geneva Conference. Saigon turned them down.

Third, some contacts between the authorities of the two zones were provided for by the Agreement in creating the Joint Commission, which was composed of an equal number of representatives of the commanders of the two parties (Art. 31). Of course, the Joint Commission was military in character and carried out military functions relating to the cease-fire, the regroupment of armed forces, and the observance of the DMZ (Art. 33). But it did ensure liaison between the two zones.

On the other hand, the Final Declaration on partition and elections not only was unsigned and thus not binding legally, but also ambiguous at least in one aspect: it did not specifically name the parties and subsequently raised some conflicts in operation and in international law as to who were the responsible parties. This was true of the southern part of the demarcation line where two authorities coexisted: the French Union forces and the State of Vietnam.

Nowhere in the military agreement nor in the Final Declaration was the State of Vietnam named. Militarily "the Commanders of the Forces of the two parties" seemed clear to everyone; it designated the French Union forces on one side and the Vietminh forces on the other, since the National Vietnamese Army in the South was negligible and incorporated into the French-led Union forces.

Politically, however, some difficulties were bound to arise. Paragraph 7 of the Declaration, for example, provided that consultations for general elections would be held "between the competent representative authorities of the two zones." Who were the "competent representative authorities" in the South? French authorities who signed the Agreement? or the State of Vietnam which Hanoi had ignored at Geneva?

Prime Minister Pham Van Dong was reported to have put the

responsibility on the French when he declared on January 1, 1955: "It is you, the French, who are responsible, for it is with you that we signed the Geneva Agreement, and it is you who will have to see that it is respected." [17]

But how could France have had the means of seeing that the Agreements be carried out when all her forces were already out of Vietnam by April 1956, that is, three months before the deadline fixed for the general elections? Hanoi did not, or could not, foresee that fatal eventuality.

Another interpretation blamed the State of Vietnam, which, it was argued, was the successor of the French and therefore had to respect the accords. Yet in 1949, when the State of Vietnam was created, its independence and territory were given back to the Vietnamese, and recognized by France. Any presumed obligation on the part of the State of Vietnam as an independent legal entity to follow French policies and to implement the Geneva Agreements from which it had dissociated itself completely was juridically questionable and politically unrealistic.

Without entering into the legal complexities of the Geneva document, let us point out that the ambiguity and shortsightedness of the provisions on partition and elections have contributed to the transformation of a "provisional military demarcation line" into a political, ideological, economic, and social wall, or "the bamboo curtain" to use a Vietnamese image symbolizing the "resistant" character of the partition.

Problems of Division

The problems caused by partition were numerous and complex, affecting every aspect of life: civil administration, social reform, economic subsistence, political structure—not to mention family separations. How those problems were handled and solved have had a great impact on the prospects of reunification. In order to simplify the analysis we will study the problems of division (1) within each zone separately, (2) between the two zones, and (3) between the great-powers supporters of each. It should be noted, however, that those problems did not always come in this order, and that frequently they occurred simultaneously.

WITHIN EACH ZONE

Within each zone the demarcation line has proved to be a good practical means to deal with military problems of regroupment of forces, of enforcing the cease-fire, and of preventing violations. On the whole the Joint Commission succeeded in ensuring an orderly withdrawal of troops partly because the regrouping zones were precise and delimited, and the provisions pertaining to military matters were clearly defined. There was no bloodbath, no major conflict, no staggering confusion.

From the economic, social, and political standpoints, however, partition created different problems in the North and in the South. In both cases these problems were handled in such a way that they kept pushing the two zones farther apart and impairing the chances of reunification.

Within North Vietnam, the division of the country had a direct and brutal impact on the economy. Economically the partition did more harm to the North than to the South, mainly because of the pattern of distribution of natural resources. The South was endowed with rich rice fields; the North had abundant raw materials for industries. Accordingly the North was heavily dependent on the South for its basic subsistence needs. The division of the country, the unwillingness of the Diem government in the South to hold economic exchanges with the North, the poor harvests which followed the Geneva Accords, and the nervousness of the authorities about the massive exodus of people fleeing south and thus depriving the DRV of useful labor, all contributed to the disastrous failure of the land reforms undertaken by Hanoi during 1954–56. About 50,000 North Vietnamese were allegedly executed and, according to one source, "at least twice as many were arrested and sent to forced labor camps.[18] Finally, a peasant rebellion occurred in Nghe An on November 2, 1956. Enraged farmers "surrounded a Commission Jeep with petitions asking that they be allowed to go south of the seventeenth parallel." [19] They were severely repressed by the Vietnamese People's Army and about 6,000 persons were deported or killed.

Thus, fear of famine and dependence on China for food supplies was and continues to be a leading factor of the Vietminh determination to unify the country under its rule. In March 1955, Phan Anh, the DRV minister of economy, stressed the economic interdependence of Vietnam and linked it with the Vietminh's fight for unity:

> "Rice. First and foremost there must be enough rice. . . . This country must be unified. They need each other economically, the north and the south. There can be no question of continued partition." [20]

Indeed, a strong and capable anticommunist regime in the South would constitute not only a military and political threat to the DRV, but also "a barrier to a vital source of food," [21] as Ellen Hammer correctly noted.

On the other hand, the outcome of this tragic land-reform experience was not only the dismissal of Truong Chinh as secretary-general of the Lao-Dong party, but also the tarnishing of the popularity and prestige which the North Vietnamese leaders had enjoyed after Dien Bien Phu. More farmers fled south. The South Vietnamese themselves felt fearful and resentful toward the repressive communist regime in the northern part of the demarcation line. This served to reinforce the division rather than to encourage movement toward reunification.

Socially, partition and the provision on freedom of movements between the two sides of the demarcation line in the three hundred days that followed the signing of the armistice did not upset the North Vietnamese structure. Very few southerners moved to the North after 1954, and those who did were mostly Vietminh cadres. Consequently North Vietnam did not have to cope with a refugee problem. On the contrary, the massive exodus of about 900,000 northern refugees to the South "gave the Vietminh its best boost toward control of the North Vietnamese countryside." [22] It helped the DRV solve its problem of rural overcrowding and freed approximately a half million acres of land for redistribution. Most importantly, the removal of the Catholic minority from North Vietnamese society made it more homogeneous and integrated.

Politically, the Catholic exodus eliminated an important core of active anticommunist opposition which could have blocked the political system. In sum, the flight of refugees helped the DRV consolidate its social and political structure under the leadership of President Ho Chi Minh and the control of the Lao-Dong party.

It is true that, as in many communist regimes, political unity in North Vietnam was obtained by the elimination of all opposition forces, and political identity was developed through skillful indoctrination by a powerful organization. However, unlike many communist countries, the DRV demonstrated an extraordinary political stability, owing to its highly effective and motivated leadership. Besides Ho Chi Minh, who was respected as a national hero, the eleven members of the Lao-Dong Politburo were comrades in arms with a common revolutionary background and a fierce determination to fight for the unity of Vietnam. Certainly the struggle for reunification and against "American imperialism" has constituted the motivating force, strength, and unity of the DRV.

Within the South, economic dislocations were less critical in magnitude and urgency than in the North. Even though roads, railways, bridges, and means of communications were damaged and cut down, South Vietnam was a viable economic entity. Economic problems at that time were caused by the ravages of war rather than by division of the country.

Nevertheless, if partition did not directly affect the South Vietnamese economy, it gradually and steadily eroded economic growth and welfare in this region. Unlike the communists, who gave high priority to economic problems, agricultural production, and land reform, the SVN governments, from Diem to Thieu, placed major emphasis on security considerations.

To maintain the partition and a viable South Vietnam, economic development was neglected and sacrificed by its leaders. Economic and social programs were subordinated to military programs for internal and external defense and anticommunist operations. Between 1956 and 1960, for example, 43 percent of all SVN public expenditures were allocated directly to the military for the support of the army and the Self-Defense Corps. Between these two years, 78 percent of all U.S. aid given to South Vietnam went into the military budget.[23] After the fall of the Diem government, the SVN economy became very artificial, relying totally on U.S. aid and subject to rampant inflation and considerable corruption. Worse, this "traditional granary of the whole Indochinese peninsula," [24] at one time one of the world's great rice exporters, began in the late 1960s to import rice from California.

Economic difficulties and bankruptcy in both North and South Vietnam point up the economic interdependence of Vietnam. In the short run and in the long run as well, partition hinders the formation of a single economically independent and viable Vietnam.

Socially, South Vietnam grappled with serious problems of population transplantation and resettlement caused by the arrival of impressive numbers of northern refugees, the overwhelming majority of whom (85 percent) were Catholic. The Diem government encouraged these people to leave North Vietnam for political as well as humanitarian reasons. The president, a Catholic from the central part of Vietnam, was unknown—almost a "stranger"—in the Confucianist South at the time of partition. Lacking popular support among the southerners, Ngo Dinh Diem sought to use the northern Catholic as his base of political power.

In effect, under the Diem regime Catholics and northern refugees dominated the governmental structure. Diem's initial cabinet in June 1954 had no southerners. The first cabinet created after the declaration of the Republic of Vietnam (RVN) in October 1955 had seven southerners matched by four northerners and three centralists, although northerners represented less than 10 percent of the SVN population, and centralists less than 30 percent.

Northerners and centralists occupied the key powerful posts in the administration. The Ministries of National Education and Foreign Affairs, the National Institute of Administration, the Special Commissariat of Civic Action, and the General Directorate of Information were considered by southerners as "northern agencies" because of their composition.

In sum, the Diem regime assumed "the aspect of a carpetbag government" [25] in its disproportion of northerners and in its Catholicism. Religious favoritism was another striking feature of the government.[26] The land-reform program did not affect the acres owned by the Catholic church. The clergy enjoyed special treatment and assistance from the government. Priests in refugee villages were sometimes more powerful than provincial officials.

The social and political impact of the refugee influx was far-reaching. Socially, the massive exodus disturbed the social structure of South Vietnam and generated social conflicts. If the Diem administration—with the help of the United States, France, and other countries—did a fairly good job in the physical task of refugee care and resettlement, it failed to integrate the newcomers into southern society. They came in compact groups, settled in small units, and even retained the names of their former northern towns and villages.

Moreover, the dominance of northern Catholic refugees in all important activities, their solidarity, their militant Catholicism, their fanatic anticommunism, the support and favoritism granted them by the government—all made them a special, separate social group which heightened the regional distinctions and rivalries in South Vietnam. Ngo Dinh Diem, anticommunist and Catholic himself, was unaware of, and blind to, the difficult coexistence between the Catholic minority of northern refugees and the Confucianist and Buddhist majority of southerners. His policies aggravated latent antagonisms and accentuated the popular consciousness of religious differences between Catholics and Buddhists. The Buddhist crisis in 1963 that brought down the Diem regime was partly a social convulsion, the culmination and crystallization of social tensions and discord stemming from the favored treatment of Catholics.

Politically, partition contributed to the creation and consolidation of a new state virtually out of nothing. As already noted, the State of Vietnam under Bao Dai had juridical status but no power, no army, and no police. French authorities exercised real control over the Vietnamese policy-making process—a fact demonstrated at the Geneva Conference where the delegation of the State of Vietnam was completely left out of the negotiations. After the Geneva Agreements were signed, many foreign observers and diplomats predicted the collapse of the Diem government in a few months.[27] Not only did it survive but it also founded, in a little more than a year, a new Republic of Vietnam (RVN) on October 26, 1955, after ousting Bao Dai in a so-called referendum held in July.

This outstanding political development, or "miracle" as some called it, would not have taken place if the country had not been divided. The new state was born out of the cold-war confrontation, out of the necessity to fill the vacuum left by the French, and out of the determination of the nationalists to challenge the communist rule and make use of massive Western assistance. As Professor Morgenthau perceptively saw it, the 1954 Geneva Conference "was beset by a number of paradoxes which have determined the diplomatic and political conditions under which the state of South Vietnam is *compelled to exist.*" [28]

Ngo Dinh Diem strongly and truly believed that, to be effective, "Vietnamese nationalism had to be free from French control." [29] He seized that unique opportunity given by the Geneva Accords to organize an alternative to the communist model. While wiping out the last vestiges of French colonial power, he succeeded in building a new state and a new political structure in the South, mostly with the help of the United States externally and the northern refugees internally.

Subsequently, those northern refugees who formed the backbone of the political system constituted the strongest obstacle to the reunification of the country. Having fled their mother land once, they would leave the country altogether if the communists took power in the South, but they would never collaborate with the DRV in the North. In bringing them south and into his administration, Diem not only accepted the partition, against which he had protested with indignation, but also sealed off the demarcation line.

Furthermore, the Diem government, in basing its political power on the northern Catholics, alienated the southerners: intellectuals and peasants as well. Most civic-action agents who served as spearheads in the government's effort to win the villagers to its side were northerners. And in the Mekong Delta, for example, they were often misunderstood, distrusted, ridiculed or rejected by the villagers because of their incomprehensible accent. The result was the gradual isolation of the government from the people, until it collapsed in 1963.

Since the fall of the Diem regime problems of leadership and political identity have continued to plague the South Vietnamese political system. However, as the war dragged on and an army grew to more than one million troops, the Republic of Vietnam became a living reality, in independent political entity with a political culture, beliefs, and attitudes divergent from those of the DRV in the North.

BETWEEN THE TWO ZONES

Relations between the two zones were seriously hampered by (1) controversy over the famous Paragraph 7 of the Final Declaration concerning general elections in Vietnam, (2) lack of mutual recognition, and (3) rigidity of their leaders' antagonistic policies, ideologies, and personalities.

The thorniest issue following the Geneva Conference was the implementation of Paragraph 7 of the Final Declaration, which provided for general elections to be held in July 1956, and for consultations on this subject between the two authorities to be held from July 20, 1955, onward. What characterized the relationship between North and South Vietnam during the post-Geneva period could be called a pathetic dialogue of the deaf.

This unbridgeable argument alternated for a year from one side to the other, Hanoi making the approaches and Saigon turning its back. In June 1955, Pham Van Dong announced that the DRV was ready to send delegates to a consultative conference to discuss elections. On July 16, Ngo Dinh Diem declared in a radio-television address that "we did not sign the Geneva Agreement. We are not bound in any way by these Agreements, signed against the will of the Vietnamese people." [30] Three days later, Dong sent notes to the International Supervision Commission (ISC) and the French and RVN governments, demanding the convening of a consultative conference. On August 9, Diem replied that conditions of freedom must be assured in the North before elections could be held. On September 21, he went further in asserting that there "can be no question of a conference, even less of negotiations [with the DRV authorities]." [31] In the meantime, Dong appealed to the co-chairmen requesting them to take measures to implement Paragraph 7.[32] In November he again asked Molotov to urge Britain to cooperate in seeing that the Geneva Agreements were respected. These actions proved fruitless. In the following year, July 1956 passed without elections and without the reunification of Vietnam.[33]

Underlying those issues of negotiations and elections has been the mutual nonrecognition between the two zones at various times. It had already existed at Geneva and became more acute after 1954. During his nine years as head of South Vietnam Ngo Dinh Diem refused to recognize the DRV as an independent state and in fact never referred to North Vietnam as the DRV but as the "Vietminh authorities" or "the communist regime of the North." Accordingly, he rejected categorically any contacts or moves made by the DRV to regularize the relationship between the two zones, pending reunification.

On the other hand, from 1955 to 1960, Hanoi repeatedly sought to develop some relations (for posts, roads, air and sea traffic, etc.) with Saigon. Probably for economic reasons, Hanoi suggested the reopening of trade with the South in September 1957 and November 1958, and proposed that remittance facilities should be established in July 1957, and in January and April 1958. In March 1958, Hanoi even proposed a consultative conference to discuss the establishment of normal relations, freedom of movement, trade, communications and the reduction of armed forces, with a view to the reunification of the country.

Saigon rebuffed all these initiatives. To this last proposal the Diem government, on April 26, 1958, imposed six preconditions that could not easily have been accepted by Hanoi: (1) let all Vietnamese who desired to do so emigrate to the South, (2) reduce the strength of the People's Army of Vietnam to the same level as that of the Army of the Republic of Vietnam, (3) refrain from all acts of sabotage and terrorism in the South, (4) cease requiring that residents of the North write favorably of local conditions in their letters to friends and relatives in the South, (5) allow all people to work in freedom to improve their standard of living, and (6) establish democratic liberties similar to those in the South.[34] It should also be pointed out that two years previously, in April 1956, the RVN refused to assume the role of successor to the French High Command on the Joint Commission, although the ISC and the People's Army High Command apparently desired it to do so. Because of this RVN lack of cooperation, the Joint Commission ceased to function in May 1956, after the French Union forces left Vietnam.

The result of this mutual nonrecognition after 1960 was total and prolonged partition and separation of the two zones. As one observer described it, "the frontier of the 17th parallel is one of the most closely sealed in the world." [35]

The difficulty of the two zones in dealing with each other was compounded by another important factor: the sharp difference between their ideologies, policies, and leaders. To Ho's socialism in the North was opposed Diem's personalism in the South. Against the one-party communist system in the North, a military regime was developed in the South. One fought for unification on its own terms, the other for maintaining partition.[36]

Their leaders' personalities also clashed or contrasted forcefully. Ho Chi Minh was a lonely revolutionary, a self-made man. Ngo Dinh Diem was a mandarin surrounded by a large family. Today, NVN leadership has remained intact, cohesive, and dynamic. Most Politburo policy makers are now in their late sixties and living with their glorious past, the history of successive revolutions against the French, Japanese, and Americans. They belonged to the independence generation of Asia, and did indeed take over the successful struggle to end French colonialism and bring independence to Vietnam. As a result, their approach at times appears ideological and doctrinaire. They have been less exposed to the rapid changes in science, technology, and development occurring throughout the world than a younger, postrevolutionary political generation might have been.

In contrast, the SVN leadership is fragmented, divided, and heterogeneous. Leaders in the South are younger in age and more varied in perspective than their counterparts in the North. They belong to the postindependence generation and display less sensitivity to the nation's colonial past. Lacking an all-encompassing ideological frame of reference and having been subject to many outside influences, they painfully search for an authentic Vietnamese synthesis of tradition and modernity.

Difference of personalities, incompatibility of goals, and divergence of ideologies transformed a difficult but tolerable coexistence of the initial years into a guerrilla and conventional war. During the first years after the Geneva Agreements, Hanoi's leaders consolidated their power in the North as they tried unsuccessfully to establish relations with the South. After 1960 Hanoi, realizing that reliance on diplomatic means was ineffectual, resorted to violence, war, and political struggle in the South. At the same time, the Diem regime grew so obsessively anticommunist, so blindly irresponsive to rural needs, and so harshly repressive toward all opposition—communist and nationalist—that it created a schism within the South itself. The convergence of Diem's actions and Hanoi's policies led to the foundation of the National Liberation Front (NLF), later replaced by the Provisional Revolutionary Government of the Republic of South Vietnam (PRG) in 1969 when the Paris peace talks began.

The existence of the NLF–PRG could be interpreted either as another case of "escalatory division" or, on the contrary, as a communist strategy for reunification. The first interpretation would take into account the indigenous formation of the NLF–PRG, the distinction of attitudes and backgrounds between northerners and southerners within the NLF–PRG, and also the different emphasis in policies between the DRV and the NLF–PRG. Indeed, the NLF kept advocating a coalition government in the South, a neutral foreign policy, and "peaceful reunification" step-by-step by means of negotiations, economic and cultural exchanges, and freedom of movement between the two zones. Again at the Paris peace talks the PRG during 1970–72 reiterated its proposal for the formation of a three-part government made up of the PRG itself; members of the Saigon regime "genuinely" standing for peace, neutrality, independence, and democracy; and representatives of other political tendencies supporting those four principles as defined and applied by the PRG.

The purpose of the coalition strategy is to build up South Vietnam, deal with the DRV on equal terms, and "proceed toward the peaceful unification of the country." In this interpretation, proceeding in that direction would be a slow, stage-by-stage process over a number of years between two sovereign states with different political structures and policies. In effect, the separation would be prolonged indefinitely, but peaceful relations could be developed between the two zones.

The second interpretation would emphasize the direct control of Hanoi over the NLF–PRG by means of the People's Revolutionary party in the South. In this case, instead of escalatory division or coexistence of the two states pending unification, we would have an automatic amalgamation of the South with the North. This could take place in a three-stage rapid sequence. First, the PRG would provide the core and power of a provisional coalition to hold elections and set up a new government of the South. Second, the PRG would in this process eliminate all opposition and gain a monopoly of power. Third, this communist regime in the South would merge with the DRV to form one unified communist government for all Vietnam.

Whether either interpretation will materialize in the future or not, the reality of a divided Vietnam for nearly twenty years has been a stalemate between the communist and noncommunist forces. The two sides have demonstrated their extraordinary capacities to survive at trial moments: NVN during the first bombings in 1965, and SVN during the Tet offensive in 1968. After passing these crucial tests of survival, we believe that neither NVN nor SVN would be doomed by further bombings or offensives. What could have changed the status quo would be the first strike or the first surprise. But it failed in both cases.

Particularly in the divided SVN, the Tet offensive, because of its brutal excesses, indiscriminate killings, and civilian massacres in Hué for example, changed the minds and sympathies of many intellectuals, civil servants, and Buddhist opposition forces toward NVN. The Tet offensive shock has added a new psychological dimension to the stalemate. However, this has been less a product of VN conflicting forces than "a reflection of the overall stalemate existing in the world" [37] among the great powers.

AMONG GREAT POWERS

The idea of partition originated with the great powers. They made it the keystone of the Geneva framework. For eighteen years their antagonistic interests and policies in the bipolar confrontation and stalemate perpetuated a "permanently temporary partition." They ambivalently paid formalistic lip-service to reunification but provided vigorous support for partition. This ambivalence of the great powers caused Vietnam's escalatory separation.

In effect, a provisional fence became a perpetual barrier. Escalatory separation converted the simple, temporary division of 1954 stage by stage into the total implacable division of later years. First, the bipolar rivalry and stalemate of the great powers established the initial conditions for devising a divided Vietnam to compromise their competing interests. Two new zones were manufactured in Vietnam to give effect to this external settlement on a temporary basis. In the second stage, the nationalist drive and political energy of each zone strove for independence and strength, and developed the characteristics of sovereign states. Consequently, the various powers helped one or the other further consolidate its position and power to deal with the conflicting consequences of division and the contending interests of the great powers. In the third stage, as these two states emerged, the great powers did not try to reduce barriers or promote peaceful contacts between the North and the South. The backing of the various great powers decreased incentives in Hanoi or Saigon for developing coexistence and interchange or finding ways toward Vietnamese unity. Finally, Hanoi and Saigon became utterly hostile and noncooperative toward one another as their partition escalated into total enmity, complete separation, and full-scale warfare. For that, the ambivalence of the great powers deserves much blame.

French governments did want to see Paragraph 7 carried out but agreed, with Washington and London, to help the South. Paris assisted in the consolidation of an independent, sovereign South Vietnam, accepted the primary initiative and presence of the United States in building up SVN, and turned over power to Vietnamese authorities in both zones.

The most telling French action in creating Vietnam's partition was to withdraw French forces entirely from South Vietnam in early 1956 before the scheduled date for the Geneva-style elections. Thereby the French government removed any leverage it might have had to bring pressure on Saigon to join in elections, and ended any semblance of remaining as the "competent representative authority" under Paragraph 7, or as "the party" responsible for civil administration in the southern regrouping zone according to Article 14a of the cease-fire agreement on Vietnam. France recognized the likely continuation of partition, and withdrew from undertaking responsibilities for any future consequences. France thus not only condoned the partition of Vietnam but also contributed to its escalatory separation.

American support bolstered South Vietnam and established an increasingly strong state in the southern zone. American policy thus made possible the continuation of southern separation and southern refusal to have anything to do with the northern government or with the political provisions of the Geneva Agreements. Strengthening the Diem government meant eliminating any prospects of 1956 elections, any understanding between Saigon and Hanoi on Vietnam's reunification, or any exchanges between the two governments. The United States contributed decisively to Diem's own nationalistic brand of escalatory separation from, and absolute rejection of, the North.

Like France, the United States nominally endorsed Vietnam's unity and favored elections under UN supervision. However, when that issue faded in the great-power context and the Saigon government rejected such elections except on conditions that Hanoi would not have accepted, the United States did not place any pressure on Saigon and acquiesced in July 1956 to no elections.

The United States over the years helped escalate partition in several other ways. It refused to accord any legitimacy or status to the DRV, insisting that Saigon represented the only sovereignty in Vietnam. Washington opposed the Soviet proposals in 1957 for giving UN membership to both Vietnams, which could have established some contact between the two zones under UN auspices and lessened the iron-clad separation imposed by Diem. Yet, after 1965, Washington treated the North as a de facto state and negotiated openly with the DRV as the sovereign entity down to the 17th parallel, while refusing to compromise its support for South Vietnam's independence. But at the Paris peace talks, Washington has endorsed reunification of the two states by stages.

Great Britain registered the only really formal endorsement of the Final Declaration and Paragraph 7, and meant to see it carried out. But London also supported the consolidation of the South to set up a "buffer zone" to help protect Malaya, Singapore, and other areas in the British Commonwealth. Thus, Great Britain had its version of ambivalence.

The issue of unification came to a head for London in 1956 when Moscow protested the threat of South Vietnam's "starting a new war in Indochina" and SVN's refusal to hold elections. The British government rejected both charges, although stating its regret over the lack of progress on fulfillment of the political provisions. In a note of April 9, 1956, to the Soviet government the British

> regard it as of paramount importance in the meantime to *preserve the peace between North and South* in Vietnam. Her Majesty's Government trust that their discussions with the Government of the Union of Soviet Socialist Republics will contribute in the first place towards the achievement of this objective and secondly towards the *eventual* achievement of a political settlement in Vietnam.[38]

Thus London put first priority on preserving peace between North and South Vietnam, and introduced the idea of "eventual unification" into the great power dialogue as a second priority.

The result of this exchange of notes was that Moscow withdrew its proposal for a new Geneva Conference. The two co-chairmen then addressed identical notes to the two states of Vietnam urging them "to make every effort to implement the Geneva Agreements." [39] Thus the Soviet and British governments acknowledged the existence of the two sovereign entities and refrained from taking or suggesting any other concrete measures to bring about reunification, then or afterward.

While giving lip-service to Paragraph 7, Moscow lacked the will to have it implemented. Higher Soviet interests lay elsewhere. There is some evidence that Soviet policy has been prepared to accept indefinite partition.

At the Geneva Summit Conference in 1955, Foreign Minister Molotov objected to any discussion of free elections in Vietnam or in Germany when his French, British, and American colleagues indicated their concern over the situation in Vietnam and their willingness to take up this important matter.[40] Partly as a result of Moscow's indifference or ambivalence, the issue of free elections and unification was dropped at that four-power level.

In 1957, Moscow went significantly further than the other great powers in an attempt to recognize and ratify the actual existence of two Vietnamese states. At the Eleventh UN General Assembly the Soviet government proposed both Vietnams for UN membership, along with both Koreas. Soviet representatives in effect disposed of the idea of Vietnam as a single state, emphasized the fact that there were "two states" in Vietnam and Korea, and advocated "the realistic approach" and "the only possible solution" of "the simultaneous admission of the four countries constituting Korea and Vietnam." [41] The United States and a majority of the UN Assembly voted down the Soviet proposal. Moscow introduced the same proposal again at the Twelfth Assembly, where it was again defeated.

Since then, Moscow has provided economic and military assistance to North Vietnam. The Soviet Union supported Hanoi's attempt to gain control of the South by military infiltration and invasion. However, it has not taken an adamant, irrevocable stand against a dual Vietnam, and as a practical expediency it has kept some negotiating ambiguity.

The People's Republic of China (PRC) has also shown ambivalence because it is the only great power physically connected with Vietnam. Chinese policy has both supported unification and contributed to division. Peking has continually called for the total implementation of the Geneva Agreements and has consistently denounced the United States for flouting or thwarting them.

Immediately after the Geneva Conference, Peking gave its unconditional support to Hanoi. It helped rebuild rail lines and repair war damages; it provided vital economic assistance; and it became the predominant great-power backer of the DRV. In mid-1972 Peking reportedly assisted Hanoi in repairing much of the damage to the railways caused by renewed American bombing.

At the same time, however, Peking also maintained close and direct liaison with the NLF–PRG, sometimes appearing to give them special status, even playing them off against Hanoi. It has given full support and prominent backing to the United Front of the Vietnamese, Khmer, and Laotian peoples. It has favored a long, protracted guerrilla war as the best way to communist victory and Vietnamese unity. These actions indicated Peking's preference for a "permanently temporary partition" which may have suited some of China's political and security interests in Southeast Asia. As Selig Harrison reported from Peking in the *Washington Post* on July 3, 1972:

> Peking would clearly feel more comfortable with a complex of Indochinese states than with a monolithic Vietnamese sphere of influence, and seems prepared, accordingly for a prolonged period of separate existence for South Vietnam.

The net result of great power interests and policies since 1954 concerning Vietnam has been escalatory separation and deferred unification. No great power saw any national interest in trying to enforce Paragraph 7 or decrease separation. The great powers were too polarized or too concerned with other interests to see any common interest in joint efforts to stop Vietnam's widening division and to prevent war. Permanent partition was an acceptable alternative for the great powers even at the cost of millions of Vietnamese lives and untold suffering.

Policy Prospects

DIVIDED VIETNAM BEFORE THE CEASE-FIRE

Unlike the two Germanys and the two Koreas, which are endeavoring to move toward rapprochement in the 1970s, the two Vietnams appear farther apart than ever. The Paris peace talks had been going on for more than four years, since May 1968, but tension between the two zones increased and reached its climax in April 1972 when the DRV launched its massive Easter offensive against the South. The two states were pitted in mortal combat and locked in fierce battles. Not only had the nature of war between the two states changed from guerrilla operations to conventional war with tanks, rockets, air power, and combat troops, but also the political issues had become more complex than twenty years earlier. To the North-South division another subdivision had been added in the South, with the formation of the PRG. An overall stalemate between the forces of outh Vietnam and the forces of North Vietnam seemed to be emerging in 972. Although this stalemate reflected the continued presence of basic sues of conflict among the Vietnamese, it nonetheless was to become one tionale for the end of direct U.S. military involvement in the war. isillusionment with a continued search for the means to resolve the onflict decisively and American domestic opposition to an open-ended volvement in an internecine struggle which might be prolonged indefin- ely had encouraged the evolution of an ever-more-restricted interpretation the U.S. role in Vietnam. Under such conditions, a stalemate became idence of the self-defensive capabilities of the South Vietnamese.

Furthermore, if the early 1970s saw an increase of tensions between the vo Vietnams, it registered at the same time a sensible decrease of tensions U.S.–Soviet and U.S.–Chinese relations. The final resolution of the ietnamese conflict continued to be illusive, but the increasing great-power etente, joined with domestic American factors and rationalized by the ccessful completion of Vietnamization, did result in a cease-fire, an ternational conference, and the withdrawal of U.S. forces from Vietnam.

THE CEASE-FIRE AGREEMENT AND INTERNATIONAL CONFERENCE

The Agreement on Ending the War and Restoring the Peace in ietnam, signed in Paris on January 27, 1973, terminated "America's war in ietnam." As stipulated in the Agreement, all U.S. military personnel and stallations were withdrawn and American prisoners of war repatriated ithin sixty days of the signing. Yet, despite the Agreement's positive hievements, the questions of peace and unity in Vietnam remain resolved. The signatories agreed to respect the independence, sover- gnty, unity, and territorial integrity of Vietnam "as recognized by the 1954 eneva Agreements." The right of self-determination of the South Viet- mese people was reaffirmed and it was agreed that "genuinely free and mocratic general elections under national supervision" would be held to termine the political future of the South. The parties reiterated that the ilitary demarcation line at the 17th parallel was provisional and not a litical or territorial boundary. Yet, as the language of the latest peace reement echoed that used at Geneva in 1954, the question remained of ow the formulas, which had been so ineffective nine years earlier, now uld be seen as a viable basis for the resolution of the substantive nditions underlying the political conflict between Vietnamese.

The most recent Agreement did go further than the earlier Geneva cord in clearly designating the parties responsible for its implementation. the case of South Vietnam, "the two South Vietnamese parties," the epublic of Vietnam and the Provisional Revolutionary Government of uth Vietnam, on the basis of "a spirit of national reconciliation and ncord, mutual respect and mutual non-elimination," were vested with responsibility for settling the question of South Vietnamese armed forces, and through a National Council of National Reconciliation and Concord, with organizing free and democratic elections. With regard to the relationship between North and South, the Agreement stipulated that reunification would be carried out step-by-step, on the basis of peaceful discussions between the two sides and without foreign interference. The time for unification was to be agreed upon between North and South, with negotiations in the interim aimed at reestablishing "normal" relations in various fields. Supervisory powers were vested in various types of joint military commissions, in the Four-Party International Commission of Control and Supervision, and in the thirteen parties participating in the Paris conference following the cease-fire. Yet, as in 1954, the agreement resolved not the problems inherent in the internal conflict, but rather the obstacles which the struggle posed to the pursuit of great-power interests. The question of whether such great-power interests might in the long run encourage a usable settlement among the Vietnamese remained unanswered.

THE FUTURE REDUCTION OF TENSION

A genuine peaceful coexistence among the great powers in Vietnam and Indochina could entail (a) a further decrease in great-power involvement and commitment, (b) a diminution in assistance to Hanoi and Saigon, (c) an increased influence of great-power détente on negotiations among Vietnamese, (d) increased pressures for Vietnamese coexistence in peace, and (e) acceptance of a political rather than military avenue to reunification. It is likely that the United States, the Soviet Union, and China would move in this direction.

Various features of this new great-power multipolarity might thus produce a better context for lessening tension and increasing cooperation in Vietnam in the future and reverse that past escalatory division that reflected a bipolar confrontation. First, competing Sino-Soviet interests could each seek to limit North Vietnam's capacities enough so that neither power would be able to gain a superior position over the other. Each having acquiesced in a cease-fire would tend to encourage negotiated settlements between the two states, and cooperative partition to the end that each power would try not to have to cope with a strong unified independent Vietnam—and Indochina—hostile to itself.

Second, the prospect of further American disengagement from military bases in Southeast Asia, especially in Thailand, as a result of a compromise in Vietnam, should induce Peking in particular to favor a "satisfactory" settlement, even if it required the indefinite prolongation of South Vietnam as a consideration.

Third, the increasing impact and attraction of Japanese economic assistance, investment, and trade could provide incentives and options for Hanoi and Saigon to balance off other great-power influences.

Finally, the growing convergence of interests among great powers and Southeast Asian states in establishing institutions and practices of regional cooperation and regional neutrality, to include both Vietnams, Cambodia, and Laos, could provide an acceptable framework for disentangling great-power rivalries and developing regional stability in Indochina and Southeast Asia.

The impact of these four features of multipolarity on Vietnam could include the reduction or ending of great-power support for escalatory separation, mutually acceptable division and eventual reunification by stages, a decrease in hostile Vietnamese confrontation, and a tendency toward peaceful coexistence in Vietnam.

The bitter divide between the North and the South, and their irreconciliable aims, are so great, however, that the great-power détente may be ineffective and coexistence with peace may remain elusive. In that not-unlikely event, it must be assumed that there would probably be a return to "no war–no peace," a long period of protracted guerrilla warfare in the South, and even some South Vietnamese air raids in the North.

Significant conciliatory steps should be taken simultaneously in the South and North. In South Vietnam, rapid economic development and effective political leadership should be vigorously promoted to deter North Vietnamese harassment or offensives. In North Vietnam, a large-scale international reconstruction program should be undertaken on Hanoi's initiative as an incentive to maintain a tolerable coexistence and the status quo. In addition, the negotiating process should offer to provide and guarantee Hanoi with interchange with South Vietnam, particularly in economic matters but also in social and cultural affairs, to regularize relationship between the two zones and to circumvent a repetition of Hanoi's unfortunate experience of the mid-1950s with a bad famine, overdependence on China, and intransigent rejection from Saigon.

Yet these steps are only intermediate (if necessary) ones. They still leave Vietnam indefinitely divided, in a state of "no war–no peace" with some skirmishes but without big and bloody conventional wars like the 1968 and 1972 offensives. They certainly do not provide a permanent settlement of any kind. In view of the inextricable overall stalemate, and the contradictory and intransigent views held by the two sides on crucial political issues such as coalition government or political compromise, it is my opinion that only absolutist and radical solutions can end the long, protracted, and violent struggle in Vietnam.

TWO RADICAL SOLUTIONS

Such drastic measures would include: (1) a military takeover by either side, which is not likely to happen; (2) an international administration of the two states that assumes a total incapacity of both authorities to handle their own affairs, as a result of the effects of a prolonged war and division and an eventual disengagement of great powers (This solution is hard to foresee because it implies a total collapse and bankruptcy of both Vietnams, which is unlikely because of the proven resiliency and vitality of the Vietnamese.); (3) a great-power "pseudo" trusteeship of each state, which is too contrary to Vietnamese nationalism to be acceptable; (4) a "ky-archy" state, meaning a federation of the three traditional "kys" in Vietnam: Nam-ky (South Vietnam), Trung-ky (Central Vietnam) and Bac-ky (North Vietnam); and (5) a Mekong Confederation that would include Cambodia, Laos, Thailand, North Vietnam, and South Vietnam.

The rest of this paper will be devoted to exploring the last two solutions. Both have the advantage of bringing about profound changes in social, economic, and political configurations by radical but peaceful means. It would be a political revolution without bloodshed and violence, if it could be worked out.

The "ky-archy" solution would alter the existing geopolitical map of Vietnam and at the same time respect the reality of practical regionalism in the country. As pointed out in the background section, regionalism in Vietnam is not only geographical but primarily historical and cultural. In his march to the South the Vietnamese mingled with the Chams and the Khmers and changed his personality, character, and outlook. The accent of speech was also modified and tradition loosened its ties in contact with the easygoing life of the sunny and fertile southern part of Vietnam. The distinction between North, Central, and South Vietnam has been the result of a long historical and political process.

Since the 1954 partition, regional cleavages have constituted a dominant feature of Vietnamese political life for at least two reasons. First, the division of the country into two parts displaced the centralists and did not give them a proper place and a proper role in the whole Vietnamese structure. The two power centers are located in Hanoi and in Saigon—not in Hué. However, the key power holders are centralists. In Hanoi, Ho Chi Minh, Pham Van Dong, Vo Nguyen Giap, and Le Duan were all born in the Central part of Vietnam. In Saigon, Ngo Dinh Diem and Nguyen Van Thieu are centralists, but the Buddhist opposition forces are also centralists. In the North are the strongest advocates of unification, since their homeland was split by the Geneva accords. In the South they either control power or oppose it, but they have great difficulty in integrating themselves into the social fabric of the South. In either case the partition did not correspond to the profound regional differences in Vietnam and created instability and rifts within each leadership with regard to crucial political issues such as unification and coalition.

Second, partition crystallized regional feelings (particularly in the South). It also created some regional paradoxes among northerners, centralists, and southerners. Northerners in the South, for instance, struggled for maintaining partition; their counterparts in the North fought for unification. Unlike the centralists in the North, the Buddhist opposition forces in the area of Hué would prefer a neutralist position between the extreme Left of the Hanoi Communist regime and the extreme Right of the Saigon military regime. Southerners would like to be let alone and resent northern and centralist rule.

Instead of a unitary state, which is a standard approach of every formula for unification, a looser, pluralistic, decentralized political structure would suit Vietnam's unique characteristics more realistically. In particular a federal-state model would preserve territorial integrity and political unity; restore the traditional diversities, historical familiarities, and cultural regionalism of Vietnam; develop economic complementarity; and give comparable gateways to the sea. A ky-archy of three regions would meet these objectives.

The ky-archy would consist of three autonomous states or regions (kys) under a federal council: Bac-ky with its 25 provinces in and around the River Delta, Nam-ky with its 28 provinces in and around the Mekong Delta, and Trung-ky with its 20 provinces composed of 16 northern provinces of the RVN and 4 southern provinces of the DRV. Under this arrangement, each ky would have approximately the same number of provinces to administer. Politically, North Vietnam could have a socialist orientation, Central Vietnam a neutralist position, and South Vietnam a mixed system. Economically, the North would concentrate on industrial projects with coal minerals resources and electric power. Central Vietnam would provide forests and fisheries and vegetables for export. And the South would provide rice, fruits, animal husbandry, light industries, and technological services. Each ky already has its own higher educational facilities. Hopefully the postwar reconstruction will provide the communication and transportation power and energy infrastructure for the three kys and for the country as a whole.

Administratively, there would be a federal government and local governments in the three regions. Matters of foreign policy, defense, economic development and coordination, higher education, common services (e.g., post office), or natural disaster would belong to the federal jurisdiction. Local governments would be in charge of police, social security, employment, local economic productions, and lower education. There would be two taxes: federal and local.[42]

Socially, freedom of movement and residence would be allowed in the three regions, although each citizen would have to comply with local laws wherever he traveled and lived.

Far from balkanizing Vietnam, a federalized ky-archy would produce much more consensus and social harmony in the pluralistic Vietnamese society than would a simple model. In the final analysis, political and social integration would be brought about not by eliminating pluralism—which could increase social anomie—but by reflecting the social and political forces from one end of the country to the other.[43]

The second solution is the creation of a Mekong Confederation. This formula would dilute the purely Vietnamese conflict into a broader regional framework of settlement. After several years of direct confrontation, hatred, bitterness, and mutual mistrust, the Vietnamese would perhaps psychologically need a larger environment to lessen the shocks of accommodation and heal their wounds. Moreover, a political settlement covering Cambodia, Laos, and Thailand would be more realistic since North Vietnamese troops have occupied sizable territories in Laos and Cambodia and waged guerrilla warfare in northeast Thailand, while South Vietnamese troops have intervened in Laos and Cambodia to safeguard their border security.

A confederated state model would respect national sovereignty, territorial integrity, and internal autonomy of the states. On the other hand, it would greatly facilitate economic development and coordination and improve the per capita and national incomes of the member states.

The Mekong Confederation would also strengthen the five states as a unit in dealing with the great powers and with worldwide economic and political forces. The confederation would reflect the modern trend toward regionalization of small states for survival and development.

The fundamental conclusion of this study is that neither a centralized unification nor a perpetual separation or division will suit the needs and aspirations of the Vietnamese people. These two solutions are offered as practical alternatives to be considered as a basis for a lasting peace and prosperity in Vietnam.

Notes

1. Telegrams from President Truman to Patrick Hurley, and from the Combined Chiefs of Staff to Truman and Churchill, in *Vietnam: History, Documents, and Opinions,* ed. by M. Gettleman, pp. 84–85.
2. Ibid., p. 89.
3. The other participants at the conference were Cambodia, Laos, and the People's Republic of China.
4. Except for Cambodia which was represented by General Nhiek Tioulong of the Khmer National Armed Forces. French Brigadier General Dietel signed for Laos and for the State of Vietnam.
5. Melvin Gurtov, *The First Vietnam Crisis* (New York: Columbia University Press, 1967), p. 73.
6. Ibid., p. 66.
7. Pham Van Dong's speech is reproduced in Philippe Devillers and Jean Lacouture, *End of a War* (New York: Praeger, 1969), pp. 206–7.
8. Ibid., p. 295.
9. Statement made by Ngo-Quoc-Dinh on May 12, 1954, quoted in ibid., p. 160.
10. Ibid., p. 280.
11. Ibid., pp. 280–82; and D. Lancaster, *The Emancipation of French Indochina* (London: Oxford University Press, 1961), pp. 332–37.
12. *End of a War*, p. 288.
13. Robert F. Randle, *Geneva 1954* (Princeton, N.J.: Princeton University Press, 1969), p. 201.
14. Dwight D. Eisenhower, *Mandate for Change* (Garden City, N.Y.: Doubleday, 1963), p. 365.

15. Randle, *Geneva 1954*, p. 353.
16. Ibid.
17. *Le Monde*, 2–3 January 1955.
18. Bernard B. Fall, *The Two Vietnams* (New York: Praeger, 1964), p. 156.
19. Ibid.
20. *The Observer*, 20 March 1955.
21. Ellen J. Hammer, *The Struggle for Indochina* (Stanford: Stanford University Press, 1966), p. 344.
22. Fall, *Two Vietnams*, p. 153.
23. Robert Scigliano, *South Vietnam: Nation Under Stress* (Boston: Houghton Mifflin Co., 1964), p. 114.
24. Fall, *Two Vietnams*, p. 291.
25. Scigliano, *South Vietnam*, p. 52. The author also pointed out that the ratio of northerners was equally high in American agencies operating in Saigon. In the Michigan State University Vietnam Advisory Group, for example, 60 of 99 national employees in 1959 were northerners. Among students, more northerners than southerners went to study in the United States.
26. Diem's brother, Ngo Dinh Thuc, was archibishop.
27. Hans Morgenthau wrote in 1956 that "in reading those articles by respectable journalists one is amazed how widely off the mark even intelligent and well-informed men can guess. It is only the lack of recollection of the public that saves their reputations." "The 1954 Geneva Conference: an Assessment," in *Vietnam*, ed. by W. R. Fishel (New York: Peacock, 1968).
28. Ibid., p. 117. Italics added.
29. Fall, *Two Vietnams*, p. 243.
30. Address reproduced in Gettleman, *Vietnam*, p. 225.
31. *Times* (London), 22 September 1955.
32. P. M. Kattenberg, "Vietnam and U.S. Diplomacy, 1940–1970," *Orbis* 25, no. 3 (Fall 1971): 822.
33. Lancaster, *Emancipation of French Indochina*, p. 372.
34. Geoffrey Barraclough, *Survey of International Affairs 1956–1958* (London: Oxford, 1962), pp. 420–21.
35. P. Devillers, "Diem and the Struggle for Reunification," in Gettleman, *Vietnam*, p. 248.
36. President Thieu's four "No's": (1) *no* coalition, (2) *no* territorial concession, (3) *no* communist participation, and (4) *no* neutrality.
37. Morgenthau, "1954 Geneva Conference," p. 121.
38. Note reproduced in Fishel, *Vietnam*, p. 124.
39. Randle, *Geneva 1954*, p. 472.
40. Kenneth T. Young, "The Geneva Machinery in Retrospect," Fishel, *Vietnam*.
41. Fishel, *Vietnam*, p. 100.
42. These are a few concrete examples; other modalities could be worked out among the regional forces themselves.
43. Vietnam covers a length of over 1,000 miles with a wide variety of terrains and climates.

CAMBODIA
LAOS

5

Cambodia and Laos

Bernard K. Gordon

FIFTEEN OR TWENTY YEARS AGO, Cambodia was known to very few outsiders—mostly wealthy tourists and French archaeologists who visited the ruins at Angkor Wat—and Laos was known hardly at all. Even Angkor itself was normally entered from Bangkok—which meant that Cambodia's capital, Phnom Penh, and other parts of the country, were rarely seen. The nation as a whole was regarded as a quaint monarchy run by an erratic and exotic prince, who earlier had been a king.

Laos was even more dimly perceived, and rarely studied, except by a few dozen orientalists and anthropologists. Indeed, Professor Bernard Fall, the French-American military historian who was killed in the Vietnam war, once remarked that French colonial policy seemed designed to preserve Laos as a museum piece, essentially untouched by the outside would and unknown to it.

In contrast, much world attention has focused on Cambodia and Laos during the past twenty years, with the result that considerable information and knowledge has come to light about the two countries. That may be the only positive development to which I will be able to point in this chapter, for a series of disasters have recently fallen to the peoples of both nations. I say "nations" because neither Cambodia nor Laos have long existed as states; both became "states," in the modern sense of that term, only recently, as a consequence of the 1954 Geneva Conference on Indochina.

"States" in Indochina

Two points are of significance here. One is that the period of modern statehood of Laos and Cambodia can be understood only as a direct and intimate consequence of the war in Vietnam. Indeed, half of their modern history as states is tied to the "second Indochina" conflict—the Vietnam war with which the United States has been so deeply involved since 1964–65. Second, the very newness of Laos and Cambodia as "states" in world politics is itself a point of central importance. For like much else of Southeast Asia, and parts of Africa, the concept of the sovereign state as an entity with clearly defined borders and a governmental structure is to Cambodia and Laos an anomaly. It is a Western-imported concept that often does not fit any local set of facts.[1]

Consequently, it is best to warn at the outset that familiar questions about government and politics, if applied to Cambodia and Laos from a traditional Western perspective, are not likely to generate useful answers. This warning applies particularly to the central concern of this book: the concept of "divided" states.

That very notion presupposes a "whole"—a state and national structure which for one reason or another has been broken up into parts. This concept does not apply very well to Laos or to Cambodia, in part because neither was ever very much of a "state," and for another reason as well. That reason is the fact that in no formal sense have Cambodia and Laos been divided into separate territorial entities and governmental structures. Unlike the two Germanies, the two Koreas, and even the two Vietnams, and despite the obvious fact that there is much division in Cambodia and Laos, their general political and international existence is still largely framed in the context of a single Laos and a single Cambodia.

This chapter will give most of its attention to Cambodia, in part because of its greater size and recent prominence, but also because of the extent to which Cambodia has been much more significant in the affairs of Southeast Asia historically, and is likely also to be so in the future. And rather than speak of a "divided" Laos or Cambodia, it will be more accurate to think in terms of their disunity, or "incoherence." For that is the primary political characteristic of both nations in recent years. They both represent an archetypical illustration of what Professor John Herz meant some years ago when he referred to the idea of the "penetrated state." [2] The borders of Cambodia and Laos have meant little or nothing to their neighbors: foreign armies, and insurgent forces supported by foreigners, have roamed and operated with great impunity within the ostensible territorial limits of both nations.

The reason for this derives from the single and compelling fact that there has not yet been a settling down of the instability left in Indochina after the withdrawal of France, brought on by their ignominious defeat at Dienbienphu in 1954.[3] That defeat was formalized by the Geneva Conference, intended to bring an end to the Indochina conflict, but which in actuality represented only a brief interlude. By 1959, open violence was again common in Vietnam, and in one form or another it spilled over first into Laos and then—beginning in the late 1960s—into Cambodia.

Cambodia under Sihanouk

The special tragedy of Cambodia is that having remained largely aloof from the war in Vietnam for so long—even at the height of hostilities in 1967–68—Cambodia finally fell victim in 1970, when the war was in its last stages. This isolation was no accident, but was instead the result of very successful diplomatic and political leadership by Prince Norodom Sihanouk. Prince Sihanouk, who lives now in Peking, and regards himself as the leader of a government-in-exile, dominated Cambodian society and politics from 1954 until March 18, 1970. On that date, he was deposed from power while out of the country.

In the intervening sixteen years Prince Sihanouk conducted a virtuoso performance as national leader—briefly as king, and then, in order to participate more actively and directly in daily politics, as prince, prime minister, and leader of a mass party-political movement known as the *Sangkum.* For this purpose, he abdicated as king in 1955, but never ceased to be regarded as monarch by the largely peasant Khmer people, in a society where many believe that royalty possesses divine and even magical power. As head of government and after 1960 (when his father died) as head of state, Sihanouk was everywhere, and appears to have had two consuming passions. One was to direct Cambodia's modernization and development, and the other was to prevent the further diminution of Cambodia's territory—a process that had begun in the thirteenth century.

For the first purpose, Sihanouk became intimately involved in every aspect of internal political activities; for example, he often personally approved the government scholarships of high school graduates who sought university education abroad—typically in France. Similarly, by building new rural schools and clinics, and by promoting rural-based "industries" in outlying areas, Prince Sihanouk sought to maintain and develop the continuing vitality of rural towns and market villages. His concern may in part have derived from a conscious desire to avoid the general movement of populations to the capital city, a trend that is common elsewhere in Southeast Asia. But the prince must also have been aware that his highly visible rural efforts contributed to his already-large popularity among the major part of Cambodia's population of six or seven million.

Indeed the single outstanding characteristic of Sihanouk's domestic style was his energy and his presence, for throughout his political career in Cambodia Sihanouk was a young man—even now he is only fifty—and barring some minor illnesses and bouts with overweight, he has been quite healthy. Thus the image that was characteristic of him during the 1960s was his arrival by helicopter at a small-town dedication, at which time he would give a speech and distribute money directly into the hands of a holiday-mood crowd.

Although the locale was a small provincial town, it was often on such occasions that Sihanouk turned his attention to the second of his major concerns: foreign policy and Cambodian security. His speeches dealt regularly with the grand issues of international politics—particularly Sino-Soviet relations, Sino-American relations, and most important, Cambodian-Vietnamese relations. To Sihanouk, these were all closely related, and just as the primary characteristic of Sihanouk's domestic style was his constant presence, so was his constant *speechmaking* the primary ingredient of his foreign policy style. Sihanouk perfectly understood that Cambodia had no power in international affairs, and to compensate for this weakness he sought to make Cambodia and its survival important to those nations whose policies, conflicts, and ambitions could both threaten and preserve Cambodia's independence and relative security.

For centuries this has not been an easy matter. In the days of Angkor, as a quick glance at any historical atlas will show, Cambodia was several times its present size. This severe decline is the result of successive invasions of the Thai and of various Vietnamese peoples, and Cambodia's present small territory is what remained when the French arrived in the mid-nineteenth century. Indeed historians generally accept the view that had France not extended its colonial protectorate to Cambodia in 1873, the Khmer people would by this time long since have disappeared as a political entity.

Sihanouk and numerous other leading Cambodians are keenly aware of this distressing historical trend and Cambodia's geography: wedged between Thailand on the West and Vietnam on the East. The prince appears to have been convinced that after the French withdrawal in 1954, a resumption of Thai and Vietnamese expansion, at Cambodia's expense, was likely again to occur. These are not imaginings; as recently as 1942, when Thailand was an ally of Japan, and French territories were under Japanese occupation, one of the first tokens of Japanese gratitude for Thai cooperation was the granting of two Cambodian provinces to Thai control.[4]

In the 1950s and 1960s, however, it was not so much the expansion of Thailand but that of Vietnam that most concerned Sihanouk and other Cambodian leaders. Accordingly, a major concern of the prince, especially when the Vietnam war resumed in a major way in 1959, was to create conditions under which both Hanoi *and* Saigon would be constrained from expanding their control at the expense of Cambodia. For this purpose the prince used a variety of techniques, but most prominent among them were his efforts to restrain both North and South Vietnam through the influence of their respective "masters." In the case of the North, the prince sought good relations with Moscow and Peking; to control Saigon, he developed cordial and friendly ties with the United States. Indeed, Cambodia was a recipient of considerable American economic and military assistance from 1955 to 1963.

Sihanouk's frank hope was that if Cambodia were seen in a friendly light by the Americans, who were then greatly increasing their influence in Thailand, and with Vietnam divided, no one of Cambodia's traditional enemies would be prepared to nibble further at Cambodia. This view, and particularly the conviction that Cambodia's best hope for security lay in the continued division of Vietnam, was widely and publicly shared by all leading Cambodians. In 1962, for example, this was a point made to me by General Lon Nol, the man who ousted Sihanouk in 1970 and has been the dominant figure in Cambodian affairs ever since.

The problem that arose, however, was that Prince Sihanouk lost faith in the ability of the United States effectively to constrain its South Vietnamese (and Thai) "puppets," and he very definitely began to suspect, by 1963–64, that South Vietnam would not be able to maintain its own independence against the will and perseverance of Ho Chi Minh. Accordingly, by the mid-1960s Cambodia under Prince Sihanouk began to adjust its foreign policy toward greater accommodation with Hanoi, with Peking, and with Moscow. To show good faith, he became increasingly critical in public of the United States, and finally brought on the termination of American aid. Similarly, in an effort to placate North Vietnam and avoid its enmity in the expected event that Hanoi would emerge victorious from the unification struggle, the prince broke relations with Saigon. All the while, since he trusted neither of the two Vietnams, he made strenuous efforts to put himself in the good graces of Chou En-lai, and because he probably did not in the final event place too much trust there either, he increasingly opened Cambodia to economic and technical assistance from the Soviet Union.

It was a difficult balancing act. Nevertheless, throughout the 1960s it certainly appeared to be achieving the major aim of preserving Cambodia's security and insulating it from the worst consequences of the war next door in Vietnam and Laos. The United States, for example, began to accept Sihanouk as a fixture—annoying but not harmful—and resisted South Vietnamese efforts either to overthrow the prince or to seek military operations in Cambodian territory. North Vietnam gave assurances, though never as ironclad as the prince sought, that it would respect Cambodia's definition of its borders, and until 1969, at least, seems to have made little use of Cambodian territory, except on a very temporary basis. And even the Soviet Union took an increasing interest in the prince—perhaps in connection with Soviet naval desires to make use of the developing port of Sihanoukville on the Gulf of Thailand.[5]

But as successful as the prince was in handling Cambodia's very difficult foreign policy requirements, his management of a number of internal problems—some with foreign policy roots and consequences—began to cause him increasing problems. In fact, in January 1970, in what turned out to be a prophetic commentary, I wrote:

> . . . the Prince can probably look forward to external conditions more favorable to Cambodia's survival than at any time since independence. He has understood and probably successfully manipulated the international environ-

ment to Cambodia's benefit—but the irony is that these relatively favorable foreign changes are taking place at *precisely that point in time when the Prince's internal authority is no longer to be taken for granted.* 1969 was the year when that became most apparent.[6]

The Overthrow of Sihanouk and Its Aftermath

The internal difficulties to which that article referred led, three months later, to the overthrow of the prince; they have been followed by three years of uninterrupted disaster for Cambodia and the denial of all the principles for which Sihanouk worked. In brief, the problems that led to his ouster were economic stagnation and decline, reflected for example in rice shortages; increasing disaffection (among the urban elite and intellectuals) with Sihanouk's developmental efforts; and probably best known, the growing presence of between 30,000–50,000 armed Vietnamese (northerners or so-called Viet Cong/NLF forces supported by Hanoi) on Cambodian territory. Sihanouk himself had become increasingly testy with Hanoi in an effort to restrict and reduce the use of Cambodian territory by northern forces, but the tiny size of Cambodia's army (then about 35,000), combined with the prince's policy of accommodating Hanoi, left him with very little leverage to deal effectively with the problem.

During the first three months of 1970, with Sihanouk out of the country, each of these problems became increasingly intractable—but it was probably rising prices and the inability of the government to deal with the Vietnamese incursions that brought events to a head. General Lon Nol had long sought and failed to gain Sihanouk's support for increases in the size and capability of Cambodia's armed forces, and in all likelihood the general was prepared, throughout the 1960s, again to accept American military assistance for that goal. Indeed the prince was fond of broadly hinting that it was best to keep him in power—for otherwise Cambodia would be run by Lon Nol and the military, who would then "turn to the Americans."

Despite these differences, Lon Nol had long been Sihanouk's most loyal and important supporter. It is my view, however, that by March 1970 (Lon Nol himself returned to Cambodia on February 18 from Europe, where he had been treated for illness), the impunity with which the North Vietnamese were freely using Cambodian territory stretched the general's tolerance to the breaking point. For in mid-March several anti-Vietnamese riots occurred in Phnom Penh and elsewhere, and Lon Nol's own vehemently anti-Vietnamese feelings contributed greatly to his willingness, finally, to cooperate with other dissidents—most prominently Sihanouk's cousin prince Sirik Matak—in arranging for the quasi-legal ouster of the prince on March 18.[7]

Cambodia's present "division" dates from that event—for the prince chose not to return to Phnom Penh, despite the offer of a Soviet jet (he was in Moscow) to fly him directly home. He went instead, as originally scheduled, to Peking, and announced that Lon Nol, Sirik Matak, and numerous others were traitors. He announced as well that he continued to represent the only legitimate government of Cambodia, and named a group of men (including some who had not been in Cambodia for years and are presumed dead) as his new cabinet.

In Cambodia, Lon Nol became prime minister, and along with Sirik Matak, the "new" government immediately established a much tougher policy with regard to North Vietnam—including a forty-eight-hour ultimatum for all foreign forces to leave the country. At the same time, American assistance was sought for a massive increase in the size of Cambodia's armed forces, and within a month, President Nixon authorized both emergency assistance and the well-known United States–South Vietnamese "incursion" into Cambodian territory.

From that point on, conditions of politics and economics in Cambodia began a steady decline, from which no rise is yet in sight. To begin with, the results of the massive American "incursion" of May–June, whatever tactical gain they may have represented for the United States, left the Cambodian government in control of far less territory after the Americans had left than before they entered. Under Sihanouk, the Vietnamese did operate with some freedom in provinces bordering on Vietnam. When the Americans entered, however, these Vietnamese forces moved much farther inland, to the point where now they control most of the north, major portions of the east, and even provinces in the west. Angkor, for example, has not been under Phnom Penh's control since 1970, and the road from the capital to rice-growing areas in Battambang Province in the northwest has been cut since sometime in mid-1972.[8] Overall, it is a very safe assumption that at least half of the territory of Cambodia is now not under government authority, and very probably an estimate of two-thirds is no exaggeration. By many accounts, the government effectively controls only the immediate area around Phnom Penh itself.[9]

INSURGENCY AND ECONOMIC DISRUPTION

Worse yet, the number of antigovernment Cambodians, loosely designated as *Khmer Rouge*, has dramatically increased from perhaps 3,000 in 1970 to 30,000 or 40,000 today. Perhaps half of these are actively under arms. Under these conditions, no society and government could be expected to perform normally, and the drastic decline that has afflicted Cambodia's economy is the best single indicator of the consequences of division. By mid-1970, for example, rubber production was in complete collapse, and rice exports were in an almost equally bad state. Overall, exports were expected to total about $46 million for the year—or about half of what had been projected.[10]

In an effort to respond to these emergency conditions, General Lon Nol decreed a general mobilization in June 1970, under which all financial resources were subject to governmental requisition. But two years later it seemed evident that despite these measures, and despite massive investments of American economic and military assistance (in the range of $200 million to $250 million annually), the economy was in a shambles. Previously, for example, Cambodia had exported commodities to Japan worth approximately $6 million annually, but by early 1972 this trade had become only a trickle.[11] In addition to rubber, the main commodities affected have been timber, kapok, and vegetable oil—and even where production has not fallen, the interdiction of roads prevents their shipment to markets for processing and export.

To a great degree, this has been the problem of rice. From time to time during the past three years, Cambodia—which frequently exported rice—has witnessed severe rice shortages. When this has affected Phnom Penh, as in late 1972,[12] the results have been riots and disturbances among troops and the civilian population. And the entire problem is further complicated because the flow of refugees to the capital has more than doubled the city's population. In response, the Lon Nol government has arranged for a 10,000-ton purchase of rice from Thailand, is hoping for a gift of old surplus rice from Japan, and already has been assured airlifts of the grain from the United States.[13] Again, the problem is often distribution and planning. In 1970, for example, when rice exports were still being targeted, the government had to announce that the goal of 450,000 tons would be reduced to only 170,000[14]—and shortly revised this to a goal of 200,000 tons.[15]

Prince Sihanouk, meanwhile, has been announcing regularly from Peking that in "liberated" areas of Cambodia, under the authority of the National United Front of Kampuchea (FUNK), both troops and the civilian population are self-sufficient in rice and meat.[16] While there is of course no way to verify his assertion, it is a fact that the government of General Lon Nol increasingly has admitted its incapacity to deal with the manifestations of economic collapse. Cambodia's unit of currency, the *riel,* was devalued early in 1972 from a rate of 55 to one U.S. dollar to a rate of 140 to the dollar, and there have been important economic disruptions resulting from the strong animosities that ethnic Cambodians (Khmers) feel for both the Chinese and Vietnamese minorities. Both groups had traditionally dominated commerce and banking, and as early as 1970, most of Phnom Penh's 200,000 Vietnamese were turned out of their homes and stores. The Chinese, who were more prominent in marketing and distribution (rather than only retailing), are regularly harassed and blamed for hoarding of commodities, and for the frequent rice shortages and price rises.[17]

REFUGEES AND POLITICAL DISRUPTION/DIVISION

Those Chinese who were able to arrange it have left the country altogether and gone to live with their cousins in Malaysia, Thailand, Hong Kong, and even South Vietnam.[18] The Vietnamese minority have been less fortunate; they were of course the initial victims of massacres that began early in 1970. The killed numbered in the thousands, and except for about 10,000 who were evacuated, penniless, to South Vietnam, many others now spend a miserable existence in internment camps in Cambodia. Many more refugees are among the Khmers themselves. In early 1972 Prince Sihanouk reported that more than 1 million peasants had been forced to leave their villages,[19] and figures provided by William Sullivan, deputy assistant secretary of state, are in the same range. Sullivan estimates that 2 million people have been displaced by the hostilities, and he identifies this primarily as the result of Cambodians fleeing from the North Vietnamese. While that is not the only reason, it is clear that about 800,000 people have moved into the Phnom Penh vicinity, and that this has considerably more than doubled the city's "normal" population and grossly strained its capacities.[20]

The same factors that lead people to leave their homes and farms and flee to the city for relative protection are also those that alienate a society from its formal governmental structure: fear, injustice, lack of confidence in authority, and sheer terror. And while a State Department official may be required to suggest that it is the North Vietnamese invasion that has led many Cambodians to run, the ethnic animosities that have characterized Cambodian-Vietnamese relations over the past several centuries make this claim foolish. Indeed, one of the deepest tragedies of Cambodia was that President Nixon unleashed Saigon's forces into Cambodia, thus placing the Khmers at the mercy of both branches of their historic oppressors. Six months after the "incursion" ordered by the President, one of Phnom Penh's most senior military leaders (General Sosthene Fernandez) had this to say:

> South Vietnamese troops rape, they destroy houses, they steal, they loot pagodas and they beat the Buddist monks. . . . My personal opinion is that if we had enough weapons it is better to avoid South Vietnamese help."[21]

This consideration—the fact that under Lon Nol Cambodia has come more under the sway of foreigners than at any time in modern history—has done the new government no good. Along with the growing evidence of Lon Nol's inability to govern effectively and to manage the economy, the result is a pattern of ever-widening support for a variety of antigovernment forces. The evidences for this are found in the extreme instability that has characterized Cambodian government since shortly after Sihanouk was removed from power, and while this essay cannot mention all the personalities and events involved, some of the main elements should be identified.

In the first few months after the ouster, the major effort of the government was to discredit the prince, establish a republic in place of the monarchy (accomplished in October 1970), and greatly expand the size of the army. For a while progress could be pointed to, but by the beginning of 1971 the first of several major cabinet crises occurred. In part these have been brought about by General Lon Nol's very bad health; he had already suffered some illnesses and injuries and these were no doubt worsened by the major offensive launched by the North Vietnamese—very close to Phnom Penh itself—in January 1971.[22] Within a few weeks, Lon Nol suffered a paralyzing stroke, and while the military situation clearly deteriorated, he was out of the country for treatment and recuperation until mid-April, at a U.S. Army hospital in Hawaii.

In his absence, the government was effectively in the hands of Sirik Matak, who was deputy premier, but who has never enjoyed a popularity among Cambodians such as that accorded General Lon Nol. In all likelihood Sirik Matak would never have been able to effect the ouster of Sihanouk alone. Complaints increasingly developed that the government was doing nothing to reduce corruption, and that some of the most notorious officials, holdovers from Sihanouk's tenure, remained in office. At the same time, Son Ngoc Thanh, one of Sihanouk's oldest rivals from early nationalist days of the 1940s and '50s, reappeared on the scene. It is likely that in this period, with the general's health very uncertain, there was much maneuvering for power among these men, as well as Lon Non (the general's younger brother) and In Tam, another leading personality.

When Lon Nol returned from Hawaii in mid-April, he probably wished to resign the premiership altogether, for he was still incapacitated and could give only a few hours each day to government business. There was too little support for Sirik Matak, however, and despite a number of other major cabinet rearrangements in 1971–72, including the accession of Son Ngoc Thanh to the premiership for a short while, Lon Nol is once again the predominant figure.[23] There is now even little pretense to democratic rule, for the general governs increasingly by decree.[24] Indeed, as recently as September 1972, the opposition Democratic party of In Tam, and Sirik Matak's Republican party, both withdrew from Senate elections that they protested had been gerrymandered by the government.[25]

The net result of these developments is to lend force to Sihanouk's regular complaints from Peking, and wherever else he travels, against the "fascist coup d'etat of the traitors Lon Nol, Sirik Matak, and Son Ngoc Thanh." [26] Son Ngoc Thanh, for example, despite his relative popularity with students and "republicans," is the subject of much apprehension because of his long years of residence in Saigon and his reputedly close connections with the United States—the CIA in particular. Sirik Matak, who appears to have been the favorite of American officials in the period since Sihanouk's ouster, is suspect in Phnom Penh precisely for that reason, and in the army and other quarters because of his royal background and associations with officials suspected of extreme corruption. And Lon Nol himself has found it necessary to take measures, including, for example, the closing of some newspapers,[27] which have weakened severely his basis of support—particularly among reformers who earlier were alienated from Sihanouk.

Given these problems, it has to be conceded that Sihanouk's credibility, particularly his claim that the "Khmer Republic" is not legitimate, probably rises in direct proportion to the extent of governmental and economic problems within Cambodia. Although it seemed in 1970 that the prince had made a serious error when he took up residence in Peking—instead of almost any other place—his statements in 1972 increasingly have emphasized that the coalition he purports to head is not exclusively communist nor Vietnamese-dominated. And of course he has taken numerous steps to buttress his claim to legitimacy, both in Cambodia and abroad. As Sihanouk argued recently:

> It has been said that we are a government in exile, yet 11 of 21 ministers reside in the country. Others are on missions abroad. We are recognized by 28 countries. Ten of the eleven ministers are *Khmer Rouge*, although they do not belong to any communist party. We have peoples' committees at village level, they elect commune and district committees, we have carried out agrarian reform [and] local capitalists have fled.[28]

Similarly, and in recognition of the fact that to many in the countryside, the monarchy is a positive factor,[29] Sihanouk has also sought to assure others that the throne is "not an enemy of democracy": "The throne is only a pure symbol of unity of patriots." [30]

SUPPORT AND LEGITIMACY: DOMESTIC AND FOREIGN

While it has to be said again that reliable information on political developments outside of Phnom Penh is scarce, a variety of noncommunist American, European, and Asian correspondents all report that support for antigovernment forces is now quite substantial. The most commonly cited figure of activists, as I suggested earlier, is not less than 30,000,[31] and judging from the proportion of territory in Cambodia not controlled by the government, Sihanouk's claim that 70 percent of the population is under the "authority" of dissident forces is probably not a gross exaggeration.[32] For it is a fact that the Lon Nol government continues to suffer military reverses which threaten to block Phnom Penh even from essential imports of fuel and food, and that foreign diplomats and observers increasingly must report that Lon Nol and his government are isolated from much of the rest of the country. Indeed, even the American ambassador was reported to say that Lon Nol is a "sick man mentally and physically." [33]

These facts have been reflected in the extent to which Sihanouk's claim to legitimacy has been accepted by at least twenty-six governments, not all of which are communist or puppets of China. His greatest success in this sphere was the acceptance of his representative at the conference of nonaligned nations in August 1972 at Georgetown, Guyana. That meeting was attended by fifty-eight nations, and the conference denied membership to Long Beret, the representative sent by Lon Nol.[34] While this action led to a walkout by several Southeast Asian nations, including Indonesia and Singapore, it is a fact, nonetheless, that Sihanouk increasingly attracts international recognition. He claims, indeed, that no less than sixty nations have accorded him de jure or de facto recognition, and that even the United States—according to Chou En-lai—is now contemplating withdrawing its support from Lon Nol.[35] The United States has denied this,[36] but it is known that American officials believe that Cambodia's republican government would stand a better long-term chance of survival were Lon Nol to step down—probably in favor of Sirik Matak and Lon Non, or perhaps other military leaders. Some reports suggest that the only consideration which so far has prevented a withdrawal of American support is concern that Cambodia's dwindling military capabilities would decline even further in the immediate aftermath of a governmental change at the top.[37]

Nevertheless, by the end of 1972 there were increasing evidences to support Sihanouk's announced belief that the time is not too far off when he will be able to return to Cambodia, possibly with the tacit support of the United States.[38] In late October, for example, a Cambodian official acknowledged that there had been several meetings, described as a "movement toward reconciliation," between government officials and representatives of the *Khmer Rouge*.[39] It is altogether likely, moreover, that Cambodian government fears about the nature of any settlement between the United States and North Vietnam will lead to more such meetings. For it is evident that Lon Nol had no prior consultation regarding the Kissinger-Tho talks in Paris,[40] and that the draft agreement described by Dr. Kissinger in October 1972 made no provision whatever for the withdrawal of Vietnamese or other antigovernment forces from Cambodia. Consequently, and as Lon Nol's situation worsens, his advisers are likely increasingly to urge a settlement with the *Khmer Rouge before* North Vietnam is free to devote more energy and assistance to Cambodia.

Conclusions and Prospects for Cambodia

In the almost three years since the ouster of Prince Sihanouk, perhaps the only gain for Cambodia that can be pointed to is that a number of individual Cambodians, including military officers, have enriched themselves considerably at the expense of American taxpayers.[41] As I have frequently mentioned in this essay, the net political result of the large American–South Vietnamese incursion in 1970 was that much more, rather than less, of Cambodia's territory has come under the control of Vietnamese and antigovernment Cambodians—who have themselves greatly increased their numbers. In this respect, and while there is still no formal division of the country, it is now more than ever probable that the next government of Cambodia will find it necessary to provide for formal participation of leftists or communists who will owe much of their loyalty to Hanoi and Peking.

The two major unknowns in this matter pertain to the role of Sihanouk himself and the Soviet Union. The USSR studiously has avoided giving support of any kind to Sihanouk in the period of his exile in China, and Russian leaders are known to have been severely disappointed that the prince made no effort to return in the immediate aftermath of his ouster.[42] In turn, Sihanouk has been extremely critical of the Soviets—he has charged, for example, that no Russian aid has been provided to the anti-Lon Nol forces, and of course he has been vehemently critical that the Soviets, although now without an ambassador in Phnom Penh, continue to be represented there. The likely explanation for this Soviet policy is a desire to avoid seeing the establishment of a Cambodian government that will be completely identified with Peking and North Vietnam; instead, we can expect that Moscow will support efforts toward the creation of a "front" or coalition government in Phnom Penh.

As so often has been the case in other instances of "divided" nations, both of Cambodia's formal poles of attraction appear firmly opposed to coalition. The prince has urged Lon Nol and the others to repair to "Honolulu, while there is still time," and Sihanouk's former colleagues in Phnom Penh have warned him that he is a traitor whose death sentence has already been announced in absentia and will be carried out should he return to Cambodia. At lower levels, however, it is likely that many other Cambodians are preparing to accept most any price—including coalition and perhaps even the return of Sihanouk—because of their greater fear of Vietnam and the Vietnamese. For once the Americans leave South Vietnam, no restraints will operate in that quarter, and the North Vietnamese will more than ever wish to make use of Cambodian "sanctuaries" in order to operate with freedom and flexibility against South Vietnam.

Certainly Moscow, and very probably Washington as well, will support a movement toward coalition, and both will want to avoid a return triumphant of the prince. North Vietnam, however, will want as much as possible to legitimate its post-Vietnam-settlement activities in Cambodian territory. For this purpose little could be better than to play the part of merely responding to the requests of a returned Sihanouk—headquartered in all likelihood near Angkor Wat. That is the outcome I judge most likely. As recently as mid-December 1972, the prince himself said that "he was remaining in readiness to join the Cambodian resistance immediately following the cease-fire," which he anticipates to be no more than a lull:

> . . . things will worsen following the cease-fire, and some day the combat will have to begin anew. There will be no true peace while small peoples determined to achieve freedom are not liberated.[43]

The conclusion to which these considerations lead, based in part on the assumption that the United States will be unwilling again to enter Cambodia and commit itself further to a government which has shown itself so frail, is that the prospects for Cambodia are for more, rather than for less division. Under the trend of present conditions we are likely to witness the formal division of Cambodia: a rump government based in Phnom Penh and dependent upon minimal American and South Vietnamese help, and a government led at least in name by Prince Sihanouk and based in Western Cambodia near Angkor, with all that those historic traditions mean. That outcome, which would represent a worsening of Cambodia's present misfortune, might be avoided were the United States to encourage Phnom Penh to accept Sihanouk's return—in an effort to bring unity to the nation. But little in the record of recent American actions in Southeast Asia suggests that so prudent a policy option will be taken up.

The Confusion of Laos[44]

For Laos, as for Cambodia, the political history of the past decade cannot be separated from the Vietnam conflict. It is geographic location alone, however, which gives Laos contemporary relevance in world affairs—for the "country" is small, landlocked, has a population of less than 3 million farmers of several ethnic groups, and produces no commodity of major commercial significance other than opium. But Laos runs lengthwise between Vietnam on its east and Thailand on the west, while its narrow northern border is with China and its southern border is with Cambodia. This sandwichlike location, and particularly the fact that the so-called Ho Chi Minh trail runs through southeastern Laos into South Vietnam, has given Laotian affairs a prominence disproportionate to any of its other features. The "trail," a number of tracks and rough roads, has represented an essential supply line for North Vietnamese and NLF forces engaged in the South Vietnam conflict.

Given the almost absolute lack of indigenous modernization in Laos, and its location in the midst of so severe a conflict as that in Indochina, it is not surprising that Laos is "divided." But the division is not formal. Instead, Laos is considered one kingdom (the Royal Lao government), ostensibly ruled by a three-part coalition of leftists, neutralists, and rightists—although much of the north and all of the east have been under communist-associated control for years. Yet as this essay was written (in late 1972), there were promising signs that these contending factions were genuinely searching for a more stable arrangement than had been seen in ten years—or in other words, since the 1962 Geneva settlements which gave modern Laos its governing structure. Since those agreements have been so formative in determining events of the past ten years, and since the present factions in Laos all refer to the 1962 Geneva agreements as the basis for a new settlement[45] it will be useful now to sketch briefly the conditions that led to and that flow from those agreements.

THE GENEVA AGREEMENTS AND THEIR AFTERMATH

The Geneva Protocol of 1962 was designed to bring an end to the instability that had characterized government in Laos since independence. As in Cambodia, this was formalized at the 1954 Geneva Conference, which provided also that upon independence, Laos should be a "neutral" state. Throughout the 1950s, however, factions associated with three princes—each brothers—maneuvered constantly (with foreign, including American, support) for preeminence, until in 1960, war broke out openly. A primary figure was a young captain, Kong Le. Allied with the Pathet Lao, his forces seized most of northern Laos before an intermittent cease-fire was agreed to, initially in 1961. Finally, along with other agreements reached earlier in Laos and at Zurich, a fourteen-nation conference met at Geneva in 1962, and the resulting Geneva Protocol affirmed the structure for the neutralist, three-part coalition government that now stands.

Under this structure the Left, in the form of the Neo Lao Hak Sat (NLHS)[46] was to be granted four seats in the new government. The right-wing faction led by Prince Boun Oum (allied with General Phoumi Nosavan) was also given four seats. To cement the structure together, a neutralist group under Prince Souvanna Phouma (the present prime minister) was granted eleven seats. The system soon broke down under both right-wing harassment and leftist actions which split the armed forces of the neutralists. In April 1963 senior leftist ministers withdrew from the capital at Vientiane,[47] and in 1964 the leftists withdrew from the coalition altogether.

The premier, Prince Souvanna Phouma, has never recognized this withdrawal as formal; instead he has kept vacant the four cabinet seats and, despite right-wing pressure, has steadily maintained the useful fiction that the coalition government continues to exist. His persistence provides for the continuing possibility of a "return" of the NLHS representatives, for they are quite reluctant to abandon, formally, the Geneva structure coauthored by the USSR.

Nevertheless, civil war has been the norm in Laos during most of the years since Geneva. Intensified attacks began in 1966, and by 1967–68 it seemed clear that the North Vietnamese were playing a great part in battles against government forces. Areas under government control were reduced steadily during that period, and by 1970 the Pathet Lao—backed by the North Vietnamese—were in control of approximately three-fifths of the nation's territory. The total number of troops with which the government of Laos must contend is between 120,000 and 145,000—of whom about 90,000 are reliably reported to be North Vietnamese. From the beginning, a difficulty has been that neither the right-wing forces nor the Pathet Lao have been willing to allow for government occupation and administration of the entire national territory. In the early 1960s, the rightists were in control of portions of central and southern Laos, while the Pathet Lao were and are predominant in the north and east and their areas of control have increased.

RECENT POLITICAL AND ECONOMIC CONDITIONS

Reflecting its greater territorial control, the leftists, organized now as a "popular front," have a great deal of internal legitimacy. This is also a function of the nature of their leadership, for the front has as members important lowland families, like Prince Souphanouvong himself, as well as the leading men of several mountain tribes. The front also includes a third group, consisting of those with some education and middle-class backgrounds, who have had ties with the Vietnamese Communists through education, other early associations, or family links. For example, the present secretary general of the Pathet Lao, Kaysone Phomvihan, as well as Nouhak Phomsavan, represent this group, and are probably more influential than Prince Souphanouvong.

These top-level links with North Vietnam have not been sufficient to prevent growing resentment of Pathet Lao troops against increasing North Vietnamese control—made worse by traditional Lao-Vietnamese differences of language and national culture. One consequence is a pattern of increasing defections to the government, with its better supplies, capability for medical treatment, and other material resources. The Royal Lao government does, after all, receive enormous American economic and military assistance. Under various AID and U.S. military assistance programs, including a heavy CIA involvement to provide for the government's armed forces, American assistance in most recent years has been in the range of $250 million to $400 million yearly.[48] Without this aid, the "government" of Laos could in no sense exist, for the level of American *economic* assistance alone (i.e., aid not directly related to military operations), is larger than the national budget of Laos.

In addition to American assistance, a five-nation consortium (known as the Foreign Exchange Operations Fund) also provides help to the Lao economy, although it should be cautioned that the concept of a national "economy" does not usefully fit the Laos environment. The bulk of the population has not been part of a monetary economy, for example, and a considerable portion of foreign assistance is devoted to the currency stabilization program—while the national currency itself (the *kip*) is regularly burned. As this suggests, inflation might be regarded as a critical problem, except that the American assistance program provides a regular backup for the Lao budget. This means that the Royal government (and some individuals) spend without traditional Western responsibility for the normal consequences of deficit financing and foreign trade imbalances. In capsule form, the unreality of the Lao "economy" is illustrated by the fact that in a typical year imports amount to $40 million or $50 million—while exports rarely exceed $6 million in value! [49]

Despite these bizarre aspects, the regular infusions of foreign assistance into Laos do appear to have promising consequences for those portions of the nation under government control. Japan, for example, has had dozens of "peace corps" agricultural volunteers in the country, and provided important capital assistance for the construction of the $30 million Nan Ngum dam on the Mekong River. That project, one of the most important efforts of the broader regional cooperation scheme that includes Cambodia, Thailand, and South Vietnam as well, is now generating electricity for use in Laos and Thailand.

Probably better known, however, is another aspect of the Lao economy which in fact *has* been disrupted by the war—the opium trade. In the wake of numerous charges (some of them moderately well supported) that the U.S.-owned airline known as Air America[50] was helping to transport opium crops, intense pressure was put on the Royal government to encourage farmers to develop alternative cash crops. Even earlier, the Meo tribesmen of the northeast, where poppy growing had been concentrated, began to move west and south in order to escape the widening occupation of the North Vietnamese and the concomitant U.S. bombing that went with it. As a result of all three factors, opium production is reported to have fallen from 100 tons in 1967 to between 25 and 30 tons at present.[51]

REFUGEES

All sources—American, Lao government, and Pathet Lao—agree that of a population of less than 3 million people, several hundred thousand have been made homeless by the ten-year war. Figures released recently by the Lao government indicated that more than 82,000 became refugees between July 1971 and May 1972 alone.[52] Other sources indicate that the figure overall is more than 900,000; the U.S. General Accounting Office, in a conservative estimate, puts the figure at between 300,000 and 400,000.[53] The Agency for International Development (AID) further estimates that 843,000 Lao are living under conditions of regular bombing in areas of Pathet Lao control—and that many of these people seek to escape from this condition as well as other difficulties, including Vietnamese oppression, the rice tax, and forced work.

This refugee population, since it derives largely from areas that for years have not been controlled by the Royal government, has put an increasingly heavy burden on Vientiane officials, which in turn has led to increasing American expenditures. The United States budgeted $15 million on refugee assistance for Laos during fiscal year 1972.[54]

A large number of the refugees are hill-tribe people whose historic homeland areas are in the region north of the Plaine des Jarres, near the border with North Vietnam. They have been displaced by the encroaching North Vietnamese; and the Meo people, in particular, have been prepared to fight in response. Indeed, General Vang Pao, who has for more than a decade been leading an irregular force trained and equipped by AID and the CIA, is himself a Meo. Casualties in this force have been very high—estimated at between 30,000 and 60,000—and the percentage of ethnic Meo troops has declined from 75 percent to about 30 percent at present. Their places have been taken by other mountain peoples—the Yao and Upland Lao—as well as by "volunteers" from Thailand.[55]

CONCLUSIONS AND PROSPECTS

The willingness of the Thai government to provide troops in Laos,[56] whether or not paid in part by the United States, helps again to illustrate the remarkably large importance given to Laos in Southeast Asian affairs by virtue of its location. For the Thai leadership clearly identifies its long border with Laos as its most vulnerable and sensitive national security interest. It fears, as have most Cambodian leaders, a resumption of Vietnamese expansion and imperialism—a process interrupted a century ago by the imposition of French colonial rule. From Bangkok's perspective —and traditionally from the viewpoint of Phnom Penh as well—the preservation of a single and unified Laos as a "buffer state" between themselves and Vietnam has been a very desirable goal.

But it is of course not Thai or other local interests that have helped to provide for the continued existence of Laos. Instead, it is the combination of American, Russian, and perhaps Chinese interests, which have so long maintained the formal existence of a single coalition government as laid out in the 1962 Geneva Protocol. Increasingly, as the Soviet Union and China have been at odds in East Asia, it has probably not seemed to be in the interest of the Soviet Union to assist communist forces in Laos that are so closely allied with Vietnam and China. The United States, of course, has found it important for a combination of tactical and political reasons to maintain the concept of a single Laos whose leaders are intent on remaining independent of North Vietnam. And China, which has given moderate support to the North Vietnamese, would probably find it preferable to have on its southern border a neutral Laos, rather than a territory that had become part of an increasingly ambitious and successful North Vietnam.

These are some of the considerations which make Vientiane so unusual a capital—for important embassies are maintained there, in close proximity, by the United States, China, Russia, North Vietnam, and Thailand—among many others. Accordingly, the Royal government is the only Lao government accorded formal recognition worldwide, and the government of Premier (and Prince) Souvanna Phouma gains legitimacy as a direct consequence. There is perhaps an analogy here with Switzerland, although economically and technologically, Laos will not for a long time be comparable. Yet, like Switzerland, Laos is a geographic expression made up of several ethnic communities. Like Switzerland in an earlier era, its continued existence appears to be sufficiently important, for larger powers, to provide a basis for optimism that Laos will survive as a political entity as well.

The question of movement toward unity or further division will depend perhaps most heavily in the immediate future on the North Vietnamese, who must have given approval to the talks begun in October 1972—just as in the past the fact that Laos did not succumb to even worse division has been owed to Souvanna Phouma's tenacity and political courage. As an informed Western analyst concluded recently, Souvanna has preserved enough of the superstructure in Laos "to persuade the communist powers to maintain relations with his government." In addition,

> his refusal to yield to the right wing and his continued appeals for talks with the Pathet Lao have made the latest exchange possible. The fact that it is possible for even preliminary talks to take place owes much to the 1962 Geneva Agreements, which provide common ground for both sides.

In both Cambodia and Laos, in other words, it appears that the prospects for division or accommodation depend heavily on formal institutions. In Laos, both sides pay at least lip-service to the agreements reached at Geneva more than a decade ago. In Cambodia, the only "institution" which might perform a similar function of attracting forces that are otherwise in much disagreement is the monarchy and the formidable personality of Prince Sihanouk himself. Yet on balance, perhaps because it is more difficult to forgive individuals than it is to accommodate to institutions, the prospects appear more bleak for Cambodia than they do for Laos.[57]

Notes

1. For elaboration on this general point, see the section on "Territoriality: Western Legalisms and Ancient Empires," in Bernard K. Gordon, *The Dimensions of Conflict in Southeast Asia*, (Englewood Cliffs, N.J.: Prentice-Hall, 1966), pp. 5–8, and chap. 2, "Cambodia and Her Neighbors," ibid. Also see the references to Southeast Asia in Adda B. Bozeman, *The Future of Law in a Multicultural World* (Princeton, N.J.: Princeton University Press, 1971); and Bernard K. Gordon, "The Uses of International Law for Issue Identification and Conflict Resolution in Southeast Asia" in the American Society of International Law, *Proceedings* of the Sixty-Sixth annual meeting, April 1972.

2. John M. Herz, *International Politics in the Atomic Age* (New York: Columbia University Press, 1959).

3. The name is that of a crossroads village near the border between northern Vietnam and Laos. The architect of the victory was General Vo Nguyen Giap, who has for years since been North Vietnam's defense minister.

4. Thailand, of course, maintained that these provinces previously had been taken from her by France, and improperly ceded to Cambodia. Nevertheless, at the end of the war, and in an effort to be restored to the victorious good graces of France, Britain, and the United States, Thailand renounced its control over these territories. No doubt there are some Thai who even today regard that return as an action taken under duress, but little has been heard of the matter in recent years.

5. For elaboration on Soviet involvement in Cambodia, see Bernard K. Gordon, "Shadow Over Angkor," *Asian Survey* (January 1969): 68.

6. Bernard K. Gordon, with Kathryn Young, "Cambodia: Following the Leader?" *Asian Survey* (February 1970): 169–76. Emphasis added.

7. Specialists disagree whether the prince's removal from office was entirely legal, within the Cambodian framework. The U.S. government and the present government of Cambodia, known now as the Khmer Republic, maintain that the prince was legally voted out of office. Others freely use the term coup d'etat to describe the event, and while that may not be entirely accurate, the action was so quick and decisive that a loose interpretation of that term seems to fit. There are some observers who hold that the anti-Vietnamese riots were instigated in order to bring about crisis conditions that would lead to the overthrow of the prince, and the fact of some army and government assistance in the riots supports that contention. Some also believe that the prince may have himself staged many of the events of January–March, in order to precipitate a crisis that would then have him called home as the savior of the nation's unity. I do not credit this view.

8. See, for example, *New York Times*, 23 October 1972.

9. The Cambodian government was recently at pains to deny a South Vietnamese military report that "more than 80 percent of the country is controlled by the *Khmer Rouges* or Khmers led by Sihanouk and authorities stated that "The Viet Cong and Khmer *Rouges* troops . . . control less than 50 percent of sparsely populated territory" (Phnom Penh broadcast, 2 November 1972). Accordingly, this estimate must reflect the most optimistic assessment.

10. *Far Eastern Economic Review*, 16 July 1970. Rubber production, it should be noted, normally has accounted for about one-quarter of Cambodia's foreign exchange earnings. See Remy Prud' Homme, *L'Economie du Cambodge* (Paris: Presses Universitaires de France, 1969).

11. *Far Eastern Economic Review*, 4 March 1972.

12. *New York Times*, 28 September 1972.

13. *New York Times*, 8 September 1972.

14. *Bangkok Post*, 18 August 1970, and reported in Bernard K. Gordon, with Kathryn Young, "The Khmer Republic: That Was the Cambodia That Was," in *Asian Survey* (January 1971): 26–40.

15. This remarkably optimistic figure was provided by the U.S. Agency for International Development (AID) in the period of 1970 when U.S. officials regularly expressed confidence that Cambodia would maintain its viability, both in economic and security terms. Indeed the *Washington Post* of 7 December 1970 reported that an AID economist had concluded that Cambodia "may survive without requiring anywhere near the $230 million in outside economic aid [earlier predicted]." In fact, of course, only the most pessimistic predictions have been anywhere near accurate.

16. See, for example, his interview with Ania Francos in *Jeune Afrique*, 26 August 1972. Similar information is being released from China. On November 8, 1972, for example, *New China News Agency* reported that "Mondolkiri Province . . . has taken on a new look [since liberation] . . . the price of foodstuffs is cheap . . . *a barrel* [20 kg.] of paddy rice costs 30 riels in the liberated zone while in Phnom Penh . . . one kilogram costs over 50 riels and is hard to get."

17. *New York Times*, 10 September 1972.

18. *Christian Science Monitor*, 14 March 1972.

19. Broadcast message from Sihanouk, from the unofficial Cambodian Information Agency, 15 February 1972.

20. All these figures must be treated skeptically, a point recently made by the General Accounting Office when asked by the Congress to assess the number of refugees in Laos and

Cambodia. The GAO adds that there is no system of accounting for refugees, who are in any event constantly moving in search of better conditions. See U.S. Congress, Senate, Committee on the Judiciary, *Hearings: Problems of War Victims in Indochina, Part II, Cambodia and Laos*, 92d Cong., 1971. Recent Cambodian government figures show an increase of 70,000 in the number of refugees in the three months following the expansion of combat activities in February. *New York Times*, 27 March 1973.

21. Quoted in the *Washington Evening Star*, 7 December 1970.

22. Attacks on Phnom Penh's airport, destroying Cambodia's air force, came on January 22, and military operations were within ten miles of the city. While it seemed possible for Vietnamese forces to take the city (though at great cost) in that period, many observers doubt that the aim was more than to demonstrate the great weakness of the Cambodian government. Because government control was so restricted territorially, it was not too much of an exaggeration to refer to Lon Nol as "Mayor of Phnom Penh."

23. For useful discussions of the several personalities involved and frequent changes of early 1972, see the discussions in the *Far Eastern Economic Review*, 18 March 1972, pp. 5–6; 25 March 1972, pp. 5–6.

24. For details see the *New York Times*, 10 and 18 March 1972, and announcements of the Cambodian Broadcast service during 1972.

25. *Far Eastern Economic Review*, 9 September 1972. The complaint of both was that the representation accorded Phnom Penh was unrealistically low—and that the probable purpose of the districting was to assure support for Lon Non, Lon Nol's brother and increasingly important confidant and counselor.

26. New China News Agency (Peking), 22 September 1972.

27. On June 22 the government closed the daily *Kamneng Pelproeuk* (announcement of Phnom Penh radio, 22 June 1972), and the *Far Eastern Economic Review*, 1 July 1972, reported the closing of *Damnoeung Pil Pruth*. In both cases the papers were charged with unfair criticism of government policy and measures. After this was written, it was learned that the Cambodian government closed four additional newspapers during the final week of December 1972.

28. From interview with Sihanouk in *Jeune Afrique*, 26 August 1972.

29. As the *New York Times*, 19 September 1972, commented on "Troubled Cambodians Miss the Monarchy."

30. Sihanouk statement broadcast by New China News Agency (Peking), 10 October 1972.

31. *New York Times*, 29 October 1972.

32. This figure was provided by Sihanouk's ambassador to Cuba, Toch Knamdeun, and broadcast by the Cuban radio, 20 September 1972.

33. Reported in the *Far Eastern Economic Review*, 5 February 1972.

34. Details of the conference on this point were reported by New China News Agency (Peking), 17 August 1972.

35. *Agence France Presse*, 4 September 1972.

36. A State Department denial is reported in the *Far Eastern Economic Review*, 23 September 1972.

37. *New York Times*, 9 September 1972.

38. Reported by Pierre Comparet in *Agence France Presse*, 11 September 1972.

39. *New York Times*, 23 October 1972. Perhaps in an effort to stress that Phnom Penh was firmly opposed to any reconciliation with the prince, the official remarked that the *Khmer Rouge* representatives participated in the meetings without Sihanouk's knowledge.

40. Lon Nol indicated this directly to a reporter; see *New York Times*, 8 November 1972.

41. This has been done in a variety of ways, not least of which is a padding, at all levels, of the reported size of the Cambodian Army in order to draw the salaries of fictitious soldiers. The result, now conceded, is that the real size of the army in early 1973 was not more than 180,000—rather than the approximately 250,000 previously assumed by the United States.

42. Statement of a senior Soviet official to an ambassador of a Southeast Asian nation posted in Washington, and reported orally to me by the ambassador in April 1970.

43. Reported by correspondent Jean Leclerc du Sablon, *Agence France Presse*, 11 December 1972.

44. This discussion has been facilitated by an earlier draft prepared by Frederick Goodhue, a graduate student in political science at the University of New Hampshire. His help, as well as research assistance in connection with compiling certain Cambodian data, is gratefully acknowledged.

45. These talks began, with much optimism, in October 1972. By the end of December, eleven sessions had been held and were continuing, though it was apparent that no major progress could be achieved until an American–North Vietnam settlement was also accomplished. This was the view expressed by the prime minister, "neutralist" Prince Souvanna Phouma, in an interview with a group of Japanese journalists and reported by Vientiane (Laos) radio, 20 December 1972. See also the *New York Times*, 27 December 1972.

46. This sometimes appears as NLHX (Neo Lao Hak Xat) and is the political organization of the communist-inspired political party or movement known as the Pathet Lao.

47. Vientiane, very close to the Thai border, is the "administrative" capital of Laos. The formal, or royal capital, is near the center of Laos, at Luang Prabang.

48. Under the so-called Symington Amendment, U.S. aid is now to be restricted to not more than $350 million per year. The aid has been used for building, currency stabilization, imports, refugee assistance, foreign education, and even direct support for the maintenance of the diplomatic representation of Laos in several world capitals. The most useful source for this information is from *Reports* and *Hearings* of the Senate Foreign Relations Committee, particularly the report dated 3 August 1971. See *New York Times*, 3 August 1971, for details.

49. Figures of $2.6 million (exports) and $46.1 million (imports) for 1971 are provided in the *Far Eastern Economic Review*, 22 May 1972. As congressional critics are quick to point out, moreover, the American effort to bring some normalcy to the Lao economy has meant that importers are under few limitations regarding what commodities will be brought in. One result is that French wines and cheeses, and Scotch whiskey, continue to be imported commercially (*New York Times*, 24 January 1972).

50. Air America is widely regarded as a transport agent for the CIA, and this point added to congressional criticism of many aspects of the U.S. involvement in Laos.

51. *New York Times*, 16 October 1972.

52. *Far Eastern Economic Review*, 30 September 1972.

53. U.S. Congress, Senate, Committee on the Judiciary, *Hearings, Problems of War Victims in Indochina, Part II: Cambodia and Laos*, 29 May 1972.

54. *New York Times*, 4 February 1972.

55. *New York Times*, 11 October 1972.

56. The number is not known; estimates suggest approximately 5,000 Thai of ethnic Lao origin.

57. Events through 1973, since the signing of the Vietnam accords in February, would seem to support this conclusion. In Laos, negotiations between the Royal Government and the Pathet Lao have proved fruitful. An interim agreement was reached on 12 September 1973 to form a coalition government under Souphanna Phouma. In October Vientiane and Luang Prabang were both neutralized, with Pathet Lao and Royal troups sharing the duties of policing the cities. The contending sides in Cambodia, however, seem unable even to agree to negotiate. *New York Times*, 13 September and 15 September 1973.

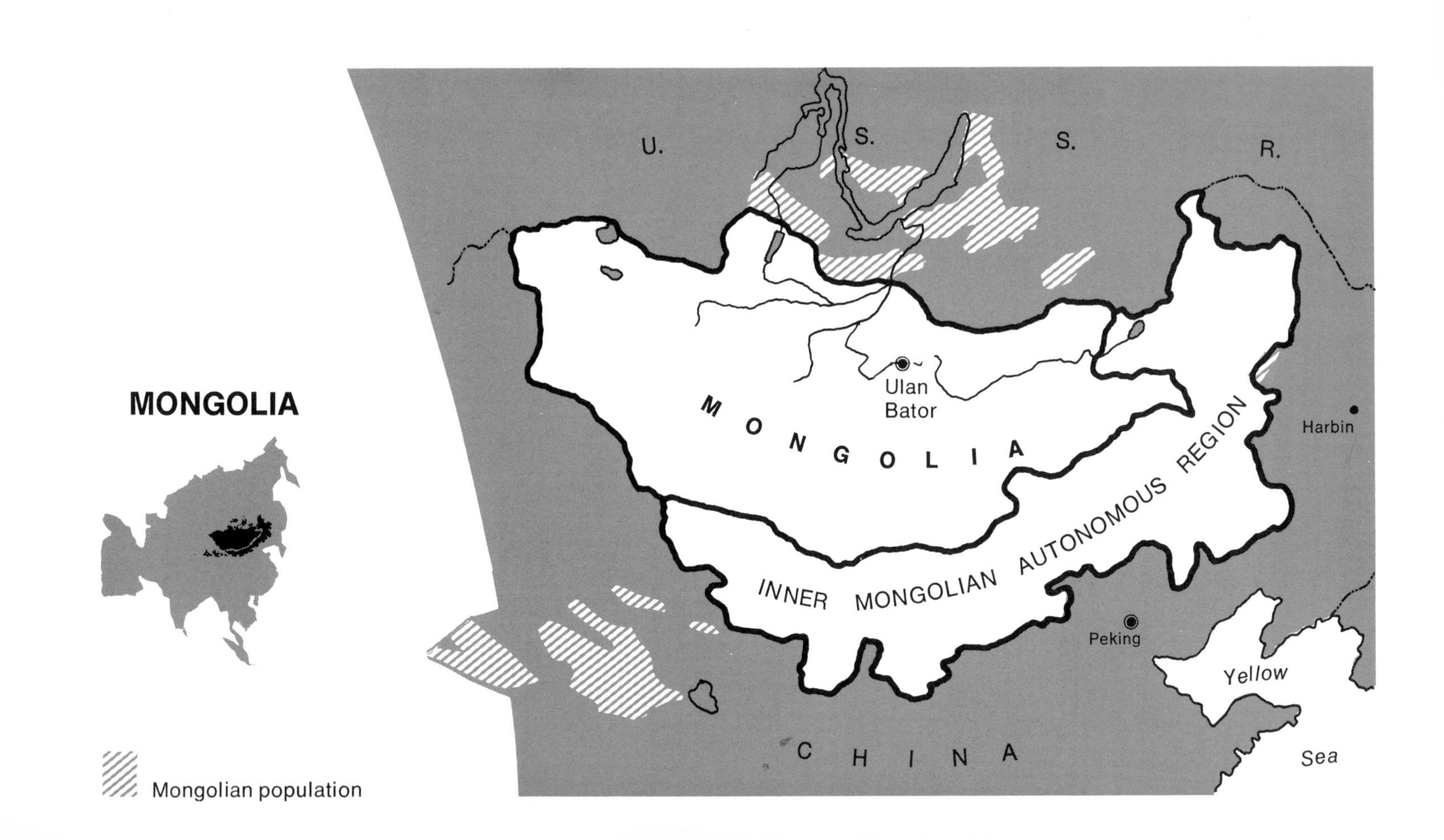
MONGOLIA
Mongolian population
U. S. S. R.
MONGOLIA
Ulan Bator
INNER MONGOLIAN AUTONOMOUS REGION
Harbin
Peking
Yellow Sea
CHINA

6

Mongolia

Harrison E. Salisbury

TO PARAPHRASE TOLSTOY, every divided country resembles every other divided country more than any unified country. But each has its own peculiar divisions, its own special problems.

Nowhere is this more striking than in Mongolia. Here is a nation unusually fragmented, divided not only into two major segments but also with a substantial portion of its people further subdivided into two more political entities.

Mongolia offers additional historical peculiarities. Indeed, it might be said that while Mongolia is a nation, it has never really been a state, at least not in the modern sense. The major division of the country is not a by-product of recent great-power struggles—although these are reflected sharply in the current Mongol situation—but originated in the deep past. In fact, objective analysis suggests that division and separation have been more characteristic of the Mongols than unity. Division seems almost to have been a natural trait flowing inevitably out of the Mongols' nomadic way of life.

The Mongols are perhaps the most vigorous of the successive nomadic peoples to arise in the great inner steppe and plateau grasslands which lie in the heart of the Eurasian land mass—the heartland, as Mackinder called it. This area spawned a succession of aggressive, horseborne nomads whose incursions periodically engulfed much of Asia and spilled over into Europe—among them the Huns and the Scythians. Mongol history, as a recorded chronicle, dates from about the sixth century A.D., but it was only at the end of the twelfth century and the beginning of the thirteenth that the Mongols became unified under the remarkable Genghis Khan. Within the space of less than a century they brought most of the known world under their subjugation—China, India, all of Siberia, Central Asia, Persia, most of the Middle East, the Caucasus, Russia, and the fringes of Europe. In 1271 Kublai Khan took the throne of China as emperor; his sovereignty ran to Indochina, Tibet, the Persian Gulf, the coasts of the Black Sea, as well as Central Asia and Eastern Siberia.

In the six hundred years that followed, Mongol hegemony shrunk steadily, reaching nadir when the Manchu conquerors of China in the seventeenth and eighteenth centuries brought almost all the unruly Mongol tribal elements under their sway and launched the divide-and-rule policy which laid the foundation for today's splintered Mongol world—notably the major division which still persists between Outer Mongolia and Inner Mongolia.

Inner Mongolia, south of the Gobi Desert and just north of the Great Wall of China, rests like a heavy necklace around the southern and eastern limits of Outer Mongolia. It fades vaguely into Manchuria with no natural delimited border, in contrast to the desert and mountains which separate it from the main body of Mongolia. Inner Mongolia has always been differentiated in degree from Outer Mongolia, largely because it is so closely connected to the natural trade routes and centers of China and because, to some extent under Chinese influence, sedentary agriculture and fixed residence in cities and villages has been a familiar way of life. Inner Mongolia fell to the Manchus as early as 1640, only a few years before the first aggressive exploratory Russian expeditions began to clash with the picket outposts of the Manchu empire along the Amur.

In the ensuing three hundred years, regardless of regime in Peking, Chinese policy has been to attach Inner Mongolia more and more closely to China. The Manchus brought the main body of the Outer Mongols (the Khalkas) under control in 1691 and the Oirat Mongols, who inhabit the western and northern Mongol reaches, in 1754. But the Manchus were careful to maintain separate rule for Inner Mongolia and Outer Mongolia and also to divide their overlordship of the Khalkas and Oirats, carefully encouraging tribal quarrels.

There are two other important groups of Mongols—the Buryats and the Uryanghai—leaving out of consideration the Kalmyks who reside for the most part on the lower Volga in the USSR, separated by thousands of miles from their fellow nationals. Both the Buryats and the Uryanghai fell under Russian domination. The Buryats are located largely east of Irkutsk and south and east of Lake Baikal. They were incorporated into the Russian empire in the late seventeenth and early eighteenth centuries under the Nerchinsk Treaty of 1689 and the Kyakhta Treaty of 1728 between the Russians and the Chinese. The Uryanghai or Tannu-Tuva Mongols occupy a remote mountain-guarded fastness tucked in at the northwest angle of Mongolia, just north of the Sinkiang-Russia-Mongolia corner. Because of its remoteness, difficulty of access, and the small number of Russians who found their way there, Uryanghai remained under nominal Chinese sovereignty until the eve of World War I. Then, gradually and informally, it was incorporated into the Russian empire where it remains to this day.

The total number of Mongols in these four political divisions is about 2.6 million, divided as follows: Outer Mongolia, 1.2 million (in a total population of 1.3 million); Inner Mongolia, 1.2 million (in a total population of 13 million); Buryat Autonomous Republic, USSR, 150,000 (in a total population of 850,000); Tannu Tuva Autonomous Republic, USSR, 110,000 (in a total population of 220,000).

In addition there are 200,000 to 300,000 Mongols scattered in small numbers in various other administrative divisions of the USSR, chiefly the Ust-Ordya and Aga Buryat National Okrugs and the Kalmyk Autonomous Republic, and in the Sinkiang-Uighur Autonomous Region of China.

The most important unit of the Mongols is obviously the Mongolian People's Republic, or Outer Mongolia. This is the only Mongol state with even nominal independence. It also is the only grouping where the population is almost entirely Mongol (97 percent). Outer Mongolia embarked on its quasi-independent course in 1911 when, with a good deal of diplomatic and moral support from Imperial Russia, it declared its independence from the Manchus (the Mongols had always contended they were subject to the Manchus, specifically, and not to the Chinese). The Mongol uprising succeeded, largely, because it coincided with the Chinese Revolution of 1911, and China was in no position to put it down.

The Russians supported the new Mongol autonomous government which, in form, was a theocracy, headed by Jebtsun Damba Khutukhtu, the chief lama, a profligate, corrupt, but astute leader who ruled as the head of a kind of junta of national unity. With the outbreak of the Bolshevik revolution in 1917 and the end of World War I, Mongolia fell into virtual anarchy, alternately occupied and fought over by White Russian adventurers, Japanese, and Chinese. Finally, with the aid of the Soviet Red Army, a Mongol Communist Movement headed by the national hero, Sukhe Bator, succeeded in establishing power. The modern state was founded November 1, 1921. It retained its theocratic form with Jebtsun Damba as nominal king-lama but power was in the hands of Sukhe Bator, his communist-led army, and his Communist party, strongly supported by the Soviet Union. With the death of Jebtsun Damba in 1924, a formal People's Republic was established and the nominal royalist-Buddhist trappings were dropped.

Sukhe Bator died in 1923 (amid suspicions of poisoning still kept alive in Ulan Bator) and his place was taken by Choibalsan who emerged as a kind of Mongolian Stalin, ruling until 1952 when he died of cancer in Moscow. Mongolia won diplomatic recognition from the Soviet Union in 1921, but in 1924 technical Chinese sovereignty was acknowledged in the Soviet-Chinese treaty signed on May 31 of that year. This anomolous situation prevailed until Chiang Kai-shek signed a new treaty with Stalin on August 14, 1945, acknowledging the independence of Outer Mongolia.

After a plebescite in October 1945, the Chinese Nationalist government accepted Mongolia's independence and announced its readiness to establish diplomatic relations. Nationalist China supported Mongolia's application for membership in the United Nations in 1946 but opposed it in 1947. Later on, Nationalist China withdrew its acceptance of Mongolian independence and insisted on China's traditional position of sovereignty over Mongolia.

The Soviet Union's relationship with Mongolia during these years became closer and closer, at least in part as a result of Japan's military activity in Manchuria and on the borders of Mongolia. Russia and Mongolia entered into a defense agreement in 1934, a defense treaty in 1936, and conducted joint operations against the Japanese near Khalkingol, in eastern Mongolia, in the summer of 1939. There, under Marshal Georgi K. Zhukov, a decisive victory was scored over the Japanese.

The rise of Communist China produced a new era in Mongol relations. Mao Tse-tung formally adhered to China's previous recognition of Mongol independence in connection with the signing of the Sino-Russian treaty of February 14, 1950. However, Mao made this acknowledgment only after first seeking unsuccessfully—according to Premier Y. Tsedenbal of Mongolia—to persuade Stalin to permit Mongolia to rejoin the Chinese sphere of influence.

The Mongolian People's Republic has an area of 1,565,000 square kilometers with a maximum length from east to west of 2,400 kilometers and a width of 1,260 kilometers from north to south. It is equal in size to Japan, Afganistan, and Burma together. It has 3,005 kilometers of frontier with the USSR and 4,373 with China. The country is largely mountainous and its average altitude is 1,580 meters above sea level. The capital, Ulan Bator, has grown with great rapidity in recent years; in 1968 the population was estimated to number 261,900, including residents of the surrounding region. In other words, more than 21 percent of the national population lives in or around the capital.

The economy of the Mongolian People's Republic is typical of that of the socialist bloc: industry is entirely in the hands of the central government, while agriculture is divided between state-owned and operated enterprises and collective farms closely modeled after the Soviet example. The principal economic differences from the Soviet Union stem from the fact that Mongolia is still largely a land of herdsmen, existing on the traditional grazing of sheep and raising of horses. The ratio of livestock per person in Mongolia is about 22 per individual—the bulk of the animals being sheep and horses. Grain economy and sedentary agriculture have been introduced, largely at Russian insistence, with the result that Mongolia is now said to be self-sufficient in grain and flour and capable of exporting a small surplus to the Soviet Union. Latest estimates of Mongolia's foreign trade indicate that 99 percent of it is conducted with communist countries, 90 percent of the total being with members of

Comecon. The Soviet Union accounts for 80 percent of Mongolia's trade turnover. Apparently a small trade continues with China. Mongolian trade with the noncommunist world is insignificant.

Traditionally, Outer Mongolia's principal relations were with Russia, with China and, particularly, with their fellow Mongols of Inner Mongolia and Tibet. Tibet is the traditional cultural and religious pole of all Mongols, linked as they are to Lhasa not only by "yellow" Buddhism but also by a common literary and cultural past. Nomadic Mongols traditionally moved with almost complete freedom over the mountain, plateau, and steppe region, traversing the Gobi Desert on pilgrimages to Lhasa or journeys to Inner Mongolia trading centers. This freedom of travel and intercourse persisted through the 1930s (except as interdicted by the Japanese) and was resumed with considerable freedom after World War II.

The cultural intercourse of the Mongols began to be impeded as early as the 1930s when the Russians introduced Cyrillic alphabets in place of the traditional vertical script (based on Tibetan) in those Mongol regions under Russian control—notably Tannu Tuva and Buryat Mongolia. In 1940 and 1941 decrees were introduced in Outer Mongolia to replace the traditional vertical script with a new Cyrillic alphabet. The war prevented the immediate implementation of the new alphabet, but in 1946 it was introduced into the schools and newspapers, and by 1950 it had become universal. Since the traditional script was retained in Inner Mongolia and, of course, in Tibet, the employment of Cyrillic in major Mongolian regions had the effect of dividing the people culturally.

Until after World War II there was relatively little economic development of Outer Mongolia. Nor was there any pressure to socialize agriculture and industry. The country remained, for the most part, as it long had been, engaged in nomadic grazing on the traditional pattern of clans and extended families. The only economic interest that the Soviet Union had shown in the area was in the utilization of Mongolia as a remount base for the provision of horses to the Red Army and as a source for providing meat and leather to the Far Eastern military forces. A railroad was built connecting eastern Mongolia with the Trans-Siberian Railway, but there was no link to China since, in Soviet eyes, Mongolia was basically a buffer against possible Japanese attack on Siberia and, therefore, not a region in which capital expenditure should be encouraged.

The victory in World War II, which eliminated Japanese influence and Japanese threat from the area and saw the rise of Communist China, brought profound changes to the Mongol world.

Inner Mongolia had been brought largely under Japanese control during the 1930s. The Japanese at first encouraged Mongol nationalism and Inner Mongolian Pan-Mongol sentiments but quickly disappointed them by imposing a basically Japanese regime.

With the proclamation of the Chinese Communist regime on October 1, 1949, Inner Mongolia became an Autonomous Region. Actually, the administrative area had been established as early as 1947—even before the whole of China was brought under communist control. It embraced an area of 1.3 million square kilometers before some recent and not completely elucidated changes. Before these changes the population had risen rapidly from 9.2 million in 1953 to something over 13 million. The capital is Huhehot; the principal city is Paotow, an important industrial center, locale of a big iron-and-steel complex, and site of some of China's nuclear facilities.

As originally set up, Inner Mongolia included some western areas of Manchuria, part of Jehol and Chahar, most of Suiyuan, and parts of Ningsia. This broad territory tended to dilute the Mongol component of the Inner Mongolian Autonomous Region. In the last two years, however, about one-third of western Inner Mongolia apparently has been shifted to two other administrative districts—Kansu Province and Ninghsia Hui Autonomous Region. At the same time, three of the eastern districts of Inner Mongolia were transferred to Heilungkiang, Kirin, and Liaoning Provinces. These transfers are believed to have reduced the territory of Inner Mongolia by nearly 50 percent and population has been cut almost to this extent. While a number of Mongols now live outside their Autonomous Region, the balance between Mongols and Chinese within the region probably is more equitable than formerly.

The economic and political system of Inner Mongolia differs from that of Outer Mongolia as does that of China from the Soviet Union. Inner Mongolian industry is organized much the same as that of Outer Mongolia, all being state owned and directed. Agriculture in Inner Mongolia, however, is based on the Chinese commune system which groups a number of individual farming cooperatives, including both sedentary farming and nomadic grazing, into one commune which also includes small industries and small towns and villages. The total population of a commune may range from 40 to 100 to 1,000 or even larger.

The establishment of the People's Republic gave a substantial impetus to Pan-Mongol sentiment. Although China policy in Inner Mongolia was carefully calculated to balance if not submerge Mongol nationals in a Han Chinese majority, China actively promoted contacts between Inner Mongols and Outer Mongols. The Inner Mongolian press continued to employ the traditional script and Inner Mongolian newspapers and books were actively circulated in Outer Mongolia.

The Chinese encouraged Mongol veneration of Genghis Khan (in direct contradiction to the Russians who excoriate Genghis Khan because of his scourge of Russia). They built a great shrine at Edzhen Khoro in Inner Mongolia to house the remains of Genghis Khan. Although there is much doubt as to whether these are, in fact, authentic remains, they are so regarded by the Mongols and the shrine was designed to attract Outer Mongol pilgrimages. The traditional Mongol pilgrimages to Lhasa were also encouraged—until the Dalai Lama fled Tibet in 1959 and the whole region was sealed off by the Chinese.

At the same time the Chinese embarked on an active diplomatic program of aid and friendship toward Outer Mongolia. An agreement was made under which 10,000 Chinese laborers were sent into Mongolia to work on construction projects in 1956, and these numbers increased to a maximum of 40,000 by 1959. The Chinese gave Outer Mongolia a 160-million-ruble grant-in-aid at the same time and followed this up with 300 million rubles in loans. The Chinese actively encouraged enlargement of Mongol-Chinese trade, sent many specialists and experts to assist Mongol economy, and encouraged young Mongols to study in Chinese universities and higher educational institutions.

These activities were carried out beginning in 1955–56 and reached a peak in 1959. During the same period the Soviet military presence in Mongolia was largely eliminated. The Chinese stressed cultural and ethnic ties between the Inner Mongols and the Outer Mongols. Ulanfu, a Mongol and head of Inner Mongolia from its foundation until the later stages of the Cultural Revolution, took a leading role in these activities.

During this period there developed within Outer Mongolia two overlapping movements. One was a Pan-Mongol movement which spoke openly but not officially in favor of uniting the Mongols of Buryat Mongolia, Outer Mongolia, Inner Mongolia, and Tannu Tuva. The other was a pro-Chinese faction which favored closer Mongol relations with China, in part as a counterbalance against the Russians, thus giving Mongolia greater independence, and in part on the theory that China was more likely to support establishment of a Greater Mongolia.

These Mongol hopes seem largely founded on wishful thinking. The idea that the Russians would have been prepared under any circumstances to permit the creation of a Greater Mongolia incorporating additional Mongol areas from the USSR seems most unreal. Soviet policy with regard to Tannu Tuva, for example, had made clear since the early 1920s that no aggrandizement of Outer Mongolia would be permitted. Soviet agents had been active in the establishment of a quasi-independent Tannu Tuva in the 1920s, and every effort either from the Tannu Tuvan or the Mongol side toward amalgamation was decisively thwarted. If any doubt had arisen as to Soviet attitudes in the 1950s it was dispelled by Soviet action in 1958. At that time, the name of the Buryat Mongolian Autonomous Republic was formally changed to the Buryat Autonomous Republic in order to deemphasize its link with Mongolia and emphasize its separateness.

The flirtation within the Outer Mongolian government and party with dreams of Pan-Mongolism and with utilizing the Chinese as a balancing power against the Soviet Union was short-lived. By 1959 the Russians had made clear to the Ulan Bator government that they would not tolerate anything other than 100 percent support of the Soviet line. Two quick purges of the Mongol party were carried out in 1962 and 1963 to emphasize this point.

By this time the Sino-Soviet split had emerged into the open and Mongolia had become a major field of contention between the Russians and the Chinese. The Russians went out of their way to demonstrate that there was no room for Pan-Mongolism (or even for any strong Mongol nationalism) under the prevailing conditions of Sino-Soviet enmity.

The first of the Mongolian purges coincided with the eight hundredth anniversary of the birth of Genghis Khan. Outer Mongolian celebration of the event occurred at the purported birthplace of Genghis Khan at Delem Boldog where speeches were given and a monument was unveiled. On the other side of the line, in Inner Mongolia, celebrations attended by 30,000 Mongols were held at the Edzhen Khoro mausoleum where the putative remains of Genghis had been placed.

This provoked a violent outburst from the Russians who not only viewed Genghis Khan as national enemy and devastator of the Russian land but as a symbol around whom contemporary Mongols might rally. They attacked the whole idea of the celebration and Tomor-Ochir, the member of the Mongol Politburo responsible for the observances, was dismissed together with a number of other high officials. Changes were also made in the Mongol military high command, and the Russians took steps to strengthen their collaboration with the Mongol military establishment which had, of course, been under virtual Soviet control for many years. A year later a further purge resulted in the elimination of Luvsantserengin Tsende, who had long been number-two man to Premier Tsedenbal. He, too, was dismissed for "nationalistic ideas."

These actions effectively eliminated from the Mongol hierarchy all known important advocates of Pan-Mongolism and, presumably, all suspected sympathizers with China or individuals who hoped to utilize the Sino-Soviet differences to promote Mongolian national aims.

At the same time, sharp restrictions on border movements were imposed. These effectively ended all contacts of any nature between Outer Mongols and Inner Mongols. And with the deepening of tension between Russia and China, all Mongol students were withdrawn from China; ordinary cultural exchanges were suspended; trade came to a virtual standstill; and diplomatic contacts were sharply reduced. By 1966 only a handful of the Chinese labor brigades sent to Mongolia to assist Mongolian development remained, and they had been isolated from the Mongol population, being housed in camps and installations surrounded with barbed wire and guarded by Mongol sentries. Many buildings which the Chinese had started remained unfinished and virtually abandoned.

Only one event ran counter to the deepening isolation of Outer Mongolia from Inner Mongolia and China. At the close of 1962 the Chinese suddenly announced the settlement, in principle, of all frontier questions between Outer Mongolia and the People's Republic. The agreement was signed December 26, 1962, just a day after a similar agreement was signed between China and Pakistan. Premier Tsedenbal went to Peking for the ceremony. Premier Chou En-lai signed for the Chinese. The agreement did not mean that the frontier had actually been delimited but that this process would take place under an agreed procedure. So far as is known, however, the actual surveying of the frontier has never occurred.

With the deepening tensions between Russia and China no meaningful moves toward collaboration on the side of the Mongols either in Outer Mongolia or Inner Mongolia have occurred. In fact, just the contrary has transpired. The Outer Mongolian frontier has become a line of contention with the Chinese. On several occasions, according to Premier Tsedenbal, Chinese military units have crossed over into Outer Mongolian territory and maintained themselves for substantial periods of time. There have been repeated incidents concerning the operation of the Peking–Ulan Bator railroad (the link to Peking was completed in 1956, that to the Soviet Union in 1949).

In the polemics between Russia and her allies and the Chinese, Premier Tsedenbal has been, perhaps, the most aggressive spokesman for the Soviet side, attacking the Chinese and specifically condemning them not only for a chauvinistic attitude toward Outer Mongolia but for "Han nationalism" in their treatment of Mongols in Inner Mongolia and other Mongol regions in the People's Republic.

Since 1969 the situation has been further aggravated by overt military tensions along the Mongol-Chinese frontier. Reacting to border incidents on the Amur and the Ussuri, the Russians in the spring of 1969 began to shift very large numbers of military forces not only to the Soviet-Chinese border but also into Mongolia. The precise numbers in Mongolia have not been revealed, but estimates run as high as 200,000 to 300,000 troops. The total size of the Soviet military establishment on the Chinese borders, including forces in eastern Kazakhstan, adjacent to Sinkiang, is now estimated at approximately 1 million men.

The Soviet command in Mongolia now comprises nuclear missile emplacements, rocket troops, jet fighter squadrons, and many mobile armored units. Permanent bases and installations have been built south of Ulan Bator and in the vicinity of the Chinese frontier and, particularly, in the easternmost projection of Mongolia, east of Choibalsan, in the region that was the staging and jump-off point of the Soviet attack on the Japanese in Manchuria at the end of World War II.

The positioning of the Soviet forces suggests that the Soviet high command would, in case of war, operate against the Chinese along a pattern similar to their successful blitz of the Japanese.

The Mongolian armed forces, in this situation, appear to have been placed under joint command of the Russians, and integrated plans for their deployment have been drawn up.

The Chinese who remain in Ulan Bator have been even further

isolated. The People's Republic has a very large embassy and compound located close to the center of the city and second in size only to the Soviet establishment. However, personnel, which once numbered 500 or 600, appear to have been cut back to less than 100. Curiously, a few hundred Chinese laborers still work in Mongolia, puttering away at small tasks—making repairs to embassy buildings, constructing small additions to hotels, and engaging in other trivial work. Why they are still there no one seems to know.

On the other side of the frontier there is a rather parallel situation. Inner Mongolia was the scene of considerable turbulence during the Chinese Cultural Revolution and, obviously because of its frontier nature, has been the object of tightened Chinese security precautions. Prior to 1967, Inner Mongolia constituted a separate defense region. In that year it became a military district, controlled directly from Peking. When the three eastern provinces of Inner Mongolia were detached in 1969, they became part of the general Manchuria defense district, probably because of better communications. The same kind of defense consideration is believed to lie behind the recent detachment of western areas of Inner Mongolia.

However, Inner Mongolia's military importance as a frontier region and an obvious initial target of Soviet attack has virtually eliminated—for the time being—the stimulation of pro-Mongol or Pan-Mongol sentiments in that area. The violent passions of the Cultural Revolution with their stress on Chinese nationalism have worked in the same direction and the elimination of Ulanfu, the leading Mongol in the Chinese power structure, has been a further blow to Mongol aspirations.

Inner Mongolia is now a zone of high Chinese security. Few foreign visitors are permitted to travel there, and for practical purposes there is no contact by Mongols in the Autonomous Region with Mongols elsewhere. The only conclusion possible as a result of the Sino-Soviet friction is that, for the time being, the Mongol national cause has been paralyzed on all fronts.

There is, however, evidence that it is by no means dead. Outer Mongolia, with tenacious stubbornness, has persisted in its course of strengthening its national presence. It campaigned arduously for admission to the United Nations and achieved that goal in October 1961. It would have won diplomatic recognition by the United States at the same time had it not been for a complex maneuver carried out by Nationalist China. A low-key campaign to win U.S. recognition has been carried on since that time. It again came close to success in the first years of the Nixon administration but the idea was put aside by Dr. Henry Kissinger for fear that it might in some way complicate the elaborate maneuvering then in progress for establishment of de facto (if not diplomatic) relations between the United States and the People's Republic.

Balked in this goal, Outer Mongolia has assiduously extended its diplomatic contacts with other powers. It has established relations with

Britain, France, Japan, and most major European countries as well as the countries of Asia and Africa. Gradually, foreign missions are beginning to be established in Ulan Bator in addition to those of the socialist bloc.

Mongolia has also been active in seeking to attract occasional international meetings to Ulan Bator—notably a United Nations women's meeting and two International Congresses of Mongologists, bringing to Outer Mongolia the leading scholars in the Mongol field from all over the world, particularly from the Soviet Union, United States, Japan, Great Britain, and Germany. The first of these meetings, held in 1959, was marked by severe tensions, probably because it was the first international gathering ever held in Ulan Bator and also, perhaps, because it was involved in some fashion in the intra-Mongol meaneuvering over the cause of Pan-Mongolism. Chinese scholars attended this meeting. The second Congress, held in 1969, had no Chinese participants. The importance of these assemblies in Mongol eyes is that they provide evidence of an independent Mongolian presence. Thus, they help support the cause of Mongol nationalism and, indirectly, that of Pan-Mongolism. Scholarly evidence of a unified field of Mongol studies provides at least an underpinning to the notion of a single Mongol state. Moreover, the meetings provide an arena for meeting Mongol specialists not only from the Western world but also from the various divisions within the Soviet sphere of influence. The Mongols are well aware of the close links between culture and nationhood.

There seems no likelihood for any early improvement in relations between the divided segments of the Mongol world. They are inextricably caught within the upper and lower millstones of the Russian-Chinese conflict. Even if relations between Moscow and Peking were idyllic, the prospects of achieving anything like unity in the Mongol world would be remote.

From the Soviet side, the policy of division of the Mongols has been practised from the early 1920s, despite the fact that during the early revolutionary period there was active Pan-Mongolism among many leading communist Mongols. But the care with which Tannu Tuva and Buryat Mongolia were segregated from Outer Mongolia leaves no basis whatever for supposing any change in attitude is likely in Moscow—even if the Soviet-Chinese frontier should again become quiet.

Not only would the reuniting of Tannu Tuva and Buryat Mongolia to Outer Mongolia be contrary to Soviet policy with regard to the Mongols, but it would also be contrary to Soviet policy insofar as other minority peoples are concerned. While paying lip-service to minority rights and minority nationalities, Soviet policy taken as a whole has always been careful not to encourage nationalism to the point at which it might become divisive. Certainly, no Soviet government (except possibly for Lenin in the earliest revolutionary days) ever supported a policy which was inclined either to weaken the Soviet national union or lead in any way to its territorial diminution. The ferocity with which Moscow has opposed any acknowledgment of Chinese territorial claims, let alone even the most minor adjustments, provides ample support for this view.

Thus, so long as the Soviet Union is presently constituted, no territorial reunion of Mongols is likely to be assisted from the Moscow side. Indeed, the contrary is almost certain—deep opposition and swift resentment of any such aspirations.

From the Chinese side, the situation seems very similar. The Chinese, to be sure, would like to see Outer Mongolia revert to the Chinese sphere of influence. But there is nothing in the record either of the present regime or its Manchu predecessor which suggests that a unified Mongolia would be likely to emerge.

To an extent even exceeding that of the Russians, the Chinese Han mass has tended in recent years to overwhelm the Mongol minority in their traditional areas. The recent redivision of Inner Mongolia—just as the original incorporation into it of outside, non-Mongol areas—is not based on any principle of Mongol unity. On the contrary, it seems to be motivated entirely by security considerations. It has seemed to the Chinese consistently that their frontier is more secure if the Mongols are thoroughly watered down with large numbers of Han ethnics. This is not a new Chinese policy. It stems from the long centuries of Chinese experience in manipulating minorities along their frontiers. Divide-and-rule was always the Chinese principle in this situation. It still appears to be.

The position of Outer Mongolia and the ability of the Outer Mongols to manipulate the situation to their advantage and to increase their independence from their Soviet protectors is harshly restricted. No movement is possible under the present situation of Sino-Soviet tension; it would simply be interpreted by the Russians as a security threat and would be summarily repressed.

The ability of Ulan Bator to maneuver in the traditional manner of a small power menaced by a powerful neighbor is also limited because of the enormous domination of the country by Soviet economy and military. Not only is 80 percent of Mongolia's trade with Russia, but she also consistently runs an adverse trade balance with the Soviet Union of hundreds of millions of rubles. Periodically, this deficit is wiped off the books by the Russians. It constitutes a vast subsidy which is designed to keep the Mongols quiet. Mongolian political life is dominated almost equally by Soviet influence. Mongol young people are trained in Soviet universities and young party activists are graduates of Soviet party institutions. Every effort is made to quench nationalist aspirations, and these efforts seem to be successful.

Mongol hopes of reaching over the heads of the Russians and the Chinese to acquire some beneficial interest or influence on the part of states like Japan or the United States seem unrealistic. The likelihood of any major Japanese interest in Mongolia is remote. Interest by the United States would be only peripheral except in the event of very great tensions with the Soviet Union. But in such a situation the Russians are in a position simply to extinguish any kind of manifestation of Mongol sympathy except that which is securely anchored to Moscow.

Even during the period of declining Manchu power, Mongolia found itself unable to win independence from the Manchus until the whole Manchu state collapsed. And this was true despite repeated Russian intrigues during the later part of the nineteenth century and the early twentieth directed at detaching Mongolia. This does not augur well for any successful Mongol effort at independence or unity in the face of a strong Russia and a strong China.

This analysis suggests that only under two sets of circumstance is Pan-Mongolism likely to be successful. The first is in the event of a cataclysmic catastrophe which produced the dissolution of the Soviet state. This, like the disintegration of the Chinese empire, would free the Mongols to move toward ethnic unity. Whether they might actually achieve it is another matter. Just as Outer Mongolia, Buryat Mongolia, and Tannu Tuva are firmly anchored in the Soviet world, so Inner Mongolia is possibly even more securely fixed in the Chinese. Nonetheless, such a cataclysm would set the stage for possible movement. (The breakup of the People's Republic would not provide the same opportunity. Inner Mongolia might then rejoin Outer Mongolia, but the combined whole would remain a protectorate of Moscow.)

The other eventuality which might assist the Mongols in achieving their aspiration would be a period of benign calm and goodwill affecting Sino-Soviet relations. There are suggestions that such a period may have occurred for two or three years after the death of Josef Stalin in 1953. At that time, large Soviet forces were withdrawn from Mongolia. So were many Soviet advisers. Collaboration between Outer Mongolia and Inner Mongolia was actively encouraged on both sides. There was even a brief revival of intercourse between Buryat Mongolia and Outer Mongolia. There have been a few hints—never confirmed officially—that the post-Stalin government in Moscow seriously considered permitting Outer Mongolia to revert to the Chinese sphere of influence. Or possibly even envisaged it as a neutral buffer zone. If such designs were harbored, they obviously were fleeting. And, in fact, even if Outer Mongolia had returned to the Chinese sphere at that time, even if it had been administratively linked to Inner Mongolia, it would still have been part of the People's Republic. And, judging by the subsequent course of events relating to Inner Mongolia, it would not have won more than a tacit measure of national independence.

This is not, however, to suggest that such beneficial consequences might not flow from a prolonged period of warm and cordial relations between Russia and China. The stumbling block is that no such development seems at all likely. The hostility between the two states may, to be certain, moderate somewhat as years advance. But the underlying suspicion, fear, and aggression are not likely to vanish to the extent that would be necessary to bring about a new era in the heartland of Asia. A far more realistic assessment is that the Mongols in their divided and separate compartments will continue in the foreseeable future to remain separate, alienated, and, in effect, little more than pawns, albeit valued ones, on the chessboard of the great powers.

Part 2

PARTITIONED COUNTRIES

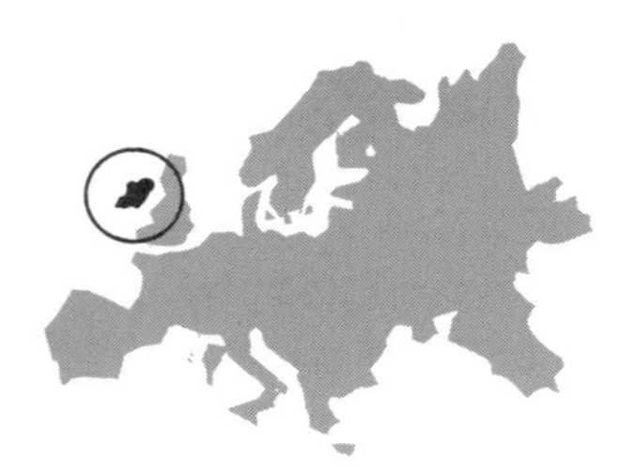

IRELAND

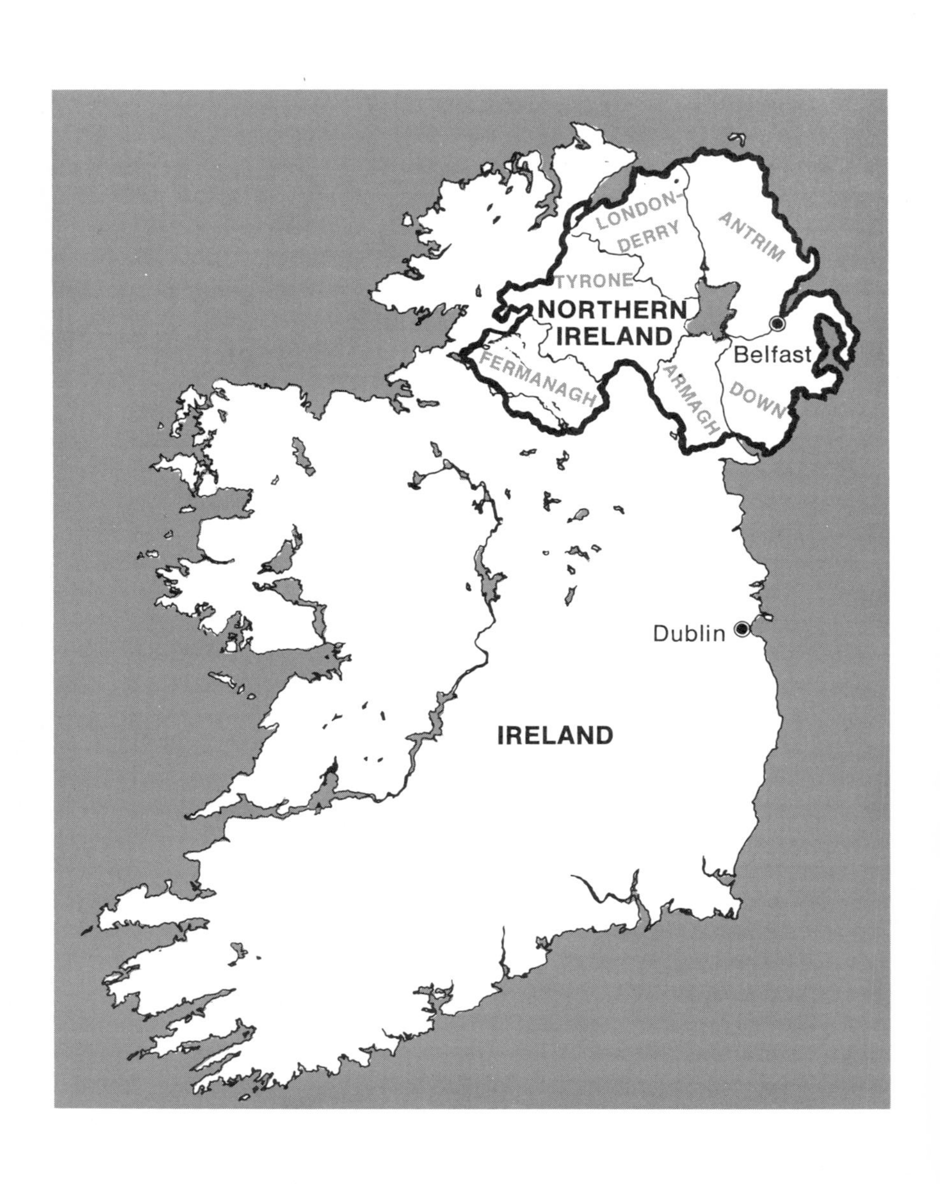

LONDON-
DERRY
ANTRIM
TYRONE
NORTHERN
IRELAND
FERMANAGH
ARMAGH
DOWN
Belfast
Dublin
IRELAND

7

Ireland

Richard Ned Lebow

IRELAND HAS BEEN DIVIDED for over fifty years, twice as long as either Germany or Korea.* As of 1973, three-quarters of the population of Ireland had been born after the partition and virtually all the leaders associated with that event have passed from the scene. Over the years, the division appeared to lose much of its political salience for people on both sides of the border. Official relations between the Republic and Northern Ireland were amicable and were actually marked by close cooperation with respect to tourism, economic planning, and security. However, events since 1968 have reversed the trend toward rapprochement and have rekindled passions that are no less intense than those of fifty years ago. What accounts for this dramatic reversal which has brought Ireland once again to the brink of civil war? What is the likely outcome of this renewed strife? Must we draw the conclusion that the trauma of division is immune to the soothing balm of time, or are the circumstances and problems of Ireland's division in some way unique?

Historical Background

The "Irish Problem" dates from 1167, the year of the Norman invasion of Ireland. For the next eight hundred years the British attempted, with varying degrees of success, to complete the conquest. Had they succeeded, the Irish, like the Welsh, would probably have become "West Britons," and

* A glossary has been provided in the appendix.

Irish problems would have been merely a footnote to European history. Ireland was never conquered, however. She was subjugated but not subdued, occupied but not assimilated; and the continuous antagonism between an insecure alien conqueror and a resentful native population gave rise to an escalating spiral of resistance and repression which left a legacy of passion and hatred that has survived to this day.

Native resistance was not effectively overcome until the reigns of the later Tudors and the Stuarts when large armies were dispatched to Ireland, which had become even more hostile to the Crown by reason of the religious differences arising from the Reformation. The British expropriated Catholic estates, subsidized the Protestant colonization of Ulster, and finally, under Cromwell, ravaged the country in a genocidal war and ultimately established effective control over all but the most outlying areas.

The key event in this final conquest was the Battle of the Boyne (1690) at which William of Orange decisively defeated an army of native Irish and Anglo-Irish Catholics led by James II, who had recently been deposed from the throne of England. This battle led to a radical redistribution of political power in Ireland which, despite rebellions in 1798, 1848, 1867, and 1916, endured almost intact until independence in 1921. Known as the Williamite Settlement, it was an attempt by a still insecure colonial regime to guarantee against future rebellion. The native Irish (i.e., the Catholic Irish with whom they were now more or less synonymous) were deprived of their remaining estates, prohibited from educating their children in Catholic schools, forbidden to own land or engage in the professions or trades, and were debarred from civil service and the Catholic religion itself was outlawed. However, it should be noted that neither the ban on Catholicism nor the right of Catholics to own land was ever effectively enforced. These acts, collectively referred to as the Penal Laws, helped to reduce the native population to a poor and illiterate peasantry outside the writ of the constitution and thus even more resentful of British rule. By the first part of the nineteenth century the most onerous aspects of the Penal Laws had been repealed; however, the mass of the Irish peasantry were generally conceded to be still the most destitute in all of Europe.

The English colonial elite, usually referred to as "the Ascendancy," was concentrated along the eastern coast of Ireland and in the cities of Dublin and Cork. Few soldiers, settlers, or administrators lived in the western, more rural part of the country, but their numbers were gradually reinforced during the seventeenth and eighteenth centuries by retired soldiers and civil servants who received large grants of Irish land as recompense for their services to the Crown. By 1800, four-fifths of the land of Ireland was in the hands of the Ascendancy, among whom were a powerful class of landed gentry allied to the Tory party in England. The Anglo-Irish elite as a whole felt neither Irish in culture, religious association, nor politics, and the gulf separating them from the native Irish was similar in most respects to the division between colonists and natives in other European colonial outposts. In fact, many of the gentry were absentee landlords who rarely, if ever, set foot in Ireland. Their estates were managed by overseers whose sole responsibility was often to extract as much profit as possible for the owners.

Given the geographic concentration of the Ascendancy as well as their numerical inferiority—they were never more than 10 percent of the total population—the government always sought to strengthen the power of forces loyal to it by encouraging British colonization of the more rural areas. The most ambitious and successful scheme was implemented in Ulster which, at the beginning of the seventeenth century, was the most backward and least British of the four provinces of Ireland. The government, anxious to break the hold of Gaelic culture, chartered the "Plantation of Ulster" and offered large grants of land to "undertakers" who were to recruit and finance settlement. The City of London, for example, undertook to plant the country of Coleraine in return for extensive economic privileges. Derry was renamed Londonderry (although all Catholics and many Protestants still refer to it as Derry) and large tracts of land were set aside for colonization by Londoners. However, it proved more profitable to lease the land back to the original inhabitants at high rents. While this policy was profitable to English investors, it was unsatisfactory to the government because few native Irish were driven from the province. Colonization was successful only in eastern Ulster, beyond the Bann River, where large numbers of Scots, anxious to resettle for both religious and economic reasons, emigrated to Ireland. Ulster thus became a patchwork quilt composed of Presbyterian Scots-Irish, Catholic natives, and above them both, a small Anglo-Irish elite. The Scots-Irish were distinct in religion and culture from both the native Irish and the Anglo-Irish and became a third force in Irish politics. They ultimately came to hold the balance of power between the other two factions, locked as they were in adversary roles.

Throughout the seventeenth century the Scots-Irish supported the British government because of both the religious passions of the time, and the very real fear of the Irish in their midst. But by the end of the eighteenth century, the beginnings of industrialization and the ensuing economic transformation of Ulster threatened to disrupt the alliance. Ulster Protestants, mostly independent farmers, small businessmen, and merchants, suffered from the same narrow mercantile policy that led to rebellion in America; in fact, the American Revolution found considerable support in Ulster. Some Ulstermen, irked by these economic restrictions and fired by the radical zeal of the times, concluded that the real interest of Ulster Protestants lay in alliance with the emerging Catholic middle class against the Ascendancy and the British government. This sentiment was by no means limited to a few intellectuals and was responsible, in part, for the rebellion of 1798, and later, for widespread Protestant support for Catholic Emancipation which was finally achieved in 1829. The dream of a united and independent Ireland in which communal differences were secondary to the political and cultural bond of Irish nationality continued to motivate many Ulstermen, among them great Irish nationalists Henry Grattan, William Smith O'Brien and Charles Stewart Parnell. But for the majority of Ulster Protestants, religion remained the dominant issue. This ancient passion, aggravated by working-class competition with Catholics for jobs and housing, kept the masses of Ulstermen loyal to the Crown and adamant in their opposition to Irish Catholic demands for reform, home rule, and later, independence.

The Struggle for Independence

By 1820, the relaxation and eventual abolition of the Penal Laws, together with the industrial development of Belfast and Dublin, led to the growth of a small but articulate Catholic middle class. Their leaders, shrewdly exploiting the widespread peasant discontent, pressured Westminster for reforms aimed at improving the Catholic position. Emancipation (1829), which had permitted Catholics to hold political office (though at the price of disenfranchising the masses), led to demands for disestablishment of the Church of Ireland (achieved in 1869), land reform (1870 and 1881), and Home Rule—the repeal of the Act of Union of 1801 and the restoration of a parliament to Ireland. The agitation for these reforms was ultimately based on a threat to escalate rural violence but was in practice generally limited to peaceful demonstrations and parliamentary appeals. The British response to Irish demands was a mixture of repression and minimal concession that served only to undermine the position of moderate Irish leaders. It helped to foster the development of revolutionary nationalism characterized by such groups as Young Ireland (1840s), the Fenians (1860s) and later, Sinn Fein (literally, "We Ourselves"). These organizations rejected any form of assimilation into British culture or political life and espoused national independence, to be achieved by revolution if necessary.

Despite the rise of revolutionary conspiracies, the Catholic moderates appeared to maintain the upper hand in the struggle to win support from public opinion. The Irish Parliamentary party, which controlled most of the Irish seats in the House of Commons, sought to hold the balance of power between the two British parties and trade their votes for Home Rule. These efforts met with success when Prime Minister William Gladstone, dependent upon the Irish for a majority, agreed to introduce Home Rule in 1886. The Home Rule Bill offered only a minimal measure of self-government but nevertheless aroused strong opposition within Gladstone's own Liberal party as well as united opposition from the Tories. It also evoked the threat of violent resistance by Ulster Protestants. The bill proved so divisive that Gladstone was deserted by a faction of his own party which crossed the aisle to join the Tories, now reconstituted as the Unionist party. Gladstone persisted, only to have the bill defeated in the House of Lords. A second Home Rule Bill, introduced in 1892, fared no better. The idea was not resurrected until 1910, when the Liberal government, led by Herbert Asquith, once again became dependent upon Irish parliamentary support, this time in its struggle to reform the House of Lords. In return, Asquith introduced the third Home Rule Bill in April 1912, the first to have any real chance of success because, in the interim, the veto power of the House of Lords had been curtailed. By rejecting a bill, the Lords could now only delay its passage for three consecutive sessions of the Commons. The introduction of the third Home Rule Bill proved to be the curtain raiser to a drama that threatened to destroy the very fabric of the British Constitution.

The Tories, still reeling from their bitter defeats over the Lloyd George budget and the reform of the House of Lords, saw Home Rule as a further threat to the diminishing prerogatives of their class. The Tory leadership decided to fight it, by extraparliamentary means if necessary. Their strategy was to encourage resistance in Ulster, and by raising the specter of civil war in Ireland, to coerce the government into dropping its support for the controversial measure. Much to the shock of Asquith, Bonar Law, leader of the Unionist party, went so far as to declare that "If Ulster resists by force, they would have the wholehearted support of the Unionists." [1] Although the Liberals dismissed this as a bluff, Ulstermen were very serious indeed and implemented measures required to make their threat a credible one. Under the forceful leadership of Edward Carson, a Dublin barrister, Ulster Protestants collected in excess of 50,000 signatures of individuals who pledged to resist Home Rule by force. Carson also organized the Ulster Volunteer Force (UVF), a paramilitary organization of about 100,000 men. The UVF drew its recruits from the Orange Lodges, received financial support from leading Belfast and London businessmen, and in a dramatic coup circumvented the British ban on the importation of weapons by landing 35,000 German rifles and 5,000,000 rounds of ammunition. By the end of 1913, Carson had both an army and shadow government which stood ready to take over the province on the day the government attempted to enforce Home Rule.

The threat of rebellion in Ulster was serious enough, but the government was shaken to its core by the revelation that the British Army was deeply implicated in the conspiracy. Asquith was outraged to learn from Sir Henry Wilson, director of Military Operations, that 40 percent of the officers were likely to defect to the side of the rebels in the event of civil war. Unkown to Asquith, both General Wilson and his superior, Field Marshal Roberts, were closely connected to the Orange cause and assisted Carson by suggesting names of retired officers to staff and train the UVF. They also supplied the force with advance intelligence about the government's plans for military moves against Ulster.

The UVF's successful defiance of the government aroused both the envy and militancy of the nationalists, who hastened to make their own military preparations. In October 1913 James Larkin and James Connolly of the Irish Transport Worker's Union organized their own paramilitary force, the Irish Citizen Army. Dedicated to the creation of a worker's republic, the leaders of the force nevertheless came to envisage national independence as the first step toward this goal. A second force, the Irish Volunteers, was organized by Catholic nationalists associated with the Gaelic League and Gaelic Athletic Association, both of which were hotbeds of nationalist sentiment. The Volunteers had no clearly defined policy but the Irish Republican Brotherhood, forerunner of the IRA, soon captured control of the force and envisaged it as the shock troops of the coming revolution.

The threat of a civil war in Ireland, with the army and Unionist party supporting the rebels, was not a situation Asquith regarded with equanimity. To forestall chaos, all the more disturbing in light of the deteriorating international situation, Herbert Asquith, David Lloyd George, and Winston Churchill sought out the leading protagonists and tried to arrange a compromise Home Rule Bill acceptable to all parties.

The most obvious compromise involved some kind of special status for Ulster. This had been envisaged by Macaulay as far back as 1833 but was first seriously mooted by Joseph Chamberlain in the 1880s when he employed partition as a tactic to demonstrate the impraticality of Home Rule. The idea was now resurrected by Churchill and Lloyd George as a possible means of averting civil war. However, the nationalists, laying claim to all of Ireland, found the idea unacceptable as did the Ulster Protestants for whom it meant betrayal of their fellow Unionists elsewhere in Ireland. Asquith nevertheless pursued the compromise scheme and in March 1914 persuaded the reluctant John Redmond, leader of the Irish Parliamentary party, to agree to an amendment of the Home Rule Bill stipulating that any Ulster country, by a vote of its parliamentary electors, could exclude itself for six years from the new Ireland after which it would be automatically brought in. Carson, speaking for the Unionists, flatly rejected the compromise. "We do not," he declared, "want sentence of death with a stay of execution for six years." [2] As the crisis deepened, it became clear that the Ulstermen were willing to sacrifice the rest of Ireland to the nationalists but would not budge with respect to Ulster. Asquith nevertheless incorporated the amendment in his bill, which was close to passage in the Commons in the early summer of 1914. At this juncture, King George, sympathetic to the plight of the Unionists, initiated a final attempt at mediation. He called a conference of the opposing leaders and asked them to consider the possibility of permanently excluding Ulster. The nationalists would not agree and the conference broke up on July 24. Passage of Home Rule and the expected civil conflict was forestalled only by the outbreak of war on the Continent in August.

War, Rebellion, Civil War, and Partition

Both Carson and Redmond pledged full support to the war effort and agreed to a compromise by which Home Rule became law but was accompanied by an act of suspension delaying its implementation for the duration of the conflict. The UVF was incorporated into the British Army and sent to France; in July 1916 it was all but destroyed in two days of fighting on the Somme. The Irish Volunteers also requested incorporation into the army as a regiment but were rebuffed by the War Office. Despite this affront, thousands of Irish nationalists enlisted in the British Army and Navy and fought in all theaters of the war. At home, the war stimulated the Irish economy and, in the opinion of most observers, Irish nationalists appeared to be willing to await the end of the war before renewing their demands for Home Rule. The more militant nationalists, already alienated from the Irish Parliamentary party, wanted independence, not limited self-government, and spurned Redmond's "collaboration" with Britain. These separatists were divided among themselves in ideology, organization, and tactics but cooperated in an attempt to discourage recruiting in Ireland. The extremists among them, the IRB and the Citizen Army, planned insurrection.

The date fixed for the rebellion was Easter Sunday, April 23, 1916. However, at the last minute the British Navy intercepted the German ship bringing arms to the rebels, thereby neutralizing effective Volunteer resistance in the provinces. Despite this setback, Pearse and Connolly decided to proceed, and the rebels, some 2,000 strong, occupied the center of Dublin without resistance. Pearse proclaimed a republic from the steps of the General Post Office and asked Irishmen to support the struggle for independence in the name of God and of the dead generations from which she receives her old tradition of nationhood. By the time the incredulous citizenry and authorities realized that an actual insurrection was in progress, the rebels were well entrenched, controlling the center of the city and some suburbs which they assiduously sought to fortify. The government, commanding only 1,200 troops in Dublin, hastened to bring in reinforcements; after a week of merciless artillery bombardment, they forced the surviving rebels to surrender.

Irish public opinion was hostile to the insurrection and the rebels' appeal to the country fell on deaf ears. In some areas Volunteers actually aided the police in rounding up suspects. However, the British government rapidly reversed this situation by executing fifteen of the rebels after summary court-martials. Connolly, badly wounded in the fighting, had to be propped up in a chair to face the firing squad. The British, in the words of George Bernard Shaw, were "canonizing their prisoners." Public anger at the rebels was quickly transformed into admiration for their idealism and courage. Asquith attempted to restore goodwill but the time for reconciliation had passed. The Easter Rebellion marked a turning point in modern Irish history because future Irish leaders, committed by the sacrifice of the rebels, could not settle for anything short of independence without invoking widespread resentment and loss of support. This became readily apparent in the first general election held after the war in December 1918. Sinn Fein, the political front of the IRB, contested every constituency and captured seventy-three seats. The Unionists won twenty-six and the Irish Parliamentary party was reduced to a mere six seats. The Republicans could now rightfully claim to speak for the majority of Irishmen.

The newly elected nationalists ignored Westminster and convened instead in Dublin in January 1919, where they proclaimed a republic and constituted themselves as the Dáil Éireann, the Assembly of Ireland. Eamon De Valera, a survivor of the Easter Rebellion, was elected president and promptly sent to the United States to plead for private and official support. British policy was marked by confusion and reflected a fear of alienating the United States where the Irish cause had received strong congressional support. As a result, the revolutionary government was free gradually to establish its control over most of Ireland. The Volunteers were reorganized as the Irish Republican Army and carried out assaults against the remaining bastions of British authority in Ireland. Effective British rule was soon limited to Ulster. There the Unionists had reorganized the UVF, which together with the B Specials, a Protestant militia financed by the British, was sufficient to overcome nationalist resistance. The Unionists equated Catholics with republicanism and sought to strengthen their hold on Ulster by driving Catholics from the province.

Lloyd George headed a coalition government that depended on British Unionist support and thus he felt compelled to reassert British authority in Ireland. He approved the imposition of martial law and dispatched troops to shore up the Royal Ulster Constabulary. By mid-1920, the pattern of ambush and counterattack had escalated into a full-scale war and Lloyd George, in need of more soldiers, created two special armies, the Auxiliaries and the infamous Black and Tans, so named for their uniforms. Both forces were recruited largely among ex-servicemen.

The war was essentially a struggle between two poorly controlled forces, each trying to disrupt the communications and morale of its opponent. The IRA claimed to have the support of the people, although this was often extracted at gunpoint, but they clearly profited from public reaction to the atrocities committed by the Black and Tans. The British government, faced with the choice of systematically conquering Ireland, which meant political suicide at home, or negotiating with the rebels, forcing the abandonment of publically proclaimed war aims, chose the latter course. A truce was concluded in July 1921, as a preliminary to treaty negotiations.

Prior to the truce, Lloyd George had tried to effect a political settlement by enacting a new Home Rule Bill (the Government of Ireland

Act, 1920) which became law in December of that year. The act, which became the fundamental law of Northern Ireland and from which de jure partition may be said to date, divided the island into "Northern Ireland," comprising six of the nine counties of Ulster, and "Southern Ireland," the remaining twenty-six counties. Each was to possess a bicameral legislature and a responsible ministry. The supremacy of the Westminster Parliament was to be preserved, and both Irelands were to elect representatives to it. Partition was not envisaged as permanent, and reunification could be effected by a simple vote of the two parliaments to merge. The act also authorized the creation of a Council of Ireland to be composed of representatives from both legislatures, to regulate national issues and to act as a possible bridge to reunification. The council was stillborn.

The Ulster Unionists disliked the surrender of their coreligionists to a Catholic government in the south but were won over by both the realization that Protestants would have a clear majority in Northern Ireland and the promise that Ulster would not be incorporated into the rest of Ireland without its consent. When elections were held in May 1921, Unionists fielded candidates, winning forty of fifty-two seats in the lower House. They promptly organized a government with Sir James Craig as prime minister.

Sinn Fein spurned Lloyd George's initiative and declared its implacable hostility to the northern regime. But it too contested the elections to demonstrate nationalist strength and won 124 of 128 seats in the south. Confident of public support, Sinn Fein accepted Lloyd George's offer to negotiate.

Lloyd George offered to concede Dominion status to the nationalists with the following reservations: Britain would maintain air and naval bases in the South; the Irish would have to limit the size of their army, maintain free trade with Britain, and contribute to the British war debt. De Valera rejected the terms as inconsistent with Irish sovereignty and the Dáil sent a new negotiating team headed by Michael Collins, Arthur Griffith, and Gavan Duffy. Lloyd George renewed his offer of Dominion status but two issues emerged as major obstacles to any agreement: the Irish would neither accept an oath of allegiance to the monarch as part of their constitution nor agree to the exclusion of the six northern counties from the new state. Lloyd George, by way of compromise, suggested a boundary commission to determine the preferences of Ulstermen and to draw the border accordingly. Reasoning that a plebiscite would award Tyrone and Fermanagh counties as well as parts of Armagh and Derry to the nationalists, making the North economically nonviable, and faced with Lloyd George's ultimatum to resume the war, Griffith and Collins persuaded their reluctant colleagues to accept the terms. The treaty, signed on December 6, 1921, created the Irish Free State, a Dominion within the British Empire but stipulated that "northern Ireland" should, by appeal of her legislature to the Crown, be permitted to remain outside the Free State and be governed according to the Act of 1920. This northern Ireland promptly did.

Postpartition Ireland

Throughout the nineteenth century nationalist ambitions for a united Ireland had been frustrated by Britain, whose power more than compensated for the numerical inferiority of the Unionist minority in Ireland. However, most British politicians realized that military might alone was unlikely to maintain permanent peace. Given the adamant refusal of Unionists to share power, and the equal unwillingness of the Catholic majority to accept inferior status, the situation moved toward a confrontation. Catholic Emancipation, Disestablishment, and land reform were all designed to forestall such conflict by attempting to placate Catholic opinion without, of course, evoking a violent Unionist response. But the need to appease Unionists meant that most reforms were halfway measures which only led to more far-reaching demands by Catholics and prompted greater insecurity and a "siege mentality" among the majority of Protestants. The third Home Rule Bill was a recognition that these other measures had failed to defuse the conflict and that the time had come for the British government to make some hard choices with respect to Ireland. Home Rule was a courageous attempt to recognize the inevitable, to cut British losses in Ireland by imposing institutional changes that would have permitted a peaceful transfer of power to the Catholic majority.

The Unionist reaction to Home Rule proved that a peaceful revolution was impossible. Any British government was therefore faced with only two broad policy options, either of them likely to provoke considerable bloodshed. They could grant extensive self-government to a united Ireland, triggering a civil war between nationalists and Unionists, or they could resist this demand, provoking a struggle with the nationalists. Had Lloyd George pursued the former policy, the Irish would at least have been able to settle the destiny of their country among themselves. The Unionists would have resisted the Home Rule Act by force, and in all likelihood the nationalists, given their numbers, would have triumphed after a bloody struggle. Those Protestants unable to reach an accommodation with the nationalist government would probably have left the country (Ireland's *Pieds noirs*) while the rest would have reached some kind of modus vivendi with the new government. In this regard it is important to note that Protestants were considered to be fellow Irishmen by most nationalists, and the new government would have probably been willing to go quite far to accommodate them.

Lloyd George, dependent as he was upon the parliamentary support of British Unionists, chose instead to crush the nationalists but was unable to do so. He nevertheless still rejected nationalist demands for independence and sought to salvage what he could for the Unionist minority through partition. The partition, in effect, gave Unionists a new lease on life by making them a majority within a separate northern state. However, by separating the six counties of Ulster from the rest of Ireland, and by including a substantial Catholic minority in the new political unit, Lloyd George ensured that the conflict which had brought Ireland to the brink of civil war would ultimately be resumed on a smaller geographic scale. Thus partition, like the other halfway measures that had preceded it, failed to resolve the key issues of discord in Ireland but merely postponed their ultimate resolution to a latter date. Moreover, by further fostering political, economic, and social divergence between north and south, partition created new difficulties, which made any future solution to the Irish problem even harder to achieve.

The Seeds of Confrontation

The border between the two Irelands was in theory designed to separate Protestant Unionists from Catholic nationalists. In practice it was an attempt to make Northern Ireland as large as possible without sacrificing a working majority of Unionists. Of the nine counties of Ulster, only four—Armagh, Antrim, Down, and Londonderry—had Protestant majorities and were the counties that Asquith had temporarily excluded from Home Rule. Lloyd George imposed a boundary that awarded the counties of Tyrone and Fermanagh and the city of Londonderry to the Unionists as well. Both counties contained Catholic majorities; Londonderry itself, 65 percent Catholic. The nationalists vigorously protested this travesty of the principle of self-determination but, confident that these counties, Londonderry, and sections of Armagh would return nationalist majorities, consented to the treaty when Lloyd George agreed to a boundary commission to redefine the borders according to the wishes of the inhabitants. The commission was finally established in 1924 but refused to conduct a plebiscite because of adamant Unionist resistance. Instead, it carried out a cursory examination of the frontiers and reaffirmed the boundary drawn by Lloyd George.

Northern Ireland, therefore, included a Catholic minority of 34.5 percent, a large enough minority to trigger the insecurities of most Protestants. These insecurities were further aggravated by the fact that the Catholics were concentrated along the long border with the Free State. This frontier, roughly equivalent to the old county boundaries, was hardly a viable frontier and is probably the most permeable border in the world—especially for Northerners who cross it en masse every Sunday because the pubs in Ulster are closed. It is 256 miles long, or three times the distance as the crow flies between Newry and Londonderry, the cities at either extremity. By way of comparison, the longest distance in the entire island is only 300 miles! Running through the middle of villages and crossing and recrossing major communication routes, it is traversed by over 200 paved roads and is almost impossible to secure. The British Army has never been able to seal it off from terrorists.

The Protestant fear of a Catholic minority with ready access to their compatriots across the border was reflected in the crescendo of sectarian violence that accompanied the creation of Northern Ireland. In 1920 the UVF, taking advantage of the struggle between the nationalists and the British government in the south, carried out pogroms against northern Catholics. In November 1920 the new Unionist regime organized the Ulster Special Constabulary. Armed by the British and flooded with recruits from the Orange Lodges, the constabulary was clearly a partisan force which set out to intimidate Catholics. In 1922, 97 people were murdered in Belfast alone, and the city was placed under a curfew that was not lifted until December 1924. In the course of this violence, over 300 people were killed; nearly 1,000 seriously injured; and more than 25,000 Catholics were driven from the North.

Northern Protestants had a comfortable majority of two to one in Ulster, and by 1924 the regime had demonstrated its ability to maintain security against threats from within and without. Given this success, it would have been wise policy to make some conciliatory gestures toward the Catholic minority in the hope of securing at least their tacit acceptance of the regime, if not ultimately their active support of the system. Instead, the Unionist party did just the opposite: it actively fostered distinctions between Protestants and Catholics and attempted to stimulate Protestant fears of the minority. The new prime minister, Sir James Craig (later Lord Craigavon), declared Northern Ireland to be "a Protestant Government" with "a Protestant Parliament for a Protestant People." Catholics, he asserted, would be "tolerated" if they obeyed the laws.[3] No attempt was made by Craig (1921–43) or his successor, Lord Brookeborough (1943–63) to integrate Catholics into the political or economic life of the country. Nor was any effort made to extend to them even the meager quality of services Unionist politicians brought to Protestant voters.

The decision to build a Protestant state is best understood as a function of the peculiar political and economic structure of Northern Ireland. Ulster had undergone rapid industrial development during the nineteenth century, most of it concentrated in the northeast where the growth of the linen and shipbuilding industries had transformed Belfast into a major metropolis. Between 1821 and 1901, the population of the city had mushroomed from 37,000 to 349,000. Much of the new population was Catholic and consisted of laborers drawn from beyond the Bann, and later from the South, who were attracted by the prospect of steady work. The Belfast industrialists, facing a severe labor shortage, welcomed the new emigrants, and most Protestants, prospering by reason of the boom, at first showed little animosity toward their Catholic coworkers.

The rapid industrialization of the province spurred the growth of a predominantly Protestant middle class, and later, of a large mixed working class which gradually asserted itself under the banner of trade unionism. Working-class leaders sought to advance the political and economic interests of their class by uniting Protestant and Catholic workers in trade unions and challenging the absolute power of the industrialists and gentry. The Tory elite sought to preserve its prerogatives by fostering sectarian strife among its opponents. The economic recession in the last decades of the century which led to increased competition for jobs and housing—sedulously fostered by the Unionist elite—and the challenge of three Home Rule Bills, each of which led to considerable communal rioting, appeared to crown their efforts with success. By the turn of the century, Protestant middle-class support for Catholic rights was restricted to a small minority of intellectuals, and the emerging Labour party had made few inroads among Protestant workers. The Orange Lodge, financed by Belfast industrialists and dedicated to the preservation of Protestant supremacy, had become the dominant institution of the Protestant working class. Fearing the imagined horrors of Catholic power (Home Rule equals *Rome* Rule) and jealous of their marginal advantages over Catholics, Protestant workers ignored their real economic interests and gave their support to the Unionist party.

While the North had enjoyed some prosperity before and during the war, partition, civil war, and a series of major strikes as well as a general decline in the market for Belfast goods led to a twenty-year economic decline. Northern Ireland had free trade with Britain, but the erection of a trade barrier by the Free State ended her lucrative economic intercourse with the South. This had serious effects on the well-being of many border towns, most notably Londonderry, which was cut off from Donegal, its natural hinterland. More important, partition disrupted transportation in both the North and the Free State because the main internal rail lines crossed the frontier at fifteen points. In the area of Clones, the principal east-west route crossed and recrossed the border six times within a distance of seven miles!

By far the most serious economic problem was unrelated to partition. Northern industry, primarily shipping, related engineering enterprises, and clothing manufacture was almost entirely dependent upon the export market. The decline in these markets throughout the 1920s and '30s led to a prolonged depression in Ulster. Unemployment (of insured workers) rose from 18 percent in 1923, the first year of real peace, to 25 percent by 1926. After a brief resurgence in the late 1920s by reason of a short boom in the linen industry, production once again declined and unemployment averaged 25 percent throughout the 1930s. Most debilitated of all was Londonderry, which even today remains the most depressed city in the United Kingdom.

Unwilling to initiate radical economic reform but nevertheless politically dependent upon Protestant working-class support, the Unionist leadership sought to circumvent any challenge to its power by maintaining and fostering sectarian conflict. The postwar depression, which further aggravated the struggle for jobs and housing, facilitated this strategy of divide and rule. During this period, Protestant and Catholic workers, struggling to overcome communal hostility in light of the steadily deteriorating economic conditions, began to collaborate in demands for radical economic change. In 1932, for example, demonstrations by Belfast workers for greater unemployment benefits and better housing led to bitter fighting with the police. The government, anxious to defuse the threat and to destroy any possibility of working-class solidarity, gave prominent support to the Ulster Protestant League which was dedicated to "persuading" all good Protestants not to employ Catholics or to work with them. Sir Basil Brooke (later Viscount Brookeborough), declared: "Many in the audience employ Catholics but I have not one about my place. Catholics are out to destroy Ulster with all their might and power. They want to nullify the Protestant vote, take all they can out of Ulster and see it go to hell." [4] Similar rabble-rousing by Lord Craigavon and other Unionist leaders had the desired effect, and the bitterness of Protestant workers was turned against fellow Catholic workers, culminating in three weeks of sectarian rioting in Belfast.

Wartime prosperity and British subsidies somewhat eased the economic plight of the North. The British Treasury, which contributed millions (£200 million in 1972) to pay for a high level of social benefits, in effect permitted the Unionist regime to circumvent meaningful reform. Westminster has also provided incentives to attract industry to the North. Nevertheless, the unemployment rate in the postwar years hovered around 8 percent as compared with 1.7 percent in Great Britain. Among insured Catholic workers it was closer to 15 percent. The difference can be explained in part as the result of a conscious governmental effort to concentrate industrial development in the northeast, the area of densest Protestant settlement. Thus between 1945 and 1966, 217 new firms (100 with one-third funding from the British government) were established in the six counties, but only 20 of these were located west of the Bann, and only 7 in Londonderry, the largest city with a Catholic majority in the North.

Pronounced differences in living standards are also apparent among those fortunate enough to be employed. In 1969, only 4 percent of those with an income of at least £2,000 per annum were Roman Catholic, a function of continuing economic discrimination. In many firms, especially family businesses, there is a strict policy against hiring Catholics. In other enterprises Catholics are restricted to jobs on the lowest rung of the economic ladder. The Belfast shipyards, for example, are the largest single industry in that city and employ 10,000 workers; only 400 are Catholic. Moreover, Catholic workers earn 20 percent less per capita than their Protestant peers. The pattern of discrimination is even more striking in the public sector which, until recently, was almost entirely the sinecure of Protestants.[5]

The depressed state of the economy and the differential standard of living between Protestants and Catholics had certain advantages for the

Stormont regime. It not only gave Protestant workers, fearful of losing their marginal advantages over Catholics, incentives to support the Unionist party but forced numerous unemployed Catholics to leave the North in search of work. Given the high Catholic birthrate, 28.3 per 1,000, the Protestant majority has been maintained only through Catholic emigration which has been twice that of Protestants. Thus, despite Protestant fears of becoming a minority, the relative size of both communities has changed only slightly in fifty years.[6] In Londonderry, for example, the Catholic population showed an absolute increase of 5.9 percent between 1951 and 1961. Without the safety valve of emigration, the increase would have been around 12.4 percent. Thus Unionist politicians have come to see economic development as a double-edged sword and Ulster remains the most depressed area of the United Kingdom.

While Ulster Protestants have been kept loyal to the Unionist party through the maintenance of sectarian conflict, the Stormont regime has employed both constitutional and extralegal means to ensure that Catholics, unalterably opposed to the status quo, remained powerless and quiescent. One of the most important devices in this respect was the rigged electoral system which facilitated fifty years of uninterrupted Unionist rule. Until March 1972, when Stormont was dissolved, Northern Irish voters elected three sets of representatives: they voted for the 52 MPs and 20 senators who comprised Stormont, responsible for the internal affairs of Northern Ireland; elected representatives to local governmental councils; and sent 12 MPs to the British Parliament at Westminister. The laws under which MPs to Westminster are elected are the same as those that apply throughout the United Kingdom. However, until 1970, elections to Stormont and local governmental bodies were governed by a complicated set of rules designed to inflate the Protestant vote and reduce the Catholic. In addition to the ordinary vote, limited companies, overwhelmingly Protestant, were under certain conditions entitled to nominate up to six extra voters while Queen's University, predominantly Unionist, was granted four seats (8 percent of the total number) in Stormont. In local elections, subtenants, lodgers, servants, and children over twenty-one living at home were deprived of the vote. About 250,000 adults, the majority of them Catholic, were thus disenfranchised. This was a significant percentage of the electorate because in 1967, for example, the total role of eligible voters (for internal elections) was only 694,484.

Equally important was the use of the gerrymander to guarantee Protestant domination of county councils. In county Fermanagh, which has a slight Catholic majority, the County Council in 1970 consisted of 35 Unionists and 17 non-Unionists. The most extreme example of gerrymandering was in Londonderry. In 1966, the city had 14,325 Catholic voters and only 9,235 Protestant voters. But housing segregation, informally enforced throughout much of the North, had the effect of concentrating almost all the Catholic voters in the Bogside and neighboring Creggan

Estates which in turn were constituted into one huge Catholic ward. Each Protestant ward, containing many fewer voters, nevertheless sent the same number of councillors to the Londonderry County Council, giving the Protestants a majority of 12 to 8. The Unionist majority on the county council was utilized to maintain residential segregation, to provide better public services to Protestants, and most important, to guarantee preferential treatment for Protestants with respect to jobs and housing. This was true of most county councils in the North. In Fermanagh, for example, the council employed 370 people in 1970; 332 of them, including all the executives, were Protestant. In the area of housing, the council built 1,589 houses between 1945 and 1969, but only 568 of them went to Catholic families. Moreover, the Fermanagh Civil Rights Association charged that Catholics were denied housing in Protestant areas of Fermanagh and were generally placed in inferior dwellings, despite the fact that they paid the same rent as Protestants.[7]

The Stormont regime also controlled its minority through the application of what Catholics call "law and Orange Order," so named because the Royal Ulster Constabulary (the RUC) has traditionally drawn most of its recruits from the Orange Lodges. The RUC and the part-time militia, the infamous B Specials, were in effect the military arm of the Unionist party. Both forces were well armed (the Specials were disbanded in 1969–70) and over the years showed little compunction about using their weapons. Their ability to intimidate Catholics was vastly faciliated by the Civil Authorities (Special Powers) Act (Northern Ireland), 1922, renewed annually until 1933 when it was made permanent. The Special Powers Act—finally revoked by Heath after the suspension of Stormont permitted the suspension of habeas corpus and sanctioned indefinite internment without trial. It empowered the government to suspend freedom of the press, search buildings and arrest people without warrant, restrict personal movement, reverse the onus of proof in trials, and dispense with holding inquests on dead bodies. The only safeguards rested with the judiciary; yet, with the exception of the first Lord Chief Justice of Ulster, who was a Catholic, the bench has been overwhelmingly Protestant and Unionist and supported the regime's actions against Catholics. Thus, in practice, Special Powers were used to deny Catholics many of the liberties and civil rights commonly associated with constitutional democracy.

The Republic

While Northern Catholics became subjects of a Protestant police state, the small Protestant minority south of the border became full-fledged citizens in the parliamentary democracy that evolved in the Free State.[8] The major conflict in the South in the aftermath of partition was an intra-Catholic one, between supporters of the treaty and opponents who wished to continue the war until full independence was achieved.

The truce of July 1921 had been negotiated between the British government and the Irish nationalists because each faction realized the futility of achieving a victory by force of arms. The jubilant reception of the cease-fire brought home the true extent of the war weariness of the Irish population, a fact not lost to Lloyd George, who stiffened his resistance at the negotiating table and threatened, if his terms were rejected, to resume the war. The debate over the treaty in the Dáil was extremely acrimonious and led to a split in the Sinn Fein movement. Griffith and Collins, expressing the sentiments of the majority, did not object to Dominion status which they perceived to be both a major concession and the foundation for ultimate sovereignty. While unhappy about the exclusion of the North, they realized that they were not strong enough to prevent this by force and regarded the promised boundary commission as the most effective means of undermining the viability of the Ulster regime. Finally, although Lloyd George's ultimatum might be a bluff, they knew the nationalists were in no position to call it and reluctantly urged approval of the treaty. De Valera led the opposition to the treaty and spoke in favor of continued resistance to Great Britain. When the treaty was approved in January 1922 (64 to 57), he resigned from the presidency. Arthur Griffith was elected in his place and in the course of the next few months consolidated the position of the new regime. The remaining British soldiers and civil servants departed from the Free State.

Many nationalists supported the position of De Valera and saw the treaty as a betrayal of the Irish cause. This sentiment led in turn to a split in the IRA with many commanders initiating hostilities against the new government. The violence escalated into a civil war in which De Valera and his supporters were pitted against Griffith and the Dáil. The war lasted until May 1923, and was fought with brutal intensity. The rebels, known as "Irregulars," were never strong enough to challenge openly the government's authority and instead relied primarily on ambush and assassination. The Dublin government countered by shooting rebel prisoners, executing more nationalists than had the British during the years of rebellion between 1916 and 1922. The conflict also claimed the lives of the most capable Irish leaders: Cathal Brugha was killed in action, Erskine Childers was captured and executed, Arthur Griffith died of a heart attack, and Michael Collins was murdered in an ambush. In the end, the Dáil, supported by a majority of the population and clandestinely aided by the British, succeeded in crushing all resistance and turned to the difficult task of building a new Ireland.

The crushing defeat of De Valera and the antitreaty faction led to their decision to reject violence and instead seek power by means of the ballot. De Valera accordingly organized the Fianna Fáil Party and was supported by all but a minority of antitreaty diehards who remained politically insignificant. Fianna Fáil's entry into electoral politics in competition with the protreaty party (reconstituted as Fine Gael) had the important side effect of blunting many of the cleavages usually found in modernizing societies. Support for each party was based primarily upon its attitude toward the treaty, for years the dominant political question in Ireland. Treaty sentiment cut completely across the normal political spectrum, and both parties thus contained within them a diversity of economic, political, and regional interests. Here an analogy can be drawn to the United States where the issue of states rights and the Civil War were the crucible from which the modern Democratic and Republican parties emerged. The American Civil War, it has been suggested, ultimately helped to blur class and ideological differences by facilitating the development of two umbrella parties, each supported by widely varied interests. As a result, the parties have strong incentives to compromise on major issues in order to appeal to the largest number of their own supporters. This is also the case in Ireland. In the late 1920s, Fianna Fáil was compelled to alter its radical republican image to increase its support among business interests, conservative workers, and the urban middle class. The party also retained its prior political base among poorer western farmers. Fine Gael, by origin a middle-class party, is today a "catchall" opposition and draws votes from laborers and poorer farmers as well. Even Labour, the major third party, has a varied constituency and, in recent years, has attracted many industrial workers and Dublin intellectuals while maintaining a core of agricultural working-class support. The major Irish parties have therefore been compelled to shy away from ideological confrontation in order to reconcile the diversity of interests represented within each party. Instead, they have concentrated on winning power and maintaining support by delivering concrete rewards to their constituencies. This pragmatism is readily apparent from the fact that Fine Gael and Labour, despite their striking differences, have from time to time formed a common electoral front against Fianna Fáil.

The key turning point in the development of a parliamentary democracy was undoubtedly the election of 1932, in which Fianna Fáil won a parliamentary majority and assumed power without resistance from defeated Fine Gael, its erstwhile opponent in the late civil war. Given the intense animosities generated during this conflict, the peaceful transfer of power to Fianna Fáil was quite a triumph for constitutionalism and contributed substantially to the legitimization of the political system. Since 1932, both parties have shared control of the government with Fianna Fáil in power for a total of twenty-four years and Fine Gael, a total of six (1948–51, 1954–57, and 1973–, in coalition with the Labour Party). With the passing of civil war leaders from the political scene and the attainment of full independence in 1949, the treaty question has lost its salience, but the Republic has been left with two major parties, each broadly representative of the nation as a whole, responsible when in power, and committed to the rules of the game of parliamentary democracy.[9]

The development of a successful democracy has also been facilitated by the underlying economic and social structure of the South. Historically, unrest has centered in the countryside, a function of a shortage of arable land for the growing rural population. The Great Famine (1845–52) and the Land Acts (1870, 1881) transformed the pattern of country life; the former by dramatically reducing the size of the rural population, the latter by creating a system of peasant ownership. Today, the equilibrium is maintained by both a system of indirect agricultural subsidies and emigration, which acts as a kind of safety valve preventing the unrest that characterized the last century. However, a high price has been paid for this tranquility. The traditional conservatism of the peasantry, the relatively small size of individual holdings, and the general lack of investment capital have all retarded agricultural modernization and output per head remains the lowest in Western Europe. Despite significant advances in the last decade, there is still great economic pressure on young people to emigrate to the cities or abroad.[10]

The gradual pace of industrial development has also functioned as a mixed blessing. The Republic has retained a high degree of social homogeneity at the sacrifice of greater affluence. Her GNP per capita is the fifth lowest in noncommunist Europe, higher only than that of Greece, Turkey, Spain, and Portugal.[11] The 1967 census revealed that 50.8 percent of the population still lived in the countryside. Dublin, with a population of 567,866 (19 percent of the total population as of 1972), possesses only a relatively small industrial working class, and in the Republic as a whole, only 30 percent of the working force are employed in industry. Of these, only 40 percent are unionized. The visitor to Ireland is struck by the impression that Dubliners, many of whom are recent emigrants from the countryside, probably maintain closer social ties with the hinterland than the residents of any other Western capital. Ireland has thus far avoided any deep class division and the familiar Western cleavages between middle and working class and between farmer and urbanite have not yet become dominant features of the society. Moreover, the numerical insignificance of minorities (Protestants comprise only 5.1 percent of the population) has permitted the Republic to escape the kinds of communal tensions that animate Northern politics. Finally, the stabilizing influence of the church must be noted. The Roman Catholic church is both conservative and powerful, and although its opposition to birth control, mixed marriage, and freedom of expression have made relations with the North more difficult, its support of the political system has acted as a strong pillar of legitimacy, especially in the early postpartition years.

While the South was fortunate in developing a viable democratic government, independence brought in its wake three major sets of problems which still remain unresolved. The most frustrating of these has been Ireland's economic dependency upon Great Britain, which in the eyes of many nationalists effectively negates the meaning of her hard-won political independence.

During the centuries of British rule, Anglo-Irish economic relations conformed to the classic colonial pattern. Britain discouraged indigenous commercial and industrial development and exploited Ireland as a source of cheap labor, inexpensive agricultural produce, and as a market for British manufactures. Leaders of all parties have been united in their desire to break this pattern, but despite fifty years of independence, the Republic's economy is still closely linked to Britain's. Real progress toward reducing this dependency has been made only in the last decades. In gross figures, Ireland more than doubled her GNP between 1940 and 1970, while cutting her yearly percentage of exports to Britain from 93 percent to 68 percent. Yet, nearly half of all Irish exports are agricultural and about 40 percent of the total yearly output still goes to Britain. Agricultural exports have been facilitated by the Anglo-Irish Free Trade Agreement of 1965, in which both countries agreed to remove all trade barriers by July 1975.[12] The agreement provided immediate unrestricted access to British markets for Irish livestock and dairy products but has seriously jeopardized many Irish industries, which now face increasing competition from British goods no longer subject to high tariffs. Irish farmers have also suffered because the British market for farm produce is cheap, a function of government policy. The Irish government hopes that the EEC market of 250 million people where farm policy is the reverse, prices being 50 percent to 60 percent higher than current British prices, will ameliorate this situation. Yet, it will be a number of years before this market is developed.[13]

The import picture is even less encouraging. In 1971 the Republic imported £350 million worth of goods from Britain: mostly cars, machine tools, and agricultural machinery. It imported an additional £25 million, primarily livestock for fattening and storage, from Northern Ireland. These purchases accounted for almost half of the Republic's imports and left the country with an unfavorable balance of trade with respect to the United Kingdom. There is little likelihood that this pattern will change in the foreseeable future because Irish industry fails to produce many kinds of machinery and electronic equipment essential to the economy. Moreover, free trade with Britain and ultimately with the other members of the enlarged Common Market will only have the effect of further discouraging Irish industrialists from attempting to produce such items themselves.

By far the greatest loss to Britain has been people. Between 1881 and 1966, the net emigration never dropped below 6 per 1,000 per annum and was usually closer to 16 per 1,000. As a result, despite one of the highest birthrates in Europe, the population of the twenty-six counties declined from 6,528,899 in 1841 to a mere 2,818,341 in 1961. Today there are 20 million Americans of Irish Catholic descent and probably over 750,000 people in Britain who were actually born in the Republic. While most emigrants have been agricultural laborers seeking employment abroad, in recent years large numbers of professionals, business executives, and artists have left the country because they found either the cultural climate or the economic situation detrimental to their careers. The government has found it difficult to stem this brain drain but has made considerable progress in reducing overall population loss. The most recent census returns show that emigration dropped to 3 per 1,000 in the years 1966–71 and that the total population rose by 94,000, or 3 percent. This suggests that Ireland has at last halted her population decline, and in the future, population migration is likely to be largely internal, consisting of movement from rural areas into coastal cities.

The second problem faced by the South has been the definition of her political relationship with both Great Britain and Northern Ireland. The Anglo-Irish Treaty of 1922 created the Irish Free State (*Saorstat Éireann*), an independent country for all practical purposes. Irish leaders were forced to accept Commonwealth status (involving an oath of allegiance to the British sovereign), special safeguards for the protection of the small Protestant minority, and the right of Britain to maintain specified military facilities in the country. Eamon De Valera and Fianna Fáil were pledged to eliminate these remaining ties to Britain and their electoral victory in 1932 led to the implementation of a new constitution. The relative ease with which this was accomplished made the bloodshed of the civil war appear even more tragic in retrospect.

The new constitution, the *Bunreacht na hÉireann,* was formally enacted in 1937, and is today the basic law of the Republic. It removed any mention of the special relationship with Great Britain but made few changes in existing political institutions beyond the creation of the office of president and recognition of the increased power of the *Taoiseach* (prime minister). De Valera, by creating the presidency, essentially established the format for a republican government but deliberately omitted any declaration of republican status for fear that this would involve a complete break with the Commonwealth, the concept of external association not yet having been accepted by Britain. He was anxious to avoid such a break in the hope that the Commonwealth tie would facilitate the ultimate reunification of the island. In expectation of this, Article 2 of the constitution declared the Free State to be sovereign over all Ireland. Nevertheless, the following article recognized the de facto division by stipulating that, pending the reintegration of the national territory, the constitution had effect only in the twenty-six counties. Given the continuing divergence of North and South, the Fine Gael–Labour coalition government of 1948 took the final step and declared Ireland to be a Republic. This became official on Easter Day 1949.

Britain had the good sense not to resist these developments and quietly acquiesced in most of Ireland's unilateral abrogations of the 1922 treaty.[14] She formally recognized the new status of Ireland in the Republic of Ireland Act, 1949, a remarkable piece of legislation which recognized Ireland as a sovereign republic but reaffirmed her special relationship to Britain by declaring that the Republic was not a foreign country nor her citizens aliens. Under this unique arrangement, Irishmen can freely emigrate to

Britain and, if resident, can vote in British elections and even hold office. In return, the Republic has granted special privileges, including the franchise in local elections, to British residents of Ireland. The Irish are thus more privileged than citizens of Commonwealth countries whose entry into Britain is carefully regulated by the Commonwealth Immigration Act.

Relations between the two Irelands were also rapidly improving until the trend was reversed by the recent troubles in Northern Ireland. In the wake of partition, North-South relations were marked by extreme hostility, and war was only averted by reason of the civil war in the South which consumed the energies of the Dáil. Nevertheless, the Dáil supplied arms to Northern Catholics and organized IRA raids across the border into Ulster. It also halted all North-South trade in an attempt to destroy the economic viability of the Unionist state. These actions failed and by 1924 both governments had reestablished internal security and had accepted a tacit truce. The truce has endured ever since and has been marred only by the semifarcical IRA campaigns of the 1930s and '50s which were officially repudiated by the Southern government.

Mutual hostility diminished only gradually. In part this was a function of the improved security position of the North and the corresponding realization by the South that reunification could not be imposed by force. This led to a situation where Southern politicians continued to pay lip-service to unity but quietly began to explore means of profiting from the status quo. This resulted in increased North-South trade and other economic cooperation. In 1950 the two governments agreed to a scheme for draining the Erne basin and constructing a hydroelectric station to supply power to both countries. In 1951 they assumed joint control over the Great Northern Railway (the main line between Dublin and Belfast) and in the following year established a commission to develop the Foyle Fisheries.

Despite growing cooperation, significant barriers to any real détente remained on both sides. The major obstacle for Northern leaders was the continuing IRA campaign against their state. The Republic had outlawed the IRA and even interred suspect terrorists during the 1950s, but Unionists still saw the Republic as a sanctuary for their enemies. They also resented the Republic's contention that it was, in theory, sovereign over all Ireland, a claim that many argued implied at least tacit acceptance of the IRA's goals. Protestant opinion, therefore, imposed severe restraints on the freedom of Unionist politicians to seek cooperation with the Republic. There were equally severe restraints on Republican leaders, a function of both nationalist shibboleths about unity and Unionist policies toward Northern Catholics. Republican politicians, like their Northern counterparts, were fearful of being charged with collaborating with the enemy.

By the early 1960s this situation had eased considerably. The terrorist campaign had been decisively defeated and the IRA appeared to be moribund. More important, a new generation of political leaders with no personal memories of the Home Rule struggle came to power on both sides of the border. These men appeared to be less bound by the hatreds of the past and tended to take a far more pragmatic approach to inter-Irish relations than had their predecessors. Captain Terrence O'Neill, the new Northern prime minister, publicly committed his administration to improve communal relations, a radical departure from the politics of his predecessor, Viscount Brookeborough, whose anti-Catholic diatribes had helped to poison North-South relations for twenty years. O'Neill's commitment to reform resulted in the return of the Nationalist party to Stormont after an absence of forty years. The party, then the major spokesman for the Catholic community, once again assumed the role of loyal opposition. These developments were carefully noted in the South by Sean Lemass, the new *Taoiseach.* While he was himself a veteran of the postpartition guerrilla campaign against the North, Lemass nevertheless became the principal Southern spokesman for improved North-South relations. In 1965, he broke all political precedent by visiting Stormont. O'Neill returned to visit and received trade concessions from the Republic. Afterward he tolerated a public celebration of the fiftieth anniversary of the Easter Rising by the Northern Catholic community, a gesture duly noted in the Republic. Unfortunately, his overture toward the Catholics cost him the support of the right-wing of the Unionist party.

The economic boom in the Republic, the Anglo-Irish Free Trade Agreement, and the real lessening of communal tensions in the North also contributed to the feeling of détente which led in turn to greater cooperation with respect to trade, economic planning, tourism, and even security. The extent of this cooperation was illustrated by an irate letter published in March 1972 by the *Irish Times*, the most prestigious paper in the Republic. In the letter, a Dubliner described receiving a parking summons in Belfast which he, of course, ignored. Upon his return home, a second summons awaited him in the post. He subsequently discovered that the Northern Ireland Traffic Bureau had forwarded the registration number of his automobile to its counterpart in the Republic which located his address in their files and mailed a duplicate summons. This, he complained, less than a month after "Bloody Sunday"! [15] It is clear that the Fianna Fáil–Unionist détente was leading to very close intergovernmental relations despite the political limitations still felt by leaders in both states. The Republican prime minister had even begun to refer to the North as "the Northern Ireland Government," in Irish eyes a clear violation of the official doctrine of nonrecognition. Had not events within the North itself shattered this honeymoon, it probably would have led to full normalization of relations.

By far the most difficult problem faced by the South has been the question of its own identity. Sinn Fein, like most nationalist movements, envisaged political independence as both an end in itself and a means to promote a renaissance of the national language, culture, and identity. But despite independence—perhaps because of it—successive Irish governments have found it very difficult to foster the growth of a unique Irish culture.

John Stuart Mill in his "Essay on Liberty" distinguished between "living" and "dead" truths; between a belief that is meaningful in the daily life of the individual because of his constant need to defend it against opposition and a belief that ceases to have any real meaning because, failing to meet opposition, it is simply taken for granted. It might be suggested that "Irishness" is increasingly becoming a dead truth, although it remains to be seen what effect the upheaval in the North will have upon the question of national identity in the Republic. For the prepartition generation, British oppression and its antithesis, independence and cultural autonomy, was very much a living truth, one that led to daily controversy, personal sacrifice, and inspiration for an impressive cultural revival. It prompted the nationalist intelligentsia to reject anything British and instead to emphasize that which was Irish. Postpartition generations, especially Irishmen born after 1940, have matured in an era of peace and growing prosperity. For most of them, the Famine, the Home Rule Struggle, partition, and civil war are ancient history. They frequently find the intense nationalism of some of their parents quite anachronistic. They have generally taken their "Irishness" for granted and display little anxiety over what the older generation perceives to be an increasing cultural erosion. Moreover, coming of age in an environment dominated by the media—British media—they have been exposed to a headier dosage of foreign cultural influence than any prior generation. It is not surprising, therefore, that young Irishmen are becoming increasingly indistinct from their British peers in terms of values, lifestyle, and culture. This is especially true in the eastern coastal cities where, aside from the use of some common expressions in the Irish language, a passion for hurling and Gaelic football, and a general (but alas diminishing) preference for stout to bitter and Irish whiskey to Scotch, the culture is best described as English provincial. In many respects it is more English than Northern Ireland and many parts of Scotland. In Dublin (*Baile Atha Cliath* appears only on postmarks) the overwhelming majority of books and magazines sold at stationers are published in Britain. British and American films have little native competition and even the famed Irish theater is a mere shadow of its former self. Foreign plays dominate the marquees and the Abbey Theater itself survives primarily on the repertory of playwrights who matured prior to the partition. The Behans aside, contemporary Ireland has failed to produce a Yeats, Synge, Wilde, or Shaw. American and British shows dominate the programming on Telefis Éireann (broadcast primarily in English) and on the BBC and ITV, broadcast from both Wales and Northern Ireland and received by well over half the population. Irish youngsters, like their Anglo-American counterparts, are likely to learn their ABCs from Big Bird and his friends on "Sesame Street"; they attend a school system that is a replica of the British system; and they assert their adolescent independence by flaunting the symbols of British pop culture. While in school they study Irish history (also British) and the Irish language, but only a fraction emerge with a working knowledge of that language despite the fact that it is required for civil service and other government posts. Compulsory study of Irish, long a national shibboleth, has recently been subject to a barrage of criticism. The Language Freedom Movement, which probably articulates the feelings of a very significant percentage of the population, opposes the artificial fosterage of the Irish tongue and seeks to remove knowledge of it as a qualification for government jobs. The government, anxious to avoid a heated controversy, has allowed the question to be debated in the Dáil but has not endorsed any proposals for change.

Nowhere is the increasing British cultural influence more apparent than in the fate of the Irish language. The percentage of Irish speakers, a majority as late as the eighteenth century, has declined precipitously. Today, 97 percent of all Irishmen use English as their daily home language although Irish remains the official language of the Republic. Only 20,000 to 30,000 people still use it as their ordinary means of expression, fewer Irish speakers than in Scotland. These individuals nearly all reside in the west of Ireland in rural pockets known as *Gaeltachtai* where the language and some elements of the earlier Celtic life style have survived the encroachments of British culture. The government has made efforts to encourage the survival of the *Gaeltacht*—it recently opened Radio na Gaeltachta—but the population of these rural areas is rapidly waning. The younger people, like their English-speaking neighbors, find it difficult to draw a decent livelihood from the barren soil of the west and are migrating into towns and eastern cities and assimilating the dominant cultural patterns. With the demise of the *Gaeltacht*, old Irish culture is dying out, and in its place British culture now predominates to a degree which the patriots of 1916 would hardly have thought possible. The transformation has led thoughtful Irishmen to ponder the irony that Britain, never able to conquer Ireland during almost eight hundred years of colonial rule, has almost succeeded during the fifty years of her independence.

Troubles in the North

On March 24, 1972, the British government assumed direct control over the affairs of Northern Ireland, ending five decades of Unionist Home Rule. The dissolution of Stormont was clearly the result of its inability to stem the escalating spiral of communal conflict which had already led to the deaths of several hundred people. The British government had made the reemergence of serious communal discord all but inevitable by including a substantial Catholic minority within the borders of Northern Ireland and giving the Unionist regime a blank check on the exercise of internal political power. Fifty years of repression bred only mutual alienation, fear, and hatred which, given the proper stimulus, finally exploded.

Conditions favorable to such an upheaval were manifest by the early 1960s: the most significant development in this respect was the gradual improvement in the economic condition of the Catholic community and the corresponding emergence of a Catholic middle class. The roots of the Catholic economic transformation can be traced to the Labour victory in the British general election of 1945. The new government was anxious to effect a redistribution of wealth in Britain and introduced educational and welfare reforms designed to raise the standard of living and improve the mobility of working-class families. The Unionist regime was hardly in favor of educational reform, national health, or increased welfare benefits; nevertheless, it was compelled to introduce such legislation in Northern Ireland by reason of the "step-by-step" principle, which committed the Stormont to keep pace with important British legislation in return for noninterference by Westminster in the internal affairs of Northern Ireland. The application of this principle resulted in the gradual extension of the British welfare state into Ireland, and most important, in the introduction of a system of national insurance conferring the same benefits received by unemployed workers elsewhere in the United Kingdom. Pensions, allowances, and National Health, largely financed through a complicated system of grants from the British Treasury to the Northern Irish government, were also introduced. By statute, no religious discrimination was permitted in the dispensation of funds and services, and the legislation thus had the immediate effect of considerably alleviating the economic plight of the Catholic community where the unemployment rate has generally been twice that of Protestants. These reforms reduced the pressure on Catholics to emigrate. Other measures encouraged them to seek upward mobility.

The most important legislation in this respect was the Education Act (Northern Ireland), 1947, which passed Stormont despite firm opposition from all parties concerned.[16] Prior to the act, only 5 percent of all schoolchildren received any public support and almost all of these were enrolled in state (Protestant) schools.[17] No money was mandated for nursery schools or medical services, and books and paper were provided for only one child in ten. The Catholic community was most directly effected by the lack of support; most Catholic parents had been unable to afford educating their children beyond the primary grades. The act of 1947 committed the state to pay all teachers' salaries in both state and voluntary (Catholic) schools as well as 65 percent of the construction and maintenance costs of these school systems. The percentage was later increased and the minimum age for completion of school raised to fifteen. Additional legislation opened higher education to Catholics by requiring colleges to be nonsectarian. By the late 1950s, a large number of Catholic students were beginning to matriculate in universities in Northern Ireland, Great Britain, and the Republic. The proportion of Catholics at Queen's University, Belfast, the most prestigious Northern school, rose from 5 percent in 1947 to 22 percent by 1960.

The emergence of a Catholic professional class and intelligentsia provided the Catholic community with a renewed pride and self-respect, and heightened expectations of upward mobility. However, these expectations were thwarted by pervasive discrimination against Catholics in all areas of economic and political activity. The resultant frustration and anger, particularly acute among university graduates, gave impetus to the emerging civil rights movement. It is very important to note that these developments occurred in an international environment sensitized to anticolonial struggles and followed the fullblown emergence of the civil rights struggle in the United States. Northern Irish Catholics, closely linked to the outside world by the media, were profoundly influenced by these events, especially the struggle of black Americans to achieve racial equality. Some Irish students had actually observed American protest marches firsthand and urged the adoption of similiar tactics in Ireland.

The first civil rights demonstrations were organized by the Northern Ireland Civil Rights Association (NICRA), founded in 1967. The association was an unwieldy alliance of Catholic groups and Protestant individuals with widely divergent goals but united by a common opposition to Unionist repression. The member organizations agreed upon a six-point program calling for one-man-one-vote in local elections, the reform of gerrymandered districts, laws against discrimination by local government, allocation of housing on a points system, repeal of the Special Powers Act, and the disbanding of the B Specials. NICRA's first attempt at direct action was in June 1968 in response to the eviction of a Catholic family from a council house in which they had been squatting in Caledon, a village of the Dungannon Rural District. The family had been evicted to make room for a young unmarried Protestant girl who was the secretary of a local Unionist politician. The eviction created a sense of outrage in the Catholic community, and Austin Currie, the local Nationalist member of Stormont, persuaded NICRA to stage a march to publicize the injustice. Despite Unionist threats to disrupt the march, it was a huge success, and to the astonishment of the organizers over 4,000 people participated. Significantly, the demonstration closed with the crowd singing "We Shall Overcome."

The second demonstration, in Londonderry on October 5, 1968, turned civil rights into a mass movement. NICRA had earlier declared its intention of marching to the center of Londonderry, a sacrosanct area to Orangemen since the lifting of the siege of Derry in 1690. The government, anxious to label the march a Catholic protest, countered by restricting the marchers to Catholic areas of the city. But the civil rights organizers were intent on defeating the government's attempt to dismiss every protest against its policies as merely sectarian and decided to proceed as originally planned. Meeting opposition at the Craigavon Bridge, the marchers began chanting American protest songs. The police, armed with batons, charged the demonstraters and injured several of them, including Eddie McAteer and Austin Currie, Nationalist members of Stormont. Several British MPs participating in the march just escaped similar treatment and publicly criticized the partisanship and brutality of the police. Their statements to the press, and the public reaction to the violence in Britain where the march had been televised by the BBC, forced the Labour government, hitherto reluctant to intervene in Irish affairs, to express concern. Prime Minister O'Neill was called to London for consultation with Harold Wilson and James Callaghan, the Home Secretary. Afterward, Wilson told the House of Commons that if O'Neill or his ideals were overthrown the government would consider a "very fundamental reappraisal" of its relationship with Northern Ireland.[18] Thus strengthened against his own diehard backbenchers, O'Neill returned home and, on November 22, unveiled a package of five reforms.

In theory, these reforms met the major Catholic grievances at that time. O'Neill promised to initiate a points system to ensure the allocation of housing solely on the basis of need, to bring in a bill to appoint an ombudsman, and to establish some kind of machinery for investigating charges of discrimination. He further promised to reform local government and with it the franchise, and to dismiss the gerrymandered Londonderry Borough Council and replace it with a Development Commission on which Catholics would be fairly represented. Catholic leaders, having a lifetime of experience with Unionist politicians, adopted a wait-and-see attitude which proved to be justified when only one of the reforms, the Development Commission, actually materialized. Nevertheless, Unionists were annoyed by the unenthusiastic Catholic response, and many were infuriated by O'Neill's dismissal of William Craig from the Ministry of Home Affairs for his part in the events of October 5. The ensuing polarization of opinion set the stage for the next round of confrontation.

NICRA was disturbed by the violent Protestant reaction to civil rights demonstrations and called for a temporary moratorium on marches. But People's Democracy, a socialist student group from Queen's University in whose leadership Bernadette Devlin was prominent, ignored the moratorium and announced a 75-mile march between Belfast and Londonderry to be held on New Year's Day 1969. People's Democracy hoped to publicize Catholic dissatisfaction with O'Neill's reforms and air demands for full adult suffrage as well as for action to alleviate unemployment and the critical housing shortage. The "Long March," as it came to be called, met resistance from Protestant extremists all along the route, culminating in the ambush of five hundred demonstrators at Burntollet Bridge outside of Derry by B Specials and followers of the Reverend Ian Paisley. The RUC did nothing to protect the marchers, who were pelted with large stones and bottles and beaten with nail-studded cudgels. A dozen or so female demonstrators were thrown into a nearby stream where several almost drowned before being rescued by newsmen. The remaining marchers reached Londonderry and were attacked again in Irish Street where, for the first time, the police squelched the violence by placing themselves between the demonstrators and enraged Protestants. By evening, however, the police, who had been drinking all afternoon, freely cavorted with the growing mob and lost all pretense of impartiality. They removed their identification badges and joined in an attack on the Bogside, the largest Catholic quarter in the city, where the Protestant mob smashed windows, broke into houses, and beat the inhabitants. For all practical purposes, this pogrom put an end to the era of civil rights marches and ushered in a more violent kind of confrontation.

In the short span of six months, Catholic activists had succeeded in provoking a crisis in the Unionist party. The moderates in the party, if indeed that term can be applied to any Irish Unionist, recognized the need to meet some Catholic demands, if only to forestall direct intervention by Westminster. More extremist Protestant opinion, a constituency nurtured by decades of virulent anti-Catholic propaganda, perceived the civil rights movement to be aimed directly at the destruction of the Northern Irish state and saw any concession to Catholics as a sellout to the "Republican enemy." O'Neill could not ignore the strength of this sentiment which was forcefully articulated in Stormont by Brian Faulkner and William Craig, both of whom hoped to bring down the government by further arousing sectarian passions. The prime minister, faced with waning parliamentary support, decided to call an election in the hope that he could offset Protestant defections by attracting the support of moderate Catholics impressed by his reforms. His gamble failed and actually led to further polarization of Northern opinion. Official Unionist candidates, selected by local constituency organizations, were in many cases, if pro-O'Neill, opposed by unofficial anti-O'Neill candidates, the reverse being the case in other constituencies where the official candidate was anti-O'Neill. The prime minister was himself opposed in his constituency by the Reverend Paisley. The returns revealed widespread Protestant support for the anti-O'Neill faction and the Reverend Paisley ran remarkably well, receiving 29 percent of the vote in a three-man race. On the Catholic side, many civil rights leaders ran for office and later constituted themselves as the Social Democratic and Labour party (SDLP). The SDLP soon supplanted the old Nationalist party as the major Catholic spokesman in the parliament.

The Northern Irish election, the success in April of Bernadette Devlin in a by-election to the Westminster Parliament, coupled with a second pogrom in Londonderry, also in April, encouraged anti-O'Neill Unionists to mount a campaign against the prime minister. Their strategy consisted of exacerbating communal tensions, thus triggering greater insecurity among Protestants and further loss of support for O'Neill. They achieved their goal by means of a bombing campaign, cleverly engineered by the Ulster Volunteer Force. Members of the force blew up post offices and utilities, including the pumping station that provided water to Belfast, but made it appear to be the work of the still largely defunct IRA.[19] The government was taken in by the ploy, declared a state of emergency, and mobilized the B Specials, provoking even more violent confrontations between activist Catholics and aroused Protestants. The rising tide of violence forced the British government to intervene again. O'Neill was called to London for a second time where Harold Wilson insisted that he placate Catholic opinion by implementing the principle of one-man-one-vote in local elections. Caught in a crossfire between his irreconciliable British and Irish constituencies, O'Neill returned home where he had difficulty in securing the acquiescence of his cabinet to the proposed reform and was forced to resign. He was replaced by Major James Chichester-Clark, minister of agriculture, who narrowly defeated right-wing spokesman Brian Faulkner (17 to 16) for leadership of the party. The new prime minister was nevertheless compelled to include Faulkner and some of his supporters in the reshuffled cabinet.

The change of government purchased several months of tranquility, but Chichester-Clark's apparent unwillingness to implement O'Neill's reform package brought Catholic demonstrators back onto the streets in June. This led to sporadic fighting throughout the early summer and culminated in a week of violence in August that threatened to engulf the country in civil war. These events, which marked the active intervention of the British Army in Northern Ireland, altered the nature of the struggle in the North.

August 12, the anniversary of the lifting of the siege of 1689, is the major Protestant holiday in Londonderry and is traditionally an assertion of Protestant supremacy. It is celebrated by parades of "Apprentice Boys" and other Orange institutions who march along the walls of the old city to the cadence of great Lambeg drums shouting insults to Catholics and throwing pennies down upon the unfortunate residents of the Bogside. Most observers of the Irish scene expected the celebrations to lead to violence, but Chichester-Clark, dependent upon right-wing Unionist support, ignored appeals by both Catholic and Protestant organizations to ban the parades. When rioting broke out, special police equipped with water cannon and armored cars were sent in to quell the fighting but instead, urged on by Orange marchers and provoked by Catholic youths, invaded the Bogside where they met well-organized resistance. The battle turned into a siege and the police began a systematic bombardment of Catholic-held areas with cannisters of C.S. gas. Catholics replied with a counterbarrage of petrol bombs thrown from the roofs of surrounding buildings. After two days of fighting, Bogsiders succeeded in repulsing the invaders and set about establishing a permanent defensive perimeter and a commune to run their internal affairs. The British government, realizing that Chichester-Clark was unable to restore order and anxious to avoid complications with the Republic, which had dispatched troops to the border, reluctantly decided to send in the British Army. The Bogsiders welcomed the soldiers and the Derry Citizens Defence Association negotiated a truce with a guarantee that neither police nor troops would enter Catholic territory. Thus, Free Derry was born. And to the fury of surrounding Protestants, the tricolor of the Republic and the Starry Plough, the symbol of the Easter Rebellion, were unfurled over its rooftops.

The "Battle of the Bogside" triggered a similar struggle in Belfast where Protestants, hearing the news of fighting in Londonderry, invaded Catholic quarters of the city. Unlike Londonderry, where the Catholic settlement is relatively compact and easily defended, the Catholic sections of Belfast are more dispersed and more vulnerable to attack. There was fierce hand-to-hand fighting with the advantage going to the numerically superior and better-armed Protestants. By August 15, when the British Army finally intervened, six people had been killed, hundreds injured, and numerous houses in Catholic areas burned out by petrol bombs. Order was only gradually restored and, following the example of Derry, the Catholic quarter of the Falls Road proclaimed itself "Free Belfast" and erected barricades traversed by checkpoints through which neither police nor soldiers were permitted to pass.

The dispatch of troops to Ireland really marked the beginning of serious British involvement in Irish politics. By convention, Irish internal affairs were the preserve of Stormont; the British government had little inclination to become involved until events forced its hand. Indeed, prior to October 1968, a full two years after Wilson's first threat of intervention, the British government had no civil servant who devoted his full-time to Irish affairs. Northern Ireland was in theory within the purview of the General Department of the Home Office, but according to the *Sunday Times* "Insight Team," the Home Office gave Irish affairs the same priority as it did control of London taxis.[20] Whitehall's ignorance was so appalling that Northern Irish officials complained of receiving communications from there addressed to "Belfast, Eire"! Thus, when public opinion and pressure from within the Labour party finally forced Wilson and Callaghan to intervene in Ireland, their policies were constructed on a base of inadequate and often incorrect information and did not have the benefit of serious prior analysis by competent civil servants well-versed in Irish problems. The government was to pay a heavy price for this inattention.

The Labour government's major response to conflict in Ireland was to pressure successive Northern Irish prime ministers to introduce reforms designed to appease Catholics and hopefully lessen tensions in the North. But the British government really had little leverage to force acceptance of their policies. The prime minister's influence derived from his ability to cut off subsidies to Northern Ireland, an act which could only aggravate communal tensions, or to take the equally dramatic step of asking Parliament to dissolve Stormont and to assume direct responsibility for Irish affairs. Wilson mooted the latter to cajole the Unionist party into accepting O'Neill's reform program, but he was unsuccessful because most Ulster politicians correctly doubted the credibility of his threat. They knew that direct intervention carried with it too many political risks for any British prime minister to assume lightly. Ireland had been the rock upon which the fortunes of the greatest British statesmen had been dashed, and ever since the fall of Lloyd George, British politicians had demonstrated a wise temerity in dealing with the affairs of that island. Moreover, the Home Office had estimated, incorrectly as Whitelaw later proved, that to enforce direct rule, assuming noncooperation from Protestants, would require a minimum of 20,000 to 30,000 soldiers and a veritable army of imported civil servants. In the words of one former Wilson minister, "Our policy therefore amounted to doing anything which would avoid direct rule." [21]

Wilson's obvious reluctance to impose direct rule actually enabled Unionist politicians to exercise considerable leverage vis-à-vis the British government. All three Northern Irish prime ministers, when confronted with British demands for reform, pointed to the opposition within the Unionist party and raised the specter of their government's collapse and replacement by extremists likely to force British intervention by recalcitrance toward the Catholic minority. The fall of first O'Neill, and then Chichester-Clark, at the hands of right-wing Unionists, gave credibility to this argument. Unionist resistance led to a political compromise which in the end helped to produce precisely the situation both parties wished desperately to avoid. Each Northern Irish prime minister endorsed some reform program, albeit honored mostly in the breech, but by doing so, provided Protestant extremists with the ammunition to undermine his ministry, moving each successive government farther to the Right. At the same time, the ministerial failure to alter the basic political structure of Northern Ireland, despite the hesitant attempts to implement one-man-one-vote, allocation of housing on the basis of need, and reform of the RUC, meant that none of the underlying Catholic grievances were alleviated. Rather, with the introduction of British soldiers into Ireland, new ones were created. This led to further confrontations between increasingly militant Catholics and more extremist Unionist regimes, ultimately forcing the British government to intervene in order to forestall civil war.

While the British government was unprepared to insist on meaningful reform, it nevertheless felt compelled to send troops to Belfast and Londonderry to restore and then maintain law and order. Whitehall had been aware for some time that such a move might become necessary, but apparently no serious thought had been given to the political implications of military intervention. This was tragic because the troops, at first welcomed into Catholic homes as liberators, succeeded within less than a year in totally alienating Catholic opinion and became, instead, the major target of Catholic militants.

The military had naturally drawn up a contingency plan for the occupation of Ireland, but General Freeland and his 6,000 troops were, like any army, poorly prepared to play the role of policeman. They were completely ignorant of the intricacies of Northern Irish politics and operated without clear political instructions from the government. The extent of their naiveté was such that at first they relied largely upon Unionist officials to supplement their meager knowledge of the Catholic minority. Much of this misinformation was quickly incorporated into a booklet, "Notes on Northern Ireland," which the army distributed to all personnel. Not surprisingly, the slim volume was superb Unionist propaganda and even contained a rather blood-chilling bogus oath of allegiance to Sinn Fein, the political arm of the IRA, that might have aroused the envy of the authors of the Protocols of the Elders of Zion.[22]

Fortunately, given the army's lack of preparedness, relative tranquillity prevailed throughout the autumn and winter of 1969. The army, despite some serious political blunders, among them an attempt to forcibly remove the Catholic barricades in Belfast, continued to draw upon the reservoir of Catholic goodwill. General Freeland nevertheless recognized that the honeymoon was bound to end unless some serious attempt was made to dismantle the mechanisms of Unionist supremacy. However, his recommendations were tabled by the Ministry of Defence and ignored by Wilson and Callaghan, who appeared to have developed a false sense of security since Ireland's disappearance from the headlines. Both men were extremely reluctant to embark upon any major programs requiring parliamentary approval. Callaghan, despite the strong recommendation of the Home Office task force now belatedly studying Ireland, refused to endorse repeal of the Special Powers Act. In the opinion of many observers, the British thus ignored a superb opportunity to cement good relations with the Catholic community.

As is usually the case in Ireland, the yearly Orange celebration provided the setting for renewed violence. Once again Chichester-Clark refused to cancel the parades; his decision was upheld by Edward Heath who had assumed office just a week before. The decision was taken in complete disregard of both the IRA's threat to come to the defense of beleaguered Catholics and Freeland's warning that should major violence erupt, as he fully expected it would, the army would be unable to control it. The new Home Secretary, Reginald Maulding, was even more ignorant of Irish affairs than his predecessor, having failed to shadow Home affairs while in the opposition. He failed to see the urgency of Freeland's final pleas that at the very least the marches should be routed away from Catholic areas. Nobody in Ireland was surprised when the Orange parade of June 27 led to rioting in which 276 people were injured. In Belfast, there were gun battles in Ardoyne and the Short Strand resulting in three Protestant deaths. That evening a Protestant mob broke through army barriers and converged on the Short Strand and by morning three more people had died and £150,000 worth of damage had been done to shops and homes in the area.

In the aftermath of the riots, both the government and the army overreacted. They were frightened by the appearance of the IRA, units of which had attempted to defend beseiged Catholics, and were convinced of the need for a show of strength. They decided on an arms search of the Catholic Lower Falls Road. This prompted fierce Catholic resistance as their small arsenal was vital for defense against Protestant mobs; three civilians were killed in the ensuing gun battle between the IRA and Black Watch and Life Guards. The army responded by imposing a curfew and conducting a second arms search which netted few weapons but enough ammunition to supply several battalions.

Unionists were naturally delighted by the news of the army–IRA clash and exploited the rising tensions to rush through a bill providing stiff prison sentences for rioters. Fully supported by Freeland, the Criminal Justice (Temporary Provisions) Act, 1970, also received the approval of the British Cabinet, despite the fact that its deliberately vague provisions mandated six-month jail terms for anyone convicted of "riotous behavior," "disorderly behavior," or "behavior likely to cause a breech of the peace." In practice, the act was directed against Catholics, and Protestant judges meted out six-month jail sentences for scribbling "Up the UVF" on Belfast walls.[23] The British Cabinet had no effective means to stem these abuses and, worse still, permitted the army to enforce the act. By December 1970, when the British finally insisted on its repeal, 269 people had been charged under the act and 109, the overwhelming majority Catholic, were brought to trial and all convicted. Catholics came to see the act as the most repressive legislation since Special Powers.

The arms searches and the Criminal Justice Act were the watershed in army-Catholic relations and facilitated the rebirth of the IRA. Prior to the army's intervention in the North, most Catholics had perceived the struggle in Ulster as an internal one with the British government playing a secondary but by no means unsympathetic role. One year later, Catholics were struggling against both the Unionists and the British government, increasingly perceived to be linked arm-in-arm, and the aim of reform gave way to the goal of destroying the Northern political system. The brutal means some Catholic extremists now adopted to achieve this end made any political solution all the more difficult to realize.

The IRA had been all but destroyed by the abortive terror campaign of the late 1950s. It had few active supporters and hardly any weapons, as most had been sold to Welsh nationalists. The defeat had prompted Sinn Fein to engage in serious self-criticism and led to its acceptance of new tactics. Terrorism was to be shelved in favor of militant political action, as a means of radicalizing Catholics on both sides of the border (Sinn Fein, it must be remembered, is equally opposed to both Irish regimes). The new IRA began to play an active role in "fish-ins" in the South where they encouraged the rural poor to occupy large estates and demand fishing rights. In the North, many Sinn Feiners supported the emerging civil rights movement and were cofounders of NICRA. Finally, in response to the demands of younger left-wing members, the organization adopted a socialist program.

The transformation of the IRA met with considerable internal opposition from many members who were dismayed to see Cathal Goulding and the Dublin leadership steer them away from direct military action aimed at reunification. Their opposition became very vocal in the summer of 1969 when the Dublin leadership failed to provide the local command in Belfast with any arms for defense of the Catholic community against Protestant mobs. The IRA, as a result, was only able to intervene in the Lower Falls area where three Thompson submachine guns, smuggled in from across the border, were used to defend Divis Street from Protestant attackers. The apparent passivity of the IRA prompted the appearance of "IRA—I Ran Away" on Belfast walls, much to the chagrin of the Belfast command. Leaders of the Belfast command now made it clear that they would split from the movement unless the Dublin leadership jettisoned socialism, endorsed the military defense of Northern Catholics, and supplied the local commands with sufficient weapons to perform this task. In the course of the next few months both sides tried to work out a compromise while simultaneously preparing for a split by recruiting rank-and-file members to their side. The negotiations fell through and the annual conference in November finalized the schism. The insurgents reconstituted themselves as the "Provisional Army Command," and Sinn Fein split shortly thereafter.

The schism was primarily in response to tactical disagreements but ideological differences also emerged between the two factions, now popularly known as "Officials" and "Provisionals." The Officials, soon all but eclipsed by the Provisionals, espouse a thirty-two-county nonsectarian socialist republic and claim to favor working-class solidarity as a means to this end. They are willing to employ selective violence but nevertheless called off their unsuccessful reprisal campaign against the British Army in May 1972 offering the rationale that it had enflamed communal passions to the detriment of working-class solidarity. The Officials have condemned the Provisionals as "Green Tories" who have brought Ireland to the brink of civil war, thus strengthening Protestant working-class support of militant Unionism. The Provisionals on the other hand have shown no sensitivity to Protestant opinion, although they admit to being frightened by the prospect of having to defend Belfast's Catholics in a civil war. Most Provisionals appear to envisage terrorism as the only possible means of driving the British from Ireland. They operate on the theory that Ulster can be transformed into a Vietnam or Algeria and the British forced to pay such a heavy price in men and money merely to maintain their limited authority that ultimately the adverse reaction of British public opinion will force the government to withdraw. Accordingly, the Provisionals are pledged to continue fighting until they achieve an immediate withdrawal of the British

Army from the streets of Ulster, acknowledgment of the right of the Irish people to determine their own political future without interference from the British government, and a total amnesty for all political prisoners and those on the wanted list.[24] Led by old-time nationalists and flooded with young but politically inexperienced recruits from western farms and Northern ghettoes, few among them appear to have devoted any serious thought to the kind of political settlement that could be made to prevail (especially with respect to the Protestants) should they ever succeed in forcing the British to capitulate.

The Provisionals dominated the Belfast IRA after the split but hesitated to commence a full-scale campaign of reprisals, despite "amateur" starts in that direction, until the Catholic population developed sufficient hostility toward the army to prompt at least their tacit cooperation with the IRA. This condition was met by the winter of 1970, largely as a result of the continuing army-Catholic clashes and the harsh application of the Criminal Justice Act. Terrorism was also facilitated by the continued existence of "no-go" areas in Belfast and Londonderry which provided the Provisionals with effective sanctuaries from which to plan operations and regroup when threatened. By the beginning of 1971 the Provisionals felt strong enough to take on the British Army and on February 6 killed the first British soldier as a deliberate act of policy. On March 10 they captured and executed three young Scottish soldiers outside a Belfast pub.

The Provisional reprisal campaign created yet another crisis in the Unionist party, which this time undermined the position of Chichester-Clark. The prime minister was under strong pressures from his party to demand firm action from Heath. His policy recommendations to the British government, illustrative of the position the Unionist leaders now felt compelled to endorse, called for the introduction of more troops, thorough arms searches of Catholic areas, total Catholic curfews, mobilization of the B Specials to act in concert with the army, and the suppression of "no-go" areas with the subsequent quartering of British troops within them. Even more frightening was Chichester-Clark's call for punitive expeditions against Catholics to be carried out as reprisals for IRA terrorism.[25] Heath agreed to dispatch another 1,500 troops but quite properly rejected the other demands. The British rebuff and public outrage at the murder of the Scottish soldiers forced Chichester-Clark to resign on March 9. Brian Faulkner, the new prime minister, proved to be a more effective advocate of extreme solutions.

Faulkner's accession coincided with a further escalation of the conflict in the North. Army-Catholic relations were marked by greater hostility as the army increasingly vented its fears and frustrations on the Catholic population. Army harassment and alleged brutality enhanced popular support for the Provisionals who now commenced a bombing campaign to drive the British from Ulster. Between March and August 1971 they exploded an average of two bombs a day resulting in the destruction of pubs, businesses, and banks. They injured over 100 civilians, killed four soldiers and wounded 29. The bombings, which the army seemed unable to prevent, strengthened Faulkner's plea for interning IRA suspects; the British Cabinet approved the initiative in the beginning of August.

Internment was conceived as a gamble and proved to be the single most disastrous throw any British prime minister has ever given to the shaky dice of politics in Ireland. The fiasco of the Criminal Justice Act should have taught Heath that he could determine the broad outlines of Irish policy but exercise remarkably little control over the all-important details. Yet, Heath once again endorsed a policy, the very implementation of which undermined the very goals he sought to achieve. He envisaged internment as a kind of surgical operation in which the army would arrest at one fell swoop the command structure and many supporters of both factions of the IRA, destroying its ability to sustain a bombing campaign.[26] Instead, Faulkner used internment to silence as many opponents of Unionism as possible, whether or not they had any connection with the IRA. The RUC prepared a list of 500 names; by their own estimate, not more than 120 to 130 were suspected gunmen, most of them Provisionals. Another 300 to 400 were classified as sympathizers. The rest were neither gunmen nor sympathizers but Catholic politicians, to be arrested because they were deemed less troublesome behind barbed wire. The army only wanted to arrest 150 people, almost all of them suspected gunmen, but by law it could only make recommendations to the Ulster government. They were quickly overruled. In the early hours of August 9 the army, acting as Faulkner's agent, set out to "lift" 450 people. By evening, 342 had been arrested, many dragged from their beds in the middle of the night. They were held without charges, which was permitted under the Special Powers Act. Ultimately, 1,576 suspects were lodged in several detention camps of which Hollywood and Girdwood, on the outskirts of Belfast, achieved the greatest notoriety by reason of the numerous and well-documented instances of beating and torture inflicted on the internees by the British Army which runs the camp.

The obvious political motivation behind internment, and the Gestapo-like tactics of the British Army that implemented it, effectively completed Catholic estrangement from Stormont, the British Army, and for many, the British government as well. In the week that followed, every Catholic area in Northern Ireland was bursting with indignation, and more than twenty people were killed in rioting. Gun battles raged in the streets of Ulster cities, thousands of dwellings were burned down, and Protestants and Catholics alike fled their homes to find refuge elsewhere in Ulster or across the border in the Republic. Needless to say, the IRA was far from destroyed. Judging from the intensification of its bombing campaign, it posed an even greater threat to security than it had prior to internment. The number of daily bombings rose from two to five and generally took a higher toll of life because of both the targets selected and the increased weight of the average explosive device. In March 1972, for example, an explosion in a crowded Belfast restaurant killed 2 and wounded 136, leaving many survivors maimed for life. All together, 174 people were killed in the six months following internment, three times the number of deaths in the preceding two years. Countless others were injured as Belfast began to resemble a city subjected to intensive aerial bombardment with the significant difference that no air-raid sirens warned of the enemy's approach.

Despite the provocations of the IRA, the army, not the terrorists, set in motion the final chain of events triggering Heath's decision to impose direct rule. The army, like its American counterpart in Vietnam, was increasingly frustrated, uncertain, and likely to overreact to any provocation. The extent of the tensions became apparent on January 30, 1972, when British soldiers killed thirteen persons and wounded sixteen after rioting broke out during a civil rights march in Londonderry. The army claimed that all the dead were snipers, but local witnesses and newsmen on the scene contended that the troops panicked and fired wildly into the crowd. The "Widgery Tribunal," subsequently established by the British government to investigate the incident, found the army to be free of blame, but the manner in which the tribunal was conducted led many independent and distinguished jurists to condemn it as a whitewash. In Irish eyes, the tribunal's judgment only added insult to injury and further inflamed public opinion.

The Irish reaction to "Bloody Sunday," as the event became known, was immediate and profound. Catholics staged new protests in defiance of a ban on demonstrations and demanded the dissolution of Stormont, now their unequivocal goal. Faulkner's inability to prevent the demonstrations or to halt a spreading Catholic rent strike further eroded his support and led to defections in both wings of his party. William Craig, more militant than even Faulkner, stepped up his campaign against the government using the same tactics employed by Faulkner to bring down Chichester-Clark. His Ulster Vanguard, a political umbrella for militant Unionist organizations, declared its intention of holding mass rallies throughout the country and declined to rule out the use of violence. Both factions of the IRA announced a further intensification of their reprisal campaigns, and the Provisionals claimed to have carried out over 300 operations in the two weeks following Bloody Sunday. The Officials captured the headlines by bombing a paratroop base in Aldershot, Dorsetshire, killing an army chaplain and six civilians. This bombing, the first IRA act of terrorism in England since the bombing campaign of 1939, created a strong sense of public outrage in Britain and a fear that further incidents might follow. In the Republic, Bloody Sunday prompted a tremendous upsurge of anti-British feeling and an angry mob burned down the British Embassy in Dublin. Responding to public pressures, Jack Lynch withdrew his ambassador from London and demanded radical changes in Ulster.

Within Britain itself, Bloody Sunday sparked an intense national debate. The British public was generally unwilling to believe that British soldiers could shoot innocent civilians or torture internees and on the whole supported the actions of the army. But public opinion polls clearly indicated that the common man's patience on both sides of the Irish dispute was wearing very thin and the government could not count on continuing support for its policy of maintaining the status quo. One Manchester porter interviewed by the *Observer* probably best articulated the popular feeling when he declared: "Pull the plug out and sink the bloody lot of 'em." [27] The leading dailies and influential Sunday papers, all of which ran large special sections on the "Ulster Crisis," were with one or two exceptions in favor of imposing direct rule or far-reaching political reforms. This sentiment was echoed in Parliament by the Labour party, and Harold Wilson himself flew to Dublin to confer with Jack Lynch. Upon his return, he committed the Labour party to the ultimate reunification of Ireland. Irish affairs continued to dominate the headlines for several weeks as the government appeared to be confronted with a choice between the stark alternatives it had long sought to avoid: protection of the Protestant regime by force or imposition of direct rule. The cabinet felt compelled to opt for the latter. The telling considerations were probably their realization that continued support of Faulkner was likely to lead to even greater violence, perhaps in England itself, and given their inability to rule Ulster by proxy, involved the continuing acceptance of political risks for a situation over which they had little control. After almost two months of intense behind-the-scenes politiking, designed primarily to retain the support of his own right-wing in light of the impending vote on the EEC, Heath announced the imposition of direct rule and the appointment of William Whitelaw, a Conservative politician and barrister, as secretary of state for Northern Ireland.

The Politics of Direct Rule

In retrospect, it is apparent that the political culture of Northern Ireland was so fragile that the civil rights demonstrations set in motion a chain of events that within the course of four years destroyed the political system and brought the country to the verge of internal war. The marches, aimed only at securing reform within the system, triggered a Unionist response out of all proportion to their threat. This in turn radicalized Catholic opinion and led to more far-reaching demands for change. At the core of the problem was the terrible dilemma faced by Unionist politicians. The party had maintained power for fifty years by first inciting, then exploiting, Protestant working-class fears of the Catholic minority. This aroused uncontrollable passions, making it impossible for any prime minister to espouse reforms without opening himself to a devastating attack from the Right. Concession became the equivalent to political suicide, as the careers of O'Neill and Chichester-Clark attest, but recalcitrance, as Faulkner demonstrated, proved to be equally disastrous because Unionist rigidity led to the re-emergence of the IRA. The gunmen on both sides set the stage for civil war and forced the direct intervention of the British government.

The British government itself bears considerable responsibility for these developments. Between 1968 and 1972, Wilson and Heath were given ample opportunity to force meaningful change on the reluctant Stormont. But both men demurred. To their credit, they did insist on the acceptance of one-man-one-vote, dissolution of the B Specials, a partially reformed RUC, and a commission to govern Londonderry, but most of these reforms were never carried out in practice and the basic political and economic structure of Northern Ireland remained unaltered until the appointment of Whitelaw. Furthermore, the government's ill-considered decisions to permit the yearly Orange marches, the Criminal Justice Act, and internment, plus the use of the army as a policeman to enforce these measures, used up whatever reservoir of goodwill Britain had among Irish Catholics. At the same time, support for successive Ulster prime ministers eroded. These actions accelerated the pace of developments in the North toward civil war. Whether through lack of insight or of courage, and certainly the Wilson and Heath administrations were noticeably short of both, the government let the situation get totally out of hand before it assumed direct responsibility for Irish affairs. Granted, most organizations prefer to postpone dramatic action until events leave them no choice, but British hesitation, in effect, all but foreclosed the political options open to Whitelaw before he was finally given the reins of power in Northern Ireland.

Direct rule, imposed in 1969 or even in Autumn 1970 (politically feasible in both instances), would have been a far more dramatic and effective action. Followed by legislation against discrimination, infusion of economic aid, and reform of the political system to guarantee minority participation, all of which Whitelaw is now trying to do, it would have placated most Catholics and undercut the IRA. Indeed, the Provisional IRA did not really exist until the winter of 1970–71. Direct rule would certainly have antagonized Unionists, but the so-called Protestant backlash was largely a fiction of Unionist politicians until the IRA bombing campaign and the subsequent advent of the UDA. The proposed reforms, especially the infusion of massive amounts of aid, would have gradually improved the security and livelihood of most Protestants and might very well have acted as a damper on Unionist militancy. The bitter pill of direct rule could have been made even easier to swallow had it been described to Protestants at that time as the one sure way of keeping Northern Ireland within the United Kingdom. This in turn would have been acceptable to Catholics, most of whom have always been suspicious of the panacea of unification and far more concerned with improving their lot in the North.[28] Organized Protestant extremists, mostly Paisleyites and noisy Orangemen at that time, could not have caused very much trouble.

By March 1972, when direct rule was finally imposed, the situation had deteriorated to the point where Britain had all but lost her opportunity to effect a peaceful political settlement. IRA terrorism had aroused sufficient Protestant anger to encourage the emergence of a powerful Protestant paramilitary organization, the Ulster Defence Association (UDA). Whitelaw must now contend with two major amateur armies whose aims are diametrically opposed and in both cases have little to do with the question of reform which so agitated Northerners during earlier stages of the conflict. To date, he has met with little success in dealing with either.

The upsurge of militant Protestant sentiment has been the most significant internal development in Ireland during the past year. This sentiment has received organizational expression through the Ulster Vanguard, created by William Craig in February 1972 to act as spokesman for the panoply of emerging militant groups such as the Orange Order, the Ulster Special Constabulary Association (retired B Specials who run gun clubs throughout the North), the Loyalist Association of Workers (first organized among Belfast dockers) and the Ulster Defence Association. Vanguard declared its immediate opposition to the appointment of Whitelaw and quickly became the major focus of anti-direct-rule sentiment. Craig demonstrated the depth of such feeling among Northern Protestants in a series of massive demonstrations culminating in a general strike on March 28. The one-day strike was supported by the majority of Protestant workers and brought Northern industry, commerce, and public services to an effective halt. Craig has since announced that Vanguard will mount a campaign to bring back a Stormont with even greater powers; failing that, it will work toward independence. He has cited the example of Rhodesia and has refused to rule out the use of violence as a proper means to achieve either goal.[29]

Vanguard's objections to Whitelaw are twofold. Militant Protestants resent his overtures toward the moderate Catholic Left and fear that this will lead to constitutional changes designed to give Catholics a greater voice in the affairs of the North. To this the Protestants remain implacably opposed. Vanguard is equally angered by Whitelaw's cautious policy toward the IRA and was especially critical of his original reluctance to send the army into Catholic "no-go" areas the continued existence of which, Vanguard claimed, facilitated the success of the terrorists. In July, to dramatize their demands, Vanguard erected its own "no-go" areas and declared its intention to maintain them until the Catholic sanctuaries were occupied. Whitelaw, fearful of the consequences of proliferating "no-go" areas, evidently felt compelled to act. On July 31 he directed the army to remove all barricades throughout Ulster. Fortunately, the army–IRA clash, which Vanguard surely wished to provoke, failed to materialize.

The Protestant barricades were manned by the UDA, until recently the military arm of the Vanguard movement and the closest Protestant equivalent to the IRA. The UDA is well armed; it appears to have close links to the Ulster Defence Regiment and draws recruits primarily from the

Protestant working class. Informed sources estimate its strength as high as 40,000 which, if correct, would make it a far greater threat to British authority than the IRA in any military confrontation. To date, the UDA has engaged in little counterterrorism of its own but has come into violent conflict with the army on several occasions. These clashes were responsible for the deaths of several people and have led to a serious deterioration of army-Protestant relations, similar to that which occurred in the Catholic community following earlier army–IRA clashes. Like the IRA, the UDA has bitterly complained of army brutality and would like to see the army withdrawn from the streets of the North. The UDA has also been involved in clashes with Catholics and has threatened to take offensive action against the IRA unless the security forces pursue their task more vigorously. While documentation on this subject is naturally difficult to procure, it is generally believed that the UDA has already commenced hostilities against the IRA and is responsible for assassinating Catholics suspected of being members or supporters of the IRA. The UDA has also participated in attempts to drive Catholics out of Protestant or mixed areas of Belfast. In July 1972 (the yearly intimidation reaches its peak in the summer months) threats to Catholic tenants and homeowners were so widespread that Whitelaw's Public Protection Agency was helpless to render effective assistance and over 5,000 dispossessed Catholics sought refuge in the Republic. Some have since returned. In October 1972, UDA and LAW split from the Vanguard movement and declared their intention of organizing a separate political party to represent the interests of the Protestant working class. The effect of this development on Ulster politics remains to be seen.

The IRA's reaction to Whitelaw was no less vehement than that of its Protestant counterpart. Both factions of the IRA immediately declared their implacable hostility to direct rule and pledged to continue their struggle against the British Army. Whitelaw was nevertheless well aware of the intense yearning for peace among Northern Catholics and initiated moves to build up this sentiment and weaken popular support for the IRA. On March 28, only four days after assuming office, he announced that the army would be prepared to scale down its activities in response to a reduction in violence by the IRA. Whitelaw also promised that, following deescalation, he would phase out the internment bitterly resented by all shades of Catholic opinion and release the remaining internees.[30] The IRA at first ignored these overtures and showed no willingness to reduce the scope of its operations. However, Whitelaw's suggestion of mutual deescalation met with a favorable response from Catholic political and religious leaders, most of whom had welcomed direct rule as a significant break with the past and urged the IRA to make some kind of reciprocal gesture. Catholic sentiment in favor of a cease-fire was further abetted by several ill-considered actions of the IRA itself. In one instance, an exchange of fire between the army and the Provisionals in Belfast resulted in the accidental death of a Catholic mother of ten. Following the shooting, a delegation of atholic women sought out Sean MacStiofain, the Provisional chief-of-aff, and urged him to offer a cease-fire.[31] In May the Londonderry :ecution by the Official IRA of a young Bogsider who had enlisted in the ritish Army acted as the catalyst for the emergence of a peace movement the Bogside. The widespread support for the Women's Peace Committee the Bogside provoked a political crisis in the leadership of the Officials; aring further loss of support, they announced a suspension of operations 1 May 30. The cease-fire was welcomed by most Northern Catholics, the ritish government, and the three major parties in the Republic. Whitelaw omised to speed up the review of Officials still interned, and most were leased in the course of the next few weeks. By June 7, Whitelaw had freed 70 internees, leaving 338 internees and 128 detainees still behind barbed ire.

The truce actually had little impact on the security situation in the orth because the activities of the Officials had long been overshadowed by e bombing campaign of the Provisionals, who still repudiated any thought a cease-fire. MacStiofain declared: "Concessions be damned. We want eedom." Any other attitude, he warned, was a betrayal of the internees, e political prisoners, and the Derry dead.[32] His attitude provoked strong atholic rejoinders. The Women's Peace Committee collected 50,000 gnatures on a petition for peace and announced that there was widespread pport for a cease-fire among the local Provisional command. The SDLP, e major spokesman for moderate-left Catholic opinion, continued to ndemn the bombing campaign, declaring that this could only lead to civil ar, and urged a cessation of hostilities. The Provisionals, clearly on the fensive, countered by offering their own peace plan, and with it, a arantee of safe-conduct to Whitelaw to come to Free Derry to discuss the ssibility of a cease-fire. They announced that they were prepared to stop e bombing in return for an end to arrests, arms searches, and the alleged rassment of the Catholic community. But they warned that the violence ould intensify if their offer was rejected.[33] Whitelaw, given forty-eight urs to reply, denounced the proposal as an ultimatum but nevertheless oved to open a dialogue with the Provisionals through the intermediary of e SDLP.[34] He correctly surmised that the Provisionals were under strong essure to reach some accommodation with him and acted to intensify this essure by issuing a new appeal for a cease-fire coupled with pledges to arantee fair allocation of jobs to Catholics, bring new investment to lster, and initiate political reforms designed to ensure "a full part" to atholics in the government of Northern Ireland. At the same time, he oved to reassure Protestants by declaring that no change would be made the border without the consent of the majority.[35] The IRA countered by nducting a "peace ballot" in the Bogside, announcing that 85 percent of e 15,000 people voting supported the proposals of the IRA.[36] On June 18 hitelaw released another fifty internees and declared that the burden for ntinuing internment rested squarely on the shoulders of the Provisionals.

Three days later he offerred further concessions, promising, if the Provisionals stopped the violence, to order Northern security forces not to move against "men on the run," to release the remaining 300-plus internees, and to review the sentences of terrorists already convicted.[37] These overtures, especially the linking of the end of internment to a cease-fire, had their desired effect. The growing strength of Catholic peace sentiment compelled the Provisionals to make the dramatic offer of a cease-fire on June 22. Sinn Fein (Kevin Street) declared that the IRA would suspend operations "provided a public reciprocal response is forthcoming from the armed forces of the British Crown." [38]

Whitelaw immediately informed a cheering House of Commons that British forces would obviously reciprocate if offensive operations ceased. By June 1972, civil violence had led to 400 deaths, 1,600 explosions, and over 7,000 injuries. Accordingly, the cease-fire was greeted with a tremendous sense of relief throughout Ulster. Only the right-wing Unionists expressed bitterness, and William Craig dismissed the cease-fire as a temporary tactical move on the part of the Provisionals.

Unfortunately, the peace was short-lived. Fighting between the IRA and the army quickly resumed. The incident that shattered the truce arose out of a confrontation between the army and a Catholic crowd trying to move a family into a house on Lenadoon Avenue in Belfast. The family, assigned to the dwelling by the Housing Authority, had earlier been prevented from taking up residence by a Protestant crowd. The army used CS gas against the Catholics; the IRA attacked the army; and the ensuing gun battle left six civilians dead, among them a priest and a thirteen-year-old girl. The Provisionals declared that Whitelaw had deliberately planned the incident to sabotage the truce. Most Catholic politicians, while critical of the army's behavior in the fracas, admit that the incident was probably engineered by the IRA to overcome the serious disaffection in its ranks caused by the cease-fire. The Belfast command, led by Seamus Twomey, had been against the idea of a cease-fire from the beginning and, it is rumored, threatened to ignore any orders to suspend operations. Whether the central leadership actually agreed beforehand to resume the fighting or had its hand forced by the independent action of the Belfast command, the effect was the same. Fighting resumed throughout the North. Moreover, the Provisionals, by offering a truce and subsequently making it appear that the army had broken it, escaped from a difficult political dilemma with most of their support intact.

Despite the resumption of hostilities, Whitelaw made attempts to renegotiate the cease-fire and even met secretly with six Provisional leaders. At this meeting the Provisionals, under obvious pressure from the extreme wing of the movement, insisted on stiffer terms for the renewal of the truce. They now demanded:

1 A public declaration by the British government that it is the right of all the people of Ireland acting as a unit to decide the future of Ireland.

2 A declaration of intent to withdraw British forces from Irish soil by January 1, 1975, and pending this, the immediate withdrawal of British forces from sensitive areas.
3 A general amnesty for all political prisoners in both countries, for internees and detainees, and for persons on the wanted list.[39]

One week later, Provisional leaders flew to London for a secret meeting with Harold Wilson and reiterated their demands. These terms still remain in effect and appear to be the minimum concessions that the Provisionals will accept in return for a cease-fire.

Whitelaw's meeting with the Provisionals, despite his earlier public assurances that there was "no question of negotiating with people who are shooting at British troops," and the subsequent modification of his peace terms, infuriated Unionists. They perceived that Provisional intransigence was reaping significant political rewards.[40] There was also dissatisfaction with Whitelaw in Britain, and numbers of Conservative backbenchers expressed severe disapproval of the secretary's behavior.[41]

The reaction to these post-truce negotiations clearly illustrates the dilemma faced by Whitelaw and Heath. They cannot accept the terms of the IRA, especially the first demand, which is the equivalent of approving Irish unification, without alienating Conservative support in the House of Commons, and more important, without aggravating Protestant anxieties in Ireland and strengthening support for militant Unionism. Concessions might even lead to open hostilities with the UDA. The Provisionals, on the other hand, are not in a position to settle for anything short of the conditions they have already enumerated without provoking a split in their ranks. In this connection it should be noted that the memories of the truce of 1920, which was exploited by Lloyd George to force Sinn Fein to accept Dominion status and permanent division of their country, act to stiffen their resolve not to agree to a premature cease-fire. Provisional leaders have alluded to this precedent on several occasions and have sworn not to repeat the error.[42]

The renewal of violence led to Whitelaw's adoption of stiffer measures toward the Provisionals. At his request, the British government on July 11 announced the dispatch of an additional 1,600 troops to Ireland, bringing the strength of the army there to 16,800. Further reinforcements brought the total to 21,000 before the end of the month. On July 14 Whitelaw demonstrated a new willingness to employ force. He dispatched 600 soldiers to the Suffolk area of Belfast to conduct an arms search in response to a shooting incident. The IRA replied by attacking army concentrations with rockets, a weapon never before used in the conflict. Whitelaw responded to these provocations in a specially televised address on July 23 in which he announced that in the future the government would lay more emphasis on the military than on the political aspects of the problem. He stated that his first objective was now "to destroy the capacity of the Provisional IRA."[43]

Following this announcement, the army intensified its activity and conducted arms searches in Belfast, Portadown, and Londonderry. The operations netted a large haul of weapons and were followed on July 30 by an assault on "no-go" areas throughout Northern Ireland. Shortly before four A.M. that morning, thousands of troops, supported by Saracen armored personnel carriers and Centurion tanks (used as battering rams) converged on "no-go" areas in West Belfast and in the Bogside and Creggan Estates sections of Londonderry. The Provisionals, despite earlier promises to defend the barricades, wisely chose not to offer serious resistance in light of popular Catholic opposition and all "no-go" areas were quickly overcome. Despite this dramatic achievement, Whitelaw's hard-line policy has proved no more successful in weakening the IRA than did his earlier tack of political initiatives. The IRA has been deprived of its fortified sanctuaries in the North, and the Army has stepped up its activities against the terrorists, but this has not led to any diminution of the bombing campaign. To date (May 1973) over 800 people have been killed in the North, more than 400 of them since the end of the truce in July 1972. An end to terrorism seems as distant as it did in March when Whitelaw assumed office.[44]

While Whitelaw struggles to render quiescent the paramilitary forces, he has pursued the parallel goal of seeking political accommodation with Catholic and Protestant moderates. To this end, he has consulted frequently with moderate leaders and has begun to implement a series of reforms designed to appeal to their constituencies. The secretary has created a Public Protection Agency to fight intimidation and halt the trend toward complete segregation in housing. He has supported the attempt by the Northern Ireland Housing Trust to devise a point system to guarantee that housing is allocated on the basis of need, independent of religious affiliation. In September, Whitelaw announced that local government elections would be held later in the autumn under a system of proportional representation. This mode of voting, long a demand of both the SDLP and Alliance parties, negates the impact of the old gerrymandered districts. The announcement was greeted enthusiastically by both parties. Whitelaw's most ambitious scheme was his call for a political conference of Irish political parties to work out a mutually acceptable constitutional framework for the ultimate restoration of regional government. The conference, held in Darlington, England, from September 25 to 27, failed to produce a consensus and is illustrative of the difficulties the secretary faces on this score.

The most important opposition parties invited to attend the conference were the SDLP, the Alliance party, and the Northern Ireland Labour party (NILP). By far the most influential of these is the SDLP which claims to represent the views of 40 percent of all Northern Catholics, although this is difficult to substantiate in the absence of elections. Whitelaw has nevertheless operated on the assumption that this is the case and has lavished much energy on building close relations with the party.

The SDLP was formed in August 1970 to advocate the goals of the civil rights movement in Parliament. The leaders of the party, while differing among themselves with respect to social policy, are united in their belief that the party should reject nonviolence and strive to be nonsectarian. Their claim to be nonsectarian is made credible by the presence in the party of Ivan Cooper, a Protestant MP from mid-Londonderry. However, Cooper, like all SDLP representatives, was elected by Catholic votes in a Catholic constituency. In practice, therefore, the party is Catholic. The SDLP opposed Stormont from its inception and called for the abolition of the Special Powers Act, the Criminal Justice Act, and the panoply of other props that kept Unionists in power until March 1972. The party would like to see Stormont replaced by a truly representative assembly and favors ultimate unification with the Republic, but only when this is supported by a majority of all the people of Northern Ireland. The party welcomed direct rule, later became the main communication link between Whitelaw and the Provisional IRA, and was credited with having played a significant role in bringing about the short-lived truce. The party has also received recognition in the Republic and, since 1969, Jack Lynch has made it his major vehicle of communication with the Northern Catholic community. The SDLP's intimacy with the British Labour party, the Republican government, and its close relations with William Whitelaw, as well as its efforts to secure a cease-fire, have caused its prestige to soar among Northern Catholics. However, the party must walk a fine line between the demands imposed upon it by reason of its need to establish a good relationship with Whitelaw and the demands made upon it by its Catholic constituency. More often than not, the two are difficult to reconcile. This has been the case with respect to internment. The party is well aware of Catholic hostility to internment and at first refused to enter into any discussions with Whitelaw until he ended internment and released all internees. But Whitelaw felt constrained to maintain internment in light of the continuing terrorism. He knew that capitulation on this issue would provoke some kind of confrontation with Unionists, only strengthening the appeal of the UDA. Both parties have subsequently modified their stands but only after conducting a tortuous dialogue aimed at preventing loss of support on either side. The SDLP finally entered into discussions with Whitelaw in April and justified its reversal as necessary to secure concessions for Catholics, especially the withdrawal of the army from sensitive areas. The party subsequently offered to abandon its civil disobedience campaign if internment was ended. Whitelaw responded by speeding up the review of internees and freed the large majority, but the SDLP refused to attend the Darlington conference until all were released. Whitelaw offered a further concession in the form of special courts to facilitate the release or trial of internees, but this was unacceptable to the SDLP which boycotted the conference. The party nevertheless submitted its own formal proposals to Whitelaw for a new Ireland, and they were discussed at the conference.[45]

Following the lead of the SDLP, the Republican Labour and Nationalist parties also refused to attend the conference because internment had not yet been ended. On the Protestant side, the Democratic Unionist party rejected an invitation to the talks. Ian Paisley, the party's chief spokesmen, explained the boycott as a response to Whitelaw's refusal to hold a public judicial inquiry into the shooting of two Protestants (allegedly by British soldiers) in September.[46] Thus four out of seven parties invited to Darlington refused to attend, effectively undermining Whitelaw's initiative. Those parties attending were the Alliance party, the Northern Ireland Labour party, and the Unionist party.

The Alliance party, unionist rather than Unionist, is nonsectarian and composed of Catholics and Protestants opposed to reunification but in favor of regional government in Northern Ireland. At the conference, the party called for the restoration of a Stormont elected by proportional representation and to operate on a committee system. Minority MPs were to be given sufficient representation on these committees to prevent the reemergence of a strictly Unionist regime. The most novel suggestion of the Alliance party was a proposal for the creation of two police forces; the first, responsible for security, to be under the control of Westminster; and the second, concerned with traffic, vandalism, and minor crime, to be controlled by Stormont. The party is against inviting the Republic to participate in talks about the future structure of the North but favors the creation of some kind of Anglo-Irish council which would enable all three governments to consult on questions of common interest.[47]

The Northern Ireland Labour party's proposals did not differ substantially from those of the Alliance party. It favored the restoration of a unicameral legislature that was democratically accountable to the population of the North and advocated the introduction of proportional representation for elections to both Stormont and Westminster. With respect to security, it favored the transfer of all police functions to Westminster and urged the British government to pass a bill of rights giving statutory expression to the police role as the guarantor of civil, religious, and political liberties in the North. The party favored consultation with the Republic but was adamant in its demand that neither unification nor border changes should be imposed without the prior consent of the majority. It urged the Republic to review the clause in its constitution claiming theoretical sovereignty over all Ireland.[48]

At the other end of the political spectrum, Brian Faulkner and the Unionist party called for a return of a strong, local, single-chamber parliament with complete jurisdiction over security. The Unionists rejected proportional representation but as a concession to the Catholic minority suggested the creation of six parliamentary committees with substantial powers, at least three of which were to be chaired by members of opposition parties. They also agreed to an end to Special Powers and internment, but demanded special courts to deal with cases of sectarian violence and terrorism. The party asked for cooperation from the Republic in defeating terrorism and proposed intergovernmental discussions on a variety of issues, especially the return of criminals. Such action by the Republic, the party claimed, could lead to the creation of an Irish intergovernmental council to discuss economic and social questions of mutual concern.[49]

The conference was productive in that the major contenders for political power in the North were forced, whether or not they actually attended the conference, to articulate specific proposals for the future government of Northern Ireland. However, the various proposals revealed a very real fear of losing support to extremists by any compromise of their often stated positions. Much to Whitelaw's exasperation, all three parties emerged from three days of talks with precisely the same positions they had held before the conference. They all agreed on the necessity of restoring some kind of regional government but could not agree on the format of such a government. It is apparent that any consensus about the future institutions of Northern Ireland is impossible in the near future. The minimalist positions of the SDLP and the Unionists, together representative of a majority of Ulstermen, are not even close enough to warrant further negotiation at this time. In the absence of such a consensus, Whitelaw has little hope of weaning support away from the extremist factions.

In conjunction with efforts to seek a political accommodation in the North, the British government has also attempted to foster an economic revival on the assumption that the stagnant Ulster economy is a major cause of political unrest. The IRA draws its greatest support from unemployed young men, and prosperity is likely to diminish their appeal. When Whitelaw assumed office there were 39,500 insured Northern workers without jobs and the overall unemployment rate was 8.8 percent. It was 10.9 percent among males. The secretary promised that the British government would give the highest priority to finding jobs for these workers and has subsequently unveiled several schemes to this end. On May 5, 1972 the government granted £35 million to the Belfast shipyard of Harland and Wolff to finance modernization of their facilities and an additional £14 million to pay prior debts. The firm is the largest employer in the North and the base of the Loyalist Association of Workers. It will now be able to compete with Japanese yards in the construction of supertankers, and new orders are expected to create 4,000 additional jobs.[50] In June the government published a White Paper in which it revealed that the subsidy to Northern Ireland would be increased £8 million for the fiscal year 1972–73. The money will sustain a higher level of services to the population. In addition to the direct grant of £133 million, a further £87 million was allocated to a loan fund to be made available to the Northern Irish government. One month later the Treasury announced another grant of £30 million, earmarked as subsidies for industrialists investing in the North. The government now pays 30 percent of the cost of plants and buildings, with higher rates applicable in areas of severe unemployment. Firms locating in Ireland also receive considerable tax advantages. Whitelaw estimates that approximately 6,000 to 8,000 new jobs will be created yearly as a result of these incentives.[51]

Londonderry is still the most depressed area of the North but the Development Commission has already begun an ambitious program of urban renewal. Their master plan, to be published later in 1973, calls for new housing, public amenities, industrial sites, and extensive city-center reconstruction. It will entail an expenditure of over £110 million, most of which will come from the British Treasury. When the commission was created in February 1969, its main priority was housing. In the past three years it has constructed more than 2,600 units and projects completion of an additional 3,750 units by the end of 1978. The commission has also carried out repair work on roads, plans a new bridge across the Foyle, and is presently constructing three new community centers and three riverside parks. In addition, £2 million is being spent on new nursery and primary schools and £1 million on the expansion of the local technical college. The main problem remains finding jobs. Unemployment, which dropped to 15 percent in Londonderry last year is now back up to almost 25 percent. The commission is desperately trying to attract labor-intensive industries employing predominantly male workers, but negotiations with several firms fell through in the summer of 1972 as a result of the renewed bombing campaign. Despite such setbacks, the work of the commission and the capital grants and loans to other Northern Irish industries and civil bodies have already begun to pay economic dividends. In 1971, 7,203 new manufacturing jobs were made available as compared with a yearly average of only 6,136 since 1967. Industrial output rose by 6.7 percent (compared with 0.9 percent in Great Britain) and industrial productivity was up 8.5 percent.[52] Economic predictions for 1972–73 are quite optimistic and an economic revival is clearly underway although the political impact of rising prosperity is not likely to be apparent for some time. The key question here is whether civil war can be averted long enough to permit the effects of prosperity to dampen political tensions.

The Republic and the Crisis in Ulster

The Republic has a deep and obvious interest in Northern problems. It has been able to exert considerable influence by reason of both its ties to Northern Catholics and Britain's interest in maintaining amicable relations with its neighbor state, third largest trading partner, and, as of January 1, 1973, fellow member of the expanded Common Market.

The troubles in Ulster are fully reported and anxiously watched throughout the Republic and have generally been treated with unexpected understanding. There has been very little public pressure on the government to intervene militarily. The strongest pressure to pursue a reckless policy arose, in fact, from within the government itself, and led to a major political crisis in the summer of 1969. Jack Lynch, it must be remembered, was particularly embarrassed by the deterioration of communal relations in Ulster because they occurred within the context of his attempt to normalize relations with the North. His policy never had the unanimous support of the cabinet and the troubles exposed Lynch to attack from the Right. This criticism became vocal in January 1969 when the "Long March" triggered Protestant attacks on the Catholic population of Londonderry. Several members of the cabinet, notably those of Northern origins, demanded that Lynch pursue a more aggressive policy toward the North. Lynch's chief protagonist was Neil Blaney, the minister of agriculture, a Northerner by birth and long an outspoken critic of the policy of reconciliation. There is evidence to suggest that the Northerners in Fianna Fáil then approached the IRA through intermediaries and offered to help underwrite the cost of military preparations to defend Ulster Catholics from attack. The funds were to come from Taca (Gaelic for "defense"), the fund-raising club of Fianna Fáil. In return, the IRA was to agree to run its Northern operations from a separate command in Belfast, thus minimizing the political risks to the Republic.[53] There is no evidence that Lynch was cognizant of these overtures but it is unlikely that Taca funds could have been diverted to the IRA without the prime minister's knowledge.

In July 1969 Lynch handily defeated the opposition parties in a general election, emerging with seventy-four seats to their combined total of sixty-six. However, Lynch, who had succeeded to the office of *Taioseach* three years before as a compromise candidate, still remained the ruler of a shaky governmental coalition. His position became even less secure when British troops entered Londonderry on August 13. Blaney, supported by Charles Haughey, minister of finance and a Northerner, and Kevin Boland, minister of local government, censured Lynch for his failure to pursue a more aggressive policy toward the North. In a series of emergency cabinet meetings, the three demanded invasion of the North and threatened to resign from the government if this was not approved.[54] Lynch opposed the invasion as foolhardy. After prolonged negotiation he managed to effect a compromise whereby the invasion was shelved and in return a new Northern Subcommittee, consisting of Blaney, Haughey, and two other ministers, was given responsibility for Northern affairs. Lynch also went on television to appeal for a United Nations peacekeeping force to replace the British Army in Ulster and revealed that the Republican Army had been ordered to erect field hospitals along the border.

The militant faction of Fianna Fáil resumed negotiations with the IRA and reached an agreement with them sometime in the autumn of 1969. At that time, £175,000 was transmitted to the IRA through the intermediaries of the Irish Red Cross and the Northern Distress Committee. However, knowledge of these negotiations soon leaked to the press and Lynch utilized the resulting scandal to sack Haughey from the cabinet, prompting Boland and Blaney to resign in protest. Shortly thereafter, Haughey was arrested and along with three associates charged with the illegal importation of arms. In October 1970 all four defendants were acquitted, but the "Dublin Arms Trial," as the proceedings became known, and the purge of Blaney from the cabinet considerably eased the pressures on Lynch to pursue a more adventurous policy toward Northern Ireland.

A second crisis developed, triggered by the introduction of internment in the North. Irish public opinion was outraged by the arbitrary arrest of Northern Catholics; anti-British feeling, hitherto fairly dormant in the Republic, became increasingly vociferous. This sentiment reached its zenith in the aftermath of Bloody Sunday when a crowd of more than 20,000 attacked and burned the British Embassy in Dublin. Jack Lynch, responding to public pressure, had an emergency telephone call with Prime Minister Heath and pulled the Irish ambassador out of London, although he did not actually sever relations. Patrick Hillery, the foreign minister, was sent to the United Nations where he condemned Britain's "lunatic policies" in Northern Ireland and declared that Bloody Sunday constituted a "new policy directed against the entire minority population of Northern Ireland" consisting of "torture, the internment of the male population and the shooting of people in the streets."[55] British Foreign Secretary Sir Alec Douglas-Home replied by telling the House of Commons, "I must give a warning to the Irish government that if they were to maintain the attitude they have taken—for example, Dr. Hillery's speeches in New York yesterday—they could do serious and lasting damage to the relationship between our two countries."[56] The imposition of direct rule and the appointment of William Whitelaw as secretary of state for Northern Ireland were received enthusiastically in the Republic and went a long way toward defusing Republican passions. Anti-British sentiment has subsequently receded and has not seriously threatened Anglo-Irish relations since.

The Irish government expressed official approval of direct rule and encouraged Northern Catholics to cooperate with Whitelaw. Nevertheless, Republican officials cannot be said to be fully satisfied with Heath's initiatives in Northern Ireland and have pressured the British government to end internment and Special Powers and withdraw the army from Catholic areas. Lynch called for Britain to establish a representative democracy in the North with effective minority participation in policy making. He is adamant in his demand that the Republic be included in any discussions about the future constitution of that province.* He also favors the creation of some kind of all-Ireland council to discuss matters of common interest.[57]

The Republic has pursued these goals within the framework of relatively amicable relations with Great Britain. Both nations deem close

* Since the completion of this paper there has been a general election in the North. The new prime minister, Liam Cosgrave, head of a Fine Gael-Labour Coalition, has indicated that his administration foresees no major departures from the Northern policy of Jack Lynch, his predecessor.

ties essential: Britain, because Republican hostility would seriously endanger her ability to effect a political settlement in the North; and Ireland, because of her economic dependence upon Britain and her desire to retain the important privileges her citizens enjoy in the United Kingdom.[58] Beyond this there is the more intangible but equally important bond of cultural and political affinity that reinforces mutual desires to maintain friendly relations. A common parliamentary heritage and "political language" have also facilitated mutual insight into and empathy for the problems faced by each set of political leaders. This in turn has been reinforced by regular consultation on all levels of government. Lynch has met frequently with both Wilson and Heath, and the British government has exercised care to keep Lynch informed of all impending policy decisions with respect to Northern Ireland.

With the exception of the Irish reaction to Bloody Sunday, both governments have been careful not to transgress the limits imposed by close relations although certain disagreements and tensions have naturally developed. Dublin resented the continuation of Special Powers and internment and the more recent plebiscite on the border. The referendum, a concession to Unionists, was designed to show that a substantial majority in Northern Ireland favor retention of the British connection. The plebiscite was publicly opposed by the Republic and by most Northern Catholics who abstained from voting. A further point of contention is the Irish demand to be included in negotiations about the future of Ulster and the corresponding British reluctance to accede to this request.

For Great Britain, the extent of the Republic's involvement in the Northern question is clearly disquieting. The British government recognizes the natural political and economic interest of the Republic in Ulster. However, it cannot help but view many Irish initiatives, for example, financial support for the Northern opposition, as unwarranted interference in the internal affairs of the United Kingdom.[59] Lynch, on the other hand, can hardly refrain from such activity and still hope to remain in power in the Republic. The British are especially annoyed by successive Irish attempts to internationalize the Northern problem through appeals to the United Nations, the United States, and Western Europe. All these moves have met with strong rebukes from the Foreign Office. Secretary General Kurt Waldheim, for example, has twice responded to Irish requests by proposing initiatives to help end the crisis. Most recently, on July 7, he offered to send Lester Pearson and Earl Warren to Northern Ireland to mediate the conflict and assist in arranging a political settlement. The British rejected both offers as interference in a domestic question.

The Republic and the SDLP have also been active in the United States. In the wake of Bloody Sunday they succeeded in arousing considerable public sympathy. Senator Edward Kennedy spoke in favor of unification and raised the question of British policy toward Ireland on the floor of the U.S. Senate. In the House, Representative Benjamin Rosenthal, chairman of the European Subcommittee of the House Committee on Foreign Affairs, organized hearings on the situation in the North and invited representatives of all Irish factions to speak. Senator Kennedy, Governor Abraham Ribicoff, and Paul O'Dwyer later secured adoption in the platform of the Democratic party of a plank condemning discrimination and repression in Northern Ireland.[60] On March 1, the International Longshoreman's Association carried out a one-day dock strike against British goods in protest of British policies in the North. The strike was supported by the Transport Worker's Union and was effective at major airports as well.

President Nixon expressed his personal sympathy for the Londonderry dead but is naturally more concerned with maintaining close Anglo-American relations and has cautioned Congress against making any sweeping declarations on the Irish problem. Secretary of State William Rogers, elaborating on the President's position, declared that the United States was in no position to intervene in the conflict.[61] Since then there has been no indication that the American government has exerted even gentle informal pressure on Britain with respect to Northern Ireland.[62]

Direct rule went a long way toward placating responsible American-Irish opinion, although both branches of the IRA still raise money among Americans of Irish descent. Both the Republic and Great Britain have requested the United States to take more active steps to squelch this support, especially the illegal importation of American arms into Ireland. The various federal agencies have apparently complied within the limits of the law. The IRA, it should be noted, has been very active in seeking international support, especially among self-styled national liberation movements. The Officials have so far received the backing of fourteen such groups, among them the Front for the Liberation of Quebec, the Revolutionary Basque Movement, and the Republican Army of Brittany.[63] The Provisionals have received encouragement from many Arab groups, and in June 1972, Colonel Khadafi, president of Libya, announced that he was supplying arms to the IRA, touching off a diplomatic crisis between his country and both Great Britain and the Republic of Ireland. None of this support, however, with the exception of American money, has been very meaningful.

The Irish government has been most successful in winning support of its case in Western Europe. It has sponsored speaking tours of Common Market countries by prominent opposition leaders which have resulted in the expression of considerable popular and editorial support for the Catholic position.[64] Following Bloody Sunday, two Italian representatives asked the Commission of the European Communities to state what action it would take to protect human rights in Ulster, and a special parliamentary subcommittee of the Council of Europe was created to investigate discrimination in housing and employment in Northern Ireland. In March 1972 the subcommittee asked Britain to permit it to send a delegation to

Northern Ireland, prompting a walkout by the British Conservative representative on the committee. The Irish government also appealed to the European Commission of Human Rights to investigate alleged British breaches of the European Human Rights Convention arising from the Northern Ireland Act, 1972, the controversial measure giving retroactive legality to British Army actions in Ulster. In October the commission, a panel of seventeen judges, one each from each member state that has ratified the Convention, agreed to hear five of the seven Irish charges.

The British government is clearly unhappy about these actions, but in reality they constitute little more than political pinpricks which are unlikely to have a major impact upon the British position in the new Europe. Whitehall is far more concerned with the activity of the Provisional IRA in the Republic, which it maintains has a serious detrimental impact upon the security situation of the North.

Unionist politicians consistently accuse the Republic of complicity with the IRA. Brian Faulkner asserts that without the "free haven of the Republic" the terrorists would quickly be run into the ground.[65] The British government has never accused the Republic of willingly providing a sanctuary for terrorists, but on several occasions it has urged the Republic to take stronger action against the IRA. Most recently, Heath raised this issue with Lynch at their meeting in Munich during the Olympic games. Heath complained that twenty-eight IRA raids had been carried out across the border in August alone, and according to official British sources, he offered specific proposals for dealing with these incursions.[66] Lynch has argued that his government has taken every action available within the law to curb the IRA.[67]

Prior to new legislation introduced in November 1972, the government had few powers to get tough with the IRA. Governmental activity was confined to the section of the Offences Against the State Act, popularly known as the "Cat and Mouse Act," under which a suspected member of an illegal organization could be detained for twenty-four hours, but had then to be released unless charges were preferred. The IRA is outlawed in the Republic but, until recently, both Sinn Fein (Gardiner Place) and Sinn Fein (Kevin Street), headquarters of the Officials and Provisionals respectively, have been permitted to operate openly. Even so, the government has invoked this act to arrest prominent Sinn Feiners in the wake of particularly dramatic outrages. Thus key Officials were arrested after the Aldershot bombing and Provisional leaders following their refusal to declare a truce in June. Both groups of leaders were subsequently released.

Lynch hesitated to introduce new legislation or special courts because there is some support for the terrorists in his own party as well as in the country at large. The Fianna Fáil front bench has frequently condemned the Provisional bombing campaign, but many backbenchers have greeted such pronouncements with mute hostility. Yet, thousands of delegates to the 1972 *ard-feis* (annual party conference) cheered the "get tough" statements of both Lynch and *Tanaiste* Childers, leading one to suspect that these backbenchers have not correctly judged the mood of the country which has clearly become more anti-IRA since the breakdown of the truce in July. Additional proof for this assertion can be drawn from the recent mid-Cork by-election which was fought largely over the government's handling of the Northern crisis and resulted in a major Fianna Fáil victory. The Labour party has also gone on record as favoring stronger actions against the IRA. Given these indicators Lynch felt he could initiate stiffer action against the terrorists. The closing down of Sinn Fein offices in Dublin in November and the new legislation making it easier for the government to prosecute the IRA and the arrest of Sean MacStiofain, Provisional chief-of-staff, is indicative of such a policy.

The most serious criticism that can be leveled against the Republic is its failure to play a more positive role in reducing Northern tensions by taking action to allay Protestant suspicions of Catholics. Such fears are certainly at the core of the conflict. Many Northern Protestants oppose full-fledged Catholic participation in Ulster political life because they suspect that Catholics, ultimately to be a majority, will undermine their civil liberties or force unification. For evidence, Unionist leaders point to the special position of the Catholic church in the Republic and its effective veto over social and educational policy. Few Northern Protestants wish to have rigid censorship or bans on contraception and divorce imposed in Ulster, and the existence of such legislation in the South has significantly strengthened the hand of militant Unionists. Northerners are also suspicious of the real intentions of the Republic, and these fears have not been allayed by either the Republic's cautious policy toward the IRA or its attitude toward unification. Northern Protestants resent Articles 2 and 3 of the Republican Constitution which declare the Republic sovereign over all Ireland. Even the SDLP has called upon Lynch to reassure Northerners on this issue. The *Taioseach* has on several occasions declared that the Republic desires unity but condemns violence and hopes to achieve unity "only in peace and by agreement with our fellow countrymen." [68] But this has a hollow ring in Northern ears in light of the Irish Constitution. The Republic would be well advised to strike out the offensive clauses and legally recognize the de facto division.

For Republicans, this is an emotionally charged issue, similar to the Federal Republic of Germany's reluctance for many years to recognize formally the Oder-Neisse line as the Polish-German frontier. Recognition of the division would go a long way toward reducing Protestant fears, without which ultimate unity and perhaps even temporary settlement of the Northern problem is impossible. Fortunately, the Republic has finally acted with respect to the special position of the Catholic church, and a national referendum in November produced a considerable majority in favor of deleting this clause from the constitution. There is speculation in Dublin that a second referendum will be held to remove the offensive parts of

Articles 2 and 3 and replace them with a statement expressing the hope that unity will someday be agreed upon by all Irishmen.

Political Settlement or Civil War?

Whitelaw has not succeeded in curbing the strength of either the Provisional IRA or the UDA. Rather, both paramilitary groups have expanded the scope of their activities, and the UDA has moved steadily toward a confrontation with the British Army. On the political front, Whitelaw has been unable to build a consensus, behind an institutional framework, for a restored regional government. Thus in many respects Irish politics appear to have come full circle to the situation that prevailed in August 1914. The significant differences this time are that the British Army is not about to support the Ulster Protestants and the Republic is of course an independent country and a third party to the conflict. Still, once again Protestant and Catholic armies stand poised on the brink of war with each other and, if need be, with the British government as well. In 1914 civil war was averted only by the German invasion of Belgium. What hope is there that such a conflict can be avoided today? What kind of political settlement could conceivably be made permament?

Both extreme solutions—restoration of a Unionist regime or unification—are clearly out of the question. Unionist supremacy, as advocated by Faulkner and Craig, would alienate all Catholics and lead to a rapid escalation of IRA violence. Unification, espoused by the Provisionals, would be equally likely to lead to civil war by reason of militant UDA opposition to such a "sellout." Moreover, unification at the present time is opposed by many Northern Catholics afraid of the economic consequences and, one suspects, by most Southern politicians who, despite their lip-service to this goal, are fearful of the impact of a large, politically articulate Protestant minority upon the "comfortable" political system of the Republic. Independence, mooted by Ulster Vanguard, is equally unworkable. And so are the various schemes for joint sovereignty popular among the Catholic Left, because of majority opposition to them. The only constitutional arrangement that appears to offer any hope of success is the restoration of some kind of semiautonomous government with specific mechanisms built in to ensure effective minority participation.

The publication of the White Paper on March 20, 1973, indicates that Heath and Whitelaw have decided to impose new institutions on the North, with or without the prior consensus of the parties concerned because they recognize that Britain cannot go on indefinitely administering the province without the participation of the governed. They recognize that the longer electoral politics remain frozen and the people of the North are denied any responsibility for their own affairs, the greater the incentive for Northerners to seek political expression on the streets. Thus, the return of some kind of responsible government is a political necessity.

The following is a summary of the main proposals of the White Paper:

1. The present status of Northern Ireland as part of the United Kingdom will continue to be guaranteed so long as a majority of its inhabitants so desire.
2. The British Army will remain for as long, and in such strength, as the situation requires.
3. Responsibility for the security forces for the administration of justice and for special powers will remain with Westminster.
4. A comprehensive new Constitutional Bill will be presented to Parliament. It is hoped to enact legislation and hold elections in Northern Ireland "without undue delay." Meanwhile direct rule will be extended for a year.
5. A new Northern Ireland Assembly of eighty members, elected by proportional representation, will develop its own rules and procedures in accordance with broad provisions laid down in the Bill. The Secretary of State and representatives of the Assembly will arrive on an acceptable basis for the formation of an Executive and the devolution of some of the powers at present held by Westminster.
6. Committees will be set up, each reflecting as far as possible the balance of parties within the Assembly. The chairman of each committee will be the political head of a Department, and the committee chairman will form the Executive. The Executive must represent both communities.
7. The right of the United Kingdom Parliament to legislate for Northern Ireland "in any matter whatever" remains undiminished.
8. The Government will bring in legislation based on its review of the Special Powers Act. Special powers will be "operative only during an emergency and with the approval of Parliament." There will be no provision for detention.
9. The Assembly will have no power to make laws of a discriminatory character, nor may any Department act in a discriminatory way.
10. The financial arrangements will be designed to accomplish physical reconstruction: to encourage investment and to work progressively towards the achievement of British standards of living, employment and social conditions.
11. There will be a Charter of Human Rights, with stringent legislative safeguards.
12. Legislation will be brought in to deal with the problem of job discrimination in private industry, following on the deliberation of a working party representing the Government, employers and trade unions.
13. The British Government is prepared to facilitate the setting up of a Council of Ireland, which may be interparliamentary as well as

intergovernmental. It proposes to call a conference representative of Westminster, Dublin and the new Assembly to discuss the question. British objectives include acceptance of the present status of Northern Ireland "and of the possibility—which would have to be compatible with the principle of consent—of subsequent change in that status."

14 Northern Ireland's representation in the British House of Commons will remain at twelve seats.

The success of such a plan clearly hinges on the response of both the Provisionals and the UDA. If both oppose implementation of it by force, the initiative cannot possibly succeed. The Provisionals are pleged to continue their reprisal campaign until the British accept their three conditions, and they have condemned the political initiative of Whitelaw. Despite the efforts of the army, IRA terrorism shows no sign of abating. It is clear that the campaign will only cease when the Provisionals lose their base of support among ghetto Catholics, without which they are at the mercy of the security forces. Direct rule significantly cut into this base of support, and both the practical termination of internment and publication of the White Paper have reduced it further. The creation of a nonsectarian government would bring still additional pressure on the Provisionals to accept a cease-fire, and Whitelaw is unquestionably banking on such a renewed Catholic backlash to force the terrorists to capitulate. Judging from his efforts to effect a truce in the spring of 1972, he will do his best to offer face-saving terms to the Provisionals, and there is certainly a chance that his efforts will meet with success. Barring any precipitous action by the UDA or the army, which the Provisionals will certainly do their best to provoke, the political initiative should lead to diminution of the bombing, although this is not likely to become immediately apparent.

The ultimate response of the UDA is more difficult to predict. It is pledged to oppose the implementation of proportional representation by force, but this claim has a ring of bluff to it. The UDA has wisely shown little inclination to take on the British Army, the only way it could effectively block implementation of proportional representation. Looking at the more optimistic side of things, UDA and LAW have begun to form their own political party, which is certainly indicative of some expectation of participation in electoral politics. Should this come to pass, the new Protestant working-class party is likely to poll a very respectable percentage of the votes, and the possibility of actually participating in governmental policy making could provide incentives for the UDA to moderate some of its positions. Moreover, should the UDA–LAW be represented in a reconstructed regional assembly, it is certain to find itself in agreement with the SDLP and the Protestant Left with respect to many economic and social policies. Common opposition to the Unionist party on such matters might gradually promote the emergence of a loose parliamentary working-class coalition among UDA–LAW, SDLP, and NILP. Ultimately this could lead to a shift in salience from sectarian to economic issues. Assuming a grace period of peace by reason of a truce, the continued influx of British capital into Ulster should lead to a drop in unemployment, better housing, and rising prosperity, all of which will further reduce sectarian tensions. These developments would lead to closer cooperation with the Republic, which in the interim, we assume, will have rewritten its constitution to remove the clauses offensive to Northern Protestants. There is still unlikely to be any significant Northern Protestant sentiment in favor of unification, and the question will probably recede in importance given closer cooperation between the two Irelands within the wider framework of the European Community. Perhaps this will ultimately lead to acceptance of some kind of joint sovereignty as now proposed by the SDLP.

The preceding account is the best of all possible worlds, and as such, it is unlikely to materialize. A more likely prediction, still on the optimistic side, would forecast continued violent conflict, with the possible extension of the Provisional bombing campaign to Britain. This latter would be a function of Provisional weakness, i.e., their inability to retain significant Catholic support for terrorism in Ulster. In this scenario the Provisional IRA would die a much slower death, and until it did, the UDA, which reflects very real security fears of working-class Protestants, would not be likely to become less truculent. Catholic-Protestant confrontations would therefore continue, and the need for the British Army to keep the peace would remain. The hope here is that, over time, the Catholic population, realizing the counterproductive nature of terrorism and profiting from the various political and economic reforms, will turn decisively against the Provisional IRA, forcing its demise. This development would in turn create strong Protestant incentives for moderation and eventually lead to the return of political stability and permit the British Army to withdraw.

These scenarios assume that the UDA will refrain from precipitous action and that the British will remain in Ulster. Neither assumption can be taken for granted. A third, more pessimistic, scenario ought to be examined as well. Unfortunately, this one, which leads to civil war, is by no means farfetched. Such a conflict could very easily arise out of a military confrontation between the UDA and the British Army. This could come about in several ways. Let us examine just two. The UDA (and possibly the Provisionals as well) could attempt to disrupt the elections and become involved in a series of incidents with the army in charge of supervising the voting. These incidents would be likely to provoke arms searches of Protestant areas or lead to other actions directed against the UDA and ultimately to a deterioration of army-Protestant relations similar to that which occurred in the Catholic community in 1969 and 1970. Army-Protestant relations are already quite strained, and further tension could certainly result in more violent confrontations. Even assuming that the UDA does not resist proportional representation by force, the new regional assembly is likely to be a house divided against itself. Sectarian feeling is running high enough to warrant the prediction that effective cooperation between Unionists of a militant stripe and the Republican Left, together a majority, is just not feasible. The parliament could therefore resemble the Reichstag during the last years of the Weimar Republic and be so ineffectual that the British might once again be forced to resume control of the province. Given such a development, or even parliamentary malaise, the Provisional bombing campaign is not apt to cease, Protestant anxieties will remain intense, and elements of the UDA are likely to take matters in their own hands, as they have already threatened, and go after the IRA. The army could not remain aloof in such a struggle and would inevitably be drawn into what would become a three-cornered conflict. Either of these situations would, at the very least, result in continuing civil conflict and army casualties.

British public opinion has already become extremely restive about the army's presence in Ulster despite the fact that, as of November 1972, only 130 British soldiers have been killed. The British public, as the Provisionals predict, may well become the determining factor on which all else turns. In March 1972 public opinion polls revealed that the overwhelming majority of the public supported Whitelaw and approved of the presence of the British Army in Northern Ireland. In October, a mere seven months later, 56 percent favored withdrawal of the army, despite the widespread realization that withdrawal would pull out all the stops and probably lead to civil war. What percentage will favor withdrawal a year from now? Should the current level of conflict continue, public opinion is likely to become more adamant in favor of "pulling out the plug and sinking the bloody lot of 'em." If the situation actually deteriorates to the point where British Protestants are shooting at British soldiers, this sentiment will become even more pronounced.[69] Prime Minister Heath will face a very difficult decision. To evacuate the army would remove the last effective restraint against civil war, but to maintain an active military presence in Ulster would be immensely unpopular and would leave the Tories open to charges of waging their own "mini" Vietnam.[70] The prime minister will not be comfortable with either alternative. Nor will the United Nations (as in the case of the British withdrawal from Palestine) be likely to provide him with a way out of the dilemma, despite the fact that a majority of the British public even now favors asking the UN to resolve the conflict. What nation would be willing to volunteer forces for a "peacekeeping" operation that will certainly sustain numerous casualties? Without such a force to give teeth to it, any Security Council resolutions that included a UN involvement would be meaningless.[71]

Several variants of scenario 3 now emerge, all of them increasingly speculative and each likely to end in civil war. Heath can either pull out the army, prompting civil war, or maintain a British military presence of up to 50,000 troops (a larger force demands either conscription, which is unfeasible, or withdrawal of British forces from the Continent). Policing the province under such circumstances would be a considerable drain on the Treasury and would be even more unpopular with the electorate.[72] Labour would probably win the election and sooner or later pull out the army. In the interim, thousands of Ulstermen would have fled the country: Catholics to the Republic and both Catholics and Protestants to Britain. Once the army is actually withdrawn, regardless of when this occurs, the Unionists will attempt to reestablish a government (or conceivably even declare independence). The Provisionals, unquestionably supported by large numbers of Catholics, will resist this by force, and the UDA will go after the Provisionals. Bloody pogroms, especially against relatively unprotected Belfast Catholics, are likely to result. The Republic can hardly be expected to remain a bystander in such a conflict, and Irish public opinion will force her military intervention.[73] Even assuming that the better-equipped Republic Army defeats UDA resistance and occupies the province, the UDA will retain effective control of Protestant urban enclaves and wage guerrilla warfare against the Irish army of occupation. The current situation would be completely reversed, with the UDA playing the role of the Provisionals (and far more effectively) and the Republican Army substituting for the British. The only real solution at this point would be the expulsion of Protestants from the North, a step not to be taken lightly by reason of the tremendous human cost involved.

The preceding analysis is both highly speculative and by no means an exclusive examination of all possible outcomes. Indeed, who in 1968 would have predicted the demise of Stormont four years later? Rather, it is an attempt to sketch in the logical alternatives which appear probable to the involved parties themselves, and in turn, influence their present behavior. The scenarios are also revealing because they bring home with dramatic impact the dilemma that currently confronts the British government. All parties to the conflict appear to be locked into historically determined roles from which the British have been unable to encourage deviation. As a result, civil war is a not unlikely possibility. Even more tragically, such a war, as is also the case in the Arab-Israeli conflict, would itself still not produce a resolution of what is likely to remain one of the most intractable conflicts of the twentieth century.

Postscript, January 1974

More than two hundred people have been killed in Northern Ireland—mostly by random terrorism—since this chapter was first drafted in Autumn 1972. Despite the bloodshed and important political developments in the Republic, Northern Ireland, and Britain, no end to the conflict is in sight. If anything, full-scale civil war has become more likely.

In the Republic a Fine Gael–Labour coalition headed by Liam Cosgrave came to power in March 1973. The new government has pursued the same Northern policy as its predecessor, including a crackdown on IRA cadres within its jurisdiction. Cosgrave has also attempted to assure Unionists that despite the still unreformed constitution the Republic favors unification only when it is supported by a majority of the people in the North.

In Northern Ireland, as predicted, the British government restored some measure of political responsibility to a new regional assembly and hopes that this measure combined with continuing economic and social reforms will bring a degree of tranquillity to Ulster. However, the new government, in existence only a few months, faces serious difficulties.

Assembly elections led to the creation of the first democratically elected local government in Ulster history, a coalition of Unionist, Alliance, and SDLP delegates. The opposition consists of Protestants opposed to both the Council of Ireland, a consultative body to be created from representatives to the Dáil and the Assembly, and cooperation with the SDLP. Naturally, the Provisional IRA and the Ulster Volunteer Force (UVF), now the paramount Protestant paramilitary organization, remain completely outside the system.

The Assembly's success depends upon continued Unionist support for Brian Faulkner, head of the coalition Executive and the major Unionist proponent of cooperation with the SDLP. Faulkner's hold over his parliamentary supporters is tenuous. In January 1974 a conference of Unionist party delegates rejected Faulkner's policy by a clear majority, compelling him to resign party leadership. He has, nevertheless, continued to preside over the Executive and to prevent major defections among his erstwhile supporters in the Assembly, although such defections are certain to occur. The political demise of Faulkner will further polarize the Assembly, making a coalition Executive difficult if not impossible to maintain.

If the Assembly becomes stalemated, the focus of politics is likely to return to the streets and the pessimistic scenarios alluded to in the conclusions become more than disquieting possibilities. The Provisional IRA, while having lost considerable support among Northern Catholics, is still an active force, as demonstrated by the extension of its bombing campaign to Britain. Protestant militancy is at an all-time high and relations between the Protestant community and the army have deteriorated dramatically. Worse still, London's ability to influence events in Northern Ireland has diminished markedly by reason of the magnitude of Britain's internal difficulties. As a result, any forceful British action, especially of a military nature, has become far more costly and is likely to be less popular than ever within Britain, a fact well known to Irish militants.

This act of the Irish drama is thus nearing its denouement. Events of the next six months are likely to have a decisive impact on the future course of the country's development.

Glossary

ALLIANCE PARTY: Founded in April 1970 and composed of individuals from the New Ulster Movement, the Northern Ireland Liberal party, and pro-O'Neill

Unionists. The party endorses the link with Britain and favors "complete and equal partnership in government and public life between Protestants and Catholics."

B SPECIALS: In November 1920 the British government organized the Ulster Special Constabulary. Three classes of the constabulary were created: Class A, for those willing to do full-time service and be posted anywhere in Northern Ireland; Class B, for those willing to do part-time service in their own locality; and Class C, reservists to be called up in case of grave emergency. The B Specials were disbanded in 1970, but a majority retained their weapons and many belong to the Ulster Special Constabulary Association, former B Specials who run gun clubs throughout the North.

DÁIL ÉIREANN: The parliament of the Republic of Ireland, first convened in Dublin by Sinn Fein in January 1919.

DEMOCRATIC UNIONIST PARTY: Organized in 1970 by the Reverend Ian Paisley and composed of former Unionists who opposed any concessions to Catholics.

FIANNA FÁIL: The antitreaty faction of Sinn Fein. Reconstituted as a political party after the defeat of the antitreaty faction in the civil war of 1922–23. The party held power 1932–48, 1951–54, and 1957 to 1963.

FINE GAEL: The protreaty faction of Sinn Fein reconstituted as Fine Gael in 1923. The party was in office between 1948–51 and 1954–57, in coalition with the Labour party. In March 1973, the coalition assumed power once again.

IRISH FREE STATE (SAORSTAT ÉIREANN): Created by the Anglo-Irish Treaty of December 1921, comprising twenty-six of Ireland's thirty-two counties. On Easter Day, 1949, the Free State became the Republic of Ireland.

IRISH CITIZEN ARMY: A paramilitary force organized in October 1913 by James Connolly, of the Irish Transport Worker's Union. Its spirit was that of revolutionary socialism and many of its members participated in the Easter Rebellion.

IRISH REPUBLICAN ARMY (IRA): Early in 1919, the Irish Volunteers were reorganized as the Irish Republican Army, the official army of the Republic, and fought against the British until the truce of July 1921. After the treaty, the IRA split into pro- and antitreaty factions; the antitreaty faction was subsequently defeated in a civil war (1922–23). A reconstituted IRA continued to oppose both Irish governments and is outlawed in both the Republic and Northern Ireland. In the winter of 1970, the IRA split into the "Provisional" IRA and the "Official" IRA. (See pp. 230–32 for discussion of this schism.)

IRISH REPUBLIC BROTHERHOOD (IRB): The dominant influence in the Irish Volunteers, the forerunner of the IRA. The IRB organized the Easter Rebellion of 1916.

IRISH VOLUNTEERS: A paramilitary force organized in December 1913 by Patrick Pearse and Eoin MacNeill. The Volunteers provided the majority of insurgents who fought in the Easter Rebellion.

LOYALIST ASSOCIATION OF WORKERS: A militant Unionist group first organized among Belfast dockworkers. LAW recently split from the Ulster Vanguard Movement and together with the Ulster Defence Association has announced its intention of organizing a Protestant working-class political party.

NORTHERN IRELAND CIVIL RIGHTS ASSOCIATION (NICRA): Founded in February 1967 by a coalition of Northern anti-Unionist groups, NICRA adopted a six-point program calling for one-man-one-vote in local elections, the reform of gerrymandered election districts, laws against discrimination by local government, allocation of housing on a point system, repeal of the Special Powers Act, and disbanding of the B Specials. NICRA was instrumental in organizing the first large-scale civil rights demonstrations in Ulster in 1968.

NORTHERN IRELAND LABOUR PARTY (NILP): Organized in 1949, it favors maintaining the link with Britain but is opposed to sectarianism in Northern Ireland. The party maintains fraternal connections with the British Labour party but is independent of it. At the 1969 election, two of its candidates were elected to Stormont.

NORTHERN IRELAND NATIONALIST PARTY: The Ulster descendant of the Irish Parliamentary party. The party, which represented the majority of Catholics in Stormont, lost its position to the Social Democratic and Labour party in 1970.

"OFFICIAL" IRA: *See* Irish Republican Army.

"PROVISIONAL" IRA: *See* Irish Republican Army.

PEOPLE'S DEMOCRACY: A loose organization of students and ex-students at Queen's University, Belfast, in whose leadership Bernadette Devlin, Michael Farrell, and Eamonn McCann have been prominent. PD organized the "Long March" between Belfast and Londonderry on New Year's Day, 1969.

ROYAL ULSTER CONSTABULARY (RUC): The police force of Northern Ireland. The force is overwhelmingly Protestant and consistently failed to protect Catholic demonstrators from enraged Protestants. The RUC is now undergoing reform designed to make it a more professional, less partisan force.

SINN FEIN ("We Ourselves" in Gaelic): Became an organized movement in 1905 and emerged as the dominant political force in the twenty-six counties when it contested the first postwar election in May 1921. Sinn Fein, like the IRA, split over the treaty question. Today, Sinn Fein (Kevin Street) is the political front of the Provisional IRA and Sinn Fein (Gardiner Place), that of the Official IRA.

SOCIAL DEMOCRATIC AND LABOUR PARTY (SDLP): Founded in August 1970, to advocate the goals of the civil rights movement in Stormont. The party is pledged to be nonsectarian and nonviolent and claims to represent about 40 percent of all Northern Catholics. Its appeal to Protestants has been minimal.

STORMONT: The parliament of Northern Ireland, composed of 52 MP's and 20 senators, until March 1972, when it was dissolved by the British government.

ULSTER DEFENCE ASSOCIATION (UDA): A Protestant paramilitary organization that became prominent in the spring of 1972. The UDA draws most of its membership from the Protestant working class and has close ties with the Loyalist Association of Workers.

ULSTER SPECIAL CONSTABULARY ASSOCIATION: An organization of former B Specials who run gun clubs throughout Northern Ireland. (*See* B Specials.)

ULSTER VANGUARD MOVEMENT: Organized by William Craig in February 1972, to act as a spokesman for militant Unionist groups. The most important of these groups are the Orange Order, the Ulster Special Constabulary Association, the Loyalist Association of Workers, and the Ulster Defence Association. In October 1972, LAW and UDA broke with the movement.

ULSTER VOLUNTEER FORCE (UVF): A Protestant paramilitary organization created by Edward Carson in 1912, to resist Home Rule. The force, later incorporated into the British Army, was all but destroyed in France in 1916. A reconstituted UVF has become increasingly prominent in recent years and, like its predecessor, is composed of militant diehard Protestants.

Notes

1. A. T. Q. Stewart, *The Ulster Crisis* (London: 1967), p. 57.
2. J. C. Beckett, *The Making of Modern Ireland* (New York: 1966), p. 432.
3. Nicholas Mansergh, *The Government of Northern Ireland* (London: 1936), p. 240.
4. Ibid.
5. For statistics on discrimination, see Denis P. Barritt and Charles F. Carter, *The Northern Ireland Problem: A Study in Group Relations* (2nd ed.; London: 1972); and Harold Jackson (for Minority Rights Group), *The Two Irelands: A Dual Study of Inter-Group Tensions* (London: 1971).
6. The percentage of Roman Catholics in Northern Ireland since partition is as follows: 1911 (34.4%), 1926 (33.5%), 1937 (33.5%), 1951 (34.4%), 1961 (34.9%), 1971 (35.2%). Given unchanging birth rates for both communities, the earliest the Catholics could become a majority is 2010.
7. Fermanagh Civil Rights Association, *Fermanagh Facts* (Enniskillen: 1969), pp. 6, 18.
8. In the mid-nineteenth century there were about 800,000 Protestants in the twenty-six counties. In 1920, there were 221,000. The size of the community has further declined through emigration and intermarriage and today (1972) there are 130,000 Protestants comprising 5.1% of the total population of the Republic. The demographic outlook of the community is not encouraging given the increasing rate of intermarriage. In 1961, for example, one-third of the Protestant men and one-fifth of the Protestant women who married that year took Catholic partners. Most Protestants reside in counties bordering on Northern Ireland (Donegal, Cavan, Monoghan, and Leitrim) and are Presbyterian. Protestants (primarily Church of Ireland) also form 9% of the population of Dublin and are well represented in Cork. Their influence is all out of proportion to their numbers. Banking, until recently, was controlled by Protestants, and they are heavily represented among the upper echelons of business management and the

professions. 6.5% of Protestants are company directors, managers, or company secretaries as compared with less than 1% of Catholics, while the proportion holding professional and technical positions is twice that of Catholics. On the other hand, they are underrepresented in the senior ranks of the civil service and almost nonexistent in the army. Only four Protestants sit in the Dáil. In the past, these figures represented a reluctance by Protestants to participate in the public life of a state in which many felt themselves aliens. This aloofness has all but disappeared among younger Irish Protestants. There is no discrimination against Protestants under law and very little informal discrimination, but most Protestants resent the influence of the Catholic church on social legislation which has led to the prohibition of divorce and the manufacture and sale of contraceptives. In the current crisis, most Protestant leaders have expressed open sympathy for the plight of Northern Catholics.

9. For many Irishmen the treaty question was officially put to rest in May 1972 when Jack Lynch announced that the army would participate in the yearly memorial to Michael Collins (leader of the protreaty military forces during the civil war) in County Cork.

10. Gross farm output increased by 27% and the number of males engaged in farm work declined by 27%, leading to an increase of net male productivity of 49%. *Irish Times,* 15 March 1972, Supplement, p. i.

11. *Irish Times,* 15 March 1972, p. 8.

12. Despite the bitter nationalist resentment over Irish economic dependence on Britain, even the IRA (farmer's sons) have been careful not to interfere with this trade.

13. In 1971 Irish exports to the EEC were £40 million. By way of contrast, imports amounted to £110 million.

14. However, the Irish refusal to honor the debt she incurred to Britain under the treaty led to economic sanctions in the 1930s.

15. *Irish Times,*23 March 1972, p. 8.

16. The Orange Lodge was so outraged that it later forced the resignation of the minister of education. The Roman Catholic church was opposed because the act brought some governmental supervision of curriculum.

17. Until the Education Act of 1930, which authorized state financing of up to 50% of the cost of constructing or reconditioning voluntary schools, Catholic schools had received no public support at all.

18. Despite this threat, no plans were made for such a contingency and the cabinet was apparently convinced that O'Neill would somehow survive. One senior minister later reflected: "If anyone had told me that we would let O'Neil fall to be replaced by someone further to the Right, and that he in turn would be replaced from the Right—well, I would not have believed it." Cited in The Sunday Times Insight Team, *Ulster* (Harmondsworth: 1972), p. 84.

19. Samuel Stevenson, self-styled "chief of staff" of the Ulster Volunteer Force, was later placed on trial for the bombings and pleaded guilty, giving evidence against other members of the force who had pleaded not guilty.

20. Sunday Times Insight Team, pp. 82–83.

21. Ibid., p. 103.

22. The relevant passage read: "I swear by Almighty God . . . by the Blessed Virgin Mary . . . by the Blessed Rosary and Holy Beads . . . to fight until we die, wading in the fields of Red Gore of the Saxon Tyrants and Murderers of the Glorious Cause of Nationality . . . and moreover, when the English Protestant Robbers and Beasts in Ireland shall be driven into the sea like the swine that Jesus Christ caused to be drowned, we shall embark for, and take, England, root out every vestige of the accursed Blood of the Heretics, Adulterers and Murderers of Henry VII and possess ourselves of the treasures of the Beasts that have so long kept our Beloved Isle of Saints . . . in bondage . . . and we shall not give up the conquest until we have our Holy Father complete ruler of the British Isles . . . so help me God."

23. The best-known case was that of John Benson, a Belfast dockworker, who was arrested for painting *No Tea Here* on a Belfast wall (a reference to the former Catholic practice of offering tea to British soldiers). The magistrate decided that this act was "an obvious attempt to intimidate people" and sentenced Benson to six months.

24. *Irish Times,* 7 July 1972, p. 1.

25. Sunday Times Insight Team, p. 249.

26. Internment was actually opposed by many Ulster police officials and by General Sir Harry Tuzo, the new GOC Northern Ireland, as impractical. They argued that unless internment was also imposed in the Republic, of which there was not a chance, it would not

destroy the IRA but strengthen it by further alienating the Northern Catholic community.

27. *Observer,* 6 February 1972, p. 7.

28. A survey conducted by the *Sunday Telegraph* (Belfast) just prior to the imposition of direct rule revealed that 82% of all the Catholics interviewed were willing to accept reform proposals that nevertheless still maintained their link with Britain. *Sunday Telegraph,* 1 March 1972, p. 1.

29. Craig's espousal of independence as a possible solution has brought him into conflict with Ian Paisley who, backed by Enoch Powell in Britain, favors full integration with Britain as the proper solution.

30. *Irish Times,* 28 March 1972, p. 7.

31. Ibid., 3 April 1972, p. 1.

32. Ibid., 31 May 1972, p. 1.

33. Ibid., 14 June 1972, p. 1.

34. Ibid., 20 June 1972, p. 1.

35. Ibid., 14 June 1972, p. 1.

36. Ibid., 16 June 1972, p. 1.

37. Ibid., 21 June 1972, p. 1.

38. Ibid., 23 June 1972, p. 1.

39. Ibid., 7 July 1972, p. 1.

40. Ibid., 6 July 1972, p. 1. Whitelaw had gone so far as to declare that he could not foresee negotiations with the Provisionals even after they had stopped their violence.

41. *Times* (London), 6 July 1972, p. 3.

42. Perhaps an analogy can be drawn here to the Vietnamese situation where the victorious Vietminh came away from the Geneva Conference with far less than it had gained on the field of battle. No doubt, the North Vietnamese leadership, with this precedent in mind, was more reluctant than it might otherwise have been, to agree to a cease-fire again without clearly defined concessions in advance.

43. *Irish Times,* 24 July 1972, p. 1.

44. A recent study suggests that 200 of the first 500 deaths were "innocent passers-by." *Irish Times,* 28 October 1972, p. 7.

45. The SDLP proposes that the British and Irish governments exercise joint sovereignty over Northern Ireland, thus satisfying nationalist demands for unification and Unionist desires to maintain the connection with Britain. Under this arrangement the North would no longer send representatives to Westminster, and within the province the Tricolour and the Union Jack would have equal status. Two commissioners, one each from Britain and Ireland, would jointly sign all legislation passed by a reconstructed regional assembly. A constitutional court composed of three judges, one appointed by each commissioner and the third, the chief justice of Northern Ireland, would adjudicate all conflicts between the Assembly and the commissioners. The eighty-four member Assembly itself would be elected on the basis of proportional representation and would have an executive of fifteen members. The chief executive would allocate departmental responsibility, subject to the approval of the commissioners. All security matters, foreign policy, and financial subventions would be the responsibility of the sovereign states. Social Democratic and Labour Party, *Towards a New Ireland* (Belfast: 1972).

46. *Irish Times,* 15 September 1972, p. 1.

47. Ibid., 8 September 1972, p. 8.

48. Ibid., 7 September 1972, p. 8.

49. Ibid., 6 September 1972, p. 1.

50. Ibid., 5 May 1972, p. 1.

51. Ibid., 6 June 1972, p. 1.

52. Ibid.

53. Sunday Times Insight Team, chaps. 5 and 11.

54. The Irish Army had devised a plan that called for a border incident to be staged as the pretext for invasion. A Republican ambulance, requested by a Catholic doctor in Londonerry, was to be fired upon while crossing the Craigavon Bridge. In response, the Sixth Brigade of the Irish Army was to secure the bridge and march into Londonderry. Meanwhile, an armored column would cross into the southeast corner of Ulster and strike at Lurgan and Toome Bridge, cutting Belfast off from the rest of Ulster. The two forces were to link up and "liberate" Belfast. The plan assumed noninterference by the British Army!

55. *New York Times,* 2 February 1972, p. 14.

56. Ibid., 4 February 1972, p. 8.

57. See, for example, Lynch's speech in the Dáil on 13 July 1972. Reprinted in the *Irish Times,* 15 July 1972, p. 9.

58. Enoch Powell has already expressed his opinion that these privileges should be revoked but there is very little anti-Republic backlash in Britain. A campaign organized by the right-wing Nationalist Front party to boycott Irish goods has met with no success whatever. Several British organizations have canceled conferences in the Republic and British soccer teams have refused to play matches in the Republic, but these decisions were made on the grounds of security and do not reflect any growing hostility toward the Republic.

59. The Republic, on the other hand, has pointed to the economic losses it has suffered by reason of violence in the North. Tourism in the summer of 1972 was down by 24% (because potential travelers confused the Republic with the North and were fearful of violence), Aer Lingus suffered a £4 million loss during the same period and in the wake of "Bloody Sunday," eighteen conferences were canceled and nine foreign industrial projects postponed. This sacrifice, Lynch has argued, clearly justifies Republican concern for Northern developments.

60. The relevant passage reads: "The voice of the United States must be raised against the terror and violence in Northern Ireland and against the discrimination, repression and deprivation which causes the awful strife there."

61. *New York Times,* 4 February 1972, p. 3.

62. Dr. Bernard Lee, executive assistant to Dr. Ralph Abernathy, president of the Southern Christian Leadership Conference, has stated that President Nixon promised Prime Minister Heath when the two met in December 1971 that he would be silent on the question of Ireland. *Irish Times,* 12 February 1972, p. 7.

63. The Officials have also received considerable left-wing student support in France, and in May 1972 the French government deported Official leaders who had come to address rallies in Paris.

64. This is especially true in Catholic Italy and France. In the latter country, Simone de Beauvoir, Simone Signoret, and Yves Montand organized petitions against internment and special powers.

65. *Irish Times,* 1 March 1972, pp. 1, 9.

66. Ibid., 5 September 1972, p. 1.

67. Ibid., 19 September 1972, p. 1.

68. Ibid., 15 September 1972, p. 9.

69. Ibid., 26 September 1972, p. 1. The poll was conducted by the Opinion Research Center for the BBC and involved a sample of 505. Mr. Roy Hattersley, a former Labour minister, commenting on this poll on the BBC program "Panorama," insisted that public opinion would be very unlikely to sustain a continued military presence in Ulster if British Protestants attacked British soldiers. "It won't be the IRA which will make the situation untenable," he declared. "It will be the people the army are supposed to be protecting from the IRA."

70. The British presence in Ulster has frequently been compared to Vietnam in the British press. The journalists have generally argued that the analogy is, of course, misleading in many ways, but given the horrors evoked in the popular mind by the mere mention of the word Vietnam, the journalistic linkage of the two situations is hardly likely to help sustain public support for a continued military presence in Northern Ireland.

71. Conceivably, Heath could seek to sell the British military presence in Ulster to the British public if British Army units were incorporated into a United Nations force to which other countries (NATO members?) made only token contributions.

72. The military presence in Ulster has already cost the British government (from August 1969 to April 1972) £22 million.

73. A third alternative for the British government might be to try to share the burden of peacekeeping with the Republic with Republican troops assigned to Catholic sectors, as once suggested by the SDLP, and British troops restricted to non-Catholic areas. Assuming the Republican government was willing to accept such an arrangement, dual occupancy would be likely to facilitate further residential segregation and perhaps lead to separate political administrations in an attempt to separate the protagonists. This, of course, would create immense problems, among them two divided cities.

INDIA, PAKISTAN

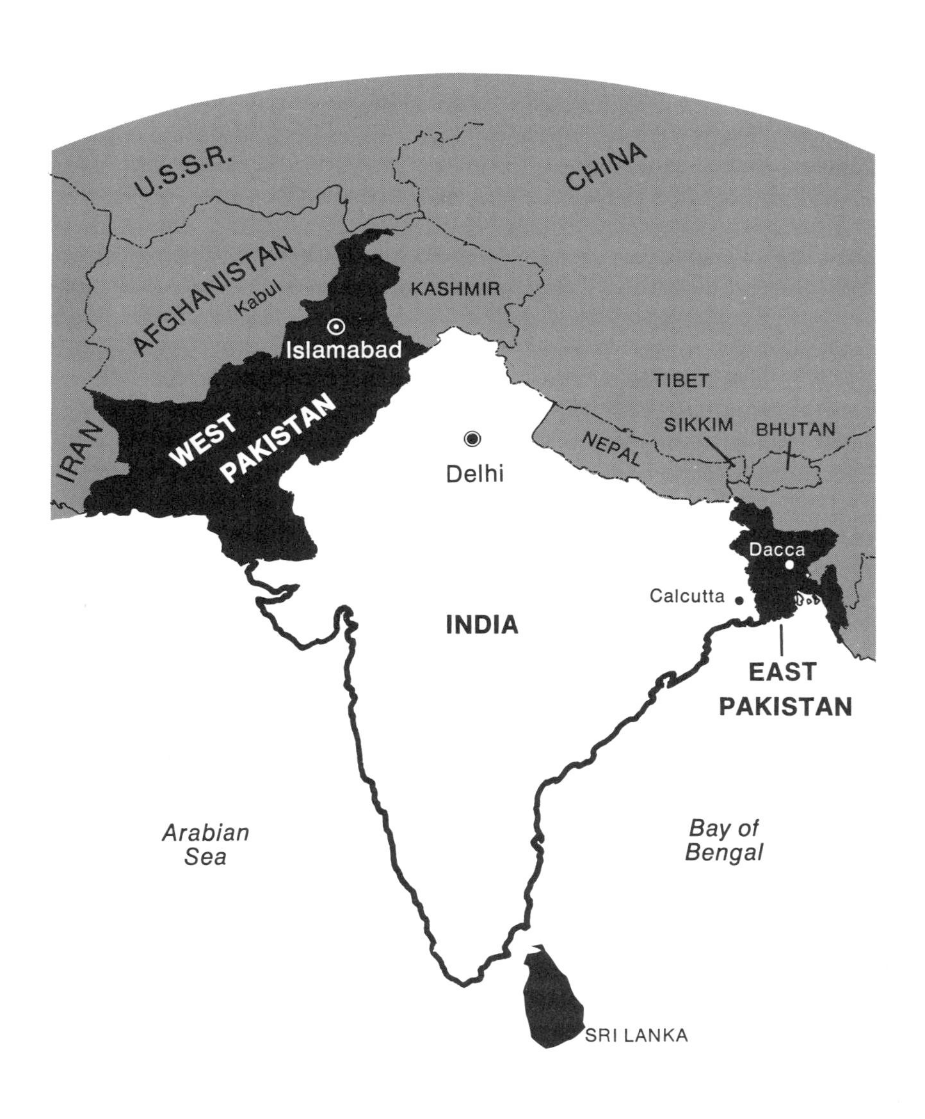

8

India and Pakistan

Craig Baxter

The Partition of India

ON AUGUST 15, 1947, India and Pakistan became independent nations, ending British rule over the subcontinent. This chapter considers the causes and results of a rare case of division in which independence and partition occurred simultaneously.

Before doing so, however, several key points must be mentioned which differentiate the partition of India from some or all of the other examples of divided nations discussed in this book.

1. Barring largely rhetorical statements from a few Indian political parties and some nostalgia in Pakistan, there is no movement in either India or Pakistan for the political reunification of the subcontinent.
2. The partition was an agreed-upon separation, reluctantly agreed-to perhaps in geographic terms by the Muslims and in "national" terms by the Hindus, but nonetheless accepted by both parties, not forced on them by an outside power or coming as the result of a postwar situation.
3. For the Muslims at least, the partition is not seen as the result of a division of a nation but rather the separation of a Muslim "nation" from a Hindu "nation" on the basis of the two-nation theory.
4. The study of the partition of India is complicated by the subsequent division of one of the successor states, Pakistan.[1]
5. The partition was made more complex by the existence within India of more than five hundred Indian princely states to which special

provisions applied and which, especially in the case of Jammu and Kashmir, continue to plague the relations between the successor states.

With this catalogue of differences in mind, the background to the Pakistani demand, the plan for partition, and the consequences of its implementation can be studied as a unique situation in which division was seen in 1947 as the only feasible answer to the question of the political aspirations of a sizable but reasonably concentrated minority wary of its future in a state in which the Hindus would have a majority had partition not taken place. The subject, on which numerous books have been written—many with the particular bias of one who participated in, implemented, or was affected by the decision—can only be treated in summary here. Much explanatory detail must be omitted.[2]

Background to Partition

At the beginning of the eleventh century Muslim raiders from Afghanistan began a series of incursions beyond the Khyber Pass into India. This marked the first round in a series of events which would culminate in control by Muslim rulers of most of the subcontinent.[3] Centering principally on the city of Delhi, a series of dynasties succeeded one another until in 1526 Babar, a descendant of Tamerlane, defeated the incumbent dynasty and established the Mughal Empire. Babar and his successors, notably Akbar (1556–1605) and Aurangzeb (1659–1707), expanded the Delhi kingdom to include a number of previously independent Muslim kingdoms to the south as well as such Hindu rulers as had survived earlier Muslim expansion. At its greatest extent the Mughal Empire encompassed all of what was to become British India with the exception of the extreme south of the subcontinent, although control was not unchallenged. Rebellion by local Hindu and Muslim adventurers was a constant source of difficulty for the Delhi government.

The Muslim, therefore, could look back from a vantage point of the 1930s to a period in which his forebears were the rulers of India. Even with the decline of central Mughal authority after the death of Aurangzeb and the arrival of Europeans at points along the coast, Muslims continued to dominate much of interior India. Local potentates such as those in Bengal, Oudh (now a part of Uttar Pradesh), and Hyderabad established themselves as at least semiindependent rulers. Subordinate to the local rulers, other Muslims acquired control of much of the land, becoming, with confirmation of their rights by the British, members of the general class of *zamindars* or landlords. There were exceptions. The Hindu Maratha Confederacy maintained its sway over western India and much of west-central India, while Hindu rulers reasserted local authority in a broad band of territory stretching from Rajasthan to Orissa. In the Punjab, the rise of the Sikhs to political leadership resulted in a kingdom under their control seated at Lahore. Although internally beset with strife, it lasted until the British conquered the Punjab in the mid-nineteenth century.

European penetration of the subcontinent began in 1498 with the arrival of Vasco da Gama at Cochin. Originally limited to coastal points, the area of European influence enlarged with the decline of the power of Delhi. At the same time, the Europeans entered into conflict among themselves. European wars were extended to India; they were principally manifested by struggles between French and British colonial armies, often in alliance with local rulers. British action against the Mughal Empire and France centered on Bengal where Robert Clive won a major battle at Pilasi (Plassey) in 1757 and began a process that would result in British control of virtually all of the subcontinent. The defeat of France in the Napoleonic wars in Europe was matched in India. Under a succession of administrations, notably those of the Marquess of Wellesley (1798–1805) and the Earl of Dalhousie (1848–56), an expansionist policy was pursued. It should be noted here, as it became important at the time of partition, that the British, whether under the East India Company prior to 1858 or under the Crown after that date, followed two different plans of expansion. One method of gaining territory was by direct annexation. Another was by agreement with local rulers under which the ruler would recognize the Crown as paramount and cede to the British certain powers while retaining local autonomy and gaining recognition as the head of a "princely state," usually with the title maharaja if a Hindu or nawab if a Muslim. By 1947, more than five hundred princely states existed within India.

In 1857 the British were faced with a major revolt, the Sepoy Mutiny, in northern India. Although the mutineers were drawn from among both Muslims and Hindus, the symbolic leader was Bahadur Shah II, the all-but-powerless Mughal ruler in whose name the British carried out the administration of northern India.[4] When the mutiny was quelled, with the assistance of native troops from the Punjab who remained loyal, Bahadur Shah was exiled to Burma and the Mughal Empire formally terminated. The East India Company was wound up in 1858 and power assumed by the Crown.

The growth of British power in a political sense was carried out in the north very largely at the expense of the Muslims. Bengal was a Mughal satrapy when it fell to the new rulers. The annexation of Oudh in 1856 was a source of Muslim grievance and a proximate cause of the mutiny. For local assistance in administering their new dominions the British turned more often than not to the Hindus who, in the eyes of the British, were both more adaptable to European methods of governance and were apparently more loyal in their employment. The anger of the rulers following the mutiny was largely vented upon the Muslims who were seen, however incorrectly, as the instigators of the rebellion and those who would have benefited most had it succeeded.[5] Although many local Muslim *zamindars* retained their holdings in the United Provinces and elsewhere, and some were rewarded for loyalty in the Punjab, it was clear that, at least for the time being, the British would look to others in the new empire.

The period of Muslim invasion, conversion, and rule—from approximately A.D. 1000 to 1857—had resulted in an uneven distribution of Muslims. Most Muslims lived in a broad belt running from the Khyber Pass and the Sind across northern India to Bengal, with majorities only in the western and eastern extremities of that belt and substantial minorities in the United Provinces and Bihar. Only three Muslim princes of importance governed outside the area, those of Hyderabad, Bhopal, and—more for his later impact—Junagadh. Relations between Hindus and Muslims had varied. The reign of Akbar saw the height of tolerance of ruling Muslim for ruled Hindu, but three generations later, under Aurangzeb, zealotry replaced tolerance and such devices as the *jizya,* a tax on non-Muslims, were reimposed. Nonetheless, communal rioting, so prevalent as independence seemed within reach, was rare, and relations between the two communities were correct if not cordial.

THE TWO-NATION THEORY

With the assumption of power by the Crown came the beginnings of a gradual movement toward the association of Indians with the running of the empire. Indians were nominated to the legislative councils of the viceroy and the provincial governors under the provisions of the Indian Councils Act of 1861. Opportunities for Indian employment at all levels of the civil service, including the prestigious Indian Civil Service (ICS), were expanded, and Indians were appointed to judicial posts. An elective principle was introduced into local administration by a series of provincial enactments following a statement by the viceroy, Lord Ripon, in 1882 that representative institutions would further the "political and popular education" of Indians.

Educated Indians were caught up in this changing atmosphere and felt a need for a formal organization to articulate their interests to the imperial regime. A number of local groups had been formed. These culminated in 1885 in the founding of the Indian National Congress. The Congress was neither a revolutionary nor a mass group at its inception. Its leadership saw it as contributing to the stability of the British regime, although the goal was increasing Indian participation in governance. A shortcoming of the Congress was the notable lack of support from the Muslim community. The founders were largely Western educated, or at least, Westernized and operated in an urban atmosphere. Only a small number of Muslims fit that description, and those few were centered largely in such entrepot cities as Bombay and not in the Muslim cultural areas of the north.

Indian Muslims had not been inactive following the British advance northward. Early movements, however, had been based more in religious traditionalism than in a modernist and political response to the British. The first truly modernist Islamic response came under the leadership of Sir Syed Ahmad Khan (1817–98).[6] Descended from the lesser nobility of the Mughal Empire, Sir Syed remained loyal to the British during the mutiny; he held appointments under the British and maintained close relationships with them. In his view the Muslims as a community suffered from hostility toward and from the British and from a rejection of Western education which the Hindus had used to achieve a higher status in British estimation. Much of Sir Syed's life was devoted to the cause of Muslim higher education and resulted in what is today Aligarh Muslim University. The institution was intended to train Muslims for service under the Crown and in so doing maintained an interdenominational stance between sectarian divisions in Islam; it admitted Hindu students and used English as the basic medium of instruction. From this beginning in modern Islamic education would spring many leaders who worked under Jinnah in the Pakistan movement.

Sir Syed, in 1883, publicly opposed the introduction of elections to local bodies. He said that the Muslims were in a permanent minority and that those few Muslims who were elected to office would owe their election to constituencies that were predominately Hindu. He added to this his opposition to the Congress as a spokesman for India, believing it to be in the hands of the Hindu middle class and unrepresentative of the Muslims. He called for Muslims to abstain from membership in the Congress and said that the new group did not view India realistically: "They do not take into consideration that India is inhabited by different nationalities." It became clear that the different nationalities of which Sir Syed spoke were Hindus and Muslims, each, in his view, with a separate heritage and a distinct future. In this lies the two-nation theory and from it grew the demand first for separate electorates and later for separate sovereignty in the form of Pakistan.

ELECTIONS AND THE MUSLIM LEAGUE

In 1892 the Indian Councils Act was revised. The legislative councils of the viceroy and of the provincial governors were enlarged; additional Indian members were included; and the powers of the bodies were expanded to include consideration, if not control, of the budget. More than this, however, the viceroy and the governors were to receive nominations for the Indian seats from recognized Indian associations. Election, in the precise sense, was not conceded. The appointing authorities could ignore the advice received, but the concept of representative Indians performing the duties of member of the legislative council was recognized.

In 1905, the last year of the viceroyalty of Lord Curzon, the huge province of Bengal was partitioned. Areas roughly corresponding to present Bangladesh and Assam became a separate province, and the remaining areas, roughly West Bengal, Bihar, and Orissa, remained under Calcutta. The division created a Muslim majority province in the east and was welcomed by the Muslim community. Not unexpectedly, the Hindu population of Bengal opposed the move and in some cases expressed their feelings by resort to terrorism.

More than annoyance to the Hindus, there was the prospect of loss of political control. The advent of Lord Minto in Calcutta as viceroy and Lord Morley in the India Office in London presaged important constitutional changes in which election to central and provincial councils was expected to play a part. Morley was determined to expand Indian participation and, unlike the archconservative Curzon, Minto worked fully with the secretary of state.

To the Muslim, elections were an inviting but disturbing prospect. Franchise qualifications were likely to be high and thus favor the Hindu, already favored in most of India by his population advantage. The likelihood was that at central and provincial levels Hindus would overwhelmingly dominate the new bodies. In December 1906, in Dacca, the Muslim League was founded "to promote among the Musalmans of India loyalty to the British government [and] to protect and advance the political rights and interests of the Musalmans of India."

The group at Dacca had not acted without preparation. In October of the same year a deputation led by the Aga Khan had called on Lord Minto at Simla and presented a memorandum to him. Assuring the viceroy of the loyalty of the Muslim community, the delegates specifically requested that the new electoral system include separate representation of the Muslim community. The proposal was that at both the central and provincial level seats be allocated for Muslims at least in proportion to their number but with preferably some weightage to ensure "adequate" representation of the minority. These seats would be filled by an electorate comprised solely of Muslims, the Hindus and all others voting in general constituencies under the assumption that Hindus would dominate and achieve their allocated proportion of the membership of the councils. The deputation left the viceroy with reason to believe that the proposal for separate electorates would be accepted.

The Government of India Act of 1909, the Morley-Minto Reforms as they are generally described, did indeed include a provision for separate electorates.[7] At central level a legislative council was established; it would include, among its 68 members, 27 members elected by Indians and 5 additional Indians to be appointed to represent special interests not otherwise gaining seats. The remaining 36 members would be officials of the government, some of whom might be Indian. At the provincial level the combination of elected Indians and appointed nonofficial Indians would outnumber the government officials included in the councils. The powers of the councils were expanded and included interpolation of officials but in no way permitted such parliamentary practices as a vote of confidence in the administration.

Lord Morley, in introducing the reforms which bear his and Minto's names, made it clear to the British Parliament that the changes were only to associate Indians with the governance and not a prelude to full parliamentary government. Yet, as Indian and British experience grew, the view of London changed. During the First World War Britain, through Secretary of State Edwin Montagu, declared the home government's policy to be "that of the increasing association of Indians in every branch of the administration and the gradual development of self-governing institutions with a view to the progressive realisation of responsible government in India as an integral part of the British Empire." No doubt much of Montagu's purpose in his declaration was to ensure Indian cooperation during the war, but it was made more necessary by developments in India including the formation of the Home Rule League, the gradual ascendancy of the extremists over the moderates or gradualists in the Congress, and the rising expectations of the liberals in India following the Morley-Minto changes. Montagu added in his statement that he would visit India as soon as possible, with the goal of formulating further reforms to be implemented after the war.

Congress opposition to separate electorates, seen as a setting in concrete of communal differences, began to moderate. The result was the Lucknow Pact of 1916 under which the League and the Congress agreed to a system of separate electorates. The agreement of the Congress resulted from its feeling that the two groups should work together toward the goal of self-government and that, to align the two organizations, the firm Muslim insistence on separate electorates must be conceded. The Muslims thereby received Congress blessing for a proportion of the seats at all levels which would be larger, in varying degrees, than the Muslim share of the population except that in no case would it constitute a majority, even in Bengal where Muslims comprised about 52 percent of the population. The Muslims also agreed not to stand for election in general constituencies, thus permitting Hindus almost assured victory in those seats. The two organizations demanded early implementation of Dominion status and received Montagu's response the following year. They added demands for greater autonomy at the provincial level and greater Indianization of civil and military services.

Prominent among the Muslim negotiators at Lucknow was Muhammad Ali Jinnah (1876–1948). No one on the Muslim side was to play a more important role in the events leading to partition than Jinnah, who was destined to become the first governor general of Pakistan. Born in Karachi into a commercial family, he traveled to London and was admitted to the bar at the age of twenty. He pursued a distinguished legal career in Karachi and Bombay and entered politics through the Muslim League, where he was to remain throughout his political career. Jinnah was not fully in tune with the older members of the League who professed loyalty to the British and opposed cooperation with the Congress. He found himself more at home with the moderates in Congress who saw a constitutional and gradual approach leading ultimately to Indian self-government. He thought the Muslims adequately protected under the Lucknow Pact. It was change within the Congress from an urban-oriented, elitist organization to a mass-based political movement that separated Jinnah from the Congress.

DYARCHY AND GANDHI

The Montagu-Chelmsford Reforms of 1919 were another step along the gradualist path toward Home Rule. The key provision was that of dyarchy, or dual rule, at the provincial level. Certain nation-building subjects were transferred to Indian control, including public works, education, and public health. These departments in the provincial administration would be headed by Indian ministers who were to be responsible to the legislative councils. Other departments were reserved to the governor; these would be headed by members of his executive council who were responsible not to the council but to the governor. The departments included finance, revenue, and home affairs. Indians could, and would, be appointed members in some province but they would, if members also of the legisltaive council, give up their elective legislative seats and become appointive official members. The legislative councils themselves were greatly expanded and elected members became a clear majority. Separate electorates were retained in accordance with the Lucknow formula and were expanded to include the Sikhs in Punjab. At central level a bicameral system replaced the viceroy's legislative council. The upper House, the Council of State, included 32 elected and 8 nominated Indians among its 64 members. The lower House, the Central Legislative Assembly, had 97 elected Indians and between 19 and 24 nominated Indians among its 135 members. Separate electorates operated as well at this level. Indian control of departments at the center was not part of the new arrangement, although the powers of the central legislature were enhanced to include debate on sensitive issues including the budget and internal security matters. Ultimate authority for legislation was retained by the viceroy.

Much had happened, however, before the new constitutional arrangements came into force following elections in 1921. A new figure appeared in the Congress who was destined to assume its leadership and transform it into a mass movement. Mohandas Karamchand Gandhi (1869–1948), a Gujarati, educated in England and admitted to the bar, had had success in South Africa agitating for the rights of Indians living there. He developed ideas of peaceful noncooperation with established authorities and believed he could achieve his ends by massive passive resistance. The depletion through death in the ranks of the moderate leaders left the field open for

Gandhi, and he soon put his new programs into operation, albeit with the misgivings of surviving members of the older leadership. Misgivings also were present in the Muslim leadership. As Sir Percival Griffith wrote: "To make the movement strong enough it must be nationwide, and this meant a mass appeal. . . . But a mass appeal in his hands could not be other than a Hindu one. He could transcend caste but not community. The devices he used went sour in the mouths of Muslims". [8] Although one of Gandhi's initial efforts was combined with Muslims, as independence drew closer the rift between Hindus and Muslims, between Gandhi and Jinnah, became unbridgeable.

During World War I the government of India had imposed certain restrictions on activities in India in the name of security. These were, if not applauded, at least understandable to the Indian political leadership; the end of the war would presumably bring about the end of the restrictions. But in 1919 the Rowlatt Acts were passed which entitled the government to detain suspected agitators without trial and permitted judges to try cases of alleged sedition without juries. Gandhi responded by calling a one-day *hartal* (general strike) which was met by arrests. The situation soon became violent. Agitation was strongest in the Punjab where Hindus, Muslims, and Sikhs joined in protest and often in violence. A number of Europeans were killed in Amritsar. There followed what is undoubtedly the darkest blot on the record of British rule in India, the Jallianwala Bagh massacre. On April 13, 1919, British-led troops opened fire on a crowd gathered in the *Bagh* (garden) from which there was no egress except the gate through which the troops—about 150 in number, two-thirds of them Indian sepoys—had entered. The toll was 379 dead and about 1,200 wounded. A governmental commission appointed to investigate the tragedy said the commander was guilty of an "error of judgment," but the act was specifically condemned both by an unofficial Indian committee and by the House of Commons.

In December of the same year the Congress held its annual session at Amritsar under the cloud of the massacre. Against opposition from Tilak and other veterans, Gandhi urged the party to cooperate with the government of India in working the new reforms. Within a year he was to reverse his stand and launch a noncooperation movement. The failure of the official commission to condemn the Amritsar action was one reason for Gandhi's turnabout. He also saw a new issue on which he might be able to unite Hindus and Muslims into a mass peaceful agitation. This was the Khilafat issue, the continuance in office of the sultan of Turkey in his religious role as caliph of Islam. Muslims in India saw the aftermath of World War I and the disturbed condition of Turkey as threatening to the position of the caliph. Although it is doubtful that the Khilafat question was of great concern to the Muslim masses, it was important to the religious leadership, who might sway the masses. Gandhi saw the issue, however, as one on which Hindus and Muslims could work together in a way that would cement the two communities to work for self-government. Congress leadership was less than enthusiastic about a noncooperation movement on the basis of the Khilafat question, but at a special session of the Congress in 1920 Gandhi won grudging approval. With this the leadership of the Congress passed formally from the old guard to Gandhi, although reconciliation was eventually effected with almost everyone. Jinnah stood among those who remained disapproving of the mass tactics of Gandhi.

In terms of immediate goals the movement was a failure. The Turks themselves abolished the caliphate. The pleas of Gandhi for passive, nonviolent civil disobedience was ignored in many places and terrorism broke out. Self-government seemed as far from realization at the end as it had in the beginning of the agitation. Congress politicians also chafed under Gandhi's injunction that the party not participate in the 1921 elections held under Montagu-Chelmsford, a situation reversed in 1923 by the formation of the Swarajist party which contested the 1924 and subsequent elections while remaining a part of the Congress. The early 1920s also saw an upsurge of communal violence between the Hindus and Muslims and appeal from leaders of both communities for peace in 1924.

Jinnah saw the violence as, at least in part, the result of the drawing apart of the two communities through the system of separate electorates. As president of the Muslim League in 1927 he offered to drop separate electorates provided other arrangements were made to protect Muslim interests. Among these were an assurance that there would be a Muslim majority in the legislatures of the Punjab and Bengal (provinces in which the Muslims were in a small majority) and that one-third of the seats at the central level would be reserved for Muslims. These would be chosen by general electorates but the seats would be reserved for members of a specified community (as is the case at present in India, with seats in Indian legislative bodies reserved for scheduled castes and tribes). The Congress rejected the offer, and what might have been a workable and reasonable proposal by one who was still very much disposed toward Hindu-Muslim cooperation was discarded. Similar suggestions made by others to the Simon Commission and at the round-table conferences held in London in the early 1930s were turned down. Disgusted with the trends in Indian politics, Jinnah retired to London and withdrew from the Muslim League in 1932.

The round-table conferences were a prelude to the Government of India Act of 1935, but earlier the Indian political leaders attempted to frame a constitutional document themselves. Prepared under the leadership of Motilal Nehru, the report was published in 1928. It called for immediate Dominion status. It also stated that all polling would be held under a system of joint electorates and that reservation of seats would be limited for the central legislature to Hindus in the Northwest Frontier Province and for Muslims in provinces in which they were a minority. At the provincial level there would be no reservation of seats in either the Punjab or Bengal, and in other provinces seats would be reserved for minorities in proportion to their population. One proposal favored by the Muslims was the separation of Sind, a Muslim majority area, from Bombay. The Nehru Report was the subject of an all-parties meeting in Calcutta in 1928 where Jinnah put forward the suggestions he had made a year earlier. They were rejected. Jinnah withdrew to join a Muslim conference in January 1929, which endorsed separate electorates on the system then existing. Jinnah, thus rebuffed, did not again put forward the proposal of joint electorates under any circumstances. Another and important aspect of Jinnah's recommendations to the Calcutta session was the grant of residual powers under the constitution to the provinces, in some of which Muslims would be in a majority, rather than at the central level, where the Muslims would be in a permanent minority.

One section of the Nehru Report, that calling for Dominion status, was opposed by Motilal's son, Jawaharlal. The younger Nehru and his associates put forward a proposal that the demand be for full independence. The demand was tempered by Gandhi, who secured agreement that the British should be given until the end of 1929 to institute Dominion government, failing which a new civil disobedience campaign would be launched. This resistance began with the salt march of 1930. The arrest of Gandhi followed and he was in jail during the first round-table conference. During 1929, Lord Irwin, then viceroy, made a statement that the 1917 Montagu declaration concerning "responsible government" was intended to mean "Dominion status." In 1931 Gandhi and Irwin agreed to call off the disobedience campaign and to release all political prisoners. Gandhi himself joined the second round-table conference. Agreement could not be reached on the key provisions of the forthcoming reforms relating to communal representation in the legislatures, and the British government itself was forced to make an award on the subject.

The 1935 Act and the Drift Toward Separation

At the Muslim League session in 1930, in Allahabad, the president was the poet and philosopher Dr. Sir Muhammad Iqbal (1877–1938). In his address Iqbal, expressing a personal view on the future of the Muslims of India, said, "I would like to see the Punjab, Northwest Frontier Province, Sind, and Baluchistan amalgamated into a single state. Self-government within the British Empire or without the British Empire, and the formation of a consolidated northwest Indian Muslim state appears to me to be the final destiny of the Muslims, at least of northwest India." It is not certain that Iqbal envisaged a partition of India in the sense that the Muslim state would sever relations with the Delhi government, but the statement is often taken as the first formulation of the demand for Pakistan. The word "Pakistan" itself first appeared during the round-table conferences in London when a group of Muslim students circulated a pamphlet advocating the combination of *P*unjab, *A*fghania (the Northwest Frontier Province), *K*ashmir, *S*ind and Baluchi*stan*. The word also has the additional meaning of "land of the pure." During the next fifteen years a variety of partition and redistribution plans would be circulated, culminating in the three-tier plan advocated by the British prior to the final partition of the subcontinent.

The outcome of the round-table conferences was the 1935 act which conceded full provincial autonomy to responsible Indian ministries. The act also provided for a federation at the central level with a form of dyarchy, provided a sufficient number of the Indian princely states would agree to join the federation. The federal provisions were never put in force as the princes did not accede to the new scheme. The separate electorate provisions were retained and expanded to include communities other than Muslims, Hindus, and Sikhs. The functional representation was also expanded and included such new groups as labor. Based on Muslim seats alone, the Muslims would not have a majority of the seats in either Bengal or the Punjab, although in the latter the almost-certain winning of some functional seats would provide a slim majority.

Elections under the new act were held in the winter of 1936–37. Congress swept to a large victory in the general seats in most provinces. It gained absolute majorities in all provinces except Bengal, the Punjab, Sind, and Assam. In Muslim seats in the Muslim minority provinces, the Muslim League, fortified by the return of Jinnah from his London exile, gained a clear majority. It was in the Muslim majority provinces, the Frontier, the Punjab, Sind, and Bengal, that the League performed poorly. In each province there was another Muslim party which held leadership. In the Frontier it was the Khudai Khitmatgar of Khan Abdul Ghaffar Khan, allied to the Congress, which dominated the Muslim vote. The Unionist party of Sir Sikandar Hayat Khan swept to victory in the Punjab as a tricommunal grouping supported by Muslims, Hindus, and Sikhs. In Bengal Maulvi A. K. Fazlul Haq led his populist Krishak Praja party to a victory in the Muslim seats. In Sind the situation was less clear, but the leading Muslim politicians contested outside the League fold. The result showed that the Muslim League in 1937 spoke only for the Muslims who lived in Hindu-majority provinces—and who presumably would feel the potential of Hindu rule much more. The League did not draw allegiance from the areas that now comprise Pakistan and Bangladesh. Jinnah would have to tackle this problem soon after the elections.

The manifestos of the Congress and the Muslim League were in general agreement except for the specifically communal demands of the League. In northern India the Congress did not oppose League nominees in the bulk of the seats. It was expected that coalitions would be formed in the United Provinces and Bihar. Indeed, the Congress before the elections felt that such coalitions would be needed as it underestimated the extent of its own ability to win in the elections and thought it would have to have the support of the League to enact its economic and social legislative program. The failure of the talks toward coalition following the election were another in the chain of events leading toward partition. Entranced by its own electoral success, the Congress placed demands on the League which were unacceptable. The Congress required that League legislature members resign from the League and accept full Congress discipline and that the League take steps which for all purposes would have dissolved the party and merged it into the Congress. The leadership of the League refused to sign its own death warrant. The Congress went ahead and formed ministries on its own, occasionally filling Muslim cabinet places with deserters from the League. Bitter Muslims placed the blame on the head of the Congress Parliamentary Board, Jawaharlal Nehru.[9]

Jinnah used the Congress rejection to rebuild his organization and to develop mass tactics among Muslims. He gained unexpected assistance from two quarters when Punjab Prime Minister Sikandar Hayat Khan and Bengal Prime Minister Fazlul Haq associated themselves with him. At the 1937 session of the party in Lucknow an agreement was signed between Sikandar and Jinnah. Under this agreement, Muslim members of the Unionist party would become members of the League and would be guided by the League in national political matters while remaining in the Unionist party in the Punjab assembly and following a tricommunal approach to the problems of the Punjab. In retrospect it seems strange, but it was pushed upon Sikandar by a growing feeling within his own party that Punjab Muslims should enter the mainstream of Muslim politics. As long as Sikandar lived (he died in December 1942), he controlled the expansion of the League in the Punjab and maintained the careful balance of national and provincial politics. The agreements with Fazlul Haq and Sikandar gave substance to Jinnah's claim that he, as leader of the League, could speak authoritatively on behalf of the Muslims of India.

In addition to the Bengal and Punjab accessions, the League began a serious program of expansion and was successful in establishing many new branches. It also found opportunity to criticize the actions of the Congress ministries. Real and imagined affronts to the sensibilities of Muslims were recorded and publicized among Muslims. Two key reports, one by the Raja of Pirpur for the United Provinces and the other by Fazlul Haq entitled "Muslim Sufferings Under Congress Rule," were given wide circulation, especially in the Muslim majority provinces where feelings of support for their Islamic brethren were generated. Congress tried to overcome these actions by issuing their own versions of the situation. The full truth was hard to find from either side. Nonetheless, the published reports, coupled with rumor, were of unquestioned effect.

Jinnah now turned to the two-nation theory of Sir Syed and to the 1930 suggestion of Iqbal and concluded that the only solution to the communal problem of India was the separation of the two nations on a geographic basis. On March 23, 1940, at the League's session in Lahore, the Pakistan

Resolution—although the word Pakistan does not appear in the document —was presented to the gathering with the blessing of Sikandar and Fazlul Haq, among others.[10] The resolution demanded that the "whole constitutional plan [be] considered *de novo*" and that the result would not satisfy the Muslims unless "it is framed with their approval and consent." It added that no plan would be workable unless it included a provision that "geographically contiguous units are demarcated into regions which should be so constituted, with such territorial adjustments as may be necessary, that the areas in which Muslims are numerically in the majority as the North-Western and Eastern zones of India should be grouped to constitute 'Independent States' in which the constituent units shall be autonomous and sovereign." It should be noted that the words "Independent States" are in quotation marks in the original and that the plural is used. This is only one point on which legal analysts of the resolution might criticize the drafting. It is not at all clear how autonomy and sovereignty can coexist. What is clear from the events and negotiations that followed is that Jinnah did not consider the resolution an irrevocable blueprint for the formation of Pakistan. It was a bargaining tool and was used as such up to the end.

BRITISH PROPOSALS DURING AND AFTER WORLD WAR II

In November 1939 the Congress ministers in the provinces resigned their offices in protest against the statement of the viceroy declaring India at war. Many Congressmen did not oppose the war as such, but were incensed that the country could be plunged into the struggle without consultation and approval by representative Indians. Jinnah greeted the Congress action by proclaiming December 22 as a "Day of Deliverance" from the oppression of the Hindu governments. The withdrawal of the Congress from parliamentary politics, compounded by the jailing of many Congressmen in 1942, left the political field to the League, the highly communal Hindu Mahasabha, and other groups inimical to the Congress.

London, concerned with the continuing political deadlock, sent Sir Stafford Cripps to India in an attempt to negotiate a settlement that would bring the Congress back into political activity. Cripps' proposal was to form an independent Dominion immediately following the war. A constitution would be adopted by elected representatives from British India and nominees of the Indian princes. Membership in the new state would not be compulsory, and such provinces as desired might withdraw and achieve Dominion status separately. The British, in the interim, would continue to be responsible for the defense of India, and the viceroy would be advised by an all-party group. Provincial governments would be reinstituted following Congress agreement to participate anew. Gandhi decribed the plan as "a postdated check on a crashing bank" and he and the Congress opposed the provisions for withdrawal of provinces. The League, which did not see its demand for an independent Muslim state fully met even after the war, also rejected the plan. Congress response was manifested in 1942 in the Quit India movement which seriously disturbed the British war effort and resulted in the imprisoning of most Congress leaders until near the end of the war.

The period of the war was one of relatively little political activity. Although he did not oppose the British war effort, Jinnah took many opportunities to establish his credentials as one who was also struggling for independence. The death of Sikandar in the Punjab and his replacement by the less skillful Sir Khizr Hayat Khan Tiwana gave the Muslim leader an occasion to extend League influence in that province which was key—the sine qua non—to any Pakistan scheme. When Khizr was elevated to the premiership in place of Sikandar, the latter's son, Sardar Shaukat Hayat Khan, was added to the ministry. Shaukat's resignation within a year and his alliance with another young scion of Unionism, Mian Mumtaz Muhammad Khan Daultana, were events that solidified Muslim support in the Punjab behind the League. It should also be noted that the League scored a victory in Bengal in 1943 when Fazlul Haq was forced out and replaced by a League ministry headed by Khwaja Sir Nazimuddin.

By mid-1945 the Congress leaders had been released and began preparations for the Indian elections expected to be held after the conclusion of the war. The victory of the Labour party in the British elections was also seen as a harbinger of more rapid political change in India. The Indian elections were held in December 1945 and January 1946. Not unexpectedly, the Congress swept to victory in all Hindu majority provinces; in those same provinces the League's percentage in Muslim seats equaled that of the Congress in the Hindu. The key provinces to the League, however, were those in which Muslims were in a majority; among these, the Punjab was most critical. The Unionist party under Khizr was almost totally rejected by the Muslims and won but a handful of seats. Following the elections, however, Khizr was able to form a ministry with his small following among Muslim members and coalition assistance from the Congress, which had swept the Hindu seats, and the Akali Dal, winner of the Sikh seats. The ministry lasted only one year as Muslim League agitation under Daultana, Shaukat, and others forced Khizr to resign in March 1947. The province was then placed under the direct rule of the governor. Sind and Bengal were able to form League ministries, but the Northwest Frontier Province remained under the control of the Congress through the Khudai Khitmatgars. Jinnah felt sufficiently confident following the elections to proclaim January 11, 1946, a day of victory.

The Attlee government in London moved quickly to attempt to sort out the Indian question. A cabinet mission arrived in India in March 1946 under the leadership of Cripps and tried to formulate a plan that would be acceptable to both Congress and League. The leaders of both groups at the time were Muslims, as Maulana Abul Kalam Azad was then president of the Congress. Azad and the Congress argued for a united India that offered safeguards for the minorities. Jinnah put forward his belief that India contained two nations, with vastly separate cultures as well as religious beliefs, and that the division of the country was the only feasible solution, although certain mutual links, established by treaty, might remain. The story of the cabinet mission has been recorded in detail elsewhere[11] but it is necessary to record two aspects of its proposals. It rejected any plan that would divide India on the basis of "weighty administrative, economic and administrative considerations" as well as the difficulties created for the Punjab and Bengal, should those provinces be divided. The loss of the hinterland of Calcutta and the division of the Sikh community between Pakistan and India were among the specific problems cited in the two provinces. As a possible solution to the problem, which would be a compromise between the Congress demand for unity with a strong center and the League demand for Pakistan, the mission suggested a three-tier system for the new government of the "Indian Union." The central government would be responsible only for foreign affairs, defense, and communications and be given the power to raise funds for the execution of these functions. All other powers would be vested in the provinces or in the princely states. The provinces might, if they wished, cede certain powers to an intermediate body which might be formed by groups of provinces deciding to work together. The mission foresaw three groups, or "sections." Bengal and Assam would constitute one section; the Punjab, Sind, and the Northwest Frontier another; and the remaining provinces would form the third group. Two of these groups would have Muslim majorities and would form, in effect, the two wings of a nonsovereign Pakistan, but would retain the unity of Bengal and the Punjab and add Hindu-majority Assam to the eastern group.[12] The mission provided an opening for the League when it proposed that the constitutional provisions be subject to review at ten-year intervals, the implication being that any province might withdraw at that time. A further safeguard stated that communal issues that might come before the central legislature would require approval of a majority of the members from the community affected by the proposed legislation.

The cabinet mission plan seems to have offered the last chance for preserving the unity of India. It was a set of compromises offered, as it turned out, to two parties who were not prepared to accept compromise. There is no doubt that, had it been implemented, it would not have provided the most efficient model of government, but it also seems at least possible that the orientation of government might have shifted from the provinces toward the center, if, and this is a large if, some feeling of mutuality developed among the groups. The plan also compromised on the question of the native states. It would have made the government a federation of British India and the states at the center, with the addition that the provinces would be under the center only through the immediary of sectional administrations.

The mission announced its plan on May 16 and included a proposal that a constituent assembly be summoned through indirect elections by the provincial assemblies and by appointment from the princely states. Of the 292 members from British India, 78 would be Muslim, a number far short of Jinnah's one-third demand, but nonetheless very close to the ratio of Muslims in the population of British India. The Muslims, however, could expect a much lower share of the 93 seats allocated to the princes.

Both Congress and the League debated the plan. On June 6 the League passed a resolution accepting it. On June 26 the Congress also accepted the plan, to the extent of agreeing to join the proposed constituent assembly. The plan and the call for an assembly were complicated by an announcement on June 16 by the viceroy, Lord Wavell, of the formation of an interim government, which would amount to a change in the method of appointment of the viceroy's executive council to permit all portfolios to be held by political Indians. The cabinet mission spent its last few days in India trying to solve the interim government problem, failed, and left for London on June 29.

As the mission left there seemed to be some hope that division in India could be avoided. Perhaps the narrative of one of India's noted historians is the best method to relate the next event: "Unfortunately, at this critical moment, when a peaceful settlement of India's future was almost within sight, it was upset by some indiscreet utterances of Pandit Jawaharlal Nehru. In 1937 his outright rejection of Jinnah's offer of a Congress-League coalition ministry ruined the last chance of a Hindu-Muslim agreement. His observations in 1946 destroyed the last chance—though a remote one—of a free united India." [13] In a statement in Bombay on July 6 Nehru said, "We are not bound by a single thing except that we have decided for the moment to go to the Constituent Assembly." [14] Jinnah called this statement "a complete repudiation of the basic form upon which the long-term scheme rests." [15] Majumdar is correct in suggesting that the chance was "a remote one," but from this date forward the bargaining ceased to be bargaining at all and turned, instead, into an exhibition of stonewalling by Jinnah until he obtained the Pakistan—however "motheaten"—he had demanded.

MOUNTBATTEN AND AGREEMENT TO PARTITION

The immediate consequential action by the League was its withdrawal of its acceptance of the cabinet mission plan on July 29 and its reaffirmation of its goal as an independent Pakistan. The League designated August 16 as "Direct Action Day." On that day, and over the next two days, serious communal rioting broke out in Calcutta which required the intervention of the army to control. It was but a prelude to the further rioting that would accompany the partition of India.

The viceroy, Lord Wavell, worked diligently but without immediate effect to form an interim government. Elections to the constituent assembly were held in July with the expected result that Congress won all but nine general seats and the League all but five of those assigned to Muslims. Jinnah refused to participate in an interim government under the viceroy's plan—which would have permitted the Congress to include a Muslim member of the Congress among its share of the posts in the coalition group. Finally, Wavell moved and installed a Congress government on September 2 with Nehru as vice chairman[16] and several nonparty members representing smaller communities. Three Muslims, two of them from the Congress, were included. On October 25 the League agreed to join, and the interim government was reconstituted to include its nominees, of whom Liaqat Ali Khan was the principal member. On December 9 the constituent assembly met in New Delhi, but the League members refused to attend. The assembly adjourned until January 20, 1947.

While these events were taking place—and the account above is very much truncated—communal rioting was spreading in Bengal and from Bengal to neighboring provinces such as Bihar. Gandhi withdrew from the political talks in Delhi and went to Noakhali in eastern Bengal on November 6. He remained there until March, hoping that by his presence some diminution of the troubles would occur. Should Pakistan be granted and the Punjab partitioned, the position of the Sikhs in the Punjab was desperate: their community would be split between the two countries. Rioting in the Punjab began in February and continued well past the date of independence.

On February 20, 1947, Prime Minister Attlee announced in the House of Commons that Britain intended to transfer power and leave India not later than June 1948. He announced also that Lord Wavell would retire as viceroy and be replaced by Viscount (later Earl) Mountbatten. The new viceroy took office on March 24 and within less than five months India and Pakistan were free.

The speed with which the new viceroy worked was a tribute not only to his ability to sort out the various facets of the problem of transferring power but also to his clear and early recognition that June 1948 would prove to be much too distant a date. Pressures for a solution—almost any solution—could not be contained.[17] Immediately upon his arrival, Mountbatten began a series of consultations with an array of Indian political figures. Notable were Gandhi, Nehru, and Sardar Vallabhbhai Patel of the Congress; Jinnah; and Sardar Baldev Singh, spokesman for the Sikhs. He put together a staff headed by Lord Ismay and including experienced British and Indian officials.

Conversations were difficult. Mountbatten found Nehru firm but engaging; he could talk freely with him. Gandhi, who spent all but the last few days of Mountbatten's viceregal period in New Delhi, was opposed to the splitting of India, but it seemed to the viceroy that political decision making in the Congress had passed out of the Mahatma's hands. He recognized that Sardar Patel commanded great influence in the party organization and skillfully used his reforms commissioner, V. P. Menon, as a means to reach Patel. But it was Mountbatten's experience with Jinnah, whom he found a difficult and cold person, which convinced him that there was no prospect of transferring power to a government for a united India. Having come to this conclusion it was necessary for Mountbatten to convince the Congress leadership that partition was the only solution, however undesirable it might appear. During April and May Nehru, Patel, and the president of the constituent assembly, Rajendra Prasad, all indicated their acceptance of partition provided Jinnah did not insist on the inclusion within Pakistan of the entire Punjab and Bengal. Jinnah protested that a Pakistan not including all of those two provinces would be "motheaten", and countered with a proposal that Pakistan be given a wide corridor through northern India to connect the two wings of the new country. That suggestion was dismissed summarily. Mountbatten clung to a last hope that the realization by Jinnah that the Pakistan he could obtain would indeed be "motheaten" would cause the Muslim leader to veer back to some plan close to that of the cabinet mission, but Jinnah did not do so. He was prepared to accept what he could get.

With this, Mountbatten caused Menon to draw up a plan under a number of "heads of agreement." The viceroy showed it to Nehru and Jinnah. Nehru accepted in writing. Jinnah, ever the cautious lawyer, gave his approval orally. Mountbatten flew to London and gained the approval of Attlee and the cabinet and discussed the plan with the opposition, including Winston Churchill who gave grudging approval. The British government and the viceroy both made statements on June 3 which detailed the plan of partition.

The Plan of Partition

It might be argued that the June 3 statement did not put forward a plan of partition but provided for a partition only when, and if, the representatives of the people of the provinces which might be included in Pakistan so decided. Nevertheless, by offering an agreed arrangement for the implementation of a decision which, by and large, was a foregone conclusion, the British statement is in essence a plan of partition.

Each province was to decide whether it wished to have a constitution framed by the existing constituent assembly (i.e., for a united India) or by a "new and separate constituent assembly consisting of the representatives of those areas which decide not to participate in the existing constituent assembly." Special provisions for the choice were set out for four provinces and for Baluchistan. For the Punjab and Bengal the legislative assemblies of the provinces would meet in two parts, one representing Hindu-majority districts and the other the Muslim majority, and each meeting would vote separately on the question of partitioning the province. In this way, one part could remain in the existing constituent assembly while the other joined the newly created one. If either of the two meetings voted in favor of partition, the province would be partitioned. The statement included a listing of Muslim- and Hindu-majority districts but made it clear that this was temporary; a boundary commission would be appointed to determine areas of contiguous Muslim and non-Muslim populations and establish a final boundary. The Sind legislative assembly was to take a vote to decide which constituent assembly it would join. In the third week of June, Bengal and the Punjab decided in favor of partition and Sind opted for Pakistan.

The situation in the Northwest Frontier Province was noted in the statement as "exceptional." It was felt that the province should be given an opportunity to reconsider its position—presumed to be in favor of a united India in view of the Congress majority in the legislative assembly—should the Punjab decide in favor of partition. Thus, dependent upon the action taken by the Punjab, a referendum would be held in the Frontier. The referendum was held in July, and despite a Congress campaign to encourage abstentions in the polling, the Frontier decided in favor of partition by a majority of those eligible to vote. The viceroy was to ascertain the views of Baluchistan, which did not have a legislative assembly, and his consultations resulted in a decision there for partition. The referendum procedure was also applied to the district of Sylhet in Assam, a Muslim-majority area contiguous to Bengal. An early-July referendum was held, and Sylhet opted for Pakistan. It was joined at independence to East Bengal, its precise boundaries to be part of the demarcation task of the boundary commission.

Although the statement did not specify a date for the transfer of power to the two new dominions, it urged all speed and said that the British government would be "willing to anticipate the date of June 1948" by transferring power "at an even earlier date." It added that negotiations must be begun immediately between (1) the successor states, (2) the successor states and Great Britain, and (3) the successor governments in the divided provinces in order to rule on the "administrative consequences." Mountbatten immediately set in motion a partition council with a range of satellite groups to determine the means and details of separation, a veritable unscrambling of an omelet. The most difficult task was the division of the armed forces, partially because Auchinleck initially said it could not be done. He was persuaded to change his view and that, too, was accomplished by agreement. By the date for the transfer only one major issue was outstanding, the report of the boundary commission headed by Sir Cyril Radcliffe; as will be noted below, that followed a few days after the transfer of power.

In London the India Independence Act, 1947, was introduced into Parliament on July 4 and specified August 15 as the date for transfer. It was passed on July 16 and received the royal assent on July 18. The act followed the statement of June 3, but it made an additional point clear: the relationship between the Crown and the Indian princely states was at an end. Mountbatten, and for India, Patel and Menon, tackled the task of relationships between the princes and the two new governments. Mountbatten appealed to the princes to accede to one of the two states—hopefully giving due consideration to the majority religion of their subjects—in three subjects: foreign affairs, defense, and communications. Accession was essentially the same as contained in the federation provisions of the 1935 act. The viceroy urged upon the rulers the need for speed; this, together with some pressure from Patel and Menon for India, and Jinnah for Pakistan, resulted in all but three of the more than five hundred rulers acceding to one of the dominions within a few weeks of partition. But the three who did not accede would form one of the postpartition problem areas.

The Consequences of Partition

On August 14 Mountbatten performed his last act as viceroy in Karachi as he addressed the body that would the next day become the constituent assembly of Pakistan. From the airport he rode in an open car with Jinnah, who was governor general-designate of the new dominion. Jinnah had received warnings that an attempt on their lives might be made, but Mountbatten decided to share the risk with the Muslim leader. To the north, in the Punjab, killing and looting continued almost uncontrolled, despite the setting up of a Punjab Boundary Force under British command on August 1.

Mountbatten returned to New Delhi in time for a midnight ceremony in which the independence of the new Dominion of India was hailed by Nehru as a "tryst with destiny." Mountbatten was sworn in as governor general of India. Missing from the ceremony was Gandhi. He was off in Calcutta residing with the Muslim League premier of Bengal, H. S. Suhrawardy, as the two tried to stem the communal violence taking place in that city. Near Delhi, and even within the city, Hindus and Sikhs were wreaking violence upon Muslims who were attempting to depart for the new Muslim homeland. The communal Hindu Mahasabha had proclaimed the day of independence a day of mourning for the vivisection of Mother India.

Clearly the first orders of business for both Pakistan and India were the restoration of law and order and the relief and rehabilitation of the countless refugees who were streaming across the borders. By the day of partition, violence was beginning to decrease in the east, but the tragedy still raged in the Punjab.[18] When the movement was completed and the killing halted by joint action of India and Pakistan, the exchange of population within the Punjab had been almost total. The 1961 censuses record but 1.9 percent of the population of Indian Punjab as then constituted as Muslim, and the number of Hindus in Pakistan Punjab as less than one-tenth of one percent. The number of Sikhs in Pakistan was too few to enumerate separately. The total exchange of population, like the number killed and missing, has been estimated with such wide variance by writers that no acceptable figure can be determined. Vast quantities of property were left behind, and the problem of restitution had to be tackled after order was established. Negotiations on compensation dragged on without a solution being reached. In the end, each country began to follow the same course. Property left behind by those who fled was used to satisfy to the extent possible the claims of those who arrived. It is unlikely that a final balance will ever be struck and settled. Refugees within the Punjab tended to become absorbed in the populations they joined, insofar as political activities were concerned. Refugees in Bengal were a greater problem for both India and Pakistan, as the resources of that now-divided province were not sufficient to meet the aspirations of the fleeing population. Politically, however, the two groups that created the most difficult problems were Urdu-speaking Muslims who went to Bengal and are now classed under the general title "Biharis," and Urdu-speakers who went to West Pakistan. Following the split in Pakistan in 1971, the Biharis became almost literally a people without a country. The Urdu-speakers in West Pakistan, especially in Sind, have not been assimilated and have claimed that they are being discriminated against. They were the victims of violence during 1972. Sindhi-speaking Hindus who have gone to India have generally rehabilitated themselves economically, but they are not a potent political group except in the few areas where they have tended to concentrate, such as some suburbs of Bombay. With the exception of the Urdu-speakers in Pakistan and Bangladesh, the refugee problem has largely been solved.

Refugees were, of course, not the only problem for those striving to restore order. Many millions of Muslims remained in India, while other millions of Hindus stayed behind in East Bengal. Communal disturbances were widespread in northern India, causing many Muslims in that area to be caught between attempting to crouch down and hide themselves or risk fleeing toward Pakistan and being subject to the clear dangers along the routes. The authorities did what they could to protect those who remained, and I have heard many accounts from Muslims of the help they received from Hindu friends and neighbors. Several reasons suggest themselves for Muslims remaining in India. One is that some Muslims did not accept the two-nation theory and desired to continue their association with India. This was largely confined to the Westernized elite groups, but it did have an impact. Another was the cost in fleeing, not only the dangers involved, but also the economic costs of giving up land, property, or position with little assurance that Pakistan would be able to provide replacements for what was left in India. In southern India and in Bengal the distinctive characteristic of speaking Urdu was not present. Muslims in these areas tended to blend in with their Hindu neighbors in matters of language, custom, dress, and diet; the only differences were those specifically required by the Quran. Communalism was rarely a problem in the south. It must be recalled, too, that the plan of partition did not call for an exchange of populations but only the grouping of areas already containing a majority of Muslims into Pakistan. The Congress had promised a secular state, and Jinnah, soon after partition, said that he foresaw a Pakistan in which the communal aspects of religion would disappear and only those which are personal would remain. The Congress statement had some effect; the one by Jinnah came too late and seemed too unlikely of accomplishment to save the situation in West Pakistan.

Even before the restoration of order, the delayed report of the boundary commissions for the east and the west were published on August 17. In the east neither country complained seriously, but the Punjab boundary was the subject of bitter denunciation by Pakistan. The July 3 plan had made a tentative assignment of districts to each new dominion and had placed Gurdaspur District among those included within Pakistan for the purposes of the legislative assembly vote on partition. The award of August 17 gave three of the four subdistrict areas (*tehsils*) to India, despite the fact that two of these three had Muslim-majority populations. Pakistanis have charged since that the initial award was tampered with and that the partition of Gurdaspur District was done in order to provide India with an access route to Kashmir. The charges seem without foundation.[19] The commission was directed to take into consideration other factors than religious majority, including physical and economic features. The boundary in the Punjab followed the Ujh and Ravi rivers through Gurdaspur District and into Lahore District. It then cut to the Sutlej River and followed that roughly to the Bikaner State border.

The division of the Punjab created a major problem between the two countries with respect to the waters of the Indus basin. Areas irrigated by the canal system lay largely within Pakistan, while the rivers feeding the system flowed through India. India did tamper with the regulators and posed a severe danger to the Punjab agricultural areas. India also wished to use the waters for irrigation projects on her side of the border. The problem festered, at times drawing the two countries close to war, until, after much negotiation and prodding by other nations, the Indus Water Treaty was signed in 1960. A division of the water was agreed upon and an alternative system using link canals and storage dams was built in Pakistan.[20]

There were other economic problems as well, most of which have not been solved and are no longer on the urgent list. For example, the jute grown in East Bengal was manufactured in Calcutta mills. Pakistan erected mills in East Bengal, and India converted some land from other crops to jute. The Punjab had been a major source of cotton for the textile mills of western India, but with the expansion of textile production in West Pakistan, all of Punjab's cotton was consumed at home. Indian access to Assam depended upon the waterways of East Bengal, but as these routes were subject to interruption, alternative rail links were developed. Pakistan required air passage across India to link the two wings and, except for the 1965 war period and the period following the Bengal crisis of 1971, these routes were generally available in return for Indian rights across Pakistan. In a broader sense, trade between the two countries has been subject to the vagaries of political relations; for West Pakistan, however, it became less important as time passed, as a version of autarky with regard to India was practiced. In the east the lack of trade relations with India was a more serious matter and became one of the grievances of the Bengalis against the central Pakistani government.

As noted earlier, the integration of the Indian princely states was troublesome for each dominion and was to create hostility, which remains, between them. Through devices which ranged from cajolery to duress, each dominion was able to go beyond mere accession on three subjects—foreign affairs, defense, and communications—and integrate the states into the political and economic framework of the country.[21] Three states, however, demurred, and one, Jammu and Kashmir, has been a cause of three armed conflicts between India and Pakistan. In Junagadh, a small state on the Kathiawar peninsula, the ruler, a Muslim, decided to accede to Pakistan despite the fact that more than 90 percent of his subjects were Hindus. The ruler fled to Karachi as the law-and-order situation broke down, and the existing administration asked India to take over the government on November 8. A plebiscite was held to regularize the action which incorporated Junagadh into India. The Nizam of Hyderabad, premier ruler in India, faced a similar situation. A Muslim, he ruled over a state primarily Hindu in population. The state was situated in the center of the Indian peninsula and was vital to communications between northern and southern India. The Nizam negotiated tenaciously, and threatened independence; but again the law-and-order breakdown caused the Indian Army to invade Hyderabad on September 13, 1948, and the state was added to India. The Nizam was given the rights and privileges of those rulers who had entered India under more usual circumstances.

The Kashmir question is so involved that only its barest points can be given here. The state has a Muslim majority, although the southern portion of Jammu is Hindu, and had at the time of partition a Hindu ruler. The ruler attempted to avoid a decision by reaching standstill agreements with both India and Pakistan, to ensure that the services and communications existing under the British would continue. The popular leader of Kashmir, Sheikh Muhammad Abdullah, was in jail. Although a Muslim, he was assumed to favor an Indian connection and would be able to carry the people of the state with him. In October tribal raiders entered Kashmir from Pakistan and seriously threatened the government of the ruler. He appealed to India for assistance. India agreed, subject to receipt of the ruler's accession to India, but this in turn was to be subject, according to Nehru, to an ascertaining of the will of the people after peaceful conditions were restored in the state. Indian troops entered Kashmir on October 27 and were soon challenged by Pakistani forces. Through the United Nations a cease-fire was arranged on January 1, 1949. The line drawn at that time remained the line of control in Kashmir, although some modifications have resulted from the conflict between India and Pakistan in 1971. Another war was fought in 1965, but the Tashkent agreement of January 1966 restored the cease-fire line. To Pakistan the question remains one of a plebiscite to determine the wishes of the people of Kashmir. To India, which claims Pakistan is the aggressor of 1948, the "legality" of the ruler's accession is not in question; successive Kashmiri governments have confirmed it, and the only point at dispute is the "vacation" of Pakistan's aggression. Nonetheless, it seems clear that India would accept the internationalization of a modified cease-fire line and the effective partition of Kashmir. To date this solution has not been acceptable to Pakistan.[22]

Kashmir, disputes over water division, and financial settlements and refugee questions have been only the manifestations of more basic differences between India and Pakistan. India has attempted to become a secular state; while this has not always been an easy task, India has made strides in integrating its vastly differentiated society, including the more than 10 percent of its population which is Muslim. The Indian political system is based upon the structures inherited from the close association with Great Britain, and through a series of regular elections, India has developed legitimacy in the eyes of its people. This is not to say that support is entirely developed internally and that external factors have not been added. Indians drew together following the conflict with China in 1962 and the wars with Pakistan in 1965 and 1971. In sum, however, it can be fairly said that India has accomplished the nation-building task it faced in 1947 and that the unity of the country and the legitimacy of the political system seem not to be in doubt.

Pakistan, on the other hand, was founded as a "homeland for the Muslims" of the subcontinent. Its raison d'être is its Islamic character and its separation from predominately Hindu India. In domestic politics there has been a struggle over the meaning of an Islamic state which pits traditionalism against views ranging almost to secularism.[23] Pakistan has not yet ingested the Westminster system of government which prevails in India and has, at this writing, not settled basic constitutional questions even for the residual Pakistan which remains after the loss of Bangladesh in 1971. Pakistan's foreign policy has tended to be responsive to India and to a fear that India might wish to reunite the subcontinent by force.[24] It has been unwilling to work with India in joint endeavors to solve problems of the subcontinent. Although left unsaid, the ability to work with India after independence might well bring into question the reason for separation. Pakistan was unable to perform the task of nation building, as was evidenced in the separation of Bangladesh, and Islam was not enough to hold the country together. The "homeland" concept is also in question as the Muslims of the subcontinent are now roughly equally divided among three nations: India, Bangladesh, and residual Pakistan. Once more, the country must face the problems it faced in 1947.

UNION OR PARTITION

Could the partition of India have been avoided? In August 1947 the answer is undoubtedly "no": in 1937 following the elections, it might well be "maybe." Ainslie Embree has called the activities of the 1920s and '30s "the politics of right mistakes" and notes that critics may suggest a number of turning points. He adds, however, that they "ignore . . . that the complexity of Indian political and social life would not have permitted any easy transition to responsible government and independence."[25] Maulana Azad is especially critical of the role of Nehru in 1937 and 1946: in his refusal, first, to cooperate with the Muslim League in provincial governments and, second, to be bound by agreements in the work of a constituent assembly. But one must wonder whether reversal of either of these actions would have done more than delay the split.

It would seem that partition stood inevitably at the end of the road toward popular government. As the elite nature first of the Congress and then of the League disappeared and ever-increasing electorates and mass politics came on the scene, the fear of the Muslim of Hindu domination and the concern of the Hindu for Muslim intransigence increased. What might have worked in a period in which the Westernized elites of both communities controlled political behavior would not work in a period in which the masses were mobilized. The error was not in recognizing that partition was inevitable, as Hindus, Muslims, and British did in 1947, but in not working together as sovereign nations after the division took place.

Appendix 1

THE PAKISTAN RESOLUTION

While approving and endorsing the action taken by the Council and the Working Committee of the All-India Muslim League, as indicated in their resolutions dated the 27th of August, 17th and 18th of September and 22nd of October 1939, and 3rd of February, 1940, on the constitutional issue, this Session of the All-India Muslim League emphatically reiterates that the scheme of federation embodied in the Government of India Act, 1935, is totally unsuited to, and unworkable in, the peculiar conditions of this country and is altogether unacceptable to Muslim India.

It further records its emphatic view that while the declaration dated the 18th of October 1939, made by the Viceroy on behalf of His Majesty's Government, is reassuring in so far as it declare that the policy and plan on which the Government of India Act, 1935, is based will be reconsidered in consultation with the various parties, interests and communities in India, Muslim India will not be satisfied unless the whole constitutional plan is reconsidered *de novo* and that no revised plan would be acceptable to the Muslims unless it is framed with their approval and consent.

Resolved that it is the considered view of this Session of the All-India Muslim League that no constitutional plan would be workable in this country or acceptable to the Muslims unless it is designed on the following basic principles viz., that geographically continguous units are demarcated into regions which should be so constituted, with such territorial readjustments as may be necessary, that the areas in which the Muslims are numerically in a majority as in the North-Western and Eastern zones of India should be grouped to constitute "Independent States" in which the constituent units shall be autonomous and sovereign.

That adequate, effective and mandatory safeguards should be specifically provided in the constitution for minorities in these units and in the regions for the protection of their religious, cultural, economic, political, administrative and other rights and interests in consultation with them and in other parts of India where the Mussalmans are in minority adequate, effective and mandatory safeguards shall be specifically provided in the constitution for them and other minorities for the protection of their religious, cultural, economic, political, administrative and other rights and interests in consultation with them.

This session further authorizes the Working Committee to frame a scheme of constitution in accordance with these basic principles, providing for the assumption finally by the respective regions of all powers such as defence, external affairs, communications, customs and such other matters as may be necessary.

Adopted by the Muslim League
Lahore, March 23, 1940

Appendix 2

POPULATION DATA, 1961

	INDIA	PAKISTAN	WEST PAKISTAN	EAST PAKISTAN
Population (in millions)	439.2	93.7	42.9	50.8
Hindu (%)	83.5	10.7	1.5	18.4
Muslim (%)	10.7	88.1	97.2	80.4
Sikh (%)	1.8	—	—	—
Christian (%)	2.4	0.8	1.3	0.3
Buddhist (%)	0.7	0.4	0.0	0.7
Other religions (%)	0.9	0.0	0.0	0.2
Urban (%)	18.0	13.1	22.5	5.2
Rural (%)	82.0	86.9	77.5	94.8

LANGUAGE DATA, 1961 (PERCENTAGE)

	INDIA	PAKISTAN	WEST PAKISTAN	EAST PAKISTAN
SANSKRITIC GROUP:				
Assamese	1.5	—	—	—
Baluchi	—	1.1	2.5	0.0
Bengali	7.7	55.5	0.1	98.4
Gujarati	4.6	—	—	—
Hindi	30.3	—	—	—
Kashmiri	0.4	—	—	—
Marathi	7.6	—	—	—
Punjabi	2.5	29.0	66.4	0.0
Pushtu	—	3.7	8.5	0.0
Oriya	3.6	—	—	—
Sindhi	—	5.5	12.6	0.0
Urdu	7.6	3.7	7.6	0.6
DRAVIDIAN GROUP:				
Brahui	—	0.4	0.9	0.0
Kannada	4.0	—	—	—
Malayalam	3.9	—	—	—
Tamil	7.0	—	—	—
Telugu	8.6	—	—	—
OTHER	10.7	1.1	1.4	0.9

ECONOMIC INDICATORS

	INDIA	(YEAR)	PAKISTAN	(YEAR)
Primary school (000)	55,930	(1968–69)	7,050	(1966–67)
University enrollment (000)	1690	(1968–69)	287	(1966–67)
GNP (billion rupees)	301,550	(1967–68)	51,048	(1968–69)
Per capita (rupees)	541.8	(1967–68)	408	(1968–69)
By sector (percent):				
agriculture	46.6	(1967–68)	66.9	(1968–69)
mining	1.0	(1967–68)	0.4	(1968–69)
manufacturing	15.4	(1967–68)	9.4	(1968–69)
construction	3.8	(1967–68)	2.8	(1968–69)
utilities	9.3	(1967–68)	3.6	(1968–69)
trade	3.5	(1967–68)	8.6	(1968–69)
services	20.4	(1967–68)	5.8	(1968–69)
other	—		2.5	(1968–69)
Agricultural production:				
rice (000 tons)	39,761	(1968–69)	13,024	(1968–69)
wheat (000 tons)	18,651	(1968–69)	6,985	(1968–69)
other foodgrains (000 tons)	35,601	(1968–69)	1,865	(1968–69)
jute (000 bales)	3,052	(1968–69)	5,881	(1968–69)
cotton (000 bales)	5,270	(1968–69)	2,974	(1968–69)
tea (000 tons)	380	(1968–69)	28	(1968–69)
Exports (million rupees)	14,132.1	(1969–70)	3,348.2	(1967–68)
Imports (million rupees)	15,674.9	(1969–70)	4,654.7	(1967–68)
Balance of trade	–1,542.8	(1969–70)	–1,306.5	(1967–68)
Defense spending:				
actual (million dollars)	1,778	(1970)	652	(1970)
per capita (dollars)	3	(1970)	5	(1970)
% of GNP	3.4	(1970)	3.7	(1970)

Sources: For population and language data, the appropriate reports of the 1961 censuses in India and Pakistan. Dash indicates data not reported; 0.0 indicates less than 0.05%. Economic data for India from *India, 1970*, an annual reference volume published by the Government of India; for Pakistan, from tables contained in U.S. Army *Handbook for Pakistan*, 1971 edition. Defense data from *World Military Expenditures, 1971*, published by the U.S. Arms Control and Disarmament Agency.

Notes

1. The division of Pakistan and the creation of Bangladesh is the subject of another chapter in the present book. This chapter will limit its discussion to matters resulting from the 1947 division and, to the extent possible, avoid what might be called the "Second Partition of India."

2. Among the books, two seem especially useful: H. V. Hodson, *The Great Divide* (London: Hutchinson, 1969), and V. P. Menon, *The Transfer of Power in India* (Princeton, N.J.: Princeton University Press, 1957). Hodson, who had access to the papers of Lord Mountbatten, was constitutional adviser to Lord Linlithgow. Menon was Hodson's successor

and a key actor during the Wavell and Mountbatten viceroyalties. For a detailed chronology see C. H. Philips and Mary Doreen Wainwright, *The Partition of India* (London: Allen & Unwin, 1970), pp. 554–83. The same work contains an excellent bibliography, pp. 584–600.

3. Earlier incursions in Sind in the eighth century did not lead to expansion as those of the eleventh did.

4. For a short analysis of the mutiny see Ainslie T. Embree, *1857 in India* (Boston: D. C. Heath, 1963).

5. See, for example, Thomas R. Metcalf, *The Aftermath of Revolt* (Princeton, N.J.: Princeton University Press, 1964), especially pp. 298–99.

6. For a much more complete treatment of Sir Syed's role, see Aziz Ahmad, *Islamic Modernism in India and Pakistan* (London: Oxford, 1967), chap. 2.

7. Three types of constituencies were delimited: general, Muslim, and special. The last provided a form of functional representation and was retained in the 1919 and 1935 acts. In 1909 such constituencies provided representation to such groups as trade associations, landholders' groups, and universities.

8. Percival Spear, "Gandhi," *Modern Asian Studies* 3, no. 4 (1969): 299.

9. Two accounts are especially important. First, by the Congress Muslim leader, Abul Kalam Azad, *India Wins Freedom* (Bombay: Orient Longmans, 1959), pp. 160–62. Second, by a leader of the League in the United Provinces, Chaudhury Khaliquzzaman, *Pathway to Pakistan* (Karachi: Longmans, 1961), chap. 17.

10. The text is contained in the Appendix to this chapter.

11. See especially Hodson, *Great Divide*, and Menon, *Transfer of Power*.

12. Under the constitutional arrangement at the time, Baluchistan was not a province but under the direct rule of the viceroy through his agent.

13. R. C. Majumdar, *History of the Freedom Movement in India* (Calcutta: Mukhopadhyay, 1963), 3: 769–70; Azad, *India Wins Freedom*, 155–62. Azad records the date as July 10, which is incorrect, and quotes Nehru as stating the Congress would be "completely unfettered by agreements" in acting in the assembly (p. 155).

14. Philips and Wainwright, *Partition of India*, p. 574.

15. Ibid.

16. Constitutionally Wavell himself was chairman. Additionally the commander in chief, Field Marshal Sir Claude Auchinleck, retained his seat in the council.

17. In addition to the Hodson and Menon works cited, particularly useful accounts include Allan Campbell-Johnson, *Mission with Mountbatten* (London: Robert Hall, 1951); and Chaudhri Muhammad Ali, *The Emergence of Pakistan* (New York: Columbia University Press, 1967).

18. Numerous accounts of the Punjab events have been published. Among the best is Penderel Moon, *Divide and Quit* (London: Chatto & Windus, 1962). Among novels which depict the events vividly are Khushwant Singh, *Train to Pakistan* (New York: Grove Press, 1956), and Mumtaz Shah Nawaz, *The Heart Divided* (Lahore: Mumtaz Publications, 1957). General Sir Francis Tuker has recorded his recollections of service in several areas of northern India and in Bengal in *While Memory Serves* (London: Cassell, 1950).

19. Hodson, *Great Divide*, pp. 352–54.

20. The story is told in Aloys A. Michel, *The Indus Rivers* (New Haven, Yale University Press, 1967).

21. See V. P. Menon, *The Integration of the Indian States* (Bombay: Orient Longmans, 1956); and Wayne Ayres Wilcox, *Pakistan: The Consolidation of a Nation* (New York: Columbia University Press, 1963).

22. Kashmir has been the subject of numerous books. For general reference see Alastair Lamb, *Crisis in Kashmir* (London: Routledge & Kegan Paul, 1966).

23. See Freeland Abbott, *Islam and Pakistan* (Ithaca, N.Y.: Cornell University Press, 1968); and Richard S. Wheeler, *The Politics of Pakistan: A Constitutional Quest* (Ithaca, N.Y.: Cornell University Press, 1970).

24. India's second largest political party has maintained a negative stance toward Pakistan and has paid lip-service to reunification. See Craig Baxter, *The Jana Sangh, a Biography of an Indian Political Party* (Philadelphia: University of Pennsylvania Press, 1969).

25. Ainslie T. Embree, *India's Search for National Identity* (New York: Alfred A. Knopf, 1972), p. 112.

INDIA, PAKISTAN, and BANGLADESH

9

India, Pakistan, and Bangladesh

Rounaq Jahan

Background

ONE OF THE TRAUMATIC EVENTS of 1971 was the disintegration of Pakistan and the emergence of the nation-state Bangladesh. The division of Pakistan into two successor states, i.e., Pakistan (formerly West Pakistan) and Bangladesh (formerly East Pakistan) is a rare phenomenon. Pakistan is only the second (the first was Malaysia) of the new states of Asia and Africa to break up as a result of its failure to integrate its plural society; and Bangladesh is the first country to emerge out of a successful national liberation movement waged against "internal colonialism" in the new states.[1] After the Second World War, a number of new states were established in Asia and Africa as independent national entities. They had "illogical" boundaries cutting across tribes and nationality groups, and contained within themselves subnational groups whose leadership aspired to lead independent nation-states themselves. Following independence, many of these states were faced with the problem of alienation of one or more nationality groups from the country's political system. These groups demanded greater participation, more autonomy, and/or secession.[2] Although ethnic-group conflicts abound in the new states, Pakistan's is a major instance in which one nationality group successfully managed to establish a separate state by breaking away from the old state.

The division of Pakistan is in some ways fundamentally different from many other cases under review in the present volume. Unlike Germany or Korea, it is not the division of a nationality group but the division of a rather artificially formed state. The division came about not because of an ideology, such as communism; or because of the dominant role played by third countries, as with Germany, Korea, and Indochina. Rather, it was the result of a successful national liberation movement waged by one nationality group, the Bengalis, who complained that the national government of Pakistan pursued a colonial policy against them. Involvement of a third country, India, came much later, when the Bengalis had already declared their independence from Pakistan. (As in other cases, however, external involvement greatly facilitated the division.) Additionally, because of the original artificiality of Pakistan, its division involved far fewer postdivision problems.

The division of Pakistan was not unexpected. When Pakistan was created by partitioning India in 1947, the viability of the new state was questioned by many. The question arose, because as one scholar aptly pointed out, "by the accepted criteria of nationhood there was in fact no such thing as a Pakistani Nation." [3] The new state was created to give the Indian Muslims a separate homeland where, in the words of the founder of the new state, they could "rule according to their own code of life, and according to their own cultural growth, tradition and Islamic laws." [4] But the Indian Muslims were concentrated only in certain regions of India. They formed the majority of the population in the northwestern and eastern provinces. So, when the time came to translate the ideological concept of a Pakistani nation into a territorial reality, Pakistan emerged with a peculiar geography. The new state was divided into two halves—West Pakistan (territory, 365,529 square miles; 1947 population, 33.7 million) and East Pakistan (territory, 55,126 square miles; 1947 population, 41.9 million) separated from each other by more than a thousand miles of Indian territory. The geographical separation between East and West Pakistan was paralleled by ethnic, linguistic, societal, and cultural differences between the two, which made the task of building a national community out of the two wings of Pakistan problematic.

The imperatives for the division of Pakistan came, first of all, from the "givens" of its social existence. The logic of geography probably played the most crucial role. The geographical separation between East and West Pakistan meant that there was little mobility of population between the two, which dictated that there be dual economic and administrative apparatus. Topographic and climatic differences that went with geographical separation resulted in different life styles in the two wings. There were also sharp differences between East and West Pakistan in demographic features (see table 1). East Pakistan, with less land, was one of the most densely populated regions of the world. The vast majority of East Pakistan's population belonged to one ethnic group—the Bengali—whereas West Pakistan's population was composed of four major ethnic groups—the Punjabi, Sindhi, Baluchi, and the Pathan. There were also linguistic differences between the two wings (see table 2). Over 98 percent of East

Pakistan's population spoke Bengali whereas West Pakistan presented a "complex polyglot." [5] Second to geography, linguistic differences between the two wings played a key role in the development of a separatist identity in East Pakistan.

Table 1
Demographic Characteristics of Bangladesh (East Pakistan) and Pakistan (West Pakistan), 1961

	BANGLADESH	PAKISTAN
Population (in millions)	50.8 (71.5[a])	42.9 (60.1[a])
Density of population (per square mile)	922	138
Urbanization (percentage)	5.2	22.5
Literacy (percentage)	21.5	16.3

[a] This is the projected 1970 population figure for Pakistan and Bangladesh. The projection was made by Lee L. Bean, M. R. Khan, and A. R. Rukanuddin, *Population Projections for Pakistan, 1960–2000* (Karachi: Pakistan Institute of Development Economics, 1968).

Source: Adapted from Pakistan, Ministry of Home and Kashmir Affairs, Home Affairs Division, *Population Census of Pakistan*, vol. 1, pt. 2, statements 2.3, 2.11, 2.14; pt. 4, statements 4.1, 4.4. The scheduled 1971 census could not be held in Pakistan due to the war, so 1961 data are used here.

Table 2
Frequency of Languages Commonly Spoken as Mother Tongue in Bangladesh (East Pakistan) and Pakistan (West Pakistan)
(Percentage of population)

LANGUAGE	BANGLADESH	PAKISTAN
Bengali	98.42	0.11
Punjabi	0.02	66.39
Pushtu	0.01	8.47
Sindhi	0.01	12.59
Urdu	0.61	7.57
English	0.03	0.04
Baluchi	—	2.49

Source: Adapted from Pakistan, Ministry of Home and Kashmir Affairs, Home Affairs Division, *Population Census of Pakistan*, 1961.

Society and culture in East Pakistan also differed from those of West Pakistan. East Pakistan's society was less stratified and more homogeneous than West Pakistan's and had few of West Pakistan's problems of tribalism, subregionalism, and feudal landlordism. Linguistic, ethnic, and societal differences led to differences in culture between East and West Pakistan. Cultural traditions in East Pakistan stressed politics and literature; those in West Pakistan tended toward military service and administration. Historical traditions in the two wings also diverged. Traditionally West Pakistan was a gateway to India; East Pakistan's historical tradition remained essentially discrete from that of the central Gangetic plains. As for the recent past, the Pakistan movement itself constituted a by-no-means-perfect common frame for the two wings. Before partition, a section of the Muslim Leaguers from Bengal wanted to establish an independent Bengal separate from West Pakistan. The 1940 Lahore Resolution, which formally put forth the Pakistan demand, in fact called for the creation of two "independent states" for Muslims in India (see Appendix 1).[6] Even religion, which was the raison d'être for the new state, was sometimes a divisive factor. West Pakistani Muslims looked down upon the Bengali Muslims as somewhat impure, Hinduized Muslims. West Pakistani leadership emphasized Islam as a public policy. Bengali leadership preferred to downplay religion since emphasis on Islam automatically alienated its 15 percent to 20 percent Hindu population.

Thus Pakistan was created as a peculiarly bifurcated state. By the accepted criteria of nationhood East Pakistan had sufficient homogeneity and identity to emerge as a separate state; all she needed was the will to incarnate her separate identity in one state. And that will was slowly developed in the twenty-four years that followed independence. The feeling of separatism grew in East Pakistan because of (1) the unequal power relationship between Pakistan's two parts and (2) the centralized economic-political-administrative-cultural policy that the central government of Pakistan followed.

After independence, the Bengalis of East Pakistan started with the disadvantage of little representation in the power elite and the dominant pressure groups of the country.[7] Pakistan began as a parliamentary democracy, but real power soon devolved onto a civil-military bureaucratic elite. This alliance ruled the country after 1954; the military were the junior partners during 1954–58 and the dominant partners during 1958–71.[8] But the Bengalis had little representation in the civil-military bureaucratic elite. In 1947 there were only two Bengalis out of a total of eighty senior civil servants. Over the years the number of Bengalis in the civil bureaucracy increased, but it was still less than 40 percent as late as 1970. Bengali representation in the military was even more marginal. In 1955 only 1 percent of the army and navy officers, and 9 percent of air force officers, were Bengali; in 1963 Bengali representation rose to 5 percent among the army officers, 10 percent among the navy, and 17 percent among the air force officers.[9] This nonrepresentation of Bengalis in the power elite meant that the Bengali elite could develop only an inadequate stake in the Pakistani political system; the numerous presence of non-Bengali civil-military personnel posted in East Pakistan was perceived by Bengalis as alien rule.

The ruling elite in Pakistan followed a policy of centralization in the hope that centralization would help unite the two wings. But the centralization policy alienated the Bengalis, because they had little share in the strong center being created. The Bengali desire for autonomy rose as the successive governments intensified their centralization efforts. The alienation of the Bengali started with the ruling elite's policy of imposing a uniformity of language and culture in the country. In the early years following independence, the ruling elite tried to impose Urdu—the language of only 7 percent of the population which was hardly known in East Pakistan—as the sole national language. This language policy was resisted by the Bengalis, and after three language movements, in 1948, 1950, and 1952, Bengali was finally recognized, in 1954, as one of the national languages of Pakistan. Though the language problem was solved, the scar remained; and the language movement marked the beginning of a Bengali nationalism in East Pakistan.

While the language policy started the Bengali sense of alienation, economic policies led to the Bengali complaint of colonial exploitation. The West Pakistani-dominated ruling elite followed an economic policy encouraging faster growth in West Pakistan, which possessed the capital city, a better infrastructure, and had a greater availability of private capital.[10] Over the years nearly two-thirds of the country's developmental expenditure, both in the private and public sectors, was spent in West Pakistan.[11] But what irked the Bengalis most was the issue of transfer of resources from East to West Pakistan. East Pakistan earned the major portion of the country's foreign exchange (in the early years as much as 70 percent of it) by exporting its primary product, jute. Its export surplus was used to finance imports to West Pakistan and develop the West wing's industries, which then found a captive market in East Pakistan. West Pakistan thus developed a colonial pattern of economy vis-à-vis East Pakistan. During the twenty-five years of Pakistan's history, the economic disparity between East and West Pakistan increased significantly (see figure 1) and the Bengalis regarded the government's economic policy as its main cause of disparity.

The gradual development of Bengali nationalism surfaced almost immediately after Pakistan's birth. Its first phase was as a linguistic-cultural phenomenon in the early 1950s, with language the central issue. It then turned into a political-economic movement in the late 1950s, with greater political autonomy and economic autonomy its concerns. Autonomy demands were first put forth in East Pakistan in 1950, in a radical draft constitutional proposal adopted by the Bengali political opposition which would have left the federal government with powers over defense and

FIGURE 1 Per Capita GNP and the Cost of Living Index in Pakistan (West Pakistan) and Bangladesh (East Pakistan), 1949–50 and 1969–70

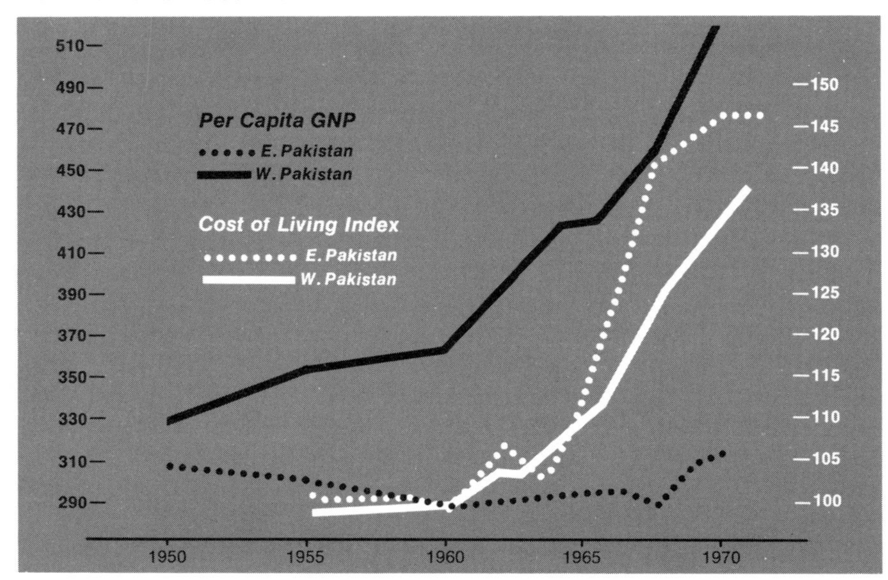

Source: Preliminary Evaluation of the Third Five Year Plan (1965–70) (Islamabad: Government of Pakistan Press, 1970), table 6.2, p. 201; *Statistical Pocket Book of Pakistan* (Karachi: Central Statistical Office, 1972).

foreign affairs only. After 1950, and until the end of the parliamentary period (1947–58), however, Bengali demands for autonomy were slightly more muted.[12] So long as the electoral process was open, the Bengalis hoped to have a dominant voice in the center because of their numerical majority.

During the Ayub decade (1958–69), Bengali political participation was restricted, and Bengali demands for autonomy became again more radical.[13] The 1966 Six Points movement, launched by the Bengali autonomist party, the East Pakistan Awami League, marked the beginning of militant Bengali nationalism. The movement not only demanded radical autonomy for East Pakistan (see Appendix 2), but extensively used Bengali nationalist symbols. Though the Six Points movement was ruthlessly crushed by the Ayub regime, the demands caught popular imagination. They were revived two years later in the 1968–69 mass movement against Ayub. At the later stage of the mass movement there was a sudden surge in Bengali separatism, and for the first time in Dacca streets one heard such slogans as "Free Bengal."

The second Martial Law of March 1969 put the lid on the mass movement, but the new military regime of Commander in Chief Agha Muhammad Yahya Khan knew that the fundamental interests of the ruling elite could be maintained only by meeting some of the demands of the mass movement. Unlike the Ayub regime, the Yahya regime (1969–72) followed a conciliatory policy toward the politicians, especially the Bengali autonomists. It acceded to their demands for holding a general direct election, and recognized the principle of one-man-one-vote, thus giving East Pakistan a majority of seats in the National Assembly in the elections of December 7, 1970, and January 17, 1971. The reconciliatory policy of President Yahya bore fruit. The Bengali autonomists decided to work through Yahya's system, despite some of its restrictions, and to uphold the unity of the country as long as they were promised participation at the central level and an enlarged share of regional autonomy.[14]

The December election of 1970 worked as a catalyst to sharpen the East-West confrontation. The election campaign focused on the autonomy issue as the Six Points program was the Awami League's major campaign theme. The autonomy issue was further escalated by the apparently almost total neglect shown by the Yahya regime to the cyclonic devastation of November 12, 1970, in the coastal region of East Pakistan, in which reportedly over half a million people died. In the National Assembly election twenty-four days after the cyclone, the Awami League won a landslide victory in East Pakistan (167 of 169 seats) and a comfortable overall majority (167 of 313 seats) in the Pakistan National Assembly. The Pakistan People's party (PPP) of Zulfikar Ali Bhutto, with 81 seats, was the second-largest party in the National Assembly. The election thus crystallized the polarization between East and West Pakistan. The Awami League, which won a national majority and an overwhelming majority of seats from East Pakistan, did not win a single seat from any province in West Pakistan. The PPP, which won the majority of seats from the Punjab and the Sindh, did not win any seats from East Pakistan or Baluchistan. In the postelection period the Awami League's national majority and its right to form a national government was challenged by the PPP on the ground that it did not win any seats from West Pakistan. In the resulting confrontation between the two major parties the ruling elite was able to maintain its position by playing the role of an arbitrator and mediator.

Bengali separatism, which was contained in the preelection and postelection periods with the hope of dominating the federal government and having a substantial measure of self-rule in the region, surfaced again after March 1, 1970, when Yahya, bowing to the PPP and Bhutto's demand, postponed the scheduled March 3 session of the National Assembly. The postponement of the session was regarded by the Bengalis as one more example of the West Pakistani elite thwarting the Bengali's rightful share in the country's political system. In the weeks following the postponement of the assembly session, spontaneous and rebellious demonstrations occurred in East Pakistan, and the Awami League leader, Sheikh Mujibur Rahman, came under tremendous pressure from other parties as well as the radicals of his own party to declare independence. Pressures from the military were also visible as additional troops were flown into Dacca. Under cross pressures, Mujib chose to chart a middle ground, and launched a nonviolent, noncooperation movement, which led to de facto transfer of power to the Awami League, thus putting pressure on Yahya to negotiate with him. The Dacca negotiations between Yahya, Mujib, and Bhutto, however, failed to produce a mutually acceptable settlement. On March 25, without formally breaking off the talks, Yahya launched a policy of military solution to the crisis, while the Awami League leaders were still waiting for a peaceful settlement. On that night, units of the Pakistani Army attacked the Dacca University campus, the headquarters of the East Pakistan Rifles and Police, and offices of the Awami League newspapers, killing numerous civilians. Sheikh Mujib was also arrested. The last hope of saving the unity of Pakistan was destroyed with the military action of March 25. On March 26, the independence of Bangladesh was declared in the name of Awami League and its leader, Sheikh Mujib.

In the final analysis, the Pakistani union could not be saved because the ruling elite in Pakistan was not willing to give up its fundamental interests, even though the election of 1970 clearly signaled the victory of the counterelites. The counterelites, with divergent power bases in East and West Pakistan (Awami League in the east and the PPP in the west) could not accommodate each other. The counterelite in East Pakistan was no longer interested in saving the unity of Pakistan, if it were to be done again at the expense of the Bengali; and the counterelite in West Pakistan did not care to save the union, if it was no longer profitable to them.

While the military action destroyed the remnants of the concept of Pakistani nationhood, the final division of the state came about nine months later, after a successful war of national liberation. It is during this period that Bengali nationalism turned from an elite phenomenon to a mass one.[15] The liberation movement first started as a war of resistance. As the news of Dacca massacres reached the districts, people rose in revolt and prepared to resist the Pakistani Army. At the time of military crackdown, roughly 70,000 armed Bengalis were in East Pakistan: approximately 6,000 regulars in the East Bengal Regiment (EBR), 12,000 to 15,000 in East Pakistan Rifles (ERP), and 45,000 to 50,000 in various paramilitary forces. In addition there were some 45,000 police. But the resistance was unorganized and uncoordinated, and the Bengalis were short of arms. In the conventional warfare that the Bengalis were fighting, the superior fire and air power of the Pakistan Army had clear superiority. Within six weeks, the Pakistan Army was able to occupy all major cities and towns of Bangladesh. Leadership of the liberation movement during this first phase (i.e., between March 25 and mid-May 1971) belonged to the Awami League; Bengali members of the EBR, EPR, and the police; and in some places, to the civil bureaucracy.

During the second phase (between mid-May and September) the long-term strategy for liberation was planned. The leadership of the movement went into exile in India and started a campaign of external publicity. A recruitment drive to the *Mukti Bahini* (liberation army) was intensified: reportedly 100,000 to 150,000 people joined. The hard core of the Mukti Bahini was composed of EBR, EPR personnel, and student volunteers. During this second phase, frontal confrontation with the Pakistan Army was avoided in favor of a guerrilla strategy. During the last phase of the movement (between October and mid-December) both conventional and guerrilla warfare strategies were used. From October on, the Mukti Bahini stepped up its activities in Bangladesh. It appeared at first that the strategy of the liberation movement was to occupy a number of border districts and set up a government-in-exile in the liberated zone.

India seemed satisfied in continuing its role of giving indirect aid to the liberation movement, i.e., providing training, arms, and sanctuary to the Mukti Bahini and giving diplomatic support to the government-in-exile. From the last week of November 1971, however, Indian involvement became more direct. On December 3, seizing the pretext of Pakistan's preemptive attack on eight Indian airfields, the Indian Army moved into Bangladesh. On December 16, the Pakistan Army, with 93,000 armed personnel and their civilian employees, surrendered to a joint Indo-Bangladesh command in Dacca. Five days later, the Awami League government-in-exile came back to Dacca and established its authority. The division of Pakistan was completed. Although Indian intervention played a key role in the final act of the division, many would argue that a direct Indian intervention was not essential for the emergence of Bangladesh. Nevertheless, an India hostile to the cause of Bangladesh would have been disastrous to the liberation movement.[16]

Because of their geographical separation, the borders of Pakistan and Bangladesh were easy to draw. In the postdivision period, both successor states started with civilian regimes. In Bangladesh, Sheikh Mujib and the Awami League assumed immediate power. In Pakistan, President Yahya was forced to resign by Pakistan's defeat and Bhutto and the PPP formed a new government. Leadership in both states professed their commitment to democracy. Sheikh Mujib in Bangladesh has established a parliamentary democracy, while Bhutto in Pakistan vowed to establish a people's democracy. Both states now claim a socialist economy as their goal but both have found difficulty in initial efforts to establish socialist economic orders. At present, both states have state ownership of key industries but permit a large degree of autonomy within the private sector. In foreign policy, both Pakistan and Bangladesh have announced a desire to have friendly relations with all major powers on a bilateral basis, though in practice neither can expect to avoid great-power rivalries.

While the division of Pakistan was accompanied by unprecedent savagery and bloodbath, the thousand-mile natural buffer zone between the two successor states minimizes many of the related problems of division.

Problems of Division

ECONOMIC DISRUPTION

Political division is usually accompanied by large-scale economic disruption. In 1947, when India was partitioned, severe economic dislocations followed. Existing communications lines and trade patterns were disrupted. Cities and industrial centers were separated from their hinterland. Factories were separated from labor, raw materials, and markets. As compared to the partition of India, the division of Pakistan involved much less economic disruption because the geographical separation between the two wings of Pakistan had already created two largely separate economies despite the ruling elite's efforts to follow a one-economy policy.[17] The division has therefore led to more short-term than long-term economic disruption.

At the present time, Pakistan is economically stronger than Bangladesh (see table 3 for the structure of East and West Pakistan's economy in 1969–70). With 61 million people and a population density of 200 per square mile, Pakistan has a well-developed infrastructure and a viable capital market. As table 3 shows, in 1969–70 only 41 percent of Pakistan's gross domestic products (GDP) came from the agricultural sector; 15 percent came from manufacturing and 30 percent from services. The annual growth rate of the GDP between 1959–60 and 1969–70 has been officially estimated at 6.2 percent. Export earnings of Pakistan also showed an upward trend. According to some observers, "on the threshold of the 1970s Pakistan seemed ready for an economic takeoff." [18] If, despite political division, economic ties with Bangladesh are restored, Pakistan's economic development probably would not be affected at all adversely by division.

Pakistan's major loss due to division was in the trade sector. East Pakisian used to earn the major portion of Pakistan's foreign exchange (see table 4). In the first decade following independence, East Pakistan's jute earned as much as 70 percent of the country's total foreign exchange. In recent years, however, East Pakistan's share of export earnings dropped to 50 percent or less. Still, as East Pakistan always imported much less than West Pakistan, her foreign exchange surplus was used to finance West Pakistan's imports. With the loss of its eastern wing, Pakistan had to limit its imports drastically. During January–November 1972, Pakistani imports totaled $599.21 million as compared with the previous year's imports of $868.04 million—a reduction of more than 30 percent in imports. Loss of East Pakistan also meant loss of a captive market, and Pakistan had to find alternative markets for the products it sold to East Pakistan. In the first year following division Pakistan did manage to sell its products abroad. During January–November 1972, Pakistani exports totaled $600.44 million as against the previous year's exports of $622.87 million—a rather insignificant

Table 3 Gross Domestic Products of Bangladesh and Pakistan, 1959/60–1969/70

	BANGLADESH 1959/60		PAKISTAN 1959/60		BANGLADESH 1969/70		PAKISTAN 1969/70	
	Rs (000)	%	Rs (000)	%	Rs (000)	%	Rs (000)	%
Agriculture	9,042	62.40	7,711	48.24	12,165	55.44	12,140	41.34
major crops	5,752	39.69	3,882	24.28	7,775	35.43	6,800	23.15
minor crops	1,287	8.88	893	5.58				
livestock, fishing,					4,389	20.0	5,341	18.18
and forestry	2,003	13.82	2,936	18.36				
Mining and quarrying	—	—	70	0.43	10	—	146	0.49
Manufacturing	912	6.29	2,018	12.62	1,905	8.68	4,675	15.91
large-scale	406	2.80	1,159	7.25	1,250	5.69	3,560	12.12
small-scale	506	3.49	859		655	2.98	1,115	3.79
Construction	224	1.54	427	5.37	1,414	6.44	1,538	5.23
Utilities	20	0.13	87	0.54	188	0.85	276	0.93
Transport, storage,								
and communications	900	6.21	921	5.76	1,319	6.01	2,079	7.07
Wholesale and retail								
trade	1,560	10.76	2,105	13.16	2,392	10.90	4,036	13.74
Ownership of dwellings	935	6.45	837	5.23	1,167	5.31	1,133	3.85
Public administration								
and defense	195	1.34	397	2.48	437	1.99	1,230	4.18
Services	701	4.83	1,411	8.82	945	4.30	2,114	7.19
Gross domestic product	14,489	100.00	15,984	100.00	21,942	100.00	29,366	100.00
GDP per person	264		355		293		481	

Source: Quarterly Economic Review, no. 1 (1972): 6, 16.

Table 4
Exports and Imports of Bangladesh (East Pakistan) and Pakistan (West Pakistan), 1959/60–1970/71
(In millions of rupees and percentages)

COUNTRY	1959/60	% OF TOTAL	1964/65	1969/70	1970/71[a]	% OF TOTAL
Bangladesh						
Imports	655	27	1,702	1,813	1,380	36
Exports	1,080	59	1,268	1,670	1,052	45
Balance	+425	—	−434	−143	−328	—
Exports as % of imports	165		75	92	76	
Pakistan						
Imports	1,806	73	3,672	3,285	2,462	64
Exports	763	41	1,140	1,667	1,324	55
Balance	−1,043	—	−2,532	−1,618	−1,138	—
Exports as % of imports	42		31	51	54	

[a] July–February only.
Source: Quarterly Economic Review, no. 1 (1972): 10.

change. Many observers, however, argue that Pakistan could maintain its level of exports by devaluing its currency and subsidizing its products; and it is still too early to say whether or not she has succeeded in finding alternative markets for her exports to Bangladesh.

According to one study (see table 6), over time Pakistan would be able to find alternative markets for two-thirds of the primary products exports and one-half of the manufactured goods formerly exported to East Pakistan.[19] Finding alternative markets for manufactured products (e.g., millwork) and primary commodities (e.g., rice and tobacco) would be difficult. Imports that previously came from East Pakistan (e.g., spices, betelnuts, tea, pulp, matches), would now cost Pakistan 650 million rupees in foreign exchange.[20] One recent analysis finds that alternative arrangement of interwing trade leaves Pakistan with an annual deficit of 110 million rupees.[21]

Division also means a loss of opportunity for Pakistani private capital to invest in Bangladesh. Though precise data is not available, over the years there had been a net capital outflow from west to east, and a related flow of interest and dividends from East to West Pakistan.[22] Following division, the government of Bangladesh nationalized all West Pakistani-owned industries. The freezing of assets in Bangladesh, coupled with continuing political uncertainty and labor unrest in Pakistan, might hinder further expansion of private-sector investment in Pakistan. In fact, after 1970 there was a sharp fall in private-sector investment in West Pakistan; indeed, between 1964–65

Table 5
Pakistan's Trade with Bangladesh 1964/65–1969/70

RUPEES IN MILLIONS	1964/65	1969/70
	EXPORTS TO BANGLADESH	
Primary commodities (all)	276	898
food grains	23	357
raw cotton	81	166
Manufactured goods (all)	576	754
cotton fabrics	176	242
cotton yarn and thread	79	86
machinery	37	66
drugs and medicine	44	54
Total	852	1,652
	IMPORTS FROM BANGLADESH	
Primary commodities (all)	47	162
wood and timber	5	12
spices	14	9
Manufactured goods (all)	489	754
tea	182	243
jute goods	104	159
paper and paper board	86	109
matches	26	45
Total	536	916

Source: Quarterly Economic Review, no. 1 (1972): 7–8.

Table 6
Trade Consequences of Pakistan, Bangladesh/Separation

PAKISTAN'S SALES TO BANGLADESH	RUPEE VALUE IN 1969–70	NEW SITUATION: EXPORTABLE	NOT EXPORTABLE
Primary commodities	900	600	300
Manufactured goods	750	370	380
Total	1,650	970	680
PAKISTAN'S PURCHASES FROM BANGLADESH	**RUPEE VALUE IN 1969–70**	**TO BE IMPORTED**	**TO BE SUBSTITUTED BY LOCAL PRODUCTS OR BANNED**
Total	900	650	250
	RUPEE SURPLUS	**FOREIGN EXCHANGE SURPLUS**	**RUPEE LOSS**
Balance	750	320	430

Source: Quarterly Economic Review, no. 1 (1972): 9.

and 1969–70 there was a steady decline in both public- and private-sector investment in West Pakistan.

Additionally, loss of East Pakistan meant loss in certain services, e.g., Pakistan International Airlines, which were developed especially to serve both East and West Pakistan. Following the division, PIA drastically cut back its services and personnel. The division left Pakistan in a relatively better position as far as public finance is concerned. West Pakistan produced the bulk of the country's tax revenue but received much less back (see table 7). Division thus leaves the four provinces of Pakistan with an increased share of tax revenue.

Table 7
Transfer of Pakistan Tax Revenue to Bangladesh
(on the basis of the 1971–72 budget estimates; Rs mn)

	ESTIMATED BUDGET RECEIPTS	LEVIED IN PAKISTAN	ALLOCATED TO PAKISTAN'S PROVINCES	NET TRANSFER TO BANGLADESH[a]
Central excise duties	2,800	2,100	1,030	650
Income and corporation taxes	1,150	920	420	320
Sales tax	800	560	340	110
Total	4,750	3,580	1,790	1,080

[a] Assuming that 20% of revenue rasied in Pakistan would still be allocated to the central government.

Source: Quarterly Economic Review, no. 1 (1972): 12.

On balance, while division involves substantial short- to medium-range economic losses for Pakistan, in the long run its losses are small. Indeed, some would argue that Pakistan stands to gain by the division, claiming that it got rid of East Pakistan just at a point when East Pakistan was turning from an economic asset into a liability. The decline in the jute market and, hence, East Pakistan's diminishing ability to earn foreign exchange, coupled with rising Bengali political demands, had made it economically and politically unfeasible to "squeeze" East Pakistan in the 1970s. Indeed, Bengali demands to transfer resources from West to East Pakistan would have become irresistible. Without the burden of East Pakistan (and her 75 million people) Pakistan stands a much better chance of becoming viable economically, provided it achieves political stability and continues to receive economic aid.

In the postdivision period, Bangladesh is clearly the less developed of the two successor states. As table 3 shows, agriculture accounts for 56 percent of Bangladesh's GDP; industries, a mere 7 percent. From 1959–60 to 1969–70, the real increase in Gross Regional Product (GRP) amounted to 4.2 percent per year, while GDP per capita increased only 1 percent a year. With tremendous population pressure, with its economy and infrastructure virtually in ruins after a year-long period of war and military occupation, Bangladesh faces a much more difficult task of economic reconstruction and development. The nine-month-long war resulted in a sharp decline in agricultural and industrial production, and a tremendous loss in both physical and social infrastructure. Estimates about war damage and the cost of reconstruction vary greatly.[23] A United Nations report put the cost at $938 million.[24]

As in the case of Pakistan, Bangladesh faces little long-term economic disruption because of division. The main economic dislocation had been in the sector of trade. In the first two years following liberation, Bangladesh found it difficult to substitute West Pakistani imports from alternative sources. The export trade also suffered. During 1972–73, Bangladesh's exports were estimated to be 30 percent lower than the level achieved in 1969–70. However, as table 6 shows, in the long run Bangladesh would be able to substitute West Pakistani imports from alternative sources, i.e., India and Japan. With the exception of tea, its exports to Pakistan can find easy markets. According to one estimate, total trade loss due to the military operations and ban on trade with Pakistan would be 600 million rupees, of which 150 million rupees (in tea trade) is a long-term loss.[25]

For Bangladesh the division also means the loss of West Pakistani private capital and a skilled managerial class. This loss also can be easily substituted by an infusion of Indian and Japanese private capital, if the government of Bangladesh encourages foreign private investment. The current policy of Bangladesh is to discourage foreign private investment, especially Indian investment, so as not to repeat the pre-1947 experience when East Bengal was a hinterland of West Bengal.

The year-long war preceding the division also had an adverse impact on the production and export of jute, the major foreign exchange earner of Bangladesh. Estimates show that 1971–72 jute production dropped by 33 percent, and the export price of jute recorded an all-time high.[26] Since the jute mills and jute exports were mostly managed by non-Bengalis, it might take some time for the jute industry to recuperate. In the international jute market Bangladesh faces stiff competition from India, and markets once lost might prove difficult to recapture. Additionally, in the postdivision period, freer trade with India might lead to an increased export of raw jute for the consumption of Indian mills, which in turn would create greater competition for the jute industry of Bangladesh.

Most observers, however, agree that in the long run the economy of Bangladesh will be better off because of division. For the first time in recent history, the resources of Bangladesh and its foreign exchange earnings will be used for its own development. Transfer of resources from east to west will stop; according to one estimate, this may increase available domestic resources by $125 million annually.[27] External assistance to Bangladesh can also be expected to increase. In the 1960s East Pakistan received roughly 25 percent (approximately $65 million annually) of the total foreign aid to Pakistan. It is expected that in the next few years Bangladesh will receive two to four times as much foreign aid.[28] Division also opened up opportunities for joint economic ventures and economic cooperation between India and Bangladesh, which would be economically profitable for both countries. Problems of flood control, water management, power, trade, and navigation could be solved by integrated economic planning. A trade agreement was signed between the two countries and a joint river commission was set up. However, the trade agreement and the border-trade pact failed to come up to earlier expectations. The high rate of smuggling embittered the economic relationship between the two countries, and trade through the regular channels was minimal. Given this setback in Indo-Bangladesh economic cooperation, it is likely that Bangladesh would be interested in reviving some of its economic ties with Pakistan, once the latter accords recognition to Bangladesh. The major dilemma faced by the economic planners in Bangladesh is whether to let India step into the vacuum created by the departure of Pakistani imports, capital, and managerial skill, or to develop an independent economy which would avoid a center-periphery relationship with India.

REFUGEE PROBLEM

A political division is often accompanied by complicated refugee problems. The division of Pakistan was preceded by one of the largest migrations of people in recent history. Bangladesh sources claim that during the nine-month-long Pakistani occupation of Bangladesh roughly 10 million people migrated to India, and another 15 million (mostly from urban-to-rural areas) were made refugees within the country. The division of Pakistan was preceded by the migration of both the Bengali and non-Bengali population; and in the postdivision period both successor states experienced another transfer of population.

The refugee problem started early in March 1971, when some non-Bengalis of East Pakistan, mostly the economically well off businessmen, left East for West Pakistan. Although there was no large-scale rioting between the Bengalis and non-Bengalis (except for one riot in Chittagong) during the noncooperation movement launched by Sheikh Mujibur Rahman, tension between the two communities had reached a near-breaking point.[29] While small in number, many non-Bengali migrants were economically powerful. It was later argued that the plight of these refugees was used by the hawks in the Pakistani ruling elite to take military action against East Pakistan.[30] Even after the military crackdown of March 25, the exodus of non-Bengalis from East Pakistan continued, while few returned to their former business in the eastern wing. The non-Bengali migrants were mostly those who could afford to get the limited space in interwing travel; at the time of Bangladesh liberation nearly a million non-Bengalis still remained there.[31] The migration of non-Bengalis from East Pakistan put pressure on the Bengalis living in West Pakistan (nearly 500,000) to leave; but, again, travel restrictions limited the number of Bengalis who could actually leave Pakistan.

It is, however, the massive Bengali migration to India, in the wake of the military action of March 25, that caught worldwide attention. Between March 25, 1971, and December 1971, an estimated 9.7 million Bengalis migrated to India.[32] At the initial stage nearly half the refugees were Muslims; later, Muslims comprise 20 percent to 30 percent of the refugees. While the Pakistani Army's policy of oppression was aimed at Bengalis in general, they also selected a number of special target groups, e.g., Awami League supporters, students, intellectuals, Bengali members of the EBR and EPR, and Hindus. It was not only a policy of genocide but also one of elitocide.

The refugee exodus to India played a key role in India's involvement in the Bangladesh cause which facilitated the final division of Pakistan. Indian leaders cited the refugee problem as the major reason for India's involvement in the East Pakistani crisis. They claimed that by driving 10 million refugees to India, Pakistan had committed a new kind of aggression against India. The East Pakistan crisis was thus no longer an internal matter for Pakistan; rather, the refugee problem had made it an international one. Indeed, the maintenance of 10 million refugees for an indefinite period of time created tremendous economic, social, and political problems for India. There were pressures on the Indian leadership for direct intervention in East Pakistan to force the return of refugees to their homeland. Indian strategic analysts argued that economically it would be cheaper to fight a war with Pakistan than to look after the refugees. It was estimated that the annual cost of maintaining the refugees would be $700 million while the cost of a war would be significantly less. (At $4 million a day the cost of the war was estimated at $68 million.[33]) Moreover, the heavy economic drainage caused by the refugees seriously hampered Mrs. Ghandi's newly promised program of *garibi hatao* (Remove poverty!), a program that had given her an overwhelming electoral victory.

The refugee burden also involved sociopolitical cost. The refugees mostly went to the neighboring states of West Bengal, Assam, Tripura, and Meghalaya. In some of these states, where local population was small in number, e.g., Tripura and Meghalaya, refugees outnumbered the local population two to one. In some places refugees (especially the Hindu refugees who wanted to settle down permanently) competed for scarce jobs. The large number of Hindu refugees was also a threat to communal harmony. It was probably the political cost which weighed most heavily with the Indian leadership. The eastern states were India's problem states. In 1971, after a number of years of military action against the Nagas, the Mizos, and the Naxalites, the Indian government finally appeared to be in firm control of the region. The existence of 100,000 to 150,000 Mukti Bahini guerrillas posed a difficult internal security problem for India. The arms and men of the Mukti Bahini were a potential source of strength to the Naxalites and other insurrectionary movements in eastern India. In addition, with the passing of time, Mukti Bahini leadership was turning more and more radical; and there was a growing fear among the Indian leadership that unless India intervened directly and forced the birth of Bangladesh, the whole eastern region of India would be engulfed in revolutionary and insurrectionary movements.

After the liberation of Bangladesh, the Bengali refugees in India went back to their country much more quickly than was anticipated. Many observers doubted that the Hindu refugees would go back to Bangladesh; yet, in spite of misgivings, the Hindus did go back.[34] The 10 million refugees returned to Bangladesh with remarkable speed and started the process of resettlement, in many cases without outside help.[35] While the Bengali refugees returned rapidly, a new group of potential refugees was created in Bangladesh, i.e., the non-Bengalis commonly called the Biharis.[36] During the first phase of the liberation movement, many non-Bengalis were killed, and during the military occupation of Bangladesh many non-Bengalis collaborated with the Pakistan Army. It was feared that the postliberation period would see a massacre of non-Bengalis. In the months following liberation, large-scale revenge killing of non-Bengalis was avoided, except for one riot in Khulna. The non-Bengalis, however, did feel threatened and a vast majority of them had to live in a few urban camps under the protection of first the Indian and later the Bangladesh army.

After the division nearly half a million Bengalis living in Pakistan opted to go to Bangladesh but the regime in Pakistan refused them permission to leave the country. The Bengalis were laid off their jobs, a number of them were kept in camps[37] and 203 senior civil and military officials were threatened with trial for treason. Obviously the Bengalis were used by the Pakistani regime to strengthen its bargaining stand vis-à-vis India and Bangladesh over the prisoner-of-war issue. In contrast Bangladesh was eager for the repatriation of the non-Bengalis living in Bangladesh who declared their allegiance for Pakistan and wanted to leave Bangladesh.[38] But Pakistan refused to take these non-Bengalis back. The repatriation issue was finally settled by a "three way repatriation agreement" reached between India and Pakistan in August 1973, by which Pakistan agreed to let all the Bengalis go back to Bangladesh and in return accept a substantial number of civilian Pakistanis and Biharis living in

Bangladesh. Under the circumstances a large number of non-Bengalis have no alternative but to live in Bangladesh and try to integrate themselves in Bengali society. Recent reports indicate that many non-Bengalis are leaving the refugee camps and are going back to their jobs and businesses and starting the process of adapting to Bengali language and culture.[39] However, many are also migrating out of Bangladesh. Similarly, many Bengalis are escaping from Pakistan. The plight of non-Bengalis in Bangladesh and Bengalis in Pakistan will result in continued tension between the two states. The government of Bangladesh looks on the Bengalis in Pakistan who opted to go to Bangladesh as its citizens for whose welfare it has to take responsibility. And though Pakistan made it clear that it does not want the Biharis of Bangladesh to migrate to Pakistan, the large number of Bihari migrants in Pakistan, many of whom have relatives and friends in Bangladesh, work as a pressure group for continuing a hostile posture toward Bangladesh. Additionally, the returning Hindu refugees may create problems for Indo-Bangladesh friendship. If a large number of Hindu refugees who migrated before 1970 want to go back to Bangladesh and claim their property, communal friction between Hindus and Muslims might flare up in Bangladesh, embitter Indo-Bangladesh relationship, and prevent close economic-political cooperation between the two countries.[40]

POLITICAL STRUCTURE

During their twenty-four-year union, East and West Pakistan failed to reach a consensus regarding the country's political system. The Bengalis wanted a democratic rule (the rule-by-majority favored the Bengalis), but the enthusiasm of the ruling elite, dominated by West Pakistan, for democracy was restrained by their apprehension of being swamped by East Pakistan's majority. After division, both successor states are faced with the task of building new political structures; and both have started with democratic regimes, charismatic leadership, and weak political organizations. Compared to Bangladesh, Pakistan has a more developed output sector. She has a well-organized civil bureaucracy and armed forces. In the past, the problem for Pakistani leadership was how to build an input sector given the developed and competitive output sector.[41] This is still the major problem facing the new civilian leadership in Pakistan.

Division, or more precisely the war preceding division, facilitated the return of civilian rule in Pakistan. The military defeat discredited and demoralized the army; three days after the surrender of Pakistani troops in Dacca, President Yahya stepped down under pressure from a faction of the military elite and handed over power to Z. A. Bhutto, leader of the Pakistan People's party. Bhutto is the first civilian to head a Pakistani government since 1958. Indeed, the permanent loss of East Pakistan might foster the growth of democracy in Pakistan, for the Punjabi elite would now have nothing to fear from democracy; in the postdivision period it comprises nearly 60 percent of Pakistan's population.

Table 8
Types of Government in Bangladesh and Pakistan

BANGLADESH	PAKISTAN
Unitary system with some amount of decentralization	Federal system with an emphasis on powerful center
Parliamentary form of government with prime minister as effective head of government	Parliamentary form of government with prime minister as effective head of government
Multiparty system (with some right-wing parties banned) with a dominant single party	Multiparty system with a dominant single party
Bureaucracy in the tradition of old Indian civil service	Bureaucracy in the tradition of old Indian civil service

Since his assumption of power, Bhutto's major emphasis has been on political survival. To accomplish that goal he has depended more on his charisma and on manipulation of symbols than on building political structures. He is following a strategy of centralization of power, a policy pursued by Muhammad Ali Jinnah and Ayub Khan before him. But Bhutto faces many more challengers to his policy. So far he has shown remarkable political agility and has often modified and adapted his policy to blunt his opponents' challenges. Bhutto became the president under a martial law regulation and prolonged martial law to facilitate his centralization of power. Under the new constitution that came into effect August 14, 1973, Bhutto is now prime minister and Fazali Elhai is president. With the chairmanship of the People's party, Bhutto continues to centralize most powers in himself.

To consolidate his postion Bhutto moved swiftly against his political opponents and the powerful pressure groups of the country. To curb the power of his chief rival, the military elite, Bhutto forcibly retired a dozen or more generals and sent a number abroad. He abolished the office of commander in chief and announced fixed tenures for the three service chiefs. While moving against the "flabby generals," Bhutto took care not to alienate the whole military complex. The defense budget was increased and priority given to replenish the lost military hardware. Bhutto also moved against the famous "twenty-two families."[42] He ordered big capitalists to declare their foreign exchange holdings, seized their passports, and imprisoned a number of leading industrialists. And to increase his party's power in the Northwest Frontier Province (NWFP) and Baluchistan, two provinces in which the PPP lost the 1970 election, Bhutto appointed PPP men as governors.

Bhutto's blitzkrieg strategy at first took different groups by surprise, but they soon recovered and mounted a counter challenge. His weak political base forced Bhutto to compromise with his opponents. Big business refused to be intimidated by Bhutto, and declaration of foreign exchange holdings was disappointing.[43] Finally Bhutto backed down, and adopted a conciliatory policy toward the private sector. The National Awami party (NAP) of Wali Khan, Bhutto's chief rival in the NWFP and Baluchistan, also started agitation demanding the removal of PPP governors and the calling of provincial assemblies into session. Again Bhutto compromised. He entered into an arrangement with the NAP–Jamaat-e-Ulema-i-Islam (JUI) alliance, which formed the majority in the NWFP and Baluchistan assemblies, and agreed to appoint alliance nominees as governors in the two provinces. At the same time Bhutto struck an alliance with Quaid-e-Azam Muslim League (QML), NAP's major rival in the NWFP. And he sent Daulatana, the chief of the Council Muslim League (CML) and PPP's major rival in the Punjab, as ambassador to London.

Bhutto was content to rule by martial law and delayed calling the National Assembly into session. But the issue added fuel to the NAP's campaign against the PPP. Finally, Bhutto called the National Assembly into session and in a surprise move withdrew martial law in exchange for opposition support of his interim constitution. The interim constitution gave Pakistan a strange mixture of presidential and parliamentary governments. The provinces were granted parliamentary systems while the federal government would follow a presidential form. The president would have a fixed tenure and would not be responsible to the National Assembly. He could be removed only by impeachment. The presidential cabinet, however, was responsible to the Assembly.

Bhutto withdrew martial law but substituted emergency rules. Though Bhutto has freed political prisoners and granted political parties and the press freedom of action, the regime has also imprisoned a number of journalists, including the editor of the leading daily, *Dawn*, for publishing adverse comments about the regime. The interim constitution indicated Bhutto's preference for a presidential system of government. However, the opposition political parties as well as a powerful section of Bhutto's own Pakistan People's party favored a parliamentary system. The constitution of Pakistan which came into effect on August 14, 1973, provided for a federal, parliamentary system of government. Though Bhutto finally granted a parliamentary and a federal form of government, the essentially strong character of the chief executive and the central government was maintained in the constitution. Key functions of the government were vested with the central government and a number of restrictions were put on the parliament's power to remove the prime minister at will. A democratic parliamentary system of government has been introduced in Pakistan after a period of fifteen years, but the new structures are still to take shape and it is too early to say whether or not the new political system will be legitimized. Available indicators do not favor democracy and civilian rule in Pakistan. Bhutto's own commitment to democracy is open to question.

He was a minister in Ayub's cabinet for eight years, and his preference for personal rule is all too obvious. The military, only temporarily discredited, is still a powerful group. The generals may be temporarily out of power, but the colonels and junior officers are watching the political scene from the sidelines, and their intervention cannot be ruled out. The PPP organizational base is weak, and the party has within its fold a number of irreconcilable groups who joined together for electoral purposes only. The PPP is already under heavy pressure from its various labor and petty bourgeoisie constituents, to deliver on election promises; its hold on its coalition is fragile. External fear of Indian invasion, internal threats to security from the Pakhtoon and Jai Sindh movements, and economic problems might lead to the reassertion of the old ruling elite and its coalition of powerful groups.

In the postdivision period Bangladesh faced a much more formidable task. She had to build simultaneously an output and an input sector—both a state apparatus and a political community. The two major instruments of a state apparatus—the civil bureaucracy and the armed forces—were in disarray and needed to be reorganized. The senior and more experienced of the Bengali civil servants were working with the central government in Islamabad, and they remain in Pakistan, though now expecting to be returned to Bangladesh. During the liberation movement some civil servants were killed, some went into exile in India, and many stayed behind. In the postliberation period, there was a great deal of confusion in the civil bureaucracy. Though the central and provincial services were amalgamated and one cleavage from the bureaucracy was removed, schism existed between those who went to India and those who stayed behind, between the "collaborators" and the "patriots," between the generalists and the technocrats, between the postliberation political appointees and the old civil servants.[44] The civil bureaucracy needed a shakeup not only to iron out its many confusions and cleavages, but also to reorient itself to the needs of an independent, democratic polity. After liberation, reorganization of services became one of the top priorities of the government and a Services Reorganization Commission was set up.

The new regime also had to reorganize the armed forces, paramilitia, and the police. Some 15,000 or more Bengali members of the various branches of the armed forces, including a number of high-ranking officers, were left in Pakistan, and they had to wait nearly two years for repatriation to Bangladesh. During the liberation movement many Bengali members of the EBR, EPR, and police were killed, and many joined the Mukti Bahini. But the Mukti Bahini also recruited heavily from student and other volunteers. In the postliberation period the most serious and immediate problem facing the new regime was how to coopt the 100,000 to 150,000 Mukti Bahini guerrillas in the various branches of the armed forces, paramilitia, and the police. After his assumption of power, one of the earliest acts of Sheikh Mujib was to call for the surrender of arms by the

Mukti Bahini guerrillas. But Mujib's government failed to launch an effective program to incorporate the Mukti Bahini into the administrative/political apparatus. Some of them were recruited into the armed forces, paramilitia, and civil bureaucracy, but their number is insignificant.

The Awami League administration has started with a priority on the input sector rather than on the output sector. The Bengali elite had long shown its preference for democracy and parliamentary rule: a major conflict with the West Pakistani ruling elite was over its demand for a freer political process. From the beginning of the liberation movement the Awami League leadership showed its commitment to political rule and the parliamentary process. When it formed a government-in-exile, the Awami League, following the practice of parliamentary systems, formed a party government. It refused to form a national coalition despite pressures of the various leftist parties. When Sheikh Mujib was released from prison and returned to Bangladesh he quickly reaffirmed his government's commitment to parliamentary democracy. Almost immediately after his return, Sheikh Mujib stepped down from the post of presidency (to which he was named in absentia while in prison) and became prime minister. He declared that Bangladesh would adopt a parliamentary and unitary system of government. The National and provincial assemblies were merged into one body, the Constituent Assembly. The assembly was called into session and a parliamentary committee was entrusted with the drafting of a constitution. Within a year after liberation, Bangladesh adopted a constitution which provided for a unitary parliamentary government and it declared democracy, nationalism, socialism, and secularism to be the four principles of state ideology. Similar to the Pakistani case, the framers of the Bangladesh constitution were eager to provide for the stability of the political system and the constitution put certain limits on the legislature's powers to remove the prime minister arbitrarily.

Though the Awami League regime granted political parties freedom of action, it has set certain parameters. Soon after liberation the government banned all right-wing parties, i.e., the three factions of the Muslim League, the Pakistan Democratic party, and the Jama'at-e-Islami, which collaborated with the Pakistani Army during the occupation. The various left-wing parties, including the Communist party, were allowed to function. Systematically, however, the Awami League government cracked down on some Far Left parties, i.e., the Marxist-Leninist factions of the Communist party.[45] Similarly, despite general press freedom, some leftist newspapers have been threatened by supporters of the Awami League, and three newspapers belonging to the Marxist-Leninist factions of the Communist party were banned by the government.

The Awami League regime is obviously following the Indian model of political development. Like India, it wants a parliamentary democracy with a single dominant party and a relatively free political process, but with restrictions on the extreme Left and the extreme Right. Nevertheless, despite the Awami League's commitment to parliamentary democracy, the new political structures face some serious problems which raise doubts about the prospects of an Indian model in Bangladesh.

Unlike the Indian Congress party, which at the time of independence was well organized and more than half a century old, the Awami League is a relatively new party with a weak organizational base.[46] Before the 1970 election, the Awami League existed mainly for an electoral victory and it contained both Left/Right and radical/moderate factions. In the post-liberation period, the party had managed to contain these divergent factions only with increasing difficulty.[47] The Awami League-affiliated student party, the Students League, was openly divided into two factions, as was the party's labor front. Like the Muslim League in Pakistan (and unlike the Congress party in India) the Awami League faces erosion of its authority from within, by irreconcilable factional differences in the party.

The Awami League also faces challenges from outside—from the different left-wing parties. The National Awami party (pro-Moscow faction) is fast developing as a responsible opposition to the Awami League, though in the elections of March 7, 1973, the League won 290 of the 300 seats, the NAP thus failing to make significant inroads. There is still no alternative to the Awami League.

However, the greatest threat to the Awami League regime and its fledgling parliamentary system comes from the thousands of armed guerrillas who belonged to various factions—ideological and nonideological—some of whom are even supporters of the Awami League. Despite Mujib's repeated pleas, a large number of guerrillas have not surrendered their arms. Armed factional fights have become rampant and seriously tax the new state's limited coercive capability. In its attempt to extend territorial control over the districts the regime has faced challenges from rival claimants to power, e.g., guerrilla leaders with strong local support, Marxist-Leninist factions of the Communist party, and even local strongmen of the Awami League.

Still, Bangladesh does possess a number of factors favorable to parliamentary democracy. It has a remarkably homogeneous and egalitarian society,[48] and faces no problem of regionalism or ethnic-group conflict (the Biharis and the tribal people constitute a miniscule minority of the total population). As the output sector is ill organized, despite the weakness of the input sector, the threat of a military intervention is remote. Mujib's charisma and personal authority remain unchallenged, and his repeated commitment to parliamentary democracy has given some legitimacy to the system.[49] There is also a broad consensus among the elite about the political system. The only open challenge comes from the Far Left, but it is still fragmented. Following the Indian example, the Awami League regime is pursuing a policy of isolating and eliminating Far Left factions and creating a national coalition that is slightly left of center. The system's most serious challenge, however, may come from the radical youth, who play a key role in the politics of Bangladesh.[50] The youth want revolutionary change, and not the symbolic gestures the regime has so far produced. The disenchantment of the youth could spell disaster for the system.

Political forces working in Pakistan and Bangladesh indicate the evolution of divergent political systems in the two countries, though both have opted for parliamentary democracy. In the next decade the civil-military bureaucracy will still have a dominant share in decision making in Pakistan, while in Bangladesh the political process will have the upper hand. As in the economic sector, a political integration between Pakistan and Bangladesh is feasible only in the context of a general South Asian confederation of states, which would include India.

IDENTITY AND HOSTILITY

One of the main reasons for Pakistan's disintegration was its failure to develop a national identity. Pakistan was created not because of an already existing identity, but because of a hope that an identity on the basis of Islam could be achieved. There were marked differences between the people of East and West Pakistan in language, literary tradition, social structure, and culture. At the time of the creation of Pakistan, regional differences between the Muslims of Bengal and those of northwestern India were overlooked as the new state was conceived as an ideological entity. But though Pakistan was created as an ideological state, its ideology was never clearly defined. After the creation of Pakistan, policy makers were busy building a state apparatus and undertaking a program of economic development, but they never seriously attempted to develop an identity that would encompass the different nationality groups that form Pakistan. The elite's quest for an Islamic state was dropped when Muslim orthodox groups pressed for a very rigid definition of an Islamic state. Though lip-service was always paid to the concept of an Islamic state, in practice the modernist north Indian Muslim culture was assumed to be the norm. Instead of trying to arrive at a synthesis between the Bengali Muslim culture and the north Indian Muslim culture, an attempt was made to superimpose the latter on the former. This led to Bengali alienation from the system. Without a common cultural unity, East and West Pakistan gradually became a "geographical grotesquerie," and separation between the two became inevitable.[51]

Division does not necessarily ease Pakistan's problem of identity. The breakaway of East Pakistan of course means that Pakistan would no longer have to attempt the difficult task of either imposing its culture on the Bengali or synthesizing two divergent cultures. But it does mean the end of the two-nation concept on which Pakistan was based. In the postdivision period Pakistan would have to build its identity on a different basis. The task is not eased by defeat in war. A defeated Pakistan badly needs faith in its destiny. Reduced to less than half its former population, it is left with an oversize army and an undersize economy. Its intellectual elite is in a cold, cynical mood.[52] The military defeat and the breakaway of East Pakistan dealt a heavy blow to some myths on which Pakistanis created their self image: the myth of the superiority of Muslims to Hindus in military power; and the dream of re-creating the Mughal past of India, when a small Muslim elite dominated the Hindu masses. The shock of military defeat, however, might ease the task of creating a new identity which is more modest, more suited to Pakistan's current realities, and which looks to the future rather than the past. Limited to a more manageable cultural diversity, Pakistan might be able to develop a more effective secular identity, in the absence of any need to emphasize Islam as the direct hold on East Pakistan. It might then be able to achieve cultural synthesis among the four remaining ethnic groups. The deemphasis on Islam would also help promote social revolution: for the first time, Pakistan would be forced to turn in upon itself, and would have to work with the one thing accessible to change—its own society and culture.[53]

The division of course makes the task of identity building much easier for Bangladesh. The Bengalis never quite understood what being a Pakistani meant—short of not being an Indian. But they do know what being a "Bangalee" means.[54] The new nation-state is developing an identity based on Bengali nationalism. Bangladesh has announced its intention to be a secular state, and it can be expected to develop a synthesis between its Hindu and Muslim cultures. In the past Bengal was successful in fostering religious and cultural syncretic movements. Sufism and Vaishnavism—both syncretic sects—had their strongholds in Bengal. In the next decade, a closer cultural cooperation between India and Bangladesh, especially between West Bengal and Bangladesh, can be expected. While division will help the natural growth of Bengali language and culture, free of any artificial constraints to Islamicize it, the militant "Bangalee" nationalism will also be reluctant to over-Sankritize it.[55] In the last two decades, i.e., after the partition of Bengal in 1947, linguistic and cultural developments in Bangladesh have been more oriented to its land and people. It has incorporated the myriad regional and "folk" cultures of the country. In the next decade, despite closer contact with the elitist "high culture" of West Bengal, the cultural development in Bangladesh can be expected to be mass oriented. Indeed, Bangladesh can be expected deliberately to shape an identity distinct from that of India and West Bengal.[56]

Division is likely to help the growth of secular cultures in both Pakistan and Bangladesh. Other forces also work in both countries against secularization. In Bangladesh, the orthodox Muslims, the supporters of the right-wing political parties banned after liberation, and the Biharis are against the development of a secular culture. These groups were staunch supporters of Pakistan, and their loyalty to Bangladesh remains in doubt. They prefer friendship and ties with Pakistan and can be expected to work as an anti-India lobby in Bangladesh. In Pakistan the old ruling elite will be against secularization, for an inward look will inevitably mean a social revolution and a loss of their power. Like Bangladesh, Pakistan also has groups whose loyalty to the state is in doubt, e.g., the Pakhtoons in the Frontier province. Both Pakistan and Bangladesh are faced with the task of fostering national identities that will encompass not only the minority groups but also those groups with uncertain loyalty to the state.

In the postdivision period, there is little possibility of close cooperation between Pakistan and Bangladesh in intellectual, cultural, societal, and political development. East and West Pakistan started with differences in society, language, and culture. Over the years they gradually grew further apart and developed two separate identities. Today there is little intellectual, cultural, and political connection between the two. Religion was and still is a common factor; but the mass killings in Bangladesh by the West Pakistani army in the name of religion negates the possibility of any pan-Islamic movement between the two countries. The issue of genocide and hostility to Pakistan still is a very emotional one in Bangladesh. In many ways it was the mass killings that gave rise to mass nationalism in Bangladesh,[57] and the genocide issue is being used to cement the psychological bond among the Bengalis. When the right-wing groups attempt to foster an anti-Indian, anti-Soviet sentiment in Bangladesh, the ruling elite uses the genocide issue to counter such a move. In Pakistan, in contrast, it is not so much anti-Bangladesh, as anti-Indian sentiments, which are being used by the right-wing opposition groups against Bhutto.

The major problem of identity building for both Pakistan and Bangladesh lies in the fact that identity in both countries depends strongly on negative factors. For Pakistan, identity was defined in terms of its differences with India. A continued hostility toward India was essential to maintain Pakistan's separate identity. In Bangladesh the Bengali Muslims in 1947 defined their identity as Muslims, separate from Bengali Hindus, and joined Pakistan. By the end of the 1960s, they had rediscovered their Bengali heritage and culture but still they defined themselves as Bengali Muslims and not as Bengalis. This failure to develop a positive self-image has led both states to emphasize hostility factors in defining their identities. Bangladesh, however, stands a better chance to develop a positive identity based on Bengali nationalism.

INTERNATIONAL ASPECTS OF DIVISION

Throughout the nine-month-long national liberation movement, Pakistan maintained that the Bangladesh issue was an internal problem of Pakistan, that it was a civil war, that the Bangladesh movement was secessionist, and that other countries and the international community had no right to interfere in the internal affairs of Pakistan. Even after the surrender of Pakistani troops in Dacca, when Bangladesh became a fait accompli, Pakistan refused to recognize the reality of Bangladesh. Pakistani leadership continued to term Bangladesh, East Pakistan. In setting Sheikh Mujib free, Bhutto hoped that some ties could be maintained between Pakistan and Bangladesh. He publicly offered Mujib the office of president, or any other office that Mujib would like to have, if he brought Bangladesh back to the union. In contrast to the Pakistan insistence on a united Pakistan, Bangladesh leadership had all along refused offers of a union and declared that the separation between the two wings of Pakistan is permanent and irrevocable. Thus, while Bangladesh recognized the fact of division and the two successor states, Pakistan refused to recognize the division and claimed to represent the people of both Pakistan and Bangladesh.

Pakistan at first adopted a policy of severing diplomatic relations with any state that recognized Bangladesh. When India and some Eastern European countries recognized the new state, Pakistan quickly severed diplomatic connections with them. However, when the Soviet Union recognized Bangladesh, Pakistan backed down from its policy and continued its relations with the USSR.[58] Similarly, when the Commonwealth countries recognized Bangladesh, Pakistan withdrew from the Commonwealth in protest but maintained diplomatic relations with Commonwealth countries. Reversing its earlier stand, Pakistan announced its intention to improve its bilateral relations with countries recognizing Bangladesh. As of October 1973, more than one hundred countries had recognized Bangladesh, with India, her client states, and the Soviet bloc countries being the first to extend recognition. Commonwealth and West European countries were the next. Of the major powers, China has not yet granted recognition, although it has indicated its interest to resume trade relations with Bangladesh.[59] The Arab bloc Muslim countries (except Iraq), deferring to Pakistan's wishes, waited a long time before recognizing Bangladesh. Bangladesh's entry into international organizations, e.g., World Health Organization and International Labor Organization, has been relatively easy and without conflict; her application for UN membership was vetoed by Peking in the fall of 1972 but a formula for eventual recognition has been adopted by Pakistan whose first step is nonopposition to UN entry.

Pakistan has not yet recognized Bangladesh. Bhutto still airs public hopes that Pakistan and Bangladesh will be able to form a confederation, in the manner of Egypt and Libya. In private, he is reported to be reconciled to the fact of division and is expected to recognize Bangladesh soon. Some of Bhutto's party men already argue in favor of recognition; and the regime is busy preparing the psychological groundwork for it. The Pakistani press has ceased calling Bangladesh "East Pakistan," and has published letters and articles favoring recognition. Recognition, however, became entangled with the prisoner-of-war question. Bangladesh refused to discuss the POW issue with Pakistan before recognition, while Bhutto insisted on having at least one meeting with Mujib before he recognized Bangladesh.

The division of Pakistan radically changed the balance of power in

South Asia in favor of India and the Soviet Union.[60] In the postdivision period India emerged as the decisively dominant power in the area. None of the other South Asian states had a force countervailing to hers. By successfully dismembering her old rival, Pakistan, in the face of opposition from two superpowers and the world community, India vindicated her claim that she is the major power in South Asia. The military victory over Pakistan, coupled with her recent economic growth and political stability, left India in a mood of new confidence. She might use her strength to keep South Asia out of superpower rivalries, thus achieving one of India's major foreign policy objectives. Unfortunately, the deterioration in India's internal affairs over the last two years seem, temporarily at least, to have sapped her strength and international capability.

The division of Pakistan also helped increase the Soviet Union's influence in South Asia. Like the other superpowers, the Soviet Union pursued a policy of noninterference in the Bangladesh crisis, but it made known its sympathies for the Bangladesh cause. The Soviet president wrote much-publicized letters to President Yahya asking for a political settlement to the crisis. During the December war the Soviet Union gave diplomatic support to the Bangladesh cause by casting two vetoes in India's favor in the United Nations. Since the emergence of Bangladesh, the Soviet presence in the new country has been very visible. Soviet prestige in India also soared. In August 1971, in the wake of the Bangladesh crisis and the Sino-American détente, India and the Soviet Union signed a treaty of peace, friendship, and cooperation which formalized the close ties between the two countries.[61] The Indians appreciated Russian arms supplies before the war and Russian diplomatic support and the presence of the Russian fleet in the Indian Ocean during the war. While strengthening ties with India and picking up Bangladesh's friendship, the Soviets took care to mend relationships with the Pakistanis. Soon after the war was over, both sides took pains to show that the "spirit of Tashkent" was back.

While the Soviet influence reached its peak, U.S. influence in South Asia reached its nadir in the aftermath of the division of Pakistan. Throughout the Bangladesh crisis the United States never publicly censured Pakistan, and U.S. policy toward South Asia was "tilted" in favor of Pakistan.[62] During the December war the United States called India the aggressor, threatened the USSR with the cancelation of the scheduled summit meeting for its support of India, and finally, near the end of the war, sent a nuclear carrier to the Indian Ocean.[63] The U.S. policy infuriated the Indians, and the relationship between the two countries, though improved by late 1973, only started to warm at the end of 1972. Thus the South Asia policy of the United States backfired as its objective of checking Russian influence in the Indian Ocean received a setback. However, the United States succeeded in regaining some of its lost influence in Bangladesh by virtue of being the largest aid donor.

Like the United States, China also backed the losing side. But while giving public support to Pakistan, China privately admonished the regime, and in fact did little materially to help Pakistan during the war.[64] In the postdivision period, China still remains Pakistan's number-one friend, without losing the interest of Bangladesh in friendly relations with China.

The Bangladesh crisis showed that, though all the superpowers were interested in South Asia, none wanted to get actively involved there. In fact, pressure from their allies—India and Pakistan—made the superpowers reluctantly take sides in the crisis, and even then they managed to avoid a superpower confrontation. Since the emergence of Bangladesh, the superpowers have again become interested in maintaining a balance and peace among the three countries. The major preoccupation of the superpowers is to reach a détente with each other. The general international milieu, plus the dominance of India, thus makes the prospects of tension reduction much brighter in South Asia.

Policy Prospects

ISSUES IN DISPUTE

The division of Pakistan is a relatively recent phenomenon, and no ties have yet been established between the two successor states. A number of outstanding issues created tension between the two countries and hindered normalization of relations between them.

First, Pakistan has not recognized Bangladesh and still claims its territory. Bangladesh has refused to establish any contact with Pakistan unless it recognizes Bangladesh first.

Second, there were in India approximately 93,000 Pakistani prisoners of war who surrendered to a joint command of Indo-Bangladesh forces. Pakistan badly needed the POWs back to calm domestic public opinion and ease pressure on the regime. Bangladesh, however, refused to talk about the POWs without a prior recognition by Pakistan. Pakistan claimed that the Pakistani troops surrendered to an Indian command so the POW question should be discussed only with India. Both India and Bangladesh authorities maintained that the POWs surrendered to a joint command and that the POW issue can be settled only with Bangladesh concurrence.

Third, Bangladesh planned to hold a war-crimes trial for some 1,500 Pakistani POWs. Pakistan was vehemently against such a trial. Pakistan has argued that a trial would inflame public opinion, threaten the security of over half a million Bengalis living in Pakistan, and undermine the civilian regime of Bhutto which represents moderate elements of the Pakistani elite and favors a peaceful settlement of conflicts between India, Pakistan, and Bangladesh. Bangladesh leadership maintained that war-crimes trials are necessary not only for moral and legal reasons but also because of domestic political considerations. After liberation, the Bangladesh regime avoided the anticipated massacre of the Biharis by promising the people that a proper trial would be held for the real culprits who committed mass killings in Bangladesh, and thus there was no need for the people to take the law into their own hands. Since liberation, Sheikh Mujib has repeatedly talked of genocide and war-crimes trials. He is now caught in his own rhetoric. It is difficult for him to back down from the trials without losing credibility with "his" people, and without appearing to be giving in under Bhutto's pressure.[65]

Fourth, half a million to a million non-Bengalis lived in Bangladesh, the majority of whom owed allegiance to Pakistan and wanted to migrate there. Similarly, approximately half a million Bengalis in Pakistan were loyal to Bangladesh and wanted to go back. Pakistan was not willing to take back all the non-Bengalis who wanted to emigrate from Bangladesh. In contrast, Bangladesh was willing to take back all the Bengalis living in Pakistan. Bangladesh was willing to exchange its Bihari population with the Bengalis in Pakistan. Pakistan was not interested in such an exchange proposal and was holding the Bengalis as a hostage against the POWs. It was using the Bengali issue to put pressure on Bangladesh to soften its position on the war-crimes trials and the POWs. There are hence complex population issues.

Fifth, there was the problem of division of assets and liabilities. Pakistan was especially keen to share with Bangladesh the liability of its interests on foreign aid. Bangladesh was willing to share the liabilities, provided the assets are also divided. Additionally, Bangladesh wanted to share liabilities in proportion to its share of foreign aid (and not the total aid). Bangladesh also demanded war reparations from Pakistan. However, issues of division of assets and liabilities and war reparation could not be discussed without prior recognition of Bangladesh. So far there had not been any direct contact between the governments of Pakistan and Bangladesh. Pakistan has shown interest in establishing economic and other contacts with Bangladesh, but the latter is going slow with reestablishing contact and is awaiting Pakistan's formal recognition.

While there had been no direct contact (or at least no direct public contact) between the two governments, third countries attempted to reduce tension between the two. Prior to and following the Simla summit conference in July 1972 between Mrs. Gandhi and Bhutto, India acted as a go-between and tried to bring both Pakistan and Bangladesh across a conference table. At the preparatory stage of the summit conference it appeared that it would be a tripartite conference between Pakistan, India, and Bangladesh. Pakistan had no objection to Bangladesh's participation at the conference, but it was not willing to offer diplomatic recognition to Bangladesh. Despite Indian pressure and persuasion to do so, Bangladesh refused to participate in the conference without prior recognition. The United Kingdom and Indonesia also reportedly tried to break the deadlock by arranging a meeting between Bhutto and Mujib in a third country.

Bhutto has expressed his willingness to meet Mujib anyplace in the world, excluding India.

The problem of tension reduction between Pakistan and Bangladesh was complicated by the fact that a third country—India—was directly involved in the tension. Tension between Pakistan and Bangladesh could not be reduced without reducing the tension between Pakistan and India. Pakistan's major enemy and major preoccupation is still India, and not Bangladesh. The final division of Pakistan was made possible by direct Indian armed intervention; and in the postdivision period, the Pakistanis remembered with bitterness their defeat at Indian (and not Bengali) hands. The issues in dispute between India and Pakistan were the POWs, Kashmir, and the Indian occupation of some 2,500 square miles of Pakistani territory in the western front during the December war. India was willing to release the POWs in exchange for a permanent settlement of the Kashmir dispute, but Pakistan was reluctant to give up the Kashmir issue which had been a cornerstone of its foreign policy.

The first step toward reduction of tension between Pakistan and India was taken by the Simla summit accord between the two countries. Both sides showed a spirit of give and take. By the Simla agreement, India gave up the territory it occupied in Pakistan's western front during the war. In return, it got Pakistan's pledge to renounce the use of force in settling outstanding disputes between the two countries. By reversing their earlier stands, Pakistan agreed to settle the Kashmir dispute by bilateral and peaceful negotiations, and India recognized that Kashmir was in fact an issue in dispute. Both countries agreed to take a number of steps to increase contact and thereby decrease hostility. Trade, communications, and cultural contacts were resumed, and both countries agreed to give up the propaganda war. No solution was found to the POW and Kashmir issues, but both countries agreed to set up a peacekeeping mechanism which would settle the disputed issues step-by-step through mutual discussion.[66] The POW and the Kashmir issues, however, need the concurrence of other parties—Bangladesh and the people of Kashmir.

The second step toward reduction of tension was taken when Pakistan and India signed an agreement in August 1973 which settled the POW and the repatriation issue. Under the agreement India and Bangladesh agreed to release all but 195 of Pakistani POWs; Pakistan agreed to let all Bengalis leave Pakistan and to accept back a substantial number of Pakistani civilians and Biharis living in Bangladesh. The 1973 agreement was the result of compromise on the part of all the three countries. India and Bangladesh gave up their earlier policy of recognition first. They agreed to the release of POWs even before Pakistan recognized Bangladesh. Bangladesh also toned down its earlier stand on war-crime trials. Instead of 1,500, Bangladesh agreed to try a much smaller number of 195. Pakistan also agreed to the repatriation of Bengalis and non-Bengalis and implicitly recognized Bangladesh, as Clause V of the agreement states that Bangladesh would participate in meetings with Pakistan "only on the basis of sovereign equality." The 1973 agreement thus broke the deadlock between the two countries and has created a climate for further accommodation between Pakistan and Bangladesh.

RECOMMENDATIONS

Both Pakistan and Bangladesh have taken a number of seemingly irreconcilable positions with regard to the issues outstanding between them. While the rhetoric of the leadership in both countries minimizes the scope of their maneuverability, some alternative policy options are still available to the two countries.

To reduce tension, Bangladesh and Pakistan might adopt the step-by-step approach, as India and Pakistan did. Pakistan is interested in resuming economic ties, and the two countries did develop some economic links over the years. Additionally, as India is now the dominant power in South Asia, Pakistan and Bangladesh—both small powers flanking India—might find it to their interest to come to an accommodation with one another. Indeed, if the present trend of anti-Indian feelings continues to rise in Bangladesh, there is a good possibility that Bangladesh would be interested in normalizing relations with Pakistan soon. On February 23, 1974, Pakistan formally recognized the government of Bangladesh.

Nevertheless, a real détente in South Asia is possible only if there is peace and cooperation among the three countries of the subcontinent. Many observers have suggested a confederation as the best means of achieving peace. But a confederation is feasible only after reducing tension and establishing mutual trust. Economic and cultural cooperation has to precede political integration. At present, neither Pakistan nor Bangladesh is interested in a South Asian confederation for fear of Indian dominance. But all three countries realize that they have to live together. They must find a mutually acceptable solution for coexistence.

Appendix 1

LAHORE RESOLUTION

While approving and endorsing the action taken by the Council and the Working Committee of the All-India Muslim League, as indicated in their resolutions dated the 27th of August, 17th and 18th of September and 22nd of October 1939, and 3rd of February 1940 on the constitutional Issue, this Session of the All-India Muslim League emphatically reiterates that the scheme of federation embodied in the Government of India Act, 1935, is totally unsuited to, and unworkable in the peculiar conditions of this country and is altogether unacceptable to Muslim India.

It further records its emphatic view that while the declaration dated the 18th of October 1939 made by the Viceroy on behalf of His Majesty's Government is reassuring in so far as it declares that the policy and plan on which the Government of India Act, 1939, is based will be reconsidered in consultation with the various parties, interests and communities in India, Muslim India will not be satisfied unless the whole constitutional plan is reconsidered de novo and that no revised plan would be acceptable to the Muslims unless it is framed with their approval and consent.

Resolved that it is the considered view of this Session of the All-India Muslim League that no constitutional plan would be workable in this country or acceptable to the Muslims unless it is designed on the following basic principles, viz., that geographically contiguous units are demarcated into regions which should be so constituted, with such territorial re-adjustments as may be necessary, that the areas in which the Muslims are numerically in a majority as in the North Western and Eastern zones of India should be grouped to constitute "Independent States" in which the constituent units shall be autonomous and sovereign.

That adequate, effective and mandatory safeguards should be specifically provided in the constitution for minorities in these units and in the regions for the protection of their religious, cultural, economic, political, administrative and other rights and interests in consultation with them and in other parts of India where the Musalmans are in a minority adequate, effective and mandatory safeguards shall be specifically provided in the constitution for them and other minorities for the protection of their religious, cultural, economic, political, administrative and other rights and interests in consultation with them

Appendix 2

SHEIKH MUJIBUR RAHMAN'S PRESENTATION OF THE AWAMI LEAGUE'S SIX-POINT FORMULA, FEBRUARY 1966.

I have placed before the country a 6-point programme as basic principles of a firm solution of the country's interwing political and economic problems.

I expected and in fact was ready to welcome criticism. But instead of criticizing the programme and pointing out its defects, if there be any, a class of people has started hurling abuses at and ascribing disruptionist motive to me. . . .

POINT 1

In this point I have recommended as follows:

The Constitution should provide for a Federation of Pakistan in its true sense on the basis of the Lahore Resolution, and Parliamentary form of Government with supremacy of Legislature directly elected on the basis of universal adult franchise.

It will be seen that this point consists in the following five ingredients, viz: (a) Pakistan shall be a Federation, (b) it shall be based on Lahore resolution, (c) the Legislature must be supreme, (d) it must be directly elected and (e) election must be on the basis of universal adult franchise. . . .

POINT 2

This point recommends as follows:

Federal Government shall deal with only two subjects, viz: Defence and Foreign Affairs, and all other residuary subjects shall vest in the federating states. . . .

POINT 3

In this point I have recommended either of the following two measures with regard to our currency, viz:

A Two separate but freely convertible currencies for two wings may be introduced, or,

B One currency for the whole country may be maintained. In this case effective constitutional provisions are to be made to stop flight of capital from East to West Pakistan. Separate Banking Reserve is to be made and separate fiscal and monetary policy to be adopted for East Pakistan. . . .

POINT 4

In this point I have recommended that the power of taxation and revenue collection shall vest in the federating units and that the Federal Centre will have no such power. The Federation will share in the state taxes for meeting its required expenditure. The Consolidated Federal Fund shall come out of a levy of certain percentage of all state taxes. . . .

POINT 5

In this point I have recommended that:

1 there shall be two separate accounts for foreign exchange earnings of the two wings,

2 earnings of East Pakistan shall be under the control of East Pakistan Government and that of West Pakistan under the control of West Pakistan Government,

3 foreign exchange requirements of the Federal Government shall be met by the two wings either equally or in a ration to be fixed,

4 indigenous products shall move free of duty between two wings,

5 the Constitution shall empower the unit Governments to establish trade and commercial relations with, set up trade missions in and enter into agreements with foreign countries. . . .

POINT 6

In this point I have recommended setting up of a militia or a para-military force for East Pakistan. This is neither unreasonable nor new. We had pledged in the famous 21-point programme in 1954 that we would give arms and uniforms to our Ansars. . . .

CONCLUSION

Now, before concluding, I want to submit a few words to my West Pakistani brethren:

Firstly, they should not run away with the idea that whatever I have stated above I have done in the interest of East Pakistan only. It is not so. In each of my 6-point programme is inherent a corresponding benefit to my West Pakistani brethren. They are sure to derive equal benefit out of their implementation.

Secondly, when I speak of East Pakistan's wealth being flown to and concentrated in West Pakistan I only mean regional concentration. I do not, thereby, mean that the people of West Pakistan have exploited us. I know there are millions like us in West Pakistan who also are unfortunate victims of this economic exploitation. . . . A leader who sincerely believes that the two wings of Pakistan are really two eyes, two ears, two nostrils, two rows of teeth, two hands and two legs of the body-politic of Pakistan, a leader who feels that to make Pakistan healthy and strong one must make each one of these pairs equally healthy and strong, a leader who earnestly believes that to weaken any one of the limbs is to weaken Pakistan as a whole, a leader who zealously holds that any one who deliberately or knowingly weakens any limb of Pakistan is an enemy of the country and a leader who is ready to take strong measures against such enemies, is the only person entitled to claim the national leadership of Pakistan.

Pakistan is a magnificent country with an uncommonly wide horizon. To be fit to become its leader one must possess a similarly magnificent heart with an uncommon breadth of vision.

Appendix 3

THE PROCLAMATION OF INDEPENDENCE OF BANGLADESH BY THE AWAMI LEAGUE ON APRIL 10, 1971

Mujibnagar, Bangladesh
10th day of April, 1971

Whereas free elections were held in Bangladesh from 7th December, 1970 to 17th January, 1971, to elect representatives for the purpose of framing a Constitution, AND

Whereas at these elections the people of Bangladesh elected 167 out of 169 representatives belonging to the Awami Leage, AND

Whereas General Yahya Khan summoned the elected representatives of the people to meet on the 3rd March, 1971, for the purpose of framing a Constitution, AND

Whereas the Assembly so summoned was arbitrarily and illegally postponed for an indefinite period, AND

Whereas instead of fulfilling their promise and while still conferring with the representatives of the people of Bangladesh, Pakistan authorities declared an unjust and treacherous war, AND

Whereas in the facts and circumstances of such treacherous conduct Banga Bandhu Sheikh Mujibur Rahman, the undisputed leader of 75 million of people of Bangladesh, in due fulfilment of the legitimate right of self-determination of the people of Bangladesh, duly made a declaration of independence at Dacca on March 26, 1971, and urged the people of Bangladesh to defend the honour and integrity of Bangladesh, AND

Whereas in the conduct of a ruthless and savage war the Pakistani authorities committed and are still continuously committing numerous acts of genocide and unprecedented tortures, amongst others on the civilian and unarmed people of Bangladesh, AND

Whereas the Pakistan Government by levying an unjust war and committing genocide and by other repressive measures made it impossible for the elected representatives of the people of Bangladesh to meet and frame a Constitution, and give to themselves a Government, AND

Whereas the people of Bangladesh by their heroism, bravery and revolutionary fervour have established effective control over the territories of Bangladesh,

We the elected representatives of the people of Bangladesh, as honour bound by the mandate given to us by the people of Bangladesh whose will is supreme duly constituted ourselves into a Constituent Assembly, and

having held mutual consultations, and

in order to ensure for the people of Bangladesh equality, human dignity and social justice,

declare and constitute Bangladesh to be a sovereign People's Republic and thereby confirm the declaration of independence already made by Banga Bandhu Sheikh Mujibur Rahman and

do hereby affirm and resolve that till such time as a Constitution is framed, Banga Bandhi Sheikh Mujibur Rahman shall be the President of the Republic and that Syed Nazrul Islam shall be the Vice-President of the Republic, and

that the President shall be the Supreme Commander of all the Armed Forces of the Republic,

shall exercise all the Executive and Legislative powers of the Republic including the power to grant pardon,

shall have the power to appoint a Prime Minister and such other Ministers as he considers necessary,

shall have the power to levy taxes and expend monies,

shall have the power to summon and adjourn the Constitutent Assembly, and

do all other things that may be necessary to give to the people of Bangladesh an orderly and just Government.

We the elected representatives of the people of Bangladesh do further resolve that in the event of there being no President or the President being unable to enter upon his office or being unable to exercise his powers due to any reaason whatsoever, the Vice-President shall have and exercise all the powers, duties and responsibilities herein conferred on the President.

We further resolve that we undertake to observe and give effect to all duties and obligations that devolve upon us as a member of the family of nations and to abide by the Charter of the United Nations.

We further resolve that this proclamation of independence shall be deemed to have come into effect from 26th day of March, 1971.

We further resolve that in order to give effect to this instrument we appoint Prof. Yusuf Ali our duly constituted potentiary and to give to the President and the Vice-President oaths of office.

[Signed]
PROFESSOR YUSUF ALI
Duly Constituted Potentiary.
By and under the authority
of the Constituent Assembly
of Bangladesh

Notes

1. I have borrowed the term "internal colonialism" from New Left writings. By internal colonialism I refer to the process of domination and exploitation of one ethnic group by another within a country. In most new states that have plural societies, early-modernizing ethnic groups dominate the power elite. Once in power, these ethnic groups follow a public policy which perpetuates their unequal power relationship with other groups. The resultant conflicts between the "haves" and "have nots" are chronic in many new states.

2. Some noted examples of such autonomy/secessionist movements are Biafra in Nigeria; Katanga in Congo; Nagaland, Mixoland, and to a lesser extent Tamilnadu in India; Shans, Karen, and Kachins in Burma; Pakhtoons in Pakistan; etc.

3. Rupert Emerson, *From Empire to Nation* (Cambridge, Mass.: Harvard University Press, 1960), p. 92.

4. M. A. Jinnah, quoted in Sharif al-Mujahid, "National Integration," in *Pakistani Nationhood* (Dacca: Bureau of National Reconstruction, 1962), p. 148.

5. Donald W. Wilber, *Pakistan* (New Haven: Human Relations Area File, 1964), p. 71.

6. When the concept of a separate Muslim nation was first advanced, there was no unanimous agreement as to its geographical composition. The first territorial demand was made on regions which now correspond roughly to the present Pakistan. Later demands were put forward for two more separate Muslim states—one in the northeast comprising Bengal and Assam, to be called Bangstan; and one in the south comprising Hyderabad, to be called Osmanistan. When in 1946 the Lahore Revolution was amended in favor of a single Muslim state in India, some Muslim Leaguers from Bengal protested. For details of the Lahore Resolution controversy, see Choudhury Khaliquzzamn, *Pathway to Pakistan* (Lahore: Longmans, 1961); Kamruddin Ahmad, *A Social History of East Pakistan* (Dacca: Crescent, 1967).

7. For a detailed analysis of Bengali nonrepresentation in the power elite, see Rounaq Jahan, *Pakistan: Failure in National Integration* (New York: Columbia University Press, 1972), chaps. 2–3.

8. J. C. Hurewitz, *Middle East Politics: The Military Dimension* (New York: Praeger, 1969), pp. 179–86.

9. Rounaq Jahan, "Ten Years of Ayub Khan and the Problem of National Integration," *Journal of Comparative Administration* (November 1970).

10. One of the most heated controversies in Pakistan was the issue of economic disparity between East and West Pakistan. Generally, Pakistani economists attributed it to the east wing's low level of development in 1947; while the Bengali economists attribute it to the government of Pakistan's economic policies. For a detailed discussion of the question, see Muhummad Anisur Rahman, *East and West Pakistan* (Cambridge, Mass.: Center for International Affairs, Harvard University, 1968); Mahbub ul Haq, *The Strategy of Economic Planning: A Case Study of Pakistan* (Lahore: Oxford University Press, 1963); Nurul Islam, "Some Aspects of Interwing Trade and Terms of Trade in Pakistan," *Pakistan Development Review* 3 (1963).

11. For a detailed analysis of public policy and economic disparity, see Jahan, *Pakistan,* chaps. 2, 4.

12. The 1954 autonomy demands of the Bengali opposition forces visualized a federal government with powers over defense, foreign affairs, and currency. The 1956 constitution provided for a fairly powerful federal government, and when the autonomist party, the Awami League, came to power in the center, its leader, H. S. Suhrawardy, defended the federal provisions of the 1956 constitution, declaring that it had granted 98% of Bengal's autonomy demands.

13. The Bengalis participated in two successive elections under Ayub's system—in 1962 and in 1964–65. After two unsuccessful attempts, it became obvious to the Bengali counterelite that Ayub's system could be changed by working through it.

14. The 1970 election was held under an ordinance called the Legal Framework Order (LFO) which laid down some basic principles of the future constitution. One of the limiting provisions of the LFO was that it vested the final power of authenticating the constitution on the president and not on the national assembly.

15. Howard Schuman, "A Note on the Rapid Rise of Mass Nationalism in East Pakistan" (Paper presented at a seminar at Columbia University, 1972). Schuman argues persuasively that the spirit of nationalism reached the mass level only after the military crackdown of March 1971.

16. This is especially the argument of the Far Left parties in Bangladesh. They maintain that India intervened militarily in Bangladesh in December 1971 to promote its own national security interests—to prevent the leadership of the liberation movement from going into radical leftist hands.

17. For a discussion of the two-economy thesis, see Rahman, *East and West Pakistan;* a. Sadeque, *The Economic Emergence of Pakistan, pt. 1* (Dacca: East Bengal Government Press, 1954); ibid., pt. 2 (Dacca: East Bengal Statistical Bureau, 1956); and *Pakistan's First Five Year Plan in Theory and Operation* (Dacca: East Pakistan Government Press, n.d.).

18. *Quarterly Economic Review,* no. 1 (1972): 5.

19. Ibid., pp. 7–9.

20. Ibid., p. 8.

21. Ibid., p. 8.

22. Ibid., p. 11.

23. Estimates about the cost of reconstruction varies. Bangladesh sources first came through with a staggering figure of rupees 20,000 million. Since then it has revised the figure to a much more modest figure of $1.5 billion.

24. "Ambassador Erna Sailer's Report on the Mission of High Level United Nations Consultants to Bangladesh (April 1972), 1:11–14. Mimeographed.

25. *Quarterly Economic Review,* no. 1 (1972): 20.

26. John Thomas, "Public Policy in the Reconstruction and Development of Rural Bangladesh" (Paper presented at the Bengal Studies Conference, May 1972), p. 4.

27. Ibid., p. 1.

28. Ibid., p. 2.

29. Even the *White Paper on the Crisis in East Pakistan* (Islamabad: Government of Pakistan Press, August 1971), compiled by the government of Pakistan, fails to list too many violations of law and order in the pre-March 25 period.

30. See the *White Paper on the Crisis in East Pakistan* for an elaboration of this thesis to defend the military action in Bangladesh.

31. The actual number of non-Bengalis is a subject of controversy. Most newspaper reports put their number at 2 million. However, the projections of population from the 1961 census figures put the number of non-Bengalis at a little over 500,000.

32. Thomas, "Public Policy on Reconstruction," p. 1.

33. Ishan Kapur, "Economic Effects of the War and the Refugee Problem: India, Bangladesh and Pakistan" (Paper available from the author).

34. Kushwant Singh, "Homecoming in Bangladesh," *New York Times Magazine,* 30 January 1972.

35. *New York Times,* 24 April 1972.

36. Though the non-Bengali refugees were generally called the Biharis, not all of them were from Bihar. The Biharis, however, constitute the majority of the refugees.

37. *New York Times,* 13 July 1972.

38. Ibid., 21 February 1972.

39. *Christian Science Monitor,* 11 July 1972.

40. Already anti-Indian feeling had risen in Bangladesh. Bengalis have begun complaining about the Indian Marwaris starting businesses in Bangladesh, the Indian Army taking away arms left behind by the Pakistani troops, Indian businessmen smuggling jute across the border, etc. See Lawrence Leamer, "Bangladesh in Mourning," *Harpers* (August 1972).

41. Fred Riggs, *Administration in Developing Countries: A Theory of Prismatic Society* (Boston: Houghton Miffllin, 1964), argues that a developed bureaucracy often hampers the growth of political institutions.

42. "Twenty-two families" has acquired symbolic importance after the chief economist of Pakistan's Planning Commission stated that the main harvest of the country's economic growth had been reaped by some twenty-two families only. See Mahbub ul Haq quoted in the *Pakistan Observer,* 3 May 1968.

43. *Quarterly Economic Review,* no. 1 (1972): 13.

44. After liberation, various cleavages developed in Bangladesh. Those who went into exile in India claimed to be the true patriots, and those who stayed were looked down upon as collaborators of the Pakistani military regime. Such sweeping generalizations and witch-hunting led one of the leading Dacca dailies to editorialize: "We are a nation of 65 million collaborators!" Conflicts also developed between the old civil servants and the new technocrats of the Planning Commission. See *New York Times,* 4 April 1972.

45. *Bangladesh Observer* (Dacca), 1–20 June 1972. The Left parties in Bangladesh—the National Awami party and the Communist—are broadly divided into three factions: pro-Moscow, pro-Peking, and Maoist. The last group, the most radical of the three, is again subdivided into a number of factions, all calling themselves the Marxist-Leninist faction.

46. M. Rashiduzzaman, "Leadership, Organization, Strategies and Tactics of Bangladesh Movement", *Asian Survey* 12 (March 1972):

47. Tajuddin Ahmad, who is the fianance minister in Mujib's cabinet and was the prime minister in the government-in-exile, is reportedly heading an Awami League faction that is in favor of closer relations with India and the USSR. Awami League factionalism is still latent, however, because nobody is in a position to challenge Mujib's authority.

48. See Peter J. Bertocci, "Patterns of Social Organization in Rural East Bengal" (Paper presented at the Bengal Studies Conference, 1968).

49. Crocker Snow, Jr., "Bangladesh: The New Nation," *Boston Globe,* 1 August 1972.

50. The youth play a key role as a political broker between the urban and rural areas. They are more politicized and more organized as compared to the other groups. Their power was demonstrated in the national liberation movement in which they played a leading role.

51. Leonard Binder, "Prospects for Pakistan," (Occasional Paper series, University of Chicago, 1972), p. 4.

52. S. M. Ali, "The Key to Peace", *Far Eastern Economic Review* 75, no. 7 (12 February 1972).

53. Binder, "Prospects for Pakistan."

54. Citizens of Bangladesh now call themselves *Bangalee* and not *Bengali* as they did before.

55. From the beginning of the twentieth century, when the Hindu-Muslim conflict intensified, each community tried to make its language communal by deliberately infusing it with Sanskrit or Arabic/Urdu vocabularies. Similar controversies arose with the Urdu-Hindi speakers.

56. Though identity in Bangladesh is defined in terms of Bengali nationalism, a territorial limit is put on that, so for all practical purposes the identity mostly connotes Bengali Muslim identity. The Bengali Muslim nationalist bourgeoisie, who were the major spokesmen of the Bengali nationalist movement, want to create a separate state of their own, free from competition and exploitation by outsiders, which includes both the Muslims of Pakistan and Hindus of India and West Bengal. Hence they are as much in favor of separating their identity from Bengali Hindus as from the Muslims of Pakistan.

57. Schuman, "Rise of Mass Nationalism."

58. *New York Times,* 26 January 1972.

59. China has recently shown interest in resuming jute trade with Bangladesh. The offer was made when the Bengali diplomats from Peking were repatriated to Bangladesh.

60. Phillips Talbot, "The Subcontinent: Ménage a Trois," *Foreign Affairs* 50, no. 4 (July 1972).

61. The treaty stipulates that neither country would enter into a military alliance directed against each other or allow its territory to be used for such purposes. In case of armed conflict with a third party, both sides would engage in mutual consultation and abstain from providing assistance to the third party. Since the early 1960s, the Soviet Union has been following a policy of having friendly relations with both India and Pakistan. Its influence with both the states was put to use in the Tashkent agreement when the USSR acted as a mediator between India and Pakistan in the aftermath of the 1965 war. After Tashkent, the Russian policy of balancing India and Pakistan became more prominent.

62. Reportedly President Nixon wanted to follow a policy in South Asia that would be "tilted" in favor of Pakistan. In January 1972 columnist Jack Anderson released to the press four documents describing the meeting of the National Security Council's Washington Special Action Group, where presidential adviser Dr. Henry Kissinger noted the President's personal preference to "tilt" in favor of Pakistan. See *New York Times,* 6–7 January 1972.

63. The United States defended its sending of the nuclear carrier to the Indian Ocean with a claim that the action succeeded in curbing Indian intention of invasion on the Pakistani Western front. Additionally it was meant to counter the presence of the Russian fleet.

64. T. J. S. George, "Peking's Pre-war Message to Pakistan," *Far Eastern Economic Review* 75, no. 6 (5 February 1972).

65. *Christian Science Monitor,* 11 July 1972.

66. For a full description of the Simla accord, see *New York Times,* 4 July 1972.

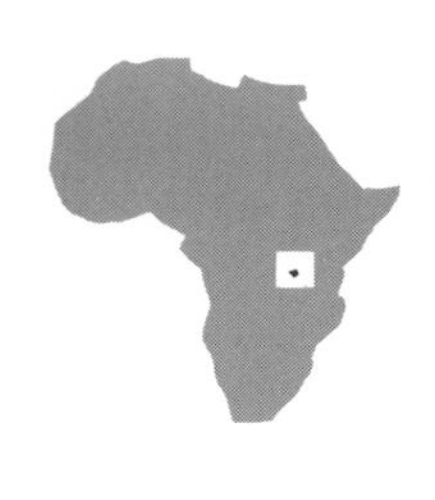

RUANDA-URUNDI

(RWANDA, BURUNDI)

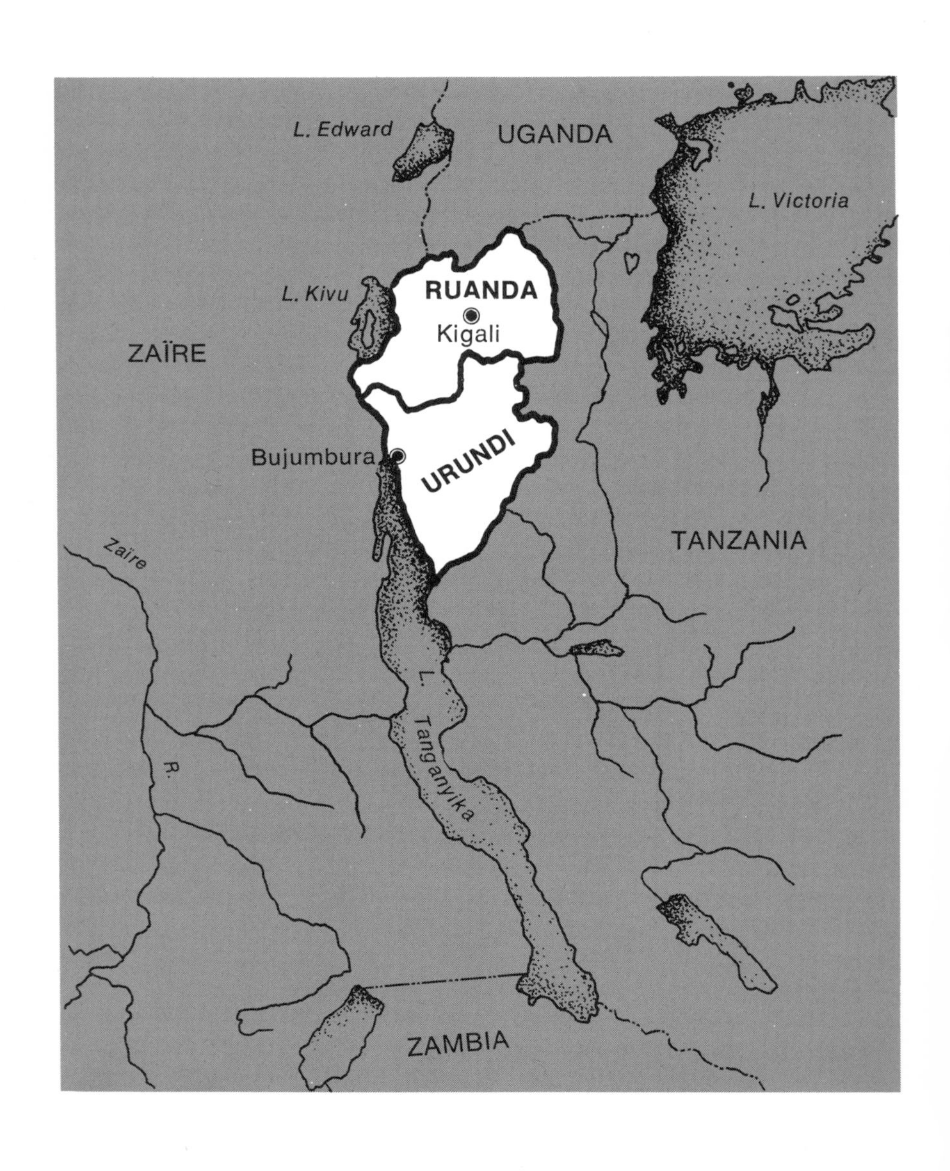

10

Ruanda-Urundi (Rwanda-Burundi)

Warren Weinstein

An Aborted Putative Nation[1]

WITH FEW EXCEPTIONS, African states are not composed of a single nation; even the least rigorous standards would exclude most states from the nation-state category.[2] Communal strife in the independent states of Africa further qualifies this statement. One need only consider the more dramatic examples: ethnic strife in Burundi in 1969 and 1972, Nigeria's two-year bout with Biafra, Zanzibar's revolution in 1964, Rwanda's revolution in 1959, the north-south split in the Sudan, recent troubles in Uganda, struggles in all countries of the western Sudanic belt where "white" and "black" segments of the population confront each other. Africa has already had several irredentist movements, the most serious being that of the Somali living in what is now Ethiopia, Kenya, and the French territory of Issas and Afars. A guerrilla war is growing in intensity in Ethiopia where Muslim Eritreans are fighting to break away from a Coptic Christian-dominated land. Another is seething in Chad between "whites" and "blacks." The list is far from exhaustive, but it suggests the degree to which African states are geographical and administratively defined units.

Unlike the experience of Zaire (formerly the Democratic Republic of the Congo [Kinshasa]) or Nigeria, where secessions have been attempted, or Uganda, where centralist republican forces have been locked in conflict with monarchists desiring autonomy for their subunits, Rwanda and Burundi lived out their colonial period in an administrative, economic, and technical union that was never allowed to grow into a political one.

Rwanda and Burundi usually inspire romantic images of dancing Watusi, the people who once ruled both these mountainous states.[3] Lying at the crossroads of Central Africa, the two landlocked states with their topography and inviting climate have had many visitors compare them with Switzerland and the Tirol.[4] Indeed, Rwanda and Burundi's natural frontiers of inaccessible mountains and rivers served as sufficient barriers to the marauding slavers of the mid-nineteenth century. Later, however, they were not to deter the curious explorers from Europe. The nineteenth-century European dissection of Africa left Ruanda-Urundi in German hands.[5] Several Germans visited the two kingdoms in the late 1800s, and German rule was officially established in the late 1890s. The Germans administered Rwanda and Burundi by indirect rule and very loosely incorporated them into the larger territory of German East Africa. The European rulers retained historical divisions between what were two separate kingdoms; they remained separate districts. The German administrators soon concluded that Rwanda was the more advanced of the two areas, and treated it accordingly. The Belgians picked up this prejudice when they took over the two districts in 1916.

Rwanda and Burundi, the indigenous-language names of these countries (Ruanda and Urundi are Swahili names) had been two mutually antagonistic political entities prior to their occupation by the Germans. Each was ruled by a traditional monarch or *mwami* (plural, *bami*). While it is not necessary to delve into the details of their respective societies, certain highlights are important for our discussion: Rwanda was a highly centralized, stratified monarchy with rather clear-cut distinctions in status between the ethnic groups that inhabited it (the ruling status group were the pastoral Tutsi; the agricultural Hutu, who made up more than 80 percent of the population, formed a low, serflike status group). Burundi was similar in makeup; it, too, had Tutsi and Hutu status groups, but the lines of distinction between them were less clear-cut. In addition, Burundi was never as centralized a kingdom as Rwanda; its precolonial political history was one of incessant secessions and internal feuding among princely lineages (or *Ganwa*) and their allies. In Burundi the mwami did not stand at the social apex above all others; he was primus inter pares among Ganwa princes.

By 1900, Ruanda-Urundi's history was tied to the fortunes of Europe. When Germany was defeated in 1919, the victorious Allies awarded Ruanda-Urundi to Belgium as a League of Nations mandate. The mandate was changed to a United Nations trusteeship following the Second World War.

Briefly, Ruanda-Urundi had never achieved any real unification under the mandate or trusteeship system. Even at the United Nations, archives dealing with the two states were kept separate. The fact that two states are ruled by one colonial authority has never been a necessary and sufficient cause to support political unification, as illustrated by the failure of a federation among the islands of the former British West Indies and elsewhere. To a large extent, the argument for unification was based on a semblance of unity achieved in the Belgian centralization of common services at the administrative seat of the Ruanda-Urundi Vice-Government General—Bujumbura. However, Belgium is guilty of having failed to Africanize the higher reaches of her colonial administration. Because of this, most officials involved at the level of common services were Europeans, not Africans. Rwanda and Burundi had two separate indigenous administrations; the Belgians never promoted any unification at this level. Even the very important Catholic church, with a following of well over one-half the total population, was kept separate, after 1922, for Rwanda and for Burundi. This was true also of the various Protestant missions that established themselves. Perhaps the Belgian and the religious authorities acted on a more realistic understanding and appreciation of the deep-seated historical divisions that stood in the way of unification.

Arguments put forward between 1957 and 1962 in favor of political unification for Rwanda and Burundi were based on several false assumptions. First, it was said that Rwanda and Burundi were somehow unified because, both as a Mandated Territory and as a Trust Territory, they were treated as one for purposes of official reporting and discussion at the League of Nations and at the United Nations. Second, it was assumed that because the two states were contiguous and had been ruled by the same colonial power, there was a historical basis for unification. Third, it was thought that because each state was composed of Hutu and Tutsi, and had seemingly similar political institutions, they ought to be unified. Fourth, there was some feeling during the 1950s and early 1960s at the United Nations, and among some students of African affairs, that unification was desirable for political and economic reasons; and that it was the proper goal to be pursued in all decolonization. This was assumed to be particularly valid for economically weak pluralist societies such as that of Ruanda-Urundi.

Although both states had traditionally been stratified mwamidoms, this was no longer true after the low-status ethnic group (Hutu) in Rwanda overthrew their Tutsi masters in 1959 and declared Rwanda a republic. The new situation was one in which the Tutsi found themselves drastically reduced in status and without political power. In Burundi the Hutu have been subjected to increased suppression by the Tutsi. Burundi remained the embodiment of a Tutsi aristocratic tradition that Rwanda's Hutu leaders had just destroyed. The Rwandan Hutu felt insecure in their success, and the continued existence of a "mwamiship" in Burundi was perceived as an indirect political, but a direct psychological, threat.[6] Rwanda's leaders feared that a continuing "mwamiship" to the south exercised a living attraction for Rwandans who might desire that the "mwamiship" be reestablished in Rwanda.[7] This, plus the presence of an estimated 119,000 Rwandan Tutsi refugees (by 1970 this figure reached 142,000), ensconced along the state's borders and poised to attack,[8] led the Rwandan leaders to maintain Belgian troops on their soil after independence as a security measure.

On the other hand, Burundi's mwami, more a paramount chief than a king in the traditional political system, felt threatened by the example Rwanda had given for his own Hutu subjects. The reigning monarch, Mwambutsa IV, had come to the throne in 1915 amid much courtly intrigue and was well aware of his kingdom's stormy history. Events in Rwanda alarmed him because there was now the added possibility of a violent fratricidal war between and among Burundi's three major groups: the royal princes, Tutsi, and Hutu. Further, this war would more likely than not be aimed at the mwami's destooling and the institutional demise of the "mwamiship," following in close repetition the social and political upheavals of Rwanda between 1959 and 1961. Burundi's internal political climate was also convulsed by the changing attitudes of Hutu and Tutsi political leaders. Both groups looked upon Rwanda's revolution with mixed emotions and mutual fear. Neither group openly wished to put Burundi through the experience of the internecine strife that had claimed thousands of lives and had caused severe socioeconomic dislocation. Important, too, was the presence of the leading nationalist politician, Prince Rwagasore, who was committed to a policy of national unity. However, Hutu and Tutsi leaders could no longer be certain of their future in an independent Burundi; their perceptual reality was strongly colored by the realization that, if it had happened in Rwanda, it could happen in Burundi.

For Belgium or the United Nations to have imposed political unification in the early 1960s would have involved forcing the existing political structures into a mold the Africans themselves opposed very strenuously. Given the political history of both states since independence in 1962, it is very doubtful that political unification ought to have been pursued as a valid goal. Militating against it were the Rwandan social and political revolution, which pitted Hutu against Tutsi after 1959; the tensions among Hutu and Tutsi and between various regional groups in Burundi; and a history of war that had kept these two societies separate for centuries. There were a few feeble attempts at unification by some local leaders, but these never amounted to much, and the traditional structures were ill suited for such a move. A major student of nationalism has hypothesized that differential treatment of certain areas, the use of indirect rule, and the very late incorporation of some peoples within the metropolitan system are significant factors of a colonial policy that emphasized ethnic cleavages and local loyalties.[9] Encouraged by the geographical limitations maintained under Belgian colonial policy, Rwandan and Burundian leaders and intellectuals highlighted their differences and developed their own particularisms to the point of two separate nationalisms.[10]

Given this climate of mutual fear, mistrust, and deep uncertainty, it should come as no surprise that Rwanda and Burundi were loathe to unite politically. Union in 1962 would have institutionalized the basic tensions that separated the mutually antagonistic political ethos that underpinned political institutions existing in either state. An imposed union in 1962 would have catapulted the Trust Territory into severe political strife and a bloody civil war if it did not naturally break up by mutual consent as soon as independence was achieved and all UN restraints effectively removed.

One or Two Nations?

It is generally accepted by informed outsiders, and by the local leaders themselves, that the high point of Rwanda-Burundi unity was achieved under alien rule. For this reason, we will look first at the Belgian colonial administration's attitude and policy toward political unification.

The shortcomings in Belgian policy and actions that were largely responsible for the political fragmentation of the Congo at independence were also present in the political disintegration of Ruanda-Urundi. Most serious was the way in which the Belgians compartmentalized the Africans they ruled for administrative purposes, thus indirectly contributing to an increased display of ethnic chauvinism among these peoples.[11] The 1954 UN Visiting Mission fully realized this when it suggested that Belgian authorities in Ruanda-Urundi balance the two territories' separate development with comparable attention given to the development of a central legislative body.[12] Summarizing failings in Belgian colonial policy, Robert I. Rotberg isolates two other relevant factors. First, the Belgian colonial administration allowed free political organization in its African territories only very late. Because of this, the channels that existed to handle the "rapid flow of articulated grievances" were the more traditional and mutually exclusive communal ones. In Ruanda-Urundi this meant the separate parallel native authorities that existed in Rwanda and in Burundi: the local mwami, the local High Council, the chiefs and the subchiefs with their respective councils, the local traditional courts controlled by these same traditional chiefs and notables. Rotberg's second factor was the open intervention in certain cases by missionaries and/or administrators which aroused or created fervent ethnic awareness. Rwanda is a ready example of the latter: several administrators stationed in Rwanda openly admitted to me that they intervened in favor of the lowly Hutu and that influential missionaries and members of the local Catholic church consciously stirred up a sense of political awareness among Hutu leaders.[13] It is now widely accepted that important figures in the local hierarchy of the Catholic church and several Belgian administrators were influential in prodding the Hutu of Rwanda to take consciousness of themselves as a group and to demand a radical restructuring of Rwandan society.[14]

Confidential official Belgian reports in the immediate after war period of the late 1940s mention unrest among *évolués* Africans. There are several serious instances of African disrespect toward European administrators. Much unrest was concentrated in Bujumbura where Burundians and Rwandans did mix, and among that new *évolué* elite that might have thought in wider Ruanda-Urundi terms.[15] In March 1955 four distinguished traditional leaders, drawn from both states, requested that the Belgian administration accept the legal formation of a political association they had formed—the Progressive Democratic Movement. Appended to their letter were the proposed statutes and a list of the forty founding members. The names read like a roster of a Rwandan and a Burundian *Who's Who*; many were destined to become leaders of their respective states.[16] In keeping with the enshrined colonial policy of no political development until economic and social development was achieved, the administration rejected this political initiative. The Belgian authorities argued that political movements might "unduly precipitate political ambitions which were out of line with [Africa's] overall social and economic development." [17] The political association that was proposed had hoped to address itself to the problems of a Ruanda-Urundi as yet undisturbed by the ethnic-status divisions between Hutu and Tutsi, which emerged in 1959.[18] It was no longer possible for such a territory-wide movement to succeed after that time.

Belgian policy, heavily weighted in favor of an initial, very limited, development at the local level, prevented a territory-wide council, the General Council, which had been expanded in membership in 1957, from becoming the seed of a federal legislature. The United Nations in 1954 had requested that this council be given increased legislative powers, that its membership be increased, and that it become the upper House of a central Ruanda-Urundi parliament. It was suggested that individual Rwanda and Burundi High Councils of State be merged into a lower House.[19] The General Council was little more than an honorific debating forum, limited to advising the colonial administration; the administration was not bound to act on its advice. The indigenous leaders were urged by the administration to regard the local High Councils as the more vital arenas in which to discuss issues relating to conditions in their territories and future policy. The Belgian administration argued that there was no effective local demand for a territorial council—this was true but it was also largely as a result of the lack of information in the Trust Territory concerning parliamentary government or the goals of representative government. The more comprehensive council also suffered because the more militant nationalists dismissed its usefulness since it had only four nonappointed members whereas the residency High Councils were totally African in their makeup and controlled by the nationalists and their sympathizers. (In 1957, the General Council's total membership was increased from 22 to 43. The number of Africans was increased to 16.[20])

After 1959, all the councils—the territorial and the residency ones—ran afoul of the local administration as they pressed for a greater say in the political reforms being planned at Brussels for the Trust Territory. By 1960 the councils had ceased to exist by the express orders and actions of the Belgian administration and were replaced by more docile bodies. There was no new comprehensive Ruanda-Urundi council, however; only councils up to the residency level.

During 1959 and 1960 the Belgian administration implemented new political reforms and held local elections in each residency. Some have questioned the validity of these elections; there have been charges that they were conducted fraudulently. Separate conferences grouping the various political parties that emerged in Rwanda and in Burundi were held in the two respective territories and at Brussels. At no time were political groups from the two states brought together. This was done later, in January 1961, at the insistence of the United Nations. By the end of 1960 the Belgians had succeeded in establishing two distinct, autonomous political regimes and the embryo of two separate nation-states replete with their own bureaucratic and administrative apparatus. At this point, Zaire (then the Congo) became independent and was plunged into political turmoil. Events in Zaire focused the attention of the UN General Assembly on Belgium's remaining possession—Ruanda-Urundi.

The United Nations intervened increasingly in Ruanda-Urundi affairs after 1960, without accepting responsibility for any policy it attempted to dictate.[21] Paradoxically, in 1961 and 1962, actions by the United Nations thwarted efforts by the Belgian administration to grant full autonomy to Rwanda and to Burundi because various member-states refused to accept the legitimacy of the governments to which the Belgians wished to transfer power.

Under terms of the trusteeship, periodic missions had been dispatched by the United Nations to visit the individual territories and then to present an official report of their findings to the international organization. From 1957 onward, UN representatives who visited Ruanda-Urundi became increasingly concerned with the lack of unity between the two parts of the Trust Territory. Concern over the importance of unification was expressed in each official UN triennial Visiting Mission report from 1951 onward. In 1957 the UN missions that toured the territory noted a growing sociopolitical breakdown in Rwanda with increasing tension between the Hutu and the Tutsi segments of the local population.[22] The Rwandan Hutu had produced a political manifesto during the preceding year. They had called for radical reforms to free them from their inferior status. The Tutsi replied with a document of their own in which they denied the very existence of a Hutu-Tutsi problem. The Belgian administration officially recognized that the problem in fact existed in official pronouncements made during 1958. What is most significant for our purposes here is that neither local Rwandan group, in pressing its demands, couched them in terms of "Ruanda-Urundi" or made any mention of Burundi. The 1957 UN mission was confronted with an undeniable emergence of strong local Rwandan particularisms. The leaders in Burundi were equally narrow in their perspectives. During 1961, at Ostend, they walked out when discussion was opened on national reconciliation in Rwanda.

The political reforms and elections staged by the Belgians during 1960 had removed the Rwandan and the Burundian nationalist parties that enjoyed strong support among the more radical Afro-Asian states: UPRONA in Burundi; Union Nationale du Ruanda (UNAR) in Rwanda. Just as these parties were on the verge of reconciling themselves with the local Belgian official authorities, the United Nations called for a general political meeting on Ruanda-Urundi to be held at Ostend. Scheduled to run for twelve days, the conference folded after four days of bitter rhetoric and mutual recriminations. Matters were left hanging. Plans for legislative elections during January 1961 were postponed to satisfy demands made by the UN General Assembly. The Belgian acceptance of this postponement and the provision for UN supervision of elections, whenever they were to be held, profoundly disappointed local political groups that had come to power in Burundi and in Rwanda during 1960. The UN observers who attended the Ostend conference left to tour the Trust Territory itself. They were received rather coolly by the local administration. Before they could begin their investigations, they were presented with two faits accomplis: a republican Hutu coup d'etat in Rwanda and indirect legislative elections in Burundi. Legislative elections were finally held in the latter part of 1961 under close UN supervision. Separate elections were organized for each state of the Trust Territory. The results in Burundi reversed the internal power configuration in favor of the anti-Belgian nationalists; in Rwanda, the results confirmed the Hutu victory of 1960 and the coup d'etat of January 1961.[23]

The more intransigent Afro-Asian states, such as Ghana, Guinea, and India, with support from the Soviet bloc, refused to accept the election results in Rwanda or the possibility of politically partitioning the Trust Territory. The General Assembly plodded along in futile pursuit of national reconciliation and simple political union, flaunting mounting opposition from the local, duly elected governments of Rwanda and Burundi. A last-ditch attempt was staged at Addis Ababa during March and April 1962. UN representatives met with those of Rwanda and of Burundi to attempt reconciliation. The United Nations was unable to bring the Rwandan and Burundian representatives to accept anything more than a rather limited economic and customs union and the maintenance of several technical common services.[24] The General Assembly's original demand for immediate withdrawal was softened. All troops were to be gone by August 1962, a month after independence, unless the government of either state requested they remain. Burundi asked the Belgian troops to leave, but Rwanda announced that it would request Belgium to maintain its paratroopers.[25]

Historic discontinuities between Rwanda and Burundi were not overcome by over sixty years of colonial rule; they had been reinforced by

Belgian policy and by indirect rule which allowed latent particularisms to grow into two separate politically oriented nationalisms. "Divide and Rule" was an important ingredient in Belgian policy. The international boundaries established between the two states represented a hesitant and begruding acquiescence in this fact by the UN General Assembly. This final solution, partition, economically unsound as it was, represented a recognition that on the political level the United Nations was unable to impose artificial boundaries in "descrambling" Africa. The final form taken by independent Burundi did not include all the territory the traditional leaders claimed—parts of "historical" Burundi had been incorporated into Tanzania when German East Africa was divided between the Belgians and the English. Rwanda had lost some territory originally claimed as part of the traditional kingdom as well.[26]

The partition of Ruanda-Urundi was received with strong reservations and dire warnings of economic and political problems ahead. The somber prospects were graphically summed up by the *Economist*: "Sure of civil war, almost certain of bankruptcy, and against the will of the United Nations, Ruanda and Urundi will triumphantly proclaim themselves separate independent states on July 1st [1962]."[27] The UN member-states whose representatives had participated in the not very effective Addis Ababa Conference (1962) felt their prestige was to some degree tied to a more successful solution. When federation was totally rejected, the United Nations was forced to accept a limited economic agreement as the only major common bond succeeding the termination of the trusteeship. As will be shown, even this minimal statement of intent to cooperate was considered unacceptable by both parties concerned. Within two years, the loose economic ties were undone and partition was complete.[28]

BALKANIZATION

Rwanda-Urundi was at best a nation with only an ambiguous "administrative" reality. Division in 1962 presented tactical opportunities to all concerned. Most important, it allowed Rwanda and Burundi to pursue mutually antagonistic social and political ethos independent of each other and, later, when events permitted, to afford them the option of seeking a modus vivendi on their own terms. Once conditions had changed and the leaders of both states felt it was in their common interest to do so, they mapped out possible avenues of technical and economic cooperation.

The serious ethnic antagonisms internal to each state, and which keep the two apart, have led the different ethnic-status groups in question—Hutu in Rwanda and Tutsi in Burundi—to seek to maximize symbolic and substantive rewards for their group in each state and to deny these to the ethnically defined adversary.[29] The mutual hostility felt for each other by the ethnically exclusive political elites of Rwanda and of Burundi precluded the adequate functioning of any effective brokerage political institutions that attempted to unite them, federal or otherwise. Readily available examples of intergroup, interethnic struggles in other countries—Nigeria, Cyprus, Iraq, Malaysia, Zanzibar, Guyana, Zaire, Sudan—suggest what might have occurred had Rwanda and Burundi been forced into political union in 1962 in accordance with the wishes of the United Nations. In the case of Nigeria political federalism as a framework failed to perform the "very reconciliation role expected of such a symmetrical system."[30] If Nigeria, with historically and administratively greater possibility for a political modus vivendi (reflected by the fact that the federation was able to survive for four years with expectations for its continued survival until 1966), was unable to sustain a loose federal system without major violence and a very high cost in lives and property, it is all the more difficult to accept the General Assembly contention that such a system could have been imposed on the two highly antagonistic states of Rwanda and Burundi. Perhaps even more indicative for Rwanda-Burundi is the tragic experience of the constitutional pluralism imposed on Cyprus. (The Cameroons provide an interesting test case. The territory was divided between the British and the French. As the issue of independence and unification of both emerged, the Afro-Asians were very divided because there was little if any ethnic or linguistic basis for unity. Nigeria was against having part of the Cameroons, administratively attached to it by the British, leave its territory.[31]) In fact, the Afro-Asians, driven by their deep fear of weakening Africa's world position by splitting up its political units into small powerless ones, stated that nothing less than a simple political union between Rwanda and Burundi would have met with their demands.

It is worthwhile, nonetheless, to pose the hypothetical question of whether or not federation was an available strategy. Had there been greater receptivity or the obverse, less obstruction, by outsiders, whether Ruanda-Urundi could have achieved a viable political federation is still questionable. Simple union and political federation alike were unworkable in this case.[32] This was true for many reasons: the activities and the influence of pressure groups and political movements in Ruanda-Urundi, insofar as they existed, concentrated more on regional or "state" governments (the residencies) than on the federal decision-making center (i.e., Bujumbura). There were some exceptions to this: the UNARU (Union Nationale du Ruanda-Urundi, 1959–61) and its supporters and various "stranger" communities stood to economically lose from partition. But these groups never achieved anything more than very marginal importance in the political development of Rwanda or of Burundi.

The competing indigenous elites of each state reinforced their regional ties at the expense of any wider identity. When there was question of establishing a definite legal nationality, Rwandans and Burundians pushed for the creation of two distinct nationalities to replace the somewhat nebulous legalism which defined them all as *ressortissants* of Ruanda-Urundi. The respective elites of each state harbored a certain resentment against the other on economic and social issues. Rwandans were very unhappy with Bujumbura's dominant position as the hub of the territory's economic activity. This was exacerbated when Belgium moved toward fully integrating the port city into Burundi at Rwanda's expense.[33] The Rwandans were also upset with a Belgian decision to create a university at Bujumbura and the construction of a lavish secondary school, Le Collège de Saint Esprit, in Burundi and not in Rwanda. Burundi's elite felt no less slighted. They chaffed at what they perceived to be an overt prejudice in favor of Rwandan development on the part of the Belgian authorities. Burundi's mwami voiced strongly his concern at a conference convened to study the standardization of Ruanda-Urundi's two principal vernaculars:

> We take this opportunity to energetically protest against certain tendencies for standardization of Kirundi and Kinyarwanda and *to the detriment of our language.* We have more than one bit of evidence to affirm that, with respect to Ruanda, Burundi has always been treated as a poor relative. For how long will such a situation continue? [34]

Whether or not the grievances of each elite against the other were well founded begs the issue. What is significant is that they existed. They reflected the fact that a national entity had existed in each of the two states before alien rule was imposed upon them. Horner suggests that Burundians had a very strong national consciousness and drew a clear distinction between Burundi and the outside world at the symbolic level. Neither of the two competing sets of elites—those of Burundi or those of Rwanda—had been made to share any meaningful experience which might have engendered confidence and loyalty to Ruanda-Urundi. There had not been any territory-wide experience of responsible self-government as occurred in the neighboring territories of British East Africa. In large part the colonial powers that held sway over Rwanda and Burundi emphasized economic development and administration; they tended to neglect political development. Belgian administrators felt no need to stem local particularisms. Indeed, their policies indicate they assured them. This only changed when local forces became politicized and threatened economic development and an established administrative routine. This change did not occur until the late 1950s and did not last a full decade.

To return to the question of federalism. R. L. Watts, in his equilibrium model, has defined a federal society as an inclusive social system "in which social forces making for diversity among differentiated communities are in approximate balance with forces making for unity." [35] Ruanda-Urundi as a unit lacked these on several levels. First, on the cultural plane, given the rather advanced state of the open Hutu-Tutsi conflict in Rwanda since 1959 which led to a recasting of the foundations of Rwandan society in a way diametrically opposed to the sociopolitical system maintained in Burundi. And economically, as Heimo, Baker and Moes have indicated, the two states were competitors. Politically, expecially after the January 1961 Hutu coup d'etat in Rwanda, the ethos that underpinned the institutions of authority and rules in either state were highly antagonistic. Historically, the two states were the heirs of a tradition of enmity, mutual disdain, and wars. Rwandan battle rituals mention the Burundians thirty times.[36] As late as 1895, only a few years before German rule over the area was effectively asserted, the mwami of Rwanda had attempted to invade Burundi but was repulsed. Linguistically, while the languages spoken in each state are very closely related, their elites took pains to emphasize and even to overstate the case for their distinctness and refused to allow any standardization of the two.

If political parties, interest groups, or elite attitudes may be considered barometers of federalism's chances for success or failure, the readings of Ruanda-Urundi from 1957 until 1966 continued to fall. This delineation takes 1966 as the mark off point of improved possibilities because it was in that year, shortly after the republicanist coup in Burundi, that the new Burundian minister of economic and financial affairs secretly visited Rwanda. In 1967, the Burundian foreign minister secretly visited Rwanda to discuss normalizing relations between the two states. He also discussed opportunities for economic cooperation and acknowledged the new regime's appreciation of Rwanda's congratulatory telegram sent upon hearing of its success in overthrowing the Burundian monarchy. Cleavages based on ethnicity, geography, and ideology, however, still kept Rwanda and Burundi apart.

As both states approached the termination of the trusteeship in 1962, the patterns of political relationships within each of these two polyethnic states were such as to be only further complicated by any political union between them. Rwanda's political system was dominated by Hutu; that of Burundi by aristocrats more widely associated with Tutsi than with Hutu. In both states there was a varying measure of tension between the two ethnic groups which continued to increase in intensity after 1961. Within Rwanda and within Burundi different groups of the same ethnic alliance were themselves divided over issues of regionalism and in terms of economic and political developmental ideologies. Ideological differences were complicated by the cold war. Burundi leaned very strongly toward the East in its foreign policy and tended to be anti-American; Rwanda was moderate in its foreign policy and pro-West. As we have argued, there was only very limited ground upon which to build a "federal bargain," and even this was handily rejected by the more politically effective and influential segments of each state's political relevant strata. Any administrative or informal structures that had grown up during colonial rule which might have formed a basis for some sort of union had been eroded away by the time the United Nations (May 1961) decided to attempt to impose its political will and have Ruanda-Urundi become a unitary political entity.

The ambivalence of various African statesmen toward political federalism is evident in the problems that have continued to plague the attempt at an East African Federation.[37] Gabriel d'Arboussier, a noted Senegalese diplomat, wrote from a perspective sobered by experience about the aborted Mali Federation that grouped his country with the ex-French Sudan:

> [T]he formula of the future is the "federation of states" and not the "federal state." [D'Arboussier stressed] the necessity of taking into account the "territorial conscience" which opposed the unitary current.[38]

This "unitary current" had gripped Africa in the euphoria of 1960–1961 when a large number of African colonies achieved independence. Senghor, Senegal's poet-president and statesman, joined others in analyzing why the Mali Federation had failed. He laid the bulk of the blame on a failure to "analyze and to understand the sociological differences between the [two] territories." Senghor counseled that the idea of political regrouping and African unity was not to be abandoned, it was to be mulled over "to be more modest, more circumspect, more realist." [39] The ephemeral Mali Federation had led Senegalese and others to recognize that they had underestimated the forces of narrower "micro" nationalisms.

These same narrow nationalisms had grown and taken on a strong political overtone in Ruanda-Urundi where German and Belgian colonial policy had emphasized the separate development of each state but had largely ignored the political content of that development. The ethnic conflict between Hutu and Tutsi, reversed in terms of the power stratification that developed in each state, precluded a comprehensive pluralist political system for Ruanda-Urundi. Any historical differences that divided the two states had been further complicated and intensified by the effects of modernization. Latent sociopolitical cleavages between Hutu and Tutsi had been made manifest in Rwanda by 1959 and in Burundi by 1964–65.

Aristocrats and Republicans: Political Breakdown

The period from 1962 until 1966 was punctuated by mutual recriminations and propaganda battles over the government radios and in the official press of each. As tensions rose in Burundi between "modernists" (generally ideologically oriented in the direction of a constitutional monarchy or a presidential republic) and "traditionalists" (those supporting the monarchy as it was, if not reinforcing it), it became more difficult for Burundi not to view the Rwandan republic primarily in an adversary role.[40] Rwanda's position as an "adversary" was rendered more intense and more threatening as ethnic tensions between Hutu and Tutsi leaders mounted in Burundi, precipitated by internal events. Likewise, as tensions increased between Hutu republican leaders and officials in Rwanda and their Tutsi opposition both within the state boundaries and in bordering states (Inyenzi guerrillas were to be found in all the bordering states for some time) Tutsi-ruled Burundi became a ready target for Rwandan enmity. Rwanda accused Burundi of supporting and harboring hostile Tutsi forces. Both Burundi and Rwanda had some good reasons to see each other as political adversaries, although they may often have indulged in exaggerating each other's intentional complicity.

A standing refugee problem remains a potential source of instability in their interstate relations.[41] There are at the moment between 150,000 and 180,000 political refugees from these two states. The bulk, 130,000 to 150,000 are Rwandan Tutsi who fled in three successive waves: (1) in 1959–60, when Hutu began to attack the Tutsi; (2) at the end of 1961 and into 1962, when Rwanda was declared a republic by its new Hutu leaders; and (3) in early 1964, after Rwanda Tutsi refugees attacked Rwanda unsuccessfully and Hutu lashed out against Tutsi still living in the country. Burundian refugees first fled to Rwanda in early 1962, after a power struggle between Hutu and Tutsi within the ranks of the then just-victorious political party, UPRONA. A second wave fled to Rwanda in 1965, a third in the spring of 1972, and a fourth in the spring of 1973. The Burundian refugees are Hutus for the large part; they have fled from Tutsi repression following unrest between Hutu and Tutsi in Burundi itself.

The refugee problem has created bad interstate relations between the two states because Tutsi refugee bands combined to plan and execute attacks against Rwanda. Hutu refugees attacked Burundi from Rwanda in March and May 1973. This problem was also caught up with the cold war in the area. The Chinese (Peking) have been very active among refugee circles. It was rumored in 1964 that the Chinese were arming and training Tutsi guerrillas. The Chinese Embassy at Bujumbura was closed when Burundi's mwami accused their diplomats of interfering in local Burundian politics. Despite this, Chinese funds were still made available to militant Tutsi refugee leaders. Rwanda and Zaire were then considered to have pro-West governments.

Relations between Burundi and Zaire reached their nadir in 1964, when Zaire's government accused Burundi of allowing Chinese-supported Zaire rebels to use Bujumbura as a base. Various Burundian Tutsi ministers of the time were said to be assisting the Chinese and their agents to supply weapons to left-wing rebels who were then rather active in eastern Zaire.

The refugee question cooled down somewhat after Burundi closed down the Chinese Embassy. In 1970, however, the refugees again became prominent when several of their leaders were arrested in Bujumbura. These men were accused of plotting together with dissident Burundian Tutsi. After a protracted trial of all the plotters, the Rwandan refugees were acquitted. Then, on April 29, 1972, a revolt broke out in Burundi, and early reports claimed that Tutsi refugees were fighting against loyalist forces. Some fighting was reported in the area where the Tutsi refugee camps are located, in eastern Burundi. The 1972 revolt, however it began, soon developed into a Hutu-Tutsi melee. Once the rebels were overcome, all Tutsi in Burundi, the refugees included, banded together to carry out a systematic repression of educated and influential Hutu throughout Burundi. In order to prevent an exodus of Hutu into Rwanda, Tutsi refugees were deployed with Burundian military and paramilitary forces along the Rwandan-Burundi border.

Zaire refugees also participated in the 1972 uprising, and many fled back to Zaire. While this experience may have strengthened relations between Burundi and Zaire, it has certainly strained relations between Rwanda and Burundi. In 1970 Burundi's ambassador (diplomatic relations were established in 1969) at Kigali, capital of Rwanda, attempted to register Burundian refugees in Rwanda in order to repatriate them. Rwandan authorities are said to have taken umbrage at this action and read Rwanda's riot act to the Burundi ambassador. Rwanda's Hutu leaders can be expected to be more suspicious than ever of Burundi. There were some rumors that in the months prior to Burundi's troubles, Rwanda's government feared a Tutsi uprising. According to one magazine, many educated Tutsi were arrested. Whether these reports are true or not, they reveal the sensitivity with which Hutu-Tutsi relations are treated in both Rwanda and Burundi. Cooperation between both states, one Tutsi and the other Hutu, can only be superficial and within the context of economic peaceful coexistence.

As a result of the aforementioned conditions, compromise between the two states until 1966 became all but impossible. Rwanda and Burundi were transformed into ideological rivals on several levels: on a more basic level of ethnic relations between the two status groups (Hutu and Tutsi) present in each state, and on a more sophisticated level of their political ethos—republican and modernists vs. monarchists and traditionalists and in terms of foreign policy alignments.[42] Divisions were not total with respect to politically relevant strata within either state, and the existence of the two offered a ready safety valve for each other's "dissatisfied." This served to siphon off some of the opposition—above all, if one thinks of the 32,000 Tutsi Rwandan refugees now in Burundi who have elected not to return to Rwanda; and of the 10,000 Hutu Burundian refugees in Rwanda (the number increased in 1972). Prominent Hutu who were involved at various times in attempts to overthrow Burundi's regime have sought and received refuge in Rwanda.

Despite mutual accusations of unfriendly acts, even criminal acts, against each other, Rwanda and Burundi were never drawn into a protracted, bloody war. Relations between Rwanda and Burundi were most strained during 1964 when each accused the other of direct armed incursions or of abetting such criminal actions. It was also at this time that relations between Burundi and Zaire plummeted, and the Western press proclaimed that Burundi was under the influence of Communist China.

In 1964 Rwanda claimed that it was twice attacked, and remained under imminent attack by Inyenzi Tutsi refugees. The attacks were allegedly followed by pogroms against those Tutsi remaining within Rwanda who were accused of sympathizing with the guerrilla invaders. Figures for the number of Tutsi killed in Rwanda range from 780 (in an official UN Report) to 25,000, depending upon one's preference for sources.[43] Burundi officially accused Rwanda of practicing genocide. On February 2, 1964, the border area between Rwanda and Burundi was proclaimed a military zone by Burundi and placed under the control of its national army. The following day Burundi's prime minister publicly accused Rwandan troops of pursuing refugees onto Burundian territory on four occasions. At the United Nations, at the Organization of African Unity (OAU), and at sessions of a special mediation committee headed by Jomo Kenyatta (Kenyan head of state) instituted by the OAU, Rwandan and Burundian spokesmen indulged in acrimonious counter accusations. Rwanda and Burundi came their closest to openly declaring war against each other.

From 1964 until late 1966, Rwandans accused the Burundian monarchy of harboring Rwanda's enemies; they protested that Burundian authorities allowed Tutsi refugees to arm themselves and to receive training in guerrilla tactics on Burundian territory. The avowed aim of these guerrillas was to prepare for future invasions of Rwanda until that country's Hutu republic was toppled and Tutsi hegemony restored. Rwanda's accusations reflected a deep feeling of insecurity on the part of its leaders. Several commentators with an intimate knowledge of Rwanda were willing to tell any who would listen that, were the Tutsi to return, they still had a good chance of winning power. These same individuals continued to point out that during the 1959 "Hutu" uprising, many who fought on the Tutsi side were *Hutu*.[44] For Burundi's mwami and his court, on the other hand, the continued success of the Rwandan political experiment (i.e., the "republic") meant increased pressure upon them to yield their power and to move toward majority rule. By 1964, and for some time thereafter, Burundi's economy was in a slump, ethnic tensions among the political elite were becoming more pronounced, and the mwami was busily shoring up his power while critically reducing that of the elected parliament and cabinet ministers.[45] Several of the more politically sophisticated Hutu were granted asylum in Rwanda when they were accused of plotting against the monarchy. Their ranks were swelled in 1965 by 3,000 refugees fleeing an abortive coup d'etat by Hutu intellectuals, civil servants, and military officers.

After independence in July 1962, Rwanda and Burundi chose not to institute formal diplomatic relations between their respective governments. The most often cited pretext was that Burundi refused to be held responsible for the personal safety of any Rwandan diplomat inside Burundi. The foreign policy pursued by the two governments drove a further wedge between them. Burundi courted the more militant, self-styled "progressive, radical" African states and was rumored to be under strong communist influence—Bujumbura had a well-staffed Communist Chinese embassy that was involved in subverting the legal governments of Burundi's neighbors. Rwanda joined the moderate grouping of French-speaking African states (OCAM). This move shortly after independence was in reaction to Burundi which veered East in search of outside help.[46] The two states often took an opposite stand on substantive political issues discussed at the United Nations and at the Organization of African Unity. One important example is the emotion-laden question of South Africa. Burundi has consistently followed a rather hard line eschewing any compromise; Rwanda's president has called for realism about any proposed economic sanctions against South Africa, and Rwanda abstained when the OAU Ministerial Council voted to condemn France, Britain, and West Germany for actual or intended sales of arms to South Africa.[47]

In November 1966, a military coup d'etat overthrew Burundi's monarchy and instituted a presidential republic. Once the monarchy was overthrown it became politically feasible for Burundi's authorities to reconsider relations with Rwanda and to probe the possibility of establishing diplomatic relations. To demonstrate "goodwill" the new government quickly proceeded to execute a cleanup operation during which the army removed Tutsi refugees from border regions to the north and made Bujumbura more secure, to allow a Rwandan embassy, among other things, to be opened. Burundi's president, Colonel Michel Micombero, met with his Rwandan counterpart, Grégoire Kayibanda, in August 1969 in Uganda, where they both were attending official ceremonies marking the visit of Pope Paul VI. They agreed to exchange ambassadors; Rwanda's ambassador arrived at Bujumbura with his staff on August 16; three days later, Burundi appointed its first ambassador to Rwanda.

Once Rwanda, Burundi, and Zaire had presidential republican regimes and a dominant single-party political system, the possibility existed for some "compatibility of the main values" held by the leadership in each state. This was achieved in 1966. However, significant factors necessary for political union between Rwanda and Burundi are generally lacking or minimal at best: "an increase in the political and administrative capabilities of the main political units to be amalgamated"; "mobility of persons"; "multiplicity and balance of transactions"; "mutual predictability of behavior." [48] In addition Rwanda and Burundi score low for those factors Deutsch has listed as significant for a looser political community, while they rate rather high for disintegrative factors. Recent documented studies of Burundi's political system poignantly evidence that its government faces increased burdens but that its capabilities for coping with these burdens has been drastically reduced. Heimo is joined by Baker in his conclusions drawn from Rwanda's economic problems that Rwanda, too, faces increased burdens with which its government may be unable to cope satisfactorily. If it is correct to assume that increased loads on the government of a state tends to induce community disintegration, then the elections originally planned for 1971 in Burundi and the drive by that state's single party to mobilize the masses politically will mean expanded political participation resulting in increased demands being placed on the political system. Were this to occur, it is more probable than not that Burundi, given its presently low profile of political development and institutionalization, would be an increasingly unstable partner in any union with Rwanda (or any other state or groups of states).[49] Recent political history underscores their instability.

In July 1971 Burundi's political situation became tense following a shakeup in President Micombero's government. The affair involved a clash between two opposing Tutsi camps divided by clan, region, and, possibly, political outlook. This latest shift in Burundi has brought to power a group with a reputation for being less moderate in their policy for internal affairs and somewhat left-wing in their foreign policy. The rift between the two groups seriously taxed what unity may have existed among Burundi's ruling elite. A political trial of those who fell from power dragged on for some time and was the basis for major criticisms of President Micombero and his regime. In the fall of 1971, Micombero responded to the increased tension by once again asserting military dominance in Burundian politics. He instituted a Supreme Council of only military officers and a smaller military committee to serve as the general watchdog over Burundi's politics and overall development. As well, for some time the Micombero regime has said it is making efforts to revitalize and revolutionize Burundi's single party and its parallel movements. Unfortunately, as the preceding indicates, these efforts have not been anywhere near as successful as anticipated. No mention was made until late 1973 of elections or a constitution, originally promised for 1971.

In Spring 1972 Burundi was convulsed by a rebellion that at the time of writing has cost between 50,000 and 150,000 lives. This revolt began as a struggle for power between two regionally distinct groups of Tutsi, but it soon became a confrontation between Hutu and Tutsi in southern Burundi. Zaire came to the assistance of Burundi's military officer-president, and the revolt was crushed. In its wake, Tutsi who felt they had come too close to a Hutu victory undertook an indiscriminate execution of all potential Hutu leaders, including primary and secondary school students and Catholic catechists. Several Belgian newspapers now warn that Burundi may soon have a Hutu uprising that will be worse than anything they have had earlier. By Fall 1972, the army, government, university, technical schools, and business community have been purged of Hutu among their ranks. Rwanda reacted and sent a strong letter in which President Karyibanda asked his Burundian counterpart to put a halt to the killing of the "little people" (Hutu).

Rwanda has also experienced internal problems. During the last elections in 1969, several prominent Hutu leaders were expelled from the ruling Parmehutu party. (Those remaining are also Hutu.) They were all old-guard revolutionaries who had since fallen out of favor and were accused of fostering regionalism in the country. In 1969 and 1971 there were unverified reports of uneasiness among the Rwandan military. In October 1971 unease was caused by the arrest of a commandant and a lieutenant in the army. The two were accused of high treason. More recently, Rwanda has had serious student unrest. In Rwanda, as in many developing nations, there are not enough jobs for all those at educational institutions. Many students are distressed by the bleak outlook they will face upon graduation. There were disturbances at the official college (a secondary school) at Kigali. In March 1972 all the secretaries-general in the governmental ministries were changed, with the exception of Information and Tourism. Nine of Rwanda's ten prefects (provincial governors) were also changed, and so were some unit heads in the army. All this created a certain uneasiness. Tensions continued to mount and ethnic fighting broke out at almost all institutions of higher learning in Rwanda during February, March, and April 1973. In part this renewed ethnic hostility was due to frustration experienced by Rwandan Hutus when they learned of the slaughter of Hutus in Burundi but were unable to do anything about it. On a deeper level, the fighting, which spread to a number of communes, was a symptom of the country's economic difficulties. Although Rwanda's government pursues a development policy, the resource base is too thin and there are not enough jobs or opportunities to go around. The Hutu began to look, with increasing anger, on the continued presence of large numbers of Tutsi in administrative posts and in private business. During the fighting, there were reports that even wealthy Hutu were attacked. The disorders spread and law and order was eroded critically, forcing the army to intervene in July 1973.

Among other disintegrative factors are several that have already received attention in the body of this chapter: an increase in ethnic or linguistic differentiation; a prolonged economic decline or stagnation (a problem common to both Rwanda and Burundi); "relative closure of the established political elite" (tending to close out Hutu in Burundi and Tutsi in Rwanda); "excessive delay in social, economic, or political reform in one state while it has already been adopted in the other" (Rwanda has had its "revolution"); and the "major failure on the part of a formerly strong or privileged . . . group, or region to adjust psychologically and politically to its loss of dominance as a result of changed conditions" (true of Rwanda's Tutsi and Burundi's monarchists with future problems in the latter if political mobilization of the predominantly Hutu masses brings about effective mass participation and real power).[50]

Economic Union: 1962–64

Following independence Rwanda and Burundi were saddled with a number of common services, and a common economic and customs union. The economic mainstay of both states—coffee—was placed under a common agency: The Rwanda-Burundi Office of Native Coffee (OCIBU). As stated above, the imposed economic ties were a legacy of Belgian policy and UN aspirations for the Trust Territory.[51]

Under Belgian rule, Rwanda had become an economic appendage of Burundi (with its port, Bujumbura).[52] In 1923, of the 145 commercial establishments in Ruanda-Urundi, only 27 were located in Rwanda. As late as the 1920s, Rwanda was still relatively isolated. The map appended to Belgium's 1923 Annual Report to the League of Nations showed the nearest automobile road went east from Mbarara in Uganda; telegraph connections had only come as far as Kabale, also in Uganda; the closest rail link to the Indian Ocean was the line between Dar-es-Salaam and Kigoma—German plans to extend their East African railroad to Rwanda went unfulfilled. The closest radio link was at Bujumbura and the only "caravan" road in Rwanda was between Bujumbura and Cyangugu—all other roads were listed as "important trails." In the 1924 Annual Report, the Belgians wrote that the normal route of evacuation for Rwandan products was through Gatsibu (Uganda) to the port of Mombasa (Kenya).

The Belgians argued that merchants tended to prefer using Bujumbura to avoid the problems of porterage that the Uganda-Kenya route involved. A Belgian post had been established at Butare in hopes that this would contribute to "drain toward Bujumbura an important part of Rwandan exports." The 1924 report registered Belgian successes: 300 tons of Rwanda's 500 total export tons had been diverted to Burundi. In 1925 Rwanda and Burundi were joined in an administrative union with Zaire. Over time, this resulted in a subordination of both states' interests to those of the larger Zaire. The leaders of both states still remember that this union led the Belgians and investors to think of Rwanda and Burundi as additional provinces of Zaire. Fears that any economic union with Zaire carried dangers of renewed Zaire economic domination continue to hamper cooperation among these three states.

The economic and technical ties between Rwanda and Burundi that succeeded independence did not survive for very long. The common services established by Belgium had never been widely Africanized. This fact limited African commitment, as no technocratic elite developed with a vested interest in continuing the common services. From a purely economic point of view, projects for the economic integration of Rwanda and Burundi could be limited at best, because both states have analagous productive structures. Each state remains dominated by its subsistance sector; each relies principally on coffee as its major earner of foreign exchange; each faces a chronic overpopulation problem; each has little in the way of natural wealth with which to finance any ambitious economic development; and, finally, both are in need of substantial foreign aid.[53] René Dumont, who studied economic conditions in Ruanda-Urundi prior to independence, concluded that they ought to think "fast . . . to economically federate in a larger African grouping." [54]

After its independence, Rwanda began to turn toward Uganda to the north and Tanzania to the east. One analyst has suggested a sociopolitical motive for what others have considered to be a rather natural move from a purely economic perspective. Russel Baker submits that Rwanda's Hutu leadership feels more naturally inclined toward Uganda because of the large number of Rwandan Hutu migrants who have worked and who continue to work in this country.[55] Shortly before 1962, Rwandans formed over 20 percent of Buganda's (a district of Uganda close to Rwanda) working force.[56] Rwanda also looked to Uganda because of growing hostility between itself and Burundi, and because political unrest in neighboring Zaire had caused a break in the normal economic flow between them.[57]

Other factors foredoomed the common services and the economic and customs union. First, there exists in Rwanda a deep-seated and often verbalized resentment of Bujumbura's (the capital of independent Burundi and a port on Lake Tanganyika) advantaged economic position: Rwanda quickly alleged that Bujumbura was favored by the Central Bank of the economic union in its handling of import licensing. Second, Rwanda and Burundi, each with a long historic tradition, manifested strong nationalistic tendencies which prevented any spirit of compromise without which there could be no free-trade area between two independent states. Third, the economic union, unaccompanied by political union, sharply contradicted the up-to-date belief that a country's monetary policy "is an essential instrument in pursuing the country's economic aims." [58] Quite apart from these factors, the imposed economic union and technical ties were tainted in that they represented the remaining vestiges of Belgian colonial rule. By April 1963 the technical common services, maintained largely in compliance with UN wishes, had disappeared. These services had included telecommunications, water and electricity distribution, and aeronautical services.

Economic deterioration between Rwanda and Burundi began to set in during the early part of 1963. Rwanda complained that the economic union was working to Rwanda's detriment. It demanded that the Central Bank divide equitably its foreign currency holdings and allow each state to husband its own share.[59] In May 1963 Rwanda was granted its request in principle, and separate licensing bureaus were established to commence operations in each state at the end of 1963. However, a final decision concerning the question of foreign exchange holdings at the Central Bank was postponed. Both states attempted to reach an agreement at Bujumbura in August 1963, and again in December of the same year. These attempts aborted and Rwanda took it upon itself to declare the economic union ended. (The following day Rwanda was invaded by Tutsi refugee terrorists —Inyenzi—operating from Burundian territory.) The immediate result of Rwanda's decision was the abrogation of the Rwanda-Burundi common currency on January 1, 1964. This currency had been the successor to the Congo franc. It was established by the Belgians in 1960, and it was pegged to the Belgian franc at par value. In March 1964 the customs and free-trade arrangement was also abrogated. The common coffee board (OCIBU) was dissolved in September and each state established one of its own.

By the end of 1964, economic relations between Rwanda and Burundi had reached their nadir; each began to look into alternative arrangements. They unsuccessfully sought to enter into the already troubled East African community. Burundi tried to establish a more active trade with Zambia and Tanzania; Rwanda turned to Uganda and Tanzania.[60] Until quite recently neither state could hope for much with Zaire because of that state's internal problems. In addition, at different points in time, both Rwanda and Burundi had very hostile relations with Zaire.

Improved relations between Rwanda and Burundi during 1967 were enhanced by friendly gestures from Zaire. Diplomatic relations between Zaire and both these states were fully restored by early 1969. Tripartite conferences grouping the three successor states of "Belgian Africa" were held at Kinshasa (capital of Zaire) in August 1966 and at Goma (Zaire) in March 1967. Intervening problems had thwarted all progress, but by 1969 cooperation was again possible. In June 1969 the foreign ministers of the three met at Kinshasa. This tripartite conference was officially opened by Burundi's president, credited with taking the initiative for convening the meetings. The ministers held discussions for three days about areas of possible cooperation. They agreed to set up three commissions, one to carry on its work in each of the three states: a political and judicial committee (in Zaire); a social and cultural committee (in Rwanda); and an economic and financial committee (in Burundi). These committees were charged with preparing the groundwork. Before the meetings ended, Rwanda suggested the three states first work on projects of mutual interest and then, at some later date, graduate to a more comprehensive union.

A tripartite summit conference was organized at Gisenyi (Rwanda) in December 1969. This conference lasted only two days; an expected agreement to organize a proposed common economic organization did not materialize. This was in large part due to Rwanda's cautious attitude. An administrator of Rwanda's National Bank explained that "hasty groupings might be economically and politically unsound and little better than the already balkanized state of Black Africa." [61] Further meetings were held in January and April of 1971. No tangible results were visible even by July 1971, when Uganda's border was suddenly closed to traffic to and from Rwanda. At that time, Burundi's foreign minister commented that the "three nations working together, we believe that we shall be able to broaden markets and harmonize development programs." A meeting of the three chiefs of state was then expected to follow shortly, but it was not held until 1973. This meeting had been decided upon during the April meeting of the three state's ministers and/or vice-ministers of Foreign Affairs. It was also suggested during the meeting that the heads of state establish a permanent cooperation committee to supervise the execution of all projects.

Rwanda's outlook at the tripartite meetings was influenced by the difficulties which then blocked progress among the member states of the Union of Central African States which approximated the union suggested between Rwanda, Burundi, and Zaire. As well, Rwanda was in the midst of a crash import substitution program to replace the considerable decrease in trade with Burundi and the loss of Bujumbura since 1964 as a supplier of necessary day-to-day goods and commodities. Rwanda had become significantly dependent on Uganda for much of its needs, and it was very doubtful the previous trade with Burundi could be revitalized. Trade with Bujumbura had also suffered because of a very high theft rate which made movement of goods through the port risky at best. (One local trader is reported to have complained that the loss of all goods in transit through Bujumbura was up to 40 percent.)[62]

Cooperation between Rwanda and Burundi ran into several other problems. Fundamentally it has been a matter of establishing sufficient mutual trust between two states, three if one wishes to include Zaire, that have been rather hostile toward each other in the past. Rwanda and Burundi have had little if any experience of normal reciprocal diplomatic intercourse and were until 1967 viewed as "enemy brothers at the sources of the Nile." [63] A continued presence of Tutsi refugees is also a problem. Now (1973) the presence of Hutu refugees in Rwanda has exacerbated this. A Belgian who visited both countries during July 1970 commented:

> Two peoples, two mentalities, two Presidents, fundamentally different. Whence delicate neighbor policy which the respective leaders are striving to improve. . . .
>
> No tension presently between Rwanda and Burundi, but *instinctive reciprocal distrust*.[64]

In the fall of 1969, Burundi experienced a reemergence of internal turmoil along ethnic (Hutu-Tutsi) lines. The government announced it had foiled an attempted coup d'etat. The accused were all Hutus: officers in the army, officials in the government, and plain civilians. The government took care not to mention the word Hutu in its statement about the discovery of a plot. There were political trials and several of the accused were executed. A few Hutu intellectuals fled to Rwanda and others abroad decided not to return to Burundi. These events were strongly influenced by the détente between Rwanda and Burundi. Several high-placed and influential Hutu may have felt the new turn of events created ripe conditions in which to make a bid for power. Equally feasible as an explanation is that Burundi's predominantly Tutsi leadership feared improved relations with Rwanda might lead local Hutu leaders to seek increased power in Burundi. It may well be that the autumn coup plot was cooked up and was meant to serve as a strong symbolic warning to impress the Hutu with the futility of resisting the government. Whatever the "factual" truth, the fact that this occurred not long after the spring and summer tripartite talks of 1969 placed a weighty question mark over any talks between Rwanda and Burundi.

At this same time, several problems of an economic order emerged. Both Burundi and Rwanda wish to have national sources of electric power. Burundi is dependent totally on Zaire at the moment and Burundi has experienced power cuts when its relations with Zaire were not very good. This has led both states to seek funds and support for their own hydroelectric dam. Rwanda is now pushing to set up a hydroelectric central on the Kagera River, above the Rusumo Falls. Rwanda turned to Tanzania; Burundi is still prospecting. The policy of both states toward their road systems is indicative of the uneasiness they have with each other and of their quest for new partners. Rwanda has placed greater stress upon improving its road connections with Uganda to the north, and Burundi has sought most to improve the roads between it and Tanzania. Rwanda, with West German financing, has constructed a bridge at Rusomo Gorge opening access to Tanzania in the east and reducing Rwanda's dependence on Uganda. Rwanda, in October 1971, had fully reconditioned a truck road linking it to Tanzania. This allowed route access to Rwanda for heavy trucks. A ten-ton ferry was put into operation on the Kagera River above the Rusumo Falls until a bridge was built in 1973.

Burundi in 1970 began to speak earnestly of improving the road between Bujumbura and Kigali, and there has been an agreement to improve telephone and telecommunications links between the two states with Dutch assistance. In April 1971 Rwanda granted Burundi landing rights at Kigali for a biweekly flight. Similar accords have also been signed between Burundi and Zaire and there are now regularly scheduled flights of Burundi's national airline between Bujumbura and Goma. As of Fall 1972 the cities of Goma, Bukavu, Bujumbura, and Kigali are all linked by air.

Most recently, relations between the tripartite states have taken a possible turn for the worse. During the fall of 1971, Zaire undertook a vigorous program of expelling jobless Africans. This measure created some ill feeling at Kigali because Rwandans in eastern Zaire were directly affected. President Kayibanda sent a special emissary to Kinshasa to discuss "communal" matters. Zaire is faced with a continued and somewhat renewed guerrilla activity in the regions bordering Lake Tanganyika. It has been rumored that these rebels have contacts in Tanzania. The Zaire government may well suspect that the Chinese (Peking) may be supporting these rebels. In light of this, it is reasonable that Mobutu was very unhappy with Rwanda's vote at the United Nations to seat the People's Republic of China and with Burundi's decision to vote similarly and also "normalize" its relations with Peking. An expected tripartite meeting was postponed indefinitely at Zaire's insistence; it was not held until 1973.

While this footdragging goes on, the tripartite states have been active in a more inclusive East and Central African Regional Grouping that recently met at Mogadishu (Somalia). Burundi and Zaire have further improved air links between their territories; however, there appears to be little real movement toward making a tripartite "Benelux" a reality. Burundi and Rwanda are negotiating to have their airspace attached to that of East Africa. The tripartite states are also engaged in discussions with Tanzania to settle a dispute concerning "Belbase" installations at Kigoma and Dar-es-Salaam. These "bases" were established following a British agreement with Belgium in 1951 to safeguard Belgian Africa's right to free transit of goods through the then British-administered ports of Kigoma on Lake Tanganyika and Dar-es-Salaam on the Indian Ocean. There are some reports, but none verified, that Rwanda has shown itself more amenable to Tanzanian views—Rwanda has relatively little to lose in the matter—while Burundi has only antagonized the interested Tanzanian authorities.

The attitude of either state toward any East African grouping has not been the same. Soon after Uganda, Kenya, and Tanzania formed the East African Community, Burundi was said to have applied for membership. Rwanda has been much more circumspect. It sent a mission to establish exactly what benefits it might derive from joining the community. Were either of the two states to fully integrate itself into an East African grouping, this would place a barrier in the way of future cooperation with Zaire. This has further complicated the tripartite discussions.

Conclusion

Movement toward cooperation, economic or political, must be preceded by some consensus or perceived need for negotiation. Separation in purely economic terms remains a basic source of weakness in that Burundi and Rwanda are very weak; both depend heavily on foreign aid, and have spent their independence years in as-yet-unfulfilled hopes of entering some broader economic community. Baker, concerning himself with Rwanda's search, argued that aligning itself solidly with any East African common market would present serious problems for Rwanda's less developed economy and its need to find a solution to its increasingly pressing problem of overpopulation.[65] In terms of outside assistance, Rwanda received $9.3 million from the IDA during 1970 to help finance the construction of a road link between its capital and Uganda. Uganda has already completed that part of the road which leads from Rwanda to the market center and transhipment point at Kampala (capital of Uganda). Burundi was given funds by the International Monetary Fund during the same year to buy badly needed foreign currency to ease payment problems resulting from lower export earnings in 1969. Burundi also obtained approval by the IMF to purchase an additional amount of currency during the 1970–71 fiscal year which is to be used to support a program to create a base for its future economic development.[66] The recent troubles may have set Burundi back several years in this respect.

A minimal perceived sense of mutual interest to cooperate did not develop among the leaders of Rwanda and of Burundi until 1967–68. This came after the feudal-like monarchy in Burundi was overthrown. Earlier distrust is not quickly disspelled, however. Rwanda is openly cautious and remains reticent at meetings between the two states, keeping all talks in a fairly conditional state of being. Political separation has allowed Rwanda and Burundi officially to close their eyes to each other's internal politics and ethnic problems. The peoples of Ruanda-Urundi had never achieved more than a shallow community, tied together in very ambiguous fashion by a Belgian administrative superstructure. A Ruanda-Urundi "nation" remained in a conditional state of becoming but was not given any assist by those outsiders who administered Ruanda-Urundi; and, whenever there were feeble attempts by the local leadership to move in the direction of common organizations and activities, these were thwarted by their European superiors. Ruanda-Urundi nationhood was a future oriented goal, it was "putative," and that goal was aborted before it could take off. In this sense, then, Ruanda-Urundi was an aborted putative nation.

It remains difficult to suggest any wholly logical or mutually satisfactory formula for a resolution of the conflicts between Rwanda and Burundi, in particular for those stemming from precolonial sociopolitical disparities and oppression. The haunting question is whether or not these two states can depoliticize their differences.

Rwanda and Burundi have so far failed to meet with minimal requirements set up in the literature that has grown up concerning integration and community building. For our purposes we will use criteria established by Karl Deutsch. Rwanda and Burundi do not meet up to what Deutsch hypothesized as necessary for a strong political union, and it is doubtful whether they could satisfy the requisites for even a looser community. Only very recently have prospects for violent encounters between the two states been generally ruled out by their respective politically relevant strata, but there is as yet no sign of a "compatibility of the main values" held by these groups.[67]

Rosalind Horner's definition of the political elite of Burundi—one we would extend to Rwanda as well—includes those social strata which competed for power. Citing Duverger's *The Idea of Politics* (1966, p. 31), Horner made the significant point that in

> the general pattern of political conflict in all states . . . "Within the dominant class [for our purposes, the political elites of Rwanda and of Burundi] there is a

minority which controls the apparatus of government, and between this minority and the majority of the ruling class there arise conflicts . . . *quite distinct* from the clashes between the ruling class and the rest of the population." [68]

The nature of the conflict within the elite in Burundi, and the manner in which an analogous conflict was resolved by Rwanda's political elite, keep these two groups basically opposed to, and too distrustful of each other to allow for, even the loosest political union. A Burundian diplomat recently addressed himself to what he has qualified as a (Belgian) "contrived" Hutu-Tutsi conflict limited to the elite, and more specifically, those dysfunctional elements of the elite more interested in personal power than in the national well-being of Burundi.[69] He suggests rather strongly that the Hutu-Tutsi conflict is not characteristic of relations between the elite and the masses of Burundi as a whole. His point is sharply disputed and questioned by Lemarchand and Tannenwald who have also written recent accounts of Burundi's political development.[70]

Whatever the reality of the situation in Burundi, the significant thing is that the Rwandan elite, confronted with a similar situation, saw it as one involving the masses and the elite in zero-sum total terms. In Rwanda the Hutu-Tutsi fought for power, each knowing defeat would be total and mean exile at best. Burundi's political elite referred to the Rwandans as racists and accused them of genocide during 1964 and on other occasions; now Burundi stands accused of genocide. The ruling Burundian elite has been more identified in terms of its Tutsi membership. Official statistics indicate that a total of more than ninety-seven major Hutu leaders were executed in 1965 and in 1969; many more Hutu were imprisoned for "racist" attitudes and activities. In May 1972, Burundi was charged with genocide by the prime minister of Belgium. This charge was made after numerous witnesses indicated that Burundi's Tutsi officials organized systematically the killing off of all educated Hutu. The Burundian government has denied these charges. Were the political elites of Rwanda and of Burundi to have commingled within a unitary political framework, Burundi's elite would have felt even more insecure to see Burundian Hutu "racists" joined by Rwanda's Hutu, thereby swamping the Tutsi in numbers alone. Nor would the Rwandan elite have been happy to be thrown together with a "Tutsi" monarchy given the fundamental insecurity of a newly born Hutu Republic which feared the magnetic pull of older, well-ingrained monarchist traditions on the bulk of its citizenry. A pluralist solution for Ruanda-Urundi's problems was out of the question given historically rooted and reinforced differences between Rwanda and Burundi. The growing ethnic split in each state further vitiated any positive prospects for pluralism as it undermined the will to cooperate among the controlling political elites in each state.

Immediate difficulties come to mind if we suggest generalizing to all Africa based on this one case study. Not all African states have stratified, ethnic-status cleavages which resemble those that have existed in Rwanda or in Burundi; and not all colonial powers refrained from creating a more integrative framework and infrastructure that were later to serve the nation-building ideologies of African nationalists in their respective territories. Nevertheless, the fragmentation that blocked the road to unity in Ruanda-Urundi is present under different guises in most African states, and Africa's nations are still being born.

Appendix

BURUNDI

Population (1970 estimate): 3.55 million
Area: 10,739 sq. miles (slightly larger than Maryland)
Population density: 326 per sq. mile (one of highest in sub-Saharan Africa)
Population growth: 2.5% per annum (at this rate population will more than double in twenty years)
Major religions:
  Christian, 70% (65% Catholic, 5% Protestant)
  Indigenous religions, ca. 30%
  Muslim, mainly in and about capital city, small %
Language: Kirundi, French

GOVERNMENT

Burundi, a one-party state, is a presidential republic with no constitution or parliament. The president, an army officer, rules by decree. He is assisted by a Supreme Council comprised of military officers. The party youth, the Rwagasore Revolutionary Youth, is a paramilitary force used to mobilize popular support for government actions and to police the country against "counterrevolutionaries."

ECONOMY

Bůrundi Franc: FBu 78.34 = U.S.$1.00
Gross domestic product (1969 estimate): U.S.$145 million
Per capita cash income (1969 estimate): U.S.$15 per year
Rural population: 90%
Salaried workers (figures are now somewhat lower than these due to execution of Hutu salaried workers in May–June 1972): 80,000 (8,000 in industry)
Foreign aid total (1969): ca. U.S.$5 million (FBu 1,301 million)
Balance of payments (1970): ca. +U.S.$2 million (FBu 584 million)
Net foreign reserves (end 1970): ca. U.S.$2.5 million (FBu 636.4 million)
SDR (Special Drawing Rights) position (as of 1971):
  Initial allocation, 2.520 million
  Second allocation, 2.033 million

Holdings (as of February 1971), 92.3% of cumulative allocation
Cost of living index (April 1, 1965 = 100%): 119.0% (1970) 119.0% (1969)

GENERAL

At least 90 percent of the people are subsistence farmers or herders. The cash economy is basically dependent on coffee production, although tea and cotton are also grown. Bujumbura, the capital city (estimates for population range between 75,000 and 130,000), has major port facilities which are underused. There is relatively little industry in the country aside from a brewery and some light manufactures: blankets, shirts, paint, soap, etc. Many plants are underemployed due to the limited market offered within Burundi. Existing light industry is concentrated about Bujumbura. The economy is very weak and in need constantly of foreign aid. During 1968, the government published a five-year development plan to run from 1968 through 1972. The inflow of expected foreign resources lagged considerably and there was a lack of follow-up in the execution of projects. More recently, Burundi has signed a five-year cooperation and commercial agreement with the People's Republic of China. China will provide Burundi with Yuan 50 million interest-free over a period of five years. (Repayment set between January 1, 1982, and January 1, 1991). The cooperation covers principal projects including four military camps. Construction on these camps has begun. In Spring 1973, Libya agreed to provide major military aid to Burundi, and Algeria is extending technical military aid to train Burundi's army. This was done to replace the Belgian military presence that was withdrawn subsequent to the civil strife between Tutsi and Hutu in Burundi during 1972 and 1973.

During 1973 discoveries of a major nickel concentration were announced, and prospecting began for oil in the offshore regions of Lake Tanganyika.

Since independence, over 85,000 refugees, predominately Hutu, have fled Burundi: approximately 40–45,000 in Zaire; 30,000 in Tanzania; and, 10–15,000 in Rwanda. The bulk of these refugees fled during and after the 1972 ethnic hostilities.

MILITARY

The latest figures are those of 1970, subject to caution since a large number of officers and men of low rank who belonged to the Hutu ethnic group were killed between 1969 and into June of 1972. Several high-ranking Tutsi officers have also been relieved of duty and some tried for treason against President Micombero's government. In 1968, the gendarmerie was integrated into the army and gendarms began to receive combat training. In 1970, the army numbered 1,600; the gendarmerie and police numbered 900. Estimates for 1973 place the army at 3,000–5,000. Defense-spending increased from U.S.$970,000 in 1966 to an estimated U.S.$2,686,000 for 1967, just one year after the military seized power. In 1970 the defense allowance increased from FBu 234.0 million to FBu 300.0 million.

RWANDA

Population (1970 estimate): 3.7 million
Area: 10,169 sq. miles (about the size of Vermont)
Population density: 350 per sq. mile (probably highest in sub-Saharan Africa)
Population growth rate: 2.84% per annum
Major religions:
  Christian, 57% (predominantly Catholic)
  Indigenous religions, 42.5%
  Muslim, 0.5%
Language: Kinyarwanda, French

GOVERNMENT

Rwanda is a presidential republic. The Constitution makes the president a powerful chief executive with extensive appointive powers. He shares legislative power with the National Assembly. The post of vice-president, provided for by the Constitution, has never been filled. The present ruling party is Parmehutu; all other parties have disappeared. The present National Assembly was elected in 1969. On July 5, 1973, Rwanda's armed forces assumed control. A National Committee for Peace and Unity, headed by General Major Habyarimana, was announced as an interim cabinet until a caretaker government was appointed by the army. The National Assembly and all activities of the Parmehutu party were suspended, but the constitution was neither suspended nor abrogated. General elections scheduled for 1973 have been postponed. When the new government was announced, Major General Habyarimana was named president and four other officers held cabinet posts in foreign affairs and international cooperation, interior and civil service, information, and youth.

ECONOMY

Rwanda Franc: FRw 85–90 = U.S.$1.00
Gross domestic product (1970): FRw 19,495 million (U.S.$194,950,000)
Per capita cash income (1970): U.S.$17
Rural population (1970): 3,553,100 (urban population, 128,260)
Salaried workers (1968): 64,600 (1969, 1,909 civil servants)
Foreign aid total (1970): U.S.$19.3 million (U.S.$5.24 foreign aid per head)
Balance of payments (1970): U.S.$4.2 million
Net foreign reserves (December 1970): U.S.$3.5 million
SDR (Special Drawing Rights) position (as of April 1972):
  Allocations (3), 6.6 million
  Holdings (as of April 1972), 21.9% of net cumulative allocation
Consumer price index (March 1967 = 100; for Kigali and Nyamirambo (December 1970) 107.5% (high-income index) 136.1% (low-income index)

GENERAL

Rwanda has one of the lowest gross domestic products in the world. Although its authorities are attempting vigorously to diversify the economy, in the past production has barely kept up with the population growth.

Coffee is the major source of foreign exchange earnings. Production fell in 1963 to 4,700 tons; in 1970 production was not expected to exceed 13,000 tons. Mineral production is a second important source of foreign exchange earnings. The value added to the economy by the mining sector increased by 50% between 1968 and 1970.

Rwanda is less industrialized than Burundi, but produces its own electric power. There are three major hydraulic power stations and four major thermal stations. In 1969 Rwanda produced 61.9 millions of kwh.

Rwanda's first five-year plan (1966–70) formally ended with a number of projects still to be completed. Only one-half of the expected private investment took place: some two-thirds of the expected public investment took place. A second five-year plan has been prepared. The government presented a National Coffee Plan and Diversification Program that sets out the agricultural policies for five years (1970–75). Rwanda spent large sums of money in 1971–72 to establish alternative transport facilities for its external trade and to build up stocks of fuel supplies.

After an exceptionally favorable performance in 1970, the economy suffered a setback in 1971. This was due to a considerable decline in the world market price of Rwanda's major exports and the closure of the country's main export evacuation route through Uganda. In the spring of 1972, Rwanda requested a Stand-By Arrangement of the International Monetary Fund.

Since independence over 143,000 refugees, predominately Tutsi, have fled Rwanda: approximately 32,000 in Burundi; 70–75,000 in Uganda; 24,000 in Zaire; and 14,000 in Tanzania. The bulk of these refugees fled during ethnic hostilities between 1959 and 1964. New refugees were added during the 1973 ethnic hostilities.

MILITARY

Despite the increase in the number of army units since 1969, the total strength of Rwanda's military army units is placed at 2,750, the air component of this is 100. (The figure for 1966 was 1,500.) In 1965, Belgium was supplying Rwanda with military assistance at an estimated cost of U.S.$280,000. In 1968, defense expenditures were estimated U.S.$3,210,000 (out of its total budget of $13.8 million). It rose to U.S. $3,879,030 in 1971.

Sources

Note: Some material is subject to further verification. Where no figures are given, it is because they are not available.

Belgium, Office de la Coopération au Développement, *OCD.*

Le Moniteur Africain, 1971–72.

Marchés Tropicaux et Méditerranéens, 1959–72.
Institute for Strategic Studies (London), Aldelphi Papers.
U.S. Government Printing Office, *Area Handbook, Burundi*, and *Area Handbook, Rwanda* (1969).

RWANDA:

United States, Department of State, *Background Notes: Republic of Rwanda*, annual.
U.S. Department of Commerce, *Economic Trends: Rwanda*, annual.
ISAR *Bulletin Statistique.*
OCIR, *Rapport de l'Exercise*, annual.
OCIR, *Plan Cafeier National et de Diversification Agricole*, 1970.
Service de l'Elevage, *Rapport Annuel.*
Service de l'Agriculture et Bureau d'Etudes, *Rapport Annuel.*
Ministry of Finance, *Annual Report.*
Bulletin Agricole du Rwanda.

BURUNDI:

United States, Department of State, *Background Notes: Republic of Burundi*, annual.
United States, Department of Commerce, *Foreign Economic Trends: Burundi*, annual.
Banque Nationale de Développement Economique du Burundi, *Rapport d'Activité*, annual.
IRUSTAT, *Bulletin de Statistique.*
Burundi, Ministry of Plan, *Bulletin de Statistique.*
OCIBU, *Rapport Annuel.*

Notes

1. For a discussion of the term "putative nation," see R. Emerson, *From Empire to Nation* (Boston: Beacon Press, 1960). pt. 2. Emerson wrote: "It might be argued that in Africa the territorial foundation has come to be of peculiar importance, not because of any traditional association between the colonial territory and the people, but because the *putative nations* (italics mine), lacking ancient roots, are defined solely in terms of colonial frontiers" (p. 128).

2. Emerson and Rustow emphasized the common will of the collective membership of a group to form a nation. (*Ibid.*, p. 95.) Rustow defined a nation as "a self-contained group of human beings who place loyalty to the group as a whole above competing loyalties." If language were to serve as the major criterion for discerning the existence of divided nations in Africa, one might argue that Somali and Pan-Somali nationalism present possibly fertile ground for a study of a divided nation. But the Somali case is not all that close to the divided nation as exemplified by the two Germanies, Vietnams, or Koreas—there exists only one Somalia and groups of Somali living in three other states where they are a distinct minority. Rwanda and Burundi, if taken separately, are linguistically homogeneous states. However, Ruanda-Urundi in hyphenated form was never considered linguistically homogeneous despite Belgian attempts to standardize the two closely related languages spoken in the territory. Rustow, *A World of Nations* (Washington, D.C.: Brookings Institution, 1967), pp. 21, 51–55,

288. See also a more recent Emerson article, "The Problem of Identity, Selfhood, and Image in the New Nations: The Situation in Africa," *Comparative Politics* 1, no. 3 (April 1969): 297–312.

3. See Ray Y. Gildia, "Rwanda and Burundi," *Focus* XIII (February 1963): 1–5. Gildia wrote that the average elevation for the two states is placed at 7,000 feet above sea level.

4. Ibid., p. 2. See also René Dumont, "Décolonisation et développement agricole au centre-est de l'Afrique: le Ruanda-Urundi," *Review du Tiers Monde* 1, no. 4 (1960): 421–45.

5. For a full discussion of the German period and of the diplomacy involved in Germany's acquisition of Rwanda and Burundi, see Roger Louis, *Ruanda-Urundi: 1884–1919* (Oxford: Clarendon Press, 1963). Ruanda-Urundi formed districts thirteen and fourteen of German East Africa (P. Chaleur, "Les étapes de l'indépendence du Ruanda-Urundi," *Etudes* 314 [September 1962]: 226).

6. "Mwamiship" as a term is a convenient shorthand symbol used to signify the ethos, structures, and processes of the "kingdoms" found in Rwanda and Burundi where the acknowledged head was or is a mwami. This office is invested with magico-religious powers and is enshrouded in a rich array of rituals and taboos. For a more complete discussion of "mwamiship," see René Lemarchand, *Rwanda and Burundi* (New York: Praeger Library of African Affairs, 1970), esp. chap. 11; and M. d'Hertefelt, A. A. Trouwborst, and J. H. Scherer, *Les Royaumes de la Zone Interlacustrine Méridionale Rwanda, Burundi, Buha*, Monographes Ethnographiques, no. 6 (Tervuren: Musée Royal de l'Afrique Central, 1962).

7. Fully cognizant of the magnetism still held by the "mwamiship," Rwanda's Hutu republicans wrote into their constitution—Article 2, "The mwami regime is abolished and may not be restored." See J. Vanderlinden, *La République Rwandaise*, Encyclopédie Politique et Constitutionelle, série Afrique (Paris: Editions Berger Levrault, 1970), pp. 28–29, 40.

8. For a discussion of the refugees and their paramilitary organization—the Inyenzi or "cockroaches"—see Lemarchand, *Rwanda and Burundi*, pp. 145–227, and Aaron Segal, *Massacre in Rwanda*, Fabian Research Series, no. 240 (London: Fabian Society, 1964).

9. Emerson, *From Empire to Nation*, p. 124.

10. In most new states it is the traditional and modern elite, however defined, who often give direction to nation-building. A major reason offered for this is the low level of political experience and participation among the masses. Emerson also suggested that differential treatment of certain areas and the use of indirect rule were significant factors of colonial policy which fostered ethnic cleavages and particularisms. See Emerson, *From Empire to Nation*, pp. 121, 150.

11. Various authors draw attention to the fact that the Belgians failed to politically integrate their territories. See H. Weiss, *Political Protest in the Congo: the Parti Solidaire Africain During the Independence Struggle* (Princeton, N.J.: Princeton University Press, 1967); R. Lemarchand, *Political Awakening in the Congo* (Berkeley: University of California Press, 1964); C. Young, *Politics in the Congo: Decolonization and Independence* (Princeton, N.J.: Princeton University Press, 1965); and A. Merriam, *Congo: Background of Conflict,* (Evanston, Ill.: Northwestern University Press, 1961).

12. United Nations, T/1168 (1954), p. 2.

13. See Warren Weinstein, "A Sea of Troubles: Decolonization in Burundi, 1958–1962" (Ph.D. dissertation, Columbia University, New York, 1970.), esp. chaps. 4, 5, 6, and 7.

14. See Lemarchand, *Rwanda and Burundi,* pp. 106–11.

15. Résidence de l'Urundi, Territoire Urbain d'Usumbura, *Rapport sur l'état d'esprit des populations indigènes*, Décembre 1948, *Mois de Décembre 1948* (6 January 1949–2 August 1949); Résidence de l'Urundi, Territoire de Bubanza, *Rapport sur l'état d'esprit des populations indigènes* (4 August 1951–10 September 1951); Résidence de l'Urundi, Territoire de Kitega, *Etat d'esprit des populations* (26 June 1950); Résidence de l'Urundi, *Etat d'esprit Usumbura* (16 June 1950); Résidence de l'Urundi, Territoire d'Usumbura, *Etat d'esprit des populations* (May 1950–12 June 1951); Résidence de l'Urundi, Territoire de Kitega. *Rapport sur l'internment à la maison de santé de Kitega de l'Abbé Antoine NTURO, prêtre indigène* (7 July 1948); and *Internement Abbé antoine TURO* (8 July 1948). (All are unpublished, typewritten documents. The author is indebted to those individuals in Belgium who made them available to him, and who requested not to be cited.)

16. Letter. Members of the Provisional Committee to the Residents of Ruanda and Burundi, 21 March 1955. (Statutes of the Democratic Progressive Movement appended to letter. Typewritten.) The names of the founding members included Grégoire Kayibanda (later Hutu president of Rwanda); P. Baranyanka and J. B. Ntidendereza (leaders of the political forces in Burundi favorable to the colonial administration); P. Mirerekano and Paul

Baganzicaha (important pro-Hutu leaders in Burundi later to go into exile and then return. They were executed for participating in an attempted coup d'etat against Burundi's monarchy in 1965); A. Muhirwa (Burundi's first prime minister after independence); P. Bwanakweli (a leading Tutsi moderate in Rwanda, the archenemy of Rwanda's mwami. Mutara-Mutara's death ultimately led to open hostilities between Rwanda's Hutus and Tutsis in 1959).

17. D. P. Rawson, "The Role of the United Nations in the Political Development of Ruanda-Urundi, 1947–1962" (Ph.D. dissertation, American University, 1965), p. 214.

18. The movement's goals were (1) to study all "political, social, and economic problems posed by the evolution of Ruanda-Urundi"; (2) "to assure the evolution of traditional customs and institutions toward a democratic conception"; (3) "to take up the civic and social education of the natives (*indigènes*)." The last two goals dealt with the wider Eurafrican context as few as yet thought Belgium would relinquish political control within only six years. Democratic Progressive Movement, "Statuts." Typewritten.

19. UN, *UN Visiting Mission to the Trusteeship Territories in East Africa, 1954, Report on Ruanda-Urundi,* T/1168, p. 21.

20. Rawson, "Role of the UN," p. 160.

21. This problem reflected contradictions which inhered in the UN trusteeship system: (1) the UN had no financial responsibility for the execution of policies it tried to impose upon Belgium; (2) nowhere did the Trusteeship Agreement state the content or direction of the terminal political goals to be pursued in Ruanda-Urundi: the agreement spoke only to the nebulous issue of social, economic, and political "development"; (3) it was never clearly established where the boundaries existed between the United Nation's responsibilities and those of the Administering Authority—Belgium. See Rawson, "Role of the UN," pp. 168–93; Weinstein, "A Sea of Troubles," passim.

22. There was also some difficulty with a minute part of the population, the Twa or pygmies. However, because they represent only 1 percent of Burundi and Rwanda's total population this group has not been mentioned.

23. For a detailed discussion of this period see Rawson, "Role of the UN," pp. 199–300; and Weinstein, "A Sea of Troubles," chaps. 4, 5 and 6.

24. The limited economic agreement included a monetary union, a customs union, joint maintenance of scientific research services established by the Belgian administration, as well as that of a common coffee board. A council on the Economic Union was the only organization joining the two states. See Rawson, "Role of the UN," p. 292.

25. A. L. Latham-Koenig, "Another Congo," *Spectators* 209 (6 July 1962): 8.

26. On the question of boundaries in African interstate relations, see I. W. Zartman, "The Politics of Boundaries," *Journal of Modern African Studies* 3 (August 1965): 155–73; Ravi L. Kapil, "On the Conflict Potential of Inherited Boundaries in Africa," *World Politics* (July 1966): 656–73; for these points as they relate to Burundi, see Rosalind Horner, "The Nature of Political Conflict in Burundi" (M.A. Thesis, University of Manchester, April 1967), passim. See also S. Touval, "The Organization of African Unity and African Borders," *International Organization* 21 (Winter 1967): 102–27.

27. "Ruanda and Urundi: UN Reconciled," *Economist* (28 April 1962): 329.

28. Rawson, "Role of the UN," p. 290.

29. D. Rothchild, "Ethnicity and Conflict Resolution," *World Politics* 22, no. 4 (July 1970): 592.

30. Rothchild, "Ethnicity," p. 612. Rothchild has summed up the Nigerian case as follows: "Recognizing the reality of . . . intersectional boundaries, the colonial power, committed to a rapid departure from the Nigerian scene, spurred the major collectivities to negotiate a modus vivendi. The upshot was a temporary institutional arrangement . . . positions became polarized as men on each side became committed to antagonistic world views, the scope for negotiation dwindled and *violent conflict became well nigh inescapable*" (pp. 602–3). Italics added.

31. For a full discussion of the Cameroon experience see Willard Johnson, *Cameroon Federation–Political Integration in a Fragmentary Society*. (Princeton, N.J.: Princeton University Press, 1970); Claude E. Welch, Jr. *Dream of Unity* (Ithaca, N.Y.: Cornell University Press, 1966).

32. Our discussion of federalism follows those who broke away from Wheare's pioneering formal-legal definition and have stressed the economic, social, political, and cultural forces that make a federal structure necessary, and by extension, possible. For a good short critical

discussion see Michael B. Stein, "Federal Political Systems and Federal Societies" *World Politics* 20, no. 4 (July 1968): 722–47.

33. J. Moes, "Foreign Exchange Policy and Economic Unions in Central Africa," *Economic Development and Cultural Change* 14, no. 4 (July 1966): 471–83.

34. Gabriel Barakana, "L'unification des langues au Ruanda-Urundi," *Civilisations,* no. 1 (1952), italics added; Horner, "Nature of Political Conflict," p. 138, quotes a myth the Rwandans have that holds the founding king of Burundi's dynasty to have been a servant of a Hutu (low status) chief in Rwanda. This myth expresses the Rwandan belief that Burundi was inferior. Numerous Rwandans and Burundians affirmed to this author that they can understand each other's language. One highly placed official put it this way, "Out languages are practically the same, but it's a question of susceptibilities." (Interviews held between 1967 and 1971.)

35. M. Stein, "Federal Political Systems and Federal Societies," *World Politics* 20, no. 4 (July 1968): 727.

36. F. E. Wagoner, *Nation Building in Africa: A Description and Analysis of the Development of Rwanda* (Ann Arbor: University Microfilms, 1971), p. 81. Rwandan history never mentions Burundi other than as a kingdom that emerged, was inferior to that of Rwanda and from time to time had violent encounters with Rwanda. Vansina, an historian, suggested that in both Rwanda and Burundi the leadership traditionally looked to events in the past to explain and understand the present. If this is still so, then the traditions of cattle raids and violent contact between both states places them in an antagonistic pattern of interaction which has prevented leaders in either state—Hutu or Tutsi—from envisaging a more positive and closer political relationship such as federation. See Jan Vansina, *L'Evolution de Royaume Rwanda des Origines à 1900* (Brussels: ARSOM, Sciences Morales et Politiques, Mémoire in 8, N.S. (histoire), T. 2, fasc. 2 *et; dernier,* 1962); Luc de Heusch, *Le Rwanda et la Civilisation interlacustrine* (Brussels: Université Libre de Bruxelles, 1966). It is most probable that even were both states to be ruled by the same ethnic group the chances for political unification between them would remain slight.

37. For discussion of the problems with which the community in former British East Africa is faced, see C. G. Rosberg and A. Segal, "An East African Federation," *International Conciliation*, no. 543 (May 1963): 1–72.

38. G. D'Arboussier, *L'Afrique ver l'Unité* (Paris, 1961), quoted in C. Wauthier, *L'Afrique des Africains* (Paris: Editions du Seuil, 1964), p. 269. For critical analysis of the Mali Federation, see William J. Foltz, *From French West Africa to the Mali Federation* (New Haven: Yale University Press, 1965); and Donn M. Kurtz, "Political Integration in Africa: The Mali Federation," *JMAS* 8, no. 3 (October 1970): 405–24.

39. L. Senghor, *Nation et Voie Africaine du Socialisme* (Paris, 1961), quoted in Wauthier, *L'Afrique des Africains,* p. 269.

40. For a discussion of "adversaries" as an analytical tool, see D. J. Finlay, O. R. Holsti, and R. R. Fagan, *Enemies in Politics* (Chicago: Rand McNally, 1967), esp. chap. 1.

41. The presence of refugees is often a destabilizing factor, especially when they are "the enemy across the border." Robert O. Mathews has suggested that Tutsi refugees had often "a sympathetic response among the people with whom they settled." Owing to this, it was quite difficult for the host countries to prevent Tutsi refugee attacks against Rwanda. In February 1964 Uganda's minister of information stated that his country was unable to control these refugees in his country. See Robert O. Mathews, "Refugees and Stability in Africa," *International Organization* 26, no. 1 (Winter 1972): 69–71. See Appendix 1 for a table of refugees and of their location.

42. If one reads the Rwandan constitution, it bluntly states that Rwanda's republic represents a symbolic break with the past. Article 2 forbids the restoration of the mwamiship; Article 7 abolishes the caste privileges of the past. At the time of his writing, Jacques Vanderlinden estimated that Rwanda's Tutsi population drastically dropped from fifteen to seven percent of the total. See Vanderlinden, *La Republique Rwandise,* pp. 26 and 28.

P. Tannenwald, "Burundi 1970: Le Prix de l'Ordre," *Revue Française d'Etudes Politiques Africaines,* no. 58 (October 1970): 75, 76. Tannenwald stressed that the violent Hutu revolt of 1959 in Rwanda served as a reference point for events that occurred in Burundi from 1962 until the time of his writing (1970). He argued that the Rwandan revolt "weighed with all its weight on the minds of the Burundians, feeding the hopes of some, terrorizing the others. . . . The Tutsi remained traumatized by the Rwandan precedent and very anxious faced with the Hutu ascent, which at times expressed itself in an aggressive manner."

43. *New York Times,* 8 March 1964, p. 18.

44. Related to the author during interviews conducted in Belgium, Burundi, and Rwanda, 1967–69.

45. Weinstein, "Burundi: Political and Ethnic Powderkeg," *African Report* (November 1970): 18–20. See W. Weinstein's forthcoming book on Rwanda and Burundi to be published by Cornell University Press.

46. See P. Whitaker and J. Silvey, "A Visit to the Congo, Rwanda and Burundi," *Makerere Journal* 9 (1964): 71–82. Rwanda's constitution (Article 39) formally interdicts communism, communist activity, or communist propaganda on Rwandian soil. One has only to think of Communist Chinese activity in Burundi, and that of North Korea more recently, to understand that this is another stumbling block in the way of cooperation between Rwanda and Burundi. See Vanderlinden, *La Republique Rwandise*, p. 30.

47. *Africa Research Bulletin* (Political) 7, no. 8 (15 September 1970): 1832–34. Rwanda's abstention was joined by nine other states: Malawi, Ivory Coast, Dahomey, Niger, Gabon, Lesotho, Madagascar. Tunisia and Zaire made reservations. *Africa Research Bulletin* (Political) 1, no. 5 (May 1964): 71–72.

48. K. Deutsch et al., *Political Community and the North Atlantic Area* (Princeton, N.J.: Princeton University Press, 1957), p. 43–69.

49. An extended discussion of political development and institutionalization can be found in S. P. Huntington, *Political Order in Changing Societies* (New Haven: Yale University Press, 1968), esp. chap. 1. For a criticism of Huntington's essay see D. Rustow, "The Organization Triumphs Over Its Function: Huntington and Modernization," *Journal of International Affairs* 23, no. 1 (1969): 119–32.

50. Deutsch, *Political Community,* pp. 43–69. See also Robert Melson and Howard Wolpe, "Modernization and the Politics of Communalism: A Theoretical Perspective," *American Political Science Review* 64, no. 4 (December 1970) 1112–30; and C. S. Whitaker, Jr., "A Disrhythmic Process of Political Change," *World Politics* 19, no. 2 (January 1967): 140–217.

51. During 1960 the Belgian authorities had drawn up economic development plans for the Trust Territory. In 1961, Common Market experts drew up a global development plan for preliminary talks to establish a common market between Rwanda and Burundi. The Belgians were very much influenced with the British East Africa model and hoped to apply it in modified form to Ruanda-Urundi.

52. The following information is drawn from Wagoner, *Nation Building in Africa* (those portions in quotes are drawn from the official Belgian annual reports made to the Mandates Commission of the League of Nations, as cited in Wagoner), pp. 63–67.

53. M. Heimo, "Réflexions sur les conditions et les perspectives du développement économique au Rwanda," *Genève-Afrique* 8, no. 1 (1968): 16. The recent discovery of important nickel deposits and offshore oil in Burundi's territorial waters on Lake Tanganyika may change Burundi's economic prospects.

54. Dumont, "Décolonisation," p. 440.

55. R. Baker, "Reorientation in Rwanda," *African Affairs* 69, no. 275 (April 1970): 145–46.

56. Ibid.

57. Eastern Zaire, the part bordering Rwanda and Burundi, was the scene of rebellions against the Zaire central government at Kinshasa. Under these conditions it became too perilous to transit this region and trade between it and Rwanda dwindled to almost nil by 1969. This trend had forced Rwanda to look elsewhere for necessary supplies: food, vehicles, replacement parts, etc. A measure of the flow of goods (mostly entrepot trade) from Rwanda to Burundi are the total transit receipts Burundi earns on the passage of these goods. In 1970 these earnings amounted to $392,000 U.S. in 1971, as a result of the closing of Rwanda's border with Uganda, the total receipts rose to $573,714 U.S. These figures clearly indicate the advantages for Burundi if closer economic cooperation and ties can be achieved with Rwanda. The benefits of routing imports through Burundi are not necessarily as attractive for Rwanda. Rwandan officials, still unprepared to return to a dependence on Bujumbura, find more direct routes transiting via Tanzania, Uganda, and Kenya appear more attractive.

58. Moes, "Foreign Exchange Policy," pp. 482–3. In his article Moes has strongly questioned the feasibility of maintaining an economic union between politically independent countries. He had in mind not only Rwanda and Burundi, but also the larger and more important economic integration schemes among the three East African states of Kenya, Uganda, and Tanganyika.

59. On November 16, 1963, Rwanda unilaterally amended a 1959 ordinance and imposed

import duties on certain goods of Burundian manufacture. The rates ranged from 2%–20%. See *Africa Research Bulletin;* see also Moes, "Foreign Exchange Policy," pp. 481–82.

60. On January 1, 1964, Burundi's prime minister announced that his government was seeking full membership in any future East African federation, and wished to join the East African Common Services Organization as soon as possible. (The "Federation" has never materialized.) Both Rwanda and Burundi sent representatives to several East African economic and technical conferences held since 1964. In 1965 they both attended a conference for East and Central African Economic Cooperation at Lusaka. See *African Research Bulletin* (Political) 1, no. 1 (January 1964): 3; idem, 2, no. 6 (June–July 1965): 317. For a discussion of ties with East Africa, see A. M. O'Connor, "A Wider Eastern African Economic Unit?" *JMAS* 6, no. 4 (December 1968): 485–493. Dr. Aaron Segal of Cornell University, who has spent some time in East Africa and has studied the Community, has indicated that Burundi and Rwanda have tended to cultivate different partners within the Community and that this had only served to further aggravate relations between themselves. For quite some time Burundi cultivated relations with Tanzania (although these are now somewhat less cordial as a result of the 1972–73 ethnic hostilities in Burundi and differences between them over the future of the "Belbases"); Rwanda had long cultivated relations with Uganda, where many ethnic Rwandans work and because they felt that Kampala (in Uganda) was a better route for import-export traffic than Bujumbura.

61. Baker, "Reorientation in Rwanda," p. 151.

62. Ibid., pp. 151–54, 149. See also "Le Marché du Burundi," *Marchés Tropicaux et Méditerranéens* 23, no. 1122 (April 1970): 1353.

63. J. Niqueaux, "Rwanda et Burundi: Les Frères Ennemis aux Sources du Nil," *Revue Nouvelle* (Belgium) 43 (May 1966): 466–81.

64. J. Carlier, "Le Rwanda et le Burundi Face à l'Avenir," *Spécial,* (15 July 1970): 14–15. Italics added.

65. Baker, "Reorientation in Rwanda," passim. Although Rwanda and Burundi have sought to enter the East African Community, there is some question whether this ever took more concrete form than seeking a rapprochement between the Community and themselves. Even were Rwanda and Burundi to join the Community, they would lack economic leverage because their import market is too small and too diffuse to be of much interest to Community states. Also, the small manufactured goods—pots, pans, etc.—that are items the East African Community states are interested in exporting are the very items on which the governments of Rwanda and Burundi want to collect import duties and taxes. There are also some reports that the Community has not been all that pleased with the way negotiations are handled by Burundi; whereas Rwandan officials, particularly since Amin closed the border with Uganda for a short time, have been said to have made themselves more amenable. However, Rwanda is a small state and its leaders are still wary of any common market where the other members are "giants" and Rwanda is the only "pygmy." I am indebted to Dr. Aaron Segal of Cornell University for having drawn my attention to the above-cited information.

66. *African Research Bulletin* (Economic) 7, no. 5 (July 1970): 1719–20a.

67. Deutsch, *Political Community,* p. 46.

68. Rosalind Horner, "The Nature of Political Conflict in Burundi." (Master of Arts thesis, University of Manchester, April 1967), p. 177.

69. See T. Nsanze, *L'Edification de la République du Burundi* (Brussels: Editions Remarques Africaines, 1970).

70. See Tannenwald, "Burundi 1970," passim; and Lemarchand, *Rwanda and Burundi,* pp. 289–497.

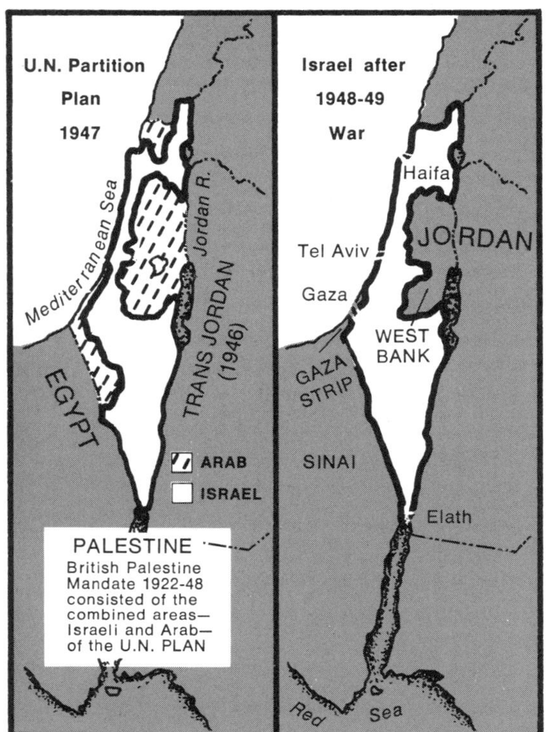
U.N. Partition
Plan
1947
Mediterranean Sea
Jordan R.
TRANS JORDAN
(1946)
EGYPT
ARAB
ISRAEL
PALESTINE
British Palestine
Mandate 1922-48
consisted of the
combined areas—
Israeli and Arab—
of the U.N. PLAN
Israel after
1948-49
War
Haifa
JORDAN
Tel Aviv
Gaza
WEST
BANK
GAZA
STRIP
SINAI
Elath
Red
Sea

ISRAEL

1974 ?

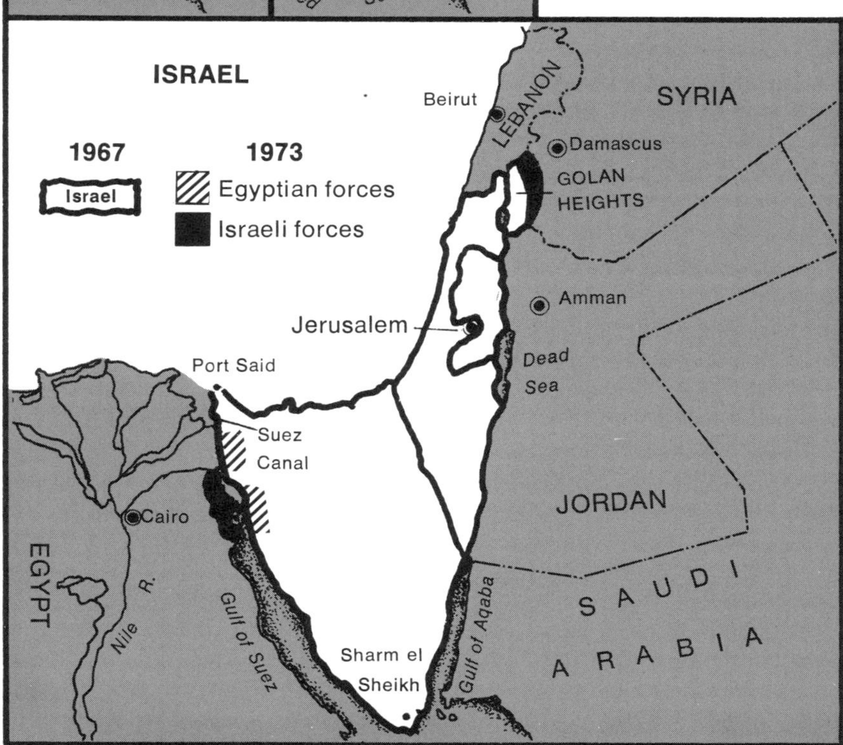
ISRAEL
1967
Israel
1973
Egyptian forces
Israeli forces
Beirut
LEBANON
SYRIA
Damascus
GOLAN
HEIGHTS
Amman
Jerusalem
Dead
Sea
Port Said
Suez
Canal
Cairo
JORDAN
EGYPT
Nile R.
Gulf of Suez
Sharm el
Sheikh
Gulf of Aqaba
SAUDI
ARABIA

11

The Future of Palestine-Eretz Israel

Gidon Gottlieb

Between Two Wars: Israeli Plans for the Future

THE YOM KIPPUR WAR has shattered Israel's view of where it stood in the area and in the world. It gave Israel a costly military victory but it also heightened Arab appetites for more successes. It opened a new era in which everything has become suddenly possible: either sitting down for talks with Israel or total war itself. In the wake of the Yom Kippur war, the prospects for a new savage round of warfare seesaw with hopes for a true settlement and a lasting cease-fire. For the first time since the creation of the State of Israel, Egypt and Jordan have agreed to enter into negotiations for a peace settlement with Israel and for the first time a settlement of the Palestinian problem is seriously contemplated.

Of the three levels of conflict, two were magnified during the war and one remained dormant: the Egyptian-Syrian surprise attack and Israel's counterpunch led to a U.S.–Soviet showdown. In dramatic contrast, the Palestinian Arabs remained at peace in Gaza and everywhere else in Palestine. The Jordan River bridge stayed open and the Jordan border was quiet. The conflict of the superpowers and the war between their regional allies failed to ignite warfare between the two peoples in Palestine (Eretz Israel).[1] Yet it is the Palestine conflict that had fed the others, that led to the involvement of the Arab world and of the superpowers. The recent history of Palestine is a record of the passionate struggle between Arabs and Jews, a record that has been told and retold no less passionately. This paper will not go over this familiar history nor over the background of the numerous dividing, demarcating, armistice, and cease-fire lines that have plowed the map of that beautiful country.

A fresh perspective may be gained by looking at the Palestine problem from the vantage point of the four major plans for the future of the country developed by responsible Israeli and Arab leaders: those of Defense Minister Moshe Dayan and Deputy Prime Minister Yigal Allon on the Israel side, and those of King Hussein of Jordan and of the Palestine Liberation Organization on the Arab side. These plans set out a framework of relevance for the appraisal of events between the Six-Day war in 1967 and the Yom Kippur war in 1973. By telling us what the leaders had in mind, the plans hold the key to an understanding of what has been attempted. Evidently, since Israel has effective control over the West Bank and the Gaza Strip, her leaders' blueprints for the future have already made their mark on the situation in the country. Theirs are the operative plans now in effect. More space is accordingly given to them here than to the Arab plans. These have by the force of events remained entirely unrealized. While some accommodation may be possible between Israel, Egypt, and Jordan, a settlement agreeable to all the peoples of Palestine remains unlikely. It is now a commonplace that as long as the vital interests of either the Palestinian Arabs or the Israelis are ignored, no durable peace in the area is possible. Despite the military defeat of the guerrilla organizations, these are likely to continue to hold a "veto" of sorts over any peace arrangements. It is, therefore, still appropriate to look at plans for the future of Palestine pressed by the Arabs and Israelis, and at options for a settlement, despite the unpromising terrain of frozen attitudes. The war-weariness of the peoples of the area is perhaps matched only by their weariness with new "solutions" and professed "settlements." Admittedly, conditions will have to change before the Palestinian dispute can be resolved, but once they do change, the basis for agreement should be ready.

In 1972 the great political debate in Israel on the future of the "administered territories" in Eretz Israel reached new intensity. The past fifty years had seen innumerable proposals for the establishment of a binational state in Palestine, for federal and confederal arrangements.[2] Now, however, established opinion in Israel is divided among the Allon plan, the Dayan policies, and the alternative proposals of A. Eliav, former secretary general of the ruling Labor party. These were precariously reconciled for election purposes in the "Gallili document." The opposition "Likud Movement," which advocates full annexation of the biblical provinces of Judea and Samaria, reflects nationalist and religious positions and reportedly also enjoys some support in the cabinet. Its position has been enhanced by the 1973 war. The great debate on the future of the "occupied (or administered) territories" is largely confined to the Israeli side. Arab opinion remains polarized between King Hussein's plan for a federated Arab state on both banks of the Jordan and the Palestine Liberation Organization's continued refusal to accept any Jewish State of Israel anywhere in Palestine. Other Arab voices are also heard from the

West Bank and the Resistance movement in support of a West Bank Palestine state.

While the intentions of the big and small powers play their part as well, only the Arab and Israeli plans concern us here. These were all developed in the period between the wars of 1967 and 1973. It is too early to tell how they will fare in the new reality of the post-Yom Kippur period.

THE DAYAN PLAN

Dayan has never outlined a "plan" as such, yet such a "plan" or policy is understood to guide the policies of the Ministry of Defense which has responsibility for the territories occupied by Israel in 1967.

The Dayan plan has remained largely inchoate. It has to be pieced together from a variety of statements, interviews, declaration, speeches, and the practices of Dayan's administration in the territories.[3] Allon has made his views public in a concise, clear manner. The importance of the Allon plan, the support which it is reputed to enjoy in the Israel cabinet, and the seriousness with which it has been studied by other governments give it saliency equaled only by the Dayan plan. The Dayan policy is based on five principles,

—Under the prevailing conditions in the Arab world, Israel must retain full military control, if need be, throughout Judea and Samaria. Israel cannot allow any other army to establish a presence there and must retain the capability to combat terrorist actions in the territories. (Israel wants to be able to combat Arab terror in the West Bank and to provide protection for Israeli settlement there without having to incur UN condemnations for every such action that would involve a border crossing.)

—Any peace agreement must provide for the right of Jewish settlement everywhere in Judea and Samaria. (Jews must have the right to live in Hebron, for example.)

—There must be a special and unique relationship between Israel and the West Bank. (There can be no closed borders anywhere west of the Jordan.)

—Israel must refrain from the inclusion of a large Arab minority in the State of Israel. (Full annexation of the West Bank and Gaza would increase Israel's Arab population by one million inhabitants.)

—When a final settlement is reached, all Israeli citizens, Jews and Arabs alike, must enjoy equal rights.

The goals set out under this plan are within Israel's reach. Israel has now achieved effective security, economic integration, and full access to all of the West Bank and the Gaza Strip. This has been done without the burden of incorporating a million Arabs into the political fabric of the state. Realization of the five principles does not require the agreement of Jordan and of the Arab states. The Dayan plan calls for immediate coexistence even as the conflict continues; it can be implemented in its entirety unilaterally by Israel. This may account for the widespread satisfaction in Israel with the growing links between Little (or pre-1967) Israel and the "administered territories."

These principles have led in their application to the creation of a bizarre, limited, tacit, de facto coalition administration, under Israel's military presence, of Israelis, West Bank dignitaries, and Jordanian protégés. Israel permits notables, elected mayors, and representatives to cross into Jordan and share demonstratively in the political life of Amman. Some ties between the two banks of the Jordan are expressed quite openly. For example, Mr. El-Khatib, former governor of Jerusalem, was provided with motorcycle escort when he reached the East Bank, and given a royal welcome. Even former Mayor Es-Shawa of Gaza, which had formerly been under Egyptian administration, was permitted to visit King Hussein in 1972 and brought back Jordanian passports for leading Gaza families, all with the acquiescence of the Military Administration. Some 6,000 West Bank officials are known to receive salaries from the Jordanian government, also with the acquiescence of the Israeli authorities. From Amman, King Hussein is known to guide the policies of his supporters west of the Jordan, to distribute his largesse to friends, and to dispatch high-ranking dignitaries on private visits. Israel has hinted it might even allow the participation of West Bankers in the Jordanian national elections, thus completing the sharing of authority over West Bank Arabs. Nevertheless, the government in Jerusalem would probably not allow the return of Jordanian civil administration before the conclusion of an agreement with King Hussein. Two additional principles thus appear to complement the other five,

—Israel recognizes the "attachment" of the people of Samaria and Judea to the political life of Jordan.

—Israel does not recognize the exercise of Jordanian civil authority in the West Bank (or at any rate will not recognize it before the conclusion of a peace agreement with Jordan).

These principles and the sweeping tide of economic integration of the West Bank and Israeli economies are more than a guide to a future settlement—they provide a key to what has already occurred in Palestine and to the existing informal pattern of relations between Israel and Jordan. The Dayan plan does not call for a change in the status quo in the territories through a peace agreement with Jordan. It puts no premium on a return of the West Bank either to King Hussein or to the Palestine Liberation Organization. The Dayan plan does nothing either to encourage the establishment of an independent Palestinian entity west of the Jordan or formal annexation by Israel. Every delay and postponement in Jordan-Israeli negotiations makes time for the continued implementation of the

Dayan plan. The plan is designed for the immediate future, for the period preceding a Palestinian settlement; to provide Israel with a policy for immediate action, not for a hypothetical future.

Essentially, this is a plan for economic and territorial integration on the one hand and for a political separation on the other. It involves

—the integration of the trade, labor, agricultural, and industrial economies of Israel and the territories;
—the removal of barriers to the free movement of persons and goods between Israel and the territories;
—the establishment of military defensive Nahal settlements in strategic areas;
—the establishment of civilian settlements of a permanent character;
—settlement in key areas to break up the territorial continuity of Arab settlement in Judea-Samaria and to encourage regional links between Arab and Jewish villages;
—the creation of urban centers rather than of agricultural settlements only. This is needed since agricultural settlements cannot meet the demands of this policy. Agricultural settlements require relatively large areas and the occupation of arable lands now owned by resident Arabs, a step likely to further estrange the Arab population. Moreover, agricultural settlements have a relatively low population density. In an area that might sustain 200 to 300 persons, it is quite possible to establish an urban center for 20,000.

For these reasons, the Dayan plan reputedly calls for the establishment of four urban centers in the hilly regions of Judea and Samaria, one each in the Hebron area (on the site of the Etzion settlements destroyed by the Arab Legion in 1948), in the Ramallah region (Beth El), in the Nablus region, and between Nablus and Jenin. These four urban centers would break up the continuity of Arab settlement in Judea and Samaria by the introduction of a significant Jewish population.[4] As a first step, this plan calls for the consolidation of land for urban development and the establishment of military camps that would secure the new towns and provide protection for the Jewish settlers.

General Dayan holds that Israel must consider itself as the permanent government in the "administered territories" and must undertake unilateral and immediate programs. There is little doubt that the Dayan plan is already in an advanced stage of implementation. The impact of the 1973 war on his influence and authority remains to be seen.

INTEGRATION OF THE TERRITORY

The economic integration of the West Bank and the Gaza Strip has posed no major problem to Israel.[5] This has come as a surprise. Before the

1967 war, Israel held only 20,600 square kilometers in Palestine and had a minority (mostly Arab) population of 400,000. In 1973 Israel controls the whole of Palestine west of the Jordan: 27,400 square kilometers with 1.4 million members of "minority groups," or 36 percent of the total population of 3.9 million under Israeli authority. The war thus led to an increase of 250 percent in the size of the Arab population under Israeli administration and to an increase of 33 percent in Palestinian areas under Israeli control. Economically, however, integration did not involve problems of the same magnitude. In 1971 Israel's gross national product reached 22 billion Israeli pounds. By way of contrast, the combined gross national product of the West Bank and the Gaza Strip for the same year was reliably estimated at 850 million Israeli pounds. This would suggest that the economies of the "administered" areas generated together less than 4 percent of the Israeli GNP, an order of magnitude that poses little difficulty for integration.

Integration of the Arab work force in the "administered territories" has also been resolved. The Jewish population of Israel is estimated at 2.5 million. The addition of 1 million Arabs has not had an economic impact proportional to the size of the Arab population. Israel's total work force is in the neighborhood of 1 million while the *total* work force of the Arab West Bank and the Gaza Strip is estimated at 180,000 persons, or only about 15 percent of that of Israel. In 1972 reports showed that up to 50,000 Arab workers from the West Bank and the Gaza Strip were employed in Israel, i.e., almost one-third the total work force of the territories. This has led to the appearance of local labor scarcity in the teritories, and it is hard to contemplate that many more Arabs could be available for work in Israel without damaging the local economies of the territories. These laborers, who are not permitted to settle on the Israel side of the pre-1967 border, or "green line," have taken home some 300 million Israeli pounds in salaries and benefits which account for nearly one-quarter of the total gross national product of the West Bank and the Gaza Strip. The influx of new monies in the territories has created an unprecedented prosperity there, largely dependent, however, on earnings in Israel.

The work force from the administered areas has been a boon to the labor-strained Israeli building industry and to the West Bankers themselves. It has brought considerable benefits to the Israel economy as a whole. While daily average earnings in the West Bank had been in the range of 7.50 Israeli pounds per day, in 1971 they averaged 11.00 Israeli pounds for Arab workers in "Little [or pre-1967] Israel." This figure is still below that paid to Israeli workers, but it has acted as a magnet on Arab laborers. In 1972, as a result of a labor shortage in the booming construction trades, Arabs were reported to be earning nearly as much as their Israeli colleagues. Integrating a 4.5 percent increase in Israel's labor force has thus been easy. Additional laborers may even have to be brought to Israel from countries such as Turkey and Iran to meet the needs of the local labor market, very much as West Germany[6] and Switzerland import foreign workers.

In agricultural matters, a common market now practically exists between Israel and the territories. The agricultural produce of the West Bank and of Gaza amounts only to some 18 percent of Israel's total agricultural production, even though the labor force employed in Israeli agriculture is estimated at some 65,000, a figure comparable to the 60,000 employed in agriculture in the "administered territories." In 1968 the Israeli Ministry of Agriculture developed a five-year plan for the West Bank. At that time the plan did not speak in terms of the integration of the two agricultural economies, rather it spoke in terms of cooperation and coordination between them. Since then, the picture has changed entirely. The introduction of Israeli agricultural methods, technical training, and advice have led to a sharp increase of average yields. Production of wheat and barley, which was about 80 kilograms per dunam, has now climbed to some 250 kilograms per dunam, with reports of yields of 400 to 600 kilograms per dunam. In December 1971 the last barriers to the free flow of agricultural produce from the territories to Israel were removed.

The resulting prosperity in the West Bank is reflected in a number of indicators: agricultural revenue has increased from 135 million Israeli pounds in 1967–68 to 226 million pounds in 1970–71. Personal income per capita has risen from 670 Israeli pounds to 1,100 Israeli pounds; the GNP of the West Bank has doubled. And, a sure indicator of rising prosperity, the number of TV sets has risen from 8,000 to 40,000. In 1971 alone, private consumption increased by some 25 percent. This process of growth continues.

Trade with the territories shows the same patterns. Figures for 1970 suggest that the West Bank sent 50 percent of all its exports to Israel, the other half going to the East Bank of the Jordan, while the Gaza Strip exported one-third of its produce to Israel. Imports to these territories from Israel accounted for 85 percent of all imports in the West Bank and 92 percent of all imports in the Gaza Strip. The trade deficit for the territories was covered by workers' earnings in Israel and remittances from workers in Kuwait and other Arab states.

The prosperity now characterizing economic life in the territories, however, developed without any significant industrial growth in the territories themselves. In 1968 the Military Administration proposed a development budget of 100 million Israel pounds. It was not adopted by the government and very small development budgets were granted. In 1972 development monies ran out in the first two months of the year.

Opposition to the full economic integration of the territories has largely come from Finance Minister Sapir. He has objected, for example, to the integration of the public services of the West Bank and Israel. Thus, the electric grid that was supposed to connect the West Bank and Israel remains at the planning stage. If the government had wanted to adopt the Dayan plan, it would, for example, have given the Israel Electric Corporation approval and support for the absorption of tens of thousands of electricity consumers on the West Bank. Instead, five years after the war, not a single town in the West Bank outside of Jerusalem is connected to the Israeli electricity-grid network. Some points on the edges of the West Bank may be connected soon, and the city of Hebron may also get its power from Israel. Within its province of authority, in dealing with public services and industrial development, the Ministry of Finance has tried to slow down the fusion of the economies of Israel and the territories. Indications are that this resistance is being overcome by the successful establishment of an agricultural common market and of a common labor force linking the territories and Israel in a chain of irreversible relationships.

The impact of the economic policies pursued in the territories is pervasive. The following report by S. Tevet, a distinguished Israeli author, reflects the trend in the West Bank in 1972:

> On 13 August [1972] the Agricultural Fair of Nablus began. The sight was in the nature of an unbelievable miracle. In Nablus, the biggest city in the West Bank, the rebellious city, the nationalist city, the city which gave rise to the school strike in 1967, that was the scene of student demonstrations in 1968 and 69, that refused to receive a loan from the Government of Israel and refused on many occasions to hold an Agricultural Fair exhibiting the achievements of Israeli knowhow and training, in the same city of Nablus you could find on one platform the Minister of Agriculture Chayim Gvati and the Mayor Haj Maazuz El-Masri watching athletic demonstrations by the students of Nablus and flag parades, with an orchestra of wind instruments dressed in white and velvet and red hats. The Haj Maazuz El-Masri greeted the visitors to the Fair and his visitors, among them the Representative of the Government of Israel. Chayim Gvati wished the farmers of Nablus and the farmers of Judea and Samaria progress and bright prospects for the future. As I stood in the crowd of the Agricultural Fair in Nablus I was struck by the change in the character of the Military Administration that no longer relies on coercion. At first everything depended upon coercion, upon the threat of military force: the shopowners strike was broken by the cancellation of licenses to do business, the transportation strike was broken by the cancellation of the bus company's license, and the non-cooperation of Nablus was overcome by economic sanctions. In 67, 68 and even in 69 when I visited the area at the request of the Military Governor, I needed an escort to go to the Casbah and to the market. I was then advised to acquire personal arms, just in case my car would get stuck somewhere. But today, in 1972, I fix my appointments alone, I arrive at the houses and offices of my hosts without escort, and my car did indeed get stuck but without incident. Those who saw me in their houses and who spoke to me did so most freely. I saw the parallel between my personal experience and the economic events: the Agricultural Fair was not imposed on the city or on its

inhabitants. The producers who showed their products did so quite freely and those who accepted the prizes (agricultural implements) from the hands of the Minister of Agriculture Chayim Gvati, did so of their own free will.[7]

The territorial integration of the Gaza Strip is also underway. Ever since Minister Gallili announced in the Knesset in March 1972 that the government would never agree to the separation of the Gaza Strip from Israel, active steps have been taken to break up the continuity of Arab settlement in the Strip. In the Rafiah area 200,000 dunams were fenced off and Jewish settlements established on publicly owned land at the southern end of the Strip. This was done over the protest of left-wing parties objecting to the brutality and harshness with which Bedouins squatting on these lands were evicted. These protests led to a Commission of Enquiry and the disciplining of senior officers. Further plans for a new town, Yamit, have also been completed at the initiative of General Dayan who faces stiff opposition to this project. In the West Bank, urban development in the Jerusalem region and in Qiryat Arba, near Hebron, on Jewish and public owned lands may be followed by another town-development project at Maale Edumin, east of Jerusalem, on the Jericho Road for which land has been dedicated. Little, however, has as yet been done to create "new facts" in the West Bank along the lines contemplated by the Dayan plan, apart, that is, from the chain of settlements in the Jordan river valley which Allon has also advocated.

Early in 1973, Y. S. Shapiro, then minister of Justice, advanced a proposal to allow controlled Israeli land acquisitions in the West Bank. General Dayan strongly supported the idea, but a major public confrontation between him and Minister Sapir and Allon then seemed unavoidable. After some hesitation Mrs. Meir, prodded by Mr. Sisco, cast her authority against the plan and a bruising intraparty fight was narrowly avoided. Before the 1973 war, the idea was included in the Labor alignments' program in the "Gallili document" which attempted to reconcile the views of Dayan and his opponents in the party.

Full pacification of the territories was secured in part by the carrot-and-stick policy adopted by the Military Administration and in part by the collapse of the resistance movements in the West Bank which followed King Hussein's military suppression of the Palestine guerrilla organizations during the Black September events in Jordan in 1970. This collapse enabled the Military Administration to emphasize liberal policies in its efforts to pacify the territories. In 1972 the territories have become more peaceful and secure than most urban areas of the United States. No violence was reported even during the Yom Kippur war. The one hundred Fatah members who surrendered to Israel in the wake of the civil war in Jordan have all been released. Ten of them were not inhabitants of Palestine and returned at their own request to Syria and Lebanon, but most stayed on in the West Bank and were employed in a variety of jobs. Some even found employment in Israel. In 1972 the former mayor of Gaza, heading a delegation of dignitaries from the Strip, requested from King Hussein that he pardon terrorists from Gaza who had been condemned to death. The position of terrorists in Jordan is ironically graver than their position in Israel, which has no death penalty for them. The number of administrative detainees has fallen off. In the first year there were thousands. By December 1972, only 140 were left.

In October 1971, 3,687 convicted terrorists remained in prisons and camps; by the end of 1972 their number fell to 2,400. The first three years after the war saw deportations of resistance activists and sympathizers. Altogether 71 personalities were deported to Jordan. Beginning in 1970 there was a reversal of the process. Deportations have now ceased and the former deportees have been permitted to return home to the West Bank. Some 50 of the 71 have returned. Among the 21 who did not, two have been appointed to the Royal Jordanian cabinet.

Economic integration of the territories does not extend to political integration. In the words of General Gazit, the Coordinator of Government Authorities in the Administered Areas, the policy is meant to introduce "practical arrangements, which some day—in ten, fifteen or fifty years—will bring a viable peace to the Middle East." He said:

> We want as many people as possible in the occupied territories to have a direct physical interest in continuing their relations with Israel. This is where they can go to work, where they can get more materials for their industry, where they can have the market for their products and where they can get certain investments for certain industries. Or it may be a place from which they will get electricity for their villages. Only by having physical contact between the two areas, can we hope—and as I said at the beginning, with a lot of optimism—that within some ten, fifteen or fifty years, some practical arrangements of peace may be achieved there.

But this policy is clearly not meant as a prelude to the political integration of the West Bank into the State of Israel. As General Gazit said,

> What we want now is that wherever a political line will be established between Israel and the Arab States—whether it be Palestine or whatever they want to call it—it will be an open and not a closed line. . . . We are trying to establish physical facts which will not permit the re-establishment of the "green line." [8]

Still, these "physical facts" must not be allowed to contravene the fourth principle in the Dayan plan, that Israel must refrain from the inclusion of a large Arab minority in the Jewish state. Dayan's answer is to permit the integration of the Arab population economically but not politically. At present, West Bank leaders play a role in the political life of Jordan at the national level and enjoy popular participation in municipal life in the territories. The policy of separation is underscored by the resolve of the Military Administration not to permit the thousands of Arab workers in Israel to settle even temporarily across the "green line" and to require them to return every day by bus to their homes and families.

Minister of Transport Shimon Peres, a close ally of Dayan, has advocated the establishment of a "Canadian type" political solution for the West Bank, which would enter into some kind of federal relation with Israel. But General Dayan has not yet made his final views on the political future of the territories known—this is an issue that is not ripe for determination. In the meantime, the political near-autonomy of the territories is psychologically encouraged by the reduction of the Israeli presence there to almost invisible levels. Out of the 8,500 government employees in the West Bank, only 196 are Israelis. Military forces are rarely seen, and the police force is made up of West Bank residents. Anwar Nusseibeh, a former Jordanian minister, has confirmed that Israel's forces in the West Bank are far smaller than those maintained there by Jordan during its rule. The sense of autonomy is further encouraged by the intense movement of people to and from the Arab world. In 1972, 161,000 "summer visitors" crossed from Jordan to the occupied West Bank. More Arabs than Americans toured Israel in that year.

Finally, a measure of genuine political autonomy has also been made possible by the scrupulous hands-off policy of the Military Administration in the municipal elections held in 1972 and by the emergence of a truly free Arab press, a unique phenomenon in the Arab world outside Lebanon.

The emancipation of one in every three Arab laborers in the West Bank from dependence upon the traditional ruling class has triggered a genuine social revolution. Suddenly cast under a foreign occupation requiring collaboration, and no less suddenly threatened in their authority over their own people, the propertied and professional classes in the territories have lost a great deal. Doctors, lawyers, landowners, businessmen, and officials, led by the Tuqans, Nusseibehs, Canaans, El Masris, and other families who occupied the apex of the tranquil social pyramid under Hashemite rule, have been brutally brought face to face with the egalitarian pressures of Israeli society and the unstylishness of their new rulers. The acute economic and class distinctions which maintained the gentle agrarian, gentrylike life style of a privileged Anglicized class have been undermined by the Israeli occupation. Their laborers now earn more in Israel, and no longer look to them for sustenance; even women begin to look for employment in Jewish areas. Positions in municipal councils in the little towns of the West Bank under military rule, journalism, the cultivation of private business interests, and Court politics in Amman are the only remaining outlets for this proud and able group that in years past ruled Palestine in semifeudal style. The alternative of resistance to Israel or to the king has proved too onerous; emigration means ultimately the loss of everything.

Squeezed by Israel's presence into participation in the political life of Jordan and the search for professional positions in the relatively less developed countries of the Arab world, West Bankers have maintained with Israel's encouragement the integrity of an educational system leading to studies in Arab universities in Arab countries. Efforts are made to encourage young Arabs in the West Bank to pursue their studies elsewhere in the Arab world, even though this means exposing them to anti-Israeli propaganda and incitement.[9] The government in Amman is allowed by Israeli authorities to make up examinations and matriculation certificates, tying the careers of young Arabs in the West Bank to life in the Arab world rather than in Israel.

The upper middle class of the West Bank, a vocal and often charming social group, enhanced in Western eyes by adherence to patrician ways and Anglo-Saxon manners, is paying the cost of Israeli occupation. They provide the only contact with outsiders, since the masses of the people remain as always beyond the pale of social intercourse. They have monopolized the voice of occupied Palestine. Yet Israel continues to rely on this class for the administration of the territories and the preservation of peace. Aware that the occupation threatens their national aspirations and their class interests by the emancipation of Arab labor, the military government has been careful not to abandon this class to the tide of social change. The military government is dealing with the local ruling class and maintains its rule through it. It did not try to use the municipal election to have them voted out of office. The old Jordanian law, which gave the vote to only some 30,000 property owners (less than 5 percent of the total population) in the West Bank, was allowed to stand without change for the elections of 1972. Effective participation in the elections was very high and reached 90 percent of registered voters in the city of Nablus. Unavoidably the elections helped the rise of a new generation unwilling to follow in the path of the elders. Inhibited by the Geneva Conventions, the Israeli Military Administration is indeed doing little directly to reform the semifeudal West Bank social structure which has allowed neither universal suffrage nor unionization, but economic upheavals and the new prosperity have already done much to shake the foundations of this society. The revolution in agricultural techniques and yields, for example, has spread Israèli influence even to rural areas.

Ironically, the leftist elements that most oppose continued Israeli occupation would objectively contribute by ending the occupation to the perpetuation of the quasi-feudal society maintained by the Hashemite king. Few can doubt that the Arab society now undergoing the most sweeping process of social and economic change anywhere in the Arab world inhabits the Israeli "occupied territories."

Mercifully, this argument is not invoked by any segment of Israeli opinion to justify the occupation. There is no missionary pretense to "sell" occupation policy, either within Israel or abroad. There is no pretense that the occupation is popular or that the West Bank Arabs welcome it to achieve the transformation of their society. Few in Israel would deny the comment by a prominent Arab personality, Anwar Nusseibeh, that "physically, we Palestinians do not suffer from Israel's occupation. However, spiritually we suffer very much."

CRITICISM OF THE DAYAN PLAN BY THE DOVES AND THE LIKUD

The success of the Dayan plan so far has swollen domestic support for the thesis that it is possible to absorb the territories without having to face the consequences of political annexation. Criticism of the Dayan plan has also been considerable. It has focused on a number of issues. First, it is argued on security considerations that the creation of "facts" in the form of a checkerboard of Jewish-Arab settlements will lead only to a desperate tangle of an insoluble character, not unlike the mix of Greek and Turkish populations on Cyprus, or the Protestant and Catholic populations in Northern Ireland. Some of this criticism is reportedly orchestrated by Finance Minister Sapir who is a leading contender to succeed Mrs. Meir as prime minister. He argues that the security of Israel is not enhanced by this pattern of development. A new generation of trained enemies, well versed in Israeli ways and ideology and familiar with the Israeli mentality and the Hebrew language, is bound at some future time to take advantage of the open borders and to spread terror deep inside Israel. From there, the Left claims, the distance to police repression, strict security measures, and other coercive moves is a short one. Nor, so Mr. Sapir and other prominent labor leaders argue, is it possible to ignore the demographic challenge posed by 1 million Arabs merely by channeling the political life of the territories toward what is happening in Amman. The issue of self-determination for West Bankers cannot be resolved in that way. Local pressures for local institutions, local universities, and eventually local autonomy and even independence will accentuate with the emergence of a leadership estranged from blood ties and family connections with the old West Bank ruling classes loyal to the king in Amman.[10]

Mapam critics in particular are concerned that the habit now being acquired by Israelis of disregarding the wishes of a large minority will lead to abuses in the "administration of the territories," particularly since the state of war can be used to justify all measures and since Black September excesses can be counted on to rally support behind the government. The Left opposition parties have linked the "irregularities" and harshness in the treatment of Arabs at Rafiah, Aqraba, Berem, and Iqrit into a significant chain of incidents, revealing a disposition to repress minority populations and to stifle criticism in Israel of that repression. The domination of Arabs and the subjugation of an alien nation are seen as betrayals of Israeli ideals that will sooner or later make themselves felt also in Israel's own political life. Powerful voices, within and outside the Labor party, claim these attitudes are linked to the widening socioeconomic gap within Israel and to the insensitivity of the government to the destiny of Israel's Oriental Jews.

Opposition to the unchecked flow of Arab laborers from the territories is swelling even within the government. Arabs are engaged in construction jobs, work as farmhands, and do a variety of manual jobs displacing Jews, so it is argued, from the manual labor that socialist Zionists have traditionally insisted must be done by Jews in a rebuilt Israel. Cheap Arab labor is seen as a threat to Israel's domestic structure and moral fiber—especially if existing patterns continue. In some trades, e.g., the building trade, 50 percent of all laborers are Arabs. Despite clear government directives to the contrary, Arab workers from the territories tend to settle in makeshift hovels near their places of work. They are paid less than Israeli workers, are not unionized, and do not benefit from the equal wages and social services available to their Israeli brethren. Critics reject arguments tending to equate the position of laborers from the territories in Israel (only 4 percent of Israel's labor force) with that of foreign laborers in Switzerland and in Germany. The new relationship between Israel and the territories, they claim, shows characteristics of neocolonial rule and cannot be compared to the situation in Europe, where foreign labor does not come from an occupied nation.

The major effect of the Black September movement's 1972 terror strikes at Lod airport and Munich has been to dampen criticism of Dayan's policies and to isolate the champions of Arab rights. Israeli liberals, who had managed to shake Israeli public opinion over the government's decision not to permit the return of Israeli Arab villagers to their homes in Berem and Iqrit near the Lebanese borders, which they had vacated during the 1948 war, fell silent once again.

No one in Israel pretends that military occupation is popular. But criticism of the Dayan policies remains rhetorical, since few Israelis would be prepared to turn the territories over to King Hussein, to the Palestinian organizations, or to launch them on a danger-ridden future of independence. The moral and ideological revulsion against prolonged occupation is a potent force in Israeli life—but a force that can find no outlet for as long as the Arab states refuse a territorial compromise as a basis for peace with Israel. Perhaps the strongest, most widely shared objections to Dayan's integration policies, however, rest on the "demographic" threat of an Arab population explosion that would erode the Jewish character of the state, a question to which we shall return.

It is necessary also to mention critiques from the opposition "Likud" and the National Religious party. These parties account for much, but by no means all, the support for the "Land of Israel Movement." They are firmly opposed to a new partition of Eretz Israel. This stand is central to their electoral program. Revisionist leaders such as Menahem Begin and Ezer Weizmann have pleaded energetically for the outright annexation of the whole West Bank and Gaza Strip and for the offer of Israeli citizenship to all their inhabitants. They object to the hypocrisy of creeping annexation, to the dangers of its excesses, and to the professed readiness of senior cabinet members, including Mrs. Meir herself, to return as much as two-thirds of the West Bank to Jordanian rule under a peace agreement. The emotional attachment and religious associations with such places as Samaria, Beth-El, and Hebron, and with the centers of the ancient Kingdom of Israel and the heartland of the Kingdom of Judea, nourish a broad alliance of poets, writers, officials, and orthodox Jews, for whom to part with any parcel of the Holy Land, now that it is finally again in the hands of the children of Israel, would be a sin in the eyes of God. The fervor and passion of this movement takes many forms. For example, a conference was held on the sanctity and unity of the Land of Israel. Arguments based on Talmudic texts were advanced to prove that even the Golan Heights were sanctified in the practice of the Elders: "The Tosseftah [to the Talmud] informs us that it is forbidden to sow, to plough or to work the Land in Syria in the seventh year. Such works are prohibited in the Land of Israel and since they were also prohibited in Syria, it is agreed that Syria is part of the Promised Land which moreover was occupied by the tribe of Manasseh."

General Weizmann, in his inimitable way, has castigated the "dwarfs of faith" who are willing to abandon parts of the Land of Israel for fear of an Arab majority. "Who is afraid of the annexation of one million Arabs?" he asked.

> All those who fear forty Arabs in the Knesset [for a total of 120 members] do not put faith in Jewish immigration, in a great increase of the Jewish population of Israel. They propose to build the State of Israel not on vision, not on a great faith, but on narrow and cramped borders. These men of little faith have something wrong with their basic Zionist understanding. The solution to the Arab problem is in the hands of Israel, and Israel cannot put it in the hands of anyone else.

Weizmann observed that some ministers already speak in clearer terms: to remain on the Jordan River; to establish civilian settlements, not just military camps, and a city in Hebron. Allon proposes another city at Maale Edumin. The defense minister supports the establishment of Jewish settlements in Judea and Samaria.

> So what is all this game about? Why is it necessary to confuse the Public? It is necessary to state to the world at large, and also and perhaps especially to King Hussein, that if he wishes to make peace with Israel the door is open, but he will not regain either Judea or Samaria. He is not the master there. He has no right to rule there and no claim of right. Even the West Bank Arabs do not

> want him there anymore after the great massacre which he made among their brothers in his country.
>
> Remain in peace in your Kingdom, this we must tell the King, and manage the affairs of your country. If you want peace—there will be peace if you do not want—there will not be any. This is not what really matters. What matters to us is peace with Egypt. And you, King Hussein, with your little country, your unimportant and unstable little country, you do not speak in the name of the Arabs of the West Bank and you have little importance in our eyes.

General Weizmann goes on to say,

> Let us state openly, loudly, clearly: this is the new State of Israel, with the Gaza Strip with Judea with Samaria with one Constitution and one law. And to all the new Arabs, that would be annexed to us, we would propose exactly what we proposed at the time to the Arabs who were with us during the Six Days War, equal conditions, equal rights to vote for the Knesset and to sit in Parliament, everything that the citizens of Israel have here.[11]

Weizmann's views stand in sharp contrast to those of A. Eliav, former secretary general of the ruling Mapai party, published in an important book, *Glory in the Land of the Living*, in the summer of 1972. Animated by a concern for the moral integrity of the Israeli position, rather than by the "demographic threat," Eliav calls for an Israeli "Balfour Declaration," this time for the Palestinian Arabs, which would declare the willingness of the government of Israel to see the establishment of an independent Palestine Arab state in the territories now occupied by Israel and east of the Jordan in the kingdom of Jordan.[12]

The fateful elections for the Knesset, which were originally scheduled for what turned out to be the middle of the 1973 war, are bound to be dominated by the conduct of the war. The heated debate on the future of the territories belongs to what now seems to be the remote prewar era. The dominant triumvirate of Golda Meir, Gallili, and Dayan find themselves called to account not only for the war they failed to foresee but also for the peace they had failed to achieve. Mrs. Meir's adviser and friend, former Justice Minister Shapiro, declared that he did not believe that this triumvirate would be able to bring peace to Israel and that it also bore heavy responsibility for the failures preceding the war. These elections will determine the future orientation of Israel at a crucial time in the nation's destiny.

THE ALLON PLAN

The Allon plan was the first major blueprint for both long-range and short-range policy planning to have been presented to the government very shortly after the 1967 war. It is based on five principles:

—the historical right to settle the land of Israel with due regard for demographic factors in the area, as the moral basis of the plan;
—the demarcation of defensible boundaries, as the geo-strategic basis of the plan;
—the maintenance of the Jewish character of the State of Israel, as the national basis of the plan;
—the promotion of a social-democratic character and basic structure for the state, as the social basis of the plan;
—the acceptability to the world of the State of Israel so constituted, as the diplomatic basis of the plan.

The future map drawn by Mr. Allon is based on these principles: the Jordan River to the Dead Sea and a median line crossing the Dead Sea from north to south must become the eastern frontier of Israel. Allon has made it plain that such a line must not be a security boundary only, it must be an effective political border as well. But it would not lead to the annexation of most of the West Bank territories lying west of the boundary. Under the plan, Israel would acquire for security purposes merely a strip of uninhabited land 14 kilometers wide in the Gilboa region and 24 kilometers wide near Hebron. This strip of land constitutes about one-third the area of the West Bank. This defense area would be immune to attacks by armored enemy forces and could withstand assaults from modern, Westernized armies. The Jordan River, which provides an excellent antitank defense, the mountain slopes between the river and the ridges dominating it in the west, the network of hills and mountains, and the few natural passes, turn this area into a major military obstacle. The West Bank areas that would be returned to Arab rule would, moreover, be demilitarized. Israeli control of the Judean desert would secure Jerusalem from guerrilla forces, while local border changes would have to be agreed upon in the Latrun region and near the Etzion settlements south of Jerusalem. Jerusalem would remain united under Israeli sovereignty. A special status over the Muslim holy places in the City would be granted to Muslim authorities. Such borders would also provide Israel with an excellent base for counterattack should hostile forces mass east of the river. They would give Israel a defensive line "against all of Asia."

Mr. Allon shows sensitivity to the national aspirations of Palestinians in the West Bank. To permit them to lead a national life of their own, whether within a common framework with Jordan or separately from Jordan, his plan provides for a corridor "for peaceful ends" linking the city of Ramallah through Jericho to the Allenby Bridge and the East Bank.

Allon considers that east of the Jordan River a Palestine community living under Arab rule already exists in Palestine. It is, therefore, wrong to claim that the Palestinians do not yet have a national home. They possess one: Jordan, east of the river, is such a national home. To call it Jordan, Trans-Jordan, or Palestine is beside the point. Allon is fond of repeating that a Palestine Arab entity has never existed. The concept of Palestine is relatively new. Even in the golden age of Islam, there was no Palestine-Arab state. Under Muslim Ottoman rule, all the territory later known as Palestine formed part of an area governed from Damascus. During British rule, Arabs in Palestine claimed for some time that they belonged to Syria. They never requested independence for the Palestine-Arab people or for a Palestinian nation, and they never claimed a Palestine citizenship. In November 1947, when the UN General Assembly adopted the Partition Resolution, there was no Palestine-Arab entity ready and able to accept the establishment of an Arab state. But, Mr. Allon concedes, we are *now* witnessing the formation of a Palestinian nation.

Allon is not hostile to the establishment of a Palestinian state in the West Bank areas from which Israel would withdraw. Shortly after the Six-Day War, he supported the grant of autonomy to West Bank Arabs without precluding the return of the West Bank to Jordan. He thinks in terms of an eventual association between either two or three states: Israel, a Palestinian West Bank and Jordan, or Israel and Jordan only, should the West Bank Arabs agree to return under the king's rule. Allon is by no means ready to disregard the wishes of the West Bank population in reaching an agreement with King Hussein. This is not simply a matter of conscience or sympathy. A stable peace must satisfy the national aspirations and pride of the Palestinian Arabs on the West Bank and must provide for a settlement of the refugees question.

Allon believes that his plan would safeguard the Jewish character of the State of Israel and at the same time preserve the geo-strategic integrity of all Palestine west of the Jordan. Like Dayan, he is unwilling to stand still and await developments in the Arab world. He advocates the continued settlement of agricultural and urban communities in the territories he has earmarked for incorporation. Jewish settlement in those strategic areas should be promoted at once and will help determine the map of the future. But just as Jewish settlements should help frame such a map, no settlement should be established in the areas that Israel would relinquish under a peace agreement. In the first five years following the Six-Day War, a chain of settlements were established along the Jordan Valley, some civilian and some semimilitary. Created in uninhabited regions, these settlements did not involve the confiscation of land or the eviction of former owners. The building of security roads and the construction of a barrier along the Jordan River system has already been completed. While Allon does not preclude the grant to Jordan of a free port in Gaza, his whole approach is based upon formal territorial boundary changes. He does not make allowances for the sharing of sovereignty or the other "complicated" arrangements preferred by Dayan. He is thus also exposed to the criticism, leveled by General M. Peled, against Dayan, that the contemplated territorial expansion of Israel is contrary to the expectation of peoples and states at this stage of history.[13] From the Likud's perspective, his plan is worse than Dayan's.

An agreement with Jordan based upon the Allon plan could become vulnerable indeed to claims resting on modern principles of international law. The Vienna Convention on the Law of Treaties provides, for example, that "A treaty is void if its conclusion has been procured by the threat or use of force in violation of the principles of the Charter of the United Nations"; and further, in Article 50, "A treaty is void if it conflicts with a peremptory norm of general international law from which no derogation is permitted and which can be modified by a subsequent norm of general international law having the same character." This provision is enhanced by another, which states that "If a new peremptory norm of general international law of the kind referred to in Article 50 is established any existing treaty which is in conflict with that norm becomes void and terminates."

Evidently, in such an international climate the conclusion of treaties providing for border changes and the acquisition of land following an armed conflict could remain the subject of international contention in the United Nations.

Restated briefly, the Allon plan provides for the acquisition of largely uninhabited territories not involving the annexation of populations; the Dayan approach is more complex. Neither contemplates a return to the pre-1967 status quo.

In many respects, the Allon plan and the Dayan plan share common features. These provided the basis for the "Gallili document." Neither General Dayan nor Mr. Allon are ready to incorporate 1 million Arabs into the political lifestream of Israel. Nor are they ready to return *all* the West Bank and the Gaza Strip to Israel's adversaries. But where General Dayan thinks in terms of continued Israeli military presence and of a lengthy, complicated transition in the West Bank leading to economic integration with Israel and political association with Jordan, Mr. Allon continues to emphasize the importance of a territorial arrangement with King Hussein. In the short run, he is opposed to economic integration and advocates cooperation and coordination instead. He is prepared to return to Jordan the inhabited two-thirds of Judea and Samaria. The central feature common both to the Dayan and Allon plans has already been implemented: the establishment of a string of settlements along the Jordan River Valley and on the heights near the Dead Sea.

THE NARROW OPTIONS

The experience of the 1973 war, the parameters drawn by the Allon and Dayan plans, and the new relationship between Jews and Arabs west of the Jordan, limit the range of peaceful solutions.

Difficulties of a "classical" solution. A "classical" solution is one based on a boundary, a partition, or some other arrangement that separates one side from the other clearly and unambiguously. The difficulty lies in the fact that the interests of Jews and Arabs in Palestine are increasingly meshed in a cunning design of mutual dependence and advantage. Moreover, the expectations of the parties and the attitudes of the international community discount every one of the classical solutions: (1) an Israeli withdrawal to the June 4, 1967, lines; (2) full annexation of the territories by Israel; (3) a settlement based upon the annexation by Israel of only the uninhabited areas of the West Bank; or (4) an independent Palestinian-Arab state in the West Bank.

A total Israeli withdrawal to the June 4, 1967, lines, with or without tangible and invulnerable security arrangements for Israel, is hardly conceivable in the present state of Israeli politics. Israel still bears the scar of the great emergency of 1967 when King Hussein's forces shelled the new city of Jerusalem and the Tel Aviv area despite Israeli entreaties that he keep out of the war. This wound was reopened by the Yom Kippur attack in 1973. Tangible and invulnerable security arrangements, moreover, would require Israeli military presence in evacuated Arab territories for some time, a presence that would necessarily be vulnerable to the goodwill of the restored Arab sovereign and to UN pressures against the stationing of military forces in foreign lands. Presence under agreement would be more vulnerable to the termination of consent than the existing presence without consent. Presence open to UN pressure could be fragile indeed, because of Israel's notorious disadvantage in the UN arena.

Full annexation of the territories, advocated by Mr. Begin and adherents of the "Land of Israel Movement" would deepen the Arab-Israel war to an extent not contemplated even by today's pessimists. It could provoke extreme responses from Jordan, the Arab world, and even from Israel's allies in the United States. The lifeline between the West Bank and the rest of the Arab world that flows across the Jordan bridges might then be severed by the government in Amman. The political backlash to annexation could well jeopardize the economic and security achievements of the Military Administration so far. It would, moreover, meet widespread opposition in Israel among those preoccupied with the maintenance of a Jewish majority in the state.

A settlement based on the Allon plan and involving cession to Israel of one-third of the West Bank's unpopulated areas would invite revisionist claims fueled by Israel's dominion over a united Jerusalem. Even if such a settlement could conceivably be extracted from the Jordanian king as part of a mutually advantageous deal including facilities in Gaza for Jordanian trade and recognition of the king's responsibility for the Palestine Arabs in general, it would nevertheless remain exposed to the implacable hostility of the Palestine resistance organizations, of Libya, and of other countries in the Arab world. The removal of Hussein, the advent of Palestine nationalist rule in Amman, or the rise of a new leadership along the West Bank could jeopardize a treaty involving the cession or lease of territory. The very nature of the concessions expected from Jordan under the Allon plan would weaken Palestinian support for a settlement involving the grant of Palestinian lands to the Jews. The Allon plan tends, therefore, to an accommodation with King Hussein, isolated as he is from much of the Arab world. That such a deal is not ruled out, despite the isolation of Jordan, reflects the solidity of the Jordanian establishment in Amman. This establishment is credited with an ability to survive even the departure of the much-threatened king himself.

Finally, an independent Palestine-Arab state on the West Bank of the Jordan, supported by men such as Mr. Shihadeh and some Israeli personalities, was bitterly opposed by the Palestine Liberation Organization and by Jordan. It has its share of enemies in Israel. From Mrs. Meir down, it is widely believed that a state such as this would remain enfeebled, crisis-prone, and exposed to social and political upheavals directed against Israel. Mrs. Meir has stated again and again that there is room for only two states in historic Palestine—one Jewish and one Arab—and that a third cannot be successfully established. After the 1973 war, there are indications that the Soviet Union was urging the PLO to change its policy and support the idea of a Palestine West Bank state, thus posing a threat to the two U.S. allies: Israel and Jordan.

A genuinely independent Palestine-Arab state would in all likelihood resist the territorial adjustments and security arrangements that Israel could conceivably extract from Jordan. It may, moreover, advance territorial claims of its own, inspired by the 1947 Partition Plan boundaries adopted by the UN General Assembly which contemplated the creation of two states west of the Jordan River, one Jewish the other Arab, and which attributed to Israel an area much smaller than even the area secured by the armistice lines in existence *before* the 1967 war. In such favorable political terrain, the spread of Arab terror could not be ruled out. On the other hand, an independent Palestinian Arab state, reasonably friendly to Israel, would be dismissed by militant Arabs and Palestinians as a neocolonial Israeli creature, a Middle Eastern Bantustan. A move in the direction of an independent Palestine entity, dismembering in effect the Jordanian kingdom, would also trigger the implacable hostility of the Jordanian ruler. Bourguiba's advocacy of the idea led to a break in relations between Tunis and Amman.

The weakness of all four "classical" solutions leaves the Dayan plan center-stage in Israeli politics, if only because it requires no Arab consent and addresses itself not to the problems of a peace settlement but to the policies preceding the still-elusive peace. It has led Dayan to discount "classical" solutions and to look for courses of actions that are certainly neither simple nor clear-cut: a Palestine regime that would be tied to Israel economically but not politically.

No Israeli initiative. The drawbacks of all four "classical" solutions, the divisions in Israeli political life, and the precarious balance of coalition politics have immobilized the Israel government. They have kept it from adopting or rejecting the Allon plan, from drawing a map or deciding on a negotiating position with Jordan. In the meantime, the Dayan plan is working to the satisfaction of the coalition partners, despite occasional rumblings from the Mapam wing of the Labor alignment. Caught between the "demographic threat" inherent in the full annexation of a fast-growing minority and the aspiration for dominion over the whole of Eretz Israel nourished by the National Religious party, the government has adopted neither the Allon nor the Dayan plan. Cabinet committees decide on security matters, on new settlements, and on other questions affecting the territories. The new settlements established in the territories have so far been largely confined to areas outlined in the Allon plan for retention. Mrs. Meir has said that under an agreement with Jordan, Israel would withdraw from many areas in the West Bank. The Allon plan has become a "minimum" for the Israel government, which is considerably worried by the demographic consequences of permanent Israeli rule in all the territories.

The strange balance and immobilism of Israeli coalition politics could thus leave King Hussein with the advantage of initiative. He is in a good position to move the Israeli government in one direction or another. The king's choice is not an easy one. It would be complicated by the readiness of the Palestinian organizations to take part in a peace conference. The most he could conceivably obtain from Israel is a peace agreement based on the Allon plan. His readiness to make a deal on the Allon lines could generate more support for the plan within the government in Jerusalem. On the other hand, for King Hussein to permit the status quo to continue would leave two dynamics unchecked: the continued ingestion of the territories by Israel, and the emergence of a new Arab leadership in the territories estranged from the king's own rule.

The context for the king's choice is a fluid one. Two dynamics—Israel absorption of the territories and the new Arab leadership there led him in 1972 to move ever more closely to serious negotiations about the future of the West Bank. From Jordan's perspective, it is difficult to determine whether the Dayan or the Allon plan is more bitter. The Allon plan calls for deep formal boundary changes, while the Dayan plan requires a deep de facto sharing of authority in the territories. Some other solution may also be hammered out on an interim basis that would contradict neither the Allon nor the Dayan plan. For example, a "coalition civil administration" in the territories might be one such outcome.

The great Israeli debate on the future of the territories revives long-dormant issues about the partition of Palestine. Annexing the territories means annexing their population as well, unless an "east Jerusalem Solution" is contemplated. (Israeli law was given effect in East Jerusalem but the Arab population has the option of retaining its Jordanian citizenship or taking Israeli citizenship.) The inhibition against annexation is not the product of world opinion nor of Arab threats nor again of any alleged principle of international law, but "demographic." It is the fear that annexation may lead to a binational state with a large Arab minority; that it would turn the wheels of fortune back to the regime advocated with passionate humanism in the 1930s by Judah Magnes and Martin Buber. They advocated binationalism as a way to avoid Arab-Jewish wars, but their position was rejected both by the Zionist movement and the Arab leadership. Now, ironically enough, binationalism again has a chance, owing to the Israeli victories which put more than one-half of the Palestinian Arab nation under Israeli rule.

Faced with the stark choice between holding onto all the "Land of Israel" at the cost of turning the country into a binational state and withdrawal from most inhabited Arab territories to maintain an overwhelming Jewish majority in the state, most Israeli leaders strongly lean to the second alternative. By the end of 1972, Mrs. Meir and Ministers Sapir, Eban, and Allon had all taken a strong stand against the inclusion of a large Arab minority. The secretary general of the Histadrut, Ben Aharon, has gone so far as to suggest that Israel should unilaterally return part of the West Bank to Jordan in order to choose her own borders with due regard to demographic factors. Even General Dayan has said that *if this* were the choice, he would not favor annexation. This position was forcefully and unattractively expressed by Mrs. Meir when she said she does not want a binational state in which she would rise every morning with the fear that yet another Arab child may have been born into it. The Israeli leadership seemed to be more alarmed by long-run prospects of communal parity than by security threats involved in territorial concessions. Whether this is still true after the Yom Kippur attack remains to be seen. The Jewish nation, a persecuted minority for millennia, is not about to become a near-minority in its homeland—maintenance of the Jewish character of the State has higher priority than the annexation of territories. No more dramatic proof of the intensity of the yearning of the Jews to live in peace among themselves as masters of their destiny can be seen than in their readiness to surrender cherished territories in the Land of Israel to achieve that goal. A Hebrew culture, a Jewish way of life, the celebration of ancient feasts, and historical continuity with biblical times have priority over the urge to rule throughout the historic Land of Israel. The Jews want some place on earth as their own, some place they need not share with outsiders, even if this means a small, cramped national home, smaller than the one they are tempted by their victories and their history to keep.

General Dayan argues that the question of annexation or no annexation is a pseudo issue. King Hussein will simply not accept the Allon plan in its entirety or even in an emasculated version that has the reputed support of Ministers Sapir and Eban. Dayan based his policy on the continued Arab refusal to compromise. Since the government of Israel is not prepared to yield *all* the territories back to the Jordanians, and thus put the most populated areas of Israel again within conventional artillery range of Arab guns, the prospects for a full peace with Jordan remain dim. Dayan holds, therefore, that the price of formalizing the peace with King Hussein would be very high and its advantages modest.

The true question, according to Dayan, is not what kind of peace to conclude with the Jordanian monarch but how to find a "durable arrangement" for Israel's relations with the territories. Relations can be stabilized, living conditions made attractive for all, a measure of friendly coexistence developed; but a formal agreement remains beyond reach. The dangers of binationalism and the "demographic" fears that agitate the establishment need trouble them neither in the immediate future nor in the fairly lengthy period that follows. The peace negotiations outlined in Security Council Resolution 338 may provide a further test of Dayan's policies. Dayan thought that peace and its "demographic" dilemmas were still some ten or fifteen years away.

The recurrence of history is bewildering. The Jews debate the future of the "territories" and Arab-Jewish relationships; the Palestinians debate the coming battle. In 1972 as in 1947 as in 1917, the Arab position remains the same:

> . . . Palestine would be an "Arab State." This does not mean that those citizens who are not Arabs would be in any sense persecuted or discriminated against, or made to feel that they are outside the full community of the State; but it means that the Government and its citizens should accept the implications of the fact that the majority of the inhabitants are Arabs and that Palestine geographically and historically is part of the Arab world.

This was the position of the Arab Office before the Partition Resolution of 1947.[14] *Plus ça change* . . . only short memories and ignorance guard against weariness in this perpetual conflict.

"No Palestinian Arab politician had ever openly negotiated with Jews and signed an agreement with them." As a result the only serious plans for Palestine (Eretz Israel) are those that could be implemented unilaterally, by each side, without recourse to agreement. Israel's new coexistence with the Arabs in the territories is still based on ultimate reliance on the Israeli Army. General Dayan, for one, has no illusions on this score. He believes that if and when Israeli forces withdraw, no Jew will have a foothold left there. Whether imposed coexistence can ever lead to genuine coexistence is anyone's guess.

King Hussein's Plan for the Future

The Palestine refusal to accept the existence of a Jewish state has been extraordinarily consistent and resilient. The rejection of the Balfour

Declaration, of the Palestine Mandate, of the 1937 Peel Royal Commission recommendations and those of the Anglo-American Commission of Inquiry of 1946 as well as of the United Nations Partition Resolution, all display consistent adherence to the position set forth by Hussein, king of the Hejaz, before the Versailles Peace Conference, when he proposed that

> Palestine be constituted into an independent state with a national government representing all the inhabitants, including the Jews; that it be expressly allowed the faculty of joining a Federation of Arab States; and that its "political and economic freedom" must in no sense or degree fall short of that of the other Arab States.[15]

The blueprint for a state in Palestine, spelled out in the Palestine National Covenant of 1968, is essentially similar to the proposal of the Hejazi king half a century ago. The Palestinian National Covenant still firmly rejects the idea that Palestine is the national home not just of the Arabs but of the Jewish people as well. It firmly rejects everything that has happened in Palestine since 1917. Neither the Versailles arrangements, nor the wars of 1948, 1956, and 1967 altered the Palestinian position. The occasional attempts by Jewish leadership to gain consent of the Palestinian Arabs, such as the decisions of the 1921 Carlsbad Zionist Congress which spoke of Palestine as the "common home" of Jews and Arabs whose upbuilding was to "assure to each of its people an undisturbed national development," [16] and many other attempts at rapprochement during the fifty years that followed, failed to modify the Palestinian position.

As far as the Palestine Liberation Organization is concerned the establishment of the State of Israel is as "null and void" as the Balfour Declaration, as the Mandate document, and as the Partition Resolution of 1947. The Palestine resistance continues to look at Jews in Palestine not as a national group, not as a people, but as individuals of a particular religious faith for whom there exist no *national* rights of any kind in any part of Palestine, however small it may be. As stated in Article 20 of the Palestine National Covenant:

> The claim of a historical or spiritual tie between the Jews and Palestine does not tally with historical realities nor with the constituents of statehood in their true sense. Judaism, in its character as a religion or revelation, is not a nationality with an independent existence. Likewise, the Jews are not one people with an independent personality. They are rather citizens of the states to which they belong.

In other words, neither the Jews nor the Israelis nor the Hebrews are entitled to self-determination, or to a national home of their own, since only a *people*, such as the Palestine-Arab people, can be endowed with these rights. The Palestinian position rests on this dogma, it rests on the refusal to recognize the right of Israelis and Jews to claim status as a people. It rests on a denial of the national rights of this ancient nation. This position remains central to the Palestine nationalist resistance and anchors one pole of Arab attitudes in their disaster-ridden rejection of the Jewish state.[17]

The intense gravital pull of the policy adopted in the Palestine National Covenant has shifted the whole spectrum of Arab politics even further away from acceptance of the Jewish national presence. Hence, any indirect or ambiguous readiness expressed by Arab states to "enter into peace agreement with Israel," is construed as the height of radical moderation bordering upon the treacherous betrayal of the Palestine cause. This is the ideological setting for appraising the relatively daring move taken by the Arab Republic of Egypt and by Jordan in their "favorable" responses to Ambassador Jarring's memorandum in 1971 in which they expressed readiness "to enter into a peace agreement with Israel."

This is also the setting for evaluating King Hussein's "historic speech" of March 15, 1972, and his plan for the future of Palestine in which he proposed that,

1 The Hashemite Kingdom of Jordan shall become a United Arab Kingdom, and shall thus be named.

2 The United Arab Kingdom shall consist of two regions:
  a the region of Palestine, and shall consist of the West Bank and any further Palestinian territories to be liberated and whose inhabitants opt to join.
  b The region of Jordan, and shall consist of the East Bank.

3 Amman shall be the central capital of the Kingdom and at the same time shall be the capital of the region of Jordan.

4 Jerusalem shall become the capital of the region of Palestine.

5 The King shall be the head of the State and shall assume the Central Executive Power, assisted by a Central Council of Ministers. The central legislative power shall be vested in the King and in the National Assembly whose members shall be elected by direct and secret ballot, having an equal number of members from each of the two regions.

6 The central judicial authority shall be vested in a Supreme Central Court.

7 The Kingdom shall have a single armed forces and its Supreme Commander shall be the King.

8 The responsibilities of the Central Executive Power shall be confined to matters relating to the Kingdom as a sovereign international entity ensuring the safety of the Union, its stability and development.

9 The Executive Power in each region shall be vested in a Governor General

> from the region, and in a regional Council of Ministers also formed from citizens of the region.
>
> 10 The Legislative Power in each region shall be vested in a People's Council which shall be elected by direct secret ballot. This Council shall elect the Governor General.
>
> 11 The Judicial Power in each region shall be vested in the courts of the region and nobody shall have any authority over it.
>
> 12 The Executive Power in each region shall be responsible for all matters pertinent to it with the exception of such matters as the Constitution defines to be the responsibility of the Central Executive Power.
>
> It is obvious that the implementation of this proposed plan will require the necessary constitutional steps and the Parliament shall be asked to draw up the new Constitution of the country.[18]

Despite ambiguous references in the speech to the "goals of liberation," presumably of all of Israel and not only of the territories lost in the 1967 war, and despite indications that Jerusalem would remain the capital of the Palestine region, his speech generated intense hostility in the Arab world. The Council of Presidents of the Arab Federation of Egypt, Libya, and Syria rejected the plan in no uncertain terms. Six characteristic reasons were adduced by Dr. El Khatib, the minister of state for foreign affairs of the federation government,

1 The plan provides favorable grounds for the implementation of imperialist designs, is intended to liquidate the Palestine people and to destroy the unity of the Arab nation.
2 The plan determines the future and the destiny of the Palestine nation in its name and in its absence.
3 The plan raises a new framework for the Palestine state intended to liquidate the Palestine problem and is opposed to the struggle of the Palestine people for the liberation of the occupied lands.
4 The plan is designed to strike at the Arab nation and to transform the Palestine problem and the occupation of the other Arab territories into a regional conflict on boundaries.
5 The United States, with its military and economic support for the Zionist forces of aggression, supports the plan.
6 This plan would block Arab efforts to find a solution that would permit Palestinian fighters to return to their bases (in Jordan).

The spokesman of the Executive Committee of the Palestine Liberation Organization leveled five accusations of his own against the king. In the first place, the PLO asserted that the people of Palestine alone can decide its own future and the future course of the Palestinian nation. Second, the Palestine resistance was created to liberate Palestine and the occupied territories while the Jordanian regime has insisted on offering itself as an accomplice of the Zionist enemy, tolerating the Zionist presence and the Israeli occupation. Third, King Hussein has been striving to establish a feeble Palestinian entity which he could control and has sought to justify the brutal massacre of members of the Palestinian people. Fourth, the king is playing in the Arab area the role of intermediary in breaking "the isolation of the Israeli wild beast" and setting it loose on the Arab nation and the rest of the Arab countries through an "Arab Kingdom."

Israel's reaction to the speech was also downright hostile. Determined to hold her government coalition together, to dispel any thoughts that a secret agreement had been reached with the king and embarrassed by statements of Secretary Rogers and Mr. Sisco about the king's impending speech, Mrs. Meir said in the Knesset:

> The announced plan of King Hussein cannot serve as a basis for an agreement with Israel. Attempts to create the impression that this is an agreed plan or that it is based upon talks with us are laughable. This whole plan is a surprising invention of its author.

The vehemence of the rejection was prompted by the news stories preceding the much-heralded speech as well as by the king's efforts to influence the impending elections in the "occupied territories." The government of Israel deeply resented the unilateral character of the proposals, the pretense to dispose without Israeli agreement of territories under Israeli control, and especially the references to Jerusalem as the capital of the Palestine region.

The king's speech served as a signal to a wave of Israeli claims. It led to Minister Gallili's statement regarding the integration of the Gaza Strip in the State of Israel, to disclosures about plans for settlement of the Rafiah area, to disclosures of the principles of the Dayan plan, and to a statement by Allon that he intended the Jordan River not merely to be Israel's "security boundary" but her political boundary as well.

In an important interview, Yigal Allon indicated that Israel's reaction to the king's proposals was motivated by his failure to refer to Israel's existence and by his omission of any reference to the need for a peace agreement. According to Allon, the king's references to Jerusalem as the Arab capital of the Palestine region could only be frivolous, while the territorial map that the king had in mind must be rejected in the most categorical terms. Allon insisted, however, that the heart of the king's proposal for a Jordanian-Palestinian federation on both banks of the Jordan does not stand in necessary contradiction to his own plan, and that he sees no reason to oppose the federal idea. The West Bank Palestine state has received no formal endorsement as yet by any Arab state or organization.

The king's proposal remains an important document. It is the only Arab initiative regarding the future of Palestine, the only authoritative blueprint except for the Palestine National Covenant.

President Sadat has so far refused to outline his views on what a settlement of the Palestine question should look like. He insists that a settlement must be made by the Palestinians themselves. Egypt's position on the future of Palestine is far from clear. It is sufficient for the purposes of this essay to note that Egypt remains disposed to sever negotiations on the question of Sinai and the "peace agreement with Israel" from the intractable question of Palestine.[19]

The Missing Plan

The peace negotiations contemplated in Resolution 338 of October 22, 1973, require some form of accommodation not only between the positions of Jordan and Israel, but also between their positions and those of the Palestinian organizations. This accommodation will be necessary whether or not the Palestinian organizations take part in any peace conference. For the Soviet Union, at any rate, is not likely to weaken its support for the "just national claims of the Palestinian people" if it can strike in this way a blow at both Jordan and Israel, the two countries most closely tied to Washington in the area.

Sophisticated discussions in Israel about the historical existence or actual reality of Palestinian nationalism and of a Palestine national home east of the river in Jordan reflect the creeping recognition by Israel of this new force in her immediate environment. Although some distinguished Israeli experts, such as Y. Harkabi, believe that the Palestinian national movement is declining, recognition of its vitality cuts across party lines and ideologies.

King Hussein's "historic speech" in which he recognizes the Palestine entity in the West Bank and offers a new association between Jordanians in the east and Palestinians in the west eloquently attests to the divisions between the two Arab populations. While more than one-half of Jordan's population east of the river is Palestinian, there is little doubt that the Palestinians now regard themselves as a distinct people. This distinctiveness purports to be more than a regional difference and can be accounted for only in terms of the wider concepts of Palestine nationalism. Palestinians and Jordanians alike are careful to leave the door open to the possibility of a future association between them. The Palestine Liberation Organization, so ruthlessly suppressed during the civil war in 1970, takes the position that "there is nothing wrong with the relationship between the two peoples [of Jordan and Palestine]; they are only threatened by the Jordanian regime and by the King himself who has always played this sinister regionalist card, and is still doing so."

A settlement with Jordan, either on the Dayan or on the Allon lines, or even along those proposed by King Hussein, will *not* meet the essential demands of Palestinian nationalism. Under the king's plan the Palestinian people would remain truncated: over 400,000 would remain citizens of Israel, 1 million would inhabit the Palestine region of a United Arab Kingdom, some 700,000 would live in the Jordan region, and 250,000 refugees would be left in Lebanon, Syria, and other countries of the Palestine diaspora. The proposed Arab kingdom would, moreover, remain under the domination of the king and his Jordanian establishment. The sizable Palestinian leadership groups that gravitate around the Palestine resistance organizations, lavishly nurtured by Libyan, Kuweiti, and other funds, are not likely to find a place in the king's scheme, even if they were so disposed. The name "Palestine" would appear on no map, and its flag would not fly at the United Nations. Palestinian institutions and life would remain subjected to federal institutions in Amman while the search for professional and political career outlets for this most advanced of all Arab peoples would lead to the continued emigration of the able to other lands. The king's plan would not quench the militant ambitions of nationalists in the resistance movement or justify the extraordinary costs of half a century of warfare. Nor would it meet the political expectations of a generation rising in the cramped horizons of a Palestine region that would remain subject to the rule of a regressive, Bedouin-led establishment in the Kingdom's capital in the barren hills of Trans-Jordan. Under the Hussein plan, Palestine would even before its emergence into independence be pressed into association and subjection to Trans-Jordanian masters. Nor would the Hashemite regime satisfy radical Palestinians who place the building of a just Arab society ahead of nationalist aspirations and who dread a return to the deadening rule of Amman.

To meet Palestine nationalist aspirations, a Palestine settlement would have to go further than either Israel or Jordan is now disposed to go. It is hard to conceive how enduring Palestinian support for a settlement could be secured without providing in some measure for:

—the establishment of an internationally recognized Palestinian entity affirming the right of the Palestinian Arab people to self-determination in Palestine;
—a common national personality for Palestinians in the three parts of Palestine (Israel, the "administered territories," and Jordan) and in the Palestinian diaspora;
—Palestinian institutions for Palestinian nationals;
—a just solution of the Palestine refugees problem;
—guarantees for the protection of Palestinian economic and political life from domination and interference by outsiders;

—a viable economy with outlets to the sea and the Arab world as well as to all other countries.

Realization of some of these goals might help vindicate Palestinian nationalist aspirations and restore the wounded pride of this Arab nation. Any Israel-Jordan arrangement aiming at stability must secure the backing of Palestinian Arabs. Any agreement on the Dayan, Allon, Hussein lines would be strengthened if provision were made for the participation of the Palestinians. Without it, all that would be achieved is an interstate accord with neither depth nor popular backing in the Arab nation. It would rest on power relationships exposed to internal turmoil. An Israel-Jordan agreement would fall short of a Palestine settlement to the extent that it fails to fulfill at least some of the basic goals of Palestinian nationalism. The question of a settlement meeting the aspirations of the Palestine Arab peoples would remain. This will be a clear challenge to any forthcoming peace conference.

The Palestine Liberation Organization and the Future: Symmetrical Perceptions and Asymmetrical Positions

The position of the Israel and the Palestine Liberation Organization reflect a certain number of symmetrical perceptions, i.e., perceptions that in their opposition reveal a degree of similarity.[20]

1 *The unity of Palestine—Eretz Israel as one country.* The question, What is "Palestine" or "Eretz Israel"? must be faced squarely. As a political entity it included at the time of the original League of Nations Mandate both the West and East banks of the river Jordan, namely all the territories presently under Jordanian and Israeli rule (except for Sinai and the Golan). The British administration in Palestine subsequently divided the mandated territory into two parts, Trans-Jordan and Palestine, limiting the application of the Balfour Declaration governing the right of the Jewish people to a national home in Palestine to the West Bank of the Jordan River only. Until the termination of the Mandate in 1948 Palestine was administered by the mandatory power as *one* territory. There never were two mandates, one west of the Jordan and the other east of the river.

Since 1917 the territorial unity of "Palestine" has remained manifest. On this, both Israeli nationalists and the Palestine Liberation Organization agree. Palestine, Falastin, or Eretz-Israel as it is known in Hebrew, has therefore long been regarded by both Palestinian Arabs and Israeli Jews to include the territories on *both* banks of the Jordan River. Under the Partition Plan of 1947, historic Palestine would have been divided into *three* states: an Arab state and a Jewish state on the West Bank as well as Trans-Jordan east of the river.

A deep change may be at hand. Reports suggest that some Palestine organizations would favor taking part in a peace conference and might support the Palestine state idea.

There is still agreement at this time among Israel, Jordan and the Palestinian organizations that there should be *no* separate Palestinian state limited to the West Bank areas occupied by Trans-Jordan in 1948 and conquered by Israel in 1967. That view is not so widely shared by the West Bank leadership.[21] Israel, the Jordanian government, and the Palestine Liberation Organization do not wish, each for reasons of their own, to see such a West Bank state emerge. On this question, however, many surprises are possible. Historic Palestine on both banks of the Jordan may therefore remain a two-state system. Within these historical boundaries, forms of association acceptable to both the Jewish and Arab peoples must be designed.

Article 2 of the Palestine National Covenant, the basic instrument of the Palestine resistance, provides

> Palestine with its boundaries that existed at the time of the British Mandate is an integral regional unit.

The article is vague on the question whether Trans-Jordan is included in the unit. The unity of "Palestine" is, however, a basic tenet of the Palestine organizations. This view is shared by the government of Jordan. At its Eighth Session in Cairo in 1971, the Palestine Liberation Organization resolved that

> Since the earliest times, a national link and a territorial unity forged by history, culture and language, tied Jordan and Palestine. The creation of one political entity in Trans-Jordan and of another in Palestine is not founded upon legality, nor upon the elements generally recognized as contributing to the establishment of a political entity.[22]

In February 1970 the Unified Command of the Palestine Resistance Movement adopted a number of resolutions to which all the various guerrilla and resistance groups subscribed. One of these stipulated,

> The Palestine struggle draws strength from faith in the unity of the people in the Palestine-Jordan region, as well as from the belief that the people of Palestine is a part of the Arab nation and that the land of Palestine is a part of Arab land.

A similar faith echoes in official Jordanian pronouncements. A Jordanian memorandum, submitted to the abortive Jeddah Peace Conference of November 1971 between the Jordanian government and the Palestinian resistance forces, proposed the following principle,

> The Hashemite Kingdom of Jordan in its two halves comprises one nation in one state. All citizens are represented by H.M. the King and the legal state authorities with their various agencies. The Kingdom is the principal base for the liberation of Palestine [territories constituting the State of Israel].

This principle was also reflected in King Hussein's "historic speech" on March 15, 1972, on the establishment of a United Arab kingdom on both banks of the Jordan River. The second of the basic principles of the proposed new plan—"the United Arab Kingdom shall consist of two regions: (a) the Region of Palestine, and shall consist of the West Bank and any further Palestinian territories to be liberated and whose inhabitants opt to join. (b) the region of Jordan, and shall consist of the East Bank"—affirms the unity of Palestine.

In his speech the king said:

> This Arab country is a country of all Jordanians and Palestinians alike. When we say Palestinians we mean every Palestinian be he in the east or west of this great world on condition that he should be loyal to Palestine and should belong to Palestine. Our call is . . . to proceed joining hands with kin and brothers to go ahead on a single path, unity in one front, clear in aims, so that all should cooperate to reach the goals of liberation and to build up the structure to which we all aspire.

This position echoes an earlier statement of 1964, before he lost the West Bank, that "Jordan with its left and right banks, is the ideal jumping ground to liberate the usurped homeland [Israel]." Anwar Nusseibeh, a Palestinian ally of the king, said recently, "The East Bank is an integral part of Palestine and belongs to us. That was the situation until 1922 when Churchill published the 'White Paper' in which he (1) guaranteed a 'National Home' for the Jewish people in Palestine and (2) fixed the mandatory borders of Palestine by transferring the East Bank of the Jordan to the Hashemite Dynasty." The Jordanian monarch formally affirms the unity of the Arab country of Palestine as the country of all Jordanians and Palestinians alike.

Hussein's assertion that Palestine is the country of every Palestinian in the world is paralleled in the doctrine affirmed by the Twenty-eighth Zionist Congress in Jerusalem held in 1972 which "declares that the right of the Jewish people to Eretz Israel is inalienable." This claim has been affirmed by the Knesset when it debated the prime minister's statement on King Hussein's speech in March 1972. On March 16 it adopted a resolution that "the Knesset affirms that the historic right of the Jewish people to Eretz Israel is inalienable."

In their dispute, the Palestine resistance, the Jordanian king, and Israel are in agreement on this basic point: Eretz Israel or Palestine is one country.

2 *The right of Jews to live in Palestine outside the boundaries of Israel and the right of Arabs to live in Israel.* The rights of Jews to settle in Palestine in the "administered territories" are recognized and affirmed by most members of the Israeli cabinet. They were included in the government's Basic Principles approved by the Knesset in December 1969: "Speeding up the establishment of security outposts and permanent settlements, rural and urban, on the soil of the homeland." The government decided, for example, to establish the town of Qiryat Arba in the vicinity of Hebron, without prejudice to the future agreed and secure boundaries with Jordan. These rights are a basic principle of the Dayan plan. The rights of Israeli Arabs to live in Israel as full citizens enjoying equal rights under the law are not contested in Israel.

The Palestine National Covenant recognizes the right of *some* Jews to live anywhere in Palestine (there would be no State of Israel under the Covenant plan). Article 6 of the Covenant provides "Jews who were living permanently in Palestine before the beginning of the Zionist invasion [in 1917] will be considered Palestinians." Harkabi has pointed out that the Article 6 reference to the beginning of "the Zionist invasion" is interpreted by resolutions of the Palestine Liberation Organization Congress to refer to the time of the Balfour Declaration in 1917.

The government of Jordan has not discussed the right of Jews to live on the Jordanian side of the frontier. However, under the 1949 armistice agreement with Israel it recognized Jewish rights of access to holy places on the Jordanian side of the armistice line and to the Mount Scopus area in Jerusalem.

3 *The rights of the Jewish and Palestinian diasporas to their country.* The rights of the Jewish people outside Israel, affirmed by the Knesset and the Twenty-eighth Zionist Congress, have been given legal effect under the terms of the Law of Return and the Israeli nationality law. The Palestinian Covenant provides in Article 3: "The Palestinian Arab people possesses a legal right to its homeland, and when the liberation of its homeland is completed it will exercise self-determination solely according to its own will and choice." Article 5 states that "The Palestinians are the Arab citizens who were living permanently in Palestine until 1947, whether they were expelled from there or remained. Whoever is born to a Palestinian Arab father after this date, within Palestine or outside it, is a Palestinian."

The Jordanian state adopted its own "Law of Return" shortly after the war of 1948, offering all Palestinians the possibility to acquire Jordanian citizenship.

The positions of the different sides, if somewhat symmetrical, are not informed by mutuality, thus:

—Neither the government of Jordan nor the Palestine Liberation Organization recognizes the historic right of the Jewish people to return to Eretz

Israel. The government of Israel does not recognize the right of "Palestinian" refugees to return to Israel.

—Neither the Palestinian Liberation Organization nor the government of Jordan recognizes the right of Jews to settle in the "administered territories." The government of Israel does not recognize the right of non-Israel Palestinian Arabs to settle in Israel.

—Neither the government of Jordan nor the Palestine Liberation Organization recognizes the right of the Jews in the disaspora to settle in Eretz Israel. The government of Israel does not recognize the right of return of Palestine Arabs to their homes.

This, however, is where the symmetry ends. *On a most vital point, there remains a basic asymmetry in the position of Israel and its neighbors:*

4 *Israel recognizes the rights of Arabs as a people to a state of their own within the limits of historic Palestine.* The government of Israel does not recognize, however, the right of West Bank Palestine Arabs to establish within the limits of historic Palestine a *second* Arab state in addition to Jordan.[23]

As already stated, the Palestine Liberation Organization does not recognize the national rights of Israelis or Jews as a people to a state of their own anywhere within the limits of historic Palestine. On this most crucial point, the position of the government of Jordan is ambiguous. On the one hand it had declared in a memorandum to Ambassador Jarring its readiness to enter into a peace agreement with Israel. On the other hand it is still committed to the liberation of the "usurped homeland."

Thus, there remains a fundamental asymmetry in the positions of Israel and her Arab neighbors with regard to the mutual recognition of the national claims of the Jewish and Arab peoples throughout Palestine-Eretz Israel.

No peace arrangement without justice to the Palestinians, no peace arrangement without security for the Israelis, no peace arrangements without full recognition of the legitimate rights of both Jews and Arabs to live as individuals *and as peoples* in historic Palestine can be either lasting or effective. The willingness of Jordan to enter into a peace agreement with Israel signifies a disposition for accommodation on a state-to-state basis. It falls short of an express recognition of the national right of the Jewish people to establish a state within Palestine—the issue that has bedeviled Jewish-Arab relations since the dawn of Zionism and which remains unsettled.

A Peaceful Solution?

The 1973 war has brought both total war and a peace settlement closer to the Middle East. It has even opened the way for a possible peace conference. But it has also deepened Israel's conviction that the Arabs remain determined to wipe Israel off the map, despite the cleverly limited Arab objectives in this latest round of fighting.

The qualified readiness of Egypt and Jordan to enter into a peace agreement with Israel was certainly not shared prior to the 1973 war by the Palestine Resistance Movement and by states like Libya and Iraq. The Palestine Covenant provides in Article 19.[24]

> The Partition of Palestine in 1947 and the establishment of Israel is fundamentally null and void, whatever time has elapsed, because it was contrary to the wish of the people of Palestine and its natural right to its own land, and contradicts the principles embodied in the Charter of the United Nations, the first of which is the right of self-determination.

It provides, moreover, in Article 9,

> Armed struggle is the only way to liberate Palestine and is therefore a strategy not a tactic. The Palestinian Arab people affirms its absolute resolution and abiding determination to pursue the armed struggle. . . .

In its 1970 accord, the Unified Command of the Palestine Resistance Movement resolved that

> Israel, by the very nature of its structure, is a closed racist society, tied to imperialism; by reason of its structure, the limited progressive forces there situated are unable to bring about the radical change which would abolish its racist and Zionist character tied to imperialism. Consequently, the goal of the Palestinian revolution is to eliminate this entity at the political, military, social, cultural trade union levels and to liberate Palestine completely.

As Harkabi observes,[25] in Palestinian eyes evil is inherent in Israel; there can be no hope for change so long as Israel exists. An "acceptable Israel" is a contradiction in terms. Therefore "the Palestine people and its movement struggle for total liberation and reject every peaceful solution . . . as well as Security Resolution 242 of 22 November 1967 which tends to the liquidation [of the Palestine Problem]." The goal is clear. It is restated in the 1970 accords:

> The goal of the Palestine struggle is the liberation of all Palestine [including Israel], in which all citizens would live with equal rights and duties, in the framework of the aspiration of the Arab nation to unity and progress.

Harkabi may yet be proved right that the Arab search for a political solution was merely a tactical device to put the blame on Israel for all the failures to reach an agreement and thus to increase her isolation in preparation for the war of 1973. The war may also have prepared the ground for a dramatic reversal in Palestinian strategy on the question of a negotiated settlement with Israel, but it is hardly conceivable that their final goal will be modified.

Despite their opposition, however, Israel and Jordan share some common perceptions that the Palestine resistance, because of its rejection of Israel, cannot share. It is not inconceivable that

—The two governments could agree, for example, that the national and ethnic character of Jewish Israel and of the Arab West Bank must be respected and protected and that peace arrangements must reflect the express wishes of Jews and Arabs to lead a separate existence free from domination or interference by outsiders.
—They could also agree, for very different reasons, on the need to prevent autonomous armed operations by Palestine resistance organizations.
—They already agree on the Open Bridges Policy enabling the Arab people west of the Jordan to maintain full relations with the Arabs east of the river and throughout the Arab world.
—They also agree on the principles of Resolution 242 of the Security Council as a basis for agreement, except for the depth of boundary modifications allowed by the resolution.
—They would agree that an agreement must be based on mutuality, fairness, and justice if such an agreement is to withstand the onslaught of those who oppose a peaceful settlement.
—The two governments could find common ground on the need to allow "self-determination" for Palestinian Arabs in the framework of a Jordanian federation. King Hussein's speech was intended to do just that. A peace agreement with Jordan, submitted to the free approval of the voters of Israel, Jordan, and the West Bank, would have deeper stability and legitimacy than an intergovernmental arrangement. It would, moreover, be an exercise of the right of self-determination by the peoples of Palestine.

This only partially outlines principles on which agreement is conceivable. But such an agreement would have to await a settlement with Egypt. On the other hand, the policies of the Military Administration in the territories provide a workable alternative to formal agreement that seems to satisfy even the inhabitants of the "occupied territories" themselves.

For the Palestinians in the territories and elsewhere, the choices are grim. The opposition of the Palestine Resistance Movement to the establishment of a "mini-Palestine" state in the West Bank has tarnished the idea. The hostility of Jordan and of Israel to this proposal have made it politically meaningless. But Soviet support for this concept and a Palestinian change of heart could well revive it. Memories of the 1970 civil war in the East Bank in which Palestinian guerrillas were slaughtered are still vivid west of the river. The West Bankers do not on the whole desire a return of Hashemite rule, especially if this means the erosion of the great economic gains made during the occupation. They also fear annexation by Israel; of this there is little doubt.

In these circumstances, and for as long as no revolutionary change takes place in Amman, West Bankers are content to endure the status quo which has the advantage of being officially characterized as "temporary."

The key to change lies, therefore, in three wholly different potential directions: (1) in the installation of a revolutionary or Palestinian regime in Amman, (2) in an agreement between Israel and Egypt that would pave the way for a Jordan-Israel accord; or (3) in court politics in Amman, should the prominent partisans of Trans-Jordanian separatism prevail and should they convince the king to sever the destiny of Trans-Jordan from the fate of the West Bank Palestinians. Such a development as well as a reversal in the positions of the Palestinian organizations could revive interest in proposals for a separate Palestinian entity in the West Bank.

An Israel-Egypt agreement is crucial for progress toward peace between Palestinians, Israelis, and Jordanians. Should Israel and Egypt fail to reach an understanding, or should a revolution in Jordan take place, another Middle East war would be likely to occur.

The consideration in this paper of model agreements between Israel and Jordan should, therefore, rest on a clear understanding that while the will to peace may now exist in Jerusalem and in Amman, this will is unlikely to be translated into political realities pending an understanding between Israel and Egypt.

PALESTINIAN VOICES

It would be unfair to the Palestinian cause to refer only to the relentless plans of the resistance organizations or to the dynastic ambitions of the Hashemite king. The PLO Covenant and Resolutions which deny all Jewish national rights absolve Israel from any effort at accommodation or compromise while the king's plan obviates the need for an accord with the Palestinian community, leaving the future of Palestine to be settled in an interstate agreement with Jordan. Yet the pulverized Palestinian community, truncated between Israeli, Jordanian, and other Arab rulers, is dominated by those two vocal parties, the PLO and King Hussein. They both share an interest in denying the emergence of spokesmen for the "silent majority" of the Palestinian people. It is an interest which moreover corresponds to Israel's own policy of opposing the emergence of a mini-Palestine state in the West Bank.

Discouraged by the Israeli occupation authorities, opposed by the king's men, and reviled as traitors by the resistance organizations, individual Palestinians have nevertheless made themselves heard in a halting and discrete debate intermittently pursued in the West Bank and in

Arab Jerusalem. Aziz Shihade, a refugee from Jaffa and now a Ramallah lawyer, has given expression to a strong current of West Bank opinion which seeks coexistence with Israel and the establishment of the Palestine Arab state that the Palestine Arab leadership had refused to set up in 1948. At that time it rejected the Partition Resolution and resisted with the support of five Arab armies the establishment of a Jewish state; it then demanded that all Palestine be Arab.[26]

The partisans of a Palestine state know well that Israel will not withdraw from the "occupied territories" before a peace agreement defines the secure and recognized boundaries. They concentrate instead on demands that without evacuating her forces, Israel should agree to a referendum to be organized and supervised by the United Nations.[27] This plan is vehemently opposed by King Hussein. As a result the mayor of Hebron, Sheikh Ali Al-Jabari, and personalities like Hamdi Canaan and Hikmet Al Masri, have been careful about the plan in order not to burn all their bridges in Amman.

A courageous West Bank personality, Mohammed Abu Shilbaya, in a recent book, *The Path to Salvation, Freedom and Peace,* recommended explicit recognition of the State of Israel with West Jerusalem as its capital, a state which would then live in peace with an independent Palestine state whose capital would be East Jerusalem. The "realistic and humanitarian nationalism" extolled by Shilbaya remains however, atypical even of West Bank attitudes that continue to take a guarded position on the national rights of the Jewish people to the Land of Israel. The cause of the Palestine state is now sustained as much by Israeli leaders like former Cabinet Minister Bentov of Mapam and intellectuals like General Peled as it is by the Arab leadership itself. The impact of renewed Soviet interest in this approach and of possible PLO support for it remains to be seen.

The Israeli administration's ban on organized political activities in the "territories" (other than municipal affairs) has not prevented the flowering of positions of all kinds. Some, like Raymonda Tawil, continue openly to reject the very existence of a Jewish state in Palestine and advocate instead "a binational democratic state." The program for a secular democratic state in Palestine has been exposed on many occasions notably by Fayez Sayegh, an able Palestine diplomat, in the service of the Kuweiti government,

> Neither an *exclusionist "Jewish State,"* existing in all or part of Palestine at the expense of deprived Palestinians, nor a *restored Arab Palestine,* in which the non-indigenous Jewish immigrants cannot aspire to have a place, fulfills the requirements of [the] vision. Neither an Arab Palestine from which alien Jews are transported wholesale or "thrown into the sea," nor an Israel from which the displaced indigenous Palestinians remain barred and still more are "tossed into the wilderness," can fit the description of that vision.
>
> Nor can a *"binational" state,* in which the barriers between the component "nationalities" are institutionalized and therefore perpetuated, promote prog-

> ress toward that vision. For a "binational" state is nothing but a coalition of once-warring communities which have come to agree to coexist as distinct communities in an ever-precarious truce and in delicately balanced structures, which preclude the possibility of the emergence of a true community coextensive with the state.
>
> Only in a *New Palestine* can the presently incompatible positions of both Parties be creatively transcended and a just peace established. The vision of a pluralistic Palestine on whose once-hallowed now-bloodied fields and hills indigenous Palestinians, Christian and Muslim, and non-indigenous Jews will live together: neither claiming the country as his alone, whether by right or by conquest, but each looking upon the land as the common domain of all. Muslim, Christian and Jew will freely intermingle to form an authentic human community, and will cooperate to set up a *pluralistic, humanistic, secular and democratic* state, of which all will be equal citizens and all devoted builders. Distinguished by fate, cultural or ethnic origin, and will nonetheless be joined together by the bonds of their common humanity, their common citizenship and their common dedication to the general good of their state.[28]

From an Israeli perspective, the realities of this program as informed by the debates of the PLO has a wholly different, sinister resonance. At its Tenth Extraordinary Session, the Popular Congress and the National Palestine Council reaffirmed in 1972 the aim of the PLO to liberate all the territory of the Palestinian homeland. The plan for a democratic secular state in Palestine has not in any way modified the resolve of the PLO to continue its armed struggle. Similarly, a PLO reversal in the Palestine state issue would not alter its final goals.

THE VIETNAM PEACE AGREEMENT—A MODEL FOR THE MIDDLE EAST?

The Vietnam peace agreement contains features that would meet with resistance if attempts were made to include them in a future Mideast settlement. This is particularly true regarding the provisions for international guarantees and for international inspection and supervision.

The Vietnam Paris Agreement reflects, however, some fundamental principles that are of direct relevance to the search for peace in the Middle East.

These principles would retain their full significance even if the Vietnam peace agreement were to collapse under the weight of violations. For they define what can be accepted as "honorable" for all parties.

1 *The unity of a country can be reconciled with the continued existence of separate states in that country.* This principle could be usefully applied in the Palestine context in which both sides affirm the unity of historic Palestine (Eretz Israel) as one country;

2 *The right of self-determination can be exercised by the people of one part of a divided country.* This principle could be usefully applied in the Palestine context with respect to the Palestinian people's right to self-determination in the areas of Palestine lying outside the agreed and recognized territorial limits of Israel.

3 *The hatred and enmity generated in a protracted war does not preclude the establishment of joint military machinery and joint commissions by the warring sides to police a cease fire to deter violations and to supervise the implementation of an agreement.* When the will to peace exists, the most unlikely events are possible. Thus, within thirty days of the bombing of Hanoi, American planes were permitted to land there and to furnish air transport facilities for North Vietnamese military personnel on their way to Saigon to participate with South Vietnamese officers in the work of Joint Military Commissions. The Four-Party and the Two-Party Joint Military Commissions are examples of security arrangements that can be implemented by adversaries within hours of a cease-fire. Joint Commissions for the implementation of security arrangements could provide the parties in Palestine (Eretz Israel) with a method of policing any territories from which Israeli forces might withdraw.

4 *The Parties to the conflict may decide to establish separate kinds of joint machinery for the disposition of security matters and for dealing with political issues. The two sets of machinery need not come into operation at the same time.* This central principle of the Vietnam agreement could assist the parties in Palestine in decoupling security arrangements from other issues. It would thus allow, for instance, the withdrawal of Israeli civil administration from selected West Bank areas in advance of the withdrawal of armed forces and the conclusion of other security arrangements.

5 *The parties to a conflict may choose to establish joint machinery for the implementation of an agreement between them rather than delegate it to an international instrumentality.* While the Vietnam agreements provide for an International Commission of Control and Supervision, it is noteworthy that the parties have resorted to joint implementation of key provisions of the agreements without reference to any international machinery and without assigning to the United Nations any role under the agreements.

6 *In a divided country the population, armed forces, and personnel of the component states are not "foreign" anywhere in that country.* The distinction between "foreign" and Vietnamese forces underlies the agreement and alone governs the status of forces from the North that may be still situated in the South. The withdrawal provisions of the Paris agreement apply to foreign forces only. Other clauses contemplate civilian freedom of movement.

This principle could facilitate the operation of Joint Military Commissions in territories from which Israeli forces might withdraw and clarify the status of nationals of the two rival states in Palestine everywhere in the country.

7 *Neither joint machinery nor international machinery established under the agreements need be stationed on a reciprocal basis in the territory of all parties to the conflict.* The International Commission of Control and Supervision and the Joint Military Commissions are to be based in South Vietnam only. This principle could obviate the need to station Joint Commissions and other control and supervision machinery for reasons of reciprocity only in territories other than those in which they would have concrete functions to perform.

8 *The parties to the conflict can meet, enter into agreements, and assume agreed functions in the territory of the adversary without prejudice to claims regarding formal recognition and the disposal of political issues.* This principle could facilitate the promotion of agreement between all parties to the Palestine conflict. It should be noted that under the Paris agreements, neither the governments in Hanoi, Saigon, nor the Provisional Revolutionary Government of the Republic of South Vietnam are called upon to recognize or accept each other's legitimacy and claims. This remains the case although North Vietnam, for example, is required to send to the South close to 1,000 military personnel and staff for the work of the Joint Military Commissions.

9 *The parties to the conflict may establish joint political machinery for reconciliation to promote concord, to perform administrative tasks and to organize elections.* The design of political solutions by joint reconciliation machinery is a model of great significance for Palestine. The principle of unanimity for the operation of joint political reconciliation machinery can be applied to reconciliation commissions composed of elected West Bank officials and Israeli and Jordanian representatives. This approach is gaining support in other situations. Joint technical machinery was established by the two German states under the December 1971 agreements between them; proposals for joint U.K.–Irish machinery for an interim solution of the Northern Ireland question were made by the Irish Democratic and Labor parties in Dublin late in 1972. Also in 1972, King Hussein referred to proposals for joint sovereignty in Jerusalem, a city which Israel is wholly determined to keep under her exclusive jurisdiction.

10 *The parties to the conflict may agree on the establishment of more than one type of line of division between them.* The Vietnam Paris agreement contemplates the creation of a cease-fire line in the South, it confirms the military demarcation line between the North and the South, and it refers to the international boundary line for all Vietnam. Each line of division serves a distinct function, with regard to the withdrawal of forces and with regard to military and political control. The Paris agreement, moreover, contemplates that the cease-fire line and the military demarcation line shall give way at an unspecified future date to the unification of the country. In the Middle East, agreement on more than one kind of dividing line could help solve questions of withdrawal, sovereignty, civilian control, demilitarization, and military control.

11 *The withdrawal of the armed forces of the parties need not be to the lines established in a previous agreement before hostilities began.* It will be remembered that the presence of North Vietnamese forces south of the DMZ has been characterized by the United States as an armed attack and an act of aggression. However, the armed forces of the North are nowhere specifically mentioned in the Paris agreement. The cease-fire in place leaves DRVN forces south of the demarcation line established in the 1954 Geneva Accord and confirmed in the Paris agreement.

12 *The parties to the conflict may agree on the nonintroduction of forces and military equipment in certain areas. Implementation of this agreement can be assured by the parties themselves through joint machinery set up for this task.* Article 7 of the cease-fire agreement limits the introduction of military reinforcements into South Vietnam. Similar provisions may be designed for areas from which Israel forces might withdraw.

13 *In the event the parties wish to involve some outside powers in a process of supervision and control, they can do so without reference to the United Nations, and without calling on the big powers.* This feature of the Paris agreements requires no elaboration.

These principles have enabled all sides in the Vietnam conflict to reach what they consider an honorable peace agreement. Whether or not the Paris agreements work, it would be difficult for the parties in the Middle East to maintain, in the wake of the Paris accords, that these principles are either unjust or dishonorable.

Evidently no principle and no text can be a substitute for a true will to peace. These thirteen principles which underlie the Paris agreement are of salient relevance in the Palestine conflict since, like in Vietnam, the parties have fought themselves to a standstill. The 1967 and 1973 wars have led the parties to an awareness that no further military solution is attainable. The Israeli leadership is fully aware that military victories are not likely to lead to changes in the Arab attitude to Israel. The leadership in Cairo and in Amman is apparently also aware that a military solution for the recovery of the occupied territories remains beyond their capability. In this stalemate a political solution alone remains possible.

But the war has also complicated matters. The Pearl Harbor style of the Yom Kippur attack has further exacerbated, if that was still possible, Israel's concern for her security. The consensus in Israel is that the desire for peace cannot be satisfied at the cost of security and that foreign guarantees, even those of the United States, are no substitute for security. The strategic depth of the Golan and the Sinai is credited with sparing Israel the cataclysm of an enemy invasion, and the country is united in the belief that the Arab aim remains the destruction of Israel.

At war's end, the Israeli leadership faced an agonizing dilemma: to shore Israel's defenses against future Arab attacks it must retain the strategic depth of the territories occupied in 1967, but to retain U.S.

protection against the very real danger of Soviet military intervention it will be required to yield most of the selfsame territories. Moreover, it needs America's help also to ensure fresh military supplies and replacements that a protracted war against Soviet supplied forces would require. This dilemma may yet prove too acute to bear and could push Israel over the brink into renewed warfare, especially as the long-term prospects of the U.S. global retrenchment would increasingly expose Israel to Soviet might. In such a conjuncture a showdown while America remains involved may be less frightening than in the forbidding future.

A revitalized leadership in Jerusalem may, however, find its way to agree to a delicate new security balance, provided Washington will not make the choices too hard to bear and that Cairo will be realistic about what a peace conference could yield. Moscow's separate interests and policies may, however, hold up any progress to an agreed settlement and perpetuate a situation that has given the Soviets such handsome political dividends in Europe and in the Arab world.

Twelve Points for a Palestine Settlement[29]

A specific model agreement between the parties reflecting these principles may be of interest. The principal points of this model are:

The parties could seek a preliminary agreement on the future status of historic Palestine–Eretz Israel and of the inhabitants of that country which would be submitted to a referendum by the two peoples of the country in the exercise of the right of self-determination. This would constitute an agreed framework within which the parties would undertake to find a just solution for the refugee problem; determine secure, recognized, and agreed boundaries; and agree on the future status of Jerusalem, leading to the establishment of a just and lasting peace.

The parties would recognize that reconciliation between Arabs and Jews in the country requires a vision of peace and justice based on a just settlement of the refugee problem, on respect for the rights of all Arab and Jewish inhabitants in Palestine–Eretz Israel within its historic limits, and on a mutual recognition and affirmation of the rights of the Jewish and Arab peoples in the country to self-determination free from the threat of force, from conquest and from dislodgement. No vision for a just and lasting peace can be imposed by force or by the threat of force, and the establishment of a just and lasting peace cannot be long delayed. Progress toward a just and lasting peace can be promoted by efforts to transcend the existing structures and normalize the relationship between the Jewish and Arab peoples on the basis of the following principles:

1 The unity of the whole of historic Palestine–Eretz Israel on both banks of the river Jordan as *one country* and one community of nations within the limits defined in the League of Nations Mandate.

2 Palestine west of the Jordan River is the national home of two peoples, the Jewish and the Arab people in Palestine–Eretz Israel.

3 Under international law, there can be two sovereign and equal states in one country.

4 The parties agree to establish a Joint All-Palestine Council of Reconciliation constituted of representatives of Jordan, Israel, and elected representatives of Palestinian Arabs. The council shall operate on the principle of unanimity. [The council shall perform civil administrative tasks in areas from which the Israeli Civil Administration shall withdraw.] It shall be located in Jerusalem.[30]

5 Nothing in these principles would preclude the establishment of appropriate forms of association between the Arab West Bank and Jordan in a manner compatible with the wishes of the two peoples in Palestine.

6 The national and ethnic character of the states in Palestine–Eretz Israel shall be respected and protected by appropriate legislation which would reflect the wishes expressed by those national and ethnic communities to lead a separate existence free from domination or interference.

7 The secure, recognized, and agreed boundaries between the states in Palestine–Eretz Israel and the status of Jerusalem shall be determined in other agreements on the basis of readiness by the parties to carry out in good faith Resolution 242 of the Security Council in all its parts and on the basis of these principles.

8 Security arrangements for territories from which Israel forces are withdrawn to agreed secure and recognized boundaries shall be established through Joint Security Commissions under separate agreements.

9 Any Palestinian Arab and Israeli Jew is in his homeland wherever he may reside in Palestine–Eretz Israel west of the Jordan. Each state shall retain the right to regulate residence requirements in its jurisdiction on the basis of these principles without prejudice to a just settlement of the refugee problem in accordance with the principles of Resolution 242 of the Security Council.

10 Citizens of the states who shall have been residents of their states for no less than [seven] years may at the same time be subjects of Palestine–Eretz Israel (e.g., citizens of Canada and of New Zealand are also British subjects). Jewish and Arab inhabitants of Palestine–Eretz Israel shall be free to elect between the citizenship of the states parties to this agreement and shall be entitled to bear Palestine or Eretz Israel passports in addition to passports of their country of citizenship. Palestine and Eretz Israel passports shall be issued under the authority of the Joint All-Palestine Council of Reconciliation.

11 No Arab or Jew who is a Palestine–Eretz Israel subject shall have the status of an alien in the state in which he is a permanent resident. Such permanent residents shall enjoy equal rights with the citizens of these states.

12 Citizens of the states parties to this agreement shall participate in national elections in the country of their citizenship.

These principles distinguish two tangled sets of problems:

—those arising about the *national* rights of the two peoples in Palestine;
—those arising about the relationship between the two *peoples,* the *states,* and the *land.*

These principles should permit a separate disposition of three aspects of the Palestine problem:

—the national right of the Palestinian Arab people to self-determination and to a national existence of their own;
—the individual rights of refugees and other victims of the Palestinian conflict; and
—the individual rights of the Arab inhabitants of Palestine throughout the country.

First, this model agreement outlines a framework for reconciliation between Israeli, Jordanian, and Palestinian claims as well as between the Jews and Palestinian Arabs.

Second, it provides for joint security machinery to promote an accord on security questions through joint military commissions, patrols, and the like. It provides also for joint political machinery to find a just solution to the refugee problem, to achieve reconciliation, perform administrative tasks, and assume, if need be, the civil administration of selected areas in the administered territories.

Third, it severs the search for agreement on the difficult issues of territorial boundaries and Jerusalem from attempts to settle the refugee problem, the creation of joint security machinery, and other matters on which early progress could be made.

Agreement on territorial issues and the status of Jerusalem would be sought either in parallel talks between Israel and Jordan or through the Joint Palestine Council of Reconciliation.

The "twelve points" model requires no particular territorial solution. It is equally consistent with the application of the Hussein, the Allon, or the Dayan plan. It severs the boundaries and Jerusalem issues on which these plans are divided, leaving them for separate disposition. Progress on the twelve points could thus be achieved without requiring a decision in favor of any particular territorial map or any particular form of association between Jordan and the West Bank.

The twelve-point model is designed on the assumption that the signature of a juridical instrument is powerless ipso facto to restore conditions of peace to the area. This could be done only in a *process* of developing and promoting conditions leading to a just peace. The joint political and joint military machinery is intended to provide instruments for the creation of these conditions of peace.[31]

With the onset of peaceful conditions through the satisfactory operation of this machinery, the salience of territorial and boundary questions would be diminished. These bones of contention, together with the question of the status of Jerusalem, may lose much of their sharpness and interest once an accord will have been reached on other issues that have poisoned relations between the peoples of Palestine.

Relatively complex constitutional and legal innovations for the separate disposition of questions involving sovereignty, self-determination, citizenship, nationality, immigration, and the status of Jerusalem should help meet the vital interests of the parties as well as dampen the emotional responses that a simple and easily communicable agreement would provoke. On highly emotional issues, complex arrangements may assist in the establishment of an atmosphere of détente. Joint machinery established by the parties for a performance of defined tasks could be designed, nevertheless, to insulate Israel and Jordan from mutual dependence that would be exposed to pressures and threats of noncooperation.

Essentially the Palestine blueprint should be in a position to meet Israeli demands for recognition of the independent, sovereign existence of the State of Israel and of Arab demands for the establishment of a democratic, secular, nonsectarian community in the whole of Palestine. The genuineness and vitality of the Arab vision for a unitary, secular nonsectarian state would be tested by the degree of cooperation between Arabs and Jews within the Palestine community. At the level of joint Arab-Israeli institutions, at any rate, the democratic, nonsectarian community could be brought into juridical existence while the independent sovereignty of Israel and of the Arab kingdom would continue unimpaired.

The value of symbols and of joint machinery designed to create frameworks for dialogue remains to be tested. So much else has been tried that there may be no harm in yet another experiment. The hard questions of security boundaries, Jerusalem, and the modus vivendi between the Arab and Jewish states would remain for separate disposition. But perhaps a tentative dialogue designed to reconcile at least the vision and program of both parties may be helpful even if other issues are unresolved. Dialogue on principles and joint machinery should now be tried.

There is something incongruous at first sight in considering models for structures common to the Arab and Jewish states in Palestine, when the immediate problems of war and peace remain so impervious to solution and while Israel remains deeply convinced of the Arab determination to destroy it. What is the utility, it can be asked, of considering common ventures when the root causes of conflict continue to fester? Encouragement can be found in the Vietnam Paris Agreement, which followed the same route.

The pattern of de facto coexistence and even cooperation, not only between Israel and the population of the "occupied territories," but also between Israel and Jordan suggests that a settlement of an associative character has in fact begun to develop. Dayan has characterized it as "creeping normalization." Whatever skeptics may object, the establishment of ventures common to Arabs and Jews is already a fact. The approach to peace in Palestine–Eretz Israel is inspired by the associative method, by the removal of barriers between peoples, not by their separation. It is an encouraging sign that the Palestine Liberation Organization printed in its Arabic language monthly a thoughtful piece by Ahmed Baha El Din, one of Egypt's most respected columnists, on the Twelve Points Model outlined in this paper.[32] It is not inconceivable that the PLO may eventually also be disposed to explore the associative approach to a settlement in Palestine.

In the intense passions of conflict, no credible *vision* of a desirable and feasible peace has yet emerged: neither Israelis nor Palestinians believe that a future settlement can bring more security than the status quo (for Israel) or more justice and vindication than a renewal of warfare (for the Palestine Resistance Movement). In this psychological deadlock, all negotiations and bargaining are perceived in Israel to lead to the erosion of a security position acquired at the cost of terrible wars. They are viewed in Palestine Liberation Organization circles as a betrayal of a just war and the heavy sacrifices already incurred. This shared perception that any settlement would be both insecure and undesirable magnifies the resistance of the parties to concessions and to the erosion of their political positions in the process of negotiations.

A credible vision of future peace that is both secure and just, stable and honorable, is required to constitute a climate in which negotiations do not merely involve the substitution of a shaky truce without security for the present security without agreement, or the substitution of a formal surrender in the place of an honorable refusal vindicating national honor. A vision of peace that the two peoples of Palestine can live with is perhaps necessary to set the stage for negotiations on the hard issues that political realists so correctly focus upon. This vision of peace must not, however, contemplate either a degree of cooperation or of friendly relations between Israel and the Palestinian Arabs that would now be regarded as utopian or distasteful.[33] It must not, moreover, lead to the postponement of negotiations on the difficult issues of boundaries and Jerusalem that could be pursued bilaterally or in the Joint Palestine Council. There may be virtues in images of the future involving a Palestine–Eretz Israel passport, of a Joint All-Palestine Council, and eventually even of a Palestine–Eretz Israel flag at the United Nations, flying side by side with the Israel and Jordanian flags. These images of national pride and national identity may deserve fuller exploration. Their impact may be beneficial—they may provide the impetus for a real start to a settlement.

The search for reconciliation formulas must take as a starting point the declared public positions of the parties. It is thus helpful to consider the program of the Democratic Popular Front for the Liberation of Palestine [FDPLP] for a democratic, secular state in Palestine at its face value along with all offers made by Israel to Jordan and to the Palestinian refugees.[34] This must be done in the lucid knowledge that many people believe that the Palestinian Organization's program is merely a euphemism for the destruction of Israel, while others believe that Israel peace efforts are merely political disguises for Zionist expansionism.

Accommodation formulas must necessarily be based upon the reconciliation of the rights of the Jewish and Arab peoples in Palestine, not merely their rights as individuals but also their rights to national existence as peoples within the narrow limits of the Palestinian territory. No asymmetrical formula denying the right to national existence of either people within a political structure of their own choosing can conceivably serve as a lasting foundation for peace in the Holy Land. Whether the refusal of some Israelis to consider the Palestinian Liberation Organization as a national liberation front is less justified than the refusal of Palestinians to recognize the Jewish struggle against the Turks and the British in Palestine as another liberation front is besides the point. Large bodies of opinion in both communities do and did regard themselves as waging a war of national liberation. This surely should be dispositive of the issue.

JOINT ARAB-ISRAELI INSTRUMENTALITIES

New juridical concepts and machinery can be developed for divided countries to help "restore" unity and unification while maintaining unimpaired the independence and sovereignty of the separate entities. They permit "having it both ways." In Palestine, such concepts could meet some demands of the Palestine Arab community.

The community of Palestine–Eretz Israel would provide a framework for an Israeli-Jordanian agreement based either on the Hussein, Allon, or Dayan plan. The community concept would fit in equally well with any of the major Israeli or Jordanian proposals. The main thrust of this concept is to ease the attainment of some Palestinian aims through the creation of a favorable political environment for reconciliation.

The establishment of a Joint All-Palestine Council of Reconciliation with defined tasks would moreover witness, on one juridical tier, the establishment of a democratic, secular community in Palestine in which Jews and Arabs alike would be able to play a role through their component states. It would leave, on another tier, the existing status and authority of Israel and of Jordan unimpaired.

A Joint All-Palestine Council of Reconciliation could be constituted on the principle of the parity of representation of Israeli, Jordanian, and elected Palestinian Arabs in the West Bank. Arrangements could be made to coopt other Palestinian representatives who might be prepared to subscribe to the principles of the agreement. The Palestine Council so constituted could also be empowered to take over gradually the civil administration of selected areas in the West Bank. It would be designed to coexist with the present authorities and to perform administrative tasks.

The Reconciliation Council would permit participation by the Palestinian Arabs in the political life of Palestine at a national level, as well as in Israeli and Jordanian politics in a dynamic situation in which the vitality of the secular democratic ideal could be tested without threatening the existence of the Jewish state of Israel. The joint Israel-Arab machinery contemplated in this model is analogous conceptually to the National Council of National Reconciliation established under the Vietnam Paris Agreement. But where the Vietnam agreement leaves the council as a transitory organ, the Palestine Council could mature into a joint governmental instrumentality. It would be intended for greater permanence and for enhanced juridical status.

In the Palestine context there would be advantages at some future point for all parties to enhance the status of the council once its effectiveness is proved, and to consider the establishment of a joint Palestine–Eretz Israel entity with international legal personality, *without* impairing in any way the prerogatives, rights, and powers of Israel and the Arab kingdom. The Palestine–Eretz Israel personality concept would have advantages that could not be derived from a Council of Reconciliation:

—advantages for Palestinian Arab nationalists in the establishment of an internationally recognized Palestinian–Eretz Israel entity rather than a mere Reconciliation Council;
—advantages for Palestinian Arab nationalists in the creation of a common national juridical personality for all Palestinian Arabs in Israel, the territories, Jordan, and the Palestinian diaspora, ending the continued fragmentation of the Palestinian people;
—advantages for Israeli nationalists in the affirmation of national rights (without prejudice to boundary questions) throughout Eretz Israel west of the Jordan and their recognition by Jordan and the West Bank Arabs;
—advantages for Israeli nationalists in defining a relationship between them and the West Bank that would avoid the "demographic" threat of the incorporation of 1 million Arabs in the state of Israel.

Israel might also benefit from setting up a joint bisovereign community in which eventual Israeli military presence in the West Bank could not be characterized as the stationing of forces in a foreign country but in a country in which both Jewish and Arab peoples have recognized rights. Israeli presence in West Bank areas would be juridically analogous to North Vietnamese military presence south of the DMZ. (The North's presence is characterized under the Paris agreement as nonforeign or "Vietnamese" presence.)

A Joint Reconciliation Council would constitute a first operational step to try out limited administrative cooperation in civilian matters between Israeli, Jordanian, and West Bank officials. Success with a

Palestine Reconciliation Council could thus pave the way to the elevation of the Palestine–Eretz Israel community to joint statehood.

The model for a joint entity of Palestine–Eretz Israel is primarily designed, however, *to explore areas that remain open for inquiry and for a dialogue between the parties, rather than as a blueprint for a political solution.* It is designed to elicit responses and exchanges between leaders searching for formulas that may help bind over and accommodate rival claims in Palestine. As a political formula, it is powerless to change political realities. But it can chart new routes for accommodation, coexistence, and ultimate reconciliation.

The joint entity of Palestine–Eretz Israel could be the final step in the development of a joint Arab-Israel reconciliation machinery. It contemplates a form of association between states unknown to traditional Western, constitutional, and political theory. It is designed as a peculiar juridical entity involving the existence of two sovereign and legally independent states within another joint structure endowed only with powers agreed upon by its component members, all three enjoying formal juridical independence as well as membership in the United Nations. In this sense, therefore, Palestine–Eretz Israel could be a paradigm for the possible accommodation of state systems in divided countries, or in countries about to be divided. It is a flexible political design within which to settle difficult political questions of who is to control what and under what conditions.

The role assigned to the United Nations in this process of accommodation is modest. In Palestine, as in Vietnam, the world organization has been perceived by one of the sides to have become the instrument of hostile powers. The UN could play a useful role, however, in undertaking collaborative efforts through the joint machinery established by Israel and the Arab kingdom. Such machinery might eventually lead to UN membership for a Palestine–Eretz Israel community alongside the existing membership of Israel and of Jordan. This perspective raises a broad qestion pregnant with implications—whether associations of states and communities of states should be granted full membership in the world organization or limited to observer status only. Membership in the UN could itself become an ingredient in the reconciliation of states rather than reflect recognition of a status achieved.

This is a subject which still lies on the periphery of investigated ideas—a subject calling for inquiry.

Notes

1. Much terminology is controversial. Thus "administered territories" or "occupied territories" or again "West Bank" or "Judea and Samaria."

2. See one very instructive study by Susan Lee Hattis, *The Bi-National Idea In Palestine* (Haifa: Shikmona, 1970).

3. Moshe Dayan, *A New Map–New Relations* (in Hebrew; Maariv, 1969).

4. Transport Minister Peres has pointed out that as of January 1973, however, there were only 4,000 Jewish settlers in the territories vs. 60,000 Arab workers in Israel from these territories.

5. For some useful data, see Coordinator of Government Operations in the Administered Territories *Four Years of Military Administration, 1967–1971* (Israel Ministry of Defense, 1971).

6. The percentage of foreign workers in West Germany is about 16 percent—some 2 million out of a work force of 12 million.

7. Haaretz daily newspaper, 8 September 1972.

8. From a speech by General Gazit at a seminar in Rehovot on April 21, 1969 at a seminar conducted by the Israel Academic Committee on the Middle East.

9. Recent offers to open a West Bank University have received the support of Allon.

10. Israel Ministry for Foreign Affairs, Department of Information, "Statements of Ministers in the Debate on the Territories Which Took Place in the Secretariat of the Labor Party" (in Hebrew; 1973). Mimeographed. A remarkable document.

11. From an interview in *Maariv,* April 4, 1972, p. 20.

12. Arie Eliav, *Glory in the Land of the Living* (in Hebrew; Am Oved, 1972).

13. Yeroham Cohen, *The Allon Plan* (in Hebrew; Hakibutz Hameuchad, 1972).

14. The Future of Palestine (London: Arab Office, August 1947).

15. George Antonius, *The Arab Awakening* (Philadelphia: Lippincott, 1939), p. 333, as cited in Ben Halpern, *The Idea of the Jewish State* (2d ed.; Cambridge, Mass.: Harvard University Press, 1969).

16. Halpern, *Idea of Jewish State,* p. 336.

17. The literature on the Arab position is considerable. See, for example, Maxime Rodinson, *Israël et le Refus Arabe* (Seuil, 1969); Anouar Abdel-Malek, *La Pensée Politique Arabe Contemporaine* (Seuil, 1970). In the latter, see in particular Baha El Din, "Redonner Vie a l'Etat de Palestine," and the chapter on Palestine. See further Hisham Sharabi, *Palestine and Israel—the Lethal Dilemma* (Pegasus, 1969) and the celebrated symposium published just before the 1967 war, *Les Temps Modernes, Le Conflit Israélo-Arabe* (Temps Modernes, 1967), for significant Arab and Israeli viewpoints.

18. For the text of the speech see *Journal of Palestine Studies* (Beirut) 166 (1972)

19. Yassin el-Ayouti, "Sadat's Egypt and the Palestinians" (November 1972). Mimeographed.

20. For an Israeli perception of Arab policies, see Yehoshafat Harkabi, *Arab Attitudes to Israel* (New York: Hart, 1972).

21. Aziz Shihedeh said recently, "to say that Jordan is Palestine is something which Jordan's people will not accept. . . . I cannot ask Jordan to renounce its sovereignty any more than I can ask Israel to renounce its sovereignty." *New Outlook 15* (1972): 9.

22. Cited in Yehoshafat Harkabi, *Palestine et Israël* (Geneva: Editions de l'Avenir, 1972), p 214.

23. This point is emphasized by the distinguished writer, Moshe Shamir, in *My Life With Ishmael* (in Hebrew; Maariv, 1969).

24. The text of the Covenant has been published in *NYU Journal of International Law and Politics* 5 (Spring 1970): 228.

25. Cited in Harkabi, *Palestine et Israël,* p. 197.

26. *New Outlook* 15 (December 1972): 8.

27. *New Outlook* 15 (March–April 1972).

28. Fayez Sayegh, *Time Bomb in the Middle East, A Palestinian View* (New York: Friendship Press, 1969), pp. 54, 70.

29. See the *New York Times* story, "A 'Commonwealth of Palestine' Is Suggested by Four U.S. Professors," 23 February 1971, p. 2.

30. In the event the Joint Palestine Council of Reconciliation were to function to the satisfaction of all parties, it would remain open for the parties to endow it with governmental status. Such a government of Palestine–Eretz Israel could apply for membership in the United Nations without prejudice to the existing membership of Jordan and of Israel. The states parties to the agreement could then further agree on the establishment of a common, multisovereign entity of Palestine Eretz Israel endowed with international legal personality. The common entity of Palestine Eretz Israel would be composed of the component, independent, sovereign, and equal states establishing it, without prejudice to the independence, sovereignty, and equality of Israel and of Jordan.

31. For some variants on the twelve points approach, see Roger Fisher, *Dear Israelis, Dear Arabs* (New York: Harper & Row, 1972), p. 125.

32. Ahmed Baha El Din, from "The Roots of King Hussein's Proposal—N.Y.U. Proposal for the Establishment of a Palestine Commonwealth," *Shu'un Filastiniya* (Beirut, in Arabic; June 1972).

Ahmed Baha El Din has published widely on the Palestine Question. The Twelve Point Model which he discusses has been developed entirely independently of any government.

33. For an excellent study of Jewish-Arab relations in Palestine, see Aharon Cohen, *Israel and the Arab World* (New York: Funk and Wagnalls, 1970).

34. See *Time Bomb in the Middle East* (New York: Friendship Press, 1969) for a discussion of the "democratic, secular, Palestine state" idea.

Conclusions

Gregory Henderson and

Richard Ned Lebow

THE IDEAL NATION-STATE is a political unit synonymous with a nationality. Such polities abound in textbooks but are rare in the real world. Most nations contain more than one nationality, and nationalities themselves are frequently divided among two or more states. A list of countries, for example, that comprise 90 percent of all the members of one ethnic group and contain a minority population of 5 percent or less would be very short indeed. Japan alone among the great powers would appear on the list, and certainly no more than a handful of newly independent countries would qualify. Division, therefore, is a basic and universal problem; and since nations have multiplied in the last generation, so also has division. Divisions and divisiveness have profound political ramifications. The desire for unification or autonomy motivates the participants in a majority of current international conflicts and has led directly to most of the wars fought since 1945.

Unfortunately for the scholar, the phenomenon of division is as varied as it is ubiquitous. This variety poses serious problems of classification and probably precludes a truly comprehensive treatment of division. Accordingly, the editors have found it necessary to impose careful limits on this study and have confined it to instances of division in which there was a period of prior political unity. In some cases, Germany and China, for example, this unity was the result of organic historical development. In others, as with the Indian subcontinent, it was imposed by force from the outside. Nevertheless, such unity, and the economic, administrative, and political structures associated with it, forms a convenient starting point for the study of division. The subsequent dissolution of these bonds is the common analytic thread binding the cases together. Group divisions solely within countries, such as the conflict between the Ibo and Hausa in Nigeria, have been excluded from study, as have the strivings for unity of ethnic groups like the Basques and Kurds, divided among several countries but possessing no history of prior structural unity.

Even within the universe of cases to be examined, considerable variation occurs with respect to both the origins of division and the patterns of political relationships that have prevailed in the postpartition period. Two distinct categories of division emerge, however. These are divided nations and partitioned countries.

Divided nations are countries with marked ethnic homogeneity, a common historical tradition and experience of successful political unity, that have been subsequently divided into two separate political units. The division is artificial in the sense that it was imposed from the outside, usually by great powers at the close of a war, or, in the case of China, has endured only by reason of great-power involvement. Germany, Korea, China, and Vietnam belong to this category of division, as do Cambodia and Laos where de facto division has emerged more recently. The division of the Mongols, once united in a single empire, belongs somewhat more exceptionally to this category, having been imposed by the great powers long ago and over a longer period of time.

Partitioned countries are divisions resulting from internal causes; by reason of ethnic, linguistic, or religious conflict between or among groups formerly residing within one political unit. These divisions are most frequently associated with the breakup of colonial empires. Thus, Austria-Hungary divided into all or part of eight states, the British Raj into five, French Indochina into four, and the Palestine Mandate into two.[1] Cyprus (de facto divided) also belongs to this category, as do other cases—Holland and Belgium, for example—not represented in this study. The editors have resisted imposing subcategorization on the basis of the kind of conflict that promoted partition because division is never the result of a single axis of cleavage. Religious cleavages in Ireland, for example, also reflect perceived ethnic differences, as they do in India and Pakistan. Linguistic differences usually have ethnic or historical overtones, and ethnic differences, as in the case of Palestine, are often reinforced by linguistic and religious diversity.

Divided Nations

The case studies suggest that the two categories of division are further differentiated from each other by the political problems that achieve prominence in the postpartition period. In particular, two different kinds of issues appear to lie at the roots of postpartition conflict in each category. With respect to divided nations these are the problems of identity and successor status.

IDENTITY

Nations generally define their identities in terms of the common traditions, history, and culture of their people. This uniqueness forms the psychological cement which binds a nation together and distinguishes it from its neighbors. Nevertheless, divided nations have found it impossible to structure their identities solely on this basis because, at the time of partition, each dyad of divided nations was to a considerable degree ethnically, linguistically, and culturally identical. Accordingly, no such claim to "national" uniqueness was possible. Even in cases where some cultural differences existed, as in Vietnam, they were perceived to be an insufficient foundation upon which to build a new national identity. Moreover, while the political elites in some divided nations have encouraged cultural divergence—the People's Republic of China, for example, has introduced a reformed script and North Korea has abandoned the use of Chinese characters—both leaders and peoples have been reluctant to renounce the notion of a common nationality, with the exception of East Germany which now claims national uniqueness on the basis of its socialist system. Willy Brandt best articulated this sentiment at the signing of the recent German agreement when he declared, in contradiction to the East German claim, that East Germany and West Germany might be separate states but their peoples constituted only one nation. The one-nation concept has been repeatedly affirmed by leaders of most other divided nations as well.

The fact that each divided nation, with the exception of the two Chinas and the two Germanies, are roughly equal in size and population, has also effectively precluded any credible claim to be the sole de facto representative of the entire nation. Leaders of divided nations have, therefore, turned to ideology as the main instrument both for structuring separate identities and justifying the separate existence of their polity. The cold war and the neat division of all divided nations into communist and noncommunist states has greatly facilitated this development. It has encouraged each side of a division to espouse its social, economic, and political truths and to lay claim to being the nucleus of a future unified nationhood. Given the sharp internal political effects of ideological confrontation, it is not surprising that despite the waning of the cold war, the intensity of ideological conflict between most divided nations endures. It is still uncertain as to how efficacious ideological differentiation will ultimately prove in structuring separate identities; initially its success seems considerable. But the level of hostility generated by such confrontation has clearly been costly to all parties concerned. It has precluded meaningful economic cooperation and necessitated exceptionally high per capita expenditures on military establishments.

SUCCESSOR STATUS

The universe immutably rules that two objects cannot occupy the same space at the same time. This physical law appears to have its political corrollary. Divided nations are splinter states of a nation with prior juridical status. Most divided nations have at some point in their history claimed to be the sole legitimate successor of the former nation-state. They have asserted legal identity with the previous national entity and have refused to recognize the de jure existence of their opposite numbers.[2] Both Koreas and both Chinas adhere to this position, as does North Vietnam; until recently, so did West Germany. East Germany and South Vietnam do not. The conflict over representation is of course, no arid legal squabble but a reflection of the goal held by each divided state claiming sole-representation status for ultimate unification through the destruction of its opponent state. The claim to sole-representation status and the corresponding effort to deter third parties from recognizing the other side is designed to buttress one's own identity and legitimacy while weakening that of the other side. The Hallstein Doctrine of West Germany carried this claim to its logical extreme by stipulating the severance of relations with any country that recognized East Germany. The economic might of West Germany gave her sufficient leverage to implement this policy and resulted in the isolation of East Germany from the noncommunist world for twenty-five years. Both Chinas and both Koreas have their own version of this doctrine.

The last few years have witnessed some easing of the diplomatic conflict between the two Germanies and, to a less-definite extent, the two Koreas, and progress has been made toward resolving the successor conflict by mutual acceptance of a "two state, one nation" solution. Given the stability and economic revival of East Germany and the corresponding desire of numerous underdeveloped countries to establish relations with it, West Germany found the Hallstein Doctrine beginning to work against its own best interests. Accordingly, it has finally been abandoned and West Germany has recognized the juridical existence of East Germany in return for other concessions. The two Koreas may be moving toward this position; the two Germanies have already entered the UN, and the two Koreas might conceivably do so. Both Chinas, of course, still adhere to their version of the Hallstein Doctrine and Taiwan refers to the mainland government as the "rebel group" while the People's Republic of China derides the Taiwan regime as the "remnant clique." Given the recent successes of the People's Republic, there is little reason to expect any similar compromise.

PROGNOSIS

The phenomenon of divided nations has endured long enough for us to hazard generalizations about the patterns of interstate relations that have emerged in the postpartition period and even to suggest some likely future outcomes. Three possible "solutions" emerge; a *solution* being defined as either reunification or mutual acceptance of the status quo and, with it, normalization of relations. The first solution, that of unification imposed through the military conquest of one divided nation by another, was tried by North Korea, the People's Republic of China, and North Vietnam but was defeated in all three instances by American military intervention. An attempt by South Korea, the United States and their allies to unify Korea by force was similarly defeated by the intervention of the People's Republic. With the possible exception of the three states of Indochina, where cease-fires are fragile, military solutions are not likely to be attempted by any other divided states in the foreseeable future.

Unification may also result from the political victory of one side over the other. According to this scenario, the internal political and economic weakness of one of the divided states leads to the collapse of its regime accompanied by strong popular sentiment in favor of unification. Unification is then accomplished without significant military resistance. Most divided states have harbored this goal and have pursued policies (e.g., propaganda, nonrecognition, sabotage) designed to facilitate it. Despite this, only in China and Indochina is such an outcome at all likely. In the case of Vietnam, the continuing inability of the South Vietnamese government to legitimize itself, and the corresponding existence of large numbers of well-organized cadres favoring unification on the terms of the North, have nourished North Vietnamese hopes of such a victory. The same is true in Cambodia and Laos. It is, of course, too early to predict the outcome of these struggles.

In the case of China, the possibility of political victory is a function of the unique structural attributes of that division. In all the other cases, with the partial exception of Germany, the disparity in size, population, and economic resources between divided states is not exceptionally great. With respect to the two Chinas, this disparity is tremendous and has ultimately given the People's Republic a decisive advantage. The emergence of the People's Republic as a great power prompted the United States, formerly the major backer of the government on Taiwan, to reconsider its China policy. The subsequent American initiatives toward détente with the People's Republic accelerated the steady erosion of Taiwan's international position. More nations now recognize the People's Republic than do Taiwan, and the People's Republic now occupies China's seat in the United Nations and affiliated international organizations. The next few years are likely to see the further isolation of Taiwan. Nixon's trip to the People's Republic, his promise to withdraw all American personnel from Taiwan, and more recently, Japanese diplomatic and economic initiatives toward the People's Republic, have all constituted profound psychological blows to the Nationalist regime. The passing of Chiang Kai-shek is likely to weaken the regime further while perhaps encouraging, for the first time, some dialogue with the mainland. It is by no means improbable that some kind of federation or even unification, largely on terms dictated by the People's Republic, will occur later in the century.

The third possible solution may be termed peaceful coexistence and has presently the best chance of emerging in the German and Korean cases. Each of the states resulting from these divisions, with the possible exception of East Germany, entertained hopes of promoting the internal collapse of its opponent and of imposing unification on its own terms. Both Koreas also made unsuccessful bids for the military conquest of the other side. These policies failing, a stalemate has emerged: each state is economically resurgent and relatively stable politically, and each receives continuing support from its respective superpower ally. Neither Korea nor Germany can realistically expect to destroy its rival; indeed, each has begun to perceive strong internal incentives for reducing hostility. The decline of the cold war and the changing pattern of superpower relations that has accompanied it, has also provided external incentives for rapprochement. Rapprochement has proceeded the furthest in Germany where the recent agreement between the two states marks a historic break with the turbulent past and may well lead to close economic cooperation and wide cultural contacts as it has led to full normalization of relations.

Within coexistence or between it and reunification lies a possible in-between zone which no nation has yet entered (with the very partial exception of the Nordic states or Luxembourg and Belgium which are not aiming at unification). This zone—not static state—would be inhabited by a number of possible federative modalities in which the chiefs of state and, perhaps, some upper bodies remain separate but consultative and under them, ministries, operating bodies, or ad hoc committees (including canals, railways, postal service, electricity, etc.) are run jointly, perhaps in or from neutral territory such as the demilitarized zones of Korea or Vietnam. Presumably, joint operation would gradually expand so that communicating coexistence would have some gradual means of developing into reunification. Kim Il-song in Korea has proposed federation before reunification and splinters of the idea are in the agreement on Vietnam. Totally alien to the old *Staatswissenschaft* theory, the various possible convergence capsules adumbrated above have the virtue of avoiding the quantum jump from two states to one, with all its difficulty and risk.

Finally, whether describable as a "solution" or not, it remains quite possible that divided nations may continue for extended periods in the state of division and hostility which has generally characterized them until today.

A PARADIGM OF DIVISION

Case studies suggest that relations between divided nations change as a function of (1) the degree of stability and legitimacy of each divided state;

(2) relations between each divided state and its respective superpower; and (3) relations between the superpowers themselves. Stated in the form of an hypothesis: *As divided nations develop internal strength and hostility between their respective superpower backers decreases, they are likely to possess greater freedom of action and seek improved relations with each other.* This process can be described in terms of stages, each marked by changes in the aforementioned variables and each indicative of improved relations between the divided states. Before describing these stages, several caveats are in order. All divided nations begin life in Stage I (intense mutual hostility) but do not necessarily pass through the other stages in the course of their existence. The dilemma of division may in fact be resolved, as was discussed earlier, by military conquest or political victory in the course of Stage I. Stage II (declining hostility) actually represents a quantum leap in the relations between divided states and is only reached as the result of a peculiar and fortuitous combination of circumstances which so far, apply only to Germany and Korea. Stage IV (unification) marks another quantum leap and, as yet, no divided nations have reached this stage.

STAGE I INITIAL DIVISION

Defining characteristic: intense hostility between units. This hostility is marked by:

1. mutual nonrecognition
2. sole claim to successor status by at least one of the units
3. intense ideological conflict
4. attempts to fortify and close the border by at least one unit
5. attempts to subvert the opponent regime through both propaganda and fifth column activity
6. possible militarization of the conflict

REASONS

External: Superpower occupation or leverage coupled with intense superpower conflict leads to the establishment or support of mutually antagonistic political elites each harboring the expectation of supplanting the other.

Internal: New regimes—especially when perceived to be puppet governments—have difficulties in establishing legitimacy and encourage interunit hostility for internal political purposes. Such hostility is usually aggravated by the existence of large numbers of refugees who seek military confrontation as their means of return home.

STAGE II MIDDLE-TERM DIVISION

Defining characteristic: declining hostility between units. This is marked by:

1. tacit or formal acceptance of coexistence and a corresponding dilution of claims to sole-successor status
2. decline in the intensity of ideological confrontation

3 decline in the salience of the border permitting a wider exchange of persons and ideas
4 decline in both overt and covert attempts to subvert the opponent regime
5 decline in mutual perceptions of the likelihood of military confrontation

Symbolic acts often associated with Stage II include:

1 exchange of visits between leaders
2 public statements renouncing military solutions to division and/or in favor of unification by common consent
3 agreements with respect to border questions, visitation, and repatriation of families
4 public recognition of the partition line as an "inviolable" boundary
5 common entrance into international organizations

REASONS

External: Recognition of a political-military stalemate between units and the counterproductive nature of hostility with respect to relations with important third parties. Decline in tensions between rival superpowers allowing greater latitude for the expression of internal pressures toward détente. In some instances (e.g., East Germany), there is actually strong superpower pressure to improve interunit relations.

Internal: Mutual success in achieving legitimacy reduces each unit's need to employ hostility as an internal political prop. Economic success has the same effect and further reduces dependence on superpowers. The successful absorption of refugees also functions to permit greater flexibility toward the other unit. Positive incentives toward détente emerge with equal salience. Chief among these are economic advantages: interunit trade and the economic benefits resulting from decreased expenditure on costly military establishments. On the political side, the populations of both units still perceive the division of families and cities as artificial and agreements mitigating these human costs of division are likely to have profound internal political payoffs for elites.

STAGE III RAPPROCHEMENT

None of the divided nations has yet entered Stage III but the experience of the two Irelands in the 1950s and early 1960s suggests the pattern of relations that is likely to prevail. Rapprochement is marked by:

1 close economic cooperation with respect to tourism, trade, and development leading to the creation of limited but joint administrative apparatus which can expand gradually
2 political cooperation with respect to common external questions (foreign aid, cultural programs, relations with neighbor states) and later, with respect to security vis-à-vis both internal and external threats
3 a further decline in the salience of the border and a corresponding increase in the mobility of persons and ideas

4 the creation of intergovernmental linkages at all levels from traffic control to security, and with it, the establishment of formal consultative machinery

REASONS

Greater internal stability coupled with a continuing decline in cold war tensions further diminishes the external and internal restraints on interunit cooperation. The passing of the generation of leaders in both units whose political career was associated with the division and initial period of intense hostility also functions to remove restraints on cooperation. With respect to positive incentives, the successful experience of prior limited cooperation is likely to be instrumental in generating popular demands for more extensive cooperation while making political elites more receptive to such cooperation. However, there are likely to be limits to this "spillover" effect that will probably halt the process of cooperation short of actual unification. These restraints, a function of the political, economic, and administrative divergence that has occurred during the span of the division, will prove very difficult to overcome. They are:

1 The existence of two independent sets of leaders and of political and administrative institutions, each with considerable reluctance to merge by reason of parochial power considerations. The fear of redundancy is especially important here.
2 The divergence of administrative procedures and values encouraging bureaucratic resistance to merger.
3 Economic disparities between states and between groups and classes present in both units are likely to motivate resistance to unification within the more affluent state and among groups and classes in either unit who occupy a favored position likely to diminish with unification.
4 Prior ideological and foreign commitments that tie the hands of leaders on both sides.
5 The opposition of communist and noncommunist systems qua systems.
6 Fear of penetration resulting in loss of legitimacy and even domestic control. This is a real fear in totalitarian regimes like East Germany which suspect that greater contact with a non-totalitarian government will lead to greater internal demands for liberalization. Perhaps this explains why East Germany has recently chosen to emphasize its national uniqueness—a measure designed to reduce the impact of post-treaty penetration from West Germany.

STAGE IV UNIFICATION (No Data)

Internal divergence and contradictory foreign commitments may remain an effective barrier to unity despite the intensity of feeling in favor of it in both units. The external restraints on unification may prove the most difficult to overcome. In the case of Germany, for example, both units are well integrated into conflicting alliance systems. East Germany is a member of the Warsaw

Pact and COMECON. West Germany belongs to NATO and her economy is integrated with that of other Western European members of the EEC. Barring the demise of U.S.–USSR rivalry and the ensuing economic integration of Europe, German unification is not likely to prove acceptable to the superpowers.

Even assuming that this stage of cooperation will be reached, it is more likely to result in a kind of loose federation than in actual unification. This might involve free mobility of persons, extensive economic cooperation and some symbolic representations of unity such as a common flag, national anthem, athletic teams and cultural organizations. Perhaps, both units might agree to a single president in whom sovereignity reposes but whose actual authority is limited to ceremonial functions.

Partitioned Countries

As legend has it, King Solomon was once confronted by two women quarreling over possession of a child. Each woman claimed to be the rightful mother and asked Solomon to award the child to her. The wise king proposed a compromise. He would cut the child in two and give half to each woman. One of the women, appalled at the thought of harming the child, pleaded with Solomon to give her rival custody of the child instead. Her concern for the child's welfare convinced the king that she was the true mother and he awarded the child to her. Ethnic groups have made similar conflicting claims with respect to territory, and like Solomon, colonial powers and the United Nations have been asked to arbitrate the disputes. Like Solomon, they have frequently offered to divide the claim between the contesting parties. Alas, none of the claimants has ever been so horrified by the thought of division as to suggest that the entire territory be awarded to its opponent. As a consequence, colonial powers and the United Nations have actually wielded the knife and divided disputed territories in two. As one might expect, such division has rarely resolved the conflict.

Partition was nevertheless intended to resolve conflict by separating hostile ethnic communities and allowing each to satisfy its demands for nationhood in separate political units. Case studies suggest that this political surgery has not proved very successful; postpartition relations between most divided groups are still marked by intense hostility; in several instances this hostility has led to war. The cases further suggest that the operation's failure was due in large part to the patients' anatomies, which made it impossible to separate the conflicting communities effectively. As a result, substantial minorities were included in one or both successor states and hostility between these minorities and the dominant communities helped promote interstate conflict. In addition, conflicting groups have rarely agreed as to where the boundary between them ought to be drawn—if indeed, they have accepted partition to begin with. This has led to bitter territorial disputes which continue to poison relations in the postpartition period.

MINORITY PROBLEMS

In every country that was ultimately partitioned, the conflicting ethnic groups were to some extent geographically intermingled. Usually this resulted from past patterns of migration, but in two cases, those of Ireland and Israel, continued intermingling represented deliberate attempts by ethnic groups to improve their security position and heighten their territorial claims. Such intermingling made it impossible to draw partition lines that neatly separated the antagonistic communities; in Cyprus, where the distribution of Greeks and Turks resembles a patchwork quilt, it has precluded the attempt at partition altogether. Each successor state was therefore left with a minority population which, in the cases of Northern Ireland and Israel, amounted to a very significant proportion of the total population.

Following partition, population transfers rectified this situation somewhat, the most notable being that between India and Pakistan which uprooted millions. Population transfer took place on a smaller scale in the Middle East, where 750,000 Arabs fled Israel and an equivalent number of Jews emigrated from Arab states to Israel, and in Ireland, where 50,000 Catholics were expelled from the North and a smaller number of Southern Protestants chose to emigrate to Britain. Major population transfers have not yet occurred between Pakistan and Bangladesh but are likely in the future, with Bengalis in Pakistan choosing repatriation and Biharis in Bangladesh opting for Pakistan.

While population transfers reduced the size of minorities in partitioned countries, they did so at the cost of tremendous human suffering and left refugees with bitter memories who have helped to keep these conflicts alive. Nowhere is this more apparent than in the Middle East where the Arab states' refusal to absorb Palestinian refugees and Israel's equal refusal to permit their return has led to their internment in refugee camps. These camps have functioned as spawning grounds of frustration and anger which have twice helped to plunge the Middle East into war. Until the refugee problem is resolved, there is little likelihood that the Arab-Israeli conflict will abate.

Significant minorities still exist in most partitioned countries. In India, the Muslim population of Kashmir wishes unification with Pakistan and has been a constant source of friction between the two states. In the Middle East, the existence of a substantial Arab minority in Israel—and, since 1967, of an even greater number of Arabs in Jerusalem, the West Bank, and the Gaza Strip—has forced Israel to implement security measures that contribute to Arab-Israeli hostility. The inhumane treatment of Jewish minorities in Arab states—especially in Iraq—has angered Israelis; public opinion polls reveal that Jewish immigrants from Arab states have the most uncompromising attitudes toward Israel's neighbors. The most dramatic example of the impact of minority problems on interstate relations is, of course, Ireland. After almost fifty years of partition, the two Irelands had finally embarked on a path of cooperation that was rapidly leading to full normalization of relations. The violent Protestant reaction to Northern Catholic demands for civil rights and the civil strife that ensued destroyed this détente, however, and once again put the two states on a collision course.

TERRITORIAL DISPUTES

With the exception of Pakistan and Bangladesh, which have no contiguous territory, no partitioned country was able to agree on a mutually acceptable border. In every instance, fighting broke out and the de facto border became the cease-fire line between the conflicting groups. Inevitably, one or both sides were dissatisfied with this line and laid claim to additional territory on the basis of historical association and/or ethnic consanguinity. In the case of Palestine, the Arab side even denies the right of Israel to exist as a nation and lays claim to the total territory of Palestine.

Disputed territories remain key sources of conflict in almost every case of partition. In Ireland, conflicting claims to countries Fermanagh and Tyrone poisoned North-South relations for decades, and many Irish Catholics still deny the right of Northern Ireland to exist at all. In the interwar years, *irredenta* plagued Eastern European politics with the splinter states of the Austro-Hungarian Empire making territorial claims on one another. Indeed, only the dominant Soviet presence in the area has brought the abeyance of such claims; should Soviet influence recede, there is every reason to suspect that Teschen, Transylvania, and Temesvar would once again become contested.

The two most violent territorial disputes are associated with the partitions of India and Palestine. In 1948 the Arab states waged an unsuccessful war to deprive Israel of her existence. In 1956 and 1967 Arabs fought to restore at least the partition line proposed by the United Nations in 1947. Arab states are now pledged to liberate the territories conquered by Israel in 1967. Israel, on the other hand, has never found her frontiers consonant with her security interests and is unlikely to relinquish much of the territory she has conquered since 1967, let alone since 1947. This dispute has already led to three wars and still dominates the politics of the region. The same is true of the Indian subcontinent where two wars have arisen from conflicting claims over Kashmir and other territory.

PROGNOSIS

Unfortunately, our authors do not express much hope of resolving outstanding issues between partitioned countries in the near future. Judging from history, this pessimism appears justified. Minority groups have usually succeeded in obtaining full equality and toleration only in periods when the majority group enjoyed economic prosperity and political security. Neither condition is likely to be met in most partitioned countries given the current intensity of interstate conflict. Thus, with the possible exception of Northern Ireland, where British intervention is promoting Catholic rights, internal communal conflict and interstate hostility are likely to continue to aggravate one another.

Nor are the passions associated with *irredenta* likely to abate significantly. Once again, only in Ireland, where the salience of the border has declined over fifty years and where joint membership in the EEC may further blur territorial division, is hope of resolution real. Territorial disputes are defused only slowly and short of dramatic resolution by war, those associated with partition are likely to be part of the international scene for some time to come. The damaging aspects of such conflicts are readily apparent. Hostility generated by such disputes demands proportionately high per capita expenditures on military establishments which in turn diminish the funds available for development. Moreover, expressions of hostility and plans for war have a way of becoming self-fulfilling and have led to a series of military confrontations in both the Middle East and the Indian subcontinent which have had a disastrous impact on the economies of several states involved and, in the case of both the Arabs and Pakistanis, have destroyed the viability of successive regimes. Defeat in war and ensuing political and economic discontent have brought political elites to focus popular discontent on foreign enemies, thus reinforcing the intensity of the original conflict. No evidence suggests that this upward spiral of hostility is about to be reversed.

General Conclusion

Recognition of the important differences between the two categories of division should not discourage a discussion of aspects of division that are common to both categories nor should it curb the search for criteria by which the dangers of division can be assessed. This unity is clearly not to be sought in the causes of division, for these are exceedingly diverse. Rather, it is to be sought in the psychological arena. The starting point of this inquiry is the realization that the cement holding social systems together is psychological. Divisions of whatever sort are thus vital though varied portions of the psychological map on which all nations and societies are inscribed.

To declare the underlying units of divisions a psychological one is clearly only a beginning. Obviously, since societies are involved, the province of study is social psychology, and since tension and hostilization within groups are modal to the problem, group dynamics ought to provide the best framework for comparative study. When this study has progressed sufficiently, some degree of measurement and prediction should become possible. For behind the diversity of division and the despair to which it gives rise lie half-seen rules and measurements of tension and cohesion, criteria of hostility and hostilization, and perhaps cool paths toward cures to be hewn eventually from the dishevelment of political history and the emotions, often the hysteria, of communal strife.

The first general conclusion to which the studies in this volume lead is that the unity of nations—probably of most if not all nations—is quite fragile, far more fragile than the nations are willing to admit. Group dynamics suggests, and our cases tend to confirm, that the cohesion of a group is inversely related to its size. Group allegiance is largely a function of repeated satisfaction gained from participation in group decisions and, if the group has common values and objectives, from sharing in the positive payoffs of group activity. The larger the group, the more difficult it becomes to satisfy disparate individual needs; increasingly sophisticated and responsive organizational structures must be developed to perform this function. On the whole, therefore, greater unities always stand in danger of being reduced to lesser, more intimate, and more interactive parts.

In speaking of greater unities easily reduced to component parts, empires like those of Rome, Spain, and Austria-Hungary, composed of many highly distinctive entities which could generate their own independence movements, come first to mind. India, Pakistan, Indochina are as easily frangible. However, the most striking examples of the frangibility of nations comes not from these obvious cases but from the division of far more homogeneous states, notably Korea and Germany. Neither of these states had internal reasons for division and both had been happily united for some time—in Korea's case, since the seventh century A.D. In both instances, division was artificial, and in Korea's case, division at the 38th parallel established a new high in arbitrariness. Yet, four new states have come from these divisions and have proved viable and indeed successful in the face of all expectations and predictions to the contrary. All four have proved more creative and energetic than the great majority of undivided nations. They are among the most rapidly developing of all the world's polities and have demonstrated beyond question that ethnic, linguistic, or religious differentiation is quite unnecessary for a successful division. Like a worm cut into two parts, each of which can crawl away and grow, peoples as homogeneous as any in the world can be divided and survive as separate units. Under certain conditions of force, of lack of recourse and of hostility, it is probable that no nation in the world could not be with some success divided. The recent signs of détente between the two Germanies and the two Koreas notwithstanding, all four states have achieved sharp identities of their own. So could, potentially, most states of the present world if they were to be divided. Certainly, there is every indication that the two Chinas and the two Vietnams either have achieved or can achieve equally striking and satisfactory new identities. So, undoubtedly, could Cambodia and Laos if two wholly separate and complete governments were to become fully operational in each part.

The latter instances point to another general conclusion also strongly affirmed by students of group dynamics: that the establishment of new and separate identities involves the institution of separate organizational structures and the success of the new identities in no small degree depends on the separateness and the fullness with which these organizations operate. In simplest operational terms, Austria was saved from division because central government for the entire country was never wholly abandoned. Against every intention except the Russians', Korea's unity was lost when separate administrations became fully operational and when the territories in which these administrations functioned were sealed off from one another. There are an infinite number of other, more subtle illustrations. In Ireland, for example, the institutions of the Catholic and Protestant churches, segregated educational institutions, and the special anniversaries and parades of each community are important components and gauges of disunity. In India, where Moslem and Hindu communities were always to some extent separate, the politicization of these identities was aggravated by the formation of the Congress party and the competition to control the legislatures of the Indian states. A completely separate identity and accompanying hostility was the clear outgrowth of the establishment of separate governments. Where no separate governments exist, as with India's remaining 40 million Muslims, identities, though distinct, are far less sharp and hostility less intense. The analysis of division is thus in a very important degree an organizational study; the level of division hostilities is importantly a function of organization.

A further conclusion is that the growth of new identities depends very much on the fullness and the intensity with which the new units and their organizations—especially their separate governments—operate. This conclusion relates to the doctrine of interaction in group formation. The formal division of a country greatly increases social and political activity. An era of crisis is born. Refugees stream across the new border, rarely in modest numbers as in Ireland, Cyprus, and Mongolia, but more often in large numbers as in Germany, Korea, Vietnam, China, Laos, and Cambodia. In some cases, heavy migration takes place in both directions, as with India, Pakistan, Palestine, and Rwanda-Urundi. The influx of refugees creates an intense demand for services separated from those of the other side and conducted in an atmosphere hostile to the other side.

The severing of integrated economies further intensifies demands for separate administrative entities. In a developed economy such as that of Germany, the diminution of major exchange through rail, road, and other means aggravated the general economic collapse of 1945 and created extensive demands on separate administrations. In Korea, the same was true when vital north-south rail, road, and shipping communications ended abruptly and, somewhat later, when the entire South was plunged into darkness with the cutting of power from the North. In economies always more separate, such as those of the two Chinas, or in the underdeveloped economies of Cambodia and Laos, or in Ireland, where communications have never really been severed, the effects have been less as have the economic demands on separate governments to create separate facilities. Developed states in this sense appear to suffer more from severance, underdeveloped states less. A medium-developed economy, e.g., Korea, perhaps suffers the most because its capacity to create viable separate economies is less than in Germany. The effort to do so is correspondingly more difficult and more damaging relative to the economy as a whole.

Economic rupture is, in short, one criterion by which to measure the relative effects and strains of division. Its impact on divisiveness cannot be measured in terms of dollar or trade damage alone but must also be reckoned in terms of the relative demands on the separate administrations whose reactive efforts deepen both the actuality and psychology of divisiveness. The political demands for separate administrations are usually quite profound and, especially in the early stages of division, outbid the rational demands of united economies. Hence, such nations as the two Koreas, the two Chinas, and the two Germanies proceeded with comparatively small outcry to duplicate facilities once obtained from the severed partner. Even in desperate poverty, Rwanda and Urundi largely ignore the clear advantages of economic cooperation. Ultimately, economic needs may prove an important channel for reunification or détente, especially in the case of medium-developed states like Korea where the expense of continuing duplication threatens greater political dependence on foreign nations.

Political activity is therefore primary in its effects on division. In all cases it appears to rise enormously in the wake of division and to function as the most basic instrument in the creation of separate institutions and of emotions which kindle the psychology of division.

Both the forms and the results of the political activity of division are impressive. Government—separate government and, usually, explicitly hostile government—in each divided part became the major objective of conflicting groups, and political parties became the vehicle by which this was accomplished. Division is, therefore, one of the chief catalysts of political mobilization and party development. In Ireland the struggle between Catholic nationalists and Protestants loyal to Britain produced major party movements on both sides, and the nationalists so effectively mobilized an impoverished and largely illiterate rural population that even in Ireland's diaspora its people have, in different national settings, maintained their reputation for political organization. The lengthy prelude to the division of Palestine was a tremendous catalyst to the rise of parties and political activity not only in Israel but in all neighboring Arab states as well. India is an even more arresting example. The formation of the

Congress party spurred the rise of Muslim political movements which mobilized the cause of Muslim separatism. These movements became the progenitors of Pakistan and continue today to be bulwarks of its cause. In an ironically similar sequence, lack of cohesion between political movements in East Pakistan and West Pakistan mobilized separatist opinion and heralded the Pakistan-Bangladesh cleavage. Political-party formation and mobilization is far less developed in Cambodia and Laos, but even here division has stimulated substantially more political activity than existed before and may well become the crucial stimulus for the development of more effective political entities with broader participation than was possible before division took place.

Party activity is perhaps the most striking form of the group-reinforcement process so basic to the building of viable national divisions. It is, of course, far from the only one and is usually the culmination of much other group activity encouraging divisiveness. Churches, for example, have played such a role in European and to some extent in Muslim culture. Their special rites, processions, and traditions have provided moral rationalizations for uncompromising and confrontatory stands. In the divisions of Ireland, Cyprus, Palestine, and India-Pakistan, one sees what may hopefully be among the last acts of this long tragedy.

The confrontatory role of churches is also apparent in descending order of importance in Vietnam, Korea, and China where religion has functioned to validate morally and ideologically the extremity of opposition to communist states by anticommunist political elites and refugees. The role of religion and church institutions as rallying points of persecuted or refugee minorities is ancient and familiar to early Christian, Jewish, Buddhist, and Muslim history. Its confrontatory role in more recent divisions, while not wholly new, has mounting significance because of both the relative ideological poverty of anticommunist nations in cold war divisions and the sheer numbers of refugees associated with such divisions. Germany has been the exception here because the refugees in West Germany are not a religious minority in any meaningful sense. This fact combined with the understanding leadership within the German church has made religion and Protestant Christianity a bridge and not a fortress of confrontatory conviction between the two Germanies.

Political party and religious activity are only the most signal and overt of refugee activities encouraging polarization. Refugees have need of, and tend to join, organizations of many kinds. Having direct experience of conditions on the other side of the division, they are liable to establish themselves as guardians of confrontation and to enter defense and control bodies. Leadership in army, police, and intelligence bodies in Taiwan, South Korea, and South Vietnam tended to be exerted by refugees. Refugees have also played marked leadership roles in the divisions of Palestine, Germany, Pakistan, and even Laos. In time of particular threat, refugees have often formed their own youth and other defense groups as in the immediate post-World War II period in South Korea and in the Middle East where Palestinian guerrillas have been a major source of continuing hostility between Israel and the Arab states. Nevertheless, the polarization induced by refugees tends to be limited largely to the refugee generation. Unless refugees, as in the Palestine situation, are kept in camps and are unintegrated into a new national society, the original spirit of antagonism is rarely inherited by their socially integrated children.

Once formed, the more intense the confrontative activity of the organizations on either side of a division, the deeper the division will run. Just as strikes and confrontation crystallize class division, conflicting contact between divided states acts as a catalyst to group division. Here, the violence of the initial break usually plays a key role. Usually the break is violent—but not always. In Rwanda-Urundi unity was putative only and a break never came. In Mongolia the break occurred in pieces and partly through migration over a long period of time. In Ireland the break occurred long enough ago to have been personally witnessed by only a thinning minority of the population and tends to merge with the violence of a long-previous and long-remembered history. In Laos and Cambodia the break is both violent and recent, but it has been less definite. At the present time, no settled borders and no fully established regimes exist in either Laos or Cambodia; thus, there are less-definite entities for emotions to cohere around. A condition not entirely dissimilar pertains in Cyprus, though the entities are more definite there and, being infinitely smaller, are far better known and psychologically grasped. In all other cases covered, the break has occurred in the last generation and has been more or less violent. It has involved the active and continued maintenance of armed forces (as, of course, it does in Cyprus, Laos, and Cambodia). In the case of Pakistan-Bangladesh alone, this condition is greatly palliated by the noncontiguity of the borders. For China, the sea provides less of a palliative.

The character of the border is another variable. The most divisive borders are unstable, illegitimate, and subject to warfare—as with the fighting lines dividing Laos, Cambodia, and, to a lesser extent, Cyprus, India-Pakistan, and Palestine. More legitimate but hermetically sealed borders which allow no friendly intercourse—as in Korea, Vietnam, and China—come next. They invoke hostility by troop concentrations, military action, or incidents while the stability of the relatively legitimized line encourages a definite psychological perception of the national entity which then forms part of the psychology of division. Borders allowing limited and controlled communication (Germany) or near-normal communication (Ireland, Mongolia, and, off-and-on, Rwanda-Urundi) probably contribute more to the tempering than to the escalation of hostility. A movement toward communicating borders is, obviously, highly desirable.

War is the ultimate expression of hostility arising from division. The threat of division to world peace is both manifold and profound. Indeed, all wars and most important military actions since 1945 have been associated with one or another of the divisions covered in this volume. The savagery of fighting between the two parts of divided countries may well exceed that between wholly foreign countries—a sad reminder that brothers make the worst enemies. During the Korean war, South Koreans told vivid stories of the cruelty of the North Korean invaders, far greater than that of the Red Chinese troops, and North Koreans frequently had more to fear from South Koreans than from American or other allied troops. In these tragedies, as in Vietnam, in the inter-Muslim slaughters of Bangladesh, and in Ireland and Cambodia, is ample evidence of the awesome dynamics of division.

Only the future politics of Korea and Indochina will show whether war between the divisions of fairly homogeneous states has any more redeeming side. It is possible that the horror of what war involves may have cathartic influences on the emotional vortices and ideological differences of national divisions. Some contact, even if usually hostile, may in some circumstances be better than none. The sight of destroyed villages and torn bodies of the same hue and birth may arouse more human feeling and pity than the flow of hostile propaganda across political boundaries. The escalation of military budgets, the wastage of scarce national resources in armies few wish to use may even arouse sobering national reactions. In Korea these reactions seem already to have begun. It is too soon to say whether war may have an ultimately ambivalent influence on the hostilities of divided countries; it is possible. For the present, however, it must still be judged the ultimate escalator of divisiveness.

Many other factors affect, or may affect, the psychological and the realistic complexes that maintain divisions. Among them are ethnic, linguistic, and religious homogeneity; population distribution; stability and legitimacy of government; distribution of natural resources; degree of development; level of education; length of historical experience; the influence of neighboring states and the great powers; ideology and propaganda. A rough and exploratory attempt to measure the impact of these factors on hostilization in relation to the cases covered in this volume has been made in the Appendix.

The relative importance of each of these factors for divisions is hard to assay. Population distribution has fairly clear importance, especially when correlated with the character of the borders involved. Dense settlement—as in Korea, Pakistan-India, and Cyprus—is an obvious intensifier of the forces discussed above. Low population density—e.g., in Mongolia and to some extent in Cambodia and Laos—tends to make hostilization forces less intense.

Ethnic and linguistic differences undoubtedly increase the possibility that a division will or may occur; they provide powerful ground for the rallying of separate groups as was prominent in the split of Pakistan and Bangladesh. Contrary to what might have been thought before World War

II, however, these differences may not greatly increase the vortex of divisiveness in states that have already been divided. Of the wars or military actions now in progress in divided countries (Vietnam, Laos, Cambodia) or in war-torn Korea, ethnic and linguistic differences are either absent or play no significant part. The last generation has proved that a divided homogeneous nation can be uncompromisingly and savagely hostile as an unhomogeneous one—if not more so.

Resource distribution and degree of development are factors that can also contribute to the emotions of deprivation. Yet, in a manner running against the grain of the Marxian thesis, it is extraordinary, on the whole, how little economic and developmental factors inject themselves into the psychological and emotional complex of national division. They are overwhelmingly rational factors, and divided nations have generally shown astonishing ingenuity in adapting themselves to imposed economic adversities. Indeed, the deprivation of a resource, a service, or a productive unit by the division of a nation appears to have an effect comparable to a similar loss caused by war. The nation is challenged to make up the loss and, in the process, often develops rapidly.

Something similar might be said for the legitimacy and even stability of government. For when a nation is lacking in these, it tends to be challenged to make up for them. Its competitiveness with its divided partner in this respect seems to be a more important contributor than economic factors to the psychology of division. Such an inference can be drawn from the strivings of both East Germany and North Korea to achieve international recognition. Recognition by foreign powers and the buttress to legitimacy it entails has been, for the two Koreas, the two Germanies, and the two Vietnams, so bitter a field of competition in the last years as to undermine increasingly their respective versions of the Hallstein Doctrine and open the prospect of widespread recognition of both parts of these divided nations.

Length of historical experience is hard to appraise, but it does appear to play a modest role in affecting the divisiveness of sundered countries. Ireland seems to be the division in which this factor has played the greatest role. Appeals to history and the creation of a myth around which people can rally and from which they are loath to retreat has been central to the Irish problem, and more than any other factor it has helped to maintain enmity after fifty years of partition. On the whole, recent experience sadly shows that countries with long histories of unity are as easily sundered as a country whose unity is brief, though they do not cleave themselves voluntarily. Whether appeals to long history will be effective as a stimulus to reunification, the example of Korea is likely soon to show. Such appeals have been rhetorically important in starting talks between the two Koreas. Were there ever to be a hope for Mongolian unity, appeals to history would certainly have to play a key role in rallying Mongols to achieve it.

The influence of great powers and of neighboring states on the achievement and maintenance of division within nations is too large a subject for adequate treatment within this conclusion, which seeks, instead, to stress the internal dynamics of division. Nevertheless, it is clear that such outside influence is great. It is decisive in divided nations; these countries can be united only with great-power consent. The influence of great powers and neighboring states on the partitioned countries is also critical. Great Britain's role in Ireland has constituted the historical reason for Ireland's disunity, and many would say that it continues so to constitute it today. The role of Greece and Turkey in Cyprus has similarly constituted the grounds for division in that island, while the role of the United Nations in peacekeeping in Cyprus continues to be vital. Rwanda-Urundi's unity was connived against by the occupying colonial power while the force favoring it has been the United Nations. Great Britain authored the plan for the partition of Palestine, and the involvement of the United States and the Soviet Union in this question through the years is deep and well known as is, of course, that of the surrounding Arab states. The interest of outside powers in the India-Pakistan division is considerable but less decisive than the former role of Great Britain as colonial overlord of the subcontinent. While Pakistan and Bangladesh might have ultimately separated in any case, the armed force of India was decisive in the actual wrenching of Bangladesh from Pakistan. In short, the role of great or neighboring powers has been decisive in all cases of division except for India-Pakistan—and even in that instance the role of Great Britain was important.

It is in the domain of ideology that the internal and external strains affecting division converge. On the one hand, ideology usually has been transmitted to divided countries by colonial powers, occupying superpowers, or interested third parties anxious to foment subversion. On the other hand, division created internal needs for ideological identification. Confrontation, crisis, strife, and the groups and institutions that division breed produced a need for organizational cement and belief in action which only ideology could provide. The communist portions of divided states such as mainland China and North Korea developed into more ideological polities than the Soviet Union itself. Ideology, in turn, bred propaganda, and divided states became propaganda states. And propaganda, having hostility as a major object, bred further hostilization.

As a result, divided countries became increasingly and rather swiftly mobilized. Beginning in early nineteenth-century Ireland, one can see this process sweeping toward its crescendo in the nearly total mobilization of the masses achieved by the People's Republic of China and by the Democratic People's Republic of Korea. A particularly interesting example of the result of mass participation is cited by Craig Baxter (chapter 8) in the case of India when Gandhi invoked a mass movement for avowedly peaceful political purposes. Problems that had been communal suddenly became national. Sentiments once localized had to be appeased in oratory and elections at the national level. The flexibility needed to avert the Muslim-Hindu crisis was overwhelmed and leadership saw its force dulled or found itself prostituted for mass ends. What was prologue to division in India became the handwriting on the wall in other cases of division.

"If it is into the waters of passion that you plunge your oar you will be borne away" ends the first sentence of a famous Japanese novel. In dividing, nations have plunged themselves and their peoples into an increasingly ideologized and politicized world. Confrontation has induced in them a quicker pace of political mobilization than has overtaken most nations. The milieu of divided countries has been one of polarization and of propaganda, sometimes of the creation of national myth and destiny. The result has not encouraged the forces of compromise and rationality needed to reduce the tensions created—let alone provide solutions to division.

It may be that we stand on the borders of a new era. The Brandt initiatives in Germany have shown a way toward compromise and rationality. Korea may be following or may find its own way. In Vietnam a war ends haltingly, hopefully enduringly. In no recent case has a state once divided reunited, nor is any state approaching unification now. For some, such as Laos and Cambodia, division may harden sooner than it recedes or yield only to traumatic armed conflict. Like Goethe's sorcerer's apprentice, the world may not be freed of the spirits it has summoned.

The path, if it is to be taken, is clear. It is the path of communication. Once organizations created out of hostilization begin to speak to each other, propaganda will recede, ideology will soften slightly, and the organizations in which separateness has inhered will change. If this communication can develop into an expanding number of joint functions and tasks for organizations on both sides of divisions, group-reinforcement processes will begin to foster unity rather than disunity. If this stage can be succeeded by attempts at reductions in armed forces, emotional tensions will ebb and prospects for rapprochement or unity will brighten. Meanwhile, the habits and institutions of disunity will be hard to overcome, and the important stories of division told here will continue to hold sober lessons on how societies behave.

Notes

1. In this sense, the countries of Indochina can be said to be doubly divided. Each is a successor state of the former French colony and each in turn is divided between rival communist and noncommunist governments.

2. See the excellent discussion of the legal aspects of this problem in John Herz's chapter on Germany.

Appendix

(1) signifies degree of presence of selected variable
(2) represents impact of variable upon hostilization

	ETHNIC NATIONAL HOMOGENEITY		LINGUISTIC HOMOGENEITY		RELIGIOUS HOMOGENEITY		REFUGEES		DEGREE OF DEVELOPMENT		LENGTH HISTORICAL EXPERIENCE		DIVISION LINE	
	(1)	(2)	(1)	(2)	(1)	(2)	(1)	(2)	(1)	(2)	(1)	(2)	(1)	(2)
Ireland	−2	+5	+4	−5	−2	+5	+2	+1	+3	+2	+5	+5	−5	+5
Germany	+4	−2	+4	−5	−3	−2	+5	+3	+5	+3	+4	−4	+4	+5
Ruanda-Urundi	−4	+5	+4	−2	−2	+1	+5	+5	−5	+1	+1	0	0	0
Palestine-Israel	−2	+4	−2	0	−4	+5	+5	+5	+1–2	+3	+5	+5	−5	+5
India-Pakistan	−3	+2	−3–4	−2	−5	+5	+5	+4	−1	−2	+3	+4	−3	+5
Pakistan-Bangladesh	−4	+4	−4	+3–4	+5	−3	+4	−4	−1	+2	−4	+4	+5	−2
Mongolia	−2	+3	−2	+4	−3	+2	+1/2	−2	−3	0	+4	+3	−3	+3
Laos	−5	+3	−4	0	−2	0	+5	+4	−4	−3	+1	−2	−5	+4
Cambodia	+2	−3	+5	−3	+4–5	−3	+3	+2	−3	−2	+5	−3	−5	+4
Vietnam	+3	−3	+4	−2	−2	+3	+5	+5	+1	+2	+3	−3	+5	−3
China	+4	−4	+3	+1/2	+4	−1/2	+5	+5	−1	−1	+3	+4	+5	−2
Korea	+5	−4	+5	−4	−1	+2	+5	+3	+2	+4	+5	−5	+4	−3

	RESOURCES DISTRIBUTION		POPULATION DISTRIBUTION		IMPORTANCE OF NEIGHBORING STATES		GREAT POWERS		STABILITY & LEGITIMATE GOVERNMENTS		IDEOLOGY		ECONOMIC SUCCESS	
	(1)	(2)	(1)	(2)	(1)	(2)	(1)	(2)	(1)	(2)	(1)	(2)	(1)	(2)
Ireland	−2	+1	−3	+2–3	+5	+3	8–4	−3	+2–3	+3	0	0	N−3, S+3	−3
Germany	−3–4	+3	−3	+4	+3	+2	+5	+5	+4	+4	+4	+4	+5	−4
Ruanda-Urundi	−5	+1	0	0	+1	−2	+2	+3	+1	+4	+2	+2	−3	−2
Palestine-Israel	−5	+3	−5	+5	+5	+5	+5	+3	A−3, J+5	+5	+1	+1	A−3, J+5	+4
India-Pakistan	−3	+3	−3	+2	+1	0	+3	−3	+3–4	−2	+1	+1	+2	+3
Pakistan-Bangladesh	−4	+4	+3	+3	+5	+5	+3	+2	−3	+4	+2	+2	−3	+4
Mongolia	+2	+1	+2	+3	same as succeeding		+5	+5	+4	+2?	+3	+3	+3	−3
Laos	+3	+1	−3–4	+2	+5	+5	+5	+5	−3	−3	+2	+4	−2	+1
Cambodia	+4	+3	+3	+2	+3	+4	+4	+4	−5	+4	+3	+3	−4	+4
Vietnam	+4	+3	+5	+2	+3	0	+5	+5	N+5, S−3	+3–4	+5	+5	+3	+3
China	−5	−3	−5	−1	1/2	1/2	+4	+4	+5	+5	+5	+5	+5	−2
Korea	+3–4	+4	−2	+3	same as succeeding		+5	+5	+4	+4	+5	+5	+5	−2

Index

"The desire for unification or autonomy motivates the participants in a majority of current international conflicts and has led to most of the wars fought since 1945."

This book represents the first published comparative investigation of countries with a history of prior unity and subsequent division. The case studies, written expressly for this volume by eminent authorities in each area discussed, fall into two categories:

Those dealing with *divided nations* which have marked ethnic homogeneity, common historical tradition, and experience of successful political unity, but have had division imposed or sustained from the outside. In this category China, Germany, Korea, Vietnam, Cambodia, and Laos are discussed.

Austria-Hungary, the British Raj, French Indochina, the Palestine Mandate, Cyprus, and Ireland are examples of *partitioned countries* divided by reason of internal differences such as ethnic, linguistic, or religious conflict after having resided in a single political unit.

Although the orientation of the work is theoretical, policy for diminishing hostilities between divided nations is proposed. Appendices provide background information to aid the reader's understanding of the studies. Maps show the present boundaries of division.